Captain Sherwood's Journals

Captain Sherwood's Journals

The Journals and Letters of Henry Sherwood
as a Teenager in Revolutionary France
and a Soldier in The West Indies and India
1790—1816

Transcribed and Edited by Tim Eaton
© 2016

First published 2016.

Amazon Create Space.

© Tim Eaton as editor of Henry Sherwood's Journals.

No part of this transcription and edition may be reproduced in any manner whatsoever without the written permission of the editor except in brief attributed quotations.

ISBN-13: 978-1536841978
ISBN-10: 1536841978

To Barbara with all my love.

Contents

Preface	1
Early life	3
Part 1—A Teenager in Revolutionary France 1790-96	5
To Miss Butt	7
1790 To France: Aged 13	8
1792 Voyage to Revolutionary Marseilles: Aged 15	9
1793 Return Voyage from Marseilles: Aged 16	15
1793 February—France at War	16
1793 September—Arrested	17
1793 September—Imprisoned	19
1793 December—Free but Pennyless	23
1795 Escape: Aged 18	28
1795 Paris	30
1795 Switzerland, Destitute	33
1795 Germany	38
Part 2— England—1795 October: Aged 18	51
1795 Home to Coventry	52
Part 3—Soldier—The West Indies 1798-1802	57
1798 A Soldier. Age 21.	58
1798 June—Sailing to the West Indies: Aged 21	67
1798 August—The West Indies	74
1798 August—Martinique	75
1798 August—St Vincent	76
1800 April —St Lucia	103
1800 August—Pigeon Island, Yellow Fever	109
1800 November—St Pierre, Martinique	111
1801 January—St Lucia	115
The Caribs	120
St Vincent—Description	125
St Lucia—Description	126
Hopes of a Return to England	147
Second Bout of Yellow Fever	152
1802 September—Transport to England,	155
Storm off Ireland	158
Plymouth and Portsmouth	163
Part 4——England—1802 to 1805	167
1802 December 13th—Ashore in England	168
1803 January 17th—March towards Shrewsbury	170
1803 February—Bridgnorth	172

1803	March—Death of Father	174
1803	June—Ipswich	175
1803	June—Marriage & Recruiting in The North	176
1803	December—Orders for Ireland	183
1804	April—Regimental Paymastership	186
1804	July—Kent	189
1805	April—Portsmouth	194

Part 5—India—1805 to 1816   197

1805 April to August Voyage to India	198
1805 August 24th Madras	208
1805 September 2nd Depart Madras	212
1805 September 14th Calcutta	214
1805 October 13th 1st River Journey, Calcutta to Dinapore, 550 Miles.	218
1805 December 4th Dinapore	235
1806 July 1st 2nd River Journey, Dinapore to Berhampore, 365 Miles.	241
1806 July 17th Berhampore	245
1807 September 8th 3rd River Journey. Berhampore to Cawnpore, 780 Miles	
	259
Benares	266
Allahabad	271
1807 November 28th Cawnpore	277
1809 January 15th Ajaighar Campaign	286
1809 March 10th Cawnpore	290
Converts	293
1809 October 25th 4th River Journey. Cawnpore to Calcutta, 955 Miles.	297
Suttee	300
Aghori Sadhu	301
Hindu Muslim Quarrel	303
1809 November 28 Calcutta Holiday	311
1809 December 19th 5th River Journey, Calcutta to Cawnpore, 1055 miles	
	316
1810 April 8th Cawnpore	333
1811 December 24th Callenger Campaign March, 140 Miles.	337
March Callenger to Cawnpore, 120 Miles.	349
1812 October 30th 6th River Journey, Cawnpore to Meerut, 250 Miles.	351
1812 November 24th Meerut	354
Christian Converts	359
Floods at Meerut	363
1814-16 The Ghurka War	366
1814 October 12th—March to Dehra Dun, 135 Miles.	366
1814 October 31st Battle of Nalapani.	375
1814 December 9th March Dehra Dun to Nahan, 120 Miles.	388
1814 December 27th Nahan, Battle of Jeytuk.	393
Surrender	410
1815 June 22 7th River Journey, Meerut to Berhampore, 1115 Miles.	416

Part 6—1815 September 25th —12 Months Leave	427
8th River Journey, Berhampore to Calcutta, 175 Miles.	428
1815 October Friends in Calcutta.	429
1816 January 2nd Depart Calcutta for England	432
1816 to 1849 Epilogue	440
Acknowledgements	443
Illustrations	444
Henry Sherwood's Timeline	445
Captain Sherwood's Travels in India—1805-1816	447
Maps	449
Sources and Bibliography	466

Preface

Henry Sherwood's 1ˢᵗ and 2ⁿᵈ Diaries, with all of Sherwood's idiosyncracies of spelling, punctuation and syntax are transcribed for publication by kind permission of the Shropshire Archivist.

This transcription is only edited to tidy the text and to add annotations, headings, notes and illustrations for publication.

The first diary is a journal, with letters, giving an account of his life from 1790 to 1795 as a teenager in revolutionary France including his imprisonment as an alien and his escape. He continued the account from March 1798 when he became a soldier, with his service in the West Indies until 1802, and in England until 1805. He married his cousin, Mary Martha Butt in 1803.

The second diary is a journal, with letters, describing Sherwood's military service in India, 1805-1816 accompanied by his wife. They travelled long distances by river and Sherwood describes battles of the Maratha and Nepal wars. They had eight children, six born in India of whom two died there. They also fostered a number of orphaned English girls in India where Mrs Sherwood started a number of schools and orphanages for British and Indian children. Mrs Sherwood became a best-selling author of over 300 books for children.

I am aware of further diaries and letters in the UCLA Library in Los Angeles. I have not had access to them.

An edited transcription of Sherwood's teenage years in revolutionary France was published in booklet form:

Bond, Andrew, ed. (1981). *The Value of Bread. a Memoir By Henry Sherwood Who, as a Teenager, Resided in France During the Years of the Revolution*. London: Saint George Orthodox Information Service.

My wife, Barbara Eaton has included some extracts from the diaries in her biography of Sherwood's wife: (2016). *Mrs Sherwood, 'So Rich in Children.'* London: Francis Boutle Publishers.

Tim Eaton, The Lizard, Cornwall, 2016.

Part 1—A Teenager in Revolutionary France 1790-96

To Miss Butt

Bridgenorth.

Dear Cousin,

You have forced me to send you this Account, but I am afraid you will be punishing yourself more than me, but that is none of my business, I have obeyed you & that is enough. I have omitted many circumstances, which I might have told you but they cannot be written. I have, as you desired, avoided mentioning family concerns more than necessary for carrying on the tale. I can assure you that, had it not been yourself that commanded it, I would not have undertaken it, for I know very well that I am incapable of doing it properly, neither have I the time. You must consider that I am employed from half after six in the Morning till eight at night, after which I am tired & not fit to write good sense or Grammar. In my Situation I never shall have occasion either to write Histories, or Voyages, or even letters except those in set forms in which the same words are always used, you must therefore content yourself with this poor performance which I only wish better because you are to read it.

I have not kept a copy myself, fearful that some time or other I might be tempted to shew it & be laughed at. I therefore beg that you will not let any one see it, & I should wish that you would burn it when read. I must also beg that you will not laugh at me yourself for I am conscious that I deserve it.

You know that, when I left you at Kidderminster, my Father placed me at Merchant Taylor's School where I remained only going twice to France till April 1790, the Year of the French Revolution. At that time I went to France as it appears to remain there altho I did not expect it at the time. My Father remained at Calais till June & then he proceeded with his Family to Bolougn, which place we left in August for St Vallery intending, as I have heard him say, to proceed to the South of France. At St Vallery my sister, Mercy, was taken ill & we could get on no further. She at length died here in 1791. &c &c &c

I am with love to Lucy,
Your Affectionate Cousin
Henry Sherwood Junr [1]

[Copy of a letter without date, but written probably in 1796. Age 19.]

---

[1] Diary of Henry Sherwood. Shropshire Archives, 5624/1.

1790 To France: Aged 13

In September 1790 My Father went to reside at Saint Vallery sur Somme, a Sea Port on the Coast of Picardy on the River Somme about 10 miles from Abbeville. The French Revolution then wore a promising appearance, particularly to those who had been accustomed to look on the American revolution as the cause of Liberty. I was too young to judge but I observed that my Father was led, in some degree to adopt the new doctrine from a difference in opinion from his Father who was a supporter of the British Government during the American Wars.

My Father had other reasons for leaving his own Country, he had been extravagant &, altho still possessing a good Income, he thought he should be able to live in greater style in France than he could in a country overburthened with debts & sunk in slavery, as he represented England to be. In June 1790 My Grandfather died & being displeased with some part of the Conduct of his family, he left his Property in very unequal divisions, a much greater part coming to me than was thought just by my Father. I was not fourteen years old & consequently under my Fathers control.[2] My Stepmother also shewed a degree of unkindness to me which made home unpleasant. Soon after our arrival at Saint Vallery my Father purchased an Eighth part of a Brig. He wished as he said to form Connections & to identify himself with <u>the Nation</u>.[3] He also bought Houses & Lands. One House in the town of St Vallery & a Benedictine Abbey at a little distance. The latter was a most Charming Spot, more like a Palace than a House. There were thirty comfortable rooms in it, & the Gardens & Grounds were laid out luxuriantly in Groves & Walled Gardens like a Noblemans domain, here I might have been happy had it not been for the constant jealousy of My Mother [sic. Stepmother] which increased so much that I could not appear in her Presence or ever dine at the table with the family. Under these circumstances I was glad of the opportunity offered of being constantly on board the Brig while fitting

---

[2] Grandfather Henry Sherwood, 'Silkman of Coventry' was wealthy with business in silk and silk ribbon in Coventry and London. Disapproving of his son's republican views, his will skipped Henry's father and after some disposals to servants, other relatives and executors he left the bulk of his estate to be divided between his grandchildren living at the time of his death, reserved for maintenance until each became 21, then as a share of the capital. His executor was Mr Lilley Smith whom Henry's father sued for maintenance of his children: *Sherwood –v- Smith* in Chancery.

[3] In revolutionary France the country was referred to as Le Nation.

for Sea & the Kindness of the Captain, who treated me as a Son of an Owner, won upon me so much that I expressed a wish to go the Voyage with him, which my Father agreed to without the least hesitation, indeed seemed very happy that it should be so. The Brig was indeed very small not more than 120 Tons & so old that she had been sold to be broken up. The Eight Share did not cost more than forty Pounds. On examination however it appeared that the Vessel was not fit for sea which caused much delay & hesitation on the part of the Owners for I believe the Captain had used influence amongst friends to procure a proper number of Subscribers & probably misrepresented the state of the Ship. So much so that they refused to pay their quota towards the repairs, these difficulties kept the Ship a Year in the Harbour sometimes fitting & sometimes dismantling, which gave me great Interest in her, & the difficulties which the poor Captain met with made him more Civil to me.

1792 Voyage to Revolutionary Marseilles: Aged 15

The Poor Fellow's perseverance, at length, over came all Difficulties & we sailed for Marseilles on the 22nd July 1792. The Bay or estuary of the Somme at St Vallery is about six Miles from the Sea & being 3 Miles across & sometimes rough in high winds I had fancied that by Sleeping on board I had become a Sailor, but I soon found the difference between a Ship at anchor & one moving. I crept under the Boat & was most miserably sick & like Robinson Crusoe, wished myself at home again. The Captain had often joked with me while in harbour by saying if you go with me you must be made a Sailor & work hard & I thought it would be a fine thing, but being sick & placed on a Watch four Hours on deck & four below alternately I found no difference between work & play, I could not reconcile myself to getting up as I fancied as soon as I got into a pleasant sleep. The first night indeed altho posted to a Watch, I was allowed to go below but my sickness was worse there than on deck. In the morning I left my Hamock & went on deck: we were close to the Isle of Wight. It looked like a Three Cornered Hatt & when the Sun arose it had a beautiful appearance. As the Sun rose higher we lost sight of the land, not because we were farther off but by reason of the Vapour rising from the Sea. The day was very fine but warm & the Sea was covered with English Pleasure boats, several with bands of music on board. I lost my sickness & began to think that the sea was more comfortable, but a Storm succeeded this Calm & we were tossed about for several days & my sickness returned. I longed for Shore. We approached, in one of our Tacks the Lands End & saw the windmills very plain. The next day we were near to Ushant & saw the light House there. The storm carried us thro the Bay of Biscay rolling us about & when off Cape Finisterre it fell Calm. The Weather was now extremely Hot, we smelt the Land & the Birds came on board the Ship. I could almost fancy myself on Shore. Off the Rock of Lisbon it was again calm & we harpooned several Porpusses & caught thirteen young sharks with a line. The Captain employed all hands in cutting up the Porpusses & Sharks, cutting the flesh into long thongs & hanging these thongs in the Shrouds to dry & in pressing out the oil from the fatt. The Frenchmen had no other food while this lasted but I could not touch it & therefore I fared Badly. One of the young Sharks seized the Dog by the foot & bit it so nearly off so that the poor fellow was thrown overboard. The Water was so transparent, that we saw the fish as in a Glass biting the bait & drew them in more by observation than feeling, indeed had time been given for their feeling the hook, I have no doubt they would have snapped off the line.

We lay becalmed off Cape Saint Vincent close in with the Shore. On the Edge of the Percipice is a large Monastry possessing a Battery, as I was told, to protect Vessels running under the guns from Sallie Rovers,[4] formerly very common about here but now seldom seen. I believe the harbour of Salee is nearly choked up. A Rock is situated in the Sea like a Sugar loaf at a very little distance, yet we passed between it & the shore, so near that we could easily have thrown a stone So as to touch it.

We had a most pleasant sail from Cape St Vincent to Cape St Lucia, where we left the land to stretch across the Bay, to make the Streights of Gibraltar. We saw Cape Spartel on the 7th Aug^t & entered the Streights in company with a Spanish Man of War. The African shore, to which we had approached nearer than to Spain, had a pleasant appearance much more inviting than the Rugged Coast of Spain. On passing along we saw a Fort which I suppose to have been Tetuan but, owing to the winding of the Streights, I did not see Gibraltar till we had nearly reached it. We still kept on the African side, Mount Atlas appearing close to us, altho I am told it is sixty miles off. The Captain jocked me about it calling it the Mount of Monkeys & giving me a Telescope bade me Observe the Animals. At first I looked out with all my Eyes, but I soon found out that he was laughing at me. The French Sailors have a Custom of (as they call it) christening a Freshman when he passes the Streights or he may purchase his toleration to heathenism. I had no money & was forced to become a Christian. I was placed in a Tub & with a Common Funnel water was poured down each Sleeve & then down my back & afterwards a bucket full thrown on my head, Gibraltar & Mount Atlas being

---

[4] Sally Rovers, the term for Moroccan pirates from the Atlantic port of Salé.

Sponsors, but which was my Godfather I do not know, it was pleasant enough in August, I should have objected much more in January. I now promised Six Livres,[5] which the Captain became responsible for at Marseilles or I might have suffered more. They dipped the Cabin boy in the Sea. The Current now sent us over to the European side close under the Rock of Gibraltar & we could see the Sentry on Europa Point. Clearing the Rock, we saw the back of the Peninsula like a Spadeful of Earth towards the Mediterranean. We saw Ceuta, an Island on the opposite shore but in possession of Spain, we kept near the Spanish Coast, the Mountains of Grenada being seen in the back ground. I felt some difficulty in believing the Captain when he told me that they were always covered with snow, we passed Malaga, which we saw & from thence to Cape Gate where the French say that the wind always changes blowing from different quarters on each side. I believe that the same wind will not carry you round which brought you there, but the sailors are ignorant of the play upon words if it is so intended. It was with us a dead Calm & the Current drove us out to sea & the Calm lasted a week, after which a breeze arose which carried us to Ivica, an Island off the Coast of Valencia, where we saw the remarkable cleft in a Promontory of the Main land which is called The Coup de Sabre de Roland, reported to have been cut in two by the famous Paladin of that Name with his sword Durandel. We were on the lookout for Turtles, I sat all day in the Fore Top looking for them, but without success, (for this place is famous for them, there being a River called The River of Tortouses here) it being a bad time of year. The next day we saw Mountserrat a mountain in Catalonia. We drifted out to sea again & towards evening saw Cabretta. one of the Ballearian Isles it is the most Western. Next Morning we passed between Majorca & Minorca with many land birds coming on board. We were nearer Majorca which had a low shore with beautiful Groves of Oranges. The eastern end of these Islands was rugged rocks, which having cleared we stretched over to the North & made Cape Rosas which is a Promontary formed by the Pyrrenees & which separates France from Spain in the whole breadth viz from the Gulf of Bayonne on the Atlantic to Cape Rosa in the Mediterranean. We had rough weather crossing the Gulf of Lyons & two days afterwards were off Toulon where we were becalmed two days in what is called a dead Calm & as there are no tides in the Mediterranean we did not move. The wind arose at the end of two days but boisterous & unfavourable, which drove

---

[5] The livre was the French unit of currency, originally a pound of silver, until 1795 when it was replaced with the franc. 24 livres/francs = 1 Louis d'or = £1 sterling, with a modern value of about £35.

us to Corsica when it changed & we reached Marseilles on the 22nd August.

A Fisherman came on board as Pilot, he related to us the dreadful Massacry at Paris on the 10th & he said the Aristocrats were hunted & seized every day. We entered a Large Rocky Bay, with several Islands in the Mouth where we observed Ships laying which we were told were performing Quarantine. These Islands appeared altogether Barren, not a blade of green to be seen. A Fort appeared on one which the Pilot called St John. He said that the Duchess of Orleans with two of her Sons were there confined. We passed close to the Rocks in very deep water. The Rugged appearance of these rocks, as we passed close under them, was tremendous: our Yard Arms almost touched them as we sailed along. The City is not seen until you enter the Harbour the entrance to which is narrow & winding. When we were fairly in the Number of Shipping appeared really astonishing & from there being no tide nor Current the water was thick & dirty & we could not tell how we had got there from being busy at the time I had not observed our course & I could not perceive any inlet.

The Fish called Pilot fish, which had followed our Ship ever since we had been in the Mediterranian died in this dirty water & floated to the surface.

The Port has a fine Effect as you have a view of its whole length terminated by a Broad fine Street, perfectly strait & the Houses 6 Stories high, are built uniformly. This street is crossed by another called the course, planted on each side with Plane trees & Fountains in the Center. This Latter is the fashionable walk on Sunday's.

The city with its harbour is surrounded by hills on the South is the Fort & Chapel of Notre Dame de Bonne Garde with the Signal Post. To this Chapel all our Crew went to return thanks for safe arrival on the first Sunday. I forgot to say that whenever we had bad weather at Sea our Captain kept a candle burning to the honor of the Lady de Bonne Garde which was always to be supernumery & not used for profane purposes indeed great care was taken that its light might not be used for any thing. The Chapel is full of Images in wax &c, & paintings of Ships in Storms, the offerings for dangers escaped or Limbs saved by the Manifest assistance of the Dame de Bonne Garde. Her Image generally appears in the Clouds in each of the Pictures offered. From the terrace of this Chapel you have an extensive view of Sea & Land but the latter apparently burnt up only bare rocks, probably the Season is unfavorable for verdure here & there in the Vallys a few stunted Firs. The appearance of the City & Harbour is very fine.

On returning to the City & while walking about, at a Corner of the Street I fell in with a Mob having Prisoners whom they were going to hang a la Lanterne. One of them was so tall that his head appeared clearly above the heads of the populace. He had no hat on & was dressed like a sportsman in a Short Shooting Jacket & Splatterdashes. He was pale but looked with contempt on the Rabble. I followed the Mob without Knowing what they were about until a Man let down a Lamp which hung across the Street & having taken it off hung the poor Man by the Rope. The mob were singing & dancing & I found myself surrounded & held by the Arm & I was afraid to attempt getting away. They hung one of the Prisoners whose name I heard was Vasque by the feet & opened his body & afterwards cut him down & dragged him round the City by his feet singing all the way. As soon as I could get away I ran off to the Ship & on my way saw several People hanging on different Lamp Cords. When I got on board I intended to keep there & go no more on Shore if I could help it.

The Captain, soon after this struck a Sailor & as the doctrine of Equality was now the order of the day the Powers in Authority decided against the Captain, & as Sailors are generally discontented all our Crew left the ship except a Boy, & the Mate & myself. We three took down all the rigging & tarred it & put it up again. This was very hard work & my hands became ingrained with Tar & dreadfully swelled. When this was finished I was sent on Shore to look for the Captain, here I also slept & had an opportunity to be at the Play every Evening. The Acting was very good & the Entrance Money very small indeed you might almost go in for nothing.

One day, while I was employed in my office of Cook, I heard a Noise in the Street & English Oaths used, on which I went out & found an English Sailor drunk & quarrelling in the Street. He either could not or would not understand the People who were trying to pacify him, upon which I addressed him in English. He suddenly turned round upon me & said, "who are you?" I answered, "An English boy" "what & serving with the French, you little Renegade you leave these French Rascalls immediately, go to England." He then went away.

Two or three days afterwards, I met the same man again, he recollected me & addressing me said, "You are the little English Boy who spoke to me the other day. I warn you to leave this City immediately, if you remain a fortnight longer you will see the blood running up to your knees in the Streets." He told me that he belonged to an English Brig in the Harbour bound for Smyrna & that the ship was employed to carry valuable goods away belonging to People of consequence & that they had chests of

Dollars sunk in the mud in the harbour at the Ship's head. I did not believe the Man for I thought such a Man could not have been trusted with such a secret but I have reason to believe he spoke truth.

The Captain of *L'Etoile Mignion* (our Ship) not being able to obtain a freight at Marseilles sailed for Cette at the bottom of the Gulf of Lyons, 30 Leagues from Marseilles, & as we sailed out of the Harbour the Citizens were attacking Fort St Nicholas which was the beginning of an act of Rebellion for which that part of France suffered severely.

All the time I was at Marseilles, the town was in a dreadful state: scarcely a day passed but that some one was not put to death by the Mob. The Sufferers were generally tried & acquited after Execution. I saw the Guillotine here first. It was carried about in procession. The Marseillois hymn was quite new at this time & I have seen the People fall on their knees in the streets with clasped hands & with all the appearance of the greatest Devotion crying, "Libertè Libertè Cherrie." At the Theater, the Actors invariably knelt & affected to pray to Liberty.

On sailing out of the Port, we were becalmed all Night, towards morning a Gulf breeze sprang up (ie a Sea Breeze). We sailed 10 Knots & reached Cette in 9 Hours. We had scarcely got into the Port before the wind increased to a Hurricane, the Harbour being much exposed to the Sea, we were in alarm all night, there is a strong current running thro' the harbour which made it the more dangerous. The Waves from the Sea actually came over the Pier into the Harbour, had we been a few hours later we must have inevitably perished for we could not have brought up any where in this Cul de Sac of a Bay, or found our way into the Harbour, the Pier being hidden.

At 8 in the Morning I was coming out of the Cabin & saw a small ship outside, it was called a Tartan in these Seas. She came safe in, as by a Miracle, & when safe within the harbour, a Shout was set up by her Crew & the People on Shore which made one thrill, a little more than an hour afterwards a Ship appeared with English Colors hoisted for Quarantine.

The Captain of our Ship had scarcely time to say, "She is lost before" she struck so close to us, that a stone might have been thrown on board but she was without & we within. The Wave cast the Ship high on the Rock & she fell on her side, but seemed fixed, beaten & almost covered by each Wave, but it so happened that she struck on the very point & it was possible almost to reach her Bowsprit under the Lee of a Rock. An English boat attempted & succeeded in getting very near & receiving the crew but was taken by a heavy sea & swamped. The Sailors saved themselves on a part of a Rock which stands in the middle of the Harbour & there remained, for neither French nor Danes would venture. Probably the Quarantine was one great reason. The Wind & Sea calmed towards evening & so quickly did they both fall that before night it was as smooth as a Pond.

The Weather was very rough all the while I remained at Cette & I understood that the Gulf of Lyons was very subject to storms. The Country round Cette seemed to be very rocky but covered with Vines, figs, Olives & all kinds of Fruit Trees. We took an English Sailor on board to replace one of our men who left us at Marseilles.

1793 Return Voyage from Marseilles: Aged 16

On the 4th of January 1793 it snowed very hard which was reckoned uncommon. On the 9th, having completed our cargoe of Brandy & Wine we sailed in company with a Brig bound to Dieppe determining to keep Company. It blew very hard when we sailed & the next morning our Companion made a signal of distress, on our going down we found that she had sprung a Leak & was making Water fast, all hands were at the Pump. The Captain begged that we would not leave her. This detained us very much as the Brig could carry but little sail & otherwise sailed badly. We had but little wind & we crept along the Catalonian Shore within view of objects on Shore from Cape Rosa to Barcelona, where we left our Companion, she going into Barcelona to repair. We almost entered the Harbour with her for she made water very fast.

The City of Barcelona appeared fine from the Sea, with a Hill to the West called Mount Joy much like the entrance of Plymouth. The Weather was very warm, altho January. The day after we had looked at Barcellona a fair wind sprang up & we were in hopes of being in St Vallery by St Blaise,[6] the wind however increased to a violent storm & we had scarcely any sail set with a high Sea crossing the Gulf of Valentia. The wind being fair we were running at 10 Knots. The night was dark when about 12 oclock the Savoyard boy at the head cried out, "a Sail" & we had scarcely time to be alarmed when a Bowsprit appeared over our deck & flying rapidly by, caught our Main Shrouds but as it did not come directly across us the bow struck our Quarter Gallery & carried it away leaving its Gib boom on board. This was a most narrow escape, a Shout was uttered by the men of both Ships & we parted in a moment: every Sailor on board put up a bit of the boom as a memorial of our escape. We knew nothing of the other Vessel or of what Country it was, our damages in the morning were found to be great. We got round Cape de Gatte in the

[6] St. Blaise: Festival on February 3.

morning, & soon afterwards saw Gibraltar we saw the Surf again against the Rock & the Sentry on Europa Point, we passed a Portugeese Fleet cruizing against the Algerenes. We were carried through the Streights with a Levant Wind which carried with it a thick Fog & as it blew strong, so we were soon clear of the land. Our Vessel was very deep in the water & we felt the Waves in the Atlantic being unable to carry sail, we were drifted to the Westward. The Vessel's planks were so open that the Water ran thro the deck & sides, my Berth was quite wet at all times, I was wet for 21 days without having a dry rag on. The storm increased so much that we lay to under our Mainsail with the tiller lashed up & the hatchways fastened down, we were obliged to watch an opportunity to run below & pull the Door after us. At the end of our 21 days the Wind abated & we got our foresail up & entered the Channel. The Fast of St Blaise arrived & we danced indeed but against our Will. We heaved the lead but I much expect that the Captain was ignorant of the soundings. We saw an English ship & made signals to her & hoisted our colors but she bore away. The Captain was very angry & said he had never found the English uncivil before. We had no observation & were afraid to advance so we lay to at night having all hands on Deck. This was Shrove Tuesday.

1793 February—France at War

At day light we saw a fishing Boat which informed us that France was at war & on being asked with whom the answer was with all the World. A high Cliff was a head of us which turned out to be Fecamp: the Fisherman said, Point D'Enfer (Hell Point). The Captain, thinking it wrong to advance as war was declared entered Fechamp & he had good reason, for the Ship would have run a great risk of being taken. On entering the Harbour I went on Shore & took a look at the Ship & she did indeed appear a wretched object. The Captain gave me leave to proceed immediately to St Vallery. I therefore set off in the diligence to Roan, [Rouen] but before I quitted the Ship, the Mate was put in prison for striking a Sailor & was in danger of being beaten by the Mob, who thought it but just & right for a Sailor to beat the Mate or Captain but the Sovreign People must not be touched by their former superiors. From Roan I passed through Dieppe & Ville D'Eu to St Vallery 22nd February 1793.

In the month of February 1793 I returned from a voyage up the Streights from Marseills to St Vallery Sur Somme. I was then Sixteen Years of Age, on my arrival I found that War had been declared between England &

France during my absence & that all communication was stopped between the two Countries. In consequence of which our remittances from England were stopped and we felt great inconvenience from the want of Money to which was added the Jealousy among our Neighbours from our being English & possessing the largest house in the town. It is well known how high the Spirit of Party at that time ran in France & what absurd tales of England & of Mr. Pitt's Emissaries were current & generally believed. We however contrived to get credit & avoid any very disagreeable dispute until April when the tradesmen of the Town became urgent for a settlement of their Accounts & not receiving what they required, they said we were spies of the English & living in a Sea Port the better to betray the Country. My Father became alarmed & returned Inland & went (I believe) to Paris.

I do not know what his plan was but he soon returned & settled in Pequiny, a Village between Abbeville & Amiens, Twelve miles from the latter town. Owing to some misunderstanding with my Father & the offer made me by an old Servant of supporting me for a short time in hopes of a Peace I remained at St Vallery. I had indeed another reason which was that at that time the French Nation was Arming in Mass & marching toward the frontiers.

Now St Vallery being a Sea Port, was considered an advanced Post & its population retained for its defence, I was consequently enrolled & stationed at a gun boat but as the gun boat was not built I received no pay (!). There being a Free Navigation School in the Town I attended it regularly every morning until the 22nd September when a Decree was passed by the National Convention for confining all Foreigners, particularly English. At this period of the French Revolution every Act of the Government was made to appear as arising from some great discovery of a Plot or Conspiracy & when put into execution by the Municipalities was always accompanied with as much Stage Effect as possible. In the town of St Vallery, besides myself & my only maternal Sister, who had also remained with an old servant of the Family, were two young English girls whose Aunt had married a Frenchman.

1793 September—Arrested

When the Decree arrived the Gens D'Armes were called out & a solemn procession set out to arrest us all. I was the only male, age 16, & my sister Margaret was scarcely 14. They seized me first. Now St. Vallery being out of the way of Grand Sights & Revolutionary Exhibitions such an opportunity was not to be missed. I was pinioned with straw bands rather I believe out of a joke than anything else & marched between two Soldiers, a Mob accompanying us to the house where my Sister lived. She they only arrested but did not insist on leading her about. They only gave her notice that she must prepare to go to prison. They left her to pack up what things she had & then the Gens D'Armes proceeded to the Uncle of the other Ladies living about a mile from the town.

The old gentleman remonstrated & said that having adopted them they ought to be considered French & the Municipal Officers seemed so little acquainted with what they were about that I have no doubt they would have released us all had it not been for losing their holiday & revolutionary Shew, they therefore did not insist on taking the two Young Ladies but returned with me singing *Ça Ira*[7] to the Town Hall where my Sister soon joined me. It was now twelve o clock & according to the French custom, dinner hour, but we had nothing to eat, indeed the Municipality had so far obeyed the decree of the Convention in arresting us, but they did not seem to know what further to do, they therefore held a consultation what further was to be done & (as there was no Prison at St Vallery) they determined on sending us to the Chief town of the District—<u>Abbeville</u>. A Gens D'Arme being ordered to conduct us was preparing so to do when my Sister complained of Hunger. She was only attended to by the Guard who gave us some bread. The Secretary, with a deputation from the Municipality went to my Lodgings & placed a Seal on all my Papers: these were only a few books on Navigation. About five o clock the Guard came to conduct us to Abbeville. He persuaded me not to take my clothes with me, giving me a dreadful account of the Prison discipline & saying I should be robbed of all I took with me & offering to take care of any thing which I might entrust to him & that I should have them safely returned to me when I regained my liberty, for he seemed to think that I could not remain in Prison long.

We were ordered to walk, but the distance being 12 Miles my sister complained that she was unable to perform the journey on foot. She was, however, answered that she must try. She begged to have a Horse by paying for it.

The Soldier went out to endeavour to hire a Horse but returned unsuccessful & we were obliged to proceed on foot at about half after five oclock before we reached the half way House, from want of food we were both much exhausted for I had eaten nothing & my Sister but little. She indeed was so much fatigued that I know not how she could have

---

[7] *Ça Ira*, the most popular revolutionary song, optimistic of success against the aristocrats and enemies of the French Revolution.

proceeded, when fortunately the Gentleman before mentioned, Uncle to the two English Ladies, had considered our situation & sent a Servant with a Horse, who overtook us here. It was now dark & the latter part of the way I felt much fatigue. On reaching Abbeville we went to the District House & to the Office of the Procureur Syndick to whom I was known. He gave an order for my being delivered over to the Concierge of the Hotel St Blimond.[8] I told him I had no food nor money to procure any. He said he would speak to Mounsieur Picot who, a Taylor remarkable for a due attendance on Religious duties, had now become an Infidel Jacobin, & for his Violent professions of love to his Country & hatred of Tyrants & the Bloody Pitt & Cobourg, was appointed Ruler of the Prisons.

1793 September—Imprisoned

At the Hotel St Blimond the Gens D'Arme delivered us over to the Concierge, who just introduced us into a Court Yard, shut the door upon us & left us. We walked about for some time in the dark, tired & hungry, but could find no way out of the Yard at length a Door opened & a light appeared, we went towards it, entered a Room in which we found a Guard of old Men sitting round a peat fire. Some Englishmen were playing at Cards on an old Butchers block which served for a Table & two or three bricks piled on each other to serve for seats. A few Spears served for Arms & to poke the fire with: these were the only furniture of the place.

An Englishman (whom I afterwards found to be a Sailor that is a Smugler) from Bolougne came up to me & asked whether I was a Countryman of his & on my saying that I was, he entered into conversation & told me that he had been confined already a fortnight. That he slept on the floor, without so much as a little straw or any covering, that he had but little money, yet he was not allowed any food. On hearing this I became uneasy as not knowing what would become of us, the whole amount of my Property being Three Livres & the Clothe's I had on. I had however put two clean shirts on.

My first thought was how I should keep my Clothes clean & in the morning I commenced operations with an attempt to wash a neck cloth, for which purpose I borrowed a bowl & began washing, but the more I washed the dirtier it seemed to become & at length, I rubbed holes in it. My sister had been placed with the Women in another part of the house.

[8] Hôtel: French term for a grand house, here a home of the Marquis de St. Blimond.

While I was at work some young English Girls, who had been in Convents for their Education, passed by & laughed at me but kindly undertook to wash for me which they did as long as we remained together.

My friend the Procureur Syndick had given an order to the Concierge to give me food at his expence until something could be settled by the District. I had hopes that this might have been continued by the Government but many other English who were in distress seeing that I was provided with food wanted to procure the same, mentioned my Name as being furnished with provision whilst they were starving. This brought out an order for One Pound of bread being issued to the Prisoners per day.

In the same Prison besides Fifty English, there were about a Hundred Nuns. The House in which we were confined was the Town Residence of the Marquis St Blimond, a Nobleman who had Emigrated. The House was old & large, but much out of Repair, on Entering by large folding doors we came into a Yard around which the House was built, we had a guard of old veterans who were paid 1/5 a day each, by the more Wealthy Prisoners, a Sentry was placed at the Gate and a space chalked out as bounds, which we were not to pass to hold conversations with Strangers at the Gate, but this was only a form for the Windows of the first floor opened onto the Place D'Arm & we could have jumped out without much difficulty.

My Clothes of which I had only those on my back, began to fail, & I procured a small quantity of Canvass from the Concierge, & sitting up in my room pulled my old Trowsers to Pieces & by them cut the Canvass into some kind of Shape. I made another pair. One day soon after my arrival A Person called to one of the English Sailors, when we were all in the Garden & asked him to shew him how to kill a Goose in the English fashion. He was desired to throw it over the wall. When it was received the Sailor chopped its head off & turning round said there it is Gillotined & now you may see how we shall all look by & bye. As there were quite as Many Women as Men present one of them fainted & another had fits, the Garden was soon in a state of the utmost confusion.

As the Winter approached, I felt the cold very severely for I had nothing but the floor of a Garret to sleep on. The House was old & the Rafters were double, one under the other, & coming down to the floor. We contrived to get a board, & putting it to stand against the lower rafter, formed a Kind of Weather board at about Two feet from the Wall, this in some measure kept the wind from me & before the Cold set in very strong a Government Depot was formed in the Stables belonging to our place of confinement & I got some straw.

There was a stove in the Room & by some accident we found a Trap door above our Room which led to the top of the House, in which was some old wood. One day they made me (as being the smallest) get thro' the door & I was Jumping on some old wood to break it when the wife of the Concierge came in & caught me. She put herself in a passion & enquired what we were doing. At first we were all silent but when she addressed herself to me, as the only one who could speak French, I answered that when we had destroyed the wood, we intended setting fire to the house. The Woman went immediately & brought in 'our little Taylor' as he was commonly called, & I was ordered with three others into a dungeon in the Common Goal, where we remained one day, after which we were brought back again.

We were now worse off than ever for fuel & felt the cold very severely. Yet we afterwards hit on a plan which was either to ring the bell violently or otherwise by some means, alarm the Guard, for it must be remembered that our Guard was composed of the oldest & poorest of the People & they were (no wonder) much alarmed at the times. On hearing the bell, they would all rush out together & we took advantage of the bustle to take their turf which was carried out of the Kitchen by a back door into the Garden & hid until an opportunity happened of carrying it into our Room. My Shoes & Stockings now were worn out which saved me some trouble in washing. I went barefoot. We were however very happy, which I have observed is often the case under circumstances of trouble, for the mind some how or other habituates itself to its condition & I do not know whether it does not particularly in youth enjoy difficulties. We found that one of our Guards understood a little of Music & could play on the Violin. He brought his Instrument & we gave him bread, a very small piece from each was enough to satisfy him, for the history of that time informs us that famine was known in France in all its horrors & therefore in some respects the Prisoner was better off than his Gaoler.

As there were many young Ladies we used to dance in the Guard room all Night. I believe I mentioned before that the Young Ladies were boarders in French Convents, how they came there I know not. We were induced to dance in this Way partly to keep ourselves warm & I must say that I felt so little my situation that I almost liked it, the truth is I fancied I was in love with one of the Young Women. We were, however, often brought to a sense of our Situation by the little Taylor who amused himself by alarming us. Sometimes he would come & say that we must prepare for Paris at other times, which touched me more, he said that the Men were to be sent to one Prison & the Women to another. At first these reports frightened us but after a time we found him out & laughed at him. Our Guards would sometimes insult us. One of them, at one time, made some insulting remark on the English, on which I pushed him backwards into the fire. He of course was indignant & threatened all the Vengeance of the great Nation. He however never took any farther Notice of it, probably fearing that he might be removed from his Station of Guard.

Another time we were all dancing & in high good humour when several of our Guards were asleep, we blacked their faces with oil from the lamp by this means a coolness arose between the Guard & us & we were obliged to keep more to ourselves. It became necessary to think of fuel, for an hour or two each day. One of our plans was to exercise with a Pike or Halbert. At the word <u>Charge</u> come down to the charge with the Pike, advance against a Turf in the Corner & then Shoulder it off to another behind us, this was always performed in the dusk before the lamp was lighted, we could of course not get much fuel this way & it may appear extraordinary that I use the word *we* as if all the English were concerned, but I must observe that I only allude to my own immediate Companions in the same Room, who were like myself utterly without Money. Most of the other Prisoners had Private Friends. Two in the room with myself were I believe Smugglers. That is one a Sailor Smuggler & one a Landsman receiver of the goods- one a Journeyman Stationer from Leeds, One a Gentleman's Servant & myself. If I am not much mistaken the Smuggler was Johnson, afterwards so well known by his Escape from the King's Bench.

Our room was a Garret but of only one Story high, with Garret Windows looking towards one of the Great Squares of the City, the Place D'Arme. In this Square whatever Troops were in Abbeville this was their place of Exercise, & all Rejoicings & National Fetes were celebrated under our Eye, at that time the French were fond of Spectacles such as a renewal of the Oath &c &c, which was continually happened of all of which we had a commanding View.

On the 22nd of December [1793] the Fete de la Raison was celebrated in this Square. The Intent was to Shew the Superiority of Reason to Religion.[9] A horrid Monster called Superstition was Painted on Canvass

---

[9] A policy of the French Revolution was dechristianization, enacted October 21, 1793, stripping of church lands, property and artefacts, and the non-juring of priests, first celebrated as a cult of the Goddess Reason at Notre Dame, Paris on November 10, 1793.

& a funeral Pile prepared, on which little Images of the Virgin & Crucifixes & all Manner of Popish trifles were hung, when a Woman of noted bad Character, an Actress & Mistress to Andre Dumont, personating the Goddess of Reason set fire to the Pile & in a Moment the Monster was consumed, the Stage Effect was to shew how quickly Superstition that is religion vanished before Reason. Yet at this very Fete & in presence of the Representative, numberless relicts were snatched from the flames by the lower ranks & preserved in spite of the Guards who perhaps felt a secret horror at the act they were employed in. Several of these very Images were shewn in our Prison in the course of the Evening & our Guards joined in cursing the Nation, meaning the Government, & wishing for the old order of things.

1793 December—Free but Pennyless

While this Mockery of Reason was carrying on, my Name was called & on descending I found my little Taylor who said that Reason required that at my Age I should not be answerable "for the Sins of your Country." I was therefore to be released. I answered that release could be of no service to me as I could not return to England & I had no means of supporting myself. The Man appeared kind & said take your Liberty at any Rate & then come back again, you can then do what you like. Seeing that my Sister, to whom the same offer was made was very anxious to accept it, I went with him to receive my Liberty in form.

He conducted me with my Sister & many other Prisoners both French & English to the largest Church in the Town, where 1 found a platform Erected in the great aisle, on which stood Andre Dumont Representative of the People, on his right hand stood the Woman above mentioned acting Goddess of Reason, behind her was an Actress, whom 1 had seen on the stage, prompting her how to act. Dumont was making a speach as I entered, he was talking of the Harlequens among the Priests while he at the same time with three large Ostrich Feathers in his hat, was out Harlequenning them. He said that there was neither Hell nor Heaven, neither Resurrection, Angel or Spirit. He said in particular that a fate attended us but he knew not from whence, or how it happened. That if God ruled the Earth with Justice, why did Louis 14th die in his bed & Louis 16 on the Scaffold. I thought & why do you stand here & why does Robespiere live & Barrère Hollot D'Herbois.[10] When Dumont had finished his address, the Prisoners who were to be released were brought up to the Platform on which stood Dumont, the Goddess of Reason & the Actress prompter. We were to go up on one side, pass over the Stage & descend on the other. To each one, some speech was address & the Goddess of Reason dressed like Minerva with a Spear in her hand touched us as in a Pantomime & our fetters fell, the only difference, that I remarked between Reason & Wisdom was that the former had on her Crest a Cock, Gallus instead of the owl, & on the Point of her Spear was the Cap of Liberty. When she moved her Train was held by four of the Municipality (Corporation) & as she passed there was an affectation of falling on the Knee in imitation of the passing of the Host in former times to the Sacrament. I have since observed that the affectation of devotion as in kneeling while a stanza of a song is sung is not peculiar to France. I have observed in England an appearance of the same devotion whilst Invoking Apollo in the hymn to that false Deity. The Woman personating this deity was an abandoned Woman, Wife to an old Man, a General Tachfire. I had the Honor of the accolade Fraternel & was declared free but at the Moment the stage shewed symptoms of giving way & I was hurried off. The Goddess however followed & I had more Notice that the rest, I was embraced & Symptoms of Pity appeared in her Goddessship for such a Youth. She condescended to ask whether I would serve the Nation on board a French Ship. I said I would never fight against my Country. Dumont spoke in favour of my Country but said it was governed by a Tyrant. I answered that there were more Tyrants than one & that Tyrant as our Ruler was, he had not shut up the French Residents in England in Prison. Dumont replied that He ought to have done so. I passed on & returned to my Prison not knowing what else to do. Having related to the English Prisoners what had passed, I asked advice & acknowledged that 1 must go on board a French ship or starve. No advice which I could follow being offered, I joined myself to the other English released, who were all of the lowest rank viz- my Companions, the Smugglers, Pocket Book Maker & Gentlemans Servant. With some others we left our Prison, the Smuggler, Pocket Book Maker, Servant & myself thinking that we ought to get to England in some way or other, but we were not one in heart. The Servant had formed Connection with a French Woman the Daughter of a Farmer who could not speak a word of English or she of French and when we came to

---

[10] Jean-Marie Collot d'Herbois (1749 –1796) was a French actor, dramatist, and revolutionary, a member of the Committee of Public Safety during the Reign of Terror—2,000 executions. Exiled to French Guiana, died of yellow fever.

France 1790-95

Fermontier in the Forest of Cressy, he would go no further, but at the same time he spaliated [?] his defection, by saying that he could escape much easyer by seizing a Boat, on the coast near, this broke up our Party, some engaged with Farmers in the Neighbourhood & I returned to Abbeville again to my Prison.

On my Arrival I was allowed my bread ration as usual & after a time a Captain Forster or I believe Lieu^t Forster, offered me his assistance, that is offered me food for my Services. With this Captain F. I lived until February. I must have been of use to him, as I was not considered as a Prisoner but could go in & out whenever I pleased, this others could not do, the confinement of the English was now much relaxed & many got their liberty some by bribing the Taylor, other by Sick Certificate which was readily given by the Medical Men. One Lady wishing to gain her Liberty had written a Letter to Mr Pijot the Taylor to which she had attached a Silver Snuff Box, but before she found an opportunity of presenting it, she lost it in the Garden, where it was found by some one who to make mischief, posted the Letter against the door of the Yard during the night. This caused suspicions amongst the English which broke out into a degree of Violence & Enmity never got over while I remained with them. This disputatious spirit led several families to wish even for French company sooner than English & probably in consequence of representations made to the Municipality, for our Taylor began now to lose his Credit. Forster was removed to the Old Colledge of the City, now abandoned by its Scholars & Professors, the Nation wanting the Services of the first in the field & Pensions of the latter to pay their Troops.

A Charge was now made on the English for a considerable Sum by way of further remuneration for the Guards who had been employed & the plea was the great lenity shewn us, whereas they, the French, had been led to believe that the English had put the french Representatives to death at Toulon, yet they had not put us to death. It had no effect to say, "well then according to your own Account, we were unjustly confined." their answer was, "well the thing is done & the Men must be paid." The English had a meeting in consequence & Sir Digby Dent, an English Admiral being the one looked up to decided that it ought not to be submitted to & so it was determined, but the Municipality frightened the old Man & he paid his Quota, the rest soon submitted on the promise that we should all be immediately released, as I really had no money, so had nothing to pay.

The Release did not however happen as it had been promised. In this Colledge there were some day students with whom I formed acquaintance & by their means was enabled to read in this Library in which were a great Number of books, all those originally belonging to the College & those of different Monasterys & of the Emigres. One of the Professors gave me permission to sleep in a Chamber of the Establishment & sent me a Pailass & Blanketts so that had I had food enough I should have been happy. I had but half a Pound p^r Diem.

Capt Forster assisted me a little & some of the Scholars also, but I did not enjoy these comforts long, for the Colledge was cleared of Prisoners & I, among others sent to a New House, the very next door to our Former abode, the Hotel St Blimond. Here I got a room to myself in which was an old Bedstead & I got still what books I wanted from the Colledge, but now we began now to be terrified by Robespier's actions, for at this time, France was in a dreadful state & this wretch was at the height of his Power.

There had been a general Massacre in the Prisons of Nante's where two English families had lost their lives: even Infants had been murdered when under two Months old but the History of this time will no doubt record these Cruelties. We were of course much alarmed. I had opportunities of seeing the Newspapers every Night, where in I read the decrees & I found that we were not in much danger of being put to death by any other process & the Prisoners had made up their minds to resist to the last any sudden attack & we had also hopes of being able to escape to the Forest of Crecy.

At this time a Prisoner was brought in, who had been confined in Amiens & he gave a circumstantial Account of the death of my Father. He described his Person, his Family & related some part of his History, where he had lived &c. I could not doubt the truth of his Assertion for what interest could he have in deceiving me. He had never written or sent me a Message since we had parted altho I had several times written to him & I began to fear that the Report was true. I wrote now to my Mother in law but received no answer from her. The Man who had related the Account of my Father's death now mentioned the Name of an Englishman in the same Prison whom he recollected as an Acquaintance of my Father's, upon which I wrote this Man whose name was Dawson & was answered by my Father himself, who said that he had never received any letter. from me.

A Report being raised in our Prison of the death of Robespiere, [July 1794] we were dreadfully alarmed for we had heard such reports having been raised before, as traps to observe how the Prisoners would behave. When we first heard this it was whispered among the Prisoners with some kind of pleasure, but we very soon began to doubt the truth & then our anxiety was to escape the imputation of having raised the report for it having been whispered in confidence it was difficult to trace it, but when the Post arrived it was confirmed with a great outcry against him & his Accomplices & particularly charging him with cowardice—but we shall hear more truly what led to his death at some future time. After the death of this Tyrant our Prisons were no longer Watched and altho we had no formal release, we walked in & out as we pleased.

This winter was very severe & many poor died from Cold. I lived with Captain Forster who contrived, by means of Jews to get some Money from England but I believe at a very great loss, the cold was exceedingly severe & I remember a Hamper of Wine being frozen altho packed in straw & placed under the Sideboard in the dining room. We had a Regiment of Hessian Prisoners in the Town with whom I made acquaintance. The old Soldiers had served in America. The famine was also very severe. I have stood for hours at a Baker's door in a Mob like the Crowd endeavouring to enter the London Play house on an extraordinary Evening & no one could get a single Pound of Bread without an order from the Municipality for to enable the Magistrates to give the Proper orders every family was registered & the Number & Names affixed to the doors of their houses in some conspicuous place, together with their ages. We were only allowed a quarter of a Pound of Black bread for each Individual. A Member of the Convention being in the Town told the poor People that they ate too much & a Poor Woman calling out that she was starving. He said I myself can live on an ounce a day. They shouted out, "we shall starve." "Well," said he, "If you die of Hunger, you will not die of the Plague." What would an English mob have said to this? The French Mob was silent.

1795 Escape: Aged 18

My situation was now very unpleasant & I began to meditate on attempting an Escape, many thoughts came into my head but I should perhaps have feared taking such a step had not my Father passed thro' Abbeville on his way to S^ت Vallery. He told me that he was determined to try to leave France & asked me to join him which I readily agreed to as I could not run the greater risk through remaining at Abbeville.

My Father's plan was to go to St Vallery & endeavour to raise Money on his Property there & succeeded but in what way I know not for I was not in his confidence. At St Vallery, my Father sent for my Sister but received her in such an extraordinary Manner that I was not in the least surprised at her declining to accompany him. I wished to have had some private conversation with her but he would not allow it, calling on me to follow him or he would disown me as his Son. I followed him not being aware of the Short Stay that he intended making & hoping that I might find another opportunity of speaking to my Sister but on leaving her it seems that he had finished his business at St Vallery for he departed for Abbeville & without delaying there passed on to Pequiny where his family had resided since the English had regained their liberty.

[NOTE *Value of Bread* has: she at once returned to the friendly nuns, one of whom was in St Vallery, & I saw her no more in France.]

We reached Pequinay on Sunday at 11 oclock in the Morning & so anxious were we to commence our retreat that every article in the House was either packed up or sold before Night & a Covered Cart hired to proceed to Paris at day light in the Morning.

Copy of the Pequigny Passport transcribed from the French:

> The Republic and La Mort District of Amiens
> Department of the Somme
> Canton and Municipality of Pequigny.

Allow freely to pass Henry Sherwood, fils, resident in the commune of Pequigny, district and department as afore said—aged 17 years, stature four feet, ten inches, hair and eyebrows chestnut, forehead medium, eyes grey, nose short, mouth medium, chin ordinary, countenance "pale"

> Has declared himself a traveller in the department.

[In *The Value of Bread* is another copy of a Pequigny Passport translated from the French:]

... in the department of the Somme & other departments of the French Republic & asks our help & assistance in the Canton of Friburg.
Delivered in the Maison Commune of the said Pequinay,
This day the 28th March 3rd year of the Republic. The said Henry Sherwood signed in our presence
Sanguir Agent Beguin off
M Sherwood fils
Montigny off. M
Have seen the citizen Enri Churrood
A Roussa 30th March Jean off M of the Guard

[A third similar document, in Darton, F. J. Harvey, ed. (1910). *The Life and Times of Mrs Sherwood*. London: Wells Gardner, Darton & Co., is a passport to travel to Amiens.]

I was despatched before at four in the morning to Amiens & the remainder of the Family came up in the Afternoon. We were badly off for food there being no bread publickly sold. Amiens was full of Prisoners of War, mostly English & Hessians. The 87th Regiment which was taken at Bergen-op-zoon was there besides many detachments & a considerable number of Officers of other Corps.

On the 1st April 1795 we left Amiens by the Paris road. I was not told where we were going & my heart misgave, I remember on reaching a hill near Amiens, & looking back on the Town, I thought of the day & wished it might not prove to be a fool's day to us. We travelled about 30 miles this day, in the same Pequiny Cart & endeavoured to stop at a farm house, but they would not receive us except we had our own bread with us. After some time we succeeded in getting admittance into another Farmer's house whose Inhabitants appeared to be friends to the Exiled King, & I believe, were inclined to receive us on that account.

The 2nd April. We moved and reached Clermont at night. Here we saw a fine old Castle on a Hill & the Duke de FitzJames's house. The fine Park & beautiful Woods which once surrounded it were greatly damaged by the wanton mischief of the Republicans.

3rd of April to Chantilly. Here in the Palace of the Prince of Condé was established a Pottery by an Englishman of the name of Potter. We did not see the Palace, it being full of English Prisoners.

1795 Paris

4th April we entered Paris by the Port St Denis. No questions were asked us at the Barrier nor indeed were our Passports once enquired for on the road. We were however informed that we should not be allowed to quit Paris without them. Paris did not appear to advantage as famine raged, we could get no Lodgings & the Bakers 'doors were surrounded by Mobs waiting their turns to receive the small allowance of bread granted to each Cityzen by paying for it. At length we were admitted into an Inn in the Rue St Denis but we had not a bit of bread the whole time we were in Paris which was three days. The City of Paris did not appear to me to be any thing equal to London. The streets are narrow & no flagged Foot Paths. The houses, in the Part where I was had no stairs case within but you went up by Stairs on the outside of the House uncovered & very slippery in rainy Weather. But the time in which I saw Paris was very unfavourable, we were all in agitation, for the horrors of the Revolution were by no means over. The very day we arrived Twelve Deputies of the Convention had been arrested. I saw the Gardens of the Thuilieries but here all was litter, the trees cut down & the basins of Water empty, the Statues defaced under a kind of Canopy lay a death like Ghastly Image of Voltaire crowned with flowers. The windows of the Louvre were all broken & Moss growing round them.

Our principal business in Paris was to obtain Passports for England, for which purpose we attended the Comittée de Salut Publick, but there were so many Persons on the same Errand, there appeared but little chance of our getting an Audience of any of the Members. By the Advice of a Friend of my Fathers, an Italian whom he had known formerly in London, we were determined to slip out of Paris if possible & make our way to Switzerland for as we had reached Paris without trouble we might in like manner reach Geneva. His advice was to take our Passage in the Boat which went regularly between Paris & Auxere in Burgundy every day. My brother James & myself accordingly took our Passage in this Boat.

My Father & the rest of the family having got out of the City by means of the Boat, soon after went on shore & took a Carriage, leaving my Brother & myself to continue our way. It rained very hard at the time of the Vessel's getting under weig^h & there being nearly 200 people on board, Market People & others, our Passports were never inquired for. Had they been asked for, I am afraid they would not have been deemed sufficient, as they were from Pequiny & simply allowed us to Travel, without any determinate Point. Indeed I now wonder how we could have ventured with such deficient documents.

I have often said that we could get no bread but I had with me a Large Cheese on which my Brother & myself subsisted never tasting bread for two days or indeed any kind of Vegetable, but simply cheese & I now know the value of Bread. At the end of two days I got on Shore & procured some bread at a farm house but only four Pounds weight.

We were four days in reaching Auxerre, 90 miles from Paris, we travelled night & day. This 4 lb of Bread was all that my Brother & myself had. We left Auxerre the same day on which we arrived & I firmly believe that the want of bread was now the impulse for my mother in law [stepmother] seemed so much overpowered, that she would readily have remained wherever the Sole of her foot could have found rest.

We passed on to Chalons sur Saone, a most delightful Country where wine was in Abundance but no bread. My remark, written about a year afterwards, was If there had been bread we should not now have been in England. From Auxerre to Chalons we travelled in a Tilted Cart & on our arrival at the latter place, the same man undertook to carry us to Geneva not much more than 40 miles for <u>one Thousand Livres</u>. The sum appeared enormous but the Livres in Paper was now sunk to so little that I have bought 100 Livres for a Small Crown or 2/6. When we had agreed for this Sum & provided for our food for the Road, we should reach Geneva without a farthing in our possession.

In our Journey to Geneva a most extraordinary providential circumstance happened. We had not advanced far from the Town towards Evening when we came to a fork in the Road. Our Auxerre Carter had trusted to meeting People on the Road but, no one appearing, he at length determined on taking the left hand & what was more curious we met no one on the road for several miles. The first house that we came to confirmed us in the Idea which we had held for some time from the appearance of the Road, that we had taken the wrong one, but it was too late to turn that night & we took up our rest at this house, it being a small Publick house, our Coachman & the People in the Common Room having well considered the advantages & disadvantages of a Return we found in the Morning it was settled we should continue our Rout & pass over Mount Jura by a more direct pass altho a more difficult one & I have reason to think that by this Providential mistake we were able to get out of France. We approached the foot of the Mountains before Evening & I was astonished at their height. I really thought it impossible to pass over them. I now speak from Memory, having no written remarks. They seemed like a Wall, to touch the Cloud. We began to ascend by a very circuitous Road cut out of the Solid Rock, we were obliged to walk & carry stones in our hands to prop up the wheels at every short distance. The Precipice on one side was so perpendicular that I dared not approach that side. We had far rather our Carter had taken two additional Horses, but I think that if it had not ventured too far to return we should have gone back, but we got over much better than we expected, for the road was in very good repair & the foundations good. At night we were on the Top of one Range & we found that Maize was the only corn grown here.

Our next days journey was short but very fatiguing for my Mother in law for her timidity was such as not to allow her to ride yet she had never been accustomed to walk, & her appearance was truly distressing. In this manner, we were three days before we descended into Switzerland. I can only remember that in one Place, we were placed in a long room with Beds running along the side like Pigeon holes, at the two sides or more properly like the Cabins on board a Dover Packet boat.

The Women wore Caps edged with fur with something like a Knitting Needle running on one side of them with little Balls at each end fitted with something like a Child's rattle & from some conversation that I held with them they appeared to be much alarmed at the idea of Spirits. These Mountains are still covered with Snow altho the Valleys in France which we had just left were in full Spring & the heat rather excessive. The sudden change from one Valley in particular was very striking. We had approached so near to the Mountains that the lower ones hid the higher & the appearance seemed as if we were only under ordinary Hills. In the Valley the Cows were uneasy from the number of flies & the reflection of the Sun against the bare rock was excessive, but on proceeding up the road we found Snow & before long the Snow began to fall with a Cold East Wind, biting in the extreme.

The inhabitants appeared very very poor & were dressed in fur. On the top of one of the Hills I remarked a small round Tower of Castle, it was remarkable as we scarcely ever lost sight of it for three days, it is said to have been built by Charles the Bold, Duke of Burgundy, in his Wars with the Switzers. When we reached the most advanced post of the French, there was a custom house but the Officer's duty seems to have been restricted to the examination of Boxes &c. They did not stop us but sent us to the Mayor to revise our Passports. The Mayor was out at supper & we passed on. It was an accident more than any thing else, our road which we had taken by mistake was thro a Country not only in itself unfavourable for Military movements, but it lead to a petty State entirely under the control of France, Geneva.

Our first thought in ordering the Cart on, was really without consideration but merely that the Cart might have some head way before we followed, but waiting a long time for the Mayor, we strolled on, scarcely knowing whether we were right or wrong until we had cleared the Frontier. The road to the highest elevation from the Village was scarcely three miles yet it took us four hours to ascend. I had never at that time seen such Mountains & was naturally much alarmed at the frightful precipices. My Brother was so so as to be incapable of walking, & we were obliged to put him into the Cart where he soon fell asleep.

The Road was narrow & in general round the Mountain, the perpendicular side was of immense height & a very few steps receeding would have precipitated the Cart from top to bottom, we carried stones in our hands to prop the cart whenever the Horse appeared to give way. At the top of this Mountain we saw numbers of Goats. The Vegetable productions: a very small quantity of Grass was peeping from under the Snow & forests of Fir trees. On the Summit of these Mountains we met a number of French Men driving Horses. They addressed us civilly with the usual salutation of Citoyen. My father could not bear this but said Mounsieur, if you please. & fancying himself clearly out of France, he pulled his Cockade[11] out of his Hatt & jumped upon it, a most inconsiderate act for we were in the power of these Men in this place which, altho not french, was certainly no other Country & we ought to have known that France controled Geneva & indeed, all Switzerland & a Band of Men in a Border district are always to be feared. They however only laughed, which shewed that the days of Terror, if indeed Terror was ever the order of the day amongst the Soldiers, was at an end.

1795 Switzerland, Destitute

The snow became now very deep, but even in this elevated Region we found a Swiss Village of St Cierge. It was Sunday & here the change was so sudden it could scarcely be believed. We were stopped by a kind of Militia with Yellow & Red Cockades who would not permit us to move thro the Village until the Protestant Service was over. I, poor foolish

---

[11] Cockade: a knot of ribbon pinned to the side of hats or lapels to denote loyalty; white for the Bourbon aristocracy, green but later red and blue for the French Revolutionaries; later giving rise to the red, white and blue of the tricoluer. At this time in Europe armies wore a colour to denote nationality.

fellow, thought this nonsense & was for abusing the Arbitrary Government.

Paper Money now was of no use & we were obliged to sell some of our Cloaths for food but here as elsewhere the Sunday was only kept by the laws & not by the People. They would buy & sell on that day. After Church we proceeded & on leaving the Village, which I found was on the descent of the Hill, we found the same kind of road as we had come up from, I believe Morges & we rapidly descended from Snow & Ice & fir trees to sun & warmth & Cherries in blossom into a very Garden, delightful in itself but more so from Contrast. Here we found fine Roads with Gentlemens carriages on them. So compleat a contrast could scarcely be conceived even had we dropped from the Clouds, no Paper Money, no dirty Citoyen's but something like regularity. But even here, every body wore a Cockade & too many had the appearance of Soldiers. We were now in the district of Lausanne & from what we now heard we wished not to leave it, except in the direct road to Germany, but unfortunately, Geneva had been pointed out as the point most easily attained & we had formed such arrangements that it became necessary to go there to find friends to enable us to reach home. I believe we had not the value of half a Crown at this time. The reports spread about here were not very consolatory. Geneva was represented as in a State as bad as France itself, which proved too true but we had no alternative & we proceeded. Towards evening, at the turning of a Road we were saluted with the French Challenge of Qui vive & saw the Tri colour flag. The surprize was great, for with oceans of advice & cautions no body had ever hinted that we must again pass thro France on our way to Geneva, but we might have known by the Map that the French Republick reached to the Borders of the Lake of Geneva. The French Officers were very civil & did not give us much trouble, they frightened me a little by pretending to suppose I was a French Recruit endeavouring to escape, but on my speaking English with all my might we were allowed to pass, the ferocity of the French soldiers was always much less than that of the Jacobins & even of the Town's People.

The gates were shut before we could reach Geneva & we halted at the English Hotel without a demi Ecu in our pockets, more than this we owed 1200 Livres to the Carter. To travellers at home this might have caused some uneasiness, & if I said it did not trouble me I should say what was not true but we had met with so many difficulties that we were not overpowered, at the same time I have remarked that I have often met with difficulties & also diseases. I have found that towards the end of your troubles you seem to feel acutely either disappointment or pain, probably because you had made up your mind to have no more of either. In the morning, my Father proceeded into the City & introduced himself to a Mr Mare, a Banker, this Gentleman, on hearing Names of Genevese mentioned by my Father, as being in some degree of intimacy, particularly the name of Lucadou, who was in partnership with Mr Troughton my Grandfather's most intimate Friend, advanced us sufficient money to pay our Charioteer & further lent us a little House in the East of the Town about ½ a mile from the City overlooking the Aar. The Bank on which this House was situated over hang the River, almost perpendicularly & on the other side in the Territory of Savoy, was a french Camp.

The Government of Geneva are always so very jealous that there is no stranger admitted to remain in the Territory above a certain time & now that time is restricted to a Week, but by the exertions of Mr Mar we were permitted to remain a Month. The City is very much confined many of the passages vaulted or at least narrow passages under houses. The Rhone running thro it is very delightful, a beautiful transparent green looking Stream. We could not judge much of the Manners of the People for the State was in disorder & the influence of the French Revolution had rendered it a very unpleasant spot to dwell in, but indeed I may accuse the French Revolution unjustly, for I am afraid that the horrors of Democracy had their chief Defenders & promoters in Geneva before they reached France. They have lost their Religion once so strict, they have destroyed their Churches & also their publick Monuments, one Representing a Duc de Rohan, merely because the French required it, & they now acknowledge that they will soon be obliged to submit to France which indeed they now do & be incorporated into the Great Nation. They are indeed treated very ill by the French, who allow no Provisions to be brought into the Territory, which as they command the whole surrounding country, they can prevent.

The Lake is a most beautiful piece of Water nearly sixty Miles long by about Twelve in breadth at Lausanne. Geneva itself is situated at the extreme point where the Lake issues into the Rhone. In old Books which I have read it is asserted that the Rhone runs thro the Lake without mingling its waters, which seems ridiculous as the Water of the Rhone is very shallow & seems nothing more than the overflowing of the Lake, it is true that Rivers run into it one even called the Rhone, but there are many others. It is also said, in these Books, that a commerce is carried on between Geneva & Lyons by the Rhone. Now the Rhone is not navigable within 12 Miles of Geneva, you may walk over it up to your knees.

We were alarmed one Night by the Ringing of Bells, the Beating of Drums &c but as the Drawbridges were drawn up we could not ascertain the Reason & we were not allowed to enter the City until Noon the next day when we found that Two of the Republican or Jacobin party had been killed during a Riot, but the Rioters had escaped before the Gates were shut. No Persons were allowed to enter the Gates without Cockades in their Hatts & I was obliged to Mount a French one. Twelve Young Men of the first families were banished for wearing as we were told Green Handkerchiefs.

6th of June [1795]. Our first remittance from England arrived, affairs were in so unsettled a state that we were ordered to leave the City. Our Friend, the Merchant, Muonsieur Desaellar, being unwilling to interest himself in our favor to procure a longer pass. We were therefore obliged to leave. The first day's Journey was most delightful, the Season of the Year fine, the fruit ripe & the Lake of Geneva unruffled on our right most delightful. The Alps appearing on the other side of the Lake covered with snow & the Jura Mountains on the Left & the intermediate space most beautiful. The lower aclevities of the Hills were covered with Vines & Mulberries & not a wave on the Lake. I do not know whether the resemblance was just but I thought of Catalonia as I had seen it from a very imperfect view, as we sailed along its Shores. We had, according to my calculation, fifteen Hundred miles to travel before we could reach England & I believe all the Money we possessed for 9 of us was less than £20. Soon after leaving Geneva we came to the French Guard Room where we had been stopped on our way to Geneva but it was now abandoned, The troops having advanced into Savoy.

This night we halted at a most delightful place called Rolle, on the banks of the Lake, the weather was fine which, of course will help to make every place delightful. I do not know whether I have a perfect recollection of places, but it struck me as being like Sittingbourne in Kent, yet Rolle was a compleat level & I think Sittingbourne is on rising Ground. Here, for the first time, we observed the white Cockade of Royalist Frenchmen worn in publick. We also saw the Green emblem of Aristocratic Geneva, for to this place the Banished Genevese had resorted in Numbers & the Towns people spoke with great detestation of the French & Genevan Jacobins.

Dined at Lausanne, a fine old town in the Commencement of the Hilly Country. The Streets very steep & narrow with fountains of Water & a running stream in the Centre; a most delightful old Town. We left the Lake about a Mile before we reached the town. The rise of the Hill presented most beautiful views. We slept at Meudon in the Pays de Vaux, a very old town taken from Duke of Savoy by the Swiss about 100 Years since, with fine fountains in the Streets & a Stream of Water running along the Middle. The fountains having a Statue of some eminent Patriot standing in the Centre. We slept in the Ancient Town Hall in a fine old Room, where was an old Picture & many old French inscriptions relating to the Capture of the City.

The next morning passed the Lake of Morat & saw the Monument enclosing the Bones of Charles the Bold of Burgundy & his Army or said to be so by the Natives which I doubt. The dress of the Peasants here is quite different from that of the Genevese. The Women wearing their Hair drawn tight from their foreheads & plaited backwards into two tails hanging down, with the addition of ribbon, to their heels. We passed a curious hanging Bridge over a most rapid River, built of wood & covered over. The Cart going over caused a tremendous motion which, added to the noise of the Torrent below, was rather terrific, it was late in the evening & we saw but little of the Bridge, indeed I should scarcely have remarked any thing extraordinary in the Bridge, only that we were told the next day that it was so. I think, however, that the Bridge must have been very long. The German language began to be spoken to the north of the Bridge. A great many English names were written on the Windows & Walls of the little Inn & we were told many English came to see the Bridge.

This morning to Berne, where we only staid to procure a Passport from the English Chargé D'affair & proceeded after Dinner. I was much pleased with Berne, the Situation delightful & the cleaness of the Streets surprizing. The Prisoners working in irons to keep them clean. A broad Stream of water running rapidly thro the Center of each with the Customary Fountains at short distances.

On leaving the City & ascending a Hill we had a fine View of it with the River almost surrounding it like a Horse shoe. From Hence to Basle, we passed thro a rugged mountainous road but money running short & not knowing where to procure more, I confess that the views were only a very secondary consideration.

The Rhine at Basle is a Noble River but I know not its breadth, having other things to think of for here we had intended stopping until our Banker at Geneva should have sent after us the next remittance from England, but, what we had expected for some time now became certain viz that there was no resting place for an Englishman in Basle. The Influence of the French was so great that no exertion on our part could obtain permission for our remaining more than Two days. Our money was now gone, & we went to every Banker in the Town to endeavour to get Cash for a Bill but they had been so accustomed to the distresses of the French Emigrés that we could not succeed in procuring Money for Bills, at last one Banker advanced six Guineas but he would not take a Bill saying that if it was paid in London it was well, if not he should lose without regret. The Austrian Ambassador advanced Ten Guineas on a Bill.

1795 Germany

We left Basle for Friborg being the nearest Town of any consequence on the road Home. Soon after crossing the Rhine we passed a camp of Austrians & could not help remarking the difference of behaviour between these Men & the Swiss. The Austrians were very civil & kind, the Swiss like the English Sulky & Rude. Liberty may be good for the Individuals but it does not make the possessors amiable. The Swiss appeared to think they were superior to the rest of the World who were Slaves in comparison to themselves. At Mid day we passed the Prince of Condé's army, our Resident Colonel Crawford was absent but it was pleasing to see the Politeness of the French Royalists.[12] Reached Friburg in the Brisgaw in the Evening.

In Friburg German is spoken & as we were unacquainted with the Language we had great difficulty in making ourselves understood. Here my Father proposed remaining until we heard from Geneva & he also drew Bills on England & gave them to a Banker who expected to have answers in the course of a Month. We took lodging for that time, but were obliged to pay in advance & having little money we felt the extreme of hunger before the Remittance from England came, for we never received any letter from Geneva.

I often walked into the Cornfields & Vineyards & eat the Ears of corn & green grapes. We sold all our Clothes & were litterally starving. From some hopes of getting relief from Colonel Crawford who was with the Prince of Condé's Army, I walked over there 12 Miles, but Colonel Crawford was at Frankford. I slept in the Guard Tent and returned.

On my arrival I found that an order had been received from the Governor to leave the Town in 24 Hours, our distress was now at its height, without Money, with 5 small children & not understanding the language, I wished myself back in France again, for there we had bread. I wandered into the Fields not knowing what to do. At length I returned

---

[12] Prince de Condé's army of émigré French aristocrats and followers was formed to fight the revolutionaries, funded by Britain at this time.

home & found that my Father had determined on going with his family to the Governor's & we set off in procession, having Mr. Wickham's passport with us. On being admitted we were shewn into a small room. The Governor soon came to us with a most savage frown, he asked what we did in Fribourg. He had our Passport in his hand & of course knew what we did there. My Father was obliged to go thro his history which having finished, the Governor began in French, "By order of His Imperial Majesty, whose Person I represent, no Stranger is to remain in a fortified Town without the Governor's permission." We explained that on our arrival we had produced our passports at the Gate & from our ignorance of the language we were not aware of any further necessity of applying to him. My Mother began to cry, upon which he slapped her on the Shoulder & in good English desired her to fear nothing & Graciously gave us permission to remain. He even lent us ten shillings until our remittance might arrive.

We were again taken before the Governor a few days later on Suspicion of taking plans of the Fortifications, but the plan appearing to be a very rude sketch of the Church, we were again released. We now felt extreme famine & had no bread in the House when the Governor's wife called & seeing our distress, sent us a Louis d'or & a Crown, when this was gone & no letter from England, we were one whole day without food. On application to the Banker, he for the first time advanced a Louis & seeing that my Mother had no Shoes on, he sent her a Pair. The next Post day I waited for the Post's arrival but no letter & I gave up all with a heavy heart. I called on the Banker, not expecting any thing, but I found £22-10 sent to me, but nothing to my Father. His Bill having been refused by my Grandfather's Executor.

No time was to be lost for if we remained the Money we had would scarcely last until we could write again to England & receive an answer & we had given up all thought of hearing from Geneva. My Father determined on advancing to Frankford immediately we should at any Rate get more money among the English & nearer home. He bought an old Landau for £6- & hiring two Post Horses we started immediately, having £15 Louis D'ors in cash. I, however, prevailed on the banker to risk £5 on a Bill of mine, with this Twenty Pounds, nine of us proceeded on a journey of 1000 miles.

A delightful country to Offenburg: here my Mother wished to pass the Night but the Innkeeper said that he had no room, probably glad to get rid of so large & apparently, so poor a family. It was fortunate on the whole for it forced us forward & altho we suffered for the Moment, when we awoke in the Morning from our Nod in the Carriage, tho tired we were between 20 & 30 miles nearer home, with the Money which our Night's Lodging would have cost us, in our Pocketts, the Young Children did not feel it.

We saw Strasburg Steeple rose & all by the light of the Moon. This is said to be the highest Steeple in the World. In the morning we entered Rastad the Capital of the Prince of Baden apparently a fine City. In the Market a large statue of the Prince of Baden, a General at the time of our Marlborough, here they refused to carry us on with two Horses, but a French Emigré wanting two the same way with some difficulty we got on.

From Rasted to Baden the Road quite strait with Rows of Fruit trees on each side to Baden. The French Gentleman kept close to us & assisted us in procuring horses at the next stage. From this to Dourlach the Road being shaded all the way by Apple Trees. The Country most level as far as the eye can reach & there being no hedges the Wheat like a Calm Sea seemed to overspread the whole Country, there was not a hill to be seen between Fribourg & Heidelbourg. We met on our road many French Deserters going to join the head Quarters of the Prince of Condé. They said that the distress of the Republican Army most most severe & that they had eaten Horses at the Siege of Mayence.

Very heavy rain came on near Bruscal, the Residence of the Bishop of Worms & we could not proceed in our open Carriage. The splendour of the Roman [Catholic] Priests & their Servants was here to be seen in all its Glory. The dress of the Bishops Servants was all covered with Lace. The Protestant States & Roman States join in all directions & the only mark of division between Worms & Baden is a Land Mark of wood. The Protestants on one side & the Romans on the other are as distinct as if they lived 1000 miles asunder. The change of Religion in Germany if not every where else was brought about by the Princes, & not by the People, I am afraid generally interested motives either accelerated or retarded the profession of Faith. France alone kept her religion in opposition to her King but Henry the 4th was not the immediate descendant of the former Kings & had been in disgrace & his Friends destroyed in the former reign.

We passed very near Manheim now in the possession of the French. At Heidelberg we waited some time for Horses, crossed a beautiful bridge at Heidelberg with three turnpikes on it. On the bridge was a statue of Charles Theodore, Elector Palatine, with Minerva on the other end. One of our Horse, a wild Hungarian, nearly threw us all into the River. The city of Heidelberg is a fine old place with Three Religions amicably settled therein viz- Calvinist, Lutheran & Roman.

The Roads now became bad, sadly cut up by the March of the Armys & we were obliged to take an additional Horse. At a Post House I heard a Man singing an English Song. He had been at St Omers at the Colledge & from thence had made his way to England & was now on his way home. We had left almost the same point & were now crossing. He said that all our English fellow Prisoners in France were released & had gone home, so it would have been better had we staid in Prison.

Passed Hessen D'Armstad but the Post House was outside of the Gate. I just looked in & saw the Parade with numerous bands of music & drilling Recruits; more than I should conceive the State would require. Reached Frankford to dinner without any money in our Pocketts. Our difficulties now if I may so say commenced afresh, we were not admitted within the Gates without great difficulty it is true we had advanced 200 miles but we were still very far from home. At the Inn the Servants would not allow us enter until the Master came home, he fearing that he should not be paid & told us we might have a Room paying a florin 20 a day for it. There were no Letters at the Post Office for us altho we had written both to Geneva & England, requesting to hear from both places, nor could we find any Banker who had heard from our Friends at either place.

We lived on Bread for a week going every day to the Post Office but no Letters. The Innkeeper became tired of us, & as the fair was approaching in which all his rooms would be wanted, he warned us to leave his hous. In this distress we knew not what to do, at the end of the week we received a Letter written by the Attorney, Mr Farr of my Grandfathers Executor, informing my Father that his Bills drawn from Geneva were all paid, but desiring that he would draw no more as Mr Smith[13] would not pay another farthing until our arrival in England.

We now lost hope as our Bills from Geneva were of no avail, for altho paid, the Banker retained the Money & we had no hope of hearing from him after so long a silence. The Banker thro whom this Letter had come, delivered it open & it appeared that he had read it. He I suppose from the tenor of the Letter that we were extravagant people & he said that, seeing us as English & hearing our Story, he might have been induced to advance us Six or Eight Guineas on a Bill but that now he could not do it, as he had warning that any Bill of ours would not be paid. After leaving him, he, of his own Accord, sent a Clerk with a present of Two Louis D'ors & advised us to try other Bankers in the City.

---

[13] Mr Lilley Smith whom Henry's father sued for maintenance of his children: *Sherwood – v- Smith* in Chancery.

My Father took his advice but no one would take our Bills, altho they all gave us something so that after paying our Bills we had Six Louis in hand. As we could not expect any more in Frankford, we again proceeded with that small Sum. Our first stage cost one Louis, of course, we could not get far with six.

It was the commencement of the Great Frankford Fair & the Road was full of Pedlars & Jews. We pushed on thro bad roads, with bad horses & without eating until the last Livre was spent, which happened at a small Village at 12 oclock at night. The Post Houses are not of necessity Inns & the one we were set down at was a private House. Fortunately the Post Master could speak French, which is no common thing in this part of Germany. We slept on the floor of the room destined for travellers to sit in while the Horses were changing, under the pretence of being over fatigued, but at five they called us to say that the Horses were ready. As the Posthorses are paid in advance, we knew not what to do. It was full thirty miles to Hessen Casel & there was no person who had any means of assisting us, as we understood, between this & that City. On the attendant wanting to be paid, we asked to see the Postmaster, but were told that he had sat up late & must not be disturbed. We sat still in the Room, every now & then, a Servant came in to say the Horses are ready. At last, I believe they thought that we did not understand them & they put the Horses to & pointed to them shewed us that we had nothing to do but pay & be off. Some fresh travellers arrived. My Mother said she was ill, on which our Horses were removed & put to the other Carriage. The Wife of the Postmaster soon saw our state & called her Husband, to him we told our difficulties & offered cloths or all that we could give him to help us on. The carriage was our own & that we offered. He not only refused, but told us his Room was not an Inn & we must immediately leave it.

My father, with his family, left the house & proceeded on foot & I stood by the carriage leaning against it & I believe crying. I stood thus for a very long time, I do not know how long. I knew not where the rest of the family had gone but I was convinced that they could not walk far, my feelings were of course much hurt. The villagers, who had heard our Story, stood round the Carriage. At length the Innkeeper wished us away & sent to a Carrier who had Spare Horses & made a bargain with him to take us to Cassel for the Carriage provided we could not otherwise pay him. The Man, having examined the Vehicle, seemed inclined to break off his bargain, while we were in the heat of Argument, Two Officers passed us, a Prussian & an Hessian. The Hessian addressed me in French & asked the meaning of what he saw. I related our present difficulties &

to prove to him that what I said was true, I gave him an Account of Colonel Bezenrod's Regiment,[14] the officers of which Regiment had been in prison with me & with whom I had been on terms of Intimacy. This Gentleman immediately interested himself for us & soon found a man who undertook to conduct the Carriage with the Family, if it could be found, to Casel. The Two Officers gave me Two French crowns, 10/-. The Man brought his Horses & I proceeded, expecting to overtake the rest of the family without going far. We soon set off & very shortly overtook the family who were not a little pleased at seeing me perched on the front of the Carriage. We were soon caught in a violent storm & wet through & were glad to get into a Jew's House to dry ourselves & pass the night for it was late in the Evening before we had procured the Horses.

The Jew gave us some good Ham for Supper & we lay on the floor in our Cloths, still wet, yet caught no Cold. The Jew was the cheapest Landlord we had ever fallen in with during our travels. On reaching Cassel, the Carrier offered to leave our Carriage if we would pay any reasonable sum for his trouble. Not being able to do so, he left us in a decent Inn sans sous.

On enquiring what English were in Cassel, we heard of only one, a Major Le Grand. Who or what he was I do not know. He either did not believe what we told him, or affected not to do so, most likely the first as from the State of France there were many distressed Persons all over the Continent. He however said that if we could prove what we had told him, he would do what he could. Now it happened that the only letter we had to shew was Mr. Farr's letter refusing to pay any Bill & of course, that would not do. Going down stairs I met a Soldier who I recognised as a fellow Prisoner & I returned with him but the word of a Private instead of doing service rather made things worse. Looking out of the window I saw a General Officer, Colonel now General Bezenrode. I ran to him but he was the Commanding Officer on the parade. He only told me to come to his House, but his manner was such that on my return to Major Le Grande, he was completely convinced. Something however, struck him with respect to my Father. I do not know what, but he did not say anything to him. There is little doubt to me now that all the cares & anxieties he had experienced had affected my Father. Perhaps remorse at having brought his Family, by his strong Republican notions, into such great Troubles.

---

[14] The Hessians were German soldiers, originally from Hesse, whose regiment served the British Army through the 18th century, particularly during the American Revolution.

Whatever it was, Major Le Grande lent me 5 Guineas saying it was as much as he could spare. On my return to the Inn, I met the Surgeon of the Regiment whom I had known intimately at Abbeville. He was very anxious to hear how we had escaped & promised to call at the Inn in the Evening & hear our adventures. He came & brought with him a Captain. They remained with us to supper, & having paid our expenses, gave me as much as they could well afford namely one guinea. They begged that we would not leave Casel the next day for they thought we might procure an Order from the Elector for a free conveyance in the Mail Cart & that, by mentioning our circumstances on Parade, many of the Officers who had known me in France might be inclined to assist us.

I do not know how it was but my Father would insist on going away in the morning, which we did and, though we arrived in Hanover the same day, all our money was expended. My Father was always sanguine & he thought Hanover was England. We found that the Hanovarians had distress enough among themselves & were as badly off, if not worse than we. After running about the whole of the next day to get help, we were obliged to sell everything we possessed, save the Cloths we had on, for a Louis D'or. By the kind assistance of an Hanovarian Major, we were accommodated with a free Carriage, nine of us in the Mail Cart to Bremen. It was my Father's intention, however, to stop at Nuremberg [Neinberg] hearing that a Mr. Duncan was British Commissary there. We were dreadfully insulted by the driver on account of our free passage & the other passengers, particularly a Soldier, behaved brutally.

We reached Nuremberg at 12 at night & my Father, being determined to stop there, allowed the carriage to proceed to the Post House before we had properly made it understood that we had no friends in the place. We were, at first, refused admittance into the Post House & it was only the Postmaster's humanity on seeing the young Children, that we were, at length, allowed to sleep on the floor. My Father had been in the Street quarrelling with the Servants of the Prince of Orange saying that as the English supported him, as an Englishman he had a right to be attended to. The Servants behaved very well on the occasion & brought him to the Posthouse. Next day we could only get Charity from Mr Duncan, who gave a Guinea & we proceeded to Bremen where we arrived with half a Crown in our Pocketts. It rained hard all the way & we were in an open Cart. We were wet thro but had no change. My Father & the rest of the family immediately walked away from the Carriage leaving me busy with the Cartman. When I looked round & saw no one of my Family, I did not know what to think or do. I dare not move lest I should lose them, for I naturally thought they would return to enquire for me. I was all the day without eating. This was the second time I had been left since we had taken our departure from Frankford. At length, tired of waiting, I set off to look for the rest of my family & after some time, I saw my Brother at the door of an Eating House, wherein was my Mother & the rest of the family. My Father had left them there & they knew no more about him than I did. In about half an hour he returned & said that he had been inquiring for Ships sailing to England & that he had found one & he expected that we should soon now be at home but he never considered that he had not a farthing to pay for the dinner his family had eaten, indeed it now appeared that he had left me & the Cart on our arrival, to avoid the Driver's application for a Present. I had not eaten all day & when I mentioned it to him he said that he could not help it. Indeed he appeared quite desperate for I afterwards found out that he had been to most of the Merchants in Bremen & had been refused assistance. Seeing him so low, I proposed to my Mother that we should go to the English Consul. We did so but we found him from Home. We saw his Brother, he declined assisting us saying that he himself was poor, but he said that there was a benevolent English Lady in Town, to whom we might apply, he would not introduce us to her but he would shew us the house, which he did. My Mother knocked at the Door & went in. I remained in the Street. It seemed that My Mother found great difficulty in making her Story believed, but after producing Letters etc. she so far succeeded to interest Lady Irvine who promised that she would, on the following day, speak to several Officers of the English Army who were expected at a Ball in Bremen. She gave my Mother sufficient to support us a Couple of days. She desired her to return at the end of that time. She said that she knew that no ships would sail to England for some time.

We immediately looked out for Some Lodgings & found One Room over a Stable to which we entered by a Ladder from the Stable. The Dunghill was under the Window & I should be glad to be able to say that that was the dirtiest part about it. We were happy in being able to pass the greatest part of the day on the Ramparts. I slept on the Straw in the Hayloft. We passed a whole week here when Count A De Harcourt brought Seven Guineas which he had collected among the Officers of the Army, but we already owed nearly as much.

A Captain of a Ship said that he would sail in a day or two & that he would take us but I do not know how it happened but my Father & the Captain quarrelled as the family were getting into the Boat & our voyage for that time all was at an end. I was absent when that happened buying Sea Stock for our passage was only to be trusted for. On my return I found my Father in charge of a Guard for fighting with the Captain. I soon prevailed on the Guard to release him. My Father appeared beside himself for altho dark we advanced to the gate, & being Challenged by the Sentry, he cried out, "Deliver up your Town to the King of England." The Sentry was very angry about it & it required some time before I could quiet him.

We went back to our old Lodging & in the morning my Father went off & hired a Boat to take us to Brock [Brake] a village on the river Weser 20 miles below Bremen where we heard there were several English Ships at Anchor. We embarked & reached Brock at one oclock in the morning. The only Inn in the Village refused to admit us from our Shabby appearance. My Father found a little Boy who undertook to lead him to a Publick House. He left my youngest brother & myself on the Warf to look after what few things we had left. We had provisions with us, being our Sea Stock which we had laid in at Bremen & there was of course more than we could carry. My Brother soon fell asleep & I covered him up as well as I could.

We remained here about two hours, at length my brother James came running towards us. It rained hard & he was advised not to come for fear of losing his way, but knowing we were exposed to the rain on the beach he would not stay in the house. We had some difficulty in awakening our youngest Brother & when we did rouse him our distress was great for we knew not how to convey our goods. At length finding some old cords in the boat used to tying up our provisions & we tied them together & loaded myself & Brothers like little Horses. It was slippery from the rain & we fell down at every step but at length at daylight we reached the Publick House & I soon fell asleep on the ground, there being no floor. This was Sunday & the House was so filled with drunken Sailors making such a disturbance we were glad to get into the fields.

I went over the Village & Hamlets near in hopes of finding a better place to Lodge in but I believe from the Shabbiness I could not procure one till dusk in the Evening when I was returning in despair & about two Miles above the River I found a House wherein was an old woman who spoke English. She agreed to let us have <u>One</u> Room but this would not do for me. I agreed to sleep in the Hayloft, having made this agreement I was so much overjoyed that I ran the whole way to my Father. I found the family still in the fields not having been able to return to the Publick house on account of the drunken Sailors.

One of my Sisters had lost her shoe in the Mud & I was obliged to carry her, when I reached the Lodgings I had taken I was really exhausted & could scarcely mount the Ladder to my Hayloft. It was now the warmest point of the year & I awoke in the night with a kind of irritation all over me, like the Pricking of Pins. I also found that I had a companion in my loft, a Danish Sailor who had been Shipwrecked.

In the Morning we learnt that there was but one Ship likely to sail very soon to England & upon applying to the Captain he required to be paid for our passage before hand & he demanded Sixteen Guineas. To comply with this was litterally impossible. My Father desired me to go to Delmenhorst, where the English Army lay. He said that I might apply to Count d'Harcourt, the Officer my Mother had met at Bremen & to enable me to get there, a horse was hired. It was always a foible of my Fathers to expect too much from Persons & I believe from seeing the disappointment he met with I have probably taken the opposite turn. He thought that being an English Gentleman that An Englishman would immediately assist him & probably from a long absence from his Country & being confined in dangerous times in France, he thought that an Englishman Abroad was a Brother to an Englishman, but I did not succeed, Count d'Harcourt did indeed behave kindly but in the first place he was not an Englishman & we had no right to expect much. He gave me a Guinea & I returned. My Horse cost me nearly that Sum as I returned along the dyke, in doleful dumps with a French Bonnet de Police on my Head & a long Black Coat one skirt torn off. My Horse with only three Legs, I must have cut a conspicuous Figure. The dyke being elevated above the common Horizon shewed me off towards Sun set in stile & the Haymakers observing my unequal gait, cried, Sneider, Sneider, myn coup. I do not quite know the meaning but the word Taylor was easily understood & I took it to myself in dudgeon.

On my Return I found an English Dragoon come down on some business to Brock. I believe he was sent to look after an English Transport by Sir Robert Lawrie. I met with him on the dyke & as a Countryman addressed him not expecting any thing from a Private Soldier. He said that He came from Birmingham & spoke of himself as of a good family, but that he had been wild. He certainly had some Education.

My Father, who was very fond of letting every one know who he was & that he was of some consequence at home, soon gave this Man to understand that he was somebody & a Warwickshire Man. The Young Soldier seemed to enter into our feelings & exerted himself with the English Captains of Transports in the Harbour who were fond of meeting in the only Inn at Brock to Drink. This Poor Soldier whose name was Thornton exerted himself much in our favor. I have since enquired about him at Birmingham but could never learn who he was.

A Serg^t Robenson of the 11th Dragoons with a Farrier of the same Regiment arrived from England, but it seems that they had landed after their Regiment was embarked & they were ordered to return in the Same Ship. To this Serg^t, Thornton applied & Robenson said He would get us to England if he should lose all that he should expend & He did so, paid our Passage to Hull & the money due to our Lodgings & we went with him to Hull where he had a Sister. On our Arrival at Hull there were letters for us with Money, & I hope my Father recompensed him. I know he repaid him.

Part 2— England—1795 October: Aged 18

1795 Home to Coventry

I was so anxious to reach my Guardian, for I had a small independency, that I left Hull the next day, but from my sufferings I had a disease on me which now broke out, an inflamatory sore throat. I reached Lincoln & would have proceeded but there was no Coach the next day to Nottingham. I therefore remained that day, my throat was so painful that I could scarcely bear it. The Landlady of I believe The Hart or White Hart shewed me great kindness & would have persuaded me to remain but I would proceed & I advanced towards Nottingham in the coach.

I became very ill indeed before we reached Newark & a Gentleman in the Coach going to Buxton, himself very ill, lent me his Coat & was very kind. While the Horses were changing I ran to the Apothecary & told my distress. The Young Man in the Shop said that I ought to Stop, but that I would not listen to. He gave me a Gargle for my Throat & would not be paid for it.

I reached Nottingham that night but here again I was unfortunate for no Coach left that place for Leicester the next day, however, I heard of one which would come into the Road about 3 or 4 miles from Nottingham & I advanced on foot for why should I find a difficulty in England walking a few miles by myself who had met with such greater difficulties abroad but without health what can be done. I fell on the Road at some distance from Nottingham & with the greatest difficulty could drag myself to a little Inn but it seemed that this small inn was situated on the Junction of the two Roads by which the Coach was to come. I had a good rest & got myself some peppermint drops which were recommended & thought myself strong by the time the Coach came. The inside was full & I mounted on top. The Weather was fine but a sudden shower came on & wet me to the Skin.

I reached Leicester & the next morning as usual no Coach to Coventry. I moved off on foot & quite exhausted reached Hinckely, here new troubles awaited me. The Assises were at Coventry & the troops moved out. All the Inns at Hinkley were full, my appearance was not in my favor & going from House to House to procure a Bed, in one Inn some Soldiers drunkenly pretended to take me for a deserter. I had been in Arbitrary Governments & I was not aware of my safety. I felt alarm & began relating my History. The Soldiers I believe thought it a good joke & finding they had got a hold on me, one said, hah, hah You have been fighting against your Country among the French for I see you are a Soldier. I felt a dread come over me & I rushed out of the house making my way across the field, in the direction towards Coventry.

At some distance, I daresay a Mile, I got into the Road by a small Publick house. It was Sunday & every one dressed in their Sunday Cloths. I had my one-skirted Coat with a Pair of Provencal Pantaloons called Catalans on. I had a French Bonnet de Police on my Head & no stockings, in this attire, it was not wonderful that they would not accommodate me in the House. The Landlord said he had no bed. I felt faint & heart broken, not more than 10 or 11 miles from home. I thought myself most cruelly used & weary with my Way & weak from my illness I fell down faint at the door. When I recovered, I found myself in the house & now I was kindly treated only some Sunday loiterers seemed to think my illness was brought on by my own fault. They spoke indeed in guarded terms & I could not quite understand them but I knew enough to be angry & hurt.

In the morning I advanced towards Coventry, within a Mile or two, I was ill, sick leaning over a Mile stone vomiting, a Chaise passed by, in which were two Ladies & a Gentleman. One of the Ladies looked out & laughed at me saying to the other something against Idle drunkards. This Lady I met the next Sunday at my Grandmother's & was by her congratulated on my return my distresses sympathised in but she did not know that I was the person she had seen on the Monday before.

Indeed my Father had made me believe that I should be disgraced if I entered Coventry in such a ragged state & even cautioned me against seeing my Relations without proper Cloaths but I had not wherewithal to equip myself. I bought a pair of Stockings at Nuneaton & advanced to Coventry. When I arrived there I had forgotten the Houses & I was fearful of going to a Stranger. I walked along the street looking in at the Windows & at length I recognised my Aunt. I knocked at the door. A Servant who had nursed me as a Child opened it & seeing my appearance said "Go to the Mayor, go." I said "I am Henry Sherwood."

This happened in October 1795. I was then eighteen years old & being under age I could not make use of my property until the 1st of January 1798 when I became of age & with the Advice of my Friends determined on entering the Army.

[Sherwood's account found in the Shropshire Archives ends here but a much edited version of the above was published in pamphlet form including a few more pages, source unknown:

Bond, Andrew, ed. (1981). *The Value of Bread. a Memoir By Henry Sherwood Who, as a Teenager, Resided in France During the Years of the Revolution.* London: Saint George Orthodox Information Service.]

Ending from *The Value of Bread*:

I knocked very lightly and & humbly at the door. It was opened & there stood Susan Sukey, as they always called her. She had been in the family before I was born. (!).

She did not know me & was shutting the door with "Go to the Mayor, go". "I.. I.. I am Henry Sherwood" I said. Of course, I was at once admitted & at once taken to bed. The Surgeon was summoned & he pronounced my disease, Scarlet Fever. I lost all recollection for days. During this time, my clothes were destroyed & unfortunately (so was) some part of the ... in my pocket which I much regretted.

Now all my troubles were over & here follows the ridiculous. My Great Aunt knew nothing of gentleman's attire & I knew little more of what was suitable to my situation; but I was to order new clothes & have my own way with unlimited means. Well, I would have blue & buff Fox's colours. I had admired it some years before when at Merchant Taylor's School. I had a recollection of a barge passing under Blackfriars Bridge, with a large party of gentlemen, thus dressed. I thought them very fine, so I would have blue & buff & nothing else.

In those days we were used to buying cloth at the woollen drapers & having it made up. So the draper was sent for with his pattern board & I chose blue, and, as I thought, buff also. Now this buff turned out to be a very fine yellow. Next, in ordering my boots, I must have a pair up to my knees. & now all things were sent home, I myself was restored to health & was to make my first appearance in public. An assistant in a ribbon manufactary was to take me under his protection, for my dear old Aunt engaged him on this account, half as a companion, half as an attendant.

This man was himself an oddity. He wore a crimson coat with hair fully powdered, a thick club knocker at the back of his neck & white cotton ribbed stockings with long quartered shoes. He carried, also, an immensely thick, short, club-like stick in his hand & he wore his hat cocked rather jauntily on one side. So I attired myself in my blue coat, yellow waistcoat & yellow knee breeches, which had immense bundles of ribbons at the knees & to which my ill-made boots joined. Away we two strutted into Coventry Park, on Sunday, &

everybody stared at us. However, I was soon told of the out of the way (unsuitable) colours of parts of my dress & they were shortly put aside.

I remained idling the remainder of the year at Coventry. My Grandfather's Executor advancing money for me, but sadly puzzled to know what to do with me. All my education had been acquired before I was twelve years old and, in the intervening years, most had been forgotten again.

My Great Aunt, Mrs. Patterson, was old, blind & quite incapable of directing me & thus I was placed in the most dangerous situation of having plenty of money at my disposal & no one to direct me how to spend it. I had, however, one steady & efficient friend, the Rev'd Gerard Andrews, Dean of Canterbury, who had married a Miss Ball, a first cousin of my Father's. This kind relative's attention & fatherly care of me was of vital importance. Whilst thus waiting to be decidedly my own Master, my cousin Mary came to London & I was, in consequence, induced to visit my Aunt at Bridgenorth as soon as I came of age, which happened on the 1st of January 1798.

[Note in the Journal, in another hand, probably his daughter, Sophia's:]

Aunt Mrs Thomasina Paterson. She was a great Aunt sister to Mr Henry Sherwood of Coventry & Wood Street [London]. The Grandmother spoken of was his Grandfather's second Wife born Mary Wedgewood sister of Josiah Wedgewood.

Part 3—Soldier—The West Indies 1798-1802

1798 A Soldier. Age 21.

While staying with the Butts at Bridgnorth, Shropshire, Sherwood met officers of the 53rd Regiment of Foot whose home base was there. On receipt of his inheritance from his grandfather at the age of 21 he decided to purchase a lieutenancy. The 53rd Regiment of Foot had been stationed in the West Indies from 1796. In 1773 at the end of the 1st Carib War on St Vincent the British had formed a treaty with the 'Black Caribs' which was depicted by Agostino Brunias (1730-1798) as the treaty was read in Jamaica by Sir William Young—or possibly General Dalrymple—and the Caribs laid down their arms.

Engraving from *Pacification of the Maroon Negroes*. Agostino Brunias.

From 1793 until 1802 during the French Revolutionary and Napoleonic Wars the British Army had up to 19,000 men in service in the West Indies to secure British interests. Of the 89,000 men—including 1,290 convicts enlisted for life—who served there about 41%, mainly NCOs and men, died of disease, mainly of yellow fever, in their first year. Overall casualties amounted to about 60%.

On the 12th of March 1798 I left Bridgenorth in a Post chaise with Lieut Stewart & Ensign Grant 53rd Regiment passed by Wolverhampton Birmingham Coventry &c to London. I had lodged Money in the hands of Messrs Greenwood Cox & Co Army Agents & I had been recommended by Colonel Thornton 1st Foot Guards to the Colonel of the 53rd Regt that I might purchase the Commission of Ensign in that Regiment now in Garrison in St Vincents in the West Indias.[15] At Coventry I called on the Attorney Mr Talor of my Grandfather's Executor Mr Smith in hopes of settling with him but I found it impossible I therefore placed my affairs in the hands of Mr Wm Bishton of Shipnal & gave him a power of Attorney to Act for me. On my Arrival in London I found that the Agents had not been so active as I had expected & that I had not got my Commission they attributed the delay to Colonel Abercromby[16] 53rd Regt but said he would be in Town in a few days. Coll Thornton was very kind and recommended my exerting myself to purchase a Lieutenancy which might now be effected in a Regiment in the West Indies as Yellow Fever was raging there & some difficulty found in filling up Commissions in that Country. And as my determination was to run all risks in the way of my Profession I ought to get on as fast as possible. I called on several Officers of 53rd Regt & made acquaintance with Captains Buckland, Rogers & Hobson besides Lieut Stewart & Ensign Grant. I ordered my Uniform, bought Swords Guns &c & fitted myself out before my Commission came out. On 22nd I saw Colonel Abercrombie who seemed to make difficulties in purchasing but I sent the Papers to General Crosbie Colonel 53rd Regt. I employed myself the remainder of the Month in drawing Flowers & learning Latin, Construing 15 or 16 lines of Virgil every day before I went out, got the Uniform of the 53rd Regt before I had a right to put it on & thought myself a very fine fellow.

---

[15] Britain's wars with France 1792-1802 included defence of British territories in the West Indies.
[16] John, later Lieut. General Sir John Abercromby, son of General Sir Ralph Abercromby.

Letter to Mrs Butt from London 19th March 1798 to Mrs Butt

I left Coventry on Wednesday Morning on the outside of the Coach & arrived here at Night & found that Mr Maskall[17] had paid Money for my Commission into the Agents hands. I have since called on the agents twice but they have not received the necessary papers from Colonel Abercromby. The Colonel is expected every day & will probably bring the Papers with him. There is no doubt but that every thing will be satisfactorily settled. I wrote to Colonel Thornton according to your advice & he asked me to breakfast with him on Saturday & I attended him & was much pleased with him, he spoke in the most Friendly manner & offered me every assistance as far as his influence went & on parting told me to call occasionally & inform him how affairs went on. I must indeed thank you for your introduction to him. I called on Mr St Quinten[18] & altho he was from home I dined with Mrs Slaney.[19] Mrs St Quinten says that she delighted with the manuscripts she gave me Batters Dream to read which delighted me extremely. Mrs Slaney is much better. I called on Mr Edwards & he told me that he would write to you immediately. I dined with Mr Andrews at St James yesterday he was very kind & desired me to come whenever I was at liberty. He also desired to be kindly remembered to you. Mr Stewart is very well & both he & Grant behave very prudently I see them every day. Stewart talks of nothing but returning to Bridgenorth he says this is the whole of his desire. I cannot say the same for I wish not to be idle but I assure you that when I left Bridgenorth I was not in the best of Spirits. I have never met with such good friends before. Captain Buckland advised me to get Regimentals as there can be no doubt of my appointment to the 53 Reg^t in a day or two & I have done so. indeed I have some hopes of a Lieutenancy but must not be too sanguine. I expect to hear from Dr Salt[20] with some advice about Botany in the West Indies. I keep a journal as you desired me but it will be poorly written but I feel some satisfaction at the hope of reading it to you some years hence when we meet in Peace. I enter my expences as you desire. I think it a good plan that by so doing I may judge of what my expences ought to be.

---

[17] Mr. Maskall, maternal uncle.
[18] St. Quinten was an aristocratic French émigré who had run Abbey Gateway School in Reading attended by Mary and Lucy Butt, Sherwood's cousins. He now ran a school in Hans Place, London.
[19] Mrs. Slaney was Mary Butt's godmother.
[20] Dr. Thomas Salt (1720-1802). Married to Alice, Dr. Butt's sister.

Pray give my Love to my Cousins. Their kindness to me shall never be forgotten. They have, I hope cured me of the worst of my faults and have been the Chief cause that I do not look upon the world in the same light that I did before. If I had not seen your family I should in all probability have become a selfish Character. I had learnt that every one for himself was a common maxim, but I hope that I am cured & it is to you & them that I owe it.

Y^r Dutiful Nephew Henry Sherwood

April   I went with Stewart & Grant to Gravesend on their way to Chatham where they are going to take charge of the Soldiers for the West Indies. I felt great regret that I could not join them on the 2nd. The Colonel signed a recommendation for me to purchase an Ensigncy in the 53rd Reg^t. Met Mr T Butt & Lord Valentia.[21] The Former did not know me, Lord Valentia wrote in my favor to General Crosbie & introduced me to Sir George Young & Colonel Colburne Sir George gave me a letter of introduction to Doctor Anderson of the Botanic Garden of St Vincents. General Crosbie was civil when I gave him Lord Valentia's letter— Colonel Abercrombie sailed for St Vincent.

Letter to Mrs Butt from London 3rd April 1798

In obedience to your last Letter I called on Lord Valentia he leaves town today & will convey this. On the day that I wrote last I was informed that the Chancery Officers refused to allow my Name to be taken out of the bill filed against Mr Smith except I gave security £400 for paying the expences already incurred. Mr Reynolds[22] & Mr Maskall have kindly stood my Friends. On Thursday Col^l Abercromby came to town & I called on him. He is a very reserved man & I was not pleased with him at first but he unbent after a time but he says that General Crosbie must sign the Papers & that he will not be in town for ten days. He is in Ireland. This lowered my spirits & a letter which I received from Mr Smith about the Chancery suit & money matters did not tend to relieve mine. I wrote to General Crosbie. I have with some difficulty found my Father. He is suffering seriously from the Chancery & can get no money but he says that he is determined to go on if he should lose his Liberty. I soothed him as well as I could & we parted good Friends.

---

[21] Lord Valentia, a friend of Dr. Butt.
[22] Mr. Reynolds had been a partner of Sherwood's grandfather in Sherwood & Reynolds.

On Wednesday Mr Grant & Mr Stewart were ordered to Chatham to the Deport. They do not much like it, the duty is said to be hard. I went with them in the Gravesend Boat. They have rooms in the Barracks & here they are to remain until they embark.

I am this day told that I am appointed to the 53rd Reg^t & ordered to join it with Cap^n Hobson therefore all is settled. I saw Mr Thomas Butt. Mr Smith says that he cannot advance me the Money for my Lieutenancy, this is hard but probably as well as it is. I had intended giving my Father what money I could spare, but when I heard him speak so strongly about Law, I thought I might as well keep the Money as give it to the Lawyers. I expect to leave London on the 20th as I hear a fleet is appointed to sail. I have only to say that I shall never forget your kindness & I hope on my return "covered with Laurels" to thank you in person.

Y^r Dutiful Nephew Henry Sherwood

12th April I am very angry at not receiving my Commission or I might have gone with him. Had my picture drawn in the new uniform of the 53rd Reg^t

18th Another Gazette out & my name not in it. & on calling on the Agents they told me that they had made some mistake.

Letter to Mrs Butt from London 18th April 1798

Commencing with a Report of Mrs Slaneys. Pray tell my Cousin that I guess by her warning me of my new Friend that she means Captain Hobson. I have only seen him twice and hope to conduct myself that none of my Friends shall have occasion to be hurt at. Mr Grant and Stewart are still at Chatham. I congratulate myself on my being alone to Study Virgil, Drawing & Field fortification. Thank my Cousins for their kind remembrances, I hope to see them again when we have Peace. I have heard from My Brother on board the Pompei at Plymouth he grumbles about Money. I dined in Company with Captain Younge & his lady. He expects to go to the West Indias. I dined on Sunday with Mr Andrewes. He begs to be remembered to you. I have almost finished the first Aeneid which considering my employment is I think a proof of my obedience to my Cousin Mary's commands & no less so to the Commands of Lucy for I have already drawn Nine Flowers better than those I sent you & I think I can say that I improve. I learn Military Mathematics, Field Fortification & the

Rules & Legislation of the Army so my time is filled up, drawing I am told will be very useful in the Army.

My Father is just as determined as ever to go on with the Chancery Suit. Just he thinks me gone which is quite as well. Mr Smith I think uses me ill. He has received an order from the Lord Chancellor to settle with me & he acknowledges that he has £400 in hand of mine yet he says Money is scarce. I have written to Mr Bishton about him. Pray give my love to my Cousins. Stewart writes me word that he is on Guard for the first time.

Y^r Dutiful Nephew Henry Sherwood

20th I called on Colonel Thornton & told him what the Agents had said yesterday. He seemed to think that the Agents were not treating me well. He said he would enquire into it & he proposed that I should meet him at the Agents office at 2 o clock. At 2 Colonel Thornton met me at Messrs Greenwood & Co's office & we found that the Commission which I had been recommended for was in dispute that is that it had been so long vacant that it was doubtful whether it had not lapsed. Colonel Thornton seemed to think that I was made a tool in the business & he told the Agents so. They said in excuse that I had confined them to the 53rd Reg^t. The Colonel told me that all Regiments were alike & advised me to enter any Regiment in which I might easily obtain a Commission. I was ashamed to say that I had purchased my Uniform & accoutrements for the 53rd Reg^t. I therefore put upon my friendship for Officers with whom I was acquainted. He treated this lightly & said that I might soon make Friends. The Agents however cleared up all things by proposing that I should purchase an Ensigncy in another Reg^t & then immediately purchase a Lieutenancy in the 53rd Reg^t & they undertook to speak to the Commander in Chief. They thought from my having been disappointed since january, permission might be given for my immediate promotion. Colonel Thornton advised me not to let so good an opportunity escape & I immediately agreed to abide by his advice. There were two Ensigncies vacant, one in the 45th one in the 57th. colonel Thornton preferred the 45th because he was acquainted with General Adean its Colonel so we agreed as to the Reg^t & I signed the necessary Papers immediately. Lieut Stewart & Ensign Grant embarked on board the *Huntingdon* Transport & all hope of my going with them now over. Grant came to London to procure some necessaries & Money from the Agents & having no leave he begged that I would call in the morning & get him a Months pay. I did so & hired a horse rode to Chatham to take my leave of them. I did not expect to see them again in England. The Transport was laying at Greenhithe above Gravesend I dined on board with several officers Captain Cameron 43 Commanding [margin note: Killed by Col Dennis in a duel] I thought the Party on board not a pleasant Party.

Letter to Mrs Butt dated London 23 April 1798

I am now going to inform you that I am not going to get my commission in the 53rd but in the 45th. I think the Agents did not behave well, it seems that after all our Trouble & expence there was no Ensigncy for sale in the 53rd Reg^t. Col Thornton has been most kind & attentive, he has lent me as much as £37 in this Purchase. I think I have prevailed on Mr Smith to let me have the money for a Lieutenancy. If I can get this settled what do you advise me. Shall I remain in the 45th or exchange into the 53$^{rd.}$ There will be no difficulty in either. I have sent you a miniature of myself in the 53rdUniform. I therefore think that I need to go into the 53rd after all, when I return I shall be so altered I think I must leave my likeness behind me. As you are my best Friend I send it you in the Above to my dear Cousins.

Y^r Dutiful Nephew HS

Letter to Miss Butt being part of the letter of 23rd April 1798 to Mrs Butt

You have most delightful weather "I suppose" for we have it to here & you have your Brother to protect you from the Cows, & other dangerous Animals, & you have me still between you and the French, you might be extremely easy. We have been in Alarm here, a plot has been discovered & we ought to have been burnt to death eer this by a Set of Republicans, I have been much frightened & have abandoned the City in consequence, I now reside in the Strand, but this is dangerous from the vicinity of the River the French may surprize us, do you know that the very day that I removed the Rascally republicans we caught close to my new Residence, Subterraneous passages, Barrels of Gunpowder, 1000 stands of Arms, French Colors, Guilioteens &c, beware, when I am gone. I have send you a Little Protector in the 53rd Uniform he will fight perhaps as well as the Original. Yr affect Cousin HS

On the 28th My Commission dated as Lieutenant 53rd Reg^t my Ensigncy only 3 days prior. Cap^n Hobson being very anxious to get out persuaded me to go with him to Portsmouth I was ready enough to join him as I found Money going away & I wished to be a Soldier indeed —

This Month I have seldom left my lodgings without reading from 30 to 40 lines of Virgil & endeavouring to draw a flower.

May 2nd 3rd & 4th   Collected in all bills, paid all Debts called on all Friends & on 4th left London at 5 in the Morning for Portsmouth. Captain Hobson had arrived before me he was at the Bleu Posts Inn where I joined him after having my Hair well powdered.

At Gosport lived my Aunt Park widow of my Uncle William Maskall now the wife of Cap^n Park one of the Lieutenants at the Haslar Hospital. [margin note: now wife of Major Park Marine Artillery] I was most kindly received. here I found a Cousin Miss Eliza Maskall, a very pleasant young woman.

After leaving Gosport Capt Hobson & myself called on General Pitt & procured an order to the Transport Agent for providing a Passage for us by the first opportunity. The Agent (Capt Patton) entered our names & said we should be provided with a passage by the first opportunity.

From this time to the 15th I employed myself every morning in reading Virgil afterwards walking with Hobson & sometimes dining & passing the Evening at Mr Parkes.

On the 15th the *Huntingdon* Transport with Stewart and Grant on board arrived. They came on shore & we all dined together & now I have again hopes that we may all join the Regiment together.

The Month ended as it began only I had more acquaintances for Stewart and Grant were often on shore & a detachment of the 85th Reg^t arrived from Bridgenorth with whom I was a little acquainted & soon became more so but no appearance of our leaving England. Stewart & Grant expected to sail every day. Convoy was appointed & no ship likely to join the fleet which could take us.

June 1,2,3,4,5,6,7,8,9   Every day we called on Capt Patton but no ship for us. The 85th Reg^t & Carmarthan Militia quarrelled at Fareham in consequence the 85 Flank Companies immediately marched away.

Sunday 10th June 1798   Mr Webb late Surgeon of the 53rd Reg^t but now a Surgeon on the Staff arrived from the West Indies & came to Breakfast with us, after Breakfast we passed over to Portsmouth & walked on the Parade at Guard Mounting, observed the Signal for the Fleet to sail for the West Indies. Hobson said suppose you go to Captain Patton & ask if he has heard of any conveyance for us, It was eleven oclock before I reached Cap^n Patton's door, on seeing me he said you are just in time there is a Victualler unexpectedly come round & she will now be able to go with the fleet, you cannot have a better opportunity if you can get there in time, at any rate I will write an order for the Captain to receive you & if you are too late it cannot be helped. I ran with my order to Hobson, he was extremely anxious to join as he had been absent very long. We therefore did not hesitate, but we made the best of our Way to a Boat. He ran over to Gosport & threw our trunks into the Boat dirty cloths and all huddled together while I ran to a Shop in hopes of getting some Stores, but it was Sunday & I could not get an ounce of any thing. I had a Pound of Tea & with this small stock we pushed off & before half after twelve o clock we were under weigh for the West Indias on board the *Prince of Wales* Victualling Transport, Captn Codd. Before 9 o clock & consequently before dark we passed thro the Needles with a fine North Easterly wind & proceeded down Channel.

1798 June—Sailing to the West Indies: Aged 21

11th June   On rising this morning we were out of sight of land with a pleasant Breeze. We had leisure to put up & Trunks & look about us. *The Prince of Wales* was a fine Ship of 300 tons with a Poop and Deck. The Main Cabin below was given the officers who were few in Number, Captain Hobson Commanding, Lieut Fleming, Myself, Ensign Shackerly brother of Mrs A 14th Regt & a Volunteer Boothby for the 53rd Regt. Fleming had some sugar I had a Pound of Tea. This was all our stock, we were therefore to trust to our Sea Rations. There was a detachment of Soldiers on board for different Regiments. The Captain could spare us a few Potatoes & a few Bottles of Port Wine, we must therefore make the best of it. Our duty was to see the Men Parade twice a day to see them clean and orderly. One Officer was on duty for the day whose business it was to see all the Hammocks on Deck & the Horlop Deck[23] scrubbed & cleaned & once a week washed with Vinager. The whole Parade with their Division. Towards evening we saw Plymouth ie The Start Point. 7 o clock being on duty saw all the Men on deck, off Falmouth. Wind North. Spoke the *Huntingdon*, all well, came near the Shore, signals making between our Convoy & the Shore. Fishing boats came off. Said that several ships were in Falmouth waiting to join us, could not come out until the Morning. Plenty of time to go on Shore & buy Stock offered to take any one & prepared to go to buy Stock dressed for the occasion & having collected all the Money in the Ship which was easily done. As I had almost the whole in my Pocket I prepared to descend the Ship's side when the Ships were seen standing out of the Harbour & a Signal was made for us to make sail & stand out to Sea, my trip was at an end & I rejoiced that I had not left the Ship, as I might have lost my Passage. I however got my Letters carried on Shore which would inform my friends of my sudden embarkation which they could not have expected from my former Letters.

13th   We got out a Boat & I went on board the *Huntingdon* to state our distress & the Officers spared us a Sheep, a Pig & 5 dozen of Wine to be repaid at Madeira – also 14 lbs of Sugar & 1 lb od Tea. Grant & Stewart well, the latter came on board & remained while the Calm lasted (ie) about an hour. We were completely clear of the Channel.

---

[23] Orlop deck: the lowest, over the bilges.

14   A very light breeze but favorable about 5 knots

15   On Duty saw Hamocks on deck, Decks cleared, men paraded, Sheep killed, 140Miles from Scilly, heavy swell

16 to 19   heavy swell no Wind on 19th Lat^{de} 45 Long^{d} 14 West. A strange sail, The *Prince of Wales* being a large light armed Ship was sent in Chase till nearly dark when we recalled

23   Advanced slowly but pleasantly Lat 37 Long 16 W

26   Light winds saw Madeira

Off Madeira. Thomas Daniell. 1810.

27   Landed at Funchal in the Island of Madeira. Walked a Mile in the Country, dirty ill built Town but looks well from the Sea. All Bustle on account of our fleet. The Street badly Paved, the Houses mostly of Wood with balconies. The Inhabitants very dark, the Hedges of Aloes, Plenty of Vines, Mulberries, Apricots Cherries Strawberries, ripe & Cheap, Dined at the Globe a decent dinner charge with Wine 12/-.

28   Walked with Stewart, came to a Convent. The Nuns ordered the Gates to be closed as we came up but seeing us peacable sold marmalade by a turnabout Waiter in the wall. Like all Hasty travellers who know the state of the natives by intuition I decide that the Inhabitants are Idle dirty Theivish disgusting &c &c &c & that they are a Mixture of I know not what, this is what I hear & must of course take for granted indeed what do I see that cannot be better gathered from Books. The difference between this & England is certainly great but I have no means of

Sailing to the West Indies 1798 69

discovering whether they are better or worse, the Climate of course is warmer, but a Stranger might think that the People of Portsmouth were more honest.

29   We began to give up our time to laying in Stock, this day I was fully employed in buying fowls, ducks Sheep & half a Pipe of Wine there was a great holyday & I got on board with what stock I had procured & was writing letters when I was interrupted by a Barge full of Friars we received them politely & gave them Wine &c they did not leave us until dark & having made fully free with our Wine. The Rocks round the Harbour were covered with statues in their best dresses with bands of mosaic, many boats full passed & repassed among the Shipping. Our Friars did not leave us till after dark.

30th I was on duty today. I was employed arranging our Sea Stores.

Letter to Mrs Butt dated Funchal Bay Madeira 30th June 1798

I sent you a letter from Falmouth by a fishing Boat in a great hurry & confusion, informing you of my embarkation in greater confusion still. I embarked on board the *Prince of Wales* Transport on Sunday in such a hurry that I had neither Bed or Provisions, you may suppose we have been uncomfortable for 18 days, but to balance this, we have a fine ship, good Cabin, & fine delightful Weather. The disagreeable part is that we are loaded with Deserters & Thieves who are bad Companions & there is some Danger. We arrived here on Wednesday last, As we have provisions to buy & the Men to watch I have had but little time to myself, what I have had has been spent walking about the Island, but never more than 3 miles inland. The Country is all Rock & Mountains, in comparison of which the Morf is a Molehill, the Hill is covered with Vines, Oranges, Lemons, Mulberries & by the Hedges of Cactus & Aloes. We have here the Plantain Tree & Cocoa Nut. The quantity of Wine exported from this small place is incredible, it is worth about 1/- p^r Bottle. Fruit is in great abundance we bought a very good desert for 8 which cost us 1/-. Mr Grant is well, I saw him yesterday, Stewart has been with me every day since our arrival, the Sea sickness has had a greater effect on him than I ever knew on any one, he was sick the whole way, & much reduced, he is now better. We walked together the day before yesterday, about a Mile, we gathered Apricoes & Mulberries & Grapes & made the Portugeeze understand us in a fashion. The Poor are very different from the lower Classes in England, they are Lazily basking in the Sun, covered with filth & Virmin, & Red Faces, Red Coats & activity, curiosity &c quite astonish them. The Women ran away, so I can say nothing of the Fair Sex only that they were brown. The Men have such villainous looks, indeed they say that it is dengerous to be on Shore after Sun set. Captain Hobhouse behaves very kindly, he comes from Yorkshire. Yapp is well, My Cousins will probably be kind enough to tell his Mother so. I wish I could send you some Madeira, it costs only 1/- per Bottle. The Nuns here are famous for their preserves & Marmalades, they say that it is better at Martinico. I hope that you or my Cousins will favor me with a Letter to St Vincents, there is nobody I delight to hear from so much as yourself, & that you should think me unsteady as you hinted in your last Letter would make me very uneasy. If I wrote thoughtlessly to my Cousin Mary it was because I had just received your letter by Mr Grant & I was in high Spirits but I forget what I said. We sail tomorrow. I hope this Letter will reach you. I will write as soon as I arrive at St Vincents, give my best Love to my Cousins, I often think of our quarrels in our Walks & I hope the time will come when we may renew them & I send a Defiance to the Cow.

Your dutiful Nephew HS

2nd Letter to Mrs Butt dated Funchal Bay, Madeira 30th June 1798:

[Perhaps an approximate duplicate sent by a different boat for security.]

I wrote to you off Falmouth in April & sent my letter by a fishing Boat, in which I endeavoured to excuse myself for my former Letters written on the hurry of embarkation. In that letter I mentioned that I had been ordered to embark on board The *Prince of Wales* Transport. In so great a hurry as not to allow time to provide either provisions or bed. You may therefore suppose that we were not badly off during a Passage of Eighteen days to Madeira but to counterbalance this we had a fine Ship, & plenty of Room & fine weather. There is indeed one great drawback which is that the Principal part of our Cargoe consists of Jail Birds ie. Men from Prisons these are not only bad companions but convey bad companions, like the Sharkes & Sucking fish. They are also dangerous being light of Finger partly no doubt from what I have observed above. We arrived here on Wednesday last but as we had Provisions to get in & and the men aforesaid to watch we have had little opportunity for observation. I have walked about the Island inland about 4 miles from Funchal. The Country is all Rocks & Mountains to which the Morf at Bridgenorth is but a Molehill as far as I have been there are plenty of Vines, Oranges, Lemons, Mulberries & the Hedges formed of Aloes. I also see the Banana or Plantain & the Cocoa Nut

Tree. The Quantity of Wine exported from this Island is almost incredible, it cost about a Shilling a Bottle. Fruit here is in great abundance & you may buy enough for a good dessert for 8 Persons for a Shilling. Ensign Grant is well. I saw him yesterday & Mr Stuart has been with me every day since we arrived here. He has suffered most severely from Sea Sickness in so much that on his arrival it was very doubtful whether his Health would permit him to continue the Voyage but he is now completely recovered. I never either saw or heard of any one affected by Sea Sickness like him for he was Sick the whole Voyage. The day before yesterday we walked into the country together, our road lay up a steep rugged hill with Vineyards on each side not so different from what I remember from the Coast of Provence & Languedoc as to excite surprize. We entered many hovells where the People seemed Dirty & Idle. We procured most excellent Fruit as Grapes & Mulberries & the Natives seemed perfectly friendly being well paid for what we took. They lay basking in the Sun & employed in a way that delicacy forbids me to mention any otherwise than comparing the occupation with Coursing. The Jealousy of the Portugese with respect to their Wives is extreme. All the Ladies of the Island are said to be shut up since our arrival & I daresay it is true. The Physiogomy of the Gentlemen is not prepossessing having a downcast look & we are told that they use a Poinard without hesitation.

 Capn Hobson is the Senior Officer on board our ship & he is very kind. Tapp is well & that I hope my Cousins will tell his Mother so. The Nuns make very excellent confiture & preserves which are sold at the Convent Gates but we are told that we may expect to find it better at Martinico. I hope you will not forget to write to me to St Vincents for I shall be anxiously looking for Letters on my arrival altho I know that it will be long before this letter can be answered. I can assure you that there is not a single Person in the World whom I regard more than you & the thought that you esteem me unsteady gives me great uneasiness. also the Letter I wrote to — [Cousin Mary] I must say I was in high spirits at the time having received letters from you by Mr Grant.

 We sail again tomorrow, I hope this letter will reach you & I will write again on my arrival at St Vincents. Give my love to my Cousins & say that I trust that if I live to bring home dried plants with me I often call to mind the sweet walks we took together & the many quarrells we have had & I hope that the time will come when we may renew them.

30th June   Went on Shore & walked about two miles up the Hill with Stewart & an officer of the 14th Reg.t We procured Mulberries & Cream at a Cottage, spent a pleasant day, On our return we stopped at a Convent & procured some marmalade at ½ English per Pound went on board to dinner & in the Evening went on Shore again to Bathe, there is a very convenient spot behind the Rock where there is no Surf & deep water. I did not go on Shore from this until the 4th July in a Boat to bathe & returned without landing. The expence of being on Shore was a sufficient reason. I had no means of judging of the Island it appeared to be a rocky dry Country with a very narrow strip between the Mountain & the Sea on which Funchal is built which is roughly paved, but the number of English Officers & a kind of Fair which our arrival caused must render the appearance & liveliness of the scene very different to what it would be at other times.

We sailed on the 4th the wind was very light. I employed myself in bottling wine. We made about 20 miles. Calm again on the 5th & we did not get a breeze until 11 oclock when we filled our sails & advanced with the *Maidstone*—

7th   Light wind today

8th   A Fine Breeze but at four in the evening a Ship in the fleet took fire & we lay too, sending boats to assist in extinguishing the fire which by assistance of all the Boats in the Fleet was got under & we proceeded.

9   One of our men on board very ill & I asked leave to get a boat out & ask assistance from the *Huntingdon*, leave being granted I went on board the *Huntingdon* & while the Doctor (Davidson) went to the *Prince of Wales* I remained on board the *Huntingdon* with Grant Lat 26.30

11th   Lat 25-20 Long West 21-20

12th   Flying fish around us, one flew on board like a herring they appeared flying around us & Bonnettas & Dolphins were seen in great numbers. Lat 24-9

13   During the night we crossed the Tropic of Cancer & entered the Torrid Zone in the afternoon we had a Nautical Christening, but it was confined to a few buckets of Water thrown by the Sailors on the Soldiers & returned with Interest. But in good humour. We are now to the South of the Sun flying fish all round Lat 20.18 Long^{dc} 24

14   We are now pretty certain of the Trade Wind which may be said to have began at Madeira but it was not called so, because it is liable to vary so far to the North but we now expect a fair Wind all the way more Flying Fish fell on board

15   Moderate Breezes   Lat   19-30   Longitude   26-30

16	Light Breezes	"	18-50	"	27-30
17	do—	"	18-10	"	28-40
18	do—	"	16-41	"	30-46.

Took a heavy Sailing Ship in Tow

19   This Morning we dropped astern to take the heavy Sailing Ship in Tow but could not find her, at length we perceived her the headmost ship in the fleet. This leads us to suspect her being behind was a trick. The breeze was pretty fresh

Lat — 15-4— Long—33   Passed close to the *Huntingdon*

20   Spoke the *Huntingdon* & asked the Officers to dinner tomorrow if the Weather fine

— 15-9 — 35-30

21   Fresh Breeze —   14-43 — 38 — Killed a pig.

22   Spoke *Huntingdon* & again invited Officers for Tomorrow if it is fine

14-16 — 40

23   Fine Weather, Stewart & Grant dined on board Long 42-18 our Lat run out

24   do — Long 44-18

25   do— " 48-25 *Huntingdon* came alongside & asked us to dinner but we hope to be on Shore soon so declined

26   Wind increased Long 50-50

27   do—   53-30

28   do —   56-8 we now reckon to be at Barbadoes 1st Aug

29   In pursuit of a strange Sail but on coming up found it to be one of our own fleet

30   Several Ships for different Islands left us Long 58-38 Wind Shifted to South & blew a Gale, the Sailors say a Tommy Cane, Harry Came's Brother, the Sea ran very high & being in the fleet we were on the look out lest we should run foul of each other it was soon over

31   Our Reckoning being out in the afternoon *Huntingdon* made a Signal for land a head but sailing till dusk we saw nothing.

1798 August—The West Indies

1   At Daylight saw Barbadoes & at ½ past 12 Landed in Bridge Town. I had a Letter to a Mr Maxwell a Merchant & asked him if he could put me in the way of seeing Mrs Sober my Cousin (formerly Jane Wall) he promised to procure me a horse after dinner. Invited me to dine with him. A very sumptuous dinner, one M^r & Mrs Maxwell & myself nine Meat dishes with all kinds of vegetables & Soup, with great varieties of uncommon fruit, at 5 o clock Mr Maxwell's Horse came, but he could not procure me a Guide & altho it was nearly dark I proceeded.

The Road was a mere track by the Sea Side. To the Westward, soon after leaving Bridge Town I came to a sandy Bay with Trees of a beautiful Green resembling Pear Trees coming almost to the edge of the water. As I rode along I picked a leaf & put it in my mouth which was observed by a Negro walking on the road who cried out, "throw away Manichineel" I immediately threw the leaf away but I found a burning in my lips which soon became sore & blistered, the man advised me The Manicheel[24] is known as a violent Poison & no grass will grow under it, it is even said that Land Crabs living under are poisoned. It was dark before I reached Spikes Town, the road to which is tolerably good & easy to be distinguished but from this to Mr Sobers Estate called Welsh Town there was only a track. From Bridge Town to Spikes Town is 12 miles. I here hired a Negroe to conduct me to welsh Town for a Dollar.

Being anxious to find out the state of the negroes I began asking my Guide what rank he held & whether he was happy. He said that he was a field Negroe a Cultivator of the Soil that he was very happy & he really seemed so, being in high Spirits, probably the gain of a dollar might have raised his spirits. I reached Welsh Town at Nine o clock & was kindly received by my Cousin.

2nd I arose at Six to see what was to be seen & I was soon followed by Mr Sober who was kind enough to walk round his Estate with me. His House was situated on the Top of a Hill surrounded by trees & he told me that he always had wind there & the Tops of Hills altho generally favoured by the breeze were less liable to the Violence of the Hurricanes than more confined situations. I observed many apparent ruins like the Round Towers or Watch Towers in Mount Jura & on enquiring what

---

[24] Manincheel: Poison guava tree.

they were he told me they were Windmills with the Sails taken down this being the Hurricane Season. The soil was covered with beautiful flowers as the Ipecacuhama,[25] Ipomea Quamoclit & Rubra, Vinca Rosea, Barbadoes Flower, fence Poinciana & many others. On returning to Breakfast at Nine I found the Table covered with Fruit, Meat, Tea, Cocoa, Coffee, Chocolate, bread, roasted Plantains enough to feed the `Ships company altho we were only three, roasted Yams, Eggs, Ham, Cold Fowls, Potatoes, Sweet potatoes. I was quite astonished, a large Table.

After Breakfast it was necessary to return which I did by the same road thro Spikes Town, the appearance of a Country so different to my own delighted me. The Road was bordered by Cocoa Nut Trees, Mountain Cabbages &c & the Fields instead of corn planted with Sugar Cane which indeed does not look very unlike Corn only higher. I reached the Ship soon after three & found the detachment drunk & riotous. I had some difficulty (being Senior Officer)in keeping them quiet. Signal to sail tomorrow morning. No waiting here for fair Winds. The Wind almost always blowing from the same quarter & Barbadoes is the first island we make being to Windward <u>that we may the more readily make whatever other Island we may wish.</u>

1798 August—Martinique

My Memorandums are now missing but <u>I find my letters that having left Barbadoes for Martinico,</u> we landed at Fort Royal where the Men were placed in an old Barrack but the accommodation for Officers was so bad that neither Lieu^t Stewart or myself would go into them. Stewart hired a small room in the Town & I took up my abode in the Tavern. Boothby a Volunteer & poor Grant went to the Barracks. Grant died on the 15th & Boothby on the 17th. I believe we landed on the 10th. This as may naturally be expected alarmed us not a little we were only nine days in Martinico & in that short time we lost half our Officers & one third of our men.

Martinico is more mountainous than Barbadoes & the Vegetation more rapid owing to the soil being more moist. Fort Royal is situated at the Bottom of a Deep & Large Bay. Fort Bourbon a Strong Fort being immediately above it commanding it & Fort Edward which latter commands the Anchorage & inner harbour called the Carenage. I was much disappointed in the fruit which did not seem equal to what I had

---

[25] Ipecacuanha: *Carapichea ipecacuanha*. Cephaeline alkaloid medical use.

expected, the Pine Apple not appearing much better than Turnips. The expence at the Tavern was very heavy my dinner cost me a Guinea. I found the Climate much more bearable than I had expected.

1798 August—St Vincent

On the 19th we were embarked on the *Favourite*, Sloop of War & we landed on St Vincents on the 21st. On joining the 53rd Reg^t in Fort Charlotte, St Vincents, I found a great relief but the Novelty of the Scene altogether precluded any thought. Before I had been 4 days in the Island I made the acquaintance with Doctor Anderson of the Botanic Garden & was much delighted with him & it.
I find no memorandums till 1st January.

Letter to Mrs Butt from St Vincent October 1798

When I wrote my last I was in low Spirits from the loss of Poor Grant but I have now recovered my Spirits & I think I can bear the climate for some time longer. It is true that I do think of home with fond delight but I am aware that at my time of life & with my prospects I must exert myself. The day before yesterday I rode about 20 miles into the Country & I thought within myself how delighted Martha would be to see hills piled on Hills with most delightful barrenness, some indeed covered with trees to the very top, in some places rugged rocks overhanging narrow paths & threatening to fall with every agitation. Sometimes our road lay by the Sea & then again ascending a Mountain overhanging the Coast the height thereof making my head giddy to look over. My Cousins would have laughed to see my companion & myself mounted on two Asses in full uniform. These animals retain their Character even in the New World & my poor Arm now aches from the frequent & unavoidable use of my Stick in beating my companion Bucephalus for we were obliged to assist each other in beating our Beasts. This Country at first sight is most beautiful, the heat however is very great & I cannot say that I enjoy rest at night, what with the heat, Mosquitoes & rats. The latter are my bedfellows & seem to live on the powder licked from my hair. I have often heard of a Mans Pig Tail being gnawed by the Rats but I always thought it a figure of speech I now find that it may be litterally true. When this letter reaches you I daresay you will be warming yourselves by a good fire in a close pent up room whilst I if I am alive shall be in a room with all my windows open, I shall be unable to bear my Coat on.

In front of my room we have a long gallery or Balcony called a Verandah, which being covered from the Sun & Weather & running the whole length of Nine Rooms forms a pleasant walk. The Officers Rooms form the Ridge of the Hill & look out on both sides to the Sea, down a precipice of about 300 Feet altho we are so immediately above the Sea that a Ball thrown by the hand will in all probability roll to the level of the Sea yet we may at least calculate the distance by the winding path at Two Miles or while a Dutchman could smoke a Pipe of Tobacco.

In front of these Rooms, across a Valley is another ridge like a Back of an Animal of much the same height. About half way up are the Houses of the Negroes, appearing at a distance like a small Camp but on going to them like Pig Sties. We have also in view many Cascades but the most beautiful appearance is a heavy shower of rain falling in large drops between us and the opposite ridge & sometimes driven before the wind like a thick cloud. Behind our Rooms is a stone Terrace about 100 Yards long on which we walk after sun sett & from which we see the Town of Kingston, its Bay with the Shipping under us.

On the opposite side of the bay a ridge over which we see, the Fort Duvernet standing in the Sea & on the Sea side of the Islands called the Grenadines. The Principal & nearest is Bequa, the whole making a most beautiful appearance for the Grass is greener, the Sea is more darkly green & the Sky is of a deeper blue than you have it in Europe.

Mr Stewart is quite well and not a little proud of being appointed to the light Company. which he has got thro the interest of his Brother for the Men justly observe that neither his figure or fashion would have entitled him to it, xcuse my illnatured remark, I have been taking two Views from this spot but also they might do for any other place as well, I only want to return home to see you, otherwise all Countries are alike.

I am ordered into Banishment next Month, that is to go with a party to Fort Duvernet about 3 Miles from this to pass my time for one month with nothing to do but fire on Ships passing who do not hoist their Colors. I shall gain rank as the Officer Commanding this Island is always stiled <u>Governor, Commander in Chief, Chief Judge</u> Civil & Military of the Rock. Sir Wm Young's Island & its dependencies &c &c &c

Letter to Mrs Butt from St Vincent 16 Dec 1798

I was not a little pleased my Dear Aunt at receiving your Letter the first I have received from England. There were other Letters by the same Packet but I broke the Seal of yours first. I had a Letter from Mr Maskall at the same time, he informs me that he has arranged a plan for getting My Sister home & I hope that he will have succeeded. Stewart is well & desires his respects to you. Hobson is stationed at Ouia & Yapp with him. Hobson came in yesterday & I saw him, looking quite as well as ever he did in England.

I am writing this on Town Guard & I cannot well speak in favour of the Hospitality of the Island for I am dinnerless. I am too far from the Mess to get any thing from thence & I cannot put my head into a Tavern for less than four Dollars. Lieu^t Palmer of the 53rd Reg^t takes this letter home. He has promised to call on you on his way to Ireland. He is the Son to the Bishop of Killala.

Pray give my best respects to Lord Valentia & tell him that Doctor Anderson has promised me some seeds & when I am to come home he will provide me with the Orphris, Orchis & Epidendrum,[26] but he says the Seapea[27] does not grow here. I can easily send any thing either to London or Bristol, from the latter place the expence of Carriage will not be much. I find from My Aunt that you are still great Botanists. I shall therefore study it more than ever. I am however sorry that I have not proper books. Doctor Anderson who has charge of the Botanic Garden here is very kind. The Distance from Fort Charlotte is too great for a pleasant walk. I continue drawing flowers & I have finished 28 & I have as good a collection of dried plants as Miss Rhodes[28] herself. I have met with five very curious Trees here, one called Pawpaw which is said to have the property of making Meat tender, the other the Manchinel which has a fruit like an apple with an Aromatic smell yet it is so deadly a poison that an Officer of ours was almost killed by only using some branches to make himself a hut, he was dreadfully swelled, he was cured by a Negroe. A Carraib Chief has made me Bow & Arrows.

1799 1st January   I commenced this Year by Marching at day light on a detachment to Fort Duvernet, otherwise called the Rock. The Command of this very disagreeable Battery is entrusted to a Subaltern

---

[26] Orphris, Orchis & Epidendrum are all Orchids.
[27] Seapea: *Lathyrus maritimus*.
[28] A botanist, Miss Rhodes is mentioned in transactions of the Royal Society of Arts.

The West Indies—St Vincent—1798-1800

Officer with Ten Men one Serj^t & one Corporal. I had been prepared for a very disagreeable service but it far exceeded what I imagined. I found my Post, a Rock situated about a Mile from the Shore. It is nearly 100 Feet nigh & so perpendicular that no possible way to the top was formed by Nature, between this Rock & the Shore was an Island called Sir Wm Youngs Island covered with wood but uncultivated & uninhabited

In former times S^{ir} Wm Youngs may have lived here or had a Summer house for there were two buildings now going to ruin on the Island. I found great difficulty on reaching my Post for the winding Steps cut in a crumbling rock & without any safeguard appeared so dangerous that My head became dizzy, this indeed did not seem so much as I ascended but when I had reached the Top I made many attempts to go down again without having the Steadiness to accomplish my object & I believe that had I had any other path by which I might descend even had it been two Miles round I should have gone round but the very Idea that I should never be able to get off the Rock without descending the Path made me accomplish it a dozen times before Night. The Top of this Rock ought be about 40 feet square on which was built a small wooden house the whole breadth divided into two Rooms, 1 for the Officer & 1 for the Men, the remaining Rock in front was formed into a level with two Guns which could be brought round the Gable of the Soldiers' room & might bear either on the Sea or Land. At about Twenty Feet down towards the Sea was a shelf or Terrace on which were Two heavy Guns 18 lbs^{rs}. The whole surface was rough rock without a bit of soil yet there were many Wild Cucumbers covering the Sides & it was over run with Rats. This place is of great consequence for it stands opposite the Bay of Callioquoia, the Town in St Vincents & completely commands it, but is so situated that a Ship bound for Kingston cannot make the Harbour without making the land within Gun Shot of the Rock, otherwise the Current would carry it past the opening of that Bay.

Wednesday 2^d During the Night I fancied that the wind was high, my House rocked & I could not get over my dread of the situation on which I was placed I expected to have been blown over but when I found that it had been a calm night my fears were stronger for if the Wind shook the house in this Calm what will it do in a Gale. But I have listed & must bear my burthen, at any rate the house has stood for 5 years & why should it fale with me.

Fort Duvernet. 2014.

Towards the Middle of the day however the wind did rise & I now perceived the great advantage of the Station for as you see it in the Margin [sketch obscured] the Wind is blowing as the arrow if you missed the Point to windward of Kingston Harbour you could not by a Jack make it without getting within Shot of the Rock. I had sent the Boat to Kingston for provisions & my whole day was employed in watching for the return. Many times the Boat appeared off the Point of the Harbour & seemed working against a heavy sea. I stood with my glass in my hand watching it until dark my eyes ached after working for a considerable time it disappeared & I was almost afraid that it was lost, my memorandums of that day give a regular account of my feelings.

As now it was driven to sea, Now it regained the Land &c &c now a Sloop appears as if going down to their assistance, now the Man at the helm of the Boat appears to wave his hatt, I am afraid they are in distress, now they go under the Land, the Surf appearing breaking against the Point. At four in the Evening it appeared again but the same success. My anxiety had worn me out & I went to bed soon after 7. The Boat arrived soon after 8. The Wind having fallen at Sun Set. I had been much alarmed for there were only Three Soldiers in the Boat & they did not understand rowing. I had no dinner, but had there been ever so much I could not have eaten, for I remembered having heard that Lieut^t Carmichael a short time before had lost a Boat with the crew coming round the same point.

3rd I went out to shoot having descended the Rock with difficulty. I met nothing but a dead Pig. Dreadfully disturbed during the Night by Rats which get into my Bed & run over me. I wake & find them pulling my hair to get at the Powder when I move they leap on the floor.

4   They Gnawed the Rope by which I had suspended a Ham to a beam & it fell in the Night. I trod among them & could scarcely recover my Property. I was obliged to send the boat again for provisions but it returned at Eleven o clock without difficulty

5   Examined my detachment. Out of the Number I have three who are sent here because they make such a disturbance in the Barracks quarrelling with their Wives that there is no peace in the Barracks. They are quiet enough here NB all Irish. Paddy Keugh, Paddy Storton & Dennis Price.

Here follows a list of my companions: Rats, Mice, Cockroaches, Fleas, Flies, Musquitoes, Sandflies, Grasshoppers, Beetles, Snakes. Crabs, Centipedes, Scorpions, Green Lizards, Guanas [iguana], Woodslaves [gecko], Black Ants, small & Large, Red Ants & White Ants & a Large Owl. These friends are very troublesome. I have procured a Hamock to sleep in which is suspended from the sides of my Room & by this means covering myself over with the Folds of the Cloth of the Hamock I am pretty secure but the Musquitoes bite thro' & the Woodslaves fall from the ceiling. I keep a Pistol loaded with Shot on the Table while I am drawing to fire at the Rats for they are seen running & routing in the dunghill under my Window like Pigs for just under my window the Men throw all the remains of their vegetables & which lie on the slope of the rock until a heavy rain clears all away.

I went fishing & caught a great many Parrott fish, they are very beautiful but not good, however with Limes & Chillie Pepper they do very well, as I have no fresh provision. I found two Mountain Strawbarries, a fruit of the Cactus about the size of a Hens Egg, the outside a most beautiful Lake Colour, the inside white with very minute black seeds like Strawberries, the tast insipid. Killed a large Woodslave & on falling its tail immediately came off as if he relinquished it voluntarily, the tail kept moving for two hours after the body was dead. They say that this animal falling on your flesh will raise a wale on your hand like the cut of a whip which burns dreadfully & sometimes becomes like a whitloe. I have often seen this appearance on a mans hand but I am not so clear whether the Woodslave was the cause.

Gathered many Cocoa Nuts on S^{ir} Wm Youngs Island.

6   This being Sunday the negroes Market day I bought Milk, 1 butt & 2 doz, I also bought yams, Plantains &c. I found the Sea Egg which I believe is a species of murex. The liquor which oozes from this animal is a most beautiful purple, the Shell is well known but it is curious it is covered with sharp needle like feelers which fall off at the least touch but are so sharp that they pierce a shoe & getting into the flesh are very difficult to extract, the beautiful regularity of the orifices to which their feelers are attached is extremely curious.

7   I went on Shore & shot a Sea Bird called an Admiral immensely large in feather but not good to eat. I bought some granadilloes, a fruit of the Passiflora Grandiflora, they are as large as my head & very pleasant and sweet. Indeed the fruits of the passiflora are among the best in the island if not superior.

 The Men cook the Rats. One fine one was cooked & I preserved the skin. I had intended eating it but I could not muster resolution.

10 Jany 1799   I was met on Shore by the Manager of S^{ir} Wm Youngs Estate who asked me to Breakfast. His name was Forgy, after Breakfast I returned to my Post and attempted to draw a Bird which I had shot. During my abode at this Station I regularly passed over the Shore every Day & attended the process of sugar making on Sir Wm Youngs Estate. I kept up my acquaintance with Mr Forgy & often went with him and a Mason named Hide who was hanging Coppers on the Estate. He had a Seine & we caught a great many Fish, as Snappers, Jacks but more particularly Spratts which we cooked & ate with Lime Juice & Chillies. Our drink was a Punch which was most easily procured. Limes grew wild & the Estate furnished Rum & Sugar, my time passed away very quickly. I shot Guana! That is one Guana & stewed it & found its taste like Chicken, it was about the size of a Cat, it lays Eggs & in many respects it resembles a Turtle. It is generally found on a branch, or basking on a Rock, the Negroes say that it delights in Music & they whistle when they see one, approaching as Boys to throw salt on a bird's tail. Some negroes affirm that they have by this means been allowed to tickle the head of the Animal & finally to secure it but I have my doubts. The Animal takes to the water from the rocks. I got a Goat whole at this Station which cost me Eight Guineas but it always gave four Kidds at a time & they produced me 12 Kidds within the year, each Kidd sold for four dollars

total 48 Dollars or nearly 12 Pounds within the year without reckoning the Milk which she gave in great quantities except 1 month ie two fortnights. I amused myself in fishing after a curious manner. I threw into the Sea several Brass wires with a Hook attached to each fastened to a Cork buoy. When the fish was caught it was curious to see the motion of the buoys. The fish caught are called langars a long fish, longer & thinner than a Herring, before I left the rock every morning I drew part of a flower. On the 16th I was obliged to fire at a Vessel because she did not hoist her Colors. The first shot is allowed but if she does not pay attention to that there is a considerable fine for the 2nd Shot.

Letter to Mrs Butt from Fort Duvernet 14 Jan 1799

I am now at Fort Duvernet or the Rock a description of which I have given in a former Letter. It is a worse station than I can describe. It is an absolute Prison & to be compared to the Eddistone Light house near Plymouth. I have a Party of Men who are chosen as the worst men in the whole Reg^t. I have now given you some of the bad qualities of my present position. Now for its advantages. Imprimis, plenty of Fat Rats of the Cattle Kind they are as Edgar expresses it small deer. Plenty of Fish, Plenty of Herbs & Trees. I care not for the Fruit, My pursuit is the blossom, health as much as you could wish & plenty of exercise for I cannot move 5 Yards without ascending Steps & the Cheapness can only be compared with that of a Prisoner in one of our Jails where if you live on the Jail allowance you will not have much to pay & I do live on my Jail allowance by which I save my Mess Bill an Established Charge of Sixteen Dollars per Month or £4- besides One Dinner per week when on guard which may be reckoned as much more & I wear what cloths I like. I endeavour to avoid expence & I think that I succeed. In time I may expect promotion & then I shall do better. Our Reg^t both Officers & men is in perfect health, they could not be better in England. It is now Xmas & I am overpowered with heat while you I daresay are shivering. The Quarters I occupy are only seperated from those of the Privates by a deal partition, they are all in good spirits singing Night & Day, sometimes rather to my Annoyance. The Ratts & Cockroaches & Lizards are sporting around me.

I am sometimes attracted from my Studies by observing the latter moving along the Roof with their backs downward & appearing to walk as easily attached to the underpart of the Beam as the fly itself. You have no doubt often observed that the candle throws a shadow on the Ceiling like a Glory round the head of the Saints towards this light the flies seem inclined to collect & here you see the lizard, watching his opportunity, lies like a Crocodile ready to snap up his victim as it approaches his Jaws. My Bed stands in a Corner with curtains made of Gauze which are tucked up with the greatest care least the Musquitoes should enter, but every precaution is sometimes taken in vain & I am delightfully serenaded all Night with a song as loud almost as the humming of a May bee & I am sorry feelingly to say that their music is not the only inconvenience. I leave off that I may go to fish by moonlight Pray excuse the Paper. Yapp is well. I have a Servant from Kidderminster Named Yapp - I am &c H Sherwood Governor of the Island of Fort Duvernet, Commander in Chief of the Forces on the Island of the Rock & Sir Wm Young &c &c &c &c

17 The Commander in Chief General Coyler passed by in a frigate & entered Kingston harbour

18th The Fleet passed from England, a most beautiful sight coming down close to my post & appearing so near that you might conceur it possible to jump on board. One of my men being rather silly attempted to get on Shore on a raft made of a door of one of the old Houses but got himself overset & was nearly drowned, when he was safely recovered we could not help laughing heartily at him for he proposed returning by land to England & did not expect to be long on his journey. He gives a curious account of what he saw at the bottom of the sea.

Made acquaintance & dined with Mr Morgan of Prospect Estate. Mr Forgy lent me a horse. I was laying in my Cott & heard the Soldiers in the next room laughing very much which made me attend to what they were about. My Friend Pat Norton who was so nearly drowned was asserting with oaths that a Lady who he knew in Ireland kept in her Park upwards of 300 Tame wild Geese that they were kept from running away by a wall 20 miles long & 12 feet high & that they made a noise that was heard 3 miles off. Norton is always making these speeches either on purpose or from the witness of his ideas. I am apt to think he does it on purpose & I am obliged to hear every thing that passes among the soldiers. I often hear some of his Wit. The other day before he undertook his Voyage he was swearing at the Country & said that if he was sure of remaining another year in the island he would be away before a month was over. Another Irish Soldier told one of ours that he himself was present at the Battle of the Boyne [1690] when a boy. He said that he stood by King James's side when an Artillery Man asked His majesty's permission to shoot the Prince of Orange but was stopped by the King who said, "you

The West Indies—St Vincent—1798-1800

Rascale would you make my daughter a Widow." Breed of sheep at Collioqua with four Horns.

Feby On the first of February my Month service at the Rock was compleated & I was relieved & returned to the Fort (Charlotte). I found the Company is this I belong the General's Company occupying the Barracks at Old Woman's Point on the same Hill on which Fort Charlotte is situated but about 100 Feet lower down. I had to go up to dinner every day. The Hill between our Station & the Mess Room was so steep that it required the greatest exertion to go up & therefore I seldom attempted it. The road round was about half a mile & we had upwards of 180 steps to go up. This was very fatiguing in the hot Climate in the middle of the day.

The Soldiers paraded near their own Barracks & only joined the other Companies on Field days when they met in Kingston or on the Beach about half Way

This Month I mounted Kingston Guard in my turn many times & when there I dined with Mr Henville, Mr Paul & Mrs Douglass. Mr Henville is Judge of the island, Mr Paul a Gentleman of Property having a Plantation near Kingston & Mrs Douglass is a Widow possessing an Estate at a Distance but living in Kingston for Security, the Part of the Island where her Estate lies having been unsettled. I bought a Goat for 20 dollars of Serg^t Shearer. Lieut^t Weston & myself walked to M^s Henville's Estate which is Inland lying towards the source of the Great heads river under the Hills. The Country here is beautifully Romantic, well wooded & green, quite to Contrast to the dry Rocky Barren hills about Fort Charlotte & the Sea.

March. I became so much reconciled to the Rock that I took Lieut^t Ponsonby's turn of duty there for a fortnight by this I found that I can live cheaper than at the Mess. I have also made acquaintance with Several Gentlemen in the Neighbourhood.

On the 1st day I dined with Mr Morgost at prospect Estate. I arrived at Two o clock & while waiting for Dinner a Young lady was playing a March in Blue Beard. I looked out of the Window over a dark gloomy Valley towards the Hills covered with high wood & could fancy that I should see Banditte rush out of the Dark & narrow paths.

Mr Warner Ottley Nephew to S^{ir} Wm Young has taken charge of S^{ir} W^{ms} Estates opposite the Rock & takes me to his house to sleep.

From this time to the 13th I passed my time at Warner Ottley's sleeping, eating, drinking & riding. Mr Otley's horses only occasionally going to the Rock leaving the Ser^t to take care of the duty, indeed he was quite as fit as myself. On the 13th a party of ladies headed by Mrs Weston came to spend the day with me, we drew the Sun, caught plenty of fish & marooned under the Trees in S^{ir} Wm Young's Island, where we cooked our provisions & drank punch. Lieut^t Weston & M^r LeCroix a French Planter related to Mrs Honville being with the ladies, we had a most pleasant day. My Time of Service was out on the 16th & I was almost sorry to return to the Fort. Bought a Horse for 184 Dollars, I drew a Bill on Mr Bishton for £100. So passed the Month of March.

I still draw plants every morning before I leave my room, indeed there is not much to attract me out of Doors. The Fort stands on a high dry Barren hill & the only ride is to Kingston & there is not much to see, I have a good many acquaintances there.

April 1799

The 2nd the Boat going to the rock was overset accident which I had been anticipating. Two white men drowned & a Negroe. I went out to Gommier an Estate of Madam Labord, La Croix's sister, where he lives. Gommier is situated under a Bluff Woody Hill which was fortified & defended by the Carraibs during the War. It was found very difficult to dislodge them, indeed they abandoned it at last from being surrounded. They returned to a Mountain covered with Wood from which a Stream of water spills. The only approach to it is by a narrow winding Path only admitting one Person with a precipice on one side & perpendicular Rock on the other. Near to this place is a Mountain called Vigie (or Lookout) It was on this Mountain that the principal Struggle took place between the Carraibs & ourselves, in two severe Battles. The first was fought by the 46th Reg^t & the Militia against the French & Carraibs. The second the 42, 53, 65th & other Corps were engaged & it was very seriously contested. Numbers were killed in this action which may be said to have ended the War, the approach to the Enemies position being up a Number of ridges from different Points, no Calculation could bring the Men to bear in a simultaneous attack, but each party was in some degree obliged to bear a brunt for a time. The party who first appeared were all destroyed, the others succeeded. On returning home we heard great shouting & perceived a Smoke over the Hill but we could not conceive the Reason, until we saw the Summitt of the Hill to our left suddenly covered with fire. We were riding along the valley, the foot of the Hill to our left, Great Heads over to our right, on first perceiving the flames we stopped to observe them but we very shortly observed that the Fire ran so fast thro the dry Canes that it became us to think of our safety, we therefore cantered off & it required hard riding to get clear of the fire, altho we had not a mile to ride. The latter part was really alarming the fire seemed to come down the Hill towards us the Canes cracking & bursting with the Heat our Horses frightened & almost ungovernable, with a River with high Perpendicular Banks to our right, we had several Ladies in company & we were all very glad when we had the River between us & the fire, the horse of the Negroes & Black Soldiers from Dorsetshire Hill working with green branches in their hands among the flames trying to beat the fire put us in mind of Devils in Hell, particularly as the Evening closed in. Our Ladies were so much alarmed as to become incapable of reason or we might have returned, but they hurried on & at last passed down to the River by a very difficult pass & ran a risk of hurling themselves & their horses but we all escaped. The Beauty of the Country I had rode thro within these few days has been most delightful, the green of the Canes, the beauty of the Woods & the Coolness of the Air with the Cascades of Water falling from the Hills made me almost wish to take up my abode here & I think I could be happy to stay was it not for friends in England, it is a very healthy part of the Country & by all I can hear, quite as much so as any part of the World.

9 On town Guard One of the Prisoners in the Goal stabbed another before my face & I could not get in for nearly an hour the factor not being found, altho I could plainly see what was passing within thro the iron bars, the Goal is a Ground floored large Room like what I remember a Cage to be in England only so much large being I suppose 30 Feet Square & all the Prisoners locked in together without any privacy, each lying down to sleep as his fancy takes him, here men, Women & Children debtors & murderers are all put in together & locked up, the factor going off with the Keys, they are like Java Sparrows in a large Cage, when the Key came, the Man who had stabbed the other threatened to murder the first soldier who entered, but on opening the door & going in he was very quiet, the man hurt was a Spanish Prisoner of war. I obtained leave on 15th to go round the Island. I set off & rode to a M^r McDonald's Estate where I passed the Evening, the Road ran by the Sea & was a continued ascent of small Hills & descents to the coast, forming a succession of bays with head lands between. The whole dry & barren with a few bushes, but more like Commons in England in very dry weather, but on passing the boundary of the Carraib Country the appearance became much finer, being a flatt & covered with Reeds & Trees. The Reeds are called Noreaus & are used by our Officers as they were by the Carraibs for building houses, the Hay as thatching & the stalks placed perpendicular tyed together make an excellent wall, beneath these Reeds the Gardens of the Carraibs, over run with weeds, still produce pines, ananas & among the forest trees we found the fruits of the Country. The Yams had propagated themselves & overrun Acres, enough to feed half the Island. It is reckoned very dangerous to pass

between Mount Young & Ouia, there being many Run away Negroes & Black Carraibs in the woods, it is said upwards of 1000. It is necessary to take an Escort from Mount Young about 16 miles to Ouia the whole distance being 37 miles from Kingston to Ouia. Near Ouia the Mountains approach the Sea & are of great height covered with wood & of a beautiful Green, the plane between these mountains & the Sea becomes of very contracted extent & full of small Rivers or Mountain Torrents, some dry at this Season, others about the Station of Ouia running all the Year the road often runs over bluffs looking down to the Sea perpendicularly 200 or more feet & in one place the whole cliff has given way & cause the road to be cut round it, but it is not six feet in diameter & without any thing to warn you becomes extremely dangerous, on looking down you see the Sea foaming at the bottom, of a Circular Hole like a deep well. The fort of Ouia is on a peninsula most beautifully situated on the Windward point of the Island, it is of moderate height & gentle elevation containing a great quantity of fine land, when compared with the Mountains around it is a Mole hill. Yet in another situation it would make a good high bluff on each side of the tongue of Land are two very fine Rivulets or Mountain Streams falling in cascades from the Mountains, in one of these Rivulets there is a delightful bath in a natural Basin overshadowed by high Trees, & on the Extreme point of the Peninsula is the finest Natural Sea Bath I ever saw or heard of. The Rocks run from the Point nearly half a mile into the Sea in a compleat plane & at the end of a natural Wall of Rock rises up as a Barrier to the Sea, the ocean always roars & beats against the Wall, & generally two or Three days in the week throws waves over, but falling gently on the land side like a Sea breaking on board ship, within the Rock is a Natural basin which is replenished by the Wave & has an outlet by which the super abundant water is carried into the sea, by this Means our bath is kept constantly replenished & constantly clear.

At this place I found almost the whole remains of the Aborigines or Yellow/Red/Carraibs now reduced to a few families not more than forty or fifty Individuals, the remainder having been destroyed by the black Carraibs. The origin of these latter is disputed some supposing them the descendents of a Guinea Ship wrecked on the Coast, others that they were simply runaway negroes from the Plantations, it however is certain that they are of Negroe Origin & that they had almost destroyed the original American Inhabitants. The yellow carraibs are of a Copper Color, Small but active rather Indolent. The Men employ themselves in fishing. The women in planting the manioc or Cassava, they make Basketts which are very neat

& they weave good Cotton hamocs but their Indolence is such that possessing food, they cannot be easily excited to work. Ouia is the Ne Plus Ultra for beyond the Mountains run down perpendicularly into the Sea. I was therefore obliged to return by the same track which I had gone & returned the 21st.

21   I forwarded to England a Box of dried specimens of flowers & drawings., I sent them by Captain Wells of the sloop *St Vincents* who kindly undertook to deliver them to Mr Maskell to be by him sent to Mrs Butt.

To Mrs Butt from St Vincents 23 April 1799

As the fleet is to Sail in a few days & an opportunity occurring of sending my collection of <u>drawings & dryed Plants</u> etc to England free of expence I am induced to avail myself of the opportunity as a heavy load of Baggage is a great hindrance in a Subalterns Haversack. I have therefore sent all my Collection in a Box addressed to Mr Maskell in London. If you do not think it worthwhile to send for them they will remain until I return. I do not think that you will find them worth seeing, but the very sight will prove that I have not been neglectful of your commands and any rate you must flatter me by saying that they are beautiful. The Shells & Jumble beads[29] I hope will please you, as I have been 50 miles to Collect them to Ouia The very extreme point of the Island. My road led thro a most delightful Country far superior to the part of the Island in our possession. It was until this few months cultivated by the Charraibs. It is now wild but I dare say Government will allot it in a Short time. It will be then cleared for it is astonishing how soon a Country in this part of the World is overrun with wood & consequently affording a secure retreat for Slaves running from their Masters & others who prefer a life of depredation to a settled state. It is computed that there are 1000 outlaws now roaming thro this Country who commit every act of atrocity on unfortunate people of any Color who fall into their hands, it is therefore necessary to have an Escort in passing thro this part of the Island.

To give you any account of the beauty of the Scenery is far above my Powers, how Marten[30] would rejoice to wander from one view to another. The only cultivated spots being the ground by the sides of Mountain Torrents. The Ridge of Mountains which like the

---

[29] Jumblie beads: bright orange-brown seed of the Necklace Tree, *Ormosia coarctata*.
[30] Marten Butt, Mrs. Butt's son.

back of a Whale runs the whole length of the Island is for the most part covered with clouds & there are not more than 2 or 3 Passages across them, in general it is adviseable to coast the island rather than attempt to cross even when directly opposite or as at St Ouia to return all round rather than attempt to go 7 miles.

One of the remarkable facts is that the Island produces no venomous reptiles while the neighbouring Islands as St Lucia & Martinique abound with them, so much so as to be a terror to the inhabitants. I am now quite fond of the Country & I should be sorry to leave it even for England at least at present. Stewart is well, Poor Yapp has drunk too much new Rum & lost his health. He is invalided & gone home. If you were here I should never wish to leave the Country.

I am in daily anticipation of being sent to Ouia a post at the further extremity of the Island about 40 Miles off.

May 20 [1799]   The Colony voted £200 as a present to be laid out in Beer & Beef for the Men of the Regiment as a token of respect. My Horse threw me by way of shewing his pleasure. I rode to a Well impregnated with fixed Air, the Water tastes like Spruce Beer.

June 5th The Company to which I belong ordered to Ouia. We embarked on board the Government Schooner in the morning & landed at Night, we passed along the Leeward of the island & consequently on the opposite side to that along which I had rode, the Mountain from Morne Rond where there is a Volcano to Ouia comes down abruptly to the Sea, covered with beautiful Woods, the Sea was rather rough for the last 3 hours prior to which the Vessel was surrounded by porpoises so thick as to seem as if we could have walked on their backs to the Shore. All my Crockery Broke.

The Officers of the Company which we relieved made a Charge for their Share of Stock viz 37 Pigs & a number of Pigeons, my share came to 4 Joes at £1-17s-4d each. The remainder of the Month passed in walking about between the foot of the Mountains & the Sea, bathing every day in fresh water before Breakfast & Salt Water afterwards, cutting sticks, supple jacks, gathering Jumbee Beads, small Pea like beads Red with a black Eye & the latter part I began to form a Garden, but my share of the 37 Pigs & Pigeons are far from good Gardeners.

Letter to Mrs Butt from St Vincents 2 June 1799

All your kind Letters have arrived safe, the pleasure which I receive in seeing the Bridgenorth postmark can only be expressed by bringing to your remembrance my high spirits which you no doubt remember. I can no longer eat, drink or sleep after hearing that a Mail is arrived at Barbadoes until it reaches this Island & then we see the Signal for the Packet, how I watch our Drum major as he goes to the Post Office & count his steps along the side of the Hill as he returns, with my Spye Glass in my hand. You are indeed in league with some thing you ought to be ashamed of or how could you ask what was become of Virgil. I acknowledge that he is very dusty but not out of respect, but Captain Hobson declared war against him on Ship board & now I really have no time to attend to him, I am even afraid to look on my Shelf where he lays for fear of his reproaches. Your Account of Poor Mr Grant's Pereginations is truly laughable tho I suppose disagreeable to himself. I wish I could see him here as the Climate would no doubt agree with him, having been accustomed to a hot climate in his Youth. Will you be kind enough to tell Mrs Grant that the 53 Rg^t still keeps its good Character. In this Island the inhabitants have voted £200 to the Privates for a dinner on the 4th of June accompanied by a Little expression of their approbation. Stewart is in possession of my late Government where he has been for a Month. I feel very proud of the remembrance of the Ladies of Bridgenorth, pray thank them all for me.

St Lucia No Letters found till July 1800 it was not lost [Sherwood's note]

July 1799   I ventured further from the Post in spite of the 1000 Men in Arms in the woods (who I believe are neither here nor there) I rode to Rabbacca & dined with Lieut^t Cameron (called the Governor) we amused ourselves turning up stones in Rabbacca River now almost dry & catching Prawns. About a mile up the river we came to a large neglected Pine apple Plantation & loading ourselves with fruit returned. We might have got a waggon load altho no one was near here, they are the remains of the poor Carraibs Gardens who might have been now here had not the French with their Revolution turned the World upside down & enticed them to attack the English. After committing great cruelties they were overpowered & carried first to a Rock near the Grenadines, afterwards to Honduras & finally to Sierra Leone on the Coast of Africa. We had scarcely left the Bed of the River & preparing our Dinner when a Storm of Rain fell in the Mountains & in less than half an hour the whole bed was full of water Rushing down with such violence that nothing could have stood against it, it was in such a Kind of flood that a Doctor Pearson was carried away with his Horse a few Months since near Callioqa. The Torrent ceased as rapidly as it rose for before we had done dinner it was almost dry again. We saw two Parrotts being the first I had ever seen Wild. They are very shy & I am told that no nest was ever taken in St Vincents or a Bird caught alive, this of course must arise from the nature of the Country in which they build. The Mountains are indeed so inaccessible that you cannot go from Rabbacca to Morne Rond, across the Hills being only 7 Miles but of necessity must go all round the Island being 60 Miles.

11   Captain Millar Lieut^t Classon & myself with Yellow Carraib Guides went over the Mountains to Chattuary. This is a bay & Valley laying to the East of the Island, formerly occupied by one of the Principal Carraib Chiefs, now entirely neglected, our Road lay thro woods so thick as scarcely to allow us a glimpse of the sky & no path whatever to be seen. The Carraibs know the way by the bark of the trees & the Bend of the higher branches for as the Wind is generally almost always Easterly, the eastern side of the Tree is clear of moss, & has an inclination towards the West.

23   Colonel Brabane ordered a sham fight. I commanded the attacking Party, was ordered to take my time of advance from a Muskett Shot but when I came to my Post I found that I was stationed on the Coast with a heavy swell against high rocks, we could not hear each other speak much less hear a Muskett at a miles distance.

26   I went up the hills in search of Water Lemons & was much bitten by insects called Bole Rouge. The Itching was intolerable but cured by Lime Juice.

Aug   Bought 11 laying Hens 11 Dollars. Much troubled with Chiquoes which is an insect which gets into the Skin of the foot & forms a bag within the flesh as large as a Pea, the Itching much like Chilblains, there is considerable difficulty in extracting them & if injudiciously done often causes bad sores.

3   I went with the Carraibs on board a Sloop at Sea, we went in a Canoe which two Men might carry on their heads yet we are 5 on board. Captain Millar one of us is a very large man, every sea washed over us & it was as much as we could do to bale out the water.

Caught a Guana & tied it up by a string, employed much in preparing a Garden, planted Maize & Chillie Pepper. Obliged to sell my Fowls, they destroy my Garden, found the Cactus Grandiflorus in flower which is uncommon, some say because it flowers in the Night only. Planted melons which were up in 3 days.

9   On the 9th we found that our Provisions began to run short for we are supplied from Kingston in the first instance but from England. The sloop appeared off the Bay but could not get in the surf running very high along the Coast. We have been out of Wine for Officers for a fortnight & there is only Rum to last till Wednesday or Cocoa & Sugar.

10   Colonel Abercromby being on a Party of Pleasure we received an invitation to meet him at Chateauaix & Captain Millar & myself went round in the Carraibs Canoe. After dinner finding that the Sloop was not arrived Millar & myself went down to Morne Ronde & Chateau Belle Air where we found the Sloop at Anchor. The Skipper seemed to trouble himself but little he said the Surf would be high all the Moon & He should not attempt coming to Ouia till the Moon changed. We therefore took possession of the Sloop & slept on board but the Accommodations were so bad that I had no rest. At four in the morning got under weigh but the breeze was so light we could not make way. We went on Shore & breakfasted with Mansel at Morne Rond, while at breakfast the Breeze freshened & the Sloop left us. We followed in the Canoe. The wind increased & blew very hard. I sat in the bow of the Canoe & the Wind blew so strong against my Neck the Sea washing over me that my teeth Chattered in my head, Millar was fully employed in bailing out the Boat & we could not move, the smallness of the Canoe being such that a very little would overset us, passing the Point of Duvalleuse we were nearly swamped & it was necessary to put into Chateauaix & put me & the Carraibs Captain Baptiste on Shore. We dried our Cloths that is my Cloaths for Baptistes clothes were easily dried & we caught some fish & cooked it & then pursued our way home where I arrived at half after three, the Sloop anchored at Ten past four & the Canoe came soon after.

I received an invitation from Colonel Abercromby to come to head Quarters to a Ball given by the Garrison to the Inhabitants which is to be on the 16th Ins^{t}. On the 14th I was prepared to ride in to Fort Charlotte but it rained so hard that I could not move. After dinner it cleared up & I was foolish enough to set off at the risk of finding some of the Torrents so swollen as to be impassible, I was fortunate enough to find them empty & I got to Fort Charlotte without any accident.

16   The garrison ball took place at Patty Charlottes tavern, all the Ladies of the Island were present & everything went off very well, at day light we marched Round the Town with the Band in front, Ladies as well as Gentlemen.

17   I was to have been at another Ball at Mr Dubois in Greatheads Valley at night but I was too much fatigued.

18   I returned towards Ouia, dined with Officers 4th West India Reg^{t}[31] at Mount Young & slept at Rabbacca at Ensign Camerons, reach Ouia on the 19th at 11 o clock.

---

[31] By the end of the 18th century, the British army had become the biggest single purchaser of African slaves. Over a 12-year period, an estimated 13,000 Africans were purchased for £70 to £80 each to serve the Crown. As combatants, Black units fought

In consequence of the expedition to Holland under Sir Ralph Abercromby Colonel Abercromby goes home & Colonel Braban is to command the Reg^t & goes to Fort Charlotte, Cap^n Millar will command at Ouia

21   Another sham fight. I took the Fort. I am busily employed every day in making a garden. Sprained my back in forcing tye tyes from the Hedge. To the end of the month I could not stand upright, resolved not to work so hard in future.

Septr The beginning of this month I must much hurt, in so much as to make me seriously inclined to sell my Commission, the Cause was this. On leaving England I had not £20 with me & I was put to great expence more indeed than was necessary from my openness of character, I advanced small sums to Officers & was not repaid, the sums that I advanced were very trifling not amounting to much over ten pounds but the expences incurred at Martinico and Barbadoes were much more and I therefore drew on Mr Bishton of Shifnal for £100 of the 200 which I had left in his hands. It however appeared that the £200 was invested in the Coventry Streets and therefore not immediately saleable there was therefore a demur on paying my Bill which was got over by the kindness of Mrs Butt. My feelings at the time were very acute & I could not understand the reasons. The Merchant to whom I had given the Bill was very kind & attributed everything to Mistake but I was attacked with Fever & much reduced in consequence & could not do my duty. Two Packets from England arrived without a single letter which made me the more uneasy. My remarks at the time were very bitter. I remained very unwell in mind and Body thro' the Month & I sold my Horse for 18 joes and 3 kidds equal to 23 Joes of £1-17. to each. Our Pay this Month was made better by 3 p^r diem, the charges made for a Rations very reduced indeed it appears that the Commissariat had originally made a wrong charge.

Lieut^{ts} Lieth & Smith came in a Boat from Teward to see us, another packet arrived but I had no letter. I lent my saddle & Bridle to a Mr Hefley & he never returned it: this was a loss of Six pounds. On the 3 a most dreadful Storm of Thunder & Rain. Our pay was again made better by an inquiry into the

---

alongside British troops in St Lucia and St Vincent before being assimilated into a British regiment. In 1799 all the individual units operating in the West Indies were combined, and called the West India Regiment. Enslaved men of African descent who were recruited for the British army in the Caribbean received the same pay, rations and punishments as white soldiers. But they were still enslaved, and subject to local slave laws. Buckley, R N, 1998 *The British Army in the West Indies* University of Florida Press.

currency. We are now to receive Spanish Dollar round for 4/8ᵈ. The disturbed State of the Country had allowed great irregularities & individuals had cut the dollars into four for the sake of change in the course of time so much was purloined from each Quarter that in some instances little more than the rim remained each person cutting away as much as he thought convenient. The pay department did not fail to take their share & only paid the Troops with the husks, this is now regulated. This is fully equal to another Six pence a day for a lieutᵗ.

Another Packet & no news. We begin to find that Ouia is a pleasant journey from Kingston & in consequence we have many Visitors which is a heavy Burthen on our Mess but not perceived by our Visitors. The two last weeks I have paid 18 Dollars for Persons I have no connection whatever who come to the Post merely as a lounge.

13   The Hogs got into my garden & destroyed all my hopes.

We were alarmed from 13ᵗʰ to 19ᵗʰ by the loss of a man coming from Kingston we thought him killed by Carraibs but he turned up on the 19ᵗʰ having lost or spent Money belonging to the officers.

Two Sloops were taken by the French between this & Kingston. Capᵗⁿ Bucklands Company relieve Capᵗⁿ Elwins., The Pigs again behaved most ungentlemanlike in breaking my Fence & eating my Indian Corn & I tried to kill one but the small shot either missed it from my blind rage or else it did not care about it.

21   A Heavy storm unroofed my House & I went into the woods to cut rafters & was bitten by a Bete Rouge,³² the bite is about as bad as that of a Muskitto & scratching makes it worse.

22ⁿᵈ·   My House irreparable. Pulled it down & carried the Materials to a better spot. Worked hard at it & so ended this month.

November   began the month with my House. MᶜCaskill severely hurt by a ground Thorn thro his leg makes our duty heavy on Guard every other Night.

3   I had a working party of 27 Men to bring thatch for my New House. Two Negroes arrived with information that Strangers would be

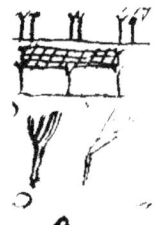

with us tomorrow. I feel angry for I have been starving myself for some time past to avoid running into debt & strangers come & drank Claret at my expence without giving thought.

We build our Hutts in the following form. Six uprights with forked heads about 6 Feet from the ground. Then Poles across lying on the forks. Then Rafters from the Pole to a

---

³² Bête Rouge, Chigger or harvest mite.

Ridge Pole. Then tying split Bamboos or rather canes like laths we take the feathery top of the Cane & breaking it thro the Lath leave the leafy part hanging outwards & tuck the stalk under the second lath within tying a second Lath on the outside which holds it all firm. Thus I built an excellent hut with two Rooms for less than Six Pounds.

On the 6th I heard from England that Mrs Butt had paid the Bill of £100 for me, I have been in great distress & even rendered ill from my feelings on the Subject. My Hut was finished & I began a Garden

9   I had to fight very hard with the Jack Spaniards, a kind of Wasp, who had taken possession of the brush wood. I made a great smoke to windward for several days & was stung & almost set my house on fire before I conquered them. Among my discoveies I was instructed how to procure the Cabbage from the Palm Trees which is nothing more than the Pith or heart of the Tender Head of the Plant it is very good & an excellent substitute for Cabbage. This day a Ball of Fire during a Thunder storm fell on the flag staff & splintered it to pieces, in all probability the Flag Staff proved the conductor & saved the Barracks. This is the Second time that Lightning or Electricity has done mischief within my observations since I arrived in the W. I. first at Old Womans Point Fort Charlotte where it destroyed a House & now the Flag Staff. Two Negroes were lately Killed under a Tree in Morne Rond. The Negroes say when it Rains, Country come Buckra, Niger Man stands stiff in a bush

13   News reached us that there was extraordinary intelligence from Europe but no particulars we were on the Fidget & Doctor Powel said he would walk to Mount Young if I would go with him, we set off at four o clock & reahced Mount Young at Eight being Sixteen Miles. The News: Seringhgapatam taken, Tippoo Sultan killed,[33] 15 Million of Money taken in the Fort: to counterbalance this we hear that the Duke of York has been beaten & driven out of Holland with Great loss. Col^l Lightburne & Captain Buckland arrived from England the latter will come to Ouia.

15   Colonel Braban arrived to take the Command, Colonel Lightburne being now in Command of the Regiment at Fort Charlotte took stock & found myself rather better than nothing having Goats &c to the value of 17 Joes. Augustin, a Carraib Chief formerly taken by Fraser came to the Post & begged to be allowed to remain. He adressed the Commanding Officer as follows, "Massa suppose me go come here me go catch Canoe up in a Buss there Yonder." Finding I cannot keep my Garden clear from othe People's Cattle I have Destroyed it & bought

---

[33] Tippoo Sultan, ruler of Mysore, India (1750-May 1799).

fowls in my defence, they will I hope give me eggs. I had eggs enough on the 3rd to sett a Hen on 13 eggs & from this time my fowls increased rapidly. Sometimes I lost a few by Opossums or manicoes & I was often called up in the night to protect them.

General Campbell the new Commandant of St Vincents notified his intention of inspecting the outposts & as I had neither Hatt Coat or Boots fit to appear at a Review I was obliged to go into Kingston. I hired the Black Carraibs to take me in their Canoe.

4th After breakfasting with Col^l Braban I left Ouia & got ducked in the Surf on getting off- The Sea being always high on this windward part of the Island. We reached Morne Rond in two Hours & I had a fine view of the Volcano called the Suffrier. The day was clear but there was no eruption, the trees towards the top seemed scorched. The carraibs told me that a Demon or Death Zombie lives there. This Zombie is a Spirit that has large flocks & Herds & Numbers of Cloths, generally of a Red Color that he often employs himself in airing his red Jacketts & covers half the Hill with them at times, that the different vents for the heated air were his Stew grates and that a favorite of the Zombie would often see each of these vents covered with a pot boiling some contained Agootees, Manicoos Guanas & other dainties. My informer had never seen the Cookery but he had often seen the Cloths hanging out to dry and he asserted that if you wished to see the Suffrier to advantage it would be advisable to offer a Bottle of Rum before you ascended it. The way to make your offering was to hide it in a Bush. If you neglected this you would be sure to put your foot into some burning hole of which there are many at the Top of the Hill. I bantered Augustine about his God loving him but he became furious & told me that black Men had Gods as well as White Men & he seemed to be carried away by his passion. I thought it prudent to change the Subject. I had a good opportunity of observing the Leeward of the Island which is much like the windward viz cultivated only a short distance from the Sea. The Inward parts being `mountainous Ridges. The Carraib County between Ouia & Mount Young apparently far the finest Country. The highest Cultivated spots are appropriated by the negroes who grow Yams, Sweet Potatoes &c. There were numerous fishing Canoes along the Leeward Coast belonging as I understand to the different Estates. In each was a Man & boy & they appeared to have caught much fish. We reached Hunts Bay under Fort Charlotte a little before four & I got up to the Mess as the Dinner was gone out. I found Buckland there who had been at Bridgenorth lately.

I spent the evening with Lieut^r Mansel & slept there.

December 1799 St Vincents

There are improvements going on in the Bay between the Fort & Kingston Town is building called New Edinburgh. I passed the day with Lieut^t Weston & found the Officers full of the Idea of going to England immediately. Lieut^t Hughes gave me some Books which were highly prized & I got them on board the Government Sloop together with my Hatt, Coat, Boots &c.

On the 7th I left Fort Charlotte & passing by Kingston saw the Militia reviewed & breakfasted with them, then left Kingston & reached Mount Young at Sun Set. Captain Dolphin 1st W. I. gave me a Supper & a Bed. Breakfasting with him the next day I proceeded & passing an hour at Rabbacca with Governor Cameron, arrived at Ouia to dinner. The government Sloop which sailed the day before yesterday was not arrived. My hands and face, particularly the Lips were peeled from the effects of the Sun— Buckland arrived. A Pig Poisoned from drinking the expressed juice of the Cassada or manioc.

I walked 10 miles to Rabbacca with our Surgeon where we slept being 22 miles. Goat Kidded 3 Kidds. Sold a Goat of my own Raising 8 Dollars, bought a share of a Cask of Madeira & bottled it had 34 bottles my share was 2 joes or £3.15. or little more than 2/- a Bottle.

1800 Jany 3

News that General Bounaparte has destroyed the Directory & with Abbe Seyes & Newbell declared themselves Triumvirs.

Impossible to sleep at Night from a Manico making love to my Fowls, this Animal is the most disgusting stinking thing I ever saw, like a pig & it has a Second or Under Belly into which its Young Creep when alarmed. It has a long tail which assists in hanging to the branches of Trees. It is extremely cunning & will throw itself down as if dead if it gets the slightest blow & will lay without Motion allowing itself to be struck with seeming to feel nothing until you have it thinking it dead, when it rises & runs off, when it lies on the Ground in this way you must seize it strongly by the back of the neck if you want to take it for if it can reach you it will bite very severely.

10   General Campbell with his staff arrived & Dined with us. We were paraded for Review at six but the General did not turn out till 8 when we were reviewed & fired 15 Rounds blank Cartridge. We had invited our Friends of the 4th West Indias Regiment to meet the General at Dinner & McCaskell & myself rode to meet them. We met Captain Dolphin, Lieut^t Cameron, Dixon & Doctor Moffat at Sandy Bay. I gave my bed to Cameron & my Hammock to Moffat & I slept on a Bench. The General & all the Strangers left us after Breakfast 11th.

Ouia St Vincents January 11

I could not sleep this night when I lay on the bench & I was much struck by the Tremendous Noise of the Sea beating against the Shore near Ouia. This indeed is the Constant noise but what we hear every day is not remarked except occasionally brought to your observation, the Surf near Ouia is sometime Tremendous, Striking against the Rocks & throwing its spray near 100 feet.

13   A Fleet appeared off, we counted 35 Sail, 5 of which were apparenty Frigates & all except Two three masted. The Fleet lay too from Sunrise till Eleven when they made sail & passed down between St Lucia & St Vincents steering North. We suppose the fleet for Jamaica. Got some Rum from the Store which the Negroes call Tiffy Taffy, Two days old Tomorrow. The Negroes are found of Repeating the Word as / Gru Gru a Fruit / Gree Gree a Tree / Tye Tye Bindweed /fum fum a Whipping / Culty Culty a Hatchet / Messe Messe Dinner

17   Being anxious to hear what the fleet was that appeared on the 13th I left Ouia for Mount Young. We were afraid of an accident having happenned to our Messenger Captain Dovers Servant was drowned last week between this & Mount Young. I reach Rabbacca & slept there.

18   Reached Mount Young before any one was up but soon roused Dixon & I found that I had missed the Man whom I had come to seek. The fleet which passed on the 13th was part of the fleet from England bound for Jamaica.

19   Breakfasted at Rabbacca & dined at Ouia.

McCaskell Doctor Powel & myself began to clear a spot of Ground to make a Garden. We worked most days, cutting up the brush wood & making a hedge. I employed myself in keeping up a large fire round the trunks of Trees which appeared decayed, picking up a Quantity of brush wood around & keeping a constant fire but I found that I did not get on as I had expected took lessons in Carraib Ma Bou y ca / How do you do. I do not think myself an apt scholar.

I planted Lemon Grass for the benefit of Society & Limes which I hope never to see in bearing.

Feby   Found the real Supple Jack[34] in the woods which has given a new turn to our exertions, now we go up the Hills every day in search of it & bring down loads it is a vine

14   while in search of Supple Jacks I heard a Horn or Conch & from that knew the runaway Negroes or Black Carraibs are not far off. Hen hatched 10 Chicks.

---

[34] Supple-jack: *Berchemia volubilus*, Rattan Vine, a climbing shrub.

Bought Hoghead wine for 15 Joes £28-2-6

21   Got my Tree down with a tremendous Crash. I had a fire burning round it for 33 days there will be fuel for the Men for some time. A fleet of 12 sailed passed to Leeward. I was unwell from over working myself & the heat in burning down the Tree.

March 1 1800 St Vincent

In pursuit of Supple Jacks, brought down 5.

7   I left Ouia to carry letters to the Post in Kingston, one for My Brother Ja^s now on board the *Neptune*. The Country parched up, the Roisseaus dry & fallen across the Road I was obliged to alight 7 times between Ouia & Rabacca & I was seven times in danger of breaking my Horses legs. I was so very ill in the Morning of the 8th that I could only proceed to Mount Young. On my arrival there Captain Naismyth was kind enough to send a Man to Kingston with my Letters. I remained this day with Dixon & returned to Rabbacca at Night & in the Morning returned to Ouia. Cameron went with me & I was only able to walk my Horse.

10th   I was ordered by the Surgeon to remain within doors but I cannot. I got to my Tree & lighted my fire round it & had apparently almost accomplished it by one o clock

11th   I succeeded in getting my Tree down today.

12th   Worked hard in cutting my Tree into logs to carry away as it lay across the Garden

13th   Went up the Hills for Supple Jacks & Zoombee Beads, brought down 58 of the latter.

16   Walked to Sandy Bay found Pine apples nearly Ripe & Water Lemons

17   St Patricks day, Irishmen drunk. The Carraibs were drunk & Insolent to me & afterwards to McCaskell. We were obliged to use some harsh measures before they would be quiet

19   The Colonel offended by my laughing at his quoting a Carraibs Commission as equal to that of an English Officer & in consequence ranged himself on their side.

21   McCaskell & myself cut down a Tree of large Zoombia beads & loaded ourselves with beads.

24th   The Officers employed for their amusement in cutting a Road to the Bathing place. Was bitten by a Jack Spaniard[35] which swelled my & gave great pain like a Wasp.

---

[35] Jack Spaniard, a West Indian wasp.

The West Indies—St Vincent—1798-1800

27th   In clearing round my House I found a great number of Soldiers in a Hole. A Soldier[36] is much like a Crab or probably more like a Lobster, they take possession of Fish Shells from the size of a Perriwinkle to that of a Conch, it is of this Animal that such wonderful Stories are related under the Name of Land Crab viz that it sets off at a certain Season of the Year in large bodies towards the Sea & that it allows itself to drop down the most perpendicular precipices. I cannot speak of the accuracy of these statements.

28   Went in search of Water Lemons but found none Ripe. A Serj^t arrived from Calcutta & reported to Captain Miller that Two United Irishmen had been drafted into the Generals Company & were arrived but that one had died on his passage & the other was a Dutchman.

April 1st The United Youths arrived in all three for the three Companies, or one for each & the Youngest upwards of 60 years old.

4   News that the Union between England & Ireland is carried. A Bull attacked a Centenel on his Post & was shot. The Wind and Sea rose so suddenly as almost to overset the fishing Boat but it was a dead Calm again in less that 3 Hours. Lines by Lt Classon 53rd Reg^t on Hearing that Buonaparte had abandoned the French Army in Egypt to General Kleber.[37]

> What! The Hero of Egypt Abandon his forces
> & sneak back to France in dispair
> Is this the result of his flaming discourses
> & the dangers he promised to share
> If Kleber can save the remains of his Legions
> From the State he so forcibly drew
> They will certainly cry who inhabit these Regions
> Da Bucra, He cleber for true
> The white man is truly clever.

[pages missing?]

April 18th 1800 St Vincents

A Schooner arrived with orders for our immediately sending in all our Baggage as we are to leave St Vincents. We are to be relieved by the 4th West India Reg^t but we do not know where we are going. I got my Baggage & 5 goats on board immediately & we, who had expected to remain Months longer quietly, in the course of a few hours, had embarked every thing we could. My Fowls 50 of which were running

---

[36] Soldier crab: a West Indian hermit crab, climbs several hundred feet up hills and rolls down to sea level for a larger shell.
[37] Jean Baptiste Kléber (1753-1800).

about my House & my House itself valued at £14 pounds were abandoned & we marched for Kingston in the morning leaving our Post absolutely abandoned.

Some hope remained that we might have got something for what we left from the Officers of the 4th West India whom we expected to meet at Mount Young but in this we were mistaken for on our march the Word was suddenly given, Shoulder Arms & we passed about 100 Men drawn up in a bend of the Road with presented Arms as we passed like two Ships passing with a fair breeze at Sea, as soon as they see each other they are separated, we went on & had not a moments time even to say good byes. We halted one day at Mount Young & the next day to Yamboo River & on the 3rd day to Fort Charlotte. The Schooner had reached before us & had landed My Goats & they were missing. As we are going off they will not again appear. My total loss in House, Fowls & Goats is 17 Joes - £31-17-6. This sum was more than all my Debts in St Vincents & I reckoned it quite as good as ready money. I was therefore obliged to draw a Bill for £20 before I could leave the Island which I had hopes never to have done again.

On Saturday 19th we embarked on board the Regular Transport the *Coromandel,* An old East Indiaman, the whole Regiment in that & the *Ocean*, for St Lucia. We lay in Kingston bay till Wednesday 23rd when we sailed & reached the Cul de Sac, St Lucia on Thursday Morning 24th April 1820. [sic. 1800]

1800 April —St Lucia

24 At 4 in the Afternoon half the Regiment disembarked, myself in the number & marched up to Morne Fortune to relieve the 87th Reg^t. I met my old acquaintance Lieut^t Gladstanes of the Buffs & he gave me Bed for the Night, others were not so well off. In the Morning I went down to the Town Castries to look after my Cloathes & hired Negroes for 2 Dollars to get them up to the Morne. The Barracks are very bad & we are two in a Room

26 This day I took to examine our new quarters, walked round the Fort, found it large covering the Broad Top of a Hill. The fortifications in Ruins, the barracks in a state of decay, the soil a wet clay, the vegetation most rapid, the brush wood coming up to the very works. There are plenty of Guns of all Sizes & Nations, Piles of old Shot, some of the Guns 68 Pounders but all the Carriages bad, in short the whole place the picture of Neglect. There is a French Imigrant Regiment the 9th West India doing duty out side the Fort & the 1st West India in other parts of the Island. The French Regiment is composed of House Negroes from Guadaloupe & far superior to the Common field Negroes, This Regiment is beyond our own West India Regiments in every thing, but Fidelity & that I should fear is not to be depended on.

St Lucia altho separated from our old Post of Ouia by a narrow Channel of less than 20 Miles is as dissimilar as if it belonged to another Hemisphere. The Soil is totally different. The productions different. St Lucia abounds with Venomous Reptiles as Serpents, Tarantulas, Scorpions. St Vincents has not one of these that is reckoned dangerous. Here are large Parrotts as large as Makaws, Wild Pigeons & the Sea is full of fish but it is very unhealthy.

27 To windward of Mount Fortune is a Mountain, much Higher, over this Hill every Morning rises a thick black Vapour which brings a damp unwholesome feel around, it is called the Black Vomit alluding to the Fever which it is supposed to induce.

Captain Elwin & Lieut^t Mansel brought a large Detachment from England, particularly united Irish & in all probability if this Island agrees with our Health as St Vincents did we shall soon be a Strong Regiment.

29 I walked to one of the out Battery's on an Iminence to the South of the Morne called the Cicerone, occupied as a Weekly detachment commanded by a Subaltern of a West India Regiment. At Present a Lieut^t

Descordel commands. He was very Polite & gives himself a very good Character which I hope is true, I have no reason to say that it is a just one.

Our Governor General Prevost[38] reviewed us. I have no great opinion of him, he seems to be such an arbitrary Gentleman & he bears that Character.

May   Captain Elwin who arrived in good Health on the 27th April is dead & the men dye very fast. Captain Stewart left for England – Two Black Soldiers 9th West India killed by a Serpent. Mansel got his Company.

The Heat of this Island is far greater that that of St Vincents & we cannot walk as we did there, but today being tired by my confinement I walked about 4 Miles & entered several plantations.

The [French Civil] War which raged in this Island was not carried on as formerly, but became a War of extermination by the rage of Royalists, or more properly speaking, People of some Property, against the Republicans, or those of no Property, whether the first should keep what they had or whether the Second should get into their places, The Latter succeeded but unfortunately the instant that they had so, they became the very persons with whom they had been contending & another set arose in their Names who in their turn took their places & contended against others, sometimes against the same who had been driven out by themselves. In this State the Invasion of the Island by the English was a real Blessing but they found half the Estates in the Island Abandoned & the Negroes either living free in the Woods or entered into different Corps as Soldiers, very few White dare live on their Estates but all huddle into Castries at Night or get under the protection of some Fort. The Land is over run with weeds & little is produced except Coffee & Cotton. The English are certainly better Masters than the French & this may be in part be proved by the different way in which the Slaves behaved in St Vincents & St Lucia. In the Former when the Masters were overpowered by the French & Charraibs, the Slaves followed them & surrounded Kingston in a State of Starvation and even fought in their behalf. In the Latter the Slaves were in Arms & Murdered every European who fell into their hands. Still as a stronger proof, the Negroes belonging to the French Planters in St Vincents, for St Vincents was called a neutral Island, forsook their Masters & joined the Carraibs.

May 1800

---

[38] Lieutenant Governor George Prévost (1767-1816). Son of Swiss-born British General Prévost, fluent French speaker, popular with French planters.

The West Indies—St Lucia—1800

St Lucia At least the Part near the Morne is composed of a Red Clay which is very productive, the Vegetation is particularly quick, but this may be owing to the Constant moisture, indeed the rapid vegetation may in some respects cause the Moisture. The greater part of the Island having been so much neglected. Should this Island remain in our possession by the Peace, there is a great reason to suppose that it will be a most valuable Colony & superior to Martinique but should it be restored to the French it will in all probability be worth nothing. The Unhealthiness I believe is owing to the want of Cultivation, at least in a great degree.

At one time the number of Putrid Human Bodies lying unburied was sufficient to have caused a pestilence. Morne des Chasseurs is a Pyramidical Hill immediately to windward of Mount Fortune & completely commanding it but in itself most difficult to take from the Nature of the ground, & might be occupied by a few Troops at any time before an Enemy with Guns could get possession. When the British Forces invaded this island under Sir Ralph Abercromby the 53 Reg^t took Morne Chabot which also commands the fort. We here lost 1 Captain & 2 Subalterns, with a great Many Men.

Morne Fortune is 1500 Feet above the sea, at the Foot of the Hill is a city of Castries (a little dirty Village) built in a Swamp at the Bottom of the

Cul de Sac, a most unhealthy situation for it is completely to Leeward & there is no tide of consequenc. The Cul de Sac towards the Town is a Putrid Mud, the Cul de Sac is defended by the Vigie on the Right & the Scorpion on the left, the former on a Hill, the latter on a level with the Sea.

There are many Venomous Reptiles on the Island of Serpents the Sele de Chien & the Sele de Crapeaux are poisonous, the latter is the smallest of a light Browne.

I stand unfortunately in the Regiment the youngest Lieut^t by which whenever I mount guard it is with an officer Senior in Rank & in consequence I always go to Town being the most disagreeable Guard & the most expensive, it must cost me 3 Dollars for Dinner or I must go without. I sometimes am invited to the General's & sometimes to the Commissaries (Mr Conways) but I am often obliged to sit under a Tamarind Tree & whistle for my dinner.

Another Man of the 9th West India Regiment bit by a Serpent & died in 2 hours. We have no amusement here but inventing News which is generally said to be brought from Martinique or some American Ship.

This Week "Surinam has been taken by the French" "The saints besieged by the French" "The *Thames* Frigate with all on board lost."

30   One of our men bit by a Serpent.

To Mrs Butt about June 1800

  My letters have been regularly unfortunate lately two have been taken to my knowledge & one sunk. I had complained of the great expence, but I am happy now to say that our Mess expences are now much reduced, it was indeed so great that our pay was scarcely sufficient to pay our Mess Bill. it was indeed so bad that all the subalterns but one left the Mess, this brought our Seniors to reason & we are now in a fair way of getting it reduced. The Regiment is now much divided 5 Companies being at Martinique & 5 at St Lucia, of the latter one Company is at Pigeon Island.

  We are in great uncertainty whether we are to join the 5 Companies at Martinico or whether they will return to us, one or the other we expect will soon happen. This state of uncertainty is not very pleasant & we are longing to be united again. It is thought that we will go to them. We think that there is little doubt of our returning to Europe as we are very sickly & few in numbers we lose on average 1 Man each day & one third of our Men are incapable of doing duty & who will be invalided & go home by the first fleet. I am sorry that I did not write to you by the last fleet but I did not then know that the former letter I had written had been lost. We have a Packett to come here but none to go away, or any post office we therefore trust to Martinique should we send letters to Martinique they run then the risk of being lost at some Merchants Shop. (I, beg pardon, Store). I intend keeping this letter until some opportunity should occur which is generally without any notice given, probably when we are in Town & the Vessel ready to sail.

July 1st The *Coromandel* Transport arrived with an order to embark 4 of the Companies 9th West India. They are to go to Dominica & bring the 7th West India here & then take the Remainder of the 9th West India to Dominica & 5 Companies 53rd Reg^t to Martinique to relieve the 14th Reg^t. I hope that the Company to which I belong will go to Martinique but we shall not know until the day before we are to embark, uncertainty keeps us on the alert.

2   The 9th Embarked at Gunfiring –

3   Colonel Lightburne has determined that St Lucia is to be Head Quarters & I am to remain The following officers go: Colonel Brabane, Captains Buckland & Hobson, Lieut^{ts} Smelt, Fraser, Grant, Smith,

The West Indies—St Lucia—1800

Stepson & Ensign McCaskell. We were obliged to call in the major's Company from Pigeon Island. General Twentyman who arrived by the last Fleet is dead at martinico. I found myself so far behind hand in money that I left the Mess intending to live on my Rations until I have paid my debts.

Col^l Crosby, Lt Col^{ls} Abercrombie (absent), Lightburne. Majors Brisbane, Brabane. Cap^{ts} Rogers, Buckland, Rhind, Dover, Stewart, Hobson, Elwin, Leslie, McMahon, Miller. Lieut^{ts} Smelt, Carmichael, Hughes, Fraser, Grant, Ponsonby, Leslie, Wynne, Palmer, Wheatstone, Grant, Smith, Weston, Lieth, Thompson, Classon, Sherwood, Gillan. Ensigns Scott, McClaskill

5th   Walked to Malcom's Battery & around by the Grand Cul de Sac. The Country low, Marshy & unhealthy but rich land. There is a River running thro the valley in which are plenty of Fish, but the Mouth is kept Chocked up by the Surf, the sides of the River are shaded by high bamboos. I found Groves of Cachoo Nutts, the Apple of which are a very pleasant acid & very beautiful to appearance, it is said to be the Apple which eve ate.

9th   Town Guard spent 4/8. We are very unhealthy four men of our Regiment died to day.

10th   The 7th West India Reg^t arrived to day.

14th   The 9th West India Sailed for Dominico & 5 Companys 53rd Rg^t for Martinico we remain as follows: 5 Subalterns, Col^l Lightburne, Captain Miller, Lieut^{ts} Carmichael, Hughes, Thompson, Erskin, Sherwood, of these 5 Subalterns we have two on duty every day & as we are in a very sickly state we cannot long do duty here we expect to follow the other Companies soon. Col^l Leslie arrived, tells us that the Ship on board of which Colonel Brisbane, Lieut^{ts} Mansel & Ponsonby was pooped in the Night & went down almost immediately, the Crew saved as it was fine weather & no one can account for the Accident except it may have been a sudden white squall taking the Ship aback. Mansel was with great difficulty saved. Accounts from Martinique sickness there lost 1 Serg^{t,} 8 Men. Took advantage of the Provision boat to see Pigeon Island where Rodney's Fleet lay during the American War. It rained so hard that I could see but little. The Island is not but a quarter of a Mile long, precipitous towards the Sea but a fine beach towards the land, there is no fresh water on the island or any venomous Reptile The Soil is sandy & from the nature of the Soil I should suppose much more healthy than the Country near Castries. The Bay called Shock Bay nearly occupies the whole Road from Gross Islet, a Town opposite to Pigeon Island. We reckon it ten miles to the Fort, a Lieut^t Grant died at Martinique he was the most popular Officer in the Regiment & of a strong constitution his death is attributed to over exertion in running up & down from St Cherres to the Mount several times each day.

To Mrs Butt from St Lucia 7 Aug 1800

We have lost in the Reg^t by death since the 24th April one Captain, 4 Serg^{ts}, 3 Corporals 51 Privates 1 Woman & 8 Children. Captain Hobson goes to Martinique Tomorrow, who will take charge of this letter, since the 7th viz 3 days we have lost Ten Men among the rest poor Cheek who was Hobson's Servant at Bridgenorth. We have now only 470 Men in the West Indies of which only 320 are capable of duty, we cannot therefore be long here. I have been walking about much & I think this Island will be most valuable when it is a little more cleared being a far better soil than St Vincents & full of Fruit, but it is dreadfully unhealthy & it is distressing to think how many poor Men have been lost in this small Fort by disease. Stewart is well & sends his best respects.

Augt I dined on the 18th Regiment with Weston, while we were sitting after dinner his only Son of Ten Years old ran out to Gather Guavas. His Mother called him back & desired him not to go into the bushes for fear of Serpents. She seemed particularly alarmed about them & made the Boy sit down but he contrived to slip out while we were talking & we heard a scream. The Mother instantly cried out "Alex is bit by a Serpent I knew it" it was true he had been gathering Guavas & was seized by a Serpent & died before 12 oclock at Night. He said that he saw the Serpents Eyes & tried to run away but could not, indeed he described the Serpent as having fascinated him & that altho he wished to run away he was obliged to advance but he was evidently in such alarm that we could not trust to what he said, every thing was done, the part was so far as possible cut out & he was rubbed with Mercurial Ointment until he died. The Serpent was killed & was Eleven foot long, it had taken the small of the leg intirely into its mouth. In the height of the distress Weston was called upon to Mount Guard, I ran out & took his Guard for him. but as soon as I had relieved the old Guard I ran down again & staid until 9 o clock when it was necessary to be with my Guard. The poor Boy did not seem in any Pain, he complained of a Numbness in his leg & it swelled very much & became black but we were not sure whether this was occasioned by the Venom of the Serpent or the friction with Mercury. As soon as the drawbridge was let down in the Morning I ran down again but found the Child dead. Weston finding himself unhappy was sent to join the Detachment at Martinico.

1800 August—Pigeon Island, Yellow Fever

31 Aug   My tour of duty at Pigeon island where I am to remain a Month in charge of the Convalescents of the Regiment. The Surgeon Batty lent me his Horse & I rode to Gross Islet where a Boat was waiting which carried me to the Island. I relieved Lieut' Hughes who returned on the same Horse — I found the Men in a very bad state, some of them being ill with Ulcers & no dressings. I wrote in immediately & represented their state & removed some of the worst to the upper battery. Captain Curry 7th West India kindly assisted me with his Men. One man died at 12 o clock.

4 Sep White washed the Barrack & cleaned them well out, wrote to the Col' & Surgeon to complain of want of medical assistance. Another Man died

5   Washed the Barrack with Vinager. The Men who were removed to the top of the Hill recovering. A Fleet passed down to Martinico. This is not the season for fleets, a Third Man died. We are out of Water, the government Schooner arrived with a supply. This arises from inattention to the Tanks which do not retain the water. A Stich in Time saves 9 but the allowances for repairs are probably not charged. The fleet which passed is from England, the 69th Reg' on Board & Probably the 6th Batt'n 60th.

11   The Garrison Surgeon arrived to inspect the sick. He says they shall be sent to the Morne tomorrow having no Medical Assistant to spare.

12   Mr Power the Quartermaster died in Morne Fortune. Rain to day we caught 36 Ton of Water which is 3 Feet Water in the Tanks.

15   The Government Schooner came & took away the worst of the sick men leaving me those who are not in want of Medical Aid viz- 2 Srg'ts 27 rank & file only three of which are capable of doing duty - We have lost 1 Officer & 16 men in 15 days out of 150.

17   Scipio & Hanibal Two Privates 7th West India fought. Hanibal beat Scipio hollow.

22   The party 7th West India Relieved Cap' Curry & Lieut' M'Lean by Cap' Hewetson & Hockiady. M'Caskill writes to me from Martinico that there is little doubt our going home immediately, indeed if we do not we shall have no men left, we are not 270 in the whole regiment & we lose more than 1 P' Diem. Cap' Stewart was taken on his passage Home after an Action of an hour with a Privateer of 20 Guns 180 Men & carried into Spain. Major Hervey 1st West India was killed in the Action.

30   I am to remain another Month. I am very glad of it, Much talk of Peace.

Oct

Saw a Brig take a Schooner, but do not know what flags they carry

4   The Brig which took the Schooner yesterday turns out to be *Drake* Kings Brig. The Schooner an English Vessel which did not know the Signals.

5   Went fishing in an open Boat, caught 12 lbs of Fish & lost the Skin from my Nose & Lips.

17th A Report prevails that the English under Sir Jas. Pulteney have taken & destroyed Ferrol with its fortifications, Stores & Shipping. Poor Hughes died this Morning of a consumption I had known him intimately for 3 Years. His Abilities were very superior but he had so great an affection of the Nerves as to have been the most unfit for the Army of any Man I ever saw, his timidity exceeded that of a delicate Woman & we had many Laughable Stories about him. Yet his wit & good humour were so great that he was much beloved. Something was on his mind which report said was having married his Father's Widow who had originally been contracted to himself but this I believe was grounded on some unconnected speech of his when drunk. He had latterly drank very hard, which probably hastened his death.

27th Wheatstone our Adjutant arrived at Pigeon Island. He has had a most violent fever & is recovering, but so weak as not to be able to stand. Col^l Brisbane promoted in 69th Captain Stewart succceeds his Majority, Lt Mansel to the Company.

Novr I was relieved by Lie^t Knight & returned to the Morne. Wheatstone went with me.

13   I was seized with the Yellow Fever & was light headed until the 23rd when I recovered my recollection I found that I had been removed by the Surgeon (Batty) to his own quarters & was there attended by him with the greatest Kindness. He gave up his own bed to me, for I had no bed of my own having always used a Hamock. I recovered as fast as I had fallen ill for on the 26th I was able to change the air to Martinico but I did not get away until the 28th when our new quarter Master (Hanso) accompanied me.

1800 November—St Pierre, Martinique

We got to Sea at 12 oclock & when cleared from the Harbour were becalmed. A singular longing came over me for porter & I drank Eleven Bottles between 12 o clock & Daylight Next Morning we got across in the Morning but the Calm continued we hired a small Boat from Fort Royal Bay to carry us to St Pierre & I drank a Bottle of Madeira on my Passage., at four we reached St Pierre & altho I could not stand in St Lucia I was able to Walk more than a mile. My Yellow face & breaking out countenance made me a hideous figure. My head having been shaved.

We entered a Taylors Shop to rest awhile & all the different fractional parts of Men fled as from the Plague. I recovered rapidly till the End of the Month, living with Mc Caskill in the Barracks by the side of a Torrent unlike those of St Vincents because never dry, but formed of immense Rocks. I did not stir out of my Barracks At First by reason of weakness but this was followed by Ear & tooth ack probably occasioned by the Mercury that I had taken.

I borrowed Mr Powel (or Assistant Surgeon)'s Horse & rode up the Hill behind our Barracks. This Hill overhangs the Town of St Pierre, on it we have Barracks for Two Companies, & here is the Signal Post & look out called the Vigie. The Town seems directly under our feet & consists of one principal street running along the Bay with a few streets diverging. This Street is reckoned Two Miles long with many well built houses of Stone. Many Vessels lay in the Bay but owing to the exposure of the anchorage the Vessels do not remain longer that absolutely necessary. Besides St Pierre is not the residence of the Chief of the Navy or Army or of the Stores or Government except the Civil Governor of the Island. Fort Royal being head Quarters. There is an American Frigate here. The Country to the North across the River is very beautiful. In the foreground is the Botanic Garden with Madam La Passeries House. Madam La Passery is Mother to the French Consuls Wife Madam Bounastes formerly Madam Beauharnais. The Cane Patches interspersed with fruit Trees has a very beautiful appearance. Our lower Barracks are almost as pleasant. The Buildings themselves are good & in front is a rapid river, the Water of which is very good to drink. Upon the whole I hope our other Companies may come here & that I may not be obliged to return to that dreadful place St Lucia. Two Merchants were taken up to day for supplying the French with provisions & Arms.

To Mrs Butt from Martinique 4 Dec 1800

I write you this short note to say I am now recovering from a most severe fever called a Yellow Fever. My Life has been dispaired of & it has been reported from one Island to another that I was dead. You may conceive that in our retired corner of the World reports spread fast & it may be that they have even reached home. I was seized on the 13th Nov & I must say that I have received the most kind attention from all my Brother Officers. On the 28th I was so far recovered from the Fever as to be able to move & I was sent to Martinique. In England where diseases are protracted it may appear strange that in so short a time I should be able to talk of death & recovery but if you were aware of the effects of the diseases in these climates you would know that 36 Hours is quite sufficient to decide on the Effect of a disease.

I am now as yellow as Gold & the Surgeons recommend my immediate return to England but I am afraid of the expence & of being obliged to return, for I fear that all hope of our return to England as a Regiment is at an end. Hobson has been very kind & attentive to me, he has a set of rooms attached to his situation & he has given them to me. We do not expect to remain stationary long but where our next Station is to be we know not.

Report which is very busy sometimes sends these 5 Companies to St Lucia & at other times brings the other 5 Companies here. We have lost 5 Officers & 120 Men in 6 months.

The order for our removal to St Lucia arrived that day 5 Dec 1800

A Report of an Insurrection in a village called Cap Pilote between this & Port Royal, 20 Miles off we do not think it of much consequence & is not intended against the English but against some old French law. We however are teased by being kept on the Alert. The Insurrection arose the following Manner, during the height of the Revolutionary War many Negroes became Officers & indeed of higher Rank in the Black Armies but when the first heat was over some of these Negroes aiming at independence were opposed by others who were attached to the Europeans, in consequence many Royalist Negroes who had gained Rank in St Domingo & Guadaloup came over to the English & had their rank confirmed among the Reg^t. One Baptiste, who had been very conspicuous & had been confirmed in his Rank of Colonel by the English & had a Pension in consequence & I understood has always conducted himself with great propriety. It so happens that his Master being in Martinique has claimed either him or his Wife & by the Capitulation of the Island the English are precluded from interfering with the Laws it seems therefore that the law is to take its course & the Colonel runs the risk of being adjudged as a common Slave, fearing this he has raised the insurrection the English altho unable to help themselves all feel much for Baptiste & we hope that some means will be found for saving him.[39]

9 I walked about a Mile & a half along the Town & weny into a Monastry of White Monks & a Church like all French Churches it is dedicated to Notre Dame de Bonne Porte. We also saw a Monastry of White Benedictine Nuns, a Brotherhood of Charity, a Sisterhood of L'Hospital. On the North of the River is the New Town which is superior to the Old one. It is joined to the Old one by a Bridge over the River. In the New Town is the Botanic Garden now much neglected. Many East Indian plants are here & I should think not fewer than 200 Cinnamon Trees. Two Ships arrived with Coals for the Troops but we have no Grates to burn them in & as far as I am able to judge we do not want them. Our Detachment has become so weak that the Militia are called on to take the duty of the Batterys alternately with the Regulars. They naturally feel this as a hardship as they are men in business & get no pay. We expect the 68th Regiment from England 2000 Strong being Two Battalions, we know not what is to become of us, we are now only 170 strong & those worn out.

14   We are informed that on the arrival of the 68th we are to return to St Lucia. A Corporal of the 14th Reg^t Named Sherwood was very angry because I did not acknowledge him as a Relation, he bears a good Character & comes from Market Drayton. We dined with the Governor (General Keppel) the Dinner was not ready till 5 o clock & as my appetite was now in good case I was not pleased. The General said that since we had done duty at St Pierre's he had no Complaints but that fromerly he was constantly teazed by Complaints from the Inhabitants against the Troops. The General also remarked that it was very bad policy to send our Irish Regiment now comprised of Raw recruits to a place like St Pierres where there is no Fort to confine the Men, who will be able to get as much new Rum as they please & will of course soon kill themselves.

19   No Cash in the Paymasters hands, I am literally obliged to live on Salt Pork & Bread.

---

[39] The 1800 insurrection against French law for former slaves serving in the army was led by a black Colonel, Jean Kina. The French would have restored him to his former master whereas British law would have kept him free. He was shipped to London, imprisoned there and after the Treaty of Amiens (1802) sent to France and imprisoned there.

24   Mounted Guard for the first time troubled with Tooth Ack

25   Dined on Morne Merail, a Letter received fro Captain Burslem 14th who is in England saying that the 88th Regiment is on its way to relieve the 14th & 53rd Regiments.

To Mrs Butt from Martinique 29 Dec 1800

I wrote to you a short note by the last Packet informing you of my severe illness & I have now the pleasure to say that I am quite recovered. The Ague which generally follows the fever is indeed to be dreaded but the Season is in my favor. We have lately heard a report which sets us all in Spirits which is that the 25th **Reg**[t] consisting of 2 Battalions is coming out to relieve the 53rd & from our very weak state it seems a likely thing. We have only 170 Men fit for duty. Should this be true I hope to see you in May or June.& we hope to be stationed in Shropshire. You will see a poor emaciated Reg[t] but one that has been always reckoned a well conducted one. General Keppel, the Governor invited us to dine with him about ten days ago & after dinner he told us & also desired the Colonel to tell the men that since he has Commanded he never saw a more regular or better behaved Reg[t] & that he was sorry that we were ordered to Saint Lucia.

I suppose you have heard by this time of the loss in Officers & Men that we have now sustained. I am higher by Six than I was on leaving S[t] Vincents & I now stand as the oldest Supernumerary Lieutenant & I hope safe from being put on half pay should Peace happen tomorrow. During my illness I received a letter from My Brother James but being very delirious I tore it to pieces. I have since been able to make out most of it & I am much pleased with it. The 67th Reg[t] are now entering the Bay & we shall soon leave here for S[t] Lucia. Col[l] Bradburn our Senior Major died yesterday.

[January 1 1801] My Birth day & not a farthing to buy a dinner but accidentally met a Ships Captain of the *Euridice* who called Classon & myself to go on board & he gave us a Luncheon which was very fortunate as we had no dinner at home.

2   The Paymaster (Sayer) received money which set us up again. The Captain of the *Euridice* took our Letters to England

5   At Two oclock Col[l] Brabane died after a Gradual waste. He was only Major in the Regiment, he had been three days dying & was reduced to Skin & Bone, he had quarrelled with M[c]Caskell & myself at Ouia, but he had no other Friends to attend him in his last moments & he seemed to feel it: he was buried in the Hospital Yard on the 6th

The West Indies—Martinique—1800-1801

11   The 68 Reg.^t arrived at Fort Royal & we are in orders to hold ourselves in readiness to embark for St Lucia.

13   The 68th Reg^t arrived, I was on guard, but immediately relieved by the Royal Martinique Volunteers, we are to embark early Tomorrow Morning.

1801 January—St Lucia

14   We embarked (ie 5 Comp^y 53rd Reg^t) on board the *Ocean* at 7 this Morning. We were relieved by 3 Companies 68th reg^t a fine Body of Men & many Officers but we see the signs of sickness, that is a great alarm about it. The 68th say that the 1st Foot 6th Batt^n 60 & 85 Reg^t are on their way to the West Indies & consequently we cannot be long e'er we are relieved.

17   We lay in the Bay until 12 This day when we sailed and at daylight on the

18   we landed at St Lucia & marched to the Morne we found the Reg^t sickly. I got my old Quarters & my Baggage carried up for a Dollar. I have a severe cold.

23   I was attached to Captain Dovers Company with the Command & Payment of it. Major Stewart arrived, says there is no chance of our going home

February 1801.

4   I was on Guard & felt most severe Cold in going my rounds at Night. I was glad to get a glass of Gin on my return. A Fleet passed we counted 56 Sail. I suppose it to be the great fleet from England which was said to consist of 200 Sail, we know of the arrival of 32 and 8. The Merchants are in alarm about the remainder. Sir Ja^s Boutems a Comptroler of the Customs of Martinico with his whole family are said to be lost.

5   The *Rosana* Brig from England arrived. She has been 3 Months from England. She brings a set of Barracks built in England for 300 Men & 26 Officers. Every part of these barracks being brought in a small Brig shews that they cannot be very substantial indeed there is not a joist or piece of wood employed much more than 3 Inches in Diameter. The Men's Barracks are each 190 Feet long. The Officer's are each Room 16 Feet by 15 & a Gallery running along the Front of each vz of Two Captains & 4 Subalterns. A Deputation of interested Persons went from St Lucia to martinique with an address requesting that General Prevost may not be removed. We understand that this was in reality formed by

himself for he has a nephew here and many friends with Negoes &c, & they are supposed to make a good thing of it. The Answer is said to be unfavorable.

On the 13th a Detachment arrived from England. Some of the men are under sentence to serve in the West Indies for Life. This is hard both on the Men & the Regiments. The Military Spirit will certainly be lowered.

16th General Prevost invited me to a Ball at Gross islet tomorrow Evening & I intend going.

17   Captain Millar & myself set off for Gross Islet & breakfasted with the General in Castries, his Boat was going & altho we had intended walking we took advantage of his Boat & went in it. We landed about a Mile before the Boat reach Gross Islet & Millar & myself went into the Woods in search of Birds, we only shot one Thrush, on our reaching the Town we could not find a conveyance to Pigeon Island & we had beau faire in firing Guns. We could not get them on the Island to attend to us, we expected to change Shrove Tuesday into Ash Wednesday.

M^{r}Nasaburre a planter came to us & invited us to dinner at his Estate, but here again we were unfortunate for from some accident our Cloths did not arrive & we were obliged to dine with the Ladies in our Shooting dress. We however found that delicacy was not the order of the day. The Gross indelicate language made use of both by <u>Ladies</u> & Gentlemen exceeded belief. I was glad to get away & I got down to the beach & hired a fishing boat to take me to the Island. At Eight I returned and supped on Lamb larded with Garlick & then to the Ball. The indelicacy here was even worse than at dinner. Songs sung by the French Ladies would scarcely have been tolerated at a Inn at Portsmouth I hope these people are the outcasts of French Society indeed I understand that many of the unmarried Ladies are Mothers & some of them have colored Children. This is the fruit of the French Equality preached in these islands. One Woman we met, a Niece of Mon^r De Longville one of the First Landholders, a fine Woman who has a large Family all born while the Mother is a Pucella[40] & every Child differing in Color from his Brother.

The Country we have been thro is very fine & St Lucia is certainly a very fine Island the Venomous Reptiles alone making it a disagreeable residence for I do not think it unhealthy except at or near Castries & the Carenage. We slept on the Billiard Table having a Negroe called the Admiral for our Pillow & went shooting in the Morning but only found one Dove. The first Estate we came to we entered & the Manager a M^r

---

[40] Pucella: maiden.

Ryan gave us a good breakfast which was very acceptable as I had eaten nothing since Supper & I was much fatigued. Mr Ryan had finished his own Breakfast but made a fresh one for us. After Breakfast we strolled about the Woods until dinner time & then dined with General Prevost at Ewings Estate. This Estate is situated in a Most beautiful Valley opening onto Chock Bay. After dinner walked to the Morne. On our arrival we found General Maitland, Colonel Shipley & others come to inspect the Building & they give us but little hope of leaving the Island, in fact our constant thought our first enquiry when we were to go away & we raised or depressed without any adequate reason.

19   Col^l Buttler 87 Reg^t came & he says that the 85 Reg^t is coming this raises our Spirits again, the Report is that the 53 Reg^t will relieve the 87th at Dominico which Reg^t will go to Barbadoes, any change will be for the better.

21   Captain Watts 7th West India arrived he says that we are positively to go away.

25   The *Fairy* Sloop arrived, took a vessel with Cattle on her passage, says the 53 Reg^t are immediately going to the Saints. I am not well.

28   It rained & I was on Guard. The clayy quality of the Soil is so tenacious that we lose the soles of our Shoes. I took off Shoes & Stockings & went my nightly rounds barefoot.

Major Stewart writes that we are also to go home.

March Capt Rogers removed to an Invalid Corps, Buckland Senior Captain some rumours of the French getting Troops out to this Country. We have no force to defend ourselves, our Men are very Sickly 125 in Hospital & we are not above 275 Strong.

I rode over the Vigie & on my return found that a Gent^n formerly an Officer in the 87th Reg^t had been taken up for accusing General Prevost of some misconduct, what it is I know not, but I find that the English Settlers are much against the General.

4   Lieut^t Weston & myself a kind of Steeple Chase, viz made our way down hill & up hill in a strait direction towards the Sea, we found ourselves at length near Tapion Battery. I had tried to carry plants in a Tin Box but the heat of the Sun was such that they were dried up before I reached home. I this day took a joint of a bamboo it more capable of resisting the excessive heat, but my poor flowers were all withered. I found great difficulty in getting a specimen to draw from.

The Gentleman alluded to on formerly belonging to the 87th has been brought before the French Magistrates but refuses to acknowledge their power to try an Englishman & he has been threatened with being put in Irons. We are at a loss to guess how it will end.

Buckland & Batty went to England. We all envy them. An expedition sailed against the Danish Islands of St Cruise & St Thomas. We had hopes of being …

[page missing 4 March 1800]

To Mrs Butt from St Lucia 16 March 1801

We are now full of business. Expeditions are fitting out against the Danish Islands. The first sailed on the 11th Ins^t supported by 10 St Croix, our hopes of our now returning home are now for the present at an end. When the bustle is over we may probably get away, but a larger extent of possession naturally requires a larger force. I am completely recovered from my late illness that I think myself well as ever I was in my life. We are now building new barracks not before they were wanted for we were before exposed to the Rain & like Mr Elwes glad to find a dry corner, the Dripping of Water has often kept me awake for hours.

March 24   The 64th Reg^t & the 1st Reg^t are arrived from England to take part in the expedition which ought to ensure us a change of quarters particularly when the Danes make Peace which considering the situation cannot be far distant. We have moved into the Barracks of the 7th West India while our new Barracks are erected.

The Orders to day were "The 53 Reg^t will <u>evacuate</u> tomorrow at Gun firing."

Col^l Lightburne taken dangerously ill. We had a good deal of fun in pulling down the Old Barracks called the Coromandel. Officers & Men enjoyed it but towards the end Lt Classon was seriously hurt which will cost his Majesty something of the Volunteer work ceased.

25th I went to Town to see Buckland & Batty off for England. We hear that there is great News from Home, a Change in the Ministry. Mr Addington succeeds Mr Pitt as prime Minister. We are now all for Peace & it is said that Lord St Helens is gone over to negotiate, some think the French will not treat thinking that we are afraid. Most people here are angry with Mr Pitt for resigning & say it will not do. I feel a Great loss at not having some Botanical Work to guide me in describing plants. I went in a Boat to a point under the Vigie in persuit of some Vincas (Periwinkles). I found two species of the Madagascar Perriwinkle, the Pink & the White. I killed a very large venomous scorpion which I preserved I am glad of it for McCaskell killed my present specimen & he threatened to take it away.

April 2nd   News of the Expedition, They have taken St Martens, St Crois, St Bartholemews: French, Danish & Swedish. We hear of Sir Ralph Abercrombie's landing in Egypt with the British Army. We hear that Major Stewart is arrived at Martinique from England. Went to the Cul de Sac to cut a large Bamboo to make drinking utensils of: its diameter was as large as a common glass Tumbler. Major Stewart arrived & says that we shall soon go home. General Prevost says that he has no doubt of our leaving St Lucia soon.

I examined a fire fly which is of a different Species from the Common ones, the Common ones have a luminous Body. This one emits its light from two round substances like eyes situated just under its true eyes. I took it into a dark room & confined it on my Book by a tumbler & I was able to read by its light as well as by a Candle as it runs along my paper it seems like a Carriage with two lamps in front. It has a great power of elasticity in its tail, for by drawing it under its breast it suddenly throws itself forward two or three yards it also strikes against the table with a very sensible blow. I have just found out I am mistaken in supposing that Serpents, Scorpions or Centipedes are produced in the West Indias & as my present information is in a good print & well bound I must believe it true. Yet I do recollect Mr Weston, Corporal McPhail, Greener, Fife & Fox & some few others who from not having read this book (Brian Edwards) allowed themselves to be killed by the imagination of such things.

I have had five Men, one Goat and one Boy under my observation dying by the Venom of Serpents. I also know that a Horse died in the Fort from the same cause. It is said that a Hog is not effected by the bite or a Serpent that it seizes & eats them & some say that Cats are not hurt, but others account for it by the extreme rapidity by which a Cat seizes the Animal about the head & kills it. The Mongoos in India is said to do the same.

12   I caught a large Serpent & stuffed it with tow, but I was afraid to inspect its head, I therefore cut it off & put it in a Vial of Rum.

15   Reports from Europe that Mr Pitt is again prime Minister & the King deranged.

16   The Invalides left for England: Reports from America say that the President has expressed a decided enmity to England & War is expected but it is hoped that the People think differently.

The Caribs

20   I employed myself in recollections & first I begin by saying that St Vincents is an island about 60 Miles in Circumference, of an oval shape. It was formerly one of those islands which European powers finding they could not conquer, (ie because they were jealous of each other & supported the Natives) agreed should be Neutral Islands. The Aborigines were called Carraibs or Carraibes of the same race as the Inhabitants of Surinam & the Spanish Main. The Islands from the Main land to the Main Land again may be easily seen from each other & in fact two Islands could be seen at a time viz. from St Vincents to the South 2 or 3 of the Grenadines & to the North St Lucia & Martinico, from St Lucia Martinico & Dominico &c &c.

The Carraibs are Short & thickset of a Copper Complexion with long black hair & very active, their countenance very pleasing, the General height of the men is under 5 feet 6 inches the women are much shorter & more inclined to Corpulency, both sexes go almost Naked, in the Water they appear amphibious. They depend on the Sea in a great measure for subsistence. Like the American Indian they are very slothful or very active, no medium. The principle game on Shore is a small kind of half Rat half Rabitt called Agootie & the Manicou or Opossum. These they sometimes hunt with Dogs & sometimes shoot with arrows. They often shoot fish in the Transparent Sea with arrows but always by judging of distances, they shoot in Air & the Arrow falls on the fish. When tired or having sufficient food they sit in doors swinging in a hamock & pushing it with their feet one side & by some post in the Room to another. They sometimes plait a kind of reed to make basketts, they weave them so neatly that they will hold water & consequently will keep out water in any weather & being light are much used by the English to carry cloths in.

Among these Yellow or Red Carraibs have arisen a Black Carraib supposed to be a mixed Race between the Negroe & Carraib women, they are more bold & robust & have almost destroyed their Copper Colored Brethren. When the Equalizing system of French was first promulgated in the West Indies the Blacks & People of Colour very naturally thought that the liberal system extended to themselves & for some little time united all Ranks in their favour. The Carraibs felt as others & not being so nearly allied as the Inhabitants of Martinique & Guadaloup, they continued to cherish the hope of universal equality after the hope was given up in the latter Islands. The consequence was that the Carraibs thought the french their real friends & being buoyed up they

The Caribs

undertook a War against the English, on the first rising of these people the horrible cruelties committed are scarcely credible, but the most remarkable circumstance is the fidelity of the English Slaves who fought for their Masters & altho obliged to retreat they followed their Masters to Kingston & remained faithful even to starvation. The end as might naturally have been expected was that the English brought fresh Troops & having conquered the Carraibs, transported the Black part of the Community to Honduras & I believe to Sierra Leona.

The Yellow or original inhabitants are left, but the destruction of this formerly populous community was brought about by the Black Carraibs & not the Europeans.

The Carraibs formerly used bows & arrows & they now have them & are very expert in the use of them, yet they are given up as an offensive weapon.

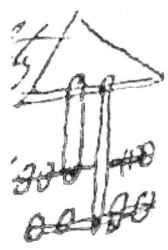

The Chiefs have a plurality of Wives & seem to part with them on very slight grounds, the woman is a compleat Slave & is made to cultivate the Land & carry water which latter is no easy job for the Hutts are generally placed on a Ridge of a Hill & every drop of Water must be carried from the Vale below. Their principal food is a paste made of Cassada or Manioc which like the Potatoe cannot be used without destroying the Crudity of its juice, the Juice is a very powerful poison. I have seen a Hog killed by drinking a small quantity of it. The Machine by means of which they express it is very ingenious, it is a loosely woven wicker basket which being filled is compressed by weights & alongated as may be seen in the Margin. They afterwards bake farina on this plater of Iron like frying pans. They also make the Plantain into a food called tum tum. They pound the Plantain in a Mortar with Chillie Pepper. Their houses a very light being a very light frame of Reed on each layer of which the double down a plantain leaf the upper ridge covering the lower one & these huts soon constructed last a sufficient time for an hours work. They are fond of keeping a fire at all times in their houses & when the weather is damp they have one under every hamock. They tye bandages pretty tight round the legs of their children & indeed round those of all the People both Men & Women, one above the Knee one immediately below & one round the ankle. This is generally Knit & fashioned on the Part, this bandage or Garter being put upon the legs of growing children causes a swelling in the joints above, they have unnatural Knees & Calves of the legs.

Their way of counting is in french & indeed more than half of their present Language which of course arises from the new Wants which Europeans gave them.

A House	Baatee	A sheep	mutton	Husband	Teriete
A Plate	assietteè	A Fowl	Cuterac	Wife	Leane
A hammock	Eyran	A Blackman	Megoro	The sea	Ballowah
A Calabash	Commodee	A European	Balencè Comba	A Dress	Coolee Habit
A Bottle	Botteil	A Caraib	Califourna	A Hat	Bonnettee
a Goat	Cabra	A Man	Abene eera	A Tree	Waiee
A Horse	Caballo	A Woman	Eniero	Cassava	Elleva
A Cow	Vacasso	A Child	Erriaraux	To eat	Stega
A Hog	Piero	Rum	Binoo or Vinoo	To drink	Stanta
Water	Louna	Wine	Duvin		
A Ship	Ocoona	How do you do	Ma bouy ca	Very well	E Nay

They reckon only to Twenty in French & then begin 20 and 5 or 6 or 15 & then two twenties.

From this short vocabulary it seems that all their furniture Cattle & is derived from France or spain. The Carraibs have two names vz one French & one Carraib, Michel, Baptiste, Philip & to which is added Yarrowby, Amouraby.

The quickness of their sight is great they point out objects long before a white man can perceive them. I can make nothing of their Religion but they certainly believe in a resurrection, Angel & Spirit, the latter is called Zoombie & is sometimes a Sylvan god & at other times a more revenant. They are full of superstition & dread fishing if they have had unpleasant dreams. They will not allow a man to lay a net in the Sea if his wife has been brought to bed within the Moon. Sometimes they appear to be predestinarians for on remonstrating with them on their endeavouring to go to Sea in a small Canoe during a Gale they said "If our friends (meaning departed) want us we shall not return, if they do not we shall"

They are all very fond of Rum & they can scarcely refrain from drinking while any remains. One day they caught a very large Snapper (a Fish) & brought it up to sell for Rum. They bargained with me for a calabash of Rum, when the bargain was made they went down & brought a Calabash which contained four Gallons. I could not have supposed there was one so large however the bargain having been made they got it filled & after dinner I went down to their Hutts to see what they were about. I found them standing in a Circle & crying from intoxication, Men, Women & Children holding each others hand singing an old French Song which they called Chansson de Misere, The words were so barbarous as not to be understood, the burthen was "O' Rochambeau! Rochambeau! Oh! Oh!" (The French Governor of the Island.) The purport was that Rochambeau had enticed them to make War on the English which was the cause of their ruin, it is however to be observed that the black Carraibs were the Poets, they kept curtseying to this tune until they could stand no longer.[41]

They generally in their songs take a child by the hand & curtseying without moving the feet cause the Child to do the same, it has much the appearance of begging. I believe they either never knew the whole purport of their french songs or have forgot it.

Their music consists of a hollowed tree or a small Barrel both ends covered with Goat Skin. The Musician seats himself astride on the instrument & beats with his Fists. When they once commence dancing they do not cease while they have liquor as long as they can stand. I never saw them dance while sober.

At this time they will sell any thing they have & send up deputations to the Officers offering to make Basketts or catch fish or do any thing the next day, if they will give them Rum but they invariably forget their promises if you lend them any thing. At certain Seasons they make an intoxicating drink of Cassada & they also ferment the Maize or Indian Corn & make a spirit of it. The Old women are employed to chew the Corn & throw it into a Vessel with water from which the Liquor is drawn off fermented & kept for use being of a very intoxicating nature. They complain of the destruction brought on themselves by the intermixture with Negroes yet so careless are they of the future that they have given their daughters as wives to the only 3 Black Carraibs remaining When the Men are inclined to be Idle, which generally happens when they are not hungry or fearing to become so they sit down & make the women eradicate every hair from their Chin Eyebrows & other parts of the Body,

---

[41] Donatien-Marie-Joseph de Vimeur, Vicomte de Rochambeau (1750 -1813). "Rochambeau, the commanding general, from the landing of Napoleon's expedition to the entire expulsion of the French, was a hard-hearted slaveholder, many of whose years had been spent in St. Domingo, and who, from the moment that he landed with his forces, treated the colored men as the worst of barbarians and wild beasts. He imported bloodhounds from Cuba to hunt them down in the mountains. When caught, he had them thrown into burning pits and boiling caldrons. When he took prisoners, he put them to the most excruciating tortures and the most horrible deaths. His ferocious and sanguinary spirit was too much for the kind heart of Toussaint, or the gentlemanly bearing of Christophe. His only match was Dessalines." (Brown, William Wells, 2014. *Clotel and other Writings*. Literary Classics of the United States, New York. p. 111).

they do indeed have a very very narrow single row of hair on their eyebrows.

They acknowledge that in former times they put to death superannuated People & those who were useless to the community. The Murders & destruction of these poor Yellow Carraibs by the more ferocious Blacks must have been dreadful, they are now so few in Number & if you ask after their ancestors or even the Father of any Individual the Answer is he was killed by the Black Carraibs.

The Women have a singular Pincushion viz a hole in the upper lip thro which there always appear a Bundle of Pin points bristling out like a number of Eaveline's [tent guyropes]. This is a very formidable defence for their Mouths. These Pins they are able to remove singly with their tongue & can even pick out any one you may require without using the fingers. This is indeed but a poor description of these People but may serve to remind me of a race with whom I may say I was very intimate, having passed many hours of almost every day for 10 months in their Company. The Black Carraibs are stouter bodied Men. They are in all probability descended from run away Slaves who wishing to distinguish their descendents from the Negroes, contrived to flatten the Heads of their Infants by compressing them between boards.

When their Numbers increased they made war on the Yellow Carraibs & having destroyed the greater part drove the remainder into the Mountains & most barren part of the Island in 1796. The Black Carraibs, encouraged by the French rose suddenly on the English & such was the surprize that no resistance was offered, the poor Whites were murdered in the most shocking and horrible manner. The Carraibs gained possession of all the Island & even of Dorsetshire Hill which overlooks Kingston. I have mentioned before that the Negroe slaves were almost to a Man faithful to their Masters. They covered the Ground between Kingston & Fort Charlotte & were in a state of starvation. Some of the Planters who had lived on the road between Kingston & the Carraib Country & with whom the Carraibs had been accustomed to lodge on their Journeys, thought themselves secure from former friendship, but those who remained trusting to these savages were all murdered. At length St Lucia being conquered some troops arrived the 53rd among the rest & soon recovered the Island, took all the Black Carraibs & transported them to an island called Rattan. It is said that the Spanish took them from there to work in the Mines. Others say that they were sent to Sierra Leone. I do not know which of the two stories is correct. The Yellow Carraibs having been less turbulent remain, but there are but few of them, residing at Masarica & Ouia. There are still some few

Carraibs in the Woods, or it is supposed so far there are doubts, Several Person have been murdered but more particularly a Mr Clapham, a Gentleman of consequence, who was fishing near Mount Young. I must own that I have my doubts for I never heard of any appearance while I was among the Yellow Carraibs & I think I must have heard of these if any, indeed Negroes might have killed Mr Clapham & attributed his death to the Carraibs since the Rising of the Carraibs & the destruction of the Estates the Planters of St Vincents.

St Vincent—Description

I go on again with the recollections of St Vincents—St Vincents is an uneven Country. The Center being high Mountains running in separate valleys towards the Sea. Between these ridges are fine valleys but generally confined to the coast. To windward or between Mount Young & Ouia, the Country is a delightful level, this is by far the finest part of the Island. There is also some fine ciaValleys between Ouia & Morne Rond, but they are detached from each other by such high bluffs as to be at present impassible & I believe always were so, they are as much seperated from the rest of the Island as if they were surrounded by Water. The Principal of these Valleys is called Challeaueux from a Family of that Name the Chief or as the Carraibs say the King of the Black Carraibs. This broken Coast may be reckoned ten Miles, the Breadth from Mount Young to Morne Rond about seven. The principal Mountains in St Vincents are Morne de Garue which is inaccessible, The Souffrier, a Volcano, it is said to have the most compleat Crater of any Volcano in the World. I am sorry that I never went up, indeed the Center of the Island is one continued Ridge which except the Worn beds of Torrents is impassible. This range is called by different Names, Near Mount Young The Rabbacca & from thence the Grand and Petit Bon Homme from thence towards Kingston, Manquoi, The Vigue, Millers Ridge & Dorsetshire Hill. The Rivers are small but during the rains they become Torrents sweeping all before them. There is not one Navigable. They are the Calonerie, Rabbacca, Ballune, Buccoma & Greatheads, there are several Mineral Springs one of which is so impregnated with fixed air as to sparkle like Spruce Beer, this is situated in Greatheads Valley. There are hot springs & Iron Springs, Sulphur &c, Kingston is the Capital situated at the Bottom of a Bay, quite open when the Wind becomes Westerly which indeed is very seldom but I have seen it turn that way & when it did The Sailors left the Ships for a Hurricane is so tremendous a Thing that having well anchored the Vessels they left them (Altho I saw this yet I am not certain whether this was general or only some particular Ship) the place from which I observed it was 2 or 300 Yards above, & I took part from hearsay. There are very few Animals or Birds but fish is very plentiful as Snappers, Red & Silver, Cavallas, Mackrell, Rockfish Grouper, Barncouta & the Rivers Mulletts Sucking Fish & a kind of young Spawn of Whiting much like what is called White Bait, we catch it on White Linnen & it is very delicate I think it is called Guzree

29   Reptiles are numerous I have before mentioned them in my Account of fort Duvernet. A General removal of Troops took place except the 53rd Reg^t. We were annoyed by this but we hope that the reason is that we are soon to go home. The two Black Regiments move from this, the 1st W. I. to St Vincents. The 7th to Antigua.

St Lucia—Description

St Lucia is situated between St Vincents & Martinico. It is said to contain more acres of sand than Martinico. In all probability if it should be ceded to the English it will become a more valuable Island. The soil is much deeper than that of St Vincents, but its having been one of the debateable Islands, has been much neglected. The Face of the Country is less rugged than St Vincents & it can be crossed in all directions yet it may still be called a very mountainous Country. The Highest Mountain is called La Soureve. The Two Petons or Sugar Loaves are remarkable objects from the Sea.

St Lucia, Piton. 2014.

They are very perpendicular & absolutely inaccessible tho many Persons have attempted to ascend them, between these Mountains there are most delightful Valleys with several Rivers not now Navigable but I think they may be easily made so. The Suffriere or Volcano is not so large as that of St Vincents, but it abounds in Sulphur. St Lucia is reckoned the most unhealthy of all the Islands & it appears likely to remain so but we have not a proper means of judging them for Castries & the Morne (that is the Principle Town & Principle Garrisson are in the most unhealthy part. It is said that the Vigie & Morne have destroyed more Soldiers than any two garrisons in the World, the Venom of the Reptiles & insects is here more powerful even the Musketo sting is dangerous which is attributed to the Nature of the Soil. The Viper is sometimes found Eleven feet long. <u>See the Acc^t of young Weston's death.</u> [see page 108 August 7, 1800] The Viper is distinguished from Snakes by the abruptness of the Point of the tail. There are more Birds than in St Vincents particularly a kind of Crow or Jackdaw which abound in the Fort & Parrots are most common in the woods. Humming Birds are very common but I never saw one smaller than a Wren. On the Morne we are not troubled much by Musquitoes but at Gross Islet there is scarcely a possibility of sleeping without curtains, it is not so in St Vincents. In the day time I could not walk in that part of the Island without my Handkerchief in my hand to drive them away. Even the Negroes carry a bough in their hand at night to switch them off. The present produce of the Island viz Sugar, Cotton, Coffee & Cocoa is so small that we scarcely see a Ship from Europe in the harbour for the produce is carried on drogers[42] to martinico. The Island abounds in fruit which seem to grow indigenous viz Orange, Pine Apples, Guavas, Cashews, Avocata Pears, Soursops, Sappadillos (Sapadilla—Naseberry), Water Lemons, Granadillos (passion fruit), Maranee (Marañon—Cashew?), besides Mangoes & Caronfies (Chironja?) which are not quite so Common.

The Principal Towns are Castries, Suffrier, Gross islet & Vieux Fort. Castries had been built on a regular plan but was destroyed in the Revolutionary War & is now only a straggling Village built of Wood one Story high. The Streets are still laid out as was intended like Washington in America & the Foundation of intended buildings in Stone are still to be seen differing in a remarkable manner from ruins being of an even height. Gross Islet is much like Castries only smaller. The streets very wide & green. Pigs, Goats & Cattle quietly grazing therein.

The Military Stations are The Morne, Pigeon Island, Souffriere, Vieux Fort, Mabouya & the Vigie. The present Garrisson consists of 60

---

[42] Droger: small West Indian coasting boat with a long mast and lateen sail.

Artillery, the 53rd Reg^t 300 strong, the 1st & 7th West India Reg^t. The Troops are stationed as follows 53 Reg^t & 5 Companies 7th W. I. the Morne, 2 Comp^{ys} 7th Vieux Fort, 1 Company 7th Mabouye, 1 Comp^y 1st W. I. Suffrier, 2 Comp^{ys} W. I. Vieux Fort. Vigie 1 Comp^y 1st W. I.. Pigeon Island 4 Compies 1st W. I..

The Harbours & Bays of St Lucia are very commodious & safe. The Principal called Carrenage is completely land locked it is very difficult of entrance as the Wind invariable blows from the Land, This is however in some respects remedied as the very general calm or rather Shelter from high lands & it is easy to turn a vessel in with a Boat. The depth of the Water is such that they lay along side the land as close as possible & the cargoe is carried out by hand, but it is very unhealthy.

Gross Islet bay is very fine having a Sandy beach not so convenient for landing goods but easyer entered which indeed can be done at all times. The entrance is defended by Pigeon Island. In this Bay Rodney lay before he fought De Grasse.

May 1st 1801.   It being now 3 Years since I had my Lieutenancy I have been calculating my Expences, the first year I spent 158£ beside my pay, the 2nd year 20£ beside my pay, the third I lived on my pay, the 1st year it is true I had to make my way out from England.

Our hopes of going home are cooled by receiving 62 Recruits.

May 8   I walked with Weston to Gross Islet in 2½ hours remained 5 Hours & returned in a Schooner. The land parched for want of Rain.

13   74 Recruits arrived for us, report of Peace with the Northern powers & that General Abercromby[43] has beaten the French in Egypt. The 7th West India embarked for Antigua. We invited the Officers to Dinner swelled my Mess Bill.

To Mrs Butt from St Lucia 20 May 1801

Statement of my weekly expences in messing	£1 -	8	
washing		4 -	8
breakfast		4-	8
	£1 -	17 -	4
My pay for 1 Week is	£1 -	18	– 2½.
My whole remaining receipt is		1/	10½ .

Can I with this provide Cloths, Servant & a Thousand other articles. I have really half starved myself yet I am now £22 in debt but I have something of a Soldiers economic turn & I will do if I can do. My Taylor

---

[43] General Sir Ralph Abercromby was fatally injured in the Battle of Alexandria, 21 March 1801, and died attended by his son Lieut. General Sir John Abercromby.

must suffer not by my non payment but the lack of orders, or as the old Joke has it when speaking of my Short Jacket It will be long enough before I have a new one. Should you see Major Buckland which I hope you will he will tell you how I get on. I should like much to see you but I do not wish to remain in England.

> We are now again in expectation of seeing England but I only wish to see you for a short time & then go abroad again.

25   A Brig arrived from England the captain says that Lord Nelson has attacked the Danes in the Baltic & taken or sunk 17 Ships of the Line & has taken Copenhagen.[44] He says that Lucien Bonaparte is in London to make peace.

31   Accounts arrived of the death of eccentric friend & Enemy, the Emperor Paul of Russia.

June 6   I walked down to the Cul de Sac Valley & ascended the River to what is called the falls which is the same as a Mill weir in England. The country was very beautiful. The River is bordered the whole way with bamboos which remind me of Brobdinag Wheat, growing apparently from a single root 50 feet high. I walked four miles & after Bathing returned. The Crashing noise of the Plants with their friction against each other & the breaking of occasional ones with the gloomy silence of the scene make the Solitary person expect to see Banditte at each opening. There are always Birds flitting about in silence, the very noise of the Bamboos is so occasional that the silence is dreadfully silent, & you almost shudder in turning round.

7   Ensign Sutherland arrived with 12 Convicts to increase the respectability of the Corps.

8   I was Transferred to the Command of Captain McMahon's Company.

15   A confirmation of a Great Battle in Egypt.[45]

18   A man bit by a Serpent today.

29   From the 18th to today a constant succession of dark gloomy days, talk no more of November in England, we had darkness visible, & the black Vomit over Morne de Chapeurs. Lightning struck the new barracks in my sight & destroyed them to the Amount of some Hundred Pounds Sterling. I was sitting opposite about 10 paces off & when the explosion took place I thought a Gun had been fired for there was no roll whatsoever.

---

[44] Battle of Copenhagen 2 April 1801.
[45] 2nd Battle of Abukir 8 March 1801 or Battle of Alexandria 21 March 1801. British defeated French.

July 1st A Vessel arrived from Martinique brings a paper with the following notification by Marshall Augereau to Holland, that Holland was no longer to consider itself a seperate State but that it was to form part of the <u>great Empire</u>. The Paper went on to state that the Dutch had revolted, that the fleet had sailed from Holland & given themselves up to the English in the Name of the Prince of Orange. The Paper further states that the English had defeated the french in Egypt & taken Cairo but with the loss of their General Abercromby

5   The Army Brig arrived suddenly calling for Two Companies 1st West india to do duty at Martinique. The sickness there is so great it is said that 16 men of the 68th Reg^t have been buried in one day. They have lost upwards of 30 Officers since they landed, among the rest a Lieut^t Col^l

9   The 1st West India falling with a camp of run away Negroes near Maboya they were totally off their Guard & singing. They consisted of about sixty mostly Women & Children. Lieut^t Roberts commanding fired among them & killed two, one of them a famous Chief Tampion who had been in the Woods 34 Years. Lieut^t Roberts then rushed before them & took 1 Man & 1 Woman together & shot them & reported that they had died of their wounds. Our Officers are very angry at this Cruelty & have expressed their feelings openly. This is not the first instance of Cruelty committed by the black Troops without orders.

This evening at Gun firing after the Gun had been fired & while reloading, from the badness of the Sponge it went off & threw both the Artillery men into the ditch, & it is thought that they will lose their sight, there was a great negligence I presume in stopping the Vent.

The *Coromandel* appeared off, with the 9th West India Reg^t which we have long been expecting. The Current is strong & the Wind low, she seems drifting like a Tub towards Jamaica. We have confirmation of the death of Sir Ralph Abercrombie on 28 March.

13   The New Officers Barracks were given over & I got one. The *Coromandel* had drifted 4 days before she got in. The 9th W. I. landed & dined with us. The Regiment is very strong.

16th I had occasion to observe the great variety of rats they ate a Serpent well soaked in Rum & corrosive sublimate, two drams of the latter had been dissolved. I saw a Frenchman dead from the bite of a small Serpent in the hand. The same man had cured many persons in cases like his own.

Aug 2   I walked with Captain Millar to the Vigie & remained all day with Lieut^t Classon.

4   News from England by which we are led to expect Peace soon. Two large Serpents were killed each having 30 Young ones in their Body's. They were much alike about 6 Feet long. The Young ones nearly a Foot. A French Lady poisoned by her Slave: his reason was hearing she might marry & her future husband not use him so well. The Lady's Character was not immaculate & stories go about not very favourable to a Captain Lauriole, 9th W. India who was her last friend. This Gentleman killed the Negroe so that the poor fellow had no trial. He, Captain Lauriole said we had no laws that he could depend on.

The largest Serpent killed near the Hospital, Eleven Feet long & had 53 Young within it, some of them 18 inches long.

Two Ships of the fleet were lost in entering Fort Royal Bay in Calm Weather, this must be attributed to neglect as the harbour was like a Pond & we understand that they sailed against known rocks with all Sail set, during the Night. Several Officers were drowned in their Cotts. Indeed the Captain of transport are often as ignorant as common Bargemen.

18   We saw an action between an English Brig & a Spanish Ship which the Brig took after an action which lasted from 12 at Night until 8 in the Morning, it must be observed, that a great deal of the fighting was at long Shot with light wind.

22   We found that the Spanish Ship mounted 20 Guns & had 150 Bound to the Savannah. The English Brig 18 Guns, Carronades.

Doctor Davidson an old friend appointed Surgeon 9th West India Regt.

I have been trying to live on my pay, but finding it insufficient I have volunteered the detachment at the Vigie, which is to be relieved Tomorrow by the 53rd. I intend living on my Rations there. I had been in orders for the Vigie, but the Detachment was not relieved & it is not known when it is to be relieved

9   I was on guard in Castries today & got nothing to eat but a bit of dry bread.

10   Removed to do duty in captain Dean's Company while Classon remains at the Vigie. The heat has been excessive these few days past. I have no doubt that a beefsteak if we had such a thing might be cooked by the Solar heat on a Gun.

22   The heat continued till this day when it rained tremendously with dreadful Thunder & Lightning.

27   I caught a very severe cold going rounds at Night. Reports of the Conquest of Egypt from the French Army. Large detachments for all Regts except the 53rd, our hopes of going home are now raised.

Octr 8   A Sham Fight between the 53rd Reg^t & 9th West India which ended of course according to orders the 9th W. I. are a very fine Corps, but nothing is so ridiculous as a Sham Fight. From this to 17th Much troubled with the Ear ack.

17   Serpents shew themselves again, they are only found after severe Rain, they probably keep in the woods & holes & in dry weather.

25   My Ear ack continued, Lieut^t Hughes with 25 Men arrived. I walked with Sanderson 9th W. I. to Pigeon Island & back which is reckoned 23 Miles

30   I went to the Vigie & slept there.

1 Oct^r [sic: 1 Nov]   Finding that Classon had no objection to being relieved I went to the Commanding Officer & told him that I was a few pounds in debt & that I could not remain in the Mess. I said that it was my turn for the Vegie & indeed for the next detachment that should an expensive detachment be ordered I must go which was unfair as Classon was on Vigie duty out of his turn where he had been for four Months, against his will. The fact seemed that they wished to keep Classon away, but on finding me determined to leave the Mess, I was put on orders to relieve Classon on Friday next.

6   I relieved Lieut^t Classon at the Vigie, the Fort is strong & might be made more so, it is not Commanded in any way & has great advantages it may be called a Presque ile being joined to the Main land by a Stream generally impassable, the only frequented path & indeed the only one capable of being used winds round a Rock upon one particular Spot of which road only two men could walk, there points a long 18 Pounder loaded with grape. We have only a Subaltern with 25 Men for Signals as it can be augmented at a moments Notice & it is in itself very secure. The Vigie cannot do much Mischief to Shipping being too high. The Tapion Battery on the opposite side of the Carenage being placed on a level with the water is of course of more use in defending the harbour.

Lieut^t Classon left me a Fish pot which is a square Bamboo trap with a small entrance thro which the fish enter but cannot return. It is on the Principle of the Common Wire Rat Traps the being bated with fruit, particularly soursops. The Fish enter & are caught, we generally throw in some broken Crockery to attract observation. I went out in the Morning to draw my Pot & found 13 Middling sized fish. I kept two for my dinner & gave the rest to the Men. The Private Soldiers are very fond of getting on these small detachments: they are to some degree independent & live more according to their own fancy but it is not right to leave them too long as it requires a time to bring them round again as to their drilling.

St Lucia 1801-1802

7 I went to my Fish Pot again but did not find a single fish. In walking along the Bay I met a Person who sold fowls & bought 5 Chickens for 3 dollars but they were very small.

8th Went to my Fish Pot again & found it entangled.

9 I went with a drag for my Pot & having got it up found 6 fish in it. Weston with Mrs Weston coming tomorrow. I therefore sunk my Pot with the fish in it. A Strong wind blew my flag staff down.

10 M^r & Mrs Weston & Captn Leslie came to see me with Mr Caskell, we had a very pleasant day. We met a Person who had just lost his Brother by the bite of a Scorpion he was bitten at 8 in the morning & died at 4 in the afternoon.

11 A Report that the People of Color in Guadeloup have risen of the French Governor & made him Prisoner. They Shot the Commandant of the Troops. I caught Ten Fish.

12th Lieut^t Knight, Erskine & Doctor Powel came to see me, passed a pleasant day. Caught only 1 Fish

13th Caught a Shark in my Fish Pot weighing 9 Pounds

15 Sunday & Market day. Went for provisions paid a Dollar for 9 lbs of Potatoes This was entirely for want of cash for I might have purchased a cask of 60 lbs for 2 dollars from an American Brig. A Logwood thorn entered my foot which is much inflamed.

16 My Foot much inflamed applied a Poultice. The Governor of Guadaloup brought prisoner to Martinique, the Negroes having rebelled. Lt Floyd & Doctor Doyle came & passed the day. Men employed getting up new flag staff.

17 A prisoner to my Foot which is much inflamed.

18 The men got up the flag staff, I could only sit in the window & see it done. Cap^{tn} Harley Engineers tells me that Preliminaries of Peace are signed, do not believe it.

19 Major Stewart came to breakfast with me, confirms Capt Harley's News. He says St Lucia is to be restored to the French, but not Martinique.

20 Lieut^{ts} Stewart & McCaskell came to see me, confirm the News & say we are to deliver up St Lucia on or before 24 January.

21 Official Notification of Peace,[46] 21 Guns fired, I rejoice at the peace but I feel for myself as I fear being put on half pay being the Senior within the scope of what is called the break vz above the peace

---

[46] In 1801 a truce was agreed which held while the Treaty of Amiens (May 1802) was under negotiation, including disposal of Caribbean islands.

establishment. I hope that something may turn up before we reach England. I am told that we shall not be relieved until the French relieve me.

22   I went to Castries & I hear that all the Inhabitants are much discontented at the arrangement of giving the Island to the French. Our Troops are delighted to be leaving such a Garrisson.

23   I went down to a Mulatoe's House under the Vigie towards the Carrenage. This man is superior in intelligence to the generality of the People of Color & he gave me some account of the State of the Island under the French. He says that Lacross the Present Governor of Guadaloup was at the time of the Revolution, a Cap^n in the French navy commanding the *Felicité* frigate & that he brought out the decree for the Abolition of Slavery & <u>for a perfect Equality</u>.[47] On his arrival he called together the Inhabitants from 12 Years old & upwards, of all Colors. He read the decree, went thro the ceremony of Embracing a certain number of Blackee's calling them Brothers & Freemen, after the Meeting he sailed away. After his departure the Planters naturally felt a great reluctance to give up their Property. The Commanding Officer himself felt some reluctance in putting the decree in force & appeared to incline to the planters. The Younger Part of the Officers who longed for promotion, intriguing with the Privates they Mutinied, a kind of civil War succeeded sometimes one part prevailed sometimes the other, & many lives were lost both in battle & by the Guiliotine. The English at length appeared off the Island upon which both parties joined against the common Enemy. They were however unsuccessful & the Island was taken. The English General Gordon was very impartial pillaging all parties alike, he completed the Ruin of the Island. He seized the rich planters & threatened to banish them but allowed them to purchase their release. I have this only from my Mulatto friend who might be a great Liar for what I know.

23   The Fort of Vigie is totally unprovided with water owing to the neglect of keeping the Cistern in repair. We have a great deal of trouble in fetching fresh water. I think the French will have some difficulty & expence in putting the Fort in repair. The Vigie now consists of a block House, octagonal, built of wood with sides planked on both sides of the timbers the intersices filled with sand which makes it musket proof. We have only one Gun serviceable vz an 18lb which is fired on a traverse carriage & stands pointed down the path which leads to the Main Land,

---

[47] Jean-Baptiste Raymond de Lacrosse (1760-1829) brought the French Revolution declaration of equality to Guadaloupe in 1795, quelling a rebellion, but later sided with the planters against the slaves. Returned in 1801 to govern.

loaded with Grape. I forgot my Fish Pot during the animating News & when I went to look for it was gone.

24 Hard rain. Report that the 9th W. I. Regt being French Royalists are immediately to go to St Vincents.

25 I walked to the Morne to hear the news: report of the day is that if Peace had not been made the 53rd Regt would have gone home in April, on dit, that the Ship *Van Tromp* was actually under orders to take us home, we now expect to go in February. In looking for an Acacea pod I was much struck with the difference of the Vegetable production between the Island & St Vincents. St Vincents is covered with Acaceas. I could never find one here, but we have quantities of dogwood & as I am now speaking of dissimilarity I must mention that this island & Martinique seem to agree with that but to differ from every other. We are here full of Serpents, Tarantulas, Scorpions &c but there are none in St Vincents that are poisonous.

The Windward part of this island like St Vincents is much more level that the Leward in appearance like the beach of the Sea gradually retires. The Centre is very Mountainous. These Mountains running towards the Sea in ridges forming head lands & high bluffs with valleys & small Bays, the passage from one to the other being very difficult, resembling the gable end of a house. The Soil of Morne Fortune is a very deep yellow clay but as you descend towards the village it is a fine rich mould: after passing Castries to the Eastward it becomes rocky & in Chock a fine Black mould, again rather swampy but very rich, this kind of soil is found for 7 Miles to Gross islet then it becomes Sandy with Rocks. The plane round the Cul de Sac is rich black mould with a river which might easily be made navigable for 4 or 5 Miles at least.

An American Brig appeared off the Island, I went on board & bought 2 Fowls for a Dollar. While the Brig lay off & on I remained on board. Jonathan[48] does not approve of the late peace. They were formerly ready enough to accuse the English of every kind of obstinacy & pride, but now they say we fought in a good cause & that it was the cause of the world & that we have abandoned a good cause. This of course arises from the fear that Jonathan will not be employed so much in peace as in War.

---

[48] Jonathan: Brother Jonathan was a term for Puritan settlers of New England, later becoming the term for Yankee soldiers.

29   I went to Castries, found Weston on Guard & remained with him, McCaskell writes me word that we are likely to go home sooner than was expected, I shot a large Agootee.[49]

Some French Commissioners arrived in the Frigate *La Pensé*. Mungo came to see me. I told Him that the French would now take St Domingo, he says they will not succeed for the General Toussaint is an Obi man & can catch Canon Balls fired at him & throw them back on the Enemy.

30   <u>A Soldiers News</u> "Well my Lads, We are going. We are to be relieved immediately by the 2 West India Reg^t. We join the French against St Domingo, the French have sent 80 Thousand Men, & we have 100 Transport & 5000 Men & we are to have half the Island, now we shall see what the Spanish will say. Well, they may say what they like, plenty of Spanish Dollars. Do you know what St Domingo is? Why it is a large Island & the blacks have taken it & murdered all the Mulatoes, but they were afraid to kill a White Man. They sent them off the Island. Well what do you think of 80 Thousand Men exclusive of the Garrissons for the island." Upon which the Orator was stopped by a question "What do you mean by <u>exclusive</u>" Upon which the Orator grew sulky said he would not enter into arguments with any of them & he went to bed.

Decem^br 3   The French Governor of Guadaloup has written to say that the Island is in a state of rebellion & requests that no assistance may be given by the English, it being Peace.

4   I was very nearly swamped in my boat in going to Castries for provisions. The French General in Guadaloup calls the People of Color Rogues, Vagabonds & Rebels, but he forgets, that it was himself that first proclaimed freedom to the Blacks which is now the order of the day to forget. (The Chief of the Mulatoes in Guadaloup, Pelagé was a Barber's Boy). He was made a captain by Rochambeau in the regiment de Antilles, he was afterwards Commandant of Gross Islet in St Lucia & being driven out by the English he went to France from whence he returned to Guadaloup with the rank of general. He has lately received orders from Home to recall the Emigrés. The difficulty was how to reconcile the old Proprietors & the actual possessors of Estates. He sided with the old Proprietors & in consequence the eléve's of the Republic rebelled & drove their Governor away & declared Guadaloup a Free & independent Republick. This might have done some time back, but now in time of peace it will not hold. Pelage will of course be obliged to submit & probably lose his Life. Guadaloup is not of itself sufficient strength to

---

[49] Agouti: a long legged rodent like a guinea pig.

defend itself like St Domingo, indeed had it not been for War in Europe the latter would not have succeeded.

6 In consequence of peace, half the Allowance for Candles is stopped.

I saw a caricature purporting to be the adventures of Johnny Newcombe – from his arrival in the west Indies until his death[50] which reminds one of many circumstances coming under my own observation.

9 A most dreadful Storm, I expected that we should have been blown away. The Flag Staff seemed in great danger, but it weathered it.

10 The French have a curious way of reckoning which must puzzle Strangers for Instance 5 Sols make 3 Dogs, 30 Sols make 12 Dogs which ought to make 18 Dogs. The fact is that 5 Sols is a real Coin & understood as such but 30 Sols is a currency & the dogs are Coins.

11 I went to Morne to hear when we were to go home. No news, Sanderson returned to pass a few days with me & take views.

12 Adj^t Hardy 9th West India came over & we made a stew with a fowl &c –

13 Two Vessels appeared to westward resembling men of war, they separated off Pigeon Island.

14 The mail arrived (News) Lord Cornwallis gone to France to settle the definitive Treaty. Lord Whitworth to be Ambassador to France. We hope soon to get away. French Merchant Ships are beginning to arrive, their destination is Guadaloup but owing to the revolution, as it is called, but more properly the rebellion, they stop at martinico & Saints. Our troops decrease in Number as we receive no detachments & death will not wait the tardy consequences at Amiens. My detachment is to be reduced to 20 Men with an Artillery man.

17 Saw the main mast of the government Schooner showing between this & Martinico. Occupied in collected seeds for Lord Valentia.

18 Busy on collected seeds as yesterday. I sent six Men away from the Post to reinforce the morne.

22 Americans arrived to carry away as much as can be done before the French arrive. I have saved in seven weeks 40 Dollars equal to £9-6-8 but I have lived on station provisions viz Salt meat varied twice a week by Fresh & my drink has been the Government allowance.

---

[50] *The Military Adventures of Johnny Newcombe by An Officer.* David Roberts 1815. Illustrated by Thomas Rowlandson.

Xmas day.   Weston, Mrs Weston, Cap^n^ Leslie & M^c^Caskell came over. It rained all day which hindered our enjoying ourselves but we passed a pleasant day.

26   A long canoe was swamped under the Vigie. The Crew saved. I observe Numbers of ships passing every day from Martinico are removing their property previous to the arrival of the French. The same thing happens in St Lucia. Most of the Negroes from the Island are gone to Trinidad. This shews a curious feeling in the human mind for altho the negroes expect to be free on the arrival of the French they yet shew great anxiety to go with their Masters before the French arrive. We have often seen the same before.

Our Boat is now so old as to be unsafe yet as the island is now considered French there cannot be a Penny expended. I therefore drew her up & caulked her myself, but she is dreadfully rotten & I fear some accident will happen.

29   A Sloop arrived & lay too off the battery without shewing her Colors. The Captain fired 3 shots but the Shot did not reach. She was loaded with Chain & tables.

This year has been particularly wet, but the Crops good. Provisions plentiful & all things getting cheaper.

1802   The 1st of January being my Birthday I observed that I seldom get a dinner on this day. 1799 I went to the Rock in St Vincents & got no dinner - 1800 at Ouia, St Vincents no dinner, 1801 St Pieres Martinique no dinner 1802 no dinner having only a bit of Cold Salt Beef & a Yam which I eat & write that I hope for better times. I cannot however say that I feel much uneasiness on the occasion. Next Year probably I may have a Plum Pudding in England.

It is true that I could easily get a <u>good dinner</u> at the Morne, to which I have an invitation but my Men would all get drunk & quarrel & fight in honor of the New Year. In the Evening a Lobster fell in my way of which I am very fond. I therefore made a tumbler of Punch & sat down to enjoy myself but my soldiers were not altogether so sober as I flattered myself my presence would have induced & I was much disturbed. The room which I inhabit is only parted from that of the Men to about 7 Foot high, above that it is all open, it may easily be conceived that I lose none of their Jokes which are <u>sometimes</u> rather coarse.

3   A Man from the Morne speaks confidently of our embarkation for England by 25th.

4   News from Europe. The Meeting of Plenipotentiaries at Amiens took place on 21 Nov. Weston says in a letter that he saw the Transports prepared to take us home.

St Lucia 1801-1802

5   The *Pensé* French Frigate mutineed & confined their Officers, application was made by the Officers to an English Frigate (the *Tamer*). She immediately laid herself along side & took the Ringleaders prisoners. The *Tamer* convoyed the French Frigate to the Saints where she now lies.

6   A Report prevails which I believe is true that the island of Guadaloup has sent a deputation to the English requesting them to take possession. The flag was instantly dismissed saying that England & france were at Peace. Being 12th day the French had great rejoicings & I went among the houses to their dances.

7   Went on board an American brig, bought a barrel of potatoes & 2 strings of Onions 3 Dollars.

9   I was obliged to attend a Court martial at the Morne. I am to be relieved on Friday.

11   It rained very hard. I found many oysters growing on the mangrove Trees. They were the first I had found & I passed most of the Evening in gathering them, they are very small but good.

12   Millar tells me that the definitive Treaty was signed 29th Nov but it so appears that the 29th Nov was a Sunday & we do not believe it. The French indeed make light of this objection but the English do not.

15   I was relieved by Lieut^t Smith & returned to the Morne.

16   A very high wind.

18   We find that it is now true that the definitive treaty is signed indeed it seems doubtful whether the diplomats have yet met. While at the Vigie I find that I have saved nearly £18 Sterling.

21   Ensign Millet arrived from England with 8 men but they say that their arrival has nothing to do with our going home, they were sent as a guard to some United Irishmen. From this to the end of the Month I was employed in botany &c.

Our Uniform is altered which is a great expence & as we think, a useless one. A report Prevails that the Congress is broken up. Bounaparte only wished to get his fleets out.

Another Report that the French are joining the English against Spain. Two Mountains to crush a fly.

6   American vessels arrived making bargains before the peace starts them out from the French islands. Poor Jonathan!

Great Rain & high winds this month but healthy.

Feby A letter from Mr Maskell says my Brother will get £500 prize money for a Danish East Indiaman taken near St Helena

5   On the 5th I was walking with Lieut Thompson we heard a Gun fire & soon after a second, on hastening back to the Fort we found that the Guns were fired from the Vigie in consequence of the Government boat having overset. The Guns were to bring a Schooner to the assistance of the People. There was on board an officer & his Mother & several Non-Commissioned officers & Privates & the sea was very rough. The schooner came down & we saw her take the boat which was bottom up in Tow but we could not see the people being too far off. We had however the pleasure of hearing that all the Europeans were saved but Ten Negroes were drowned, This is very extraordinary as there were two white women but the same thing happened in St Vincents. Do not the Blacks trust too much to swimming & neglect the Boat which might keep them above water even when capsized. The French Officers shewed but little feeling on the occasion for they called out Sergt Grant of ours a fool for risking his life to save an old Woman, altho she was the Mother of one of their Officers an Ensign Colombier.

Our Officers were very angry & immediately entered a subscription for Sergt Grant.

8   News from England about the middle of January the Definitive Treaty is not yet agreed, but the French have sent a large fleet to St Domingo. We begin to fear that the regiment will not go home as we had expected.

10   I went to Town to dine with the Bearcrofts with whom I have some acquaintance lately. The Elder is Comptroller of the Customs, the sons are nothing, the older is son to Counceller Bearcroft. The weather was so bad that I could not get back. I therefore slept at Mr Bearcroft's house being situated in the valley to the east of the Morne. I did at length reach the Morne but not till after parade nor without the greatest difficulty, the old road being grown over & wet.

It seems certain that the Danish & Dutch West India Islands will be immediately given up, by which there will be Two European & one Black regiment unemployed: we may be relieved immediately.

12   Lieut Weston & Mrs W. arrived from Antigua, it is said that all the islands are unhealthy. St Lucia now escapes which is a great Wonder.

16   A General order directing the 53rd Regt to be sent home immediately so that the Peace has in reality detained us. We now expect to sail by 19th April.

18   Our heavy luggage is ordered to Town which seems as if it was intended immediately to send us away. Weston gave me a Matress, I had never possessed one before, having slept in a hamoc or in my Cloths this 4 years

St Lucia 1801-1802

21 A Report that 13 Transports are arrived from England to take home the [Regt]

I took a long walk by the old French Hospital loaded myself with Cashews & returned across Cootes Bay. Three men of the Regiment died to day

25 A very high wind & a Sloop driven on Shore off the Tapion, it was laden with Cotton & had 6 Negroes on board, 5 were drowned. The one saved was drifted into a Cave under the Tapion from which it was very difficult to get him out there being a tremendous Sea breaking into its mouth.

26 A French Sloop arrived, wanted to sell Wine but was refused permission

27 Report that the definitive Treaty was signed on the 27 January, 500 French have arrived at Guadaloup & landed without opposition.

February has been rather dry with high winds. Healthy except with Colds & Sore Throats.

March I had a severe sore throat. The Regiment Reviewed on 4 by Genl Prevost. The General of course praised the Reg^t & got a dinner which all eat & the Subs pay for, a Mulatoe Carpenter died from a Serpents bite.

6 Attempted to ascend Morne de Chapeaux but found the bushes so much grown we could not succeed, killed a large Serpent. The Troops employed on working parties carrying stores to Town to embark, also all the English ordnance.

We very clearly saw Dominique to day clear of Martinique which proves the Maps wrong which all place Martinique in a line between us & Dominique.

A Ship appeared off & Hughes, McCaskell & myself went on board to see if we could get any provision for our passage home. We found the Vessel a Ship from Bordeaux laded with wine which she is not permitted to sell. The Captain very civil, we remained two hours on board.

15 Ensign Sutherland was bit by a serpent in the Foot. The piece was immediately cut out & he suffered much pain. He is not considered in danger but he will be ill for a long time to come even should he save his Life.

The Heat on 17-16th was intense then after a Shower it was so intensely cold we were obliged to cover ourselves well up, in consequence colds & sore throats are common. I have a bad one.

20th My Throat so bad I could not do duty. I passed the day with Sutherland who suffers severely

21   We are required to advance 35 dollars cash towards Sea Stock

23   I was not able to dine at the Mess till today. Lieut Smith left us for St Vincents. We do not expect that he will join again, he has an Uncle in St Vincents

24   A Report prevailed that the treaty was likely to be broken off. We were employed in mounting Guns again, the outlying pickets again Mount & War is the order of the day. The 43 Reg^t is expected at Martinique from England.

27   On dit that Admiral Gautheaume is arrived with a French fleet & that he came a head to report to the British Admiral. Peace is again the order of the day.

28   Several Ships apparently of the line passed down, we suppose the French & English

30   No News of the definitive treaty as late as 20 Feby from London

31   Strong report that we are to keep Martinique & St Lucia in lieu of Trinidad if so we think it will be a great gain, St Lucia I believe is of greater consequence than Trinidad. March has been hot, dry & healthy.

April 1802   I suffer much from a relaxation in my Throat which has now lasted Three Months as I caught it in coming from the Vigie on the 13 January, being wet.

2-3   An order arrived for discharging all men enlisted for limited Service viz during the War. These Men came from the 79th & 109 Reg^{ts} who had engaged to serve during the War only. Excessive drought, the well within the Fort is dry. I feel very unwell but I cannot bear missing my duty if I can bear it in any way.

7th I was for duty to day. Accounts of the French in St Domingo having received a severe beating it is said that they have lost 6000 Men. The Report from Private Source says that the French General Huinbert has applied to the English in Jamaica for Assistance.

12th Our Reg^t gave a Division to General Prevost & his Staff.

Strong reports are received every day, against the definitive treaty being signed in fact it is not wished here

News from England, The death of the Duke of Bedford

15   General Vansillart arrived to Command. News of Horrid Mutiny of the 8th West India Reg^t in Dominica. The Negroe Soldiers (of which this & all other West India Regiments are composed) rose on their Officers & European Noncommissioned Officers & murdered every one.

The Governor of the Island, Johnson, who is also a Colonel of the Reg^t called out the 68th Regiment & attacked the Mutineers killed 300 Men.

Notwithstanding his exertions the blame is laid on him & will, I have no doubt, always remain so.

The Governor of Guadaloup being a refugee in our Islands is supposed to have instigated the Negroes. The reports concerning the regiment are so various & contradictory that altho I took them down at the time I have since thought, they are unworthy of Credit & have erased them, this seems certain that on the breaking out of the Mutiny, they murdered all the Officers they could catch & the Serg[ts] & Drummers, several Officers threw themselves down precipices among the rest the Surgeon & his wife who remained on a rock nearly all night & were fortunately seen by the Shipping before they were discovered by the Blacks & so excaped. The Guns which the Negroes brought to bear on the Vessels in the Bay actually drove them to Sea, among the Vessels was a frigate & a Sloop of war. These foolish people had only possession of the Fort 48 Hours when they were overpowered by the 68th Rg[t] altho they fought furiously yet they were all destroyed. This is a dreadful business but it is consoling to think how inferior the Blacks even when drilled under every advantage are to Europeans.[51]

17 April 1802   My Sore Throat becomes in a very Alarming state with ulcers in the roof of my mouth & around my Gums. I have no pain with it which the Surgeon says is more alarming.

News from Dominico, the Mutineers 8th West India killed 1 Captain, 1 Lieu[t], 1 Ensign, 2 Commisssaries, 1 Artillery Officer. We do not know the reason for their Mutiny but it is said that Governor Johnson or Major Gordon made the Soldiers work on Private Estates (their own) & paid them nothing. It is even said, with held their Government pay. On dit that some officers abandoned their wives, but this I hope not true. One in particular is mentioned. Nearly 100 of the Men did not join but swam off to Shipping & in all probability a Minority only were concerned but overcame the rest by the sudden & unexpected manner of the rebellion. We think that there is no doubt of the Guilt of the Col[l] Major & probably the Paymaster, but the latter is thought merely to have acted weekly.

---

[51] A plaque at Fort Shirley on Dominica reads: 'On this spot the mutiny of the 8th West India Regiment broke out on 9th April 1802 and lasted three days. This plaque is in memory of those members of the regiment who were killed or executed in their fight for freedom. As a result of their actions here some 10,000 slave soldiers in the British Army were freed in 1807. It was the first act of emancipation in the British Empire.' The Mutiny Act of 1807 led to the freeing of all slave soldiers prior to the 1808 Abolition Act.

The Grenadiers were the Ringleaders & fired on the 68th. The Europeans charged with bayonets & destroyed them, after all it seems to have been an unpremeditated business a mere ebullition of anger from a withholding of pay.

18   General Vansillart our new Governor dined with us to day. My Throat still in a Bad way.

19th I was advised to try the astringent juice of a Cachew Apple to my Throat & I find great relief. Fresh accounts from Dominico which give in addition to the Names of Officers already known to have been killed in the Mutiny, Cap^n Casson, Lieut^{ts} McKay & Rivington, Cap^n Burr was taken Prisoner but some hopes are still entertained of his being alive.

20th Report now says that much blame is attached to the Officers 8th W. I. but I now know so much of the world as to perceive that blame is put on the one that can bear it ie dead Men. A Liu^t named Barton is said to have been killed. The Report says that Major Gordon the Commanding Officer was wounded & escaped in the following manner. He was with the Adjutant in the orderly room when some men ran in & told him that the light Infantry were in a state of Mutiny. He went out with the Adjutant to enquire into the report & at the door were fired on by the Light Company. The Adjutant was killed & the Major wounded. The latter reentered the house & passing thro found his horse standing behind the Room. He mounted & rode off.

21 to 28   It rained so continually that we could not be reviewed by the general altho we were in orders for a review every day & kept in a state of preparation until 10 o clock every morning not excepting Sundays. This was tiresome & will not be of any service at the Review, at the end of the time the Review was postponed by orders on Acc^t of General Vansittart having sprained his Ankle.

29   An American Brig brought a Barbadoes Paper in which was an extract from the London Evening Star announcing the Signature of the definitive Treaty of Peace. The Paper is of the 15 March.

May 2 Two Ships appeared off. One full of Troops, we were in hopes that they were the French but they went off—we afterwards heard that the Ships had the Mutineers of the 8th West India on board with a detachment of the 11th Reg^t guarding them. The Commanding Officer says that upwards of 200 Mutineers were killed in the Action. 65 were buried in one hole & 60 in another. The Reasons given for the Revolt are 1st a Fatigue Party being employed by the Colonel to drain a Marsh, his own Property, without any extra Pay; 2nd A Report raised by some incendiary that at the Peace they would be sold as slaves.

5   A large Frigate passed down, we hope she brings the Difinitive Treaty

We hear from Martinique that the Frigate was the *Latona*, the Treaty of Peace was signed on the 27th March.[52] An official Report of the Mutiny of the 8th W India arrived. The number of Officers killed is not as great as we had heard, there were 1 Cap^n 2 Lieu^{ts} + 1 Commissary 1 Serg^t Major, 1 Serg^t 1 Drummer 1 Artilleryman (Cameron, McKay Wastings + Laing)

Note added Jan 1803: 5th May last entry
[Odd comment as journal resumed at 5 May 1802]

To the end of 1802

Having written thus far I was seized with a Yellow Fever which I never properly recovered until the Island was given up to the French in September, during my extreme illness my great fear was that the French would come before I was able to move but it pleased God to give me strength to get on board a Ship near a Month before the arrival of our New Friends. We reached England in December after being in the greatest danger off the Coast of Ireland & driven into a Bay called Squince near the Staggs & Castle haven on the North Eastern extremity of the Island, we were again driven into the Cove of Cork & again into Plymouth were we performed quarantine. I quitted my journal during this time, first on Acct of illness afterwards for want of opportunity for most of our Men being dead or Transferred we were stowed seven Officers, 2 Ladies & 3 Children in the small Cabin of a 300 Ton Ship & had not room to move. No one can conceive the Distress of Gentlemen on board a Transport under such circumstances at times it is bad enough but when the full strength of Officers for a Regt is quartered with 20 Privates the accommodation must be bad indeed. On Parade at Portsmouth I had on Parade of my Company 2 Officers, 2 Sergts, 1 Corporal & 1 Private.

5 May 1802   We have not yet received an Account of the signing of the definitive of Peace but we hear that a French force of 500 Men have arrived at Guadaloup which we naturally suppose could not have been allowed if Peace had not been settled.

6   General Richpanse (A Republican General) is arrived at Martinique as Commander in Chief of the French West Indias & report says (which General Richpanse by no means contradicts) that General

---

[52] The Treaty of Amiens was signed 25 March 1802.

Goulet is on his passage with 10,000 Men to take possession of the Islands but we say, "Crede" To day we have had an instance of the cruelty of a French planter to his Slave, he placed him under a reversed Copper & allowed him to die there. The same Man whipped a poor Girl nearly to death for allowing the Cows to break from her & run into a Cane patch. General Prevost it seems has no power over this Man as he shelters himself under the French Laws which were granted by the capitulation of the Island the Mans Name is O Neal.

9th Official Accounts arrived of the Signature of the Definitive Treaty of Peace of Amiens on the 27th March.

11   A Vessel arrived to carry away the Stores &c to St Vincents. The French are said to have landed at Guadaloup 2500 Men.

12   The Stores are being carried down to embark.

15   News from Guadaloup, 3000 Men landed under Richpanse. Pelage the Mulatoe General surrendered his Command & the Troops marched towards Basse Terre but were attacked on their rout by the Mulatoe & Negroes under a Mulatoe Name <u>Grace</u>. The Action continued for 4 Hours. The European French conquered but with loss, Grace & his Party kept possession of basse Terre where they murdered all the Europeans & Whites, they even fired on the Ships in the Harbour. Basse Terre is now besieged by the European French

23rd News that General Le Clerc a Republican & Brother in Law to the Chief Consul Bonaparte with a large Army of French can scarcely maintain himself in St Domingo, it is even said that he has left the Island Incog to report the state of the Colonies to the French Government.

24   A Man of the 53rd Reg^t bit by a Serpent & died early on the Morning of 25th. Brian Edwards says that there are no venomous Serpents in the W. I. Islands during this Month we have had great numbers of Bees swarming about the Morne & the Soldiers have actually hived 20 Hives. I have heard it asserted that Bees do not store honey where there is no Water but I can assert that this is false as we have a great quantity of Honey & Wax.

St Lucia Morne Fortune June 1802   On the 1st a Dispatch arrived from the French General Richpanse[53] Governor of Guadaloup announcing that he had overcome & destroyed the Rebel negroes & acknowledging the kindness of the British Officers.

A Report that the Negroes of Guadaloup having got possession of Fort Matilda determined to defend themselves to the last but finding that they

---

[53] General Antoine Richpanse (1770-1802). Governor of Guadaloupe, 1802, re-established slavery. Died of yellow fever.

St Lucia 1801-1802

were in want of provisions they attempted to force their way thro the French blockading army in which attempt 300 succeeded. The Remainder consisting of 500 Men were driven back. Their Commander called Delgrace blew himself & them up by placing some barrels of Gunpowder under the Room in which they were & then placing a trail to it. The 300 who escaped are now in the woods but without ammunition.

Hopes of a Return to England

Price of Provisions in the West Indias
A Full grown Fowl 1 dollar or 6/9[54] a Duck 9/- Guinea Fowl 9/- Goose 12/6 to 15/- Turkey 12/6 to 15/- Eggs 2^d each Fish 6^d P^{ld}Pork 1/- Pr Pound Mutton 1/- Butter 1/6 Tea 13/6 Beef is not sold Potatoes American 25/- Pr Barrels, Wine 4/6 a Bottle porter 1/3 since the signature of the definitive Treaty some articles have fallen at least one half.

4th 5, 6 We sent 20 Invalides to England. We hear that the French will relieve us in a Month at farthest. McCaskell arrived from Martinique & says that the Definitive Treaty was ratified 23rd April & Peace proclaimed in London on 26th. We shall probably soon go home. An Ensign of the 3rd or Buffs shot his Captain & then himself this creates a great deal of talk. 2 Lieut^{ts} 37th Reg^t tried & broke

7 I was employed with 450 Men in carrying Gunpowder away. We put in on board a Sloop near the Tapion. We made two turns to day.

8 450 men employed again at the same work.

16 A severe shock of an Earthquake felt, I was writing at a desk & I felt it so severely as to get up from my Chair & seize the Table as a support. The Barracks rocked like a Ship at Sea & the Slight beams seemed to work on their pegs backward & forward. I expected the house to come down. Something however must be allowed for the sudden & uncommon feel which passed away before I had time to consider what was going forward, the instant it stopped I ran to the door & it seemed that every officer did the same, we all appeared like a parcel of Pigeons putting our heads out of our respective doors with every single hair on end. The well within the Fort which had cost a great deal of Money lately was quite destroyed but our wooden barracks only rocked to & fro, giving to the Motion/ they are all fastened together by pegs.

[54] British currency then £-s-d, pounds, shillings and pence. 12 pence = 1 shilling, 20 shillings = £1. Thus 6/9 = about 34pp.

17th   We are anxiously looking for the return of the Government Schooner from Martinique for by it we expect to gain some intelligence relating to our Return to England. We have no doubt as to our almost immediate return, but the manner of it we are anxious to learn

We had Parrots for dinner today. I have omitted to mention this before, the bird is very good food & so esteemed by the French but it is not eaten in the English Islands.

19   The Government Schooner returned & brought a general Order requiring that all soldiers belonging to the 53rd Reg^t who should wish to remain in the Islands should immediately give in their names.

20   One Hundred & forty men volunteered for the 37th Reg^t but we expect the 60 of these will not be thought fit for Service, indeed I think we have not so many Men in the Reg^t if the whole of these are received & 96 men who are sentenced to serve in the W. I. for Life we shall have but few Men to take home. We have orders to hold ourselves in readiness to embark for England at an hours notice.

21   Orders received to send away our Volunteers & all Men enlisted for Limited Service, the Ships *Southampton* & *Gaiety* are arrived to carry them away.

22   I was on duty to embark the Volunteers we sent away 182 Men including 7 men who are discharged as limited Service Men.

24   Transferred 6 men to the Artificers we have 282 Men left. Dreadful thunder & Lightning. The officers of the *Southampton* perceived the Shock of the earthquake when they were half way between Martinique & St Lucia & thought they had struck on a rock. The same thing happened to Ships off Portugal in the famous earthquake at Lisbon. By a Schooner from Martinico we hear that the French have taken possession of Tobago & St Martens & that we may expect them in a fortnight they are said to be likely at Guadaloup.

2   We hear that the French General at Guadaloup has certified to General Vantissart that he will be ready to take possession of this island in a fortnight.

3   We hear that the *Melpomene* Frigate & *Highland Lass* are appointed to carry the 53rd Rgt to England & it is expected that we shall sail in 3 weeks.

4   I went to gather Cashew nuts. This is the first fine day we have had for a long time.

On the 7th Ensign Millar & myself found a Bee's nest in our old Gun (very apt to Sampson "out of the Strong came forth Sweetness." We courageously determined to put our hand into the Lion's Mouth but being over bold we took the wrong time of day as we were afterwards told. As it was we attacked it with a Bundle of Matches but the Bees who were out of doors attacked us & soon made us run glad to make our escape. One of the Band was passing down the road as we ran from the wood & he offered to go & bring out the Comb which he succeeded in without difficulty, how he did this I cannot understand, he had formerly been a Juggler or Merry Andrew.

We hear that the French are to arrive on the 18th. We have received orders to be paid to the 24th prior to our embarkation. The Paymaster is to retain Sufficient Money in hand to provide vegetables to the 18th. We have subscribed 18 Dollars each to purchase Sea Stock, I say subscribed but there is no option, it has been stopped from me. I have not half a Dollar left. The schooner Officers altho themselves raised from the ranks are ready enough to say that no one has any business in the Army who cannot afford to live like a gentleman. There is always an exception for Scotishmen who are by right entitled to certain emoluments, as to payment of a Company &c which in our Reg^t is never to be given to an Englishman even should the Captain be of that nation.

12   Many disagreeable reports are in circulation viz that the French have lost so many Men in Guadaloup by disease that they will require all the forces from france to maintain themselves there & that they cannot take possession of the Islands now in possession of the English, but last night a Vessel arrived which says that official reports have been received that 2500 Men have actually sailed from France to take possession of these Islands. If this is true we may embark on Sunday or Monday Next.

14   News that the French cannot be here till next month. The 10th August is the day now mentioned. It was some time since mentioned that Tobago had been given up to the French but it appears that it was not so altho reported by Authority. The story is this. In referring to my Account of Guadaloup, La Crosse was overflowed by the People of Color under a Mulatoe named Pelage. The intention seems to have been to have rendered the Island an independent state in imitation of St Domingo. Unluckily for Pelage the Peace between Great Britain & France deprived him of any chance of success. He therefore endeavoured to place himself under the power of the English stating that he had only taken charge of the Island for England, but our Government would not take the Island under their protection. He therefore endeavoured to make his Peace with France trying to represent his own conduct as being favourable to the Government. When the General Richpanse arrived he immediately joined him & claimed a reward from him. The Second in Command named Degrace had not so clear an Idea of the Power of France when at

peace with England, endeavoured to maintain himself but was soon reduced, Pelage now boasting much of his attachment beset the new Governor with troublesome claims upon which Richpanse appointed him Governor of Tobago & sent him to take possession but having got him on board Ship he dispatched him for Europe or perhaps a still longer voyage or may be a profounder one, this seems to be the History of the occupation of Tobago as reported some time back. It is said by some that the French have supplied the Spanish mines with Men from among their insubordinate citizens.

15   Captain Leslies Servant in cleaning his master's boots was bit by a Scorpion within the boot. He instantly tied a string round his finger so as to stop the Circulation of the blood & ran to the doctor who was found at a very short distance off, not above 200 Yards, Yet his Arm was so much swelled that it was thought adviseable to amputate the Finger which had been bitten.

18   A Report now prevails that the French will not be able to take possession of these Islands until after the Hurricane Months.

19   I went to day to eat a kind of Cherry (Malphequia) to madam Labatte's & to examine the Tree. It is a beautiful Tree bearing Fruit & blossoms all the year round of the Class Decandria, Triguinia, All the flowers which I gathered were withered before I got them home(Mem, I am not an Enthusiast)

21   A General order is received for the reduction of Supernumary Officers by this order every regiment on the Home Establishment is entitled to Eleven Lieutenants. I stand 12th therefore liable to be placed on half Pay & of course I shall go on half pay should no change occur immediately which I have no reason to expect. An opportunity is offered to all Supernumeraries to accept of vacancies in Reg^{ts} not ordered home & Major Stewart sent to me to say that he can procure for me the choice of Vacancies in any Reg^t remaining in the Islands. I feel a great loss how to act. I do not like to remain, & I do not like to be placed on half Pay.

22   After taking some time to consider I determined to go to St Vincents & see what chance I might have of settling myself there. I therefore went to <u>my Friend</u> Major Stewart & asked for leave of absence. My <u>Great Friend</u> finding that this would not benefit his Countryman (for the resignation must be immediately given in or the vacancies would be filled up) told me that he knew <u>I was the Eleventh Lieutenant by the Adjutant's being considered a Supernumerary officer</u> & when orders came out that day I found that one order could not have been known without the other. I afterwards found that he had played the same trick with $Lieut^t$ Hughes in hopes of succeeding with one of us that he might

bring in a Junior Lieut', Lieu' McCaskell merely because he was a Scotsman, I must however do justice to McCaskell & say that he was totally ignorant of the Scheme & would not, I am convinced, have been concerned in such a business. I must also say that the Major's Brother was very indignant & told both Hughes & myself of the Scheme as soon as he found it out, & that in an open Manner. I was sent for to translate a Letter received from General Richpanse, the Governor of Guadaloupe, to our Governor. The purport of it is this, that should the Negroes under the Idea of being free on the arrival of the French shew any symptoms of insubordination, he begs that the Governor will let him know & that he will immediately send a force & reduce them to order! Mirabile! We do not want French assistance neither do the Negroes want to learn Gallic Subordination. The Frenchman talks much of our wise & just administration. This indeed is something new, we have not been in the habit of hearing such acknowledgements from these Revolutionists,

25   Captain Millar gave me a most beautiful St Lucia parrot which he had wounded but the wretch makes such a noise I am afraid I shall never be allowed to take him home.

27   The Government Schooner arrived from Martinique. There is no immediate prospect of the French coming.

29   A Party at the Mess & the Officers were drinking hard. Captain Miller proposed to me to leave the Mess to go Mr Campus's (a French Planter living in Mother Cole's hole as we call the valley beneath us) who intends going out in the morning in a small Schooner to amuse himself in tow Fishing. With some difficulty we made our excape & got to Mr Campus's where we were regaled with Land Crabs & Calleloo & new Rum & a Bed being spread on the floor we betook ourselves to rest, but rest would not come. Millions of Muskitoes attacked me & before Morning I was scratched & swelled in such a manner as scarcely to be recognised, yet I am not Johny Newcome (O what I suffered) never on the Guard bed at Castries was I bit in any degree like it, I was relieved when at 3 o clock the house was in motion to prepare for the sport. We went to the bay & found our Schooner a long boat decked something like a Catalonian fishing boat. We proceeded to Sea & tacked & tacked & tacked till one o clock but Fishy would not come & be killed, but the Lion would come & burn & I had not a bit of skin on my lips or Nose, we saw fish leaping around us but no Catchy, at One we returned to dinner. The Coast which we passed along had a most beautiful appearance, from the remains of cultivation shewed what it had been before the Revolution & what it might still be. The great & rapid increase in vegetation with the quick growth of large umbrageous bees renders it

very unhealthy but I believe it was not so when once brought into cultivation, it is true that the attempt by allowing the Sun to draw up the moisture renders it pestilential, but with proper precautions such as not sleeping to Leeward of the new turned up soil & working as much as possible to windward & eating before work is begun I daresay it may become healthy again, but we can advise this & not take precautions ourselves.

August Heavy rain on the 3rd. Two French Officers arrived. An Artillery Officer & an Engineer, they say that the French will arrive in a fortnight.

4   I breakfasted in Company with the Republican Officers at General Vansittarts, they appear polite Gentleman like Men.

10   A report prevails that the *Van Trump* Transport with the whole 3rd Reg^t or Buffs sunk on her passage home & only Col^l Blunt saved.

Second Bout of Yellow Fever

1 Sepr 1802   I had just written the above [on 10th August] when I was taken again with the Yellow Fever & did not leave my bed till 28th I cannot describe what I suffered for the very thing I had been looking for so long a time was now to me an object of the greatest dread, viz. Should the French come & relieve the Regiment while I am confined to my bed, I did indeed suffer most dreadfully. I now begin to eat soaked bread in tea & sit in a Chair, with my head shaved, my gums sore, & a Night Cap on. I hear the news & hope for a few days respite before I go on board Ship & eat Salt Pork & hard biscuit with Gums softened by Calomel. Report has killed General Richpanse the French General & General Greenfield the English General & raised rebellion in all the French Islands. I am appointed to the Major's Company. This is my first Independent Step (I mean) having a Company from which I cannot be removed except to another. I am now high enough to have the Command of a Company.

4   I feel rheumatism in my Legs & cannot yet walk, my ankles are swelled & the otherwise small of my leg is larger than the Calf. We are informed that our Transports are coming.

6   The Doctor sent me to Pigeon Island for Change of Air. Capt Miller who is also unwell with an Ague accompanies me. General Vansittart is kind enough to lend me his canoe. The day was delightful & we reached the Island when the sick man Miller having the ague on him stripped & plunged into the sea to dive for Crabs & what is most extraordinary it did him good. Pigeon Island is now deserted &

overgrown with Grass. I remain weak. My left Leg quite unable to support me without a stick.

8th A Major Haffey, Doctor Gilchrist, Capt Lindsey & Capt Carmichael came & spent the day with us.

10th My Leg so weak I cannot walk across the room without the aid of a Stick.

12   We went to Gross Islet & dined with Mr Nazabour, An Irish Gentleman dined with us & asked us to dine with him tomorrow a most gentlemanlike Man we were much taken with him & he sends horses for us.

Sept 13th Gross Islet, St Lucia. At Six we went on the Shore & found the Horses waiting on the Beach. We went up to Mr O Neals but what was our astonishment to find that this is the very person who is said to have been so cruel to his Slaves, to us he appeared the Mildest most Gentlemanlike obliging Man we had seen for a long time. This Gentleman I mentioned in May last.

Millar, O Neal & some other Gentlemen went out shooting. I was not able I therefore remained read in Paul & Virginie. Curiosity tempted me to go out of doors & I enquired among the Negroes what kind of Master M^r O Neal was & they spoke very strongly in his favour. How is this to be accounted for. I heard him speak kindly but I still fear the Acc^t it is too true, he has been brought up in the uncontrolled liberty of Arbitrary Power, passion overcomes him & Pride will not allow him to acknowledge his error. We shudder at him even while under his roof & partaking of his hospitality he will give you all he has at one moment & shoot you the next. It was Ten at night before we could get away, & I will never go again, it is indeed probable I shall never have an opportunity.

14   Stewart came over to see us by which we were furnished with an excuse for not going to Mr Nazaboor's to dinner, we did not like our Company & Miller was as much pleased as myself. Stewart remained with us during the Night & gave us reason to expect a Party of Officers from the Morne who, having been 3 years on the Island, now begin for the first time to think it would be advisable to see something more of the Island than Castries & the Overlooking Mountain the Morne. We waited all the Morning but no Officers appeared at last Stewart & myself went to Gross Islet & heard that the French were arrived at Martinique. Soon afterwards two large vessels were seen steering from Martinique.

16   A Frigate & Two Large Vessels entered the Carenage our hearts beat & our Chairs would not hold us. The Spy Glass was constantly at our Eyes surely it must be that the French are arrived, we have no boat

large enough to carry us away & we are not able to walk for News. We are Prisoners—At 3 o clock the General's Canoe came.

It is true we are going home, we embarked in the Canoe & returned to the Morne. The French are not actually arrived in S\.^t^ Lucia they are at Martinique, the Ships are our Transports to take us home. My State of Health is such that I feel very weak & not fit to go into the bustle, now going forward, our Baggage is embarking, all is fermentation, no regular food, nobody cares for it.

18th 19th 20th all confusion. Hurry, bustle. I cannot stand it & I feel overpowered & evidently becoming ill my strength is going. The Surgeon says I must embark immediately.

21st I have been ordered on Board the *Endeavour* lying in the Carrenage, on embarking I immediately perceived a change for the better but why nobody can say. The Mind probably was satisfied at being embarked for England & I really think I should have refused to go on Shore again at any risk.

The French arrived this Evening in Ships of War, full of Troops, low in the water, Dirty & hung round with Cabbages all singing Republican Songs. Poor fools they know not what they have to go thro. The Frigate broke from her moorings & ran foul of us, we lost our Main Top Gallant Mast & the Frigate (The *Castor*) was damaged. I felt alarmed being Nervous & sick. All the 21st was passed in waiting for two Transports to take the 9th West India Reg.^t^ away. This is very injurious, as the 9th W. I. are Royalist French & the Republicans are insulting them by singing obnoxious Songs.

22   The *Highland Lass* Transport arrived for the 9th W. I. but is not sufficiently large. The *Warrior* is expected, surely the French Royalists should have been sent away before.

23   Instead of preparing for Sea our Ship has warped up nearer the Land. There may be good reason for it, but the reason given is the fear of the Equinoxial Gales, it being the New Moon on Sunday 26th

24   The *Warrior* arrived. The 9th W. I. embarked, & the remains of our baggage, Ladies &c.

26   The French landed about 500, part of the 82 & 87 Demi Brigades, few of them marched up the Hill, they seem old men or Boys & have no Military appearance.

27th The 53 Reg.^t^ evacuated the Morne at daybreak & we were all embarked by 7 o clock as soon as they were embarked the French flag was hoisted & a Salute fired, but it began inauspiciously. They blew away their Artillery man who was torn to pieces.

1802 September—Transport to England,

We are on board the *Endeavour* Indiaman, Transport, Major Stewart, Cap^n Carmichael, L^{ts} Stewart, Thompson, Knight & Sherwood, Ensign McCaskell, A Surgeon Gilchrist, Grenadiers, Light Company, Majors Carmichael & Mansel's Companies, Band &c, one third of the Officers & Men to be always on deck. The French Commadore will not permit us to Sail until the 29th on Account of the Moon, this I say without knowing better for I cannot conceive what the French have to do with it, I presume he is the bugaboo. But they need not make use of the Mumboo Jumboo, as we have a better reason, viz a detachment of the Reg^t under Lieu^t Weston, not yet come in from Suffror.

28   Some of our Officers who have been on Shore & they report that the French are very insubordinate & are being drunk about in the Streets, the Inhabitants of Castries express themselves openly to be dissatisfied with the exchange.

29th We sailed this morning at daybreak with a light breeze, our Men were becoming very unhealthy in the Carrenage, there being no current, & a Swamp directly to windward, two Men died during the Night

30   We passed close under Martinique yesterday Evening & this day we are becalmed under Dominique, which we see very plainly. A Man & a Child on board died today.

Octob^r Becalmed all day under Guadaloup. We saw many pleasant plantations & apparently fine houses. The *Crown* sails so slowly that we were obliged to bear down to her twice today.

2   A Moderate Breeze, this morning to windward of Montserrat saw Antigua but could not weather it, a man died, at 12 becalmed off St Johns Antigua, it rained hard. The *Crown* much to Leeward

3   A moderate Breeze during the Night, but the *Crown* was so far behind we did not make much of it. We were off Barbuda, 1 woman died.

4	Nearly Calm.	Lat 19.18	Long 61-11
5	Two men & 1 Woman died.	Lat 19.54	Long 61-10
6	Calm	Lat 20.33	Long 60-43
7	A Man died,	Lat 21.12	Long 61

8   A Man died, fresher breeze, Met a Brig from Boston bound to Martinique, out 14 days   Lat 22.16   Long 60

9   Two Men died

11   Two Men died, Wind strong from E.S.E   Lat 25.35   Long 61

12   Woman died, Calm all yesterday   Lat 26.12   Long 61

13   Three Men died   Lat 27.33

14   A Good Breeze, but we have drifted far to the westward spoke an American Schooner 7 days from Antigua, they have had a Severe Gale from the North carried away her Main Top mast we have excaped this Gale.   Lat 29.7

15   Ensign Sutherland died of the Yellow Fever, he was a stout Young Man aged 18, a native of the West Indies, it has been truly alarming the number of deaths, since we sailed, the total number 28 in 16 days.   Lat 30.44

16   Good Breeze   Lat 32.19   Long 61-30

17   The Cold is very great & our West India Cloathing is not sufficient. We are not provided with warm Cloathing owing to our uncertainty of the time of embarking & also the want of Money. I have only Nankeen Pantaloons

18   I was glad to be able to purchase a pair of Slop Sailors Trowers from the Captain, a man died   Lat 35.40 Our longde keeps the same

19   The Crown spoke us & stated that their Sick were now getting better & ours the same, & we find the Wind setting from the West. West we turn our course homewards having conversed a Short time we gave 3 Cheers& directed our Cours for England we had been steering North, we now turn West.

20   A Man died   Lat 38   Long 57

21   Lat 38.55   55.24

22   Lat 39.54   52-30

23   Lat 40-16   48-24

24   Last Night the Sea ran high & the wind strong. The Captain came on deck very drunk & found fault with the Steering, he took the Helm himself & threw us in the wind & was very near to carry away our Masts & poop us, the Waves coming into the Cabin Windows. The Wind increased to a Gale & we lost sight of the Crown Lat 41.27   Long 45

25th   It fell Calm with a great swell   Lat 42   Long 42-40

26   No appearance of the Crown   Lat 43-21   Long 39-54

27   A Yellow Hammer came on board exhausted & soon died, our nearest Shore is Newfoundland, nearly 300 Miles

28   A Foggy day no observation our Long reckoned 33.30 we do not care for Latitude now.

29   Long 29-3

30th   Long 28

31   Long 26.30

1 Nov   A Storm   Long 23.3

From 2 in the Morning until the 6th a heavy gale with dark weather no observation, the dead Lights in & we of course in darkness which is not a little disagreeable having 9 officers & two Ladies in a small Cabin. Several Land Birds were blown on board during the Gales but died on reaching the Ship.

6th   The weather became Calmer but with a heavy swell, & rain all day

7th   A fine day & I took advantage of the Sun to open my Trunks & air my Cloathes. I found my Humming Birds & dryed Animals destroyed by the damp & my best Laced Jacket eaten by the Moths, & Cockroaches, we are in latitude 46.42 & Longitude computed 16-19

8   We had light Breezes from the E. S. E.   Lat 46.48   Long 15

9 Very heavy gale from the East. No observation, spoke the Ship *Grant* from Jamaica to London out 65 days, when we spoke her it was blowing hard & we saw the Gib Torn in pieces & while we were laughing at the Ribbons flying about our own Fore Topsail was split & flew about in narrow Slips, the wind fell on the

10th   Lat 48.36   Long 11

11th We ran a good course until Morning when by our computation we ought to find soundings. Sounded with a line of 130 Fathoms & found no bottom, we are of course to the Westward of our reckoning.

12   Spoke the Bremen Brig Dorothée Louise from St Thomas's to Hamburg out 56 days, her longitude is 9-30. The wind Easterly & of course against us

13   Rough Sea & dark weather. Sounded found bottom at 75 Fathom white sand at night again sounded 60 fathom white sand with specks, we were hoping to see Scilly but not perceiving the light we tacked & stood to Sea till Midnight

14   Then stood in again very dark & supposing we had drifted to the Northward of Scilly stood out again at 8 o clock

15   Fair clear all day observed latitude to the North of Scilly 57 Miles, Long by Soundings 7-30 which agreed with an American from Newcastle

in America for London: we thought from Newcastle in England & being in want of fresh provisions asked if they had any to spare, they answered yes & we sent a boat on board, but we were both mistaken for it seemed that they understood we were in want of provisions generally & of course Water & we thought it was a coaster from Newcastle upon Tyne for London, it is true we could not account for her being so far to the Westward but not knowing of any Newcastle in America we did not put things together. The Capn Callender had hoisted water on deck & on our Boats arrival & things being explained Capn Callendar said he would spare us what he could. We had asked for Porter & he thought we said Water. We got a Pig from him & 2 dozen of Wine & a few Potatoes & Pumpkins which were lowered into the Boat, but when they were to be paid for he positively refused to receive a farthing. On the Return of the Officers we immediately subscribed to send him a Piece of Plate value Six Guineas & a half To be presented to him in London. No sight of Scilly   Lat 49-51. Soundings 75 fathom Grey Sand.

Storm off Ireland

17   Becalmed all day but at night a strong Breeze from the S. S. E. with which it was impossible to weather Scilly. The wind soon became a Gale, when we found it necessary to run before it, the Coast of Ireland being directly under our Lee, we expected to make the Cove of Cork. We took in all Sail except the Fore Top sail yet we ran before the Gale 8 Miles an hour. The Captain had marked our situation at 12 oclock & calculating at the Rate we were going McCaskell & myself were afraid of being on the Shore before daylight & from our knowledge of the Captain we had no confidence in him, & so convinced were we of the danger that on relieving watch at 12 oclock we could not conceal our anxiety from the Commanding Officer, Major Stewart. We therefore awoke him & told him our ideas. He got up & called for the Captain, Spread the Map on the Table & McCaskell & myself pointed out the evident danger of what we were doing. Yet the Captain out of opposition still said we had

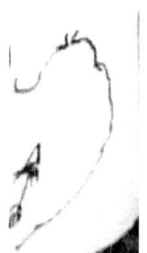

plenty of room. As a Sailor he probably thought it right to despise our knowledge. At length to quiet the Major he promised to lay to at 4 o clock & we went to our Cabin as I got into my Berth I said to McCaskell four oclock will be the time, he must not delay. Having had the first watch I soon fell asleep & was awoke by a most dreadful Cry. I ran on deck in my Shirt & saw a Head Land of a great height overhanging the Ship, the Sea was beating against it & the foam of the Ships way seemed to join the foam of the Breakers, it was ½ past four. The Captain threw himself on the deck & roared out like a Boy when beaten & when spoke to. cryed out, "We are lost we are lost." the first Mate was below, the Second Mate cried out, "Put up the Helm." He did not say which way, we were running before the wind as direct as it could blow, the Helm was put up but not I believe as he intended for we now stood to the Eastward. The Wind now blew exactly on Shore & we saw the Rocky Shore as it appeared close, to us, the Foam seemed all round us, there was no light, & at ½ past 4 on the 17th Novr it was quite dark after some time anxious watching we cleared the Land & saw no more of it in half an hour it appeared again as in the Margin our course being as the Arrow there was now to all appearance no hope the wind blew on Shore a perfect hurricane no one on board knew the Coast, The Captain lay crying on the deck, the Chief Mate never came up, the 2nd Mate was the only active Man, (it afterwards appeared that the Captain & Chief Mate had been drinking all Night & laughing at the Landsmen's fears & supporting each other in a foolhardy daring) & he joined himself to the Major & our officers & took the Command, in which he took great responsibility in himself but acted like a good Sailor. When he saw the land ahead he evidently saw that we could not weather it & it became a question whether we should wear Ship, for tack we could not, or run the Ship on Shore in the hopes of finding a Spot in the Bottom of the Bay. We found we could not get the Ship round, & our last resort was to run the Ship on Shore, the place chose was the nearest place to the Bluff head as it appeared, we thought it was higher land than the rest, & judging from what we were in the habit of seeing aboard expected a Sandy Beach within it, we therefore hoisted more sail & stood as near to the wind as we could to give ourselves another chance of clearing the point but we drifted inwards & all hope of saving the Ship was over when instead of finding a beach we passed on thro a Channel narrow & seemingly full of rock yet we passed thro, & so rapidly that we had not time to think of getting an anchor out or in all probability we

should have let go the Anchor under the Lee of the Island. On clearing this Channel we found ourselves in another Bay & by this time day began to break, we saw the Shore & two Rocks a head & just under our Lee another rock with the sea beating against it, sometimes it was covered at other times stood a Mountain, we now saw our danger & determined on tacking to recover the Shelter of the Island & Providence befriending us, the Ship answered her helm & we tacked but it was a very anxious moment, we soon got under our Island & seeing a Bay to Leeward ran in, in doing this we seemed to slide down the side of the rock as a Cork would do in an agitated bason of water we anchored. The band began to play & we scarcely knew whether we were drowned or not, the Bay turned out to be Squince bay.

I must again repeat from a better knowledge of the Land our situation & what we have escaped. The Head Land which we made at ½ past 4 o clock was called Dundiddy Head & having at the time cleared the head land we found ourselves in the Bay of Ross, the next Head land was Ragged Island & having passed between it & the Shore the Piramid Rocks a head were the Stag's, the Rock under our Lee was called Black Rock near Castle Haven, & on our return we could not weather Caracanamen Rock & ran into Squince Bay, we are now as completely land locked as in the Carenage at St Lucia but our exit seems doubtful as the entrance is extremely narrow & the Island closely opposite. Many gentlemen came on board & said that they had never seen a Ship in the Bay before. A Ship called the *Plymouth* had once anchored in the passage between Ragged Island & the Main but lost the anchor & was nearly on Shore in getting clear.

We have taken a wild Irishman on board as a Pilot to get us out & Pilot us to Cork, his name is Tim Haggerty & a funny fellow he is, he says that God must have been before the Ship, behind the Ship above the Ship, beneath the Ship & must have stood at the Helm. The Gentlemen of the Neighbourhood say much the same, we have received many civilities from them particularly from a Mr Townsend of Castle Townsend & a Mr Matthews.

19 Novr At Sea Irish Channel.   A Calm & we commenced warping the Ship out of the Bay. Mr Matthews remained on board, with his boat assisting. Mr Matthews's son says that the Inhabitants are abusing the Man who made a Signal for us to anchor & they say that if we had not done so they might all have had Red Jacketts on. The Poor here have a much more savage look than the Carraibs in the West Indias.

A Coasting Vessel called a Hooker passed us says that a vessel described like the *Crown* is in Crookhaven. With great difficulty we warped out & sailed with a scant breeze. Mr Matthews now took his leave, the fear of some accident induced the Captain to steer for the Cove that our Ship's bottom may be examined as no one went on Shore we can say nothing for the Irish except that we thought them Savages.

Our Voyage was close to the Shore we saw the Houses, one of them belonging to a Sir John Feah. Tim Haggarty says that provisions are cheap & that the poor live on Potatoes, that they cost 2/- per C^{wt}. We bought a small fowl for 6^d Butter, Eggs & Milk very cheap. Beef is sold for 5^d per pound & Mutton for 6^d – a small Sheep might be bought for 10/6

20th Towards 7 oclock last evening the Wind freshed & it soon increased to a Gale, we lay to under Fore top Sail till after 6 this morning, most part of the Night we had Kinsale Light house to guide us but we lost sight of it towards the Morning most likely from the light going out as our Captain did not wish to go away from it, it might however have been the sudden rising of a fog. The day broke with heavy fog the wind blowing very strongly in Shore, we stood in for the Coast which we did not see until within 2 Miles, we were then opposite the Entrance to Cove but our Captain was alarmed & poor Tim Hagerty Bothered & he did not know whether it was the Cove or not, he knows the Coast he says very well when he is in a fishing Boat, but not in a Ship, we were so uncertain of our situation that we tacked & stood to Sea but the Tub made so much lee way we found ourselves going on Shore side foremost so that we had no alternative but make for the apparent Cove which turned out to be the true one, when we bore down we were under Carlisle Fort in a Quarter of an hour. At 9 oclock we were at Anchor, the wind still increased & it rained dreadfully hard we were none of us able to get on Shore but we were very glad to be in safety.

21 Sunday   Stewart, Thompson, Gilchrist & myself went on Shore to Church. The Cove appeared a dirty disagreeable place, & the Church a Mile off we walked to the Church, after Church we walked to the Barracks, which are good, the Nottingham Militia are doing duty there. An American Ship came in the Captain says he spoke the *Crown* going into Cork Haven having suffered damage in the Storm.

22   I examined the returns of the Reg^t found that the Reg^t
Landed at St Lucia in 1796   857 Men
joined between 1796 & 1802   824
                                 1681

	1681		[editor's %][55]
died	805	-49 %	
deserted	39	-2.5 %	
Invalided	306	-18 %	
Discharged	9		
Transferred	194	-11.5 %	
	-1353	-80.5 %	
	328		
But we have only	-307		
Leaving	21 unaccounted for.		

It rained all day & I remained on board

23   We hear that a Brig was lost off Dundeddy Head on the Morning of the 18th about the same time that we were there, we must have been very near her at the time, all on board perished. The Colors of the 17th Regt were washed on Shore we therefore conclude that some officers of that Regiment were on board. The Stern was washed on Shore by which it was known that the Vessel was the *Mary* of Liverpool & the Merchants here know that a Vessel of that name was bound to London from Limerick, there was a quantity of Butter washed on Shore.

24th   General Myers the Commanding Officer has ordered us to Sea as soon as the Ship is repaired, this is the matter of course. The General mentions having received a report from Cap^n Miller announcing the arrival of the *Crown* in Crook Haven & expects to be ready on Friday 26th

25   A Circumstance has happened on this Coast within a few days which shews the Savage State of the Inhabitants, it appears that a Lieu^t Lapsley of the 17th Reg^t was on board the *Mary* of Liverpool lost on the 18th & that he had reached the Shore in safety but was murdered by the Natives near Clomkelty: two men of the Neighbourhood of Clonkelty are taken up on suspicion.

27th   We are not ready for Sea until today when we dropped down opposite to the barracks to prepare for sailing in the Morning, from our present anchorage we have a fine view of the Cove which appears to be 8 or so Miles in depth. I never saw so beautiful a piece of Salt Water in my life, but the weather is so fine that any place would look well.

28   The Mate & Captain have quarrelled so violently that they are both gone on Shore to state their Grievances & his Majesty's Service &

---

[55] Of 89,000 British soldiers and NCOs who served in the West Indies 1793-1798 43,747 49% died of yellow fever and similar hazards and 15,505 17.5% were discharged unfit for service. At 49% and 18% the 53rd Foot were typical.

his majesty's Money is to be neglected / the former by the by is neglected, the latter is not so

29th   We got under weigh at day break with a light North wind, the Tide being in our favour we soon got to Sea, when we had a Charming view of the Shore with the Seat of Colonel Roach pleasantly situated on the Shore <u>but without Trees</u>, every thing looks bare. I understand that plantations are now making & some years hence it may be different.

30   Light Easterly Breeze, this Evening we are 30 Miles to the westward of Scilly.

1 December 1802   The wind fair but light Lat by observation 49.30 Sounding 62 Fathom which gives us between 20 & 30 miles S.W. of Scilly. At Eight at Night we saw the Light, Stewart & myself sat on the round Top till midnight watching the Light & our course thro the water, we saw The Lizard Light before 12 oclock.

Plymouth and Portsmouth

2   The Wind increased during the Night & came from the South, at day light it blew a hard Gale, the Start Point was under our Lee but rather a head, we stood on till Ten oclock hoping to weather it but perceiving that the Ship from her little hold in the Water made much Lee way we had no hope of clearing Portland The Storm now was very furious & our Captain decided on making Plymouth, at which Port we arrived at 3 oclock, as we went up the Bay the Ship rolled in such a manner that we expected the Masts to go overboard. We got in safe to the Homeage. The Waves as we were going in appeared to heap themselves into little Hillocks, not as the generally do into rolling waves but this by which means the Ship seemed to rest on the apex of a wave & rolled off like a Tub bringing the gunwales into the flood. We had no sooner anchored than the Health officer came on board & put us under Quarantine.

3   It blew such a gale all Night that we were heartily glad to be in harbour even here we had high waves & some houses were blown down. We find that there is no account of the *Crown*'s having arrived in England, indeed there is a report that she has been driven into Scilly. We are now laying at Anchor between Mount Edgecombe & Plymouth close by a Monument said to have been built to the honor of Lord Mount Edgecombe & the appearance of the Land is beautiful & I hope to Land & see it when the Quarantine is taken off

4   A Rainy day all day nothing new. No account of the *Crown*, being in Quarantine still we saw no one or heard anything till the 9th when we heard that the *Crown* was safe at Portsmouth.

11   Remained in Quarantine till the 11th when we were released at 6 oclock in the Evening & the Wind & tide being favourable we immediately sailed so that we had no opportunity of seeing the Shore. The wind held fair all night & at 8 o clock we made the Isle of Wight.

12   The wind being North we could not make the Needles — at 11 oclock we were off St Catharines Point & 12 off Culverhead we are not above 2 Miles from Land & we go thro the water at the Rate of 3½ Miles per hour yet we make no way owing to the Tide. We have a fine view of the Shore & I set Two objects on Shore by which I see we neither gain or lose. At six at Night the Tide turned & we advanced. I went to bed according to my custom when I had no watch & when I awoke I heard no noise on deck. I crept up the stairs & found that I had never awoke while the anchor had been lowered & that we were at Anchor at Spithead & I hope our Voyage is ended.

Part 4———England—1802 to 1805

1802 December 13th—Ashore in England

At day break a boat came off with Vegetables for Sail & I obtained leave to go on Shore to see Cap^n Park[56] at Haslar. I found them all well & kind I was pressed to stay but could not as I had promised to return. My Cousin Elize [sister Margaret's daughter] was in Nottinghamshire. My [half] Brother James is I find on Board the *Hussar*, at Sheerness serving out his time as Midshipman. On my return to Portsmouth I found the *Endeavour* had entered the Harbour with the Tide & we were ordered to Land tomorrow Morning & occupy Hilsea Barracks.

14 The pleasure of walking on Shore after being at Sea 12 weeks is delightful & we could scarcely any of us keep quiet on board this Evening.

15 We landed & marched to Hilsea where we found the other 5 Companies

16 Our Rout is for Shrewsbury after remaining here for cloathing & rest. I asked leave for 3 days to go to London & received it.

17 Left Portsmouth at 5. Breakfasted with Mr Reynolds who seemed pleased to see me, went to Mr Maskell. I stated to him that I was much in want of Money being £25 behind hand & having a compleat new equipment to provide.

I have a reversion of a Considerable Sum on my Fathers death, he advized that I should apply to my Father & between us dispose of the Principal & he undertook to communicate with him, he has reason to suppose that there will be no difficulty, as my Sister has already done the same & received £430.[57]

18th I called on Mr Andrews at the Rectory St James's & found that Mrs Butts family were well at Bridgenorth which much delighted me, as I had not heard from them for some time.

19 My [half] Brother John called & conducted me to my Father's. My Father did not behave well to me, but I refrained from answering &

---

[56] Captain Park, Sherwood's maternal aunt's second husband.
[57] Reversion of funds on Father's death: probably the value of his mother's marriage settlement which would have been held as part of father's own possession until his death, subject to father's disbursing it earlier. Until the Married Women's Property Acts of 1870 and 1882 women's earnings (1870) and assets and property (1882) were owned by the husband.

England—1802-5

gladly escaped from his house, before we parted he became more calm & kind, but insisted on having half of the amount for which the Property might sell. He offered to Lend me Money.

20   Mr Maskell strongly advised me to Borrow £50 of my Father but I refused, but on M^r M- begging me to do so & thinking it right to attend to his advise I wrote to my Father. My Uncle had a Large Party to dinner.

21   Called on Mr Reynolds who most kindly enquired into my Affairs & hearing what I was about to do remonstrated & even offered to Lend me what Money I might require & he pointed out the great loss that I should have that I thankfully accepted his offer & he lent me £70. My Father never answered my Letter & I left London most highly gratified by the great kindness I had met with from my friends particularly from Mr Reynolds.

22   On arriving at Hilsea I found myself attached to the Light Company an honor I had not expected but not the less pleasing as it had been called for by my Seniors.

23   My Honor is but of Short duration but I had it which is sufficient. I am wanted to Command a Company & for which I am to receive £20 Pr Annum Extra. I leave the Light Company to take the permanent Command of the Majors Company. I am promised the Command of the Light Company the 1st Vacancy & I am allowed to retain my Green Feather & Wings, honors are showered upon me.

24   My Aunt Park was kind enough to send to enquire after me I therefore went to Haslar Hospital to see her, I breakfasted with her & afterwards called on all my old friends in Gosport & I received a very pressing invitation to dine with my old Friend Mr Merrit Stewart of the Hospital, Tomorrow it being Xmas day, but as I am on duty Tomorrow I cannot accept his kind invitation, I might indeed exchange duties but then I could not ask the same favour again so soon as New Years day which is my Birth day & my Aunt intends keeping it in her own house.

1803 January 1st Remained Quiet in Barracks & on 1st January I went to Gosport & dined with my Aunt & spent a very pleasant day. Between 1st & 17th I often went to Gosport & saw my Friends who were very kind to me, on the 16th I walked with Miller & some other Officers on the Road to Chichester & we visited Purbrook house, now neglected the Family having been absent for some years & every thing looks in a state of decay— On returning we heard that the Jolly Boat of the *Neptune* was capsized in a Squall, 2 Midshipmen & 5 Sailors drowned. The Midshipmen were Brothers.

1803 January 17th—March towards Shrewsbury

At half after 8 This Morning marched from Portsmouth for Bridgenorth, the Weather was frosty. The road quite hard. The first six miles we coasted the Bay, on our Right the Portdown Hills. The Number of Ships of War laying in the Bay & Roads remind us of the Power of Britain. We left Porchester Castle on our left, where were said to be 10.000 French Prisoners. We breakfasted at Fareham & proceeded to Wickham where part of the Regiment were to halt. The division to which I belonged advanced, the Country becoming Common & Waste Land to Waltham. Many of the Men had to retrace their Steps some Miles having been relaxed from long Service in the Tropics they felt this <u>unnecessary</u> hardship. This being my first March I felt angry & irritated, custom will reconcile all. My Company was so much scattered that I could not find my Men & I spent ½ a Crown out of 6^d a day, viz my dinner 10/- My pay 5/8. March 15 Miles.

18   Our pleasant travelling on frozen ground was at an end, the Thaw had taken place with drizzling rain. The roads wet & bad thro Commons & Waste to Winchester 10 miles before we entered the Town the Colonel gave us goose for not attending the Mess which is a hardship as he has the Mess at head Quarters & consequently makes it worth the Servants while to attend, but we poor Subs, can get no attendance at our Inns if we expend nothing, he however promised to pay the Inns on the Road. Winchester a fine Old City, it was dark before we got our dinner.

19   Marched at 7. The road bad & it was dark each step above my feet in the mud, I was much tired being forced to keep the track of the wheels. To Andover 16 Miles

Halt 20

21   I was on the Baggage Guard & coming before the Regiment to Luggeshall called for Breakfast. No Milk, I got 4 Eggs: with 2 I made the Mixture for my Tea & the other two I ate by which I got Credit for having eaten all the Eggs in Luggeshall. We had frost again & the road was very rough, Luggeshall is a most paltry village yet sends two Members to Parliament. To Everly where was head Quarters, it began to rain. 52 Men & all the Officer's quarters in an Inn, The Men with some difficulty got into a Stable. The March 12 Miles

22   Rain, our March over Commons about ½ way then thro a forest with many Deer to Marlborough. Wet roads. The Head Quarters Dukes Arms the Subs at the Castle dined at Dukes Arms against the Grain = 12 Miles

England—1802-5

23   Halt, went to Church. The Castle Inn an old Castle of a Nobleman & the Big Wigs dined with us today but did not like it as they were obliged to call for something at their Inn.

24   A Wet day, after 5 Miles found the Country improve. My Division halted at Cricklade

25th A very severe frost which was pleasant to those in Motion tho I must own that I did not like the Cold wind, the Poor creatures on the Baggage Waggons suffered severely & a Child was frozen to death, Mr Valentines. As we approached Cirencester we found a drunken Sailor asleep in a ditch he was roused or in all probability he would soon have lost his life. We got him into the first house as he was so drunk that he could not keep up with us. Cirencester is a very old Town Caern Cester. Here the Earl of Gloster had a Strong hold in Stephens Reign, here the Duke of Essex & Earl of Surry were taken in Henry the 4^{ths} time & here Prince Rupert sustained a siege in Charles's time. It was a jacobite Town at the Revolution we were told that there were many Roman buildings worth seeing but the snow came on so very hard that we could not see them. Our Dinner at the Kings Head was very bad, both as to quality & cooking.

27th The Wind from N.E. was very cutting with Snow as we advanced along the Ridge of Hills I thought my nose & Ears were gone. We rather ran than walked over a very rough road, for the Snow drifted from the Highway the wind being high, we breakfasted at Birley. The Number of the Men frightened the Land lady & she was glad to get rid of us, indeed there was no room within doors for half the Men. We ran down the Road to Cheltenham, the Snow being now about a foot thick & Slippery for the latter part of the Reg^t. There were several amusing tumbles.

I was on Guard but could get no Guard Room. We passed the night in the Market house dreadfully cold. The Hall being narrow & the wind high the snow drifted thro. In the Morning we hired a Stable & locked the Baggage up which kept me employed & we are to halt here for some days to cure the bile but I much fear that the drain from our pockets will rather increase than diminish our bile, we halted till 31st.

On Saturday 29 there was a Ball. The excuse was a Compliment to the Reg^t the real reason can be easily guessed. I did not like the Compliment but our Big Wigs pretended that it was a compliment & as in duty bound I went. The Gentlemen were almost all composed of Officers 53^t Reg^t & there was no lack of Ladies. A Clergyman was the Master of Ceremonies who required that we should break up at 12 it being Sunday but as he had notified this early in the Evening the Ladies & Gentlemen contrived to put the clock back. The Gentlemen must have gone half way towards the deception or it would not have passed.

31   Marched at daylight, The Weather being frosty & pleasant we reached Tewksbury by 10 o clock. I now became anxious to have a few days at Bridgenorth. I asked the Colonels leave to go on & it being granted I engaged a return Chaise to Worcester & while the Horses backed I visited the old Abbey to see the spot where so many persons of Note were buried after the Battle of Tewksbury. There is only a Brass plate over Prince Edward Son of Henry the 6th which does not even mention the Year of his death. The Man who shewed the Church said that he was a Prince put to death by Oliver Cromwell.

1 Feby I slept all the way to Worcester & I slept again there & at 6 oclock 1st Feby proceeded by Coach to Kidderminster where I was at School in 1789. The Town seemed to have shrunk into nothing since my Time, I could not I thought jump thro the Town hall in a hop Step & Jump, formerly it was a building of great consequence in my Eyes.

1803 February—Bridgnorth

I reached Bridgenorth at 2 it being nearly 5 Years since I quitted it. I ran to my Aunts House full of pleasing thoughts but was met at the door by the old Servant keeping the door in her hand half shut as if fearing a Thief. She knew me but said she would call somebody down, at length I was admitted into the Hall when a Young Lady, Miss Congreve, came down and told me that My Aunt & Cousin Lucy had a dangerous Typhous Fever & that one Servant was dead. I own that I felt much hurt at my reception & I said that having served so long on the West indias where the Yellow Fever carried off so many I did not feel the Dread of the fever, after some time my Cousin Mary came down with a formal Courtesy & after staying a few minutes I took my leave wishing that the Regiment would arrive that I might proceed to Shrewsbury, all my fond hopes of meeting my friends seemed in a Moment at an end.

4th The Regt arrived & at 6 o clock on the 5th We marched for Shrewsbury, where we arrived at 3 o clock 20 Miles on My Road I heard that an Officer was to be sent recruiting to Bridgenorth my inclination still led me there & I applied to the Colonel to be sent on that duty which was immediately granted.

6   Attended St Chad's Church

7&8   Settling Company Accounts which being finished I proceeded on 9thby Coach to Bridgenorth & I know no more of Shrewsbury than that it

England—1802-5

is full of Houses & there is an Inn there you can get a Bed & food by paying for it. I reached Bridgenorth at 11 & took charge from this to the 22nd I procured one Recruit & sent him to Shrewsbury. His name Saml Bourne.

24&25   Remained & was fully employed in paying my Company, when I had procured the proper receipts I gave them over to Major Stewart. I returned to Bridgenorth by Wenlock enlisted a recruit but he deserted on the road.

26   Mr Marten Butt my Cousin came & I find he is shut out of his own house as well as myself which in some degree reconciles me, he slept at my Lodgings & explained the Prophecies of the revalation of Daniel so clearly that I can now tell what will be the end of all these Wars & that there will be an end of all things very soon.

March 4   I left Bridgenorth to see [grandmother] Mrs Sherwood & [great aunt] Mrs Patterson of Coventry. I left on Foot & walked 6 Miles when a coach to Worcester overtook me. The day was fine & I got on the Top. Dick Weston was recruiting at Kidderminster, I dined drank Tea & supped with them Then walked over the Town & looked at all my School Boy haunts which all seemed changed for the worse. The Fields are no longer so long or broad as formerly. I called twice at my Old School Master but did not see him, passed thro Birmingham to Coventry, saw Mrs Sherwood & Mrs Patterson. They were both (particularly the latter) very kind. It snowed on 7th but I walked to Peter Hall & dined with Mr Congreve. I ran back (it freezing) 6 Miles in one Hour. Coventry as formerly full of parties each one being able to settle the Affairs of the Nation yet most of them unable to manage their own private concerns, Politics run dreadfully high.

12   I remained till the 12th when I left at nine & passing thro Birmingham reach Wolverhampton at 3. Classon who was recruiting forced me to remain till tomorrow promising to walk with me to Bridgenorth.

14 15, 16   Classon & I walked to Bridgenorth & on 15th He returned – on the 16 I enlisted Joseph Webster & sent him to the Reg^t.

22   I walked to Arly to spend the day with Mr Thos Butt. Miss Congreve & my Cousin Mary were there & I returned with them in the Chaise, On my return I received Letters from most of the Officers saying that the Regiment was ordered to Bridgenorth & requesting me to procure Lodgings, the Reg^t is expected Tomorrow. I got Lodgings for the Col^l, Major Adj^t & Paymaster & Surgeon

25   The regiment arrived & my Recruiting ends in one Month. Many Officers remain Years on this duty & I had hoped at least to have

remained a few months. I walked to Arley & met my Cousin Marten & returned with him, on our return a conversation happened which I think will be the means of altering my situation. [This may have been Marten's intimating that Sherwood's cousin Mary and aunt Mrs Butt might be receptive to a proposal of marriage. Ed.]

1803 March—Death of Father

1st April   Received a Letter acquainting me with the sudden death of my Father at Clifton on the 25th March. In consequence of my Fathers death it will be necessary to proceed to London & Mr Woodhouse the Trustee of my Fathers second Marriage settlement will be in Town in a fortnight. I have applied for leave, in the mean time I pass my time with my Cousins in the most pleasant manner.

15   Having obtained leave of absence I left Bridgenorth with my Cousin & Miss Congreve we dined at Arley & afterwards I proceeded with Miss Congreve & my Cousin Lucy who was unwell to Hagley. We stopped there & walked in the Park.

16   Breakfasted at Birmingham & arrived at Peter Hall at 6 o clock.

18   To London, on outside of Coach by Night it rained hard & was very Cold.

20   Dined with the Rev Gerard Andrews who was very kind

22   I received £735 from a share of my Mother's Settlement & immediately returned to Peter Hall which I reached at 8 in the Morning of the 23 found Lucy much better.

24   Left Coventry & reach Bridgenorth at 6. My Cousin Mary at Badger & the weather cold.

May   The Reg^{t} at Bridgenorth until the 17th when an order arrived to march for Ipswich, Circumstanced as I was I felt this move severely but I must submit.

19   To Wolverhampton. 20 Birmingham. 21 Meriden & halt. I borrowed Cap^{n} Mansels Horse & rode to Peter hall & returned.

23   To Lutterworth, dined at Peter Hall thought of Miss Congreve's song "Tis hard to be parted from those with whom we for ever could dwell"

24   To Harbro – 25 to Thrapstone – 26 to Huntingdon – 27 To Cambridge -28 to Newmarket, 30th to Bury – 31 Needham, This day Piercy contrived to throw my Horse on his back, he fell on my Leg, but did not hurt me much.

1803 June—Ipswich

June 1 To Ipswich, I have no eyes, Ears, tongue or Pen to see, hear, speak or record, all being left at Bridgenorth. I was allowed Lodging Money there being no room in Barracks. I could not get Lodgings under 16/ a week& I only receive 6/- from Government.

Lord Paget commands the force assembled here which consists of the 7th & 18 Dragoons, the 24th, 35th, 53rd & 69th Foot, The Cambridge & Two Battalions of Suffolk Militia all these Regiments having no other amusement Piercy & myself went to the play. I am appointed one of the Mess Committee.

4 A Full day. Lord Paget gave the word to all the Troops which he did in a very fine stile, but the Cavalry Horses were very unsteady at the firing.

5 We did not go to Church this Sunday there being no room for the Troops.

6 Six oclock drill with most of the Garrison on Parade till 12 & 2 Inspection of Arms, 3 Parade till 5 & at 6 Drill till 8.

7 As Yesterday, we had Litterally no time for food, yet I must acknowledge that it is not the intention of the Commanding Officers, but the fact is that certain Independent Orders have been given out by the Commander of the Troops & the Commander of the Reg[t] & as neither of them ever attend, they do not know (in all probability) what they are about.

8 General Rain interfered & gave us a Holyday

9 All Captain Lieutenancies abolished, the Captain Lieutenants becoming Captains of Companies, the Field Officers losing their Companies, the Senior Lieut is to get his Company by raising 50 Men, for each of which allowed £5 by Government which seems an inferior proceeding as Many Lieut[ts] from circumstances will find it easier to raise than others, & indeed the very capability is in itself a mark of the unfairness of the proceeding. As a Recruiting Lieut has an evident advantage over one who has served with his Reg[t] being accustomed to the Subject. There are Lieut[s] of 1793 in old Reg[ts] & Lieut[s] of 1800 in New raised ones who stand equal in this arrangement — & again a Scotsman or an Irishman has a great advantage over an Englishman as recruits are easier got by their Friends.[58]

---

[58] The 53rd Foot raised a 2nd Battalion at this time which was to serve in the Napoleonic Wars while the 1st, Sherwood's, went to India.

1803 June—Marriage & Recruiting in The North

10   A Camp is to be formed & we are ordered to prepare for it. From this to 24th at Ipswich, was mustered & then got a fortnights Leave to Bridgenorth. I was married on the 30th & passed the Night at Hagley.[59]

July   My uneasiness now is the idea of going away for my leave expires on the 7th but I obtained leave til the 24th. The 20th I was obliged to leave Mrs Sherwood & return to Camp at Bromswell near Ipswich here I was only allowed to remain 3 days when an order was received to send 3 Captains 3 Subalterns 10 Sergts 10 Corporals & 10 Privates to York. I was the first for duty & not sorry to go for I found the Camp Cold & unpleasant. The *Sydney Smith* is laying in Horseley Bay near us with a Frigate & two Sloops of War. When I found myself in orders for York & a Party of Men going to March I immediately conceived that I might spend a week at Bridgenorth & overtake the Party before it arrived at York. One Captain & one Subaltern are ordered with the Men, the others are to make the best of their way. As I am not the Subaltern for Duty I interpret the order to mean "go by Bridgenorth". I therefore set off immediately & stopped at Woodbridge for the London Coach in which I proceeded & from London to Coventry Birmingham and Bridgenorth. I Met Dr Salt in the Church Yard who was astonished to see me. Mary was at Badger but expected to night & I had the pleasure of seeing her at Ten oclock. I passed the day at Oldbury with Mrs Butt & Mary & I fancy that I am formed for retirement & wish for a Cottage, no Duties, no Promotion—on Monday I was again put to it for I dare not remain longer. I passed thro' Wolverhampton, Litchfield, Derby, Sheffield to York & on my arrival found that I could as well have waited a week longer as there were no orders for us.

8 Augt 1803   From 3rd to 8th nothing to do but walk about the Town, on the 8th an order arrives for me to proceed to Wetherby a village on the Great North Road 16 Miles from York. My duty is to receive men balloted for the Army of Reserve.[60] I am to send these Men as I receive them to York. I left York at 2 oclock for Tadcaster with Mansell, here, not finding an opportunity to proceed to Wetherby, I walked about by the Side of the River & was delighted with the beauties of the place, but

---

[59] Marriage to cousin, Mary Martha Butt (1775-1851). Mrs Sherwood became a best selling author of over 300 books for children. See Eaton, Barbara: *Mrs Sherwood 'so rich in children'*. London 2016.

[60] Additional Forces Act, July 1803: Army of Reserve of 15,780, for war with Napoleon, the Treaty of Amiens of March 1802 having broken down by Britain's declaration of war on France in May 1803.

England—1802-5

at the same time most unhappy wishing M`rs` S. was with me to see this fine spot.

9   I passed on to Wetherby passing thro the beautiful Village of Thorpe Arch: the Village seemed so inviting I wished myself clear of the Army & Settled there. On arriving at Wetherby I find that there are so few Men to be called out in this Village that it must be a mistake sending me here, as this is an Entire dependence on Knaresboro, where there is another Officer, My Junior indeed, but having a separate command the beautiful walks about here are charming & if I had my wife here I should be delighted. Just before Dinner the Waiter brought me a Message from a Lad who is at School at Thorpe Arch saying that if convenient he would join me at dinner & that he had a Hare, I accepted his advances & he soon appeared, a very fine Lad, but I was astonished at him, he drank a Bottle of Wine without its appearing to have any effect on him, I expressed my astonishment but he said it was his custom at home, but that he should not be allowed it at School. He was now returning from the Holydays. The Young Gentleman had his Snuff Box & took Snuff in Stile. He wished to smoke but I prevailed with him to take a walk. We walked by the River side & I was pleased with the Young Man's remarks. What have Parents to answer who bring upon their Children in this way?

10   I took Lodgings in which I am to be boarded for 21/- per week.

11   Walked to Tadcaster, met Piercy & M`r` M`c`Caskell & my Poney & rode back. On my return I found my [half] Brother James, whose Ship now lies at the Mouth of the Humber. I have not seen him since I left England. He has been serving as a Midshipman this six years in many climates.

12   James[61] & myself went to Knaresboro. He could not ride & I was much amused by his Sailorlike Horsemanship.

14   To Church, rather shocked at finding in one of David's Psalms, the word <u>Israel</u> changed to <u>Brittain,</u> we had a Loyal Sermon "Fear God & honor the King & follow not those who are given to change<u>"</u>

15   Ordered immediately to proceed to Doncaster & place myself under the Command of Captain Platt 50 Reg`t`. I immediately sent my Recruits to York & my Party to Doncaster & then set off with my Brother to York we rode & tyed & reach York at three oclock, found Piercy, Rees & M`c`Caskell, & we are quite at a loss what to do. The confusion in all the Offices about this Army of Reserve seems perfectly ridiculous not one officer that I have met with knows what he is about &

---

[61] Sherwood's half brother James Taylor Sherwood served as a boy on *HMS Naiad* in 1805 and was later reported to have died at the Battle of Navarino in 1827.

I find Officers sent to places where no drawing is expected, & on the Contrary, chief places without an officer, the head Quarters at York had got about 100 Men.

Tuesday I rode to Tadcaster, Piercy accompanied me, we dined with Mansel & after dinner rode to Ferry Bridge & found the Landlord very uncivil from my wearing a RedCoat which annoyed me not a little.

17 Augt Left Ferrybridge at Six. The Country delightful. The Crops on the Ground very luxuriant. I breakfasted at the Redhouse & reached Doncaster at 12 oclock. immediately called on Captain Platt who asked me to dine, but I find that I am not to be under his orders, but to act for myself. I understand Cap^n Platt has written to the War Office saying that he is incapable of taking accounts "Your Petitioner will ever Pray" what do you mean, write "your petitioner will ever Fight." Glew a Lieut 53 & Killingly an Ensign 53rd Regt say the same, & I do think that if many others had followed their example it would only have saved confusion in Accounts, for it certainly is not required that an Officer should be able to undertake so complicated a business. I had cause afterwards to find that no allowances would be made for Ignorance, many an officer lost money to such a great amount as scarcely to recover it, some I believe never did. Lieutt Glew introduced me to a Lodging with himself here I am boarded for 20/- a week at a Mr Turners, a respectable Shoe Manufacturer. In the Evening Cap^n Platt took me to Parade & introduced me to 200 Ragged Rascalls, without even a list of Names, he said that he took all that came & that he gave them no money, nor did he care about them. They were all clamorous for Pay & made claims. I told them that I would have nothing to say to them until they were regularly delivered over & all claims settled prior to my receiving them. This I believe will be a difficult matter as I am likely to have a sinecure place for some time as I am decided not to take unsettled accounts on myself.

Augt 18 1803   I went to Parade the Men at 10 this Morning. Lord Eardly came there & teazed me not a little. He seemed kind but he gave me a lesson on our duty in such an extravagant manner that we could scarcely contain our laughter in his presence. He was dressed so slovenly & looked so dirty that it was disgusting. He was so over kind that he would not leave us until we had taken tickets for Ashe's Concert which I grumbled at as I had no wish to spend my money in that way. I went to the Concert but was not at all amused.

Saturday 20   I was ordered to the Town Hall to receive Ballotted men for the Army of Reserve. All seemed confusion. Men were sworn in for the Militia who ought to have been sworn for the Army Reserve & in the

England—1802-5

opposite way & when I remonstrated I was told that they must go on. I objected to the Ages of Men & to their Country & to their profession. My orders were not to receive men above 40, Irishmen or Sailors yet all these kind of recruits were sworn in without attending to my remonstrances. I therefore walked away & left the Magistrates to act for themselves.

Monday 22   I took my recruits to the Race Ground, merely to keep them out of Mischief, as I have no assistance, but I made them stand at ease & called to attention.

23   Orders received from Col^l Wood for me to march my enrolled Men to Sunderland by the most convenient rout. Lt Glew & Ensign Killingly 53rd Reg^t to accompany me. I am left to my own judgement as to the Rout, but I am to march Tomorrow Morning.

[Margin Note: because I afterwards found that all the known routs were occupied – by the War Office]

I numbered my Men as they stood on Parade 350 but I never had a Roll of them & knew no Names, on application to Cap^n Platt he promised to furnish me with a Roll before Night, which he did not do. I waited till late at Night but no Roll came —

24   At five the Roll beat by Cap^n Platt's orders & I went out but he had no Roll & he ordered me to march. Cap^n P. had provided plenty of Baggage Waggons, full of Women. I asked him who was to pay for them. He said Government. I told him it was no such thing, Government only allowed Waggons, for Carriage of Arms & as we had none, no Waggons were allowed by the Regulations he however insisted & as my Superior Officer I was obliged to obey but I discharged all but one at Ferrybridge. I had ordered a Parade to take a Roll of my Men at Ferrybridge, but unfortunately I fell in with another party & my Men were sent to Pontefract, Knottingly & Brotherton & I could not collect them but hope to succeed Tomorrow.

25 Augt 1803   Marched from Ferrybridge to Wetherby. I was some time collecting my Men but on the whole I got on better than I expected with my reserve army. Reserve Army or Pickle Army. I found 7 old Sg^{ts} — 2 old corporals, 1 drum^r & 333 Prostitutes as they are called (substitutes). I halted & breakfasted at Aberford. A most beautiful Country (but this is a fine Season)! Arrived at Wetherby got my Men into Quarters & they had eaten their breakfast when a Drum was heard & I ran out & found a large Detachment under Captain Wallace of the 53 Reg^t marching in. He had sent on no Serg^t for Billetts & was quite unexpected, at first I only laughed at the thought that he would find no room, but on comparing Routs I found that Wetherby was his Rout for today while mine was

discretionary. I was therefore obliged to turn out of Quarters. My Men got their Breakfasts for nothing. The Party under Wallace were obliged to go without & my men bivouac'd under Haystacks—& bore it with good humour.

25   I march to Rippon to keep clear of Wallace whose Rout pointed out Boroughbridge, breakfasted at Boroughbridge. Ripon is a very Romantic looking Town with a Fine old Abbeyminster. The Inkeepers seemed pleased to see us which is not usual.

27   Marched to Bedal & arrived at 8 o clock. I was much pleased with the Country which is well wooded & the peculiar beauty of the small Rivers which are rapid & crossed by stepping stones, the water being delightfully clear.

28   Halted & mustered my Men 327 Present. I had hoped for some assistance from Glew & Killengly but Glew had led away the young Ensign who was not above 50 Rutting with the Landlady's Daughters at the Inn for which my friend Glew was peculiarly fit tho not a beauty.

29   To Richmond. The Wind unpleasantly high & lots of Dust. The Wild beauties of the Country very attractive. The old ruins of the Castle built by Fitzsomebody son of the Conqueror. The narrow walk round which, overhanging a small river at a great height in a Windy day, is was rather alarming.

30   March towards Darlington lost my road & found myself on the banks of a river with a ferry. A Scene of confusion ensued, many of my Men forded the River, others got onto the Ferryboat, owing to my ignorance of their Names & the want of a distinguishing dress I was quite at a loss, the Ferry Man stormed, my Men laughed & I was glad to escape by paying the Passage of my Men at a halfpenny each. On arriving at Darlington I had reason for being pleased with my march for I found that it had been the intention of the Men to refuse passing the borders of their County under some plea of not having received the Marching Guinea as they called it, the meaning of which I neither know or care to know but being in Yorkshire as it were by surprize their plan was so completely knocked up that they could not find an excuse ready at any other place. I daresay we should have got on without much difficulty as my Men were of a laughing order & I agreed with them, yet it is not pleasant to try an experiment of even a shew of Mutiny.

31   A Long March 18 Miles to Durham. I had hoped to have halted to Breakfast at a fine Inn 9 miles on the Road but the Landlord came out with his waiters en Robe de Ceremonies with a deputation of Waiters Chamber Maids & others to petition that I would not halt my Ragged Regiment at a lone House. I saw there was some reason in what they said

I therefore advanced 3 Miles further to a Village & breakfasted. Pleased with Durham, its Walks, its Castle, Palace & Cathedral, with its History of St Cuthbert.

September 1   We marched from Durham & reached Sunderland at 12 o clock. We were immediately placed in Barracks, still keeping the Command of the Men, I was employed in hiring furniture for my room, which is easily done as there are always Hucksters near Barracks ready to hire, or sell furniture. The Barracks are situated near the Sea which has a low sandy Beach. They are of wood, 2 stories high & good & are intended to contain 1500 Men. They are now full of Detachments like my own under Officers of different Corps. Both Cavalry & Infantry taken from all the recruiting Parties. These parties consist of a number varying from 100 to nearly 400, mine is the largest being 372 men.

One of our first Plans was to form a Mess & I was employed to procure a Messman. Most of the Officers of our Regiment who left Bromwell Heath with me are arrived & several Fresh Officers lately appointed to the regiment, it being now formed into two Battalions. Piercy, Giles, Thursby, Mansel, Balders & other Captains have joined & we have got up a Mess having each subscribed 10/6 for utensils & we pay 10/6 p^r week each.

7   We find that the Regiment broke up camp at Bromswell on the 6th & are marching this way & may be expected on the 26th. I rode every day on the different roads round Sunderland, generally with Piercy & Mansel. The Country is flatt & bare of Trees, but the River is fine & Iron Bridge a work of wonderful Art.

10   Col^l Scrogs our 3 Lieut^t Col^l joined us today.

11   Mrs Wheatstone arrived from Camp, I got Lodgings for them, Rode with Ximenes, Piercy & Mansel, crossed the River about 5 Miles above Sunderland & visited Lord Strathmore's House at Hilton it is a fine place for a Ghost, but we got some good fruit.

14   Dined with Ximenes- a fine stiff breeze & a Fleet of Colliers appeared waiting for the Tide, I went down the Pier to see them Enter which they did as soon as the Signal was hoisted to inform them that there was water sufficient. I never saw such confusion for they all rushed in together without waiting & were jammed together at the entrance coming upon each other without the slightest fear such bumps, such cracking, such Hallooing, sails tore, yards broke, shrouds torn from the blocks & even Booms carried away, it was a perfect babel, there were about 50 of them.

15   Cap^n Inglebury a new Officer 53rd Reg^t brought in 150 Men.

25   I went to Durham on the 25th to meet the Regiment. They were arrived & I staid with them & marched on the 26th with them to Sunderland. I find that the arrival of the Regiment does not take off my responsibility, I have my Pickled Detachment still (Reserve Present Pickle) as a separate Command. I had paid them up to 24th being certain that I should have been clear of them, & I had hoped for a few days leave to meet Mrs Sherwood on her way to Sunderland but I am disappointed & in that not a little.

3 October   We began to form our flank Companies from the Army of Reserve, we have (of course) Two Light Companies & as I belong to the 1st I had enough to do. In forming our 2 Battalions we are what is called Chequered ie- The Senior Capn to the 1st battalion the 2nd to the 2nd & so on, by which means I am with the 1st battalion Piercy is my Captain. As before our first business was to cloth the Men & size them & prepare Rolls &c so that it was the 14th before our drills began but when they did begin it was in earnest, we formed before day light on a cold Eastern Beach & never left till Dinner & then again at 3 till 6.

Mrs Sherwood arrived on the 11th in safety but we have no accoutrements for the Men, they exercise with a firelock only & at the work <u>Load</u> they slap their Hinder parts instead of the pouch. I have the Command & payments of the Light Company.

October 31st   Visited Roland Burdon Esqre of Castle Eden. We remained 3 days. There are but few Trees in Durham & I was told that the reason is that the land being let on lives, Tenants have no Interest in planting.

Nov 5   Drank Tea with Doctor Pailey Author of Pailey's Evidence,[62] he was very kind to us, he is somehow related to us but I do not know how. We were kept very hard at our drills the remainder of the Month & our Baggage sent away. The Wise Men of Gotham have more fear for our Baggage that for all the Good People's property in Sunderland.

Decr   Deep snow from 5th to 10th a repetition of the Confusion on the 14th Sepr with the addition of a Gale of Wind setting in Shore. The Sea was dreadfully rough & the bowsprits seemed to go for nothing, being shivered to pieces one after the other as if made of a single Match. One Brig entirely dismasted, two others one Mast each, 20 bowsprits gone, within the Year I have paid my Regimental Taylor 49.19.6 this does not include Colored Coats, Leather Breeches, Blue Pantaloons.

15   Ten Officers ordered Recruiting.

---

[62] Paley. *Natural Theology or Evidences of the Existence and Attributes of the Deity.* 1803.

1803 December—Orders for Ireland

23   At 12 o clock at night an order arrived for the Regiment to march to Carlisle to embark for Ireland. The March to commence at 8 o clock which accordingly took place by divisions. 2 Companies marched on 24 & on Sunday 25. The march continued no halt is allowed, The Detachment to which I belong marched on Monday the 26th. At the first notification of our March we were all alarmed at the suddenness of it & the hurry of the removal naturally prepared us for some dreadful Rebellion in Ireland, I therefore thought Mrs Sherwood would be better at home but she preferred going with us & so did all the Ladies of the Regiment. Mr Scott the Surgeon who goes in the same Division proposed that Mrs Scott & Mrs Sherwood should follow each day's march in a Post Chaise which I gladly agreed to.

26   We marched at 8 oclock in the Morning for Newcastle. The Commanding Officer, The Two Flank Companies & Cap^n Turners. The Road wet, the Country barren & gloomy, we arrived at Newcastle at 12 o clock the Ladies followed us. It rained all the afternoon so meaning that I could not see the Town but it had some good Streets & fine houses in it.

27   Our March Today being a very long one we marched at four oClock, we had a Moon, but the Road was very wet & rough, it seemed unusually long before day light. The Men said that there was good bottom in the road if you could find it. The Road itself is an old Military road originally paved. We were not far from the Picts Wall all the way & we breakfasted at Harlow Hill on the Wall. We perceive a great difference in the manners of the Inhabitants & in the price of provisions. We had a good breakfast with Ham, plumb Cake & Eggs with very good Cream for which we paid 1/- each, from hence 1½ Mile on the Military road where we struck off to the left, the views very fine but covered with Snow, The Village of Corbridge pleasantly situated, we halted at Hexham on the Tyne. The Estate of Erringtons to the North of the River is well wooded, which is a wonder to us, I think of Tewksbury but whether there is any real resemblance so that the battles fought there bring them together in imagination, is more that I am able to say, we were so much tired that we were glad to get our dinners & dry feet. The Ladies soon afterwards came up. They seemed pleased with their journey. It rained all the Evening, if there was any but there was very little day to be perceived.

28   Marched at 7 to Haltwistle the views fine & the Country better. We were continually falling in with the Tyne whose banks are beautifully romantic The Country apparently barren but we found plenty of provisions & very cheap. A Large fowl costing 8^d Haltwistle is but a very

small place but very much noted in border story, the Featherstonehaughs having a seat here.

29   From Haltwistle to Brampton a short March but an unpleasant one, we were up to our knees in water at Glenwelt but we there got on the Military road again, the Country a wide Heath we had a very extensive prospect but neither Trees nor houses. The View was bounded by high Mountains on all sides, several Old Forts & Castles at different distances. On arrival at Brampton a very unexpected order met us Ordering us to halt, we are at a loss to account for this so sudden an order & conjecture is afloat we suppose the French have Landed, on the Coast that we have left.

30   Brampton is a very pretty place, on the outside of the Town is a fine conical Hill covered with Firs, it has the appearance of an Artificial Elevation but it is not preserved. From this Hill we have a fine view of the Mountains of Westmoreland on the one side & Scotland on the other. From the great rain there is an appearance of many Rivers but it is likely that they are only the remains of floods.

Jany 1804   Remained at Brampton from the 30th December to 3rd January when we marched for Carlisle. It was a frosty Morning & we soon reached our destination. We found other parts of the Regiment, but we nave no further orders & are quite at a loss as to our next point & there is a probability of our halting some time. On the 4th I went to look for Lodgings & not being able to succeed in procuring room sufficient for the Scotts & ourselves, Scott proposed that we should each provide for itself, he therefore seized on one & I fortunately was immediately offered rooms with a Lieut^t Andrews & Mrs Andrews. We remained in these Lodgings making one family with the Andrews's but I had a violent pain in my face & a swelling in my Lip which alarmed me, it formed a bag of blood & the Surgeon thought it might be necessary to perform the operation of eradicating it with a knife but we first tried to burn it away with Caustic & after some time succeeded. The Castle of Carlisle is a fine old Ruin. Lieu^t Ford the <u>Governor</u> was attentive to us as far as he could but being only a Lieu^t on half Pay with a wife could do. He kindly undertook to point out the beauties of the view, but he was not master of his subject for he pointed to the Scottish Hills for Skidaw & he talked of meandering Streams "Oh he could talk, Ye Gods he could talk." We had a heavy fall of Snow but it soon gave way to rain, before the Month was out the Number of Troops caused a feeling of Burthen on the Town & 4 Companies were marched to Cockermouth leaving 6 behind & 4 Companies 2 Battalion.

England—1802-5

Feb'y 2   Orders received for separating the Battalions, all Men enlisted under the Act for embodying the Army of Reserve who will not extend their services voluntarily are to be embodied in the 2nd Battalion, all the disposable Men to the 1st Batt'n.

The Officers are required to use all their influence to prevail on the Men to volunteer for general service in consequence of this order all kinds of rioting & drunkenness was encouraged, but it did not succeed for we did not procure 20 Men & these no doubt would have volunteered without it.

9   We were ordered to hold ourselves in readiness to return to Hexham to receive the 6 Companies of the 2nd Battalion who are to come on to Carlisle by which means we expect to have the 1st & 2nd Battalions separated distinctly.

10   General Grey arrived & gave orders for putting in force the order respecting the final separation of General Service Men & Limited Service Men. This was ordered to be done so suddenly as to create great confusion. We ie the 1st Battalion is to march in the Morning. The Men, 70 to be given over, the Arms accoutrements &c to be examined & their accounts made up. But I must say that I was prepared with all these accounts, with 70 Men before the 2nd battalion could give me 11 Men & that I had not so much Money to receive an account of the Debts of 70 Men as the 2nd Battalion brought against 11 Men & at last I was obliged to remain behind to receive the Accounts of the 2nd Batt'n which could not be completed till the 13th when I left Carlisle, passing thro' Brampton where was a very hard frost & the Chaise moved pleasantly along, we stopped at Haltwistle for the Night. Here we find Major Buckland & Lieut McCaskell with Volunteers from 2nd to 1st Battalion.

14   At 12 oclock reach Hexham. Andrews had procured Lodgings for us in an old House apparently built during the Wars of York & Lancasteer very pleasant but more calculated for Summer than Winter.

15   General Grey inspected the Reg't. I have a very bad Ear ach & the review made me worse so much so that I suffered most excruciating pain until the 29th & became deaf, but on the 29th Two large abcesses broke in my Ears & in part relieved me but I did not recover my hearing, during this time viz the 25th the Regiment marched to Morpeth but I was too ill to go with it.

March 1st   We left Hexham with Mrs Andrews, passing thro Cambo, The Country delightful the weather Cold & the ground covered with Snow, but we observed beautiful Parks & many fine houses, 3 close together vz Lord C Ainsley, Mr Trevillian & Sis Wm Lorrain's. We had some refreshment at Cambo & proceeded to Morpeth. Near Morpeth the Country is very romantic by the side of the River Wansbeck. There are still some buildings to remind us of the Borders vz. Ruined Watch Towers & old Castles. One I particularly remarked & I think it must be Mitford with the Ruins of a Bridge near it. At Morpeth we found good Lodgings provided for us by the kind attention of Lieu^t Thompson.

6   We do not expect to remain long here, I am very deaf & I begin to fear that I may not recover as my mother was deaf.

8   Mrs Sherwood & myself took the opportunity of calling on the Ladies of the Regiment, this delightful weather lasted till the 18th when we had snow & severe frost again.

Snowed 18, 19th, 20th, 21st, 22nd. & 23rd which latter day we expected a thaw but the easterly wind blew again with snow which continued to the end of the Month, on 31 General Grey reviewed us & buttered us as usual.

1804 April—Regimental Paymastership

Mr Todd Paymaster intending to resign, I applied for leave to London to endeavour to obtain the appointment. The Col^l Lightburne having kindly offered his interest he gave me a Letter to the General (Crosbie).

April 1st 1804   It is this day 9 years since I looked back from the Windmill above Amiens when leaving a French Prison, that I said am I not going on a fools errand & again this day when leaving Morpeth in the Coach to ask for the Paymastership of the 53rd Reg^t I again ask the question. I am concerned that human nature has great superstition in it & altho we may affect to laugh at vulgar proverbs many feel a kind of awe from them which they are unable to conquer. The real difference between boldness & Courage is said to be that boldness is ignorant of danger while Courage calculates & prepares itself for the Trial, so in superstition, those who defy Ghosts & old Proverbs are the soonest led to terror while the one acknowledging the weakness of his Nature prepares himself by reason for the conquest of his fears. Our Coach only reached Newcastle this Night. On the 2 proceeded for London as we passed Durham we found that the Spring was less advanced than it had been at Morpeth. The price of provision also rose every step that we advanced & I was surprized to hear from Scotsmen that from Morpeth to Edinburg the same was remarked by which it sees if I am rightly informed that in the Narrow Isthmus Provisions are cheaper than any where in Brittain. We reached London at 4 o clock on the 4th April. I immediately proceeded to Hackney to ask Mr Maskall if he would be security for me if I could obtain the Paymastership & having obtained his consent I immediately returned & proceeded to Battersee to Mʳ Reynolds to ask from him the same favour which he also agreed to, I returned to Hackney to sleep completely tired.

5   I sallied out again & called on Greenwood Cox & Co & after waiting two hours for an audience I shewed my letters of recommendation but I met with a very cool reception, indeed as nearly as possible a positive refusal. I therefore wrote to Colonel Lightburne & wait the result.

10   A Letter from Colˡ Lightburne desiring me to call on General Crosbie & state my claims to him. I went & with a great deal of trouble in which I owe much to Colonel [sic] Crosbie 22ⁿᵈ Regᵗ & Mʳˢ General Crosbie. The old General was prevailed on to sign a recommendation which as soon as he had done he became very kind & chatty & invited me to his house & began to complain of the Government which had neglected him &c. Selfishness soon drove me away & having obtained the signature required I gave it in to the Secretary at War's office & finding that there was no further need of my presence it was the 17ᵗʰ before I could settle every thing I then returned & reached Morpeth on the 20ᵗʰ. I then gave my resignation as Lieuᵗ. We had much snow until the 23ʳᵈ & very cold. Mʳˢ Sherwood was confined on the 20ᵗʰ with a daughter.[63] The Light Company to which I belong having been removed to Tynemouth, I expected by sending in my resignation to be allowed to remain & did remain till the end of the Month, the Spring very backward, & no leaves appearing. I bought Capⁿ Giles's Gig.

May   I find this description of Morpeth. It is situated in a warm Valley & is watered by the Wensbeck, the Town Hall was built by Lord Carlisle in 17ᵗʰ C —The Cross in 1699 by the Honᵇˡᵉ P. Howard & Lord Bellaford. The Parish Church is half a Mile from the Town & is a rich Living. There is a Chapel of ease in the Town in which Service is performed in Winter when the Parish Church is closed, for the Service is never performed in both places during the same period. There is the remains of a fine Castle now in ruins, it is built on a high ground overlooking the Town & enjoying a fine view. There is however an artificial Hill or Mound at a little distance overlooking the Castle, probably raised by an Enemy. The Original Lords of the Castle were named Morley meaning as I am told a Hill & Morpeth a Valley under the Hill.

---

[63] Mary Henrietta Sherwood, their 1st child.

9   On the 9th when I expected nothing less than to see my name in the Gazette as paymaster I was disturbed immediately after dinner by a sudden Regimental order to proceed to Tynemouth to join my Company as it is said that my presence cannot be dispensed with. I did not know my own value before. I must acknowledge that I did not feel at all pleased with this discovery of my own efficiency but as major Stewart could not do without me I said "need will when the devil drives."

10   I therefore moved off at 8 o clock on the 10th, Andrews accompanying me to Newcastle in my own Gig which Andrews drove back & I proceeded in a Chaise to Tynemouth where I arrived at Night & was comfortably taken out to a drill at daylight on the sands below Tynemouth & kept till one oclock.

12th May   We were at drill from 6 in the Morning till one which is carrying it too far. At Night I was on Pickett going my rounds. I met Parker who had walked from Morpeth with a bond for me to sign as Paymaster, I lay all night, alarmed & uneasy at the great undertaking. I signed the Bond & sent Parker back in the Morning.

13   The Regiment is to leave Morpeth & join us soon at Chirton Barracks near North Shields. An old House which is fitted up with births in the Nature of apple racks from Top to bottom every room having steps built one above another like the shelves in a Cloths press which the Men are to be packed in each small room of about 16 feet square is to contain 38 Men, there does not appear room enough for the number to stand clear of the beds which reach to within a few Inches of the ceiling. Let People talk of Goats or Prison Ships but let them also see Chirton Barracks.

The Old Castle of Tynemouth is a fine old Ruin on Peninsular Bluff.

14   Drill from 9 till 1, tired for the day

15   I was excused drill

16   General Grey drilled the Flank Companies & marched the Light Company 53rd Regt in Echelon into the Sea to our waists before he perceived it & then as an excuse for his error said he did it on purpose to teach them not to fear Water. This Evenings Gazette put Ensign Parker into my Lieutenancy & I am a Gentleman at large. I immediately asked leave to return to Morpeth & finding a return Chaise for Newcastle I proceeded & from thence on the Coach to Morpeth & arrived at 7 in the Morning found the Family in bed but well.

17   The Weather now is very fine & the walks delightful by the side of the Wansbeck both above & below the Town, in the Blue Bell Wood the Lady's Chapel Wood.

England—1802-5

June 1st   My name appeared as Paymaster 53rd Regt in the Gazette & I was very busy in taking charge of the Paymasters Accounts. This fully employed me till the Regiment marched on the 14th for Chirton Barracks. We were sorry to leave Morpeth where we had met with much kindness. Before we left, a Family of the Town, Mr Henry formed a plan for our seeing Bothall Castle which is a fine old Ruin 4 Miles down the River. We were delighted with the beauty of the Spot to be sure the time of year is in favour of the beauties of nature. Our drive lay thro a beautiful wood near the River all the way, about ½ way we passed the Ruins of an old Chapel dedicated to the Virgin, from which the wood takes the Name of the Lady's Chapel Wood. A Tree has grown thro the walls & in all probability it will soon be down.

We also went to Stannington Village on the London road, the living of which was held by the late Mr Thos Butt, we went into his house, it must be pleasant in summer but in winter very dreary.

15   Left Morpeth. Mrs Scott, Mrs Sherwood & a maid servant in a Chaise Massowden & Self in my Gig. I procured pretty good Lodgings at 1 Guinea a Week in Shields which is dear considering that the sea Bathing Season is approaching. All the Regiment is now in one House, the Officers, receiving Lodging Money provide for themselves. I had some difficulty in making up my first Monthly account but I succeeded pretty well. We have had fine dry weather but what is called backward. The Fire was necessary until the end of the Month. We had few vegetables.

July   July set in with Cold weather. 1 Camp was formed at Blyth of three Militia Regts vz 2nd Stafford 2 Derby & Westmoreland. Mrs Sherwood & myself visited the Light House on the point of Tynemouth Castle Keep, it is a triangular revolving light which as it turns shews darkness & light 3 Times in one revolution like a Dumb waiter. From the Lighthouse we had an extensive Coast view Northward to Newbiggin between which place & Tynemouth are Cullercoats, Hathly Blyth & Seaton. To the South we could only see about 4 Miles, The View up the Tyne, with the Shipping &c was very fine

1804 July—Kent

We have orders to hold ourselves in readiness to go into Camp & it is reported that the East Essex Militia & ourselves are to encamp together. On the 20th An order arrived for our forming a Camp & we drew Bat & forage in consequence. I received an allowance of £20 to prepare for encamping. The East Essex came into Tynemouth, & we were busy in preparing when to suddenly an order arrived for us to embark in 2 Transports & to proceed to Ramsgate in Kent. This is not pleasant. Mrs Sherwood has decided on going to London by Sea, at this fine Sea & I have taken a passage for her on a Vessel which has accommodation better than a Transport can afford. Mrs Whittery Wife of Lieu^t Whittery will go with her. She pays One Guinea & a half for herself & one Guinea for the Servant

On the 30th The Regiment embarked & what is rather singular, we sailed in the same Ship (the *Crown*) which brought us from the west Indias. On the 31st we sailed. Mrs Sherwood cannot get off till tomorrow.

August 1st The wind at first was slack but at 7 o clock on the 1st Augt in the Morning it freshened. At 10 o clock we crossed Robin Hood's Bay & received plenty of Fish on board remarkably cheap,

2   I lost my watch which I suppose caught in the rigging it was my Grandfathers & I feel its loss. At 12 we were off Scarboro Castle & passing Hamboro head, stood to Sea. At 12 at night we saw Cromer light & at 7 in the Morning Yarmouth, we passed Lowestoft. By the shore saw people playing Crickett.

3   At 12 on the 3rd we anchored off Broadstairs near Lord Kieth's House & at 9 at Night arrived at Ramsgate harbour having been 3 days from South Shields.

Saturday 4th August   At 4 oclock in the Morning the Regiment disembarked at Ramsgate. I took part of a Chaise with Major Stewart & Cap^n Mansell & proceeded towards Barham Downs, The sudden change of climate was I think more than I have ever seen in so short a time, we were in Shields on the Evening of the 31st July & now at 4 oclock in the Morning of the 4th Augt in Kent. The Corn is quite ripe & some cut. We left it green, not even in the Ear. The Hay Harvest at Shields scarcely begun, Cherries, Gooseberries, Currants, here all gone & at Shields not ripe.

Breakfasted at Sandwich & stopped 2 Hours, reach Barham Downs at Twelve o clock & were shot out of our Chaise on the Common not knowing where the Camp was to be. The day was fine & I lay down with my desk under my head & my Portmanteau by my side, alone, for Stewart & Mansell had gone back to meet the Regiment. At 3 the Regiment arrived but we had no Tents or food. Add to this rain came on. The Guards vz 1st & 3rd battalions of 1st Reg^t lay on the Ground but we saw nothing of them. Major Marly of the Staff Corps did all that he could to assist us, our Tents were up at 12 at Night

Sunday Our Tents which were pitched irregularly during the Nightm were taken down & repitched & so much difficulty was there in drawing straight lines that we had them Pitched & repitched 3 or 4 Times before the Staff were satisfied. I like regularity, but in a lean Country, Monday would have done as well as the Sabath. The Officers 53rd Reg^t found a small Publick House near us where we dined it is called Black Robin, just at the 61st Mile Stone. Our Camp is on good ground but Cold. The 53rd Reg^t right on the 61 Mile stone. Water is not near us otherwise it is pleasant.

9th A Letter from Mrs Sherwood by which I find that she had not sailed on 2 August.

10 It blew hard. Mr Whitting &myself were alarmed for our wives but in the Evening we heard of their arrival at Woolwich.

13 The Wind has been so high as to throw down most of the Tents with a Cold disagreeable Rain. Mrs S. wrote to say she wished to see her friends in Worcestershire while we live in Canvas Bags & so it is agreed.

21 The Duke of York reviewed our Camp & the Brigade in Canterbury. The Field Day (or Review) was completed of the following Regiments, Blues, Greys, Two Batt^{ns} Guards, 18th, 53rd & 61 Foot & Nottingham Militia. The Duke came on the Ground before One o clock.

29 Dined at the Artillery Mess & met Lieut^t James of the Scots Greys who was Prisoner with me at Abbeville in 1793/4/5. We had a good deal of conversation respecting our fellow Prisoners. This Month Cold wet & uncomfortable, the few last days more pleasant

7th Sep^t 1804 I rode with Stewart, who was this day notified as Cap^n in the 24th Reg^t, to see Dover. I must acknowledge that not being an Engineer I can not give an opinion on the New Works except so far as to know that they will cost <u>Money</u>. 68 Pound Carronades are mounted where I should think they can do little execution. The day was hot & heavy we could see no distance, no part of France was visible. I have a tooth ach & my duties not calling me to be in Camp I have taken lodgings in Canterbury & removed there on the 10th

12 Stewart left us to join the 24th. I feel a good deal at leaving this my oldest Army Friend.

15 I lost a 5£ note on my way to Camp which has made me low & angry with myself I had been stinting myself & saved £8 this last Month & I foolishly lose £5 of them. I took out my pocket book on the Road to give Sg^t Downie some money & I presume that it blew away.

I received a present of £5 from Mr Burton. I am much displeased with my own conduct I gave way to my Companions & then during the Night on my Bed I am unhappy.

27 The weather considerably colder with rain but it is said to be partial, no rain having fell on the other side of Rochester, or at Dover.

October   On the 1st in the Evening having obtained leave of absence for a few days I left Canterbury for London at eight o clock & sleeping all the way reached London at 8 o clock in the Morning of the 2nd & proceeded to Hackney but Mrs Sherwood was not arrived. I breakfasted & returned to London looking into every Coach that passed but I missed her, for on arriving in Town I found that M^rs S had gone to Hackney. I found her there on my return.

6   Went by water to Battersea to see M^r & Mrs Reynolds & passed the Night

7   Returned on the 7th Visiting Miss Rawdon at Hans Place. M^r H Quinten had left.

9   Returned to Canterbury, breakfasted at Dartford & reached Canterbury at 8 at Night. Lieu^t Thompson promoted, Cap^n Miller promoted to a Majority in the 6th Foot. I went with Thompson to see him off. The Regiment feel the Cold very severely in Camp

14   Major Mawby from the 18th Appointed Lieu^t Col^l.

Nov^r   The West Kent Militia passed thro. The weather getting cold, we find the expence of living here much greater than at Shields. Meat 7/- P^r pound, little Mary cut two teeth & can stand alone being 7 Months old.

December   The Month set in Warm but wet. I should this Month have been a Captain, had I not been Paymaster.

5   Colson, Andrews & Mrs Andrews arrived from Ireland with their relation, Ensign Hays The weather towards the end of this Month with Snow on the Ground 3 days.

January 1805 Canterbury

The beginning of the Month mild, say a Lilac in Bud — Sir Ed^rd Dinnington died.

The end of the Month cold with Snow

February   Set in with the frost & Snow. [Mrs Sherwood's] Sister Lucy was detained till the 16th by the Cold, on that day she arrived.

24   We were removed from Canterbury to Reading Street Barracks near Tenterden. I left Mrs Sherwood & her Sister in Canterbury & proceeded with the Regiment the 1 days March was to Ashford 15 Miles. I was at School here & had anticipated great pleasure in seeing the old spot but it was not so. My Old Schoolmaster Mr Stoddart was still alive

but the School much fallen off. Ashford is much altered mostly owing to Barracks being built. I walked over the Ground on which I had so often played pointing out every Spot to my Friend McCaskill but every house & every field seemed reduced in size. The School Room was much reduced. I fancied it a Church, upon the whole I was quite disappointed. We dined with the 1st West York. The gooseberry bushes were becoming green. We feel sorry to leave Canterbury.

March On the 1st we marched to Tenterden by a New Military road. The Country about Tenterden is beautiful but our Barracks are at the extreme edge of the fine Country, being on the declivity of the Hill leading to Romney marsh. The Views on each side of the road are very extensive & the Country well wooded.

I took lodgings at Tenterden and on the 5th Returned to Canterbury for Mrs Sherwood. On the 7th Mrs Andrews Mrs S. & Lucy returned with me to Tenterden. Towards the middle of the Month the weather became Mild, we have many pleasant Walks, the Violet, Primrose, ranunculus & Periwinkle's full bloom the Gooseberries & Currants in leaf. On the 21st in the Morning I was riding to Reding Street I met some of our Officers who informed me that an order was arrived for our March Immediately to Portsmouth, there to embark. I had enough to do to pay the Men who march Tomorrow.

Mrs Sherwood bears the news very well & we have made up our minds to go to London on our way to Portsmouth. In the mean time we are very busy packing up, we leave Tenterden with regret.

26th March 1804   Miss Lucy Butt, Mrs Sherwood the Maid & little Mary[64] left Tenterden in a Diligence for Maidstone where we passed the Night. We found Maidstone a better place than we had expected. The Diligence is a cheaper conveyance than a Post Chaise & being a regular Coach has always horses ready. We reached London at 12 o clock & went to Mr Andrewes's at the Rectory House, St James's. We were glad to find that our destination was the East Indies. Mrs Sherwood was decided on going with me & we are to leave little Mary with her Aunt. We had enough to do to prepare cloths &c I could only remain Two days in London & then I took leave of Lucy & the little Mary, a long farewell & who knows whether we shall ever meet again.

---

[64] Mary Henrietta, 11 months old. They would not see her again until 1816.

1805 April—Portsmouth

28   I left London for Portsmouth at 5 oclock 28th. Mrs Sherwood is to follow when it is known how, where & when the Reg^t is to embark. I reached Portsmouth about an hour before the 1st division of the Reg^t arrived. We are to occupy the Hilsea Barracks until our embarkation.

April   On the 1st The Ships to carry us out were named vz. *Warley, Ganges, Cumberland, Devonshire* & half of the *Exeter*. These Ships are in the Downs & expected every day.

Captains Wheatstone, Thompson. Lt Russel, Younghusband, Parker, Rees, Massowden, Stone, Ensigns McDougal & Price with 70 Volunteers from the 2nd battalion arrived from Ireland

8th Mrs Sherwood arrived. Col^l Mawby, Captain Coultman & Lieu^t Groombridge arrived. We were dreadfully busy, we embarked on the 23rd & sailed on the Morning of the 24th.

Part 5—India—1805 to 1816

1805 April to August   Voyage to India

On the 23rd of April Mrs Sherwood and myself embarked on Board the Honourable East India Companys Ship *Devonshire*[65] to proceed to India with H^s M^s 53rd Reg^t.[66]

On the 24th The *Blenheim*[67] of 74 Guns made the Signal to get under weigh and we sailed for the Needles with a strong wind from the East. We Anchored at Seven at night opposite Yarmouth in the Isle of Wight. We did not expect to sail so soon & were quite unprepared. Our Cabin[68] which we hired from the Carpenter was so far forward as the Main Mast, the entrance being before the Pump Handle. It was just the width of One Gun and room for a single chair, our Cot was slung cross ways over the Gun but it could not swing, there not being height sufficient. In entering the Cabin which was only made of Canvas we were forced to stoop under the Cot there not being one foot from the head or foot of the cot to the partition. The Ship was so light on the water that she lay down so much we could not open our Port & had no scuttle. The water from the Pumps ran through our Cabin & M^{rs} S as a young sailor was so sick she could not hold her head up. This was an enviable situation yet no person who has not been at sea can conceive even half of the Inconveniences.

---

[65] *Devonshire* 1804-1814, 821 tons, East Indiaman, 5 East India Company voyages.

[66] The Honourable East India Company (EIC) (1600-1857) recruited and maintained its own army in India which grew from a European guard force of an officer and 30 soldiers in 1652 to 1750, 3000 regular troops; 1763, 26,000; 1778 67,000. These were mainly locally recruited Indian sepoys with British officers trained by the Company at Addiscombe Military Seminary and a few British NCOs. They were run as three separate armies in Bombay, Madras and Bengal with the Bengal C-in-C in overall command. The C-in-C was also permitted to be Governor General so the Company effectively ruled 90 million Indians. The Company paid native troops well and maintained a number of long term care establishments for invalid veterans. The British crown lent regiments to the EIC to help with the expansion of territories. Henry Sherwood's 1st Battalion, 53rd Regiment of Foot was sent to Bengal in 1805 and fought in the second of the Anglo Maratha Wars in Bundelcund and the beginning of the Anglo Nepal War in the Himalayan foothills, leaving in 1816. By 1824, the Company's armies included about 170 native and 16 British regiments.

[67] *HMS Blenheim* 74 gun, 749 tons, Royal Navy Ship of the Line.

[68] Cabins on the gun deck were typically about 8 feet square with canvas framed walls, demountable for gunnery action. A cannon took up about half the floor space with a hung cot or hammocks over the gun.

Voyage to India 1805

On the 25th it was a beautiful morning with a fine light Easterly Breeze we passed through the Needles. This is the second time I have come through & both times in such fine weather. It is a fine sight passing with a large Fleet, and it would be doubly so if it was coming to England instead of going away. The *Blenheim* struck the Ground in going out but soon got off again. We are fearful she must have received a shock.
Margin note: She sunk in 1806 supposed near the Cape & every Body Perished probably she was hurt here.
At Twelve o clock we saw the Bill of Portland and kept it in sight all day.

26.   The wind still light and fair we were abreast but not in sight of the Lizard.

27th   At 12 oclock we were in Latitude 48.32 & Longitude 6.30. We spoke a Ship which mentioned that the French Mediterranean Fleet had passed Gibralter on the 6th Instant, they consisted of Eleven Ships of the Line & Seven Frigates. Soon after the Admiral made a signal that an Enemy was in sight and Altered our course to the Westward. Mrs Sherwoods Sickness is very violent. The wind this evening fell off to the S.W.

28th   A Stiff Breeze from the W.S.W. which increased to a Gale with a rough Sea. Mrs S suffers very much.   Long 8-5 Late 48-15

29th   The Weather more moderate but the Sea has a very heavy swell, the Ship rolls much & of course Mrs S very unwell.   Long 9 Lat 49-13

30th   A fine moderate day, Mrs S. better. The Admiral made a signal last night for an enemy in sight to the S.W. He also spoke a Sloop of War. We suppose the report of the French Fleet is confirmed.   Lat 48-14 Long 10-30 West

1st May   We had a very fine Breeze which carried us smoothly 6 Miles an hour & from the easy Motion Mrs S is settling ... [page frayed]... *Cumberland* & saw several of our Officers in good health

2nd   The Breeze continues but rather fresher. We ran 7 Miles an hour the last 24 Hours, the Sea rather rougher & Mrs S not so well.
                              Lat 44-54   Long 15-46

3rd   A disagreeable Calm all day. Mrs S very unwell.
                              Lat 43-2   Long 17

4   The former part of the day Calm   Lat 42-37   Long 18
The wind rose towards the Evening. Capt Giles & McCaskell went on board the *Hope* and brought me a parcel from Vernon. All the Officers on board the *Hope* well.

5th   Sunday Divine Service   Lat 41-14   Long 20.
The Wind rose in the Evening & at 12 at night it blew so strong that we

lost our Fore Topmast & Main Top Gallant Mast. This disabled us so much that at Daylight the fleet was nearly out of sight. The *Greyhound* Frigate however missed us & came to our assistance & sent six men on Board but the Sea was so rough & we rolled so much nothing could be done except clearing the broken Masts We lay in this way until near One o clock, When a strange Sail appeared which we soon made out to be a Sloop of War much larger than the *Greyhound*. We were rather alarmed & the *Greyhound* sent for her Men back. The Frigate still approaching under easy sail, We found she was the *Immortalité* Cap^n Owens on a Cruize but intending Immediately to proceed to England. Cap^n Owen offered to stay by us until we could repair our damage. The *Greyhound* proceeded after the Fleet. I wrote Letters to all my Friends to send by the *Immortalité*. The Sea became calmer Towards the Evening.

A Fleet of East Indiamen at Sea. Nicholas Pocock. 1803.

7th During the night we had much Lightning & there was every appearance of bad Weather. At Day light it cleared up. We saw the Fleet about Twelve miles a head Laying to, we had no observation today but we suppose we must have drifted to the North.

8th   This Night we had a great swell of the Sea the Ship rolled much & Mrs Sherwood was very sickTowards Evening a fine Wind & we set off after the Fleet all damage being repaired at the Rate of 5 1/2 Miles an hour.   Lat 40-19   Long West 21-57.

9th	The Breeze continued all night with a heavy swell		
		Lat 38-10	Long 22
10th	Calm & then a fine fair Breeze	Lat 36-31	Long 21-2
11th	Fine Weather & fair Breeze	33-47	21-3
12	Fine Steady Weather	31-17	22-0

We begin to feel Warm, this being Sunday we had Divine Service

13th I have been looking about me at the passengers & my Accommodation until now when I began to have nothing to do. I will therefore explain our Situation on Board the *Devonshire*. In the first place our Cabin which I pay the Carpenter 30 Guineas[69] is exactly as I described it the first day with this addition that our Side called by Sailers the Starboard side has since our departure been the Leeward side & is likely to continue so all the Voyage which we found the following inconveniences. Our Ship, in the Sailors Language is very crank ie very light on the Water & we carry a great deal of sail consequently we lay so much down in the water that the Port cannot be opened, we are therefore in constant darkness. The Ship is also very light which is not a favourable circumstance as new and tight ships must have much putrid water on board which is pumped up at our Cabin Door and every four hours we are floated by it, the Partition being canvass & so forward among the Men our Ears sometimes suffer amazingly. The Deck where Mrs Sherwood is constantly obliged to sit you have several inconveniences but they are much more bearable than below. The wind & the rain is not very disagreeable in this Climate. We have as Fellow Passengers. Coll Rumby of the Madras Native Cavalry his wife and a little child in the Starboard half of the Round House, Lt Coll Kerr of the 2nd Ceylon Regt with his Wife on the Larboard Side. Major Buckland has the Starboard Awning Cabin & the Captain the Larboard do. The other Passengers are Three Miss Layards on Matrimonial Expeditions[70] consigned to their Brothers on Ceylon, Mr Balmain a Madras Civil Servant Mr M Kerrill a Madras Writer and the following Officers 53rd Regt Capn Giles & Lay & McDougal & Surgeon McIntire Nineteen Cadets for Madras One Free Mariner and the Ships Officers making Forty Four Persons who dine at the Captains Table. We Breakfast at 8 that is we scramble for Tea about 40 of us when the Table cannot hold above 23.

---

[69] A ship's carpenter would have been paid between £3 and £5 a month so 30 guineas (£31.50) for a 4 to 6 month voyage was a considerable bonus.
[70] The EIC facilitated the transport of respectable women as potential wives for men serving long years in India: known as 'the fishing fleet' and if unsuccessful 'returned empty.' de Courcy, Anne. (2012). *The Fishing Fleet, Husband-hunting in the Raj*. London: Weidenfeld & Nicholson.

We dine in Two divisions the Cadets at One o clock we at Three. We may sup at Nine but I have not troubled them for Supper. We have a Cow on board and they make Bread but not enough for all. Mrs Sherwood who was very ill at first is getting better & she has a good Sea appetite. We were this day in   Lat 29-41   Long 22-10

14th   The former part of the day Calm but afterwards a fine Breeze which we think the Trade Winds   Lat 27-26

15th   Lat 24-42   Long 23-7

16th   Lat 22

17th   Lat 24-17   Long 25

18th   We passed under the Sun and lay to for a Bad Sailing Ship.   Latitude 19-2

Sunday 19th We had Divine Service. We saw St Antonio one of the Cape DeVerd Islands distant about 20 Miles at which distance we remained all day but proceeding parallel. It appeared Rugged & They looked like West India Islands. One in particular which had a great semblance to Pigeon Islet off St Lucia West Indias or [page frayed ?]

22nd   Cloudy day with frequent Calms & squalls no observations.

23rd   The Wind contrary we tacked several Times during the day. Divine Service performed. We were nearly run foul of by the Ship *Ganges*, in one of the Tacks during the Night.   Lat 27-46   Long 26-30 W

24   Strong Swell, with a high wind from S.E. Lat 29-5   Long 26

25   The Wind & Sea abated   Lat 30.31   Long 26-30

26   The Wind fair N.W. but light we make 3 ½ Miles per Hour   Lat 31-22   Long 26-32

27th   A Fine Breeze A Sailor fell overboard and notwithstanding every exertion drowned.   Lat 32-51   Long 24-41

28th   The North West Wind increased during the Night and from four o clock in the morning we ran 8 Miles an hour   Lat 33-49 Long 21-57

29th   Fine N.W. Breeze   Lat 34-41   Long 17-57

30th   We ran 311 Miles this 24 Hours   Lat 35-1   Long 13-54

July 1st The wind S.W. & we lay to for the bad sailing Ships. The wind blowing strong   Lat 35-5   10-38

2nd   More moderate. We saw many Birds called Albatross.   Lat 35-17   Long 8-5

Voyage to India 1805

3rd   The Weather as we approach the Continent of Africa gets very cold, this brings winter with drizzling rain the days are short & uncomfortable.

4th   The wind fair but moderate   Lat 36-41   Long 2-15
5th   Passed the Meridian of London   Lat 37-8   1-0 East
6th   37-23   5-30 East
7th   37-28   9-30

8th   A strange sail in sight which was visited by the Frigate. This is an Event in the Fleet, the Cold increases very much and is very uncomfortable something like a raw November day in England
                                              37-30   13-3

9th   The strange Ship yesterday was a Friend   Lat 37-30 S Long 15-40 East

10th   The Weather very cloudy & disagreeable the Ship surrounded by Birds the Principal of which were the Albatross the Gannet & the Pintado Bird. We crossed the Longd of the Cape of Good Hope but we had no observation

11th   A Heavy swell with repeated squalls & then dead Calm Mrs Sherwood was very unwell. A Ship appeared near the Fleet which had much the appearance of an Enemy which seemed to sail very well & to manoeuver Cautious by she left us at Sun Set. The Moon was totally eclipsed   Lat 36-48   Long 22-58 East

12th   This was a very fine day & the Fleet for Bombay Company their course laying through the Mozambick Channel or between the Island of Madagascar & the African Continent. We are to proceed eastward until we get into 70 Degrees eastwards & then we sail North & a little to the East

13   Fine Weather   Lat 37-20   Long 29-25

14   A very fine day until the Evening when the whole Atmosphere was darkened it seemed that the whole fleet was enclosed in a Large dark Cloud and a dead Calm. We saw the Ships heads laying in every direction. The swell arose without wind the Ships roled tremendously. The Thunder burst forth & vivid streams on Lightning every now & then caused light nearly equal to day, at other times during the night it was so dark you could scarcely see two yards.   Lat 36-38 3 3-30

15th   A Light Breeze & clear   Lat 36-57   Long 35-30

16th   This morning we found a very long heavy swell without any wind The swell increased and towards three o clock we were surrounded by innumerable perfect water Spouts, they came so much among the Fleet that we were obliged continually to Fire Great Guns to burst them which was continued until about 10 at night when the wind increased violently from the south East that all sail except the Gib & Storm Stay sail was taken in, it blew a perfect Hurricane. The upper Deck Guns to Leeward were in the Water. The Ship drifts to the West & we can only see Eight Ships of the Fleet. The wind began to abate about Three o clock and we made a Little sail. The wind still blows from the St East.

   Lat at 12   36-39   Long 37-52.

18th During the Night the wind & sea fell surprisingly this morning it was nearly calm but the sea has still a Long swell. We are rather behind what we were on 16th Lat 36-33 Long 37-40

19th A fine Breeze. We find we have parted from Two Ships of the Fleet in the Storm, the One is the *Coutts*, with Part of the 67th Reg^t on board, the other the *Dorsetshire*, with 3 Company 53rd Reg^t under the Command of Cap^n Thursby. The Fleet lay to from 10 o clock till 12 to collect but these two Ships could not be seen. Lat 38-20 Long 40-13

20th A Fine but rather strong Breeze. Lat 36-24 Long 43-18

21st A heavy gale of wind & rough Sea. We lost two other Ships, probably they took advantage of the gale to run away hoping to arrive before us.   Lat 36-58 Long 47-21

22nd More moderate but very cold with hail & sleet Lat 36-26

23rd   Lat 36-1 Long 53-29

24th Little wind   36-6   56-14

25th A fine Breeze the Ship *Dorsetshire* which parted Company in the first storm joined again.   36-36   59-23

26th Light Breeze   Lat 36-23

27th Fine Breeze   36-1   Long 65-5

28 An unpleasant squally day with Clouds & Rain

29 The Weather Rather clearer & the wind fair We began to run to the Northward.   Lat 33-3 Long 72-23

30th Fine Weather   Lat 30-18 Long 74-23

31st The Weather getting much warmer Lat 28-51 75-23

August 1st Nearly calm.   Lat 27-31 Long 76

2nd   — 26-48 —76-59

3rd   —25-40

4th   — 25-14 — 78-25

5th The Weather since yesterday at 12 o clock very squally with dark clouds & Rain. We had no observation

6th   Moderate wind from the South with Rain & Cloudy. Towards Mid day the Wind increased, soon after Dinner, on the weather clearing a little we saw three strange Ships as if coming from India, by reason of the haze they were close to us before they were perceived. A Signal was made from our Admiral that the Three Strange Ships were suspicious. One of the Three Strangers lay to while the othe two came down & passing close to the Rear, we had scarcely time to form our conjectures what they were, when they hoisted French Colours & began to fire, the alarm was instant & we began to pull down all cabins erected between the Last Gun & the forepart of the Ship to clear for Action, our Cabin was demolished and in less than five minutes every thing thrown in heaps into the hold, the Ladies were tumbled after them & our Guns prepared. We found that One of these Ships was a Seventy Four or Eighty Gun Ship the other a large Frigate. At the beginning, the Ship on board of which we were was one of the nearest, and Three Shot passed through our Sails, but as we advanced the Large Ships fell back & the Battle soon became unequal. One of the Indiamen singled out the Frigate and would have Fought her but after a Few Broadsides the French went off, in fact they were as much supprized as ourselves & that they found themselves among us so suddenly that they were without any plan.

7th   We passed the night uncomfortably having no cabin & we could clearly see the French Lights, at a little distance & about Midnight they sailed a head & crossed us, getting to windward, and at Daylight they appeared preparing to renew the Action, we could perceive that the Frigate had met with some Damage and that she was changing her Masts, the Third Ship which was a Merchantman was not in company. Several Times they bore down as if to attack, but always stop'd out of reach of the Guns. Our Admiral followed by some Indiamen made a shew or persuing them but they did not go far. We have little doubt but that had our Bombay part of the Fleet, with the *Greyhound* Frigate been present we should have taken the Frigate as she semed partly disabled.

                                                    Lat 19-5   Long 80-52

8th   At Day Light the Enemy was not in sight, it was nearly calm & we sent on board different Ships to enquire what damage had been done. The Rigging of the *Hope* & *Cumberland* was much cut. A Mr Cook on board the *Blenheim* was killed, a Man of the 67 Reg^t was killed on board the *Ganges* and a Lieu^t 53rd Reg^t lost both his Leggs in the *Dorsetshire*. From the *Hope* was brought an Ode to Bramha & an Epigram on the Action written by Cap^n Fraser which I copy as I rather like the ending of the Ode.

Ode to Bramha

1
Hail Monarch of the Promised Land
Bright Region of Renown
Come Greet us with a Friendly hand
Our various wishes Crown

2
Alas we leave our Native Shore
And all its bliss forgo
Then Bramha deign thy gifts to pour,
Ah! Cheer the Strangers Woe

3
As Ganges rols his Sacred Stream
So Peaceful & Serene *
Thus may our days unruffled seem
In the Great Stream of Time
*The writer of course had not seen the Ganges.

4
May Health that our smiling Guest
Attend our Festive Board
May Glory fire the Patriots Breast
And wield the conquering Sword

5
But let not all Golconda's Guns
Be granted as our Doom
No! Bring us only Golden Dreams
Unless Hygeia Come

6
Yet what O Bramha what art thou
Thou canst not hear our prayer
In Hindustan to God we'll bow
The Christians God is there

7
O Lord what a fuss, what a terrible Noise
Is made about Fighting that Black Guard Linois[71]
But oh, had we taken that troublesome Elf
We might all hold our Tongues, That would speak for itself.

---

[71] Admiral Charles-Alexandre Léon Durand Linois, a French Admiral who campaigned against British trade in the Indian Ocean in 1803-4, had failed to engage another East India fleet when they bluffed their power.

Voyage to India 1805

(It has since appeared that Linois suffered severely and was glad to get away)

We saw no more of the French but it is ascertained by those who have been thro these Seas before that the Man of War was the *Marengo* of Eighty guns & the Frigate the *Belle Poule* of 40 and the third an English East Indiaman a prize. This was the *Brunswick* East Indiaman

                                                       Lat 17-14 Long 80-48 E

10th   We had a fine Breeze   14-29   81-9

11th This morning a strange Sail appeared which seemed waiting for we expected the French. The Admiral went a head & we were all prepared, however she proved to be the Ship *General Stuart* which separated from the fleet on the 21st July and fortunately did not see the French. We still miss the *Coutts* which we lost on 18th July & the *Warley* which parted on the 21st. We are anxious about them as we suppose them behind us. The Coutts had lost a mast when we last saw her, it appears the *General Stuart* must have passed a head of us while we were sailing under easy sail & formed in fighting order, of course we could not make much way   Lat 11-55   Long 82-11

12th   Strong Breeze with heavy squalls of rain   Lat 9-11   Long 82-41

13   6-24   83-6 as yesterday

14   Heavy Rain a man fell from the Foretop but somehow or other he rolled from sail so Sail that he fell on the deck with only a Bloody Nose.   3-39

15   The Wind fell & we had only occasional squalls.

                                                          Lat 1-46   Long 83-16

16   We recrossed the Line and entered 16 Miles within the Northern Hemisph

17   We had some very severe squalls with Rain Lat North 2-41

18   We had the most uncomfortable day since our Voyage began, we had alternate Calms & very heavy squalls in which the Ship seemed to lay all one side in the Water, called by the sailors on her beam Ends in the sea quite smooth from the Neighbourhood of the Indian Continent.

                                                         Lat 5-41   Long 83-21

19th The Wind steady and very Light. The Sea as smooth as a pond We saw several Snakes swimming round us, and we were looking out for Ceylon which we ought to see, & indeed we fancied we did see it. It must here be observed that our Longitude is merely an imperfect calculation of supposed currents, and calculated rates of sailing corrected by a difficult observation of the Sun & Moon therefore very imperfect. We are in Lat

8-14 and our Long suppose 83, which might be between 50 & 60 Miles East from Ceylon, and as it is very high Land it might be seen

20th   We had a Good Breeze & we must have nearly cleared Ceylon and we approach the Continent   Lat 9-41   Long 80-35

21st   We saw Land, we had a Light Breeze and squalls

22nd   At Day Light we were off Pondicherry distance about 6 miles. The Town looked beautiful & the Sea was calm, we coasted along with a Light Breeze the Shore Low & woody. We saw the palm Trees, Little Villages. The sight of land after 4 Months puts us all in spirits we are all packing up and fidgeting looking at the Shore

We are calculating the distance to Madras asking the Sailors if we can get in to Night, watching the Sails to see if they fill with the Wind. We see many Boats anchored about two Miles from the Shore but the People are so stupid they will not come on board to tell the News. We sat down to Dinner but could not eat, some one running out every minute to see how we get on. We see Numbers of Snakes & Sharks and a great many Butterflies.

23rd   At day Light we were closer to Madras, we could see the masts of the Ships in the Bay, as we approached the Land appeared delightful the Sun shone on the Shore which appeared covered with Palaces through a Glass we could see Black Men as carrying what they tell us is a Palankeen. We see several men sitting in the sea on a small Log of wood more than a mile from the Shore, as we get nearer the Fort shews itself and further on is a kind of suburb and a Palace which they say is the custom house. We came to Anchor at Ten o clock, when some of the Blacks almost naked as when they were born came along side riding on a Log of wood scarcely four Foot Long. Some of them brought Letters well secured from the Sea in a conical cap, it appeared that the surf is so very rough that they are obliged to dive under the Three first waves not long after we anchored several Boats full of Natives appeared Dressed in muslin & marked in different parts of the face with yellow or white streaks or spots, we passed the remainder of the Day in asking questions.

1805 August 24th Madras

[The following appears to be a later account, apparently from a letter]

On the morning of the 24 August 1805 I got into a Boat to go on shore, our Ship was anchored in smooth Water & all around looked Calm, the Sun shone bright on the Land the Water as even as a Lake, nothing indicated any difficulty landing. It is true we heard a roaring near the Shore & saw breakers there but not more than I have seen on other shores, the Boat I was in was one used for landing Ships Cargoes, very large but instead of being put together with nails it seemed to be sewed & was pliant like a leathern boat. I should not have thought from its apparent weakness & unwieldiness that it was most unlikely to contend with a heavy swell. The Ship laid rather more than a Mile from the Shore & when we left her side I was almost inclined to think either that the old Indians had been quizzing or that there was something peculiar in the day, as we approached the Shore the noise of the Surf increased & the Helmsman called to stop rowing where we lay a few minutes I presume to gain strength & watch our opportunity many other boats were around us is the same state. At length a Word was given & I never heard such a jabbering as was set up, each boatman screaming as loud as he could & pulling away. I put my fingers in my Ears & away we flew on the Top of a Mountainous Wave. This Wave passed quicker than we did & soon we saw another following but here again we lay to as before in silence for a short time, every now & then a White foaming wave threatned to over whelm us but they so managed that we lay comfortably in a trough of the Sea, at length the Word was again given, the jabbering recommenced & we flew over a Second wave & rested as before & again proceeded we came on the Top of a Wave Bump upon the Shore. I know not how I got out for hundreds of People were on the beach, they seized the Boat & with shouts & screams dragged us high & dry, but not before a Wave had sprinkled us thoroughly. I was not allowed to get quietly out for I was seized on by half a dozen People & pulled on Shore like a Bale of Goods.

24th   This morning I went on Shore in a Boat called a Mussalla Boat.[72] I had heard a bad account of the Surf & was astonished to see the Ships anchored in such calm waters, I began to fancy the Indians had been quizzing yet the make of the Boat seemed very curious, it being sewed together & seemed as Loose as a hide of Leather. As I approached the shore however I began to perceive it was no joke. The Roaring of the waves became tremendous the Boat Men stopped as if to prepare & then began to howl & scream or rather keep a kind of horrid time to the oars pulling very short. We rose in an instant as if on a mountain the Boat standing thus [sketch]

[72] 'Mussalla Boat' musoolla, a surf boat, of flexible frame and skin.

Madras Landing. Engraving after J B East. 1856.

we were hurried along & left by the Wave three times at the third we struck the Shore with a shock which nearly threw us all out. Now about 100 persons seized the Boat & pulled us up on the Shore but not before we were overtaken by one more wave which gave us a Ducking. I went to a Tavern and got a Breakfast & hired a Palenkeen[73] it is formed as in the Margin [obscured sketch] & carried by four Men. I got in but could not balance myself. I sat uneasy & was afraid of falling. I wished to get out & walk but it was so hot. I landed close to the Custom house which is situated in the Black Town. It is a fine Building. The Bearers carried me to the Fort at about the Rate of 5 Miles an hour. The distance appeared more than a Mile, I first went to the Pay Masters Office & I found the Regiment is to Land Immediately The Fort is low & the Houses encrusted with a fine white Mortar made with shells burnt which takes so good a Polish that they appear to be built of Marble, they look very Grand. I went into a Coffee House within the Fort which had the appearance of a Large Publick Exchange. It seemed as if it belonged to Government but I knew no one whom I could ask I returned again through the surf which seemed even worse than landing as in Landing you have the advantage of running away but on going off the Noise in itself is enough to alarm you & the Blows given by the waves make the

---

[73] 'Palenkeen' palanquin.

Boat quiver, in fact it is impossible to give an Idea the feeling is nearest allied to sliding on the Sea. You seem raised & hurried along with violence & then you get a severe shock the Boat either Laying with the head up so /) following a wave or driven before it thus (\ and the wave pursueing you as if determined to rush over you.

I brought Mrs Sherwood on shore and got a Barrack apartment which was very Large & consisted of Two Rooms but without any Furniture it had more the appearance of a Small Church we immediately got the Room furnished with a bed and made ourselves as comfortable as we could hoping for a Little enjoyment but on the next day 25th we received an order to embark again & on board the same Ship for Calcutta as soon as possible. Mrs Sherwood & myself went two or three days after landing to call on the Miss Layards our Fellow Passengers, they were with Doctor Anderson, Physician General at the Garden House about Two Miles as I guessed from the Fort. We went in Palankeenes in the Morning to Breakfast, it was nice & cool & the road shaded with Acacia & in some places fenced with Prickly Pears and Aloes and some Trees which I did not know. Doctor Andersons House was built open encrusted with the fine Chunam[74] (Mortar) After breakfast we called on his Son in law a Mr Young who is building a Beautiful palace it is all raized on smooth high Polished Chunam Pillars about 7 Foot from the Ground or probably more & is on a grand scale, it is flatt Roofed & surrounded by Palm Trees. The Season for Fruit is not come & what there was was very bad. The prices of Provisions we found to be a fowl in English Money about six Pence, a Leg of Mutton 7 Pence, Bread by the small loaf 2½ But the fowls are not so large as pigeons & the Mutton not weigh above 4 lbs the Quarter, The Eggs are like Pigeon eggs, Vegetables are out of season & Fish scarce.

I cannot be a judge of the Place from the short time I remained on Shore. I was obliged to make up a great many white Jackets & Pantaloons which are worn in India & I paid Three Rupees per Piece for nankeen, the Taylor worked fast but he could not get on without a pattern & I was told they can imitate very well but they have no invention, the Story goes so far as to say that an Officer sent an Old Coat as a Pattern to make a new One & that the old one was patched at the Elbow, the Taylor thought it necessary to put a patch upon the new one. Lieu^t Whittery being already tired of the Country was made an exchange with an Officer of the 73rd Reg^t & returns to England immediately. I wrote home to all my Friends by him.

---

[74] Chunam: lime, here used for a lime plaster made from calcined shells or limestone pounded finely and worked to a highly polished surface, very durable.

1805 September 2nd   Depart Madras

We embarked on the 2nd September on board the *Devonshire*, the same Ship which brought us from England & I got a better Cabin, it was one of those on the Quarter Deck under the Awning on the Starboard Side. We embarked 33 Officers and 7 Ladies

3   We got under weigh with very little wind in company with the Ships *Castle, Eden, General Stuart* & *Preston* under Convoy of the *Greyhound* Frigate. We proceeded up the bay. Mrs Sherwood is as sick as when she left England the first time. We soon lost sight of Madras.

4th   A Strong Wind with dark Clouds, we could only get a bad observation & we suppose our Latd to be about   14-36 N

5th   Rain all day with moderate Wind and a swell

6th   It rained but the Sun was caught about 12 o clock as it peeped through a watery cloud & we believe our   Latd 18-10

7th   A Fine day very hot.   Latd 19-30   Long 87-30

8th   At Day light we saw a Brig & a Country Boat and we made a signal for a pilot which was not answered they ran away towards Twelve we saw Three Ships the Frigate spoke to one, in the Evening we saw point Palmiras and we anchored at Night in Balasore Roads, all the night, at Day Light on the 9th we saw Point Palmira and soon after a small brig & Two Boats, we made signals for a Pilot, the Brig came & spoke the Frigate. At Twelve o clock we saw 7 Pilot Boats coming down & we got a Pilot on board there Lat^d was 21-3 fine clear weather. We came to an Anchor at night on the Edge of a Bank called the Eastern Sea Reef out of sight of Land.

10th   At Day Light we had considerable difficulty in getting the Anchor up, the Bottom being thick heavy mud brought down the Ganges, as we advanced Trees seem to rise out of the Water which was very much discoloured & full of Branches of trees floating. The Island of Sangor on which these trees grow is very low and covered with Brush wood, our Pilot says it is full of Tigers. He says it is noted for being a place of Worship where the Hindoos assemble at certain seasons to bath in the sea, that several devote themselves to death going into the Sea to be devoured by Sharks, he says he has known 30 carried away in a day so it seems that the worshipers never take precautions against tigers but suppose they are highly favoured by their God if a tiger seizes them. They also make vows that if their God will grant them so many Children they will sacrifice One at a Certain Age to the Sharks at Sangor or to an

Idol near Point Palmiras called Juggernaut.[75] He says that some years ago he was informed that a very fine Boy was to be sacrificed to the sharks & that he attempted to save him by going near the place in a Boat & carrying him away when he should be thrown into the water but altho he remained all day they were so careful he could not catch him. The Boy cried much, it appeared he was devoted being a Seventh Son of a Woman who had been barren some years.

In this island M[r] Munroe was seized by a Tiger, he was on Shore sitting with Another Gent[n] with Guns in their hands when a tiger sprung on M[r] Munroe & seized him by the Head, was carrying him off as a Fox does a Goose, the other Gent[n] fired on the Tiger who let M[r] Munroe fall but he had died almost immediately. The Tide carried us along & we passed several Ships at Anchor at Sangor. The Tide turned at 12 & we anchored close to a Low Point covered with brush wood & called Onud Point. The Natives came down the River in great numbers with Fruit, Fowls Eggs & they asked a Rupee for six Ducks. At 7 o clock on the 11th we again proceeded keeping close to the right hand of the River along a Low Muddy bank covered with reeds & Brush Wood, we could easily throw a stone on Shore. We anchored at Diamond Harbour. Large Ships go higher.

The Shore seems covered with Vultures and a Large Bird called an Adjutant which is something like the figure in the margin [sketch] & stands 4 Feet high its head seems raw & it has a large bag hanging down from the bottom of his Throat which holds his provisions.

A Sailor fell over board & was carried away & drowned immediately. We have only lost one Soldier in all our Passage from England.

Sep 12th   Remained on board in expectation of an order for the Regiment to Land, but found that it would require four or five days for Boats to be sent down and it was very unpleasant laying in a River at Anchor without being able to go on Shore for the Banks were deep mud, & when you got on Shore you find nothing but Brush Wood. I asked leave to go up to Calcutta, which having obtained I hired a small 8

---

[75] Juggernaut: a very large wagon bearing a figure of the god Krishna at Puri. Self-sacrifice: suicide, being crushed by the wheels.

oared Boat called a Panchway to take me to Calcutta, I am to pay One Guinea for it, the distance is 50 Miles.

13th The Boat which we hired yesterday did not come and we waited for it until the Tide was a considerable way up when we became impatient and called another. It was about Eleven oclock when we got clear of the Ship and at One The Tide beginning to Turn we stopped at a Tavern at Fulta. The River Bank was low all the way & covered with Brush wood, with numbers of small Hills, and herds of Cattle. The tavern was very comfortable. At first it appeared to me like a Gent^{ns} House & I thought there was some mistake. Mrs Sherwood heard a Buffalo & thought it was a Tiger coming to carry her away. I thought the place so pleasant after being at Sea I could willingly have remained. We got a Good Dinner & Tea with Two Bottles of wine, the Remains of which we put into the boat to comfort us on our passage, the expences were 13 Rupees which amounts as our Guineas go to £1-8. At Ten o clock at Night the Tide turned & we proceeded towards Calcutta.

1805 September 14th Calcutta

At Three o clock on the 14th we lost the Flood tide. We anchored off a small village. The river about as broad as the Thames at Putney. When the Sun arose I tried to make the boatmen understand that they must proceed, the current did not appear very strong. I tried all I could to make them comprehend me & at length by signes I got off. The Current was stronger than I had expected and it was 9 o clock before we saw the Fort. The Boatmen stopped and here again I was lost for the Men to talk to me and I to them but we could not understand each other at last I pushed the Boat from the Shore & pointed to the Town, said, "Calcutta."

 Still we did not understand each other, and we lay in the middle of the Stream for an hour, we did not advance and the heat was extreme. I made all the signs I could and the Boatmen talked so fast I was really quite angry and uneasy,

At length about 12 o clock I espied a Boat with a White man on board & I now found all that the people wanted was to know where I wished to go to & that where we first stopped was as near to the Fort as our present Situation, this being settled we crossed the River & my Trunks being seized by the Custom House Officers I gave Mrs Sherwood in charge to a Black Man who carried an umbrella & I followed my Trunks to the Custom House. The Officers of the Custom House immediately gave me up my Trunks & I soon reached the Crown & Anchor Tavern where I found M^rs S in good Quarters & we got a good Breakfast at 2 o clock. There we remained quiet at the inn (The Crown & Anchor) where we were for 24 Hours.

Old Fort Gaut, Calcutta. T & W Daniell. 1810.

On the 15th after Breakfast I went to Fort William and got a Barrack Room & with the Assistance of a Banyan or Native Broker I got a Bed & a Couple of Chairs & a Table, and M^rs S was settled to her satisfaction in a few hours. On the 16th I went to the Pay Masters Office to learn what I had to do. I saw nothing On my Road but the Government House which appeared very grand. People say it is larger than any European Palace. The Squares of Fort William & Calcutta are full of those Birds called Adjutants they are so tame that you pass close to them and they do not stir, their heads are bald with Two little Eyes, they look like some crows. Any Person who Kills one in Calcutta is severely fined, as they destroy the dead Bodies which are all thrown into the River, and they eat all putrid meat. I have not seen them described in any Book of Natural History.

On the 17th The First division of the Regiment landed and we find that the 67th Regiment which came with us from England and landed at Madras has followed us. This will probably move us as there is not room for two such Reg^ts in Fort William. I find myself overloaded with work which has accumulated on board ship. I have 15 Times 3 Muster

Rolls[76] of the Regiment to write & my Serg.t is not well. I tried a Black writer but he makes so many Errors I am afraid to trust him. I am therefore obliged to confine myself to writing and I scarcely moved out of the Room except early in the morning, until the 29th when I dined with M.r Dashwood. They live very Luxuriantly.

The Servants which I have engaged are 14 in number & I class them as follows

1 Kitmidgar 9 Rupees. He goes to market, oversees the Cook & waits at Table but he will not carry home what he buys and always charges about the value of a Penny for a Porter called a Coolie, like Boy

1 Musalchy 4 he cleans dishes & carries a lantern & is the Kitmudgars right hand man.

1 Beastie 4 Water Carrier

1 Matranir 4 A Woman who sweeps the Room &c.

1 Sirdah Bearer 6 He takes care of your Cloaths & cleans Boots

1 Mate d.o 5 Assists to clean Boots & takes care of Cloaths and sometimes assists Bearers to carry the Palankeen

5 Bearers 20 They carry me about in a Coffin

1 Washerman 7

1 Sircar 16 The banker to take care of my money

1 Cook 7

Total 82 Rupees Per Month or £10-17/2 Sterling yet I have not the number which I must have. A Palankeen is absolutely necessary as a European cannot walk in the Sun he would be liable to be struck Dead. There is not one of these servants that can possibly be dispenced with. The Private Soldiers are not allowed to go out of Doors between the Hours of 8 in the morning & five in the Evening. A native is born in a certain station & he would sooner die than do any thing which he was not born to do, or at least they say so. The Kitmudgar is a Mahomidan & probably a descendant of the Tartars yet he knows nothing of his Religion and he will not eat with a Christian. The Sirdar is a Gentoo[77] & he would not on any Account touch meat yet his business is to clean Boots. Now I cannot see the difference between touching Meat and touching the Skin. The Musalachy is of Low Cast he cleans Plates yet he pretends to say he will not clean a Boot, a whimsical circumstance occurred one Evening, I gave out a Wax Candle which I

---

[76] Muster Rolls: Sherwood's paymaster register of officers and men who were mustered for payment monthly.

[77] Gentoo: term for a non-muslim Indian.

had brought from England and I observed a great fuss among the Servants which I could not account for as the Kitmedgar (who speaks English) was absent. I heard the Sirdah calling the Musalchee but he was out and I could not get my Candle Lighted until the Kitmedgar came in when they pretended they should lose their Casts if they touched Tallow. I explained to them that it was wax and all went on very well. Their distinction of casts is much against their being converted to Christianity for they are brought up in the belief that in whatever situation they are born there they must remain & that they must not even rise from a lower to a higher Cast, and they will allow Christ is the God of the White men, should any One become a Christian he must leave all his Friends no one will eat with him.

Fort William is a well built regular fort on the left Eastern Bank of the most westerly branch of the Ganges, the Barracks are very large & commodious. As a captain I have two very large & convenient Rooms, the only thing against them is the great noise which is always made the whole being in One House with a Publick Gallery which is filled with Pedlars, Servants and Officers exactly like the Exchange. From our Windows we see a fine Grass Plot and an avenue of Trees with walks, always kept clean. The 67th Regiment arrived and are ordered immediately to proceed upwards of Five Hundred Miles to a place called Danapore on the Ganges near Patna.

I had an opportunity of seeing a great Hindoo Festival which they called Pujah [margin note Durgah Poojah] I went into one of their Houses at the Far end of which was a Frame on which stood a Woman (Goddess) with a Spear in her hand treading on a Kind of Devil, before these Images were numbers of Naked Boys howling a kind of song as hard as their throats would allow them & dancing in a terribly horrid Manner, to the Music of Tum Tums (a kind of Drum) and horns or Trumpets. It required you to hold your ears. In another place we saw a Dancing Girl. She moved one foot as we keep time and sang or rehearsed something going around the room & stopping opposite persons who were sitting on Benches round the Room she seemed to address them all. I sat myself down like the rest & she came & made a song at me, after which I received some Atar of Rosses for my Handkerchief. I understand this God or Goddess is worshipped three days & then he or she is abused & thrown into the River. I was so busy I could not go out but Mrs Sherwood saw him Thrown into the River.

An order is arrived that We are to proceed up the Country & not the 67th Regiment this will be so suddenly that we shall scarcely have time to prepare. As the Boats are collected for the 67th Reg^{t}.

1805 October 13th   1st River Journey, Calcutta to Dinapore, 550 Miles.

I had the Rheumatism and was laying on my couch in great pain, when the Sirdah came and neaded my knees and drove it away. My time is now fully taken up in getting Money & providing myself with a conveyance and we have no time to spare.

I got a Pinnace[78] with Two Rooms and Lt Andrews wishes to go with me we have taken him in. Our Bed Room is large enough for two couches and our Trunks. Lieut Andrews sleeps on a couch in the outward Room and we have a kind of Lobby where the White Servant stays.

A Pinnace with a Panchway in front. Balthazar Solvyns. 1807.

[78] Pinnace: a keeled boat with sail; crew of 16 to 20, sail, row or haul.

1st River Journey—Calcutta to Dinapore 1805-6

On the 13th October the 53rd Regt embarked & we sailed with the Tide. I now begin to look about me. We were in so great a hurry that we leave two Officers sick behind us and Captain Erskine died. He joined the Regiment at the same time that I did (in August 1798) and never was ill in the West Indias. As we pass Calcutta we were reminded of London, the Shipping I suppose brought it into our minds.

Octor 13th   As soon as you get clear of Calcutta the banks are frequented by the Brahmins Dead Bodies, and every few Yards is the remains of Funeral Piles or Bedsteads in which the Body has been brought to the River side but the unburnt Bodies floating down is still worse, some of them are stranded, and the Wild Dogs and Vultures eating them, thus the whole Bank is covered with human Bones, sometimes we see them floating, with Crows resting upon them and eating them. We anchored this evening close to a Dead Body which was very offensive, but we cannot get it removed, nor can we find a place free from them.

Cremations, and remnants, on the Ganges. 2015.

14th   The Current runs strong against us & we advance slowly we came to an Elegant Palace the Country House of the Governor General it is a fine Stone Building. We passed the Body of a child which is going to be burnt. It is laid on a hurdle of Bamboos there are three men forming a

Pile. The Child lays at a distance and the people appear very unconcerned. We stopped for the night near a small Village about 15 Miles from Calcutta here is an Indigo Factory & a Powder Magazine.

15 We again advanced, the Shore is fine & Flat, we came near Chandernagore & saw many ruined Houses which formerly belonged to the French among the rest one which is said to have been the first which was built on the Present plan, it belonged formerly to a Monsieur Le Chavalier, once Governor of Chandernagore about half after Nine we got opposite Chandernagore it brought to my remembrance Old Sir Digby Dentwho used to Talk of its capture.[79] He served either in the *Kent* or *Tiger* when it was taken by Admiral Watson in 1755 or 1756. There were then three Ships of the Line before it & now they tell me that a small loaded Brig could not get up, but I doubt it. We anchored a little further on near some Stables belonging to the Company[80] it is here they keep their Elephants. They are the first I have seen in the Country, there are only Two in the Yard, one Large and one small, the others are gone to bring provisions for themselves. Three Large ones soon arrived, One very large who knelt down & a Man tied a kind of Mattress on his back and then got upon it. They returned in about an hour heavily Loaded. I sent over to Chandernagar to buy Bread, Meat &c &c & when it arrived we again proceeded and soon came to a very fine looking town Belonging to the Danes it seems to mock the ruins of the French City they called it Chinsura, if I understand right. It rained almost all day. The Natives here seem very religious for we continually pass them standing up to their knees in the Water holding Beads in their hands & praying like this, bowing to it & throwing water on their heads, they are not in the least disturbed by our Boat. The Banks of the River are now Deep Mud, and in many places covered with Bamboos. In some places are large Marshy commons with Acacia growing & Asclapias Favota. We often meet Morinda, papa Palma Christa, several Cassias, Poinciana, Vinca & numerous Convolvulus Many palm Trees of different kinds & plenty of Plantains. The Plantain & the Shadock are the only Fruits and we have no kind of vegetables at this season except Onions.

The Birds flying about are a White Bird with long legs which seems like a Starling to be fond of the cattle, they tell me it is called a Paddy Bird & is not fit to eat, here are vulture Adjutants, several kinds of hawks & Kites, Crows innumerable, a good looking Bird about the size of a Thrush called Minoe, it is not good to eat, we see many snipes. There are

---

[79] Battle of Chandernagore, 17th March 1757. Colony taken from the French by *HMS Kent* & *HMS Tiger*.
[80] The Honourable East India Company, commonly referred to as 'The Company.'

1st River Journey—Calcutta to Dinapore 1805-6

numbers of Wild Dogs & Jackalls which howl so much during the Night they hinder our sleeping, We stopped for the Night at a small Village near Hoogly. Mr Andrews & myself went on Shore but as we advanced into the Village the Inhabitants ran into their houses & shut the Doors, but as soon as we passed they opened them again & followed us but except one or two who seemed more bold than the rest when we turned they all scampered off as hard as they could run.

16th October. The Banks of the river today are much clearer from Brush Wood, Bamboos & reeds. I shot a white Bird with long legs & a very long Bill, it was not good to eat. We Got a very favourable wind and I continued in advance until late in the Evening and completely lost the remainder of the Fleet, indeed I have not seen the great Body since yesterday but I saw a few straggling Boats. We Anchored near a low marshy common & when the Candles were brought in we had numbers of Insects which nearly extinguished them but they did not bite & White Ants which become blind and fly towards the light they swarm round it in such numbers that the Tables are soon covered. They fight each other & continue to pull each others wings off, they appear as a mass and soon after disappear without any person being able to discern what becomes of them you see nothing but wings left, during the night we were much disturbed by Jackalls which howled close to the Boat & continually woke us.

17th   The Fleet[81] appeared I therefore did not move, It rained a good deal & we lay at anchor by a broad Common on which grew quantities of Esclapias Favota [82][?] & a species of Cavia[83] called king Weed also a few stunted Acacias[84] called in India Baubles the thorns of which ran into my Leg & caused an Instant Numbness which alarmed me but it soon went off. The Fleet did not appear.

18th   The Weather cleared but no Fleet appeared until Evening it appears they were obliged to halt one day to form into regular order. The Colonel leads the Van followed by the Interpreter, & then the Major Adjutant, Quarter Master, Pay Master then the Officers of the Grenadiers followed by the Grenadier Company and each company according to seniority. The Rear brought up by the Light Company each Company distinguished by a Color & in this state we proceed, the

---

[81] The Regiment's fleet of about 100 boats carrying about 1000 men, some wives, plus servants and camp followers stretched about 2 to 3 Miles.
[82] *Esclapias [Favota?]* Indian Milkweed.
[83] *Cavia,* Cuphea Hisssipifolia, False Hissop.
[84] *Acacia mimosa* – Bauble tree.

Colonel making Signals like a Man of War to his Convoy, we must extend near Two Miles & we move like a Duck followed by Ducklings.

20th   At Day light the Signal for sailing being made (ie) Three Guns & the Union at the Main we advanced but only made four miles & stopped at a village called Mirzapoor. This day we only proceeded Three Miles by the Map[85] owing to the Winding of the River & the Current.

21st   Our Leadmost Vessel got a ground and delayed us almost the whole day. The country is very low and the River winds so much that we anchored within a quarter of a Mile of our last Nights station. Here is a Pagoda something like St Pauls on a small scale which we have been close to these last two days.

22   We still see the pagoda at Midea from the Place we anchored at night.

23rd   We came to the Village of Gondpalla.

24   Parachee, I went on Shore shooting. The Country fine and many Mangoe Groves. I could see nothing to shoot but a Crow.

25   Cossaralpoor, Great Number of Mangoes. I shot snipes & Doves.

26   The Country now becomes very pleasant. The Mangoe Groves cover half the Country. We passed the Village of Cutura, which is celebrated for Brass. We find great difficulty in making ourselves understood even by the Kitmidger who professes to speak English. Whenever we ask a question which he does not understand he always says, "yes." We asked him how far it is to Plassy, his Answer was Cutura before, he meant to say One day before Cutura, the next to Plassy.

27   Plassy. This Village will be memorable for Lord Clives[86] Victory over Suraja al Dowla[87] Nabob of Bengal from which we may date the English Power in India. According to Gholaum Houseen Khan[88] this Battle was fought on Thursday the 5th of the Mahometan Month of Shawail in the year 1170 which is the Christian Year 1756. The nabob moved with a Large Army against the English army (who were not above 5000 and most of those were natives). The Flames of battle were Lighted up. As Europeans and the English in particular were celebrated for skilful

---

[85] Sherwood refers elsewhere to the Map of the Ganges system by James Rennell FRS, 1786. See Maps.
[86] Lord Clive, Major General Robert Clive, (1725-1774) 'Clive of India' responsible for The East India Company's gaining supremacy over much of India for the British crown.
[87] Siradj ul Daulah, (1733-1757) last Nawab of Bengal 1756-1757, lost Bengal to Clive's forces at the Battle of Plassey in 1757.
[88] Ghulam Husain Khan (1727-?) historian: *Sair al-Muta'akhkhirin* (c. 1783) (A History of Modern Times) (*A History of the Mahomedan Power in India*)

management of Artillery, Col.' Clive began his Attack with a Cannonade so unremitted and Instantaneous as confounded the sight of his oposers and overcame their faculties of hearing.

He informs us that the Action was principally sustained by a Part of the Army under Meer Muddin[89] who being Killed by a Cannon Ball, the Treachery of Meer Jafficer succeeded in prevailing the nabob to order Moin Laal[90] (who still continued the Action) to retreat. It is said by the English that lord Clive did not intend to fight but was drawn into it by an Officer of Artillery, however it is clear that that day put us in possession of Bengal, formerly there was a palace at Plassy and it was noted for large Groves of Mangoes but they say the late Nabob felled most of the Trees & the River having altered course has swept away the Field of Battle. I saw many jackals and we have some reason to think that a Pack of them are following the Boats for the Offalls and that they will accompany us to Dinapore. They are not shyer than Dogs & they go in large Packs Howling all night long.

28th   We were moving all day but at night we found ourselves still at Plassey, near a large house belonging to a Grandson of a Servant of M.r Hastings[91] they call him Rajah But I do not know what the meaning of rajah is for he cannot be a Prince.

29th Oct.   We passed some most beautiful spots & Groves of mangoes. I employ myself all day in copying my muster Rolls and in the Evening M.rs Sherwood, Andrews & myself stroll about among the Groves and I carry a Gun in case any Birds appear. We in General bring home 2 or 3 Doves & I this day shot a Wild Duck. It cannot be expected that so large a fleet can be provided with provisions from the Villages: we therefore brought from Calcutta Poultry of all Kinds, salt & dried Meat and Biscuits and a Dove is now & then acceptable. We are to prepare by sending on to the great Towns to increase our Stock whenever an opportunity occurs we see numbers of Wild geese & Ducks Flying about but at so great a height there is no getting at them. We passed through a New Cut in the River which saves several miles.

30th   We reached a bend in the River within sight of a principal Military Station called Berhampore.

31st   We reached Berhampore this morning but the Fleet anchored on the other Side, here are very large & commodious Barracks for upwards of 1400 Europeans, but now unoccupied. The Station formerly protected

---

[89] 'Meer Muddin' Mir Madan Khan, one of the nabob's generals at Plassey.
[90] 'Moin Lal' Mohan Lal, one of the nabob's generals at Plassey.
[91] Warren Hastings (1732-1818) Governor General 1773-85.

our Factory at Cossimbazar[92] & was a check on the great City of Moorshedabad the Residence of the Nabobs of Bengal, the Country through which we have passed is very rich & so populous that it seems like one continued Village. We remained at anchor near Berhampore until the 3 of November in which time I wrote Letters both Private & on business to every person with whom I correspond. In the evening we walked out on a raised Dyke shaded by Trees which ran along the River as far as we could walk or see, it was very pleasant as the Heat at this Time of the year is very moderate. I only crossed the River once to take my Letters to the post office & I did not see the whole Cantonment.

3rd November   We proceeded from Berhampore and passed Cossimbazar which is not at present on the Banks of the River but it was formerly The Bed of the River has now taken a direct line from Moorshedabad. I suppose it to be about 6 miles by water from Berhampore to the beginning of the City which lies on the Eastern Side of the River. Our Fleet kept the Western bank which is a kind of Suburb. The Number of Boats opposite the town was very great but the magistrates had ordered them all to move to the East Bank otherwise we should have been detained some days with so large a fleet as it is necessary to pass every Track Rope over the masts of the boats at Anchor. As it was we got on but slowly & we reached the opposite shore about half way through Moorshedabad – This City has been the residence of the Sabahs or Nabobs of Bengal but I do not know when it was built but I find in 1739 an Adventurer named Mirza Mahomet Ali,[93] killed his Relation & Prince Soferaz Khan[94] & usurped the Government & by Means of Bribery contrived to get himself confirmed by the mogul, he sent a Million of Rupees, and Seventy Hundred Thousand Rupees value in Jewels as presents, he lived to a good old age & left his grandson as his Successor a wild young man who attacked the English, took Calcutta and put the English in the Black hole, he once wished to prevail on his Grandfather whose Assumed name was Aleverder Khan to attack the English. The Old man made him this Answer. My Son if you Kindle a Flame you know that even on Land it is difficult to extinguish it, how much more difficult will it be to put out the Sea if on Fire. The Young Surajah Dowla however set fire to the Sea & was destroyed. The English

---

[92] Cossimbazar EIC Factory, a fortified silk trading station built 1652 for English merchants.
[93] Mirza Mohammad Ali, birth name of Ali Vardi Khan (1671-1756) Nawab from 1740.
[94] 'Soferaz Khan' Sarfaraz Khan, (after 1700-1740) Nawab of Bengal 1727 and 1739-1740. Killed in battle by Ali Vardi Khan.

placed Jaffier Ali Khan[95], on the Musmud but soon after deposed him & placed in his room Cossim Ali[96] his Son in Law. Cossim was placed in an awkward situation. The Companies servants for their private advantage inserted in the Treaty that all the Covenanted servants had a right to trade duty free, this soon gave rise to a quarrel for the English sold their protection to every Black Merchant who would pay for it & the duty in the nabobs Dominions were likely to be reduced to Nothing. Cassim complained, but Private interest prevailed even against positive orders from England & the consequence was a War in which Cassim murdered all the English in his Power at Patna & in the end he was expelled & Jaffier Ali reinstated but with very limited power, which was even less in the reigns of his three Sons, and is now a meer Nominal Power, under his Grandson who calls himself the Lion of War. They say he feels hurt at his situation & is constantly Drunk.

Near Gangwaugh Colly on the River Hoogly. T & W Daniell. 1810.

We crossed the River in a small Boat (Mrs Sherwood, Andrews & myself) we entered a Pagoda in which was an Idol with an Elephants head a big Belly & Number of hands. [Ganesh] The blacks threw themselves on the Ground before him & struck their foreheads against the Ground. It appears that the Inhabitants were much frightened at us as we were

---

[95] 'Jaffier Ali Khan' Mir Jafar Ali Khan (1691-1765) Nawab of Bengal 1757-60 & 1763-65. Supported by East India Company.
[96] 'Cossim Ali' Mir Kasim Ali Khan (?-1777) Nawab of Bengal 1760-1763 deposed by East India Company.

followed by at least 500 People who vanished in an Instant when we turned towards them & appeared again in our Rear. The City seemed nothing more than an assemblage of little sheds about six feet square here we see silver smiths with a little fire of Charcoal making Silver ornaments, the whole apperatus not worth Six pence. Thay Blow the Fire through a Bamboo tube. Brasiers are at work in the same way. We now and then saw a house rather better, but nothing more than a kind of porch, such as are often at the entrances of churches, these better kind of houses are occupied by Bankers, Money Changers & Men who sell Cloth Muslin &c. We were shewn a God manufactory. They make their Gods of straw & then plaster them over with clay leaving the Sun to bake them, here we saw (As our interpreter informed us) Durgah the Wife of Seib riding on an Ostrich. The Ostrich seemed well done, but the Ladies Eyes are all very long. Seib himself had a movable jaw like a pair of Dutch nut crackers. I asked leave to touch him which was allowed. We are told that these Gods are to be worshiped in about Ten days & then thrown into the River. We met in the Narrow streets a large Elephant with Three Men on its back & altho they say they are quite harmless yet there is something in the first appearance which rather alarms.

4th November. We passed Bernagur a Town on the Western banks of the Hoogly it is much better than the City opposite the houses in Gardens full of Flowers, the Principal, Poinciana and Balsams with a few Vinca. We got a great many into our Boats. We entered a narrow cut which takes off a long Angle in the River, and anchored at Dysabad, here a Man came with Fruit & Vegetables pretending they were a present from the nabobs Secretary but he required a present of a rupee in return, I believe he only imposed upon us.

5th of November we passed a fine Country to a few Miles below Jungipore

6th We stopped at Jungipore, here is a large house belonging to a Brother of Lord Dalhousie, he invited the Col.l to Dinner.

Jungipore As we halted to day & I had little to do I will describe my Boats. In the first place the Pinnace has a verandah where the European sits, a Hall Sixteen Feet long & 14 Wide, and a Bed Room 12 Feet square, the Vessel itself is about the size of a Gravesend Boat[97] but formed for the Ganges, the Rooms being built very high above the Body of the Boat. She is drawn by 16 men who on

---

[97] Gravesend Boat: Thames sailing barge.

1st River Journey—Calcutta to Dinapore 1805-6

Occasion Row 16 Oars. The upper works are latticed all round and you may open the whole, next to the Pinnace I have a cooking Boat, which is formed like a Cottage built on a Boat and in this our Servants live. She is calculated to carry 24,000 [lbs.] Weight we have also a small Canoe a Panchway to carry us from our large Vessel. The Larger ones are not allowed to move out of the Ranks. The Expences for the use of these three Boats from Calcutta to Dinapore is Sixty pounds Sterling, the Distance being calculated according to an average 450 miles for Six Weeks.

7 We proceeded & Anchored near Gheriah, here a great Battle was fought between the English & Cossim Ali's Troops which seemed to be the destruction of all Cossim's plans.[98] Agreeable to Rennals[99] map we ought to be near the Great River but the Boat Men say we are yet several days off it appeared to me that we are going more to the westward.

8th We passed (if I understand right). Sooly which lies on the Ganges agreeable to the Map but we do not see any appearance of a large River than the one we are upon which is very shallow we can scarcely get the Boats along. We stopped to day near a Village called Moangange

9th We proceeded all day to day & about four o clock we were just at the entrance of the Hoogly. I believe we have travelled from Jungapore at least 26 Miles or probably 30. The Map lays it down as only 10 but the River winds very much as we often saw the rear of the fleet (which ought to be Three Miles behind us) just across a Field.

10th The opening of the Hoogly is very narrow & the current strong we entered the Ganges early this morning but we were suprized to find it not above half a Mile broad. We had been given to understand we could scarcely see across however I found that we were opposite an Island & near a Village called Pockyria this explains the distance between Jungipore & the Ganges as we have entered the River 14 Geographic Miles West of this old opening & I understand that almost every Year the Ganges makes a fresh opening. The hoogly is dry here from the end of December to the beginning of June. We find ourselves only Six Miles below Ouda Nulla famous for its siege in 1763. The river widens very much & runs straiter and not so rapid as the small River, great numbers of Ducks and Geese fly over our Heads but they are very high. The

---

[98] Battle of Geriah, August 1763. Mir Kassim.
[99] Major James Rennell (1742-1830) Surveyor-General of Bengal, 'Father of Indian Geography.' 1776 Map of Ganges basin (Calcutta to Benares), scale 1:816,000. 1786 Map of the Ganges catchment, scale 1:400,000. Rennell's survey was the basis of atlases in 1794 and 1804 but none found online include all placenames as given by Sherwood as on a map.

boatmen say we shall have good shooting soon. Col.[l] Mawby received a present of Fruit & Fish today. He sent half a Fish which weighed when whole 10 lb it had the appearance of Salmon but eat like Cod.

11th   We continued to have large Islands in the River & we could seldom get a view of the breadth indeed I believe we never did get a distinct view. We passed Ouda Nulla but I did not see it and we stop.[d] about half way to Raja mahal.

12th   We reached Rajamal. The Ruins of the Palaces are very fine they have been partly swept into the River & lay in heaps we found great difficulty in passing as the current rushed so violently past the Ruins. Andrews & myself went on Shore to examine the Ruins, we found a large palace as they tell us built by a Soubah of Bengal 500 Years ago, some of the Rooms are in good repair. One in particular which was the place of private worship is coated with white marble and beautifully inlaid with Persian Letters in black marble but the place being so neglected travellers have picked out whole sentences. I endeavoured to get one of the letters out but it was so firm I could not succeed. We saw the remains of many Palaces, Mosques, Gateways &c. There was also a large Caravansarai and a very large Well which must have been very old, as a Great Tree grew out of its sides & sent its roots to the bottom in search of Water.

13th   Cap.[n] Lambourn invited us to breakfast in the old Palace, he took his Table on Shore & took possession of a Balcony of the Palace which is over the River, we had as fine views of our fleet which were all day passing the Ruins and we found we must remain all Day. Colonel Mawby sent for his Dinner & we remained in our Quarters. From Cap.[n] Lambourn who has been 27 Years in India I endeavoured to learn as much as I could of India. I learnt from him that at a little distance on the other side the River lays the Ruins of a very large City called Gour & the remains are still very grand but all ruins are alike a mixture of Pagodas over run with Shrubs, Trees &c. with Mosques & Gateways in fact just like Rajamal only larger, it is now dangerous to go to Gour the place is infested with Wild Hogs, Tygers & Serpents and it is particularly remarked that the Hogs delight in inhabiting the Mahomedan Mosques, he says that since his remembrance the River has carried away many buildings at Rajamal & that it seems as if it was endeavouring to force its way to the south and that it now takes a Southerly direction 20 Miles from where it did when he came to the Country. Cap.[n] L Wishes to prove Palabothra to be Patna, from the Resemblance of Pale Pana, Patnam &c meaning a City near a Warf or Passage across a river but as Patna has only retained its first name of City I do not know if he is right, it appears from him that the River Goan formerly entered the Ganges at Patna, that

1st River Journey—Calcutta to Dinapore 1805-6

the only reason against this is that the distance from the Sea & from other places does not agree but the Antients do not seem to have a good idea of distances in India. A very fine Ridge of Woody Hills approach the River near Rajamal, the Inhabitants of which are a distinct race to all appearances, they are shorter & thicker set. They have no Casts and seem naturally Enemies to the Lowlanders with whom they were formerly always at war & I am told that numbers of English Officers have been killed or wounded in different expeditions undertaken against them.

Augustus Cleveland's house, Bhaghalpur, now a university faculty. 2015.

M[r] Cleveland[100] who was stationed in the Civil Service at Banglipore [Bhagalpur] has contrived to gain them over so completely that we can now depend on them better than any Natives & a Corps has been raised who do all the duties in the past. A Company of them were on duty armed with Bows & Arrows with which they are so expert that they very soon knocked a Rupee down which was placed against a Tree about 50 Yards off & the fellows went off & all got drunk with the money which was given them. When drunk they did not appear quarrelsome but laughed without ceasing when they found they could not walk. They believe themselves to be descended from the first created of men who

---

[100] Augustus Cleveland (1754-84) Collector of taxes and judge, Bhagalpur, Bihar.

were originally seven & these 7 were placed in the Hills of which those of Rajamahal are a part. That their Ancestor, the Eldest falling Sick, the others disputing among themselves, separated, carrying their provisions with them which they had collected. The Two Eldest (after the sick one) Loaded themselves with all kind of provisions & went a long way off. The 2 next could not find quite so much particularly they could not find any Pork, they did not go so far. The 2 Youngest had only a little Rice, they therefore settled immediately under the Hills. The Eldest Brother however recovered & finding himself stripped, ordered his descendents always to make war & get the rest of the world. They soon found the descendents of the 2 Middle ones in the Afgawns & Mahomedans but they could hear no living of the 2 Eldest until the European appeared. They had also a tradition that the descendants of the 2 eldest would reconcile them to the rest, this was of great use to Mr Cleveland but they never mention any thing of women being created.[101]

November 14th We advanced today about Ten Miles and Anchored near a Village of Invalide Seapoys, the Government have lately given Pensions & uncultivated land to many invalids & Men who have served a certain time, it is said they keep the Country in order. The natives being very fond of Pillageing each other & murders are constantly committed for the most trifling gain.

We saw the Print of a tigers Foot in the sand. It was Immensily large, this part of the Country under the Hills is very much frequented by them. The Mountaineers it is said formerly used to think they had entered into a treaty with them & they of course never killed them except the Tigers broke the treaty by hurting one of them, it was then the custom to send round the Villages & the Inhabitants would collect & hunt the Tigers until they had one or more as retaliation after which they thought they had given them a proper lesson they returned to their heits & the treaty was supposed to be in force again. The English have now caused a deadly war by giving a Reward of Ten Rupees for every Tigers head brought to a Collector & it is extraordinary how many are now killed. Wild Boars are very common—the English Gentlemen are fond of Hunting them which is very dangerous as they will rip up a Horse if the Rider does not spear the Hog in time, they say a Boar will fight a Tiger & sometimes has been known to kill it. The Rhinosceros is also common about this part of Bengal.

15th Novr We this day advanced to Sicely Gully a very pretty Village The Hills about it are well wooded we scrambled up a Hill on which is a

---

[101] Sauria Paharia, a tribe in the hills, from Son River, west of Patna.

1st River Journey—Calcutta to Dinapore 1805-6

Mosque probably the remains of a Fort which guarded the Pass for here is only a very narrow passage between the Hills & the River, the word Gully means a Pass, from the top we had a beautiful extensive view of the North West of the River and the fine Country it brought to my remembrance the West Indies and with a little fancy I made it like the View of Chock bay & Pigeon Island from the Vigue St Lucia

16th We coasted all day along Sandy Island & were much troubled with the sand which blew about.

17th We reached Pointy a very pretty place, the Country like Sicely Gully

18   Halted at Bidersroon or Patten Gotly. We were taken by the Boatmen up a very steep Hill to see a Cavern which they say has no bottom. One of our Guides said he had advanced near a Mile into it. We were too much afraid of Serpants, that we only looked in & Mr Hays would go in but it was so close & hot that he was glad to return

19   Passing the Point of Pattergotly we saw numbers of figures carved on the Rocks, some very large we soon came to Cilgong, here are 2 or 3 Islands in the Middle of the River formed of Immense Rocks, some Fackeers have taken possession of one of them. We advanced to a Sand bank & anchored near another Seapoy Invalide Colony

20th We crossed to the northern bank of the River.

21st We reached as near Banglypore as the Great River would allow us and we stopped under a kind of Common. Banglipore lays on a smaller Channel which is only navigable some part of the Year. I bought a Pea hen which had been Shot & we thought it good eating there are great numbers wild in all Bengal.

22nd Our Fleet remained all day to collect & also to give the opportunity to repair any damage but I did not stir out. The sandy plain had nothing to tempt me

23rd We advanced & soon entered a small Channel, our course was more Southerly for 4 or 5 Miles after which we stood more to the west this Channel is not laid down in the map. We stopped again at a Seapoy Colony, they seem to line the shores.

24th This day we had some delightful prospects, the Country was very fine, particularly at Jangara,[102] where there is a high Bold Rocky Island rising abruptly in the Middle of the River. There seems to have been a Castle on it but it is now inhabited by Fackers. The Bank of the River advanced boldly towards the Island & only allows a narrow passage for

---

[102] Jangara island, now a popular mainland pilgrimage site.

the River which is very rapid, the Shore is formed of large masses of rock most of them carved into Gods & Goddesses.

Our Boatmen were obliged to scramble over these rocks and they had great difficulty in pulling the Boats, several times the Eddys took us & whorled us round striking us against the sides, putting us in some Danger, we just moved far enough to give room for our Rear & we stopped at a Village where we found very large Mangoe Groves. I gathered the Zombie beads[103] the first I had seen in India. We saw a number of Partridges.

Jangara by Sherwood above. In 2014 below.

25.   The river very shallow we are sometimes on one side & sometimes on the other, altho we track slowly on the Southern sides but our Boatmen are up to their waists in water & in general keep the middle of the River, & sometimes are nearer the land on the North Shore.

26th   This morning we came to Sittacund here is a hot spring worshipped by the natives. I went to it. We found the Bramins had got

---

[103] Zombie or Jumblie beads: bright orange-brown seed of the Necklace Tree, *Ormosia coarctata*.

possession of it. I could scarcely hold my hand in it, it was clear & bubled up in the Centers as if boiling, the poor natives purchased permission to wash away their Sins & some brought a quantity of Water away with them. I am told the water is the same as at Bath. The Tradition of the origin of this Water is that Ram (who is one of Vishnoos Incarnations) lost his Wife who was seized & detained by Ravun the Giant of Ceylon for Ten Months. Ram however destroyed Ravun & regained his Wife, who to prove herself chaste jumped into Boiling Water & came out safe, the Water has been boiling ever since. On a Hill a little distance from the well is a Building which resembles an English Church it is seen from a great distance. It was built by an Officer lately in Siddeahs Service who lives on a Pension given him by the English, I believe his name is Beckett.

27 November. This morning early we reached Monghyr. This Place is known in the History of the Mogul Empire. This Fort is very large & seems to have been regular, it is now Ruins. We saw One side of a Wall & a ditch. The Antient Subahs made Monghir their Residence & we hear of it several times, as being the Fort where the unfortunate Brothers of the Moguls have withstood more fortunate Brothers, Cassim Ali Resided here when he was planning the quarrels with the English. Monghir is noted for all kinds of Iron Work & a Gun Manufactory also cabinet making. The Monghir Black Wood Chairs & Couches are in general use. Here are also numbers of Birds for Sale Parrots & Mountain Miners, the Miners learn to speak possibly better than any other Bird, they are about the size of a Black Bird with Two Yellow fleshy substances on each side of the head like Ears

28th We got a fine Wind to day & we sailed rapidly along for 24 Miles we reached Pipiliah, during our Run to day we lost sight of the Mountains, the Country is now quite flat but pleasant very rich & numbers of Mangoe Trees.

29th The Wind failed today & we were much detained by the frequent shallows. We halted at a very dirty Village called Machiah inhabited mostly by a low cast of People who feed Hogs. We bought a sucking Pig & our Boatmen pretended great horror at our bringing it into the Boat, but I believe it is all Affectation, during the Night we had a tremendous Thunder Storm, and heavy Rain. Capn Lambourne says he never saw such a Storm in November since he has been in India 28 Years.

[Margin note This is all nothing I shall have occasion to remark that we must not believe what old Indiamen say.]

30th The Current strong & the River shallow, we reached a Seapoy Colony very pleasantly situated, here is an Officers house called a

Bungalow but it is only inhabited for a day or two at a time when the regulating Officer goes round. This Colony has been long settled and is composed of a Subidah (Black Captn) 4 Jemmidahs or Black Lieutenants & 20 Noncom Officers & Privates, their houses are very neat & surrounded by Gardens, they form a great contrast with the other natives.

Dec 1st We passed by Bar in the middle of the day & consequently I could not get out of the boat & the Channel of the River was so low I did not even see a trace of it. Bar is by some supposed the Palibothra of the Greeks, but it seems only from its agreeing in Instances, which probably are erroneous.

2nd As we approach the end of our Journey I left the Fleet & went forward after the Colonel who left us. On the 30th we anchored at a distance from a Village & the Boatmen told us we must be on our Guard all night we therefore placed a Guard. Andrews, myself & my Servant Parker. We loaded our Fowling Pieces & Pistols, but we were not disturbed.

3rd Late this Evening we reached Patna having travelled 20 miles.

4th I got up early to see the Famous City of Patna, our Boat had halted during the night in the suburbs, we entered the City by a flight of Steps and we proceeded along a narrow street or Bazar, the houses on both sides full of Shops, we walked through this Bazar nearly Three Miles, every Body seemed full of business & small shops of about 6 Foot square, where were Braziers, Silver smiths, Sweetmeat Makers & particularly Table Cloths & and Towels for which Patna is famous. Wood work is also cheap. They work here with a lighter Colored Wood called Sissoo, we purchased Two Seats for Children with Birds & Beasts they cost about a Shilling a piece. The Streets are Terribly dirty & we could not see any very fine buildings, there were many remains of Old mosques & Pagodas built of Bricks very small & thin & the Old Walls which are washed by the River have rather a fine appearance. The Gauts or Warfs are mostly of Stone & have formerly been short like Salliports. The Walls are all of an immense thickness. Our Boat overtook the Colonel and we reached Dinapore late in the Evening.

1805 December 4th   Dinapore

5th   Andrews & myself went into the Cantonement of Dinapore to look for Quarters.

We found the Cantonement a Noble place which put us in mind of some publick Building at home. It is composed of two Squares the Principal one is just 750 Yds within the Barracks, it is an oblong square, the One Long Side towards the South & West is a long range of Soldiers Barracks of One Story Capable of holding near 2,000 Men. The opposite side is Officers, in the Exact Centre of which is the Ruin of a very large House built for the Commandant but now going to ruin as Government do not think it worth while to repair it. Government have sold all the Officers Quarters as they find it better worth their while to allow the Officers House Rent than to keep up such large Quarters at their expence, a Captain Receives 90 Rupees per Month to find his own Quarters which is very liberal, I hired a very nice Quarter for 60 Rupees—it contained Eight rooms, with Servants Houses & cook Houses detached. I soon got my goods on shore & I was quite settled to dine on Shore. I now wrote all my Friends in England. We heard of Peace being made with Scindeah & Holkar[104] is driven into the upper Country we have no prospect of moving soon. We like Dinapore but our men are getting unhealthy. We lost 15 Men the first 14 Days. The weather gets very cold & we are glad to shut up our Houses & light a fire, almost all houses have one room with a fire place in it. Dinapore is reckoned one of the cheapest parts of India, we buy the smaller fowls for a Rupee 3 or 4 Large Roasting Fowls 7 Rupees a lean Sheep 12 Annas a Quarter of Fat Mutton half a Rupee. Butter forty ounces per Rupee Eggs 100 per Rupee. And we contract with a Gardener to furnish as many vegetables as we want for 4 Rupees per Month. Bread is 22 small Loaves for a Rupee. My servants are the greatest expence amounting to an Average to 115 Rupees per month, or £14.7.6. My Pay Allowance per 30 Day Month is 506 Rupees or £63-5. On the 15th we were invited to Dine with a major at Dinapore, it is of little use to write what passed each day as I scarce had any thing but our own parades to which I walk in the Evening & during the day I am busy with Accounts. Mrs Sherwood was brought to Bed of a son on the 25 December.

---

[104] Scindeah & Holkar: Shrimant Daulat Rao Scindhia (1779 -1827) Maharaja of Gwalior; Yashwant Rao Holkar (1776-1811) Maharaja of Indore, both Marathas.

1806 My Little Boy was Baptized Henry[105] by the Rev[d] Doctor Stacy Chaplain to the Station. He is an Oxford man & rather Elderly with a family of Eleven Children, he has only been three years in India. The weather got warmer towards the end of the Month. The Trees in Cantonements shed their leaves, a curious instance of the Superstition of the Natives happened. I employ a native Money changer to avoid receiving Bad Money this man whose name is Mootie Ram or the Pearl of Ram is rather elderly he tells me that his wife had a vision that it is necessary she should go on Pilgrimage to the Temple of Juggernaut, which is by the Sea in Orissa near the Entrance of the Hoogly.

The Husband & wife therefore set off at 12 Hours notice on a journey which must have taken them six months.

I bought a carriage drawn by Two Bullocks. The Bullocks of India have a Hump on the Shoulders. We hear that Holkar has made a Peace & Lord Lake[106] is returning from the Field. The end of this month is very cold and almost all the Trees are without Leaves.

February

This month Set in with Rain very cold which is said to be unusual at this time of the year. We begin to have greater plenty of Fowls & Vegetables Potatoes are as good as in England the weather gets warmer & we have frequent squalls of wind as the month advances which blows the dust about. I remarked an Assemblage of swallows as it is in England at this Season. I do not recollect when I first perceived them but they are now very common. It is possible I may have overlooked them before. The Trees begin to bud. I purchased 20 Sheep the best of the Flock at 12 Annas per Sheep. I remarked that all the Sheep here are black & nearly all the Cows light colored approaching to white. The heat increases towards the end of the Month & we are preparing for the hot Winds by making what they call Tattas[107] which are made of the shoots of a kind of Odoriferous Grass something like a thin door mat on a frame with these we are to close the windows and doors on the North West side of the House & to keep them wet the wind coming through them cools the whole House & Stronger the Winds

---

[105] Henry, Sherwood, 1st son, (25 Dec 1805 Dinapore-25 Mar 1807 buried at Berhampore).

[106] Gerard, 1st Viscount Lake (1744-1808) C-in-C India 1801-1805, 2nd Anglo Maratha War.

[107] Tattas, open-weave mats hung over open windows and kept damp to cool the house by evaporation.

Dinapore 1805-6

blow the cooler the House will be, the mornings & Evenings are getting very pleasant they were formerly rather cool.

March

The Month of March set in with a few windy days rather warm but it got cool again. The Trees became beautifully Green. The Principal Tree here is the same which I once & only once met with in the West Indias & Weston told me it was Lilac, however it appears to be the Neem, or Melica,[108] it is very common and has a pretty flower with a pleasant smell.

Golghar Granary at Patna, built 1776 for 138,000 tons of grain. 2015.

On the 26th Mr Rickets the Collector of Bihar,[109] to whom was brought Letters from Mrs Dashwood in Calcutta, invited me to dine. He sent over an Elephant for Lt Groombridge & myself & we boldly mounted on its back, the motion is very unpleasant. At Bankipore 8 miles from Dinapore is a large Granary called a Gola, it is built like the Dome of St Pauls it has

---

[108] Neem, or Indian lilac, Azadirachta indica, mahogany family, Meliaceae.
[109] Mordaunt Ricketts (1786-1862). East India Company service in India from 1802-1830 rising to Resident (Ambassador) to the court of Ghazi ud din Haider King of Oudh at Lucknow and his son. Dismissed for corruption having considerably greater funds than his salary could produce, dismissal upheld by Enquiry 1831, pension refused 1836 despite appeal. Case used as a warning to EIC employees.

never been used and it has so good an Echo that it repeats 32 Times and it acts exactly as the whispering Gallery at St Pauls.

We dined with Doctor & M^{rs} McNabb who are mentioned in Bissats life of Burke. This is the Mahomedan Holydays called Mohurrum, to commemorate the death of Hosseen the Son of Ali who was starved in the desert. The Streets are full of wild looking Fellows all drunk carrying Banners & representations of Tombs smiting their breasts & calling out in a melancolly voice oh Hosseen Hoseen. The English Soldiers & even the Blacks when they speak English call it Hopson Jopson. [Hobson Jobson]^{110} Mr Keating, Chief Judge of the Court of Appeal for the Division of Bihar has much scandalized the Christians by building a Mosque & openly protecting the Mahomedans & paying a number of mahomedan Priests, he is even suspected of believing the Mahomedan Religion he is a poor Glutton who has reduced himself as much by eating as noted others do by drinking.

I received a Letter on the 29th from my Uncle Maskall^{111} dated London 24 Sepr all well and no News. I saw in the Newspaper an Acc^t of a House having been discovered in Crowle Wood Worcestershire under ground supposed to be the retreat of some sheep stealers it strikes me this house has something to do with the Ghosts which we used to hear infested Abberly Hill.

A Portugese Ship arrived which saw the English Fleet entering the Bay at the Cape of Good Hope & that as she came away she saw the French Frigate that attacked our Fleet on the 6th August last The Portugese does not know if the English succeeded as (to use his own words) he thought it best to be out of Harms way — Vegetables received are in great plenty this month, Cabbage Artichokes Cauliflowers &c &c & fruit is coming in.

April

Mr Rickets invited the whole family to spend a week at Bankipore & we set off on the 6th in the Bullock carriage, Garden Chairs & Palankeen. We met with much civility from Mr Rickets & the other Gent^n residing at Patna. Major Stuart & Doctor McNabb. Mr Rickets has a number of men employed cutting a kind of Pebble just like Scotch Pebbles, they are found in the River Loam. The Weather begins to be very warm & all wood work if not very well seasoned or covered with cloth, cracks & warps astonishingly. In Mr Hills Shop a large Pier Glass cracked from

---

[110] Hopson Jopson: Hobson Jobson, title of 1886 book of Indian terms and words used by Europeans.
[111] Mr Maskall, Sherwood's maternal uncle.

Dinapore 1805-6

Top to Bottom & the Glasses break on the table. We returned to Dinapore on the 12th.

On the 20th The Hot North West Wind blew, but we were kept cool by the Tattas if you only put yourself in the draft it seemed like crossing the mouth of a heated oven.

On the 22d the Wind was Easterly & not much of it, except for about half an hour every day when we had violent North West Squalls. We received a Letter from Lucy[112] brought by Capn Thomas a Brother of Mrs Whitmore My Old English writing desk was so much contracted by the heat that it could not be opened.

May

During the Month of May the People told us we were to have hot winds so bad that we could not move out however we were disappointed as the Wind blew from the East with occasional squalls, which brought on Showers of Rain. A Large Fleet arrived from England. They took the Cape of Good Hope[113] on their way out.

June

It began to Rain in Showers on the 2d and on the 6th it rained very violently. I wrote home Publick & Private Letters. It is reported that the Regiment is immediately to go down the River to make Room for some Regt which is leaving the Field. On the 9th I rode over to Bankipore to see Mr Rickets. The Rains had been so heavy that we could scarcely get our Horses over the road between the Barge & Bankipore. We have no Official orders to go to Berhampore but the reports are as strong as ever. The Poultry during the heats of April & May get swelled heads & die. We hear that 125 Men have Volunteered to the 53rd Regt from the 75th Regt which is ordered home.

The Official order at length arrived for our proceeding by Water to Berhampore as soon as Boats can be collected. Mr Rickets was kind enough to hire me a Sixteen oared Budgerow.

This is different from a Pinnace in being Flat Bottomed & rising high in the Water it is said to be more dangerous in windy weather but safer when they run aground as they draw so little water, I am to pay Monthly wages of 8 Rupees per Oar & to take it for the Trip that is to allow One Month for altho we shall probably go in a week yet they calculate the distance to be One Month which is averaging with and against the Stream. Mr Rickets has invited us to spend a week with him. I therefore

---

[112] Lucy Lyttelton Butt (1781-1858), Mrs Cameron. Mrs Sherwood's sister.
[113] Battle of Blaauberg, January 1806, the British won the Cape from the Dutch.

did all my business by the 30th & got leave to drop down before the Fleet, it has rained almost every day in June.

1806 July 1st   2nd River Journey, Dinapore to Berhampore, 365 Miles.

A Budgerow. Balthazar Solvyns. 1807.

On the first having settled all my business Mrs Sherwood & myself embarked on a 16 Oared Budgerow & in the afternoon we dropt down the River to Deega to make Mrs Stacy a call. Doctor Stacy was not at home but Mrs Stacy made Mrs Sherwood pass the Evening & stay to Dinner. The River has a very different appearance now to what it had when we came up in Decr. The whole bed is not covered with water, you can occasionaly distinguish what the Boats are on the opposite side.

On the 2nd we reached Bankipore and we were kindly received by Mr Rickets. We Heard from the Colonel that the Regiment were positively to sail on the 6th. The wind was however so high from the East that we that we thought it impossible they could attempt the move & I engaged myself out to Dinner. We were astonished to see the whole fleet in the midst of the River about Ten o clock. They appeared like a fleet in a Gale of Wind they could not advance against the Wind notwithstanding the current, the Waves ran as high as the Sea., It seems to have been an ill judged attempt for after losing two Boats they were obliged to run for the Shore & it seems to have been at the risqué of losing all the fleet.

On the 7th the Wind was still high & it took the whole day to repair the damages of yesterday. On the 8th the Wind was more moderate but when our Boat got into the River it rolled so bad we were afraid of her sinking & when we had reached Patna, the River opening to the eastward & losing all protection from the Shore we lay rolling 3 Hours the current attempting to drive us down while the Wind with equal violence drove us up. We lay there without making above ½ a Mile, however a lull for about half an Hour allowing us to cross the River we entered a smaller channel which runs on the North side completely sheltered & we were carried 30 Miles to about Ten Miles above Bar.

9th   The Wind while Easterly but more moderate. At 9 oclock we passed in sight of Bar. We saw some Ruins but mostly hid among the Palm Trees. In 2½ hours more we passed the Seapoy Village mentioned on the 30th November. In One Hour & ½ passed Mochiah & we soon had a view of the Mountains in the Back Ground & the Island formed in the bend of the River. We stopped at Diriapore a few Miles below Mochiah. The Country from the River is very beautiful the Rains having made it all Green and those ugly sand Islands on which we were accustomed to anchor on our Way up were now covered with Water. I dined with McCaskell.

10th   We moved very early in the morning it is rather a grand sight, by the Light of the Moon it seems upwards of 100 Boats floating down so large a River without a sail set, it puts me in mind of a fleet passing the Needles. I have not often mentioned that you cannot go out of Doors except in a Palenkeen after Sun rise or before Sun set for which reason the Whites in Bengal Generally are up & do most of their out Door business before or at halflight it is the only pleasant time of Day. We get a chair on the Deck of the Budgerow & sit enjoying the Prospect which varies about Six Miles an hour from 4 until 6 o clock after which we are obliged to seek shelter below. As we came opposite the large Island the two Currents parted & I happened to be the headmost boat to the North. I was sucked into the Northern Channel, while almost all the Fleet kept the South there were only the Budgerow & two Men's Boats which followed me. At 8 o clock we passed Papiliah. The fleet had a better passage in the Southern Channel as from the first I joined nearly the last, about One o clock we saw Mongheri. We kept the Shore & soon passed by a Ruin of a Large Brick Bridge over a Nulla. It had a pretty appearance there was an old Pagoda near it which was quite in Ruins. We passed Monghir & had a fine view of the Walls toward the Ganges, it must have been rather strong against Native Troops. We halted about Two Miles below Monghir, just where we stopped coming up, here are some beautiful lanes which reminded us of England.

11th   We passed through Sittacund at Daylight. The appearance of Mr Beckets house on the Ridge is pretty, it is seen from a great distance & of course they must have a very extensive View from it.

We soon came to Jangara where the Rock is in the Middle of the River, it is reckoned very dangerous as the river narrows so much it requires all the Boatmens exertions to keep clear, if you struck it the Boat would certainly be Knocked to pieces, we were fortunate in a wind from Jangara Rock to the entrance of Boghipore Nulla was 2½ Miles. We kept sailing about forty Miles further until we came opposite Boglipore. One oclock we passed Boglipore but not in the small River & at Two oclock crossed the River. In One hour more we saw Colgong distant about 16 Miles, we continued about six Miles South East & and Anchored on the left Bank of the River, the Country flat, marshy with long Grass.

12th   At a Quarter after five we moved on, the River winds very much. We steered S.S.E. 6 Miles, E. 3 Miles & One Mile of continued Winding from E. to E.N.E. when we passed the Islands at Calgory. The Hills here are very romantic being covered with large Trees and Mr Glass has a very fine Bungalow on a hill which looks like a Northern one in England & a Park. In Two hours we reached Pattergolly where we saw the Cavern on our way up. Nothing can appear more beautiful than the Right hand shore of the River, all the way from Mongheri Ridges of Hills covered with fine Trees & here & there a huge bold Rock projecting from the River. At Bidushroor it is at least three Miles across, we crossed it & then steered E. 6 Miles then E.S.E. 6 Miles which brought us opposite Pointy, here is a Tomb erected to a Mr Middleton. They say he had a vision that he was to die at such an hour & nothing could persuade him against it & he did die. The Story as it is told me resembled Lord Littletons Ghost. From Pointy East South East 8 Miles and Anchored on a low Bank opposite Tiriagully. This place was formerly the King of Bengal's. Gully means a PASS & this is a very narrow one, a small fort on the Hill being difficult to defend it from a large Army such as the Moguls had.

13th   At Seven oclock this morning we passed TiriaGully here is the Mosque & Fort on a Hill to guard another strong pass & a Bungalow for the occasional residence of the Officer appointed to the Command of the Invalides. From Tiriagully to Siriagully is Ten Miles nearly East with a slight Bend or bay to the South between Two Points. About 5 Miles below Siriagully we turned South and sailing 13 Miles passed Rajamahal at a Quarter after Twelve. As we passed Rajamal it had a very beautiful appearance the water being quite up to the Ruins and we were in the Middle of the River. From Rajamal we steered South East Twelve Miles & then E.S.E, 12 Miles. We entered the Hoogly and anchored at Moangange. The River was very rapid & we had not room for all our boats we found ourselves very uncomfortable. We were closing up till near Ten at night & several Boats not able to stop themselves ran foul of others & were likely to do mischief. The Stream carried us upwards of 52 Miles.

14th The Small River winds very much we often seemed to be close to the Boats which were several Miles from us. I reckon that we went 36 Miles in 16 Geographical Miles. I mentioned the Black Men & I find I have for my family Fifty Seven, with more the number of Women & Children. We passed Jungipore & halted about four Miles below. Mr Hannays house at Jungipore strikes you, it seems a fine house. The Country here is low & Marshy but is the proper Country of Indigo. The Indigo manufactured by the River almost the whole way to Moorshedabad. The Wind rose very much in the Evening from the South East.

July 15th The wind blew very strong & we were whirled by the Stream running one way & the Wind blowing the other. My Budgerow got into a bay & I could not get out for above an hour. When we were just clearing a head land the wind took us & blew us back. The whole Fleet seemed in the same way & now & then we ran foul of each other Had it not been that the River was narrow we might have sunk some Boats but the Wind had not the power it would have had in the great River we were obliged to bring up in the opposite Shore from Digrabad, here we found a number for Mulberry groves & Silk Worms & Mangoe Groves .

16th The Wind was very high all the night & still continued however we moved on till we came to the Mouth of the Dysabad Nulla. But the Entrance only admitting one Boat we rushed on each other & soon choaked up the Entrance. The River here takes a very long sweep & the Nulla or Cutt is made shorter the Passage several Miles when I found that the Mouth of the Cut was choaked up I disengaged my Boat as well as I could determined to go round but I had not proceeded far before we saw another cut which we entered & got out before the fleet who were muddled together & could not act. The Cut through which we passed had been choaked up by the sand but the River had forced itself through again this year, about seven oclock we reached Bernaghur opposite Moorshedabad, inhabited by Rajapouts, the wind died away & we had Rain. The Stream carried us rapidly by Moorshedabad, we arrived at Berhampore at Eleven o clock, having dropt down with winding about 308 Miles in 8 Days.

We learnt on landing at Berhampore that the fleet from England had arrived. We got good Quarters but Damp.

1806 July 17th   Berhampore

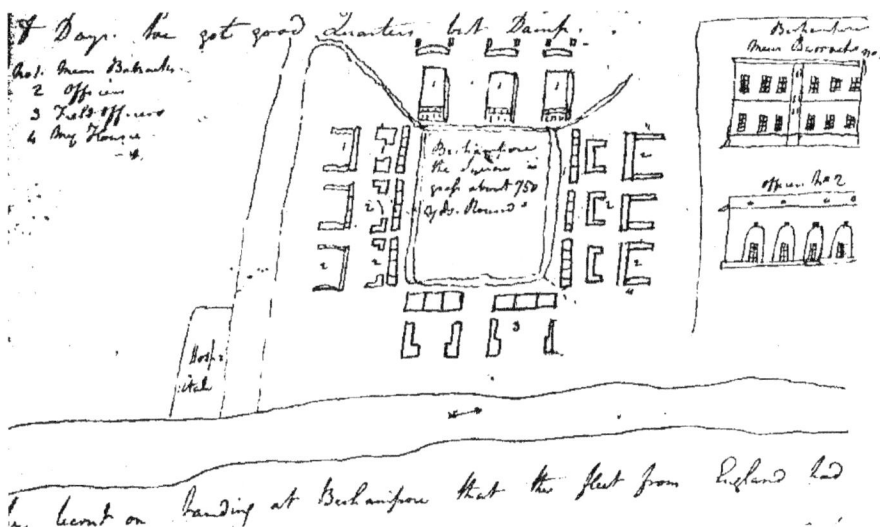

17th   I received Letters from England, the Postage came to upwards of Two Guineas owing to them having been directed to Madras. I dislike paying it only from this reason: that had any of my Letters reached home they would have been directed to Calcutta, I therefore fear my Letters sent in October last did not reach home as the *Medusa* Frigate arrived in England on the 19th Jan[y] & M[r] Maskalls letter is dated 21st. February.

18th   We received One Hundred & Thirty Men who Volunteered for the 53rd Reg[t]. from the 75th Reg[t]. H. M. 75th Regiment passed down to embark for England. We find provisions here about the same price as at Dinapore. Servants Wages rather higher however as I do not require quite so many it will come to the same.

It rained every day to the end of the Month.

August

The Commander in Chief (Lord Lake) arrived here on the 4th on his way to England. It had been intended for the 53rd Reg[t] of which he once was Colonel to invite him to Dinner but the Civil & Military Officers in the Company's Service had written up & engaged them before us. However he will remain Tomorrow on purpose to dine with us which he had not intended.

5th   The 53rd Reg[t] gave a Publick Dinner to the Commander in Chief & all the Civil & Military Servants met him. We sat down to Dinner upwards of One Hundred. We had a very pleasant Evening. Lord Lake frequently mentioned the 53rd on the Continent[114] & made a Speech & twice drank to our old acquaintances. Lord Lake is a fine Old Man of 63 (but I am sorry to say that his life is rather loose for his Age) he has much the appearance of a Frenchman. After Dinner we had a Ball & Supper.

On the 9th The 25th Light Dragoons passed by on their way to Madras to Relieve the 19th L Dg^s who go home. They were to have dined with us but passing in the Morning they could not stop. We heard of a Mutiny at Valloris in the Carnatic.[115] One or Two Seapoy Regiments murdered their Officers & attacked & killed many Men of the 69th Reg^t. said to be 180 & 18 Officers. The Reasons for the Mutiny are kept secret but the General opinion is that Tipoo's[116] Sons who were confined at Vallore were at the bottom of it. I wrote to Mr Maskall, Mrs Butt & Marten.[117] The River rose so high that it is at least 5 Feet above the Country & it is only retained from flooding by the Banks & we are afraid they will give way the Water has not been so high since 1801 when it overflowed & carried away thousands of Inhabitants. It has now risen within Six Inches of the top of the Embankment. The Natives huts are very low laying all along under the Bank & remind you of Pigs Sties.

12th This day the Bank broke about Two Miles below Berhampore. The Water flowed like a River & inundated the Country so much that we had scarcely time to embank our own Cantonement & we are now like an Island in the midst of the Sea, fortunately where it burst there were no Inhabitants & the Noise frightened the Neighbours so that they all escaped & ran far Inland or towards the Cantonements. They however lost every thing except their live stock. I walked down the Bank & saw the Poor creatures collecting their goods & carrying them on Rafts from one height to another. We fortunately had no Wind and the Furniture of a Native is not worth much. We saw Curious fishing today, at One of the openings through which the Water was rushing violently several Persons held Nets who caught the fish as they were hurried through & sometimes the Fish in attempting to avoid the extreme rapidity of the current leapt on Shore & were knocked down by persons who waited for them with sticks. The Instant the Fish found themselves drawn into the violent

---

[114] A 2nd Battalion of the 53rd Foot had been recruited in 1803-5 for the Peninsular War.
[115] Vellore Mutiny, Karnataka, 10 July 1806, against sepoy uniform regulations, leather in hats conflicting with Hindu and Muslim cleanliness codes. Instigated by the sons of Tippoo imprisoned at Vellore. Almost successful but a rescue led by Col. Rollo Gillespie prevailed.
[116] Tippoo, Sultan of Mysore (1750-1799).
[117] Rev. John Marten Butt (1774-1846), Mrs Sherwood's brother.

stream they attempted to leap out. When the Nets were instantly thrown under them or a good Blow of a Stick knocked them down, great Numbers were killed in this Manner.

The Water kept increasing around us & we began to fear that our Cantonements would be soon overflowed we are now considerably under the Level of the Water and the Road from Cantonements is two feet at least flooded, every thing is damp in our House. But we suffer little in comparison. The Whole fine Country round is covered with Water the poor Ryots[118] are laying in Cantonements & their Cattle nearly starving. The Cattle die very fast & A great Mortality among the Natives is expected, had such a thing happened in England The whole Country would have been destroyed but here a small quantity of Rice will suffice a Man a long Time, & the upper provinces will be enabled to supply this & besides this very flood will be the cause of a more plentiful Harvest in a few months. After the 24th The Water did not rise & by the 31st altho the River still kept above the level yet the Water which covered the Country began to sink into the Earth or evaporate.

September

We received an Invitation from the Nabob of Bengal[119] to see Illuminations & Sup on the 11th at Moorshedabad. I believe it is some ceremony on the River having passed its height. The Island of Cossimbazar is so low that it would not be extraordinary if some year, it is entirely destroyed by the Ganges, had the Bank broke just above Moorshedabad the loss would have been very great. The Natives have a Tradition that Bengal was formerly Sea & they say that a Rajah who lived many centuries ago at the Foot of the Rajahmahal Hills had a very Religious Daughter who going Down to the Ganges with her Earthen Pot to perform Pujah, the Gods were so pleased with her prayers that Waves came & took her Pot carrying it with the stream a short distance when it stopped and soon collecting round it the floating Grass & small branches it formed a small Island which has been gradually increasing into Bengal.

11th Early this Morning Mr & Mrs Hanson, Mrs Sherwood & myself hired a Budgerow for the day & proceeded towards Moorshedabad, we had a very pleasant sail up & we arrived about One oclock. After eating our Tiffin we walked into the City we saw nothing but a common Bazar & the principal manufacture was shoes, finely embroidered in Gold or Silver.

---

[118] Ryot: peasant tenant farmers.
[119] Babar Ali Khan (c.1778-1810) Nabob or Nawab—a Mughal viceroy—of Bengal.

 They are made with the Toe curled & pointed upwards. I bought a very smart Pair, Scarlet & Gold for Two Rupees. The day was very hot & there were so many Boats come to see the Shew that we could only get a place under a Bank which was open to the west we were much troubled by the Evening Sun. The amusement began as soon as the Sun set, by the Poorer Musulmen offering small Paper Ships bearing lighted Lamps, these they launched into the stream & allowed them to sail away until the light burnt out or the wind overset them, these ships were mostly formed like Peacocks which is the Mahomedan emblem, at Seven oclock we went to the Nabobs, he was seated under a very large Tent or Porch, he was surrounded by a Multitude of attendants & some dismounted Cavalry & his Courtiers, he received us very generously & shook our hands, he appeared to rise from his Sofa with great difficulty. Report says this is occasioned by the great quantity of Spirits that he drinks, he is rather a good looking man but with a kind of dull Melancholy Air, they told us he was not above 28 Years old. We took our seats & were served with Wine & Water cooled in Ice. A Nautch (or Dance & Song) was being performed by a Woman & Two Girls but they only moved their hands & feet & we were told it constantly repeated what a Great man is the Nabob &c. The Nabob did not seem to attend to them and, when they retired, there rushed in about a dozen pretended fools or Jesters playing all manner of Tricks some of which were not very delicate. The principal Story which they acted was a Trial before an English Judge respecting a horse. One of them represented the horse frisking about & trying to commentate Neighing. The Two claimants alternately endeavoured to get on his back & he (as far as I could understand) endeavoured to throw the unjust one. They afterwards wanted to make a Road for the Nabob & the Chief Fool lay the rest down in a Row and then walked upon them when he had strutted for some time one of them put up his hand & tripped him up which caused a roar of laughter from his Highnesses Courtiers, the nabob himself did not seem to notice them at all but smoaked his Hooka with great Apathy. Immediately after these jesters went away, an elderly man appeared as if covered with Blood with a spear running through his Body. I was so taken with surprize that for an instant, I believed it was realy a Man who had been wounded & was coming to complain, for his Countanance was very grave & seeming more like a steady Soldier than a Buffoon after this man had stood before his Highness a few minutes some singing Men came & I understood they repeated to the nabob "You are a greater Man than your Father but not so rich, many great white Gentlemen are come to pay their respects to you, some on Horses Some in Chairs, some in Boats & Budgerows and

some in Palankeens. At Nine oclock a Signal Gun was fired to give notice that the fire works were to commence, we therefor went into a Gallery of the Palace overlooking the River. The Crowd all moved together & it was not without difficulty that we could push through them we however at last got a seat. The River appeared almost covered with Fire. The Bank opposite the palace was covered with the Representation of a Fine illuminated Palace upwards of a Quarter of a Mile long. The Frame had been made of Bambooes and seemed a very regular Building. Large Castles Ships & Forts Floated down the River from which was a constant discharge of Fire works, it was really very Grand, but the Noise stunned you, as the nabobs Guns were firing all the time. No Illumination in Europe could be compared to this. At Ten oclock we sat down to Supper. Two Young Men presided at our Table. I do not know who they were, some persons told us they were the Nabobs half Brothers others said they were his Sons. They were very fine Boys. One of about fourteen & the other about seven. They seemed as if they had never used a Knife or Fork before. The Supper was abundant but very badly cooked. There was plenty of Claret Madeira & Hock. After sitting about an hour we were dismissed by each person receiving a Collar of the Flowers of Jassamine & a little Attar of Roses put in our Handkerchiefs. On the whole the Fire works were very Grand, the Nabob very civil and every thing very Stupid. The Nabob has an Income of 16 Lacks of Rupees. P^{er} Annum (£190,000) but this is to maintain his whole Family & all his descendants of Jaffier Alli Khan. The Last Nabob but one received 70 Lacks P^{er} A (£875,000) I returned to Berhampur during the Night.

I wrote home on the 15th. The Batchelors of the Regiment gave a Ball & Supper on the 25th. We sat down to Supper 105 and nearly as many went away before Supper was served up, The Fleet from England arrived but I received no Letters. One Ship (*The Lady Burgess*) was lost on a Rock near the Cape de Verd Islands, probably our Letters were on board. This Season very mild but our Regiment is very sickly & the Men have died very quick.

Octo^r 1806

There was nothing extraordinary in all this month, the mornings & Evenings begin to get cool & the River fell over 30 Feet

November

The weather gets very cool & Pleasant as the month advances. I wrote home by the *Mercury* Packet. A Detachment of 80 Men arrived from the 2^d Battalion [53rd Foot] with Two Officers, Lieutenants Stoney & Bowyear.

December

The Emporer of Hindostan Shah Allum[120] died at the Age of Eighty One [sic.], he is succeeded by Shah Acbar. The Life of Shah Allum has been very unfortunate. When Shah Zadeh or Heir Apparent he escaped from the Vizier Gazardeem Khan & fled to Sujah Dowlah Nabob of Oude who persuaded him to attempt the Conquest of Bengal, which at that time was in great confusion, it being just after the English had placed Jaffier Khan on the Musnud. He entered Bahar towards the end of 1758 but he had undertaken a task he was unequal to. He found he must retreat, after failing in an attack on Patna. He lay with an Army on the Borders of Bahar & Oud, & the English did not think it advisable to attack him. His Father Allum Geer the 2nd was murdered in 1759 & He was proclaimed Emperor by the King of Cabul Abdalla who had at that Time possession of Delhi & all the Country to the North & West of Amr Anopriseer, he made the Nabob of Oude his Vizeer & sent him to Delhi, but he himself (being now Mogul) thought he should find it easy to drive the English out of India. He laid siege to Patna a second time but was defeated by the young Nabob Meeran Son of Jaffier, & Major Caulland, he was however saved for the Time by the death of Meeran, who was killed by Lightning in his Tent. In the Mean Time, the Nabob of Oude, or more properly the Afgawn King of Cabul had defeated & broke the Mahratta forces at Panniput. Major Carnac however now advanced against him & defeated him in January 1765 upon which he was obliged to surrender to the English who allowed him a Pension of Three Milions Sterling & gave him Allahabad as his residence, here he might have remained happy under the English protection but he was too restless he therefore after residence of five years endeavoured to prevail on the English to reinstate him on the Throne which they declined & endeavoured to disouade him from attempting it, but he was obstinate & having entered into a treaty with the Mahrattas he advanced towards Delhi in 1771 and was placed on the Throne but merely as a Pajeant being sometimes a Tool in the Maharattas who dragged him about that they might destroy their Enemies under pretence of His Majesty's wishes & sometimes he escaped from them, was used by One Noble against another until the year 1788 when he was made Prisoner by Gholaum Cawdor Khan[121] who stabbed out his Eyes with a Dagger. Scindeat the Mahratta came to his assistance & put Ghalaum Cawdor to death & seemed to Treat the old man with some kindness but he was nothing but a State Prisoner & treated with little respect for when Lord Lake took Delhi he found his Palace gone to ruin & himself in poverty. He

---

[120] Shah Alam II (1728-1806) 15th Mughal Emperor.
[121] 'Gholaum Cawdor Khan' Ghulam Qadir Khan, a Pashtun enemy of the Mughals.

remained under the English protection unto his Death, it is extraordinary how he lived to such an age having gone through so much, but the Chinese & Mogul Emperors are naturally long lived. Shah Allums Eldest Son died at Benares in September 1788, he had placed himself under the protection of the English and did not live to know how his Father was Treated by Gholaum Cawdor. The Present Emperor Ackba Shah[122] is the Third Son & Succeeds from his Fathers wish. Both The Eldest Jahan Buckt & the Second Furkinda Buckht have left Children.

The Weather is now getting very cold & vegetables plenty. I wrote home & was just in time for the *Euphrates* a running Ship on board of which Cap^n Thompson proceeds to Europe. General Palmer gave a Dinner Ball & Supper to all the Station on Xmas day. A Chaplain arrived for the Station, his name is Parson from near Lichfield. Mrs Plowden invited us all to a Ball the 29th & all the Married Officers dined with me on the 1st January being New Years day & my Birth day 30 Years old.

January 1807

January was cold & Pleasant, I drove Mrs Sherwood out in a Gig every Evening.

February.

No News worth Mentioning except the Accounts from Europe of the Invasion of Prussia by France & Mr Fox's death. The *Euphrates* sailed for Europe 23rd January & a Fleet on 24 Feb^y.

March

The Weather got warm with Showers of Rain and dark cloudy days, the *Margaret* Packet arrived from England but I did not receive any Letters— she sailed the 15 Sepr last. We heard that the Ship *Skeldon Castle* has a very large Packet of Letters & that she may be expected every day on the 10th, 11th 12th & 13. The Wind blew very hot & on the 14th The Thermometer in the Shade was at 97. This is very unusual. On the 15th the Glass fell considerably & did not rise above 87 the remainder of the Month & in general below it.

[Margin note:] Mrs Sherwood confined, a daughter][123]

We hear that Buonaparte carries all before him I wrote home by the Ship *Fortune*, we had Rain in quantities in March.

1807 April

Two Ships arrived from England (The *Union* & *Matilda*) They sailed from Portsmouth in Company with the *Skeldon Castle* but parted company off

---

[122] Akbar II (1760-1837) Mughal Emperor.
[123] Lucy Martha (March 25, 1807 Berhampore-September 2, 1808 Cawnpore) buried at Cawnpore.

the Cape of Good Hope these two Ships being obliged to stop there where they remained a fortnight. We are alarmed for the safety of the *Skeldon Castle* as she sailed for India direct & has not been heard of. We received a Detachment from the 2nd Battalion under Lieut^t Young and Ensign Daley.

On the 11th the Cheruck or Swinging was performed this is a Religious ceremony of the Hindoos[124] but I believe only the lowest or moved Casts swing. Several of these poor People had prepared themselves the day before by having an Iron Bar as large as a small spit thrust through their Tongues. The first Man who made his appearance was a Carpenter who had worked for me. The Priests laid him on his Back & inserted Two Iron hooks into the Flesh under the Muscles below the Shoulder Blades by which he was to hang, near him was a Pole between Twenty and

Thirty feet high, crossed by another Pole which was so fixed that it admitted of being lowered & run round, from the Two ends were cords, to one of which these Iron Hooks were fixed & the Populace seized the other, raised the Poor man up near Twenty Feet from the Ground & hurried him round like Horses in a Mill, whilst the Poor fellow threw flowers to the crowd assembled under him. I however observed that the first who appeared did not remain long nor were they whirled round with great velocity, probably they paid the Priests, however after wards some of the lowest Casts came intoxicated with opium and These when swinging Sang & Kicked & were whirled as fast that they seemed like Birds flying, the velocity with which they went threw them entirely from their Center, it was horrid to see them. One in particular was so drunk that altho he could scarce draw his Breath from the Quick Motion clapped his hands & kicked & when the People below wanted to take him down he roared & kicked like a little petted child when taken from a swing & they were obliged to let him drop & then he began beating all round him, I thought he must have had a Devil. I was very much afraid that the Muscles could not have borne the weight added to the velocity & had they broke the Man would certainly have been killed, but I was told it never happened, but sometimes the Rope or Posts did & that the Man was in general killed. The most extraordinary thing was that I did not see any Blood, but there was no deception as our Surgeon examined the Back. We think they had numbed the flesh by some Herbs. The Country round us is now very distinctive, as the natives take up so little Room & build their huts of straw touching each other & probably covering a Mile of Ground.

---

[124] 'Cheruck' Charak Puja, still performed in West Bengal in April 2015.

Berhampore 1806-7

Charack Puja.

We have great reason to think that the Straw merchants & Thatchers wilfully set fire for we observe that whichever way the wind blows The Fire always breaks out on the windward side and as the wind blows at this season of the year very strong the destruction is immence. On the Evening of the 16th the Bazar which lies to the South of Cantonements was perceived to be on Fire on its Eastern side. The Fire raged diagonally & burnt all before it until it reached the River and on the 20th the wind having changed to the North West. The fire broke out again at the River side & destroyed the remainder of the Bazar shows $^{16th}X^{20th}$ the directions that the Fire took, The Wind blowing on the 16th to the South East and on the 20th from the N. E. The flames on the last day were so Rapid that altho the fire happened in the middle of the day 25 Persons were burnt to death & many very much wounded & the Bazar was completely destroyed that not one hut stood. I walked over the Ruins in the evening, the Traces of the Streets could scarcely be discovered, the wretched Inhabitants were smoking sitting on the half extinguished Rafters of their late huts mostly half drunk or stupid with Opium during the violence of the Fire we observed many Birds hovering over & suddenly falling in. The Consequences of the whole Villages in Europe being destroyed would be dreadful but here it is of little consequence the hut is not worth above 2 or 3 Rupees & the only furniture a Bedstead worth about half a Rupee some of the Richest have a Brass Pot but most of them use earthen ones not worth above a Farthing. The Man in general at the sight of Fire catches up his Bedstead & Pot & sometimes runs back and Brings away what is called the Chopper, this is not more than a Frame of Bamboos thatched which is easily carried and is in fact the whole house. The Number 1 in the margin is baked mud and the N° 2 is the Chopper it is bought for about Two Shillings ready made & all that the natives do is merely to place N° 2 on N° 1. It is of so little consequence that the Seapoy Barracks always stand as N° 1 through heat & rain & when a Regiment arrives each Soldier buys his Chopper which are always to be found ready made. When the Regiment leaves a Station they invariably burn their huts or the Bazar People uncover them in a few hours. The Natives can sleep & most of them from choice do sleep out of Doors at this Season. In fact Bengalese often set fire to their own houses to destroy the Vermin but the Richer Merchants suffer severely.

More than £25,000 Sterling in Cloth & Grain is supposed to have been destroyed in these Two fires. The Flames were so particularly rapid on the 20th that a strong Woman running down the Street was caught by the flames & killed.

The Natives of Bengal are very subject to Putrid Fevers. The fires are a great preventative for they have scarcely any Remeddy, they in general attempt to starve the Fever, in general 4 die out of 5 that are attacked. M' Belsham in his History of the Reign of George the 3rd [125] tells a fine Story but as different from the Truth as light from darkness, he attributes the diseases & depopulation to the English Government & gives as a reason that the Famines destroy the dead & that the Putrid Bodies caused infection but M' B ought to have known that the Hindoos never do bury their dead & that 3 out of four are always exposed to the holy River. The Bengal Capitals as long as history can trace back have been frequently depopulated by the Plague. Gour Tandah & Moorshedabad have been frequently left desolate & the damps alone of Bengal with the low living easily accounts for it. The Natives in speaking say that in One year the Fever carried away in Moorshedabad Twelve Annas the meaning of which is that as a Rupee is composed on Sixteen Annas. Three fourths died in some of the Villages scarcely a human being was left & in one of them was only a poor old Woman who was attacked & killed by a Jackall. Yet it seems wonderful that Bengal is so very populous, but it must be remembered that Children always marry as soon as they attain the age of

---

[125] Belsham, William: *Memoirs of the reign of George III*, 6 Volumes, London 1793-1801.

Berhampore 1806-7

10 or before it & that Two Generations of Europeans are equal to 4 of Hindoos. They have Children at 12 years old and a woman does not wean One Child until she has another. This is curious probably if ascertained the Numbers of little Children is wonderful & I often have heard the Officers express their suprize at finding a populous Country which has been destroyed with fire & sword only a few years before Mr Belsham talks in raptures of Bengal in its former peaceful State (I presume before Tigers & Aligators or Musquitoes were invented) when the happy Artisan seated under the delightful spreading Trees with the Peacocks on the Branches, their wives or Family either singing or playing or some instrument. I only mention this from Memory but I am sure his description is even finer but he knows nothing about it. As far back as History goes Bengal was oppressed & unhealthy either Pillaged by Moguls, Mahrattas or Rebels and probably before that was covered with impenetrable Jungles full of Tigres Serpents & Musquitoes & also it seems likely from the Present embankment of the River which is kept up at great expence by the English that it could scarcely have been inhabited in the Ruins however from the History of the Century before the English became Master of it, it certainly was in a terrible state.

On the 25th we had a most violent North West Wind with hail, my Kitmudgar brought me half of a Brick & said it hailed stones as large. My last Ten Months expences Receipts & savings have been as follows

	Servants Wages	Housekeeping	
In July 1806	109		80
Aug	115		80
September	116		80
October	114		80
November	111		80
December	110		80
January 1807	122		80
February	113	1	10
March	117		80
April	117		80
	10/113/8		83

The Servants being on an Average per Month for the Ten Months 113.14
Housekeeping do   83
Wine &c &c   50
Houserent   55
Total Expences for 1 Month =   302 This 302 Rupees is equal £37—15.

My average Receipts have been 506 Rupees Pay and allowances which makes a saving of 204 which Sum in General brought me by favour of Exchange between Calcutta & this 214 Rupees Calcutta Bills. The Interest also on this money saved amounted One Month with another to 36 Rupees—making a clear saving of 250 Rupees or in Sterling Money £31—5. Per Month or Per Annum £375. I must also remark that we endeavoured to make the 80 Rupees per Month pay all the house expences & Cloaths but it ran out on the 8th Month. The Wine also was not allowed to exceed as when I drank too much I went without on the next.

May

This month set in with heavy squalls of Wind & rain & between the squalls very hot, but the Thermometer is scarcely ever below 92 in the shade. The Reports in circulation are very many & Contradictory we hear that Buonaparte has entered Prussia, that a great Battle has been fought. The King of Prussia is killed & Buonaparte missing.

I received a small Box of Letters which arrived by the *Margaret* Packet but had been neglected in Calcutta their were so many Letters & among the Rest we find that Lucy was married to Mr Cameron on the 12th June.

Our Conversation is much about the Ship *Skeldon Castle* which was seen off the Cape of Good Hope on the 12th of December last but which has not been heard of Since. Reports are continually raised, sometimes she has been in one Place & sometimes in Another, but I fear she has gone to the Bottom, for we certainly must have heard something certain in so long a time. It rained almost every day this Month which People say is very extraordinary, on the 28th I wrote to Mr Maskall [uncle] & Old Mrs Sherwood [step-grandmother] of Coventry.

June

The first four Days of this Month were so oppressive we could not Sleep. The River had risen but it now falls again on the 5th it threatened rain & a heavy shower fell towards the Evening, the Thermometer in the Shade from Eleven to four is 92 the Weather just as hot until the 10th both Frequent Showers. The White men very subject to sore Throats & violent Colds. On the 18th a very unexpected order arrived for the 53rd Reg^t to prepare to proceed to Cawnpore by Water when the 22nd Regiment which is ordered to Berhampore arrives, but it appears the 22 Regiment are still at Multra we cannot therefore move until August— On the 13th The River begins to rise it rushes down with great violence. It seemed much on the 13th &14th. The River fell again altho the Showers continue with an Easterly wind. The Closeness of the Air was very oppressive yet the Thermometer was never above 90. We are to expect

Berhampore 1806-7

Two Ships from England (the *Devagnis* & *General Stuart*) They parted Company off the Cape with Two Ships which arrived at Bombay. We hear that Monte Video in the River La Plata has been taken by the English. We also hear that some severe Battles have been fought in Poland & that Buonaparte has been severely wounded in two places. On the 24th we received Letters from England dated in October & November all well, we hear from Mrs Andrews 53rd Reg^t that Marten has got two Livings & from Mrs Cameron we hear that he is married & she doubts he has Two Livings but merely employment, or as if we knew all about it. The River did not open completely until the 26th. We hear that Lord Minto[126] is appointed Governor General & may be expected daily. Report still speaks of the great Victories of the Russians over the French but I am at a loss to conceive why when the French are so completely beat that they always advance & the Russians retire. They say that a Russian Army of 55,000 Men beat a French Army of 90,000, that they killed 4,000 & took 30,000. Bounaparte they say made his Escape with his personal Staff severely hounded, & pursued by the Russians who mistaking one of his Aida de Camp for himself took him Prisoner which gave Bounaparte time to escape & intrench himself near Marienburgh. This report has been near Two Months in circulation yet we see no Official Report. I own I do not quite believe it for all the Accounts agree that the French are still advanced as far as Jhorn & Koenigsburg. I am much Troubled with Boils as I was at this time last year, the River Rises Rapidly & the heat is very oppressive.

July

This month began with heavy rain & heat we heard Lord Minto is arrived at Madras. We also hear that the *Blenheim* of 74 Guns (which was our Convoy from England) sunk of the Cape & Sir Thos Troubridge & every person on board perished. We heard from Cawnpore that the 22nd Regiment marched from Multra 28th of June we may therefore expect them the Middle of August. It is exceptionally hot this month. My Poor Little Boy feels the heat so much that he falls away every day & Poor little fellow he was taken from us but like a Candle going out. We were kindly assisted by every One & Mr Parson the Chaplain thinking Mrs Sherwood would like to remove from her House was kind enough to offer his which is situated in a Garden out of Cantonements & is rather more lively.

---

[126] 1st Earl of Minto (1751-1814). Governor Gneral 1807-1813.

Aug^t

I wrote many Letters home the beginning of this Month To all my Friends in Worcestershire & to Todd. We received letters from England, Marten wrote on the 20th January which was continued by his wife to 18th February. It rained very much on the 17-18th & 19th. The Country became flooded on the 20th & 21. The Rain actually fell nearly 3 Perpendicular Feet on the surface of the land. His Majestys 22nd Regiment arrived on the 23rd. But the Boats on which they came are so much damaged that we cannot move for some time. Major General St Ledger, provisional Commander in Chief is expected every day, on the 28th he arrived. The 53rd Regiment gave a Dinner Ball & Supper to the Station preparatory to having it we had also a review. Major Mansel arrived from England with Cap^{ns} Wallace & Andrews, Ensigns Horsely, Harrington, Emery, Currie, Constable & Green & 300 Men.

1807 September 8th   3rd River Journey. Berhampore to Cawnpore, 780 Miles

On the 8th the 53rd Reg't left Berhampore for Cawnpore. I remained behind for Money but on the 9th I sailed with a fine Easterly Wind & soon overtook the Regiment which was halted to place themselves in order about Three Miles above Berhampore. On the 20th we passed Pointy and halted about Three Miles further on. The Heat today was very oppressive, the Thermometer in the shade as high as 97 without a Breath of Wind.

21st   We had some little difficulty in passing Colgong today, we anchored at the Mouth of a small River about 3 Miles further on. A M'r Glas son of Doctor Glas sent us a very acceptable present of vegetables Bread & Butter. The House which I mentioned in our Journey down does not belong to him & I believe is not inhabited, there is a Bungalow at the Point of Colgong where we saw a White Man & Woman probably Indigo Planters.

We reached Baglipore on the 22nd. The first thing I did was to dispatch Letters to all my Friends in England which I had been preparing since we left Jungipore they are to go either in a Fleet or by the Running Ship *General Stuart* which is soon to sail as a Packet. Doctor Glas with whom I became acquainted at M'r Parsons's House at Berhampore invited us to his house but he had not a spare Room we therefore brought our Pinnace down & Anchored close under his house as we are to stay some days.

We were much pleased on the 23rd to meet with M'r Cromelin, a Cousin of M'r Dethicks of Bridgenorth, we knew his Children in England. He was passing down by Dawk[127] to Calcutta. We were much pleased with him & the more so as we hear he is a Methodist, which is as much as to say he believes in Christ & says his Prayers. We remained the whole day with Doctor Glas & also the 24th & I called on Cap'n Lumsden & Littlejohn whom I knew at Berhampore. The Country about Banglipore is the most pleasant in India. The high Hills are not very close but there is rising Ground all about and it is green & well wooded. Doctor Glas says he can see the high Mountains of Tibet, the Antient Imans covered with snow from his front verandah but while we were there the weather was cloudy. I learnt from Doctor G. who has been many years in India

---

[127] 'Dawk' Dak, postal and passenger relay system of bearers, palenquins or horses.

that murder is very common among the Innocent Hindoos, how very ill Europeans reason when they talk of the poor Innocent Gentoos who will not shed the Blood even of vermin. They are certainly timourous but very cruel even to their sacred Cows which they treat as bad as any savage drover & with regard to each other the Stories which I have heard (& Firmly believe) of their Thefts & murders are enough to shock an Englishman. There are now Fourteen Men in Banglipore Goal convicted of cruel murder for Trifles & it is only four months since there was an assize. The Number of Murders between Pattergolly & Banglipore as related to us by Doctor Glas almost exceeds belief, it appears that 17 dancing Girls were strangled a short time since merely to get ornaments on their Toes & a Man murdered a Child for a ring of Silver which was round her Ancle weighing One Ounce. There are the little Innocent Black Lambs, Tigers are very common about Colgong, they come down to the River for water & are constantly killing the Cattle, they certainly tell some tough stories concerning them.

25   We sailed from Banglipore this Morning with a fair wind and passed Jangara, we anchored at the Village so exactly at the spot I did the Journey in 1805 that my Boat was exactly opposite a Bush with the Zombee Beads but they were not ripe this Year.

On the 26th there was but little wind & we crossed the River & halted at Gogary, on the 27th the wind was again fair & we passed Monghir we halted at an early Hour about Two Miles further on. We were afraid the Colonel would not have stopped which rather annoyed us as we had calculated all along on buying Chairs at Monghir. We were therefore in so great a hurry in passing the fort that we purchased them rather dearly, however I am not much displeased with my Bargain. I bought a dozen handsome Black Wood Chairs for 30 Rupees, a pair of Sophas for 16 Rupees and an iron Stove for Twelve. Also an Iron Cast Tea Kettle which we thought the best in the world for 5 Rupees. On the 28th the Breeze was strong and we made the same way exactly that we did in 1805, halted much in the same place at Popihah, The Journey up the Country at that time seemed as if I should describe it now, the only difference in the water being higher & a better Wind. The Bank under which we anchored during the night was falling & very dangerous which I presume caused our moving on the 29th altho it blew a Gale of Wind, about half an hour after we sailed my Cookery Boat overset in the Middle of the River, it was with some difficulty we saved the People and not before I threatened to fire at a Boat which was passing to make them stop & assist me. I did not lose above 100 Rupees but we were just to great inconvenience. The wind increased so much that we were obliged to Anchor on a Sand bank & we passed the night very uncomfortably and on the 30th It was so bad and the waves rising our Boats struck on the Shore I expected to go down every instant. Towards midday Lieut' Groombridges Budgerow which lay between us and the Shore beat the Bottom out & sank & Seven Soldiers Boats were dashed to Pieces at four oclock it was so bad we were obliged to trust to the river & we got under sail with difficulty however we found an entrance of a small Nulla into which we all ran & found shelter for a night during which the wind fell.

October the first we got a small uncovered boat to carry my Goats & cookery Utensils to Patna & the weather being moderate we crossed the River & Reached Mochiah on the way we Picked up whole Boats load of Soldiers & women which had been wrecked yesterday. They had made a Tent of the Boats sail. On the 2nd about Six Miles above Mockiah we came under the Point of a high sand Bank past which the River ran so rapidly that the Head Boat could not pass without extreme difficulty & we were all stopped waiting our Turn. The Bank was also falling which makes it very dangerous. One of the Boats in our Front full of Soldiers in endeavouring to pass was taken by the Current & whirled round but the stream was rapid that it overset. I never saw any thing so shocking as it rolled by us it several times rolled over like a Ball & the Soldiers Heads were seen on each side endeavouring to disengage themselves. We were for some time in the greatest Anxiety for we could not prevail on the Black Boatmen to assist & altho I ordered a small Panchway of my own to go immediately to their assistance they would not but sat unconcerned, fortunately the Boat drifted on Shore & a Portugese soldier drowned, all this Time the Innocent Hindoos were laughing & eating without shewing any concern.

This sight so alarmed us & the prospect of the great violence of the Stream induced all the Married Officers to go on Shore with their Families. Mrs Sherwood went on Shore & we walked until we might reach smooth water, when we landed at Ten oclock it was not very hot but soon after the Sun burst out & I never found any thing so hot. We were in a Marshy Common coverd with Reeds at least Twelve feet high the Sun darting down perpendicularly on our heads. The Bank was even now & then a soft Mud in which Mrs S. lost her Shoe. We had all the Soldiers Wives with us & I suppose we walked in this distressing way near Two Miles and when we cleared the Jungle we could not for a River but were obliged to sit on the Burning Sand until One oclock when our Boat arrived & we got on Board, providentially we felt no bad effects. Seven Boats were overset Two Soldiers & many Blacks drown passing this Bank & we even think it is fortunate it was no worse. I never saw so awkward a place. Almost all the Officers walked & the Men were obliged to assist in dragging their own Boats, all my Servants, which were Eleven in addition to the Boatmen could scarcely drag my Boat round, on the Third we reached Bar, & we are happy to find that we do not suffer from the walk yesterday. We saw some fine old Ruins at Bar, particularly an old Mahomedan Burial Ground. We remained at Bar on the fourth to repair the damaged Boats & we made a kind of Tent by Hanging a Carpet in a Grove to four Trees. Major Mansel, Cap^n & Mrs Piercy & ourselves joined our Tiffins together & passed a very pleasant day, we also dined & passed the Evening in Piercys Boat.

5th We had a very strong current with a falling Bank but being prepared there was no great danger however we were from 5 oclock until Twelve going Three Miles. We saw the Soldiers & their Wives walking. We only made five Miles the whole day.

On the Sixth we passed Futwa & saw the Ruins of a very fine old Bridge over a Nulla. Futwa is famous for napkins & Table Cloths we bought some. The Price for Table napkins from 2 Rupees to 2½ per Dozen, 7½ foot Table Cloths 2 Rupees each. 11 Feet 3 Rupees and 15 Feet 5 Rupees, the Napkins which I bought were 2 Rupees 4 Anna per Dozen. We halted at Jaffir Khans Gardens, Memorable for having been defended for a considerable time by a small Party of English. We found the Gardens to be a square within Brick Walls of a considerable height & some strength but now going to ruin. The inside full of Guava & Sugar apple Trees but running wild & Choacked with weeds. At a little distance from the Garden we saw a very neat Pagoda belonging to the Priests of Vishnoo it was built of a hard stone which is very clean. The enclosure in which it stands is mostly flagged with these stones through which the water ran in every direction and it was planted all over with different variegated Balians [?]. Near the Pagoda we saw two Country Houses belonging to Patna Bankers. They have their Gardens much like the old fashioned Citizens Gardens near London as represented in Pictures 100 years ago. The Houses are nothing more than an open Verandah.

8th At Day Light Mr Hanson & myself landed intending to walk towards Patna we passed many ruins of large Tanks & Garden houses and after walking Three Miles we reached the City. After Breakfast I again landed & walked all through the City but could see nothing more than a common Bazar. We halted for the Night about half way between Patna & Bankipore under the Judges House. Mrs Sherwood & myself went to call on Doctor McNabb who we found well. Mr Rickets was in Calcutta & Major Stuart has removed to Dinapore. On the 9th we reached Deiga & halted a little below the nabobs House. I walked into Dinapore to the Revd Martyn.[128] I brought a Letter to him from Mr Parson. M^r M would walk back with me to call on Mrs Sherwood & he begged we would stay at his Quarters while we remained at Dinapore. M^r & Mrs Robinson (whom we met at Mr Parson's) were there. On the Morning of the 10th after calling on Major & Mrs Stuart we went into Cantonements to Mr Martyns with whom we were much pleased. We were introduced to Major & Mrs Young of the 25th Native Infantry[129] who were very civil & invited us to Dine Tomorrow but I was sorry to find that it is the Colonels intention to move Tomorrow Morning. On the 11th It being Sunday we went to Church to hear Mr Martyn who gave us a very striking Sermon after which we Breakfasted with Major Young & proceeded after our Boats in Palenkeens.

The Fleet had made so much way & the Road by the River was so bad that we left our Palankeens & went on board Cap^n Wheatstones Boat which was passing & when the Boats halted at night we regained our own. We stopped about Two Miles above Surpour.

On the 12th & 13th we did not move. I got a good Fish. On the 14th we crossed the River opposite the mouth of the Soan and halted at Muckun Gunge, on the 15th we entered the Chuprah Nulla in which we found Rapid Water. We passed Chuprah about 9 oclock. We saw Two Muggs Boats rowed by 24 Men each, they are like the Common Panchway but so long & narrow & without a Keel that they are very unsteady on the Water & require a great deal of management. There is not the least bit of iron used in making them. These Boats are often Pirates. The Muggs live in the Mountains to the North East of Chittagong & until lately they were always making incursions on the Bengalese but they are now kept in order by the fear of the English, at half after Twelve o clock we again entered the Great River & halted at a Custom house, which was in Ruins near the Mouth of the Gogra River which runs from Oude, here is a large Stone House & Stables which we understand are built for the Poosa Stud. We were alarmed by a Large Leak having sprung in our Pinnace & we got all our furniture out but we soon got it stopped, however had it happened in the Night it would have been very dangerous, the Water was rushing in very fast & the Bank was Steep, at Seven oclock on the 16th we crossed the Gogra & soon afterwards the Ganges, the River is now very

---

[128] Rev. Henry Martyn (1781-1812). See Eaton, Barbara: *Letters to Lydia: 'beloved Persis'* 2005; a biography of Henry Martyn.

[129] The Indian army started life in the 17th century when the East India Company recruited local personnel to guard its interests. These forces were organised into units in the mid-18th century. Indian military men or 'sepoys' were recruited throughout the subcontinent. Native regiments were led by British officers. National Archives: *Fighting for the Empire.*

shallow & we have barren sand Banks. We had however a little Breeze in our Favor & we reached Selimpore in the Evening having a good days work considering the Windings of the River.

The 17th we did not make much way & anchored under a very disagreeable High Bank

On the 18th The River was very low & in endeavouring to get round a point the Quarter Master & myself crossed the River but we were not followed by the Rest of the Fleet, the consequence was that we soon left the Fleet far behind & we halted for One hour & a half until The Rest by following our example overtook us. We were again obliged to cross in the Evening & we halted in one of the most beautiful Natural Parks I ever saw. It was full of little Plots of Trees Like Noblemens Parks in England.

On the 19th The River became so full of Shoals that we could scarcely get along. We passed a long sand bank on which were planted Poles with Flags on them which I find is intended to mark the Ground for a large Fair to be held here on the next Full Moon. We saw an old Devotee of some Religion either Mahomedan or Hindoo, he was sitting under a Tree, he is said to be a very holy Man. I suppose he will collect a great deal of Money at the Fair. We anchored about 8 Miles below Buxar & dined with Colonel Mawby.

On the 20th a Man came with Letters among the rest was one to Lieut' Andrews which we knew to be M^{rs} A^s writing we therefore took the Liberty of opening it & we found within one for Mrs Sherwood. At One o clock we arrived opposite Buxar. I did not cross over the River to see the Fort. I was told there was nothing worth seeing. Buxar was formerly a Frontier Garrison between The Bihar & Allahabad Districts & here was One of the Most famous Battles fought which gave the English the Country. [130]

At Eight o clock the 21st we sailed with a fair breeze but very slight we passed the Caramnara River this may be called the Rubicon of the English. Our Government were in a great doubt whether they should pass it or not & when it was passed The King & the Vizier were brought down. The waters of the Caramnara are reckoned very unholy by the devout Hindoos if the Smallest drop should touch a Pilgrim on their return from Worshiping at any of the Celebrated Temples he loses all his Trouble, they are therefore very careful not to touch it. The Inhabitants of its banks are however exempted. We very soon got under high Banks with a very rapid Stream. I never saw such Tremendous looking Banks.

---

[130] Battle of Buxar 1764.

They were I suppose Twenty Feet high and hanging over in a dreadful way, had it been a Month or six weeks ago I scarcely know how we could have passed them it has been continuously falling but now it seems in most places to have formed a Ledge by the Pieces which have fallen & the upper part which falls now rests on this shelf, there are however still several very dangerous Places in one of which Captn Coultons Budgerow was nearly overset by a Slice falling after passing this Bank the Colonel led us into a kind of Cul de Sac which having entered some way we could get no further & it would require some caution to get out as the Boats pressed on each other & the place was very narrow, we therefore halted to make arrangements for Tomorrow, when my Boat Brought up we had a Rocky Bank along side at least 20 Feet high & we had no means of getting on Shore but from the Mast.

On the 22nd we found great difficulty in getting out of our scrape & we were obliged to return by moving the next Boat first we had to return upwards of half a Mile and it took us Three hours to regain the Shore opposite where we had Anchored, we however made eight Miles & Anchored under a high bank covered with Bauble Trees (Acacia Mimosa) within sight of Gazepoor.

On the 23rd we had a nice breeze & we passed Gazepoor which has the Appearance to have been a Fine old Palace but we passed on very quick with a good Breeze which rather died away by the Time we reached the European Quarters. Mrs Cromelin sent her servants to Beg that we would anchor and dine with her but as Tomorrow is the 24th & I must muster the Regiment I made an excuse & followed the Colonel Three Miles further than her House. When we halted we received Three kind Messages with presents of Meat & Vegetables & a kind invitation to call if ever we came near them. We are very sorry that we could not see Mrs Cromelin & she bears a particular Good Character as is very steady Good Religious Woman which is not common in India. I mustered the Regiment this Morning & we proceeded a considerable way & Anchored on a Sand Bank.

[new page]

This begins our Passage up the Ganges 14 Miles above Gazepoor.

The 25th of October. The Fleet of Boats moved on about fourteen Miles and Anchored under a disagreeable Sand bank. I found myself very unwell, I believe from eating Cucumber.

The 26th This morning we had a little wind which assisted us but we could only go about 12 Miles. The Banks of the River were very pleasant with several small tipes of Trees. We saw some Monkies, they came down to the River side and did not appear to be frightened by the

Dandies[131] some of them even remained under the Drag Rope. The place where we Anchored for the night was under a high Bank, the Country round was pleasant & well cultivated and the Great Road to Benares ran near the River & seemed very good. We dined with Cap[n] Piercy & met the Col[l].

The 27 We had the same small Breezes to day which brought us within 6 Miles of Benares. We had a view of the Minarets of the Principal Mosque. We found a Large Stone Tank at the Village. The Fleet are not to stop at Benares to avoid confusion I therefore procured Leave to proceed before to see this famous City.

Benares

28th   About 2 Hours before Day Light I quitted the line of Boats and approached Benares before it was light. The City appeared to be illuminated and had a very pretty appearance as we came near we found the cause to be the Numbers of Hindoos who were performing their ablutions, they each brought a small lighted Lamp which they leave on the Stone Steps leading to the River. The whole bank of the River may be said to consist of Flights of Stone Steps some of which are very beautiful and I daresay are at the Least 60 Perpend[r] feet high some much more, most of these are on sand but they have a very grand appearance. The first place I visited was the Mosque with the Minarets in the Mosque in the shape of it, I understand it was built by Aurangab[132] on the Ruins of a Hindoo Temple. It stands on the most elevated part of the Bank and has a very good high Flight of Steps to the River, my head is not a very good one & I was afraid to go down them, they are very narrow & each step particularly high, it seemed like a precipice I dare say the Ground

round the Mosque was 60 feet above the River. The Mosque itself is nothing more than a porch, I walked round it in expectation of finding some Body to it but I was disappointed. In the Evening I again returned and with Captain Coultman went to the Top of the Right hand minaret we found 64 narrow steps to the Top of the Porch and 50 more within the Minaret. I believe each step may be reckoned at

---

[131] Dandies: boatmen.
[132] Aurangzeb (1618-1707) 6th Mughal Emperor, built the Grand mosque. The two tall minarets of the entrance gate became unsafe and were shortened and later demolished after one fell.

10 Inches therefore the bottom of the open part at the Top must be about 180 Feet above the River but this is only conjecture. I believe it rather more than less, from the Top the City & Country appeared to great advantage it put me in mind of a Panorama. I do not think that London from the Top of Sᵗ Pauls had a finer appearance: probably our large Fleet of Boats set it off. The narrow Streets were much in its favour as we could only trace them between the flat Terraced Houses but we could scarcely see the Bottom. The River & Flat well Cultivated Country appeared Beautiful. The Town of Benares and all Indian Towns are so different from those in Europe that no comparison can be made, the Streets are narrow, the houses very high with dead walls almost touching at the Top and the only openings outwards are more like loop holes in Towers than Doors or Windows. In these uncomfortable Streets you see Hogs, Sacred Bulls, Naked Fakeers, Pariah Dogs, disgusting objects of deformed men women & Children, processions, howlings, in fact you may suppose yourself in the Devils House. The Naked Fakeers are Horrid they walk about the Streets without a rag on, both Men & women & Glory in their Nakedness. We were insulted by one who came down to the Boat side & we were obliged to shut our windows I took my Horsewhip to one but I was afterwards told it was very dangerous. I afterwards went to the Principal Hindu Temple. Here I found them Worshiping Mahadis under the Form of a Black Stone, this is the most indelicate worship I ever heard of you have a very good Idea of this Temple when you see Bilinsgate Fish Market the Priests were constantly employed scattering Flowers & water about which being constantly trod on made it like a Fish market. The Black Stone was in a kind of Stone Trough[133] and partly covered with water & Flowers several priests were round it ringing bells and hallo'ing for Charity. Several Bramine Bulls were walking about and eating the Flowers. They made so much noise altogether that I was glad to stop my Ears & run away. There was small marble Ape and a Statue of a Woman which they said sometimes eats but I could not go near it. I could just see that her face was Gilt. As I did not understand the language of course, I may be mistaken in what I understood from the People. We went through the different Bazars which are as well supplied as any in India they are all distinct, the great numbers of shawls, Jewels, fine Cloth & Muslins are really astonishing. Amrat Row the Son of Ragonat Row or Ragoba[134] is here and they say he has near 10,000 Mahrathas with him, some Persons think it is dangerous

---

[133] The Lingam and Yoni representing the male and female sexual organs are widely worshipped.
[134] 'Amrat Row' Amrut Rao (c1770-1824). Maratha nobleman.

to allow so many in that rich City but I believe Gov^t knows how far he can be trusted.

29th We left Benares at four o clock this Morning to overtake the Fleet which passed us yesterday. The Illuminations appeared even to great advantage on this side the City it appears as if studded with small Stars. The Revd Mr Corrie a Friend of Mr Parsons sent a boat from Chunar to meet us with a present of Bread & Vegetables' which were very acceptable. As the day Broke we heard a confused noise of Horns, cracked Drums and nondescript Instruments enough to frighten any Body. I believe these are from the different Places of Worship to assemble the Mahometans to prayers. We only reached Ramnaghur today.

This was the Fort & residence of the Rajah of Benares & here I believe Chet Sing[135] lived who was deposed by Mr Hastings, it is not above Two Miles above Benares on the opposite side of the Ganges. The Fort seems the most compleat of any we have met with in the Country, but we could not see it to judge.

Gateway at Ramnagar Fort. 2015.

They would not admit us inside and the outward walls are encrusted with mud Houses belonging to the lowest servants. The Village of Ramnaghur itself appears to have been very regular in former Times. There was a

---

[135] 'Chet Sing' Chait Singh, Maharaja of Benares, deposed by Hastings in 1781.

very broad Stone built street Leading from the Principal Gate of the Fort which was crossed by another equally as well built and a large square in the center but all this Street was filled up in the same way with these ugly mud huts. The present Rajah has merely a nominal Power, but he likes to keep up his status, in the Balcony which is over the outward Gate of all Indian Houses, he had his Band which consists of Bad Drums and Horns which make a horrid noise, he had a few Large Trees near the outside gate and Two Panthers or Hunting Tigers, the Latter were not confined but walked about with their Keepers, also a small Leopard.

30th As we passed the Fort this Morning we found that it appeared to much greater advantage towards the River where there is no room for Huts to be built, it is built of stone and has a fine Entrance by a large Flight of Steps from the River. The banks of the River are rather high & shortly afterwards the River becomes broader & shallow, we found some difficulty in passing some sand Banks. In the Evening we reached an English Cantonement called Sultanpoor half a Regiment of Seapoys are stationed here, I should think it a disagreeable place. The Country being flat & Sandy.

31st A little before day light this morning I got into a small Boat called a Panchway and went a head of the Fleet to Chunar Ghat to call on the Revd Mr Corrie a Friend of Mr Parsons's. I reached this strong Fort about 7 o clock. The Hills here come down to the River, Chunar is very strong rising abruptly from the River, Mr Hastings saved himself here from Rajah Chat Sing when the English besieged it they were repulsed by the Viziers Garrison who rolled down large round stones on the Storming Party which swept all before them, they called these stones Mist Wallows (ie Drunken Fellows). The Stone of Chunar is very hard and is used to make Grindstones & Mill Stones &c. There are Piles of these stones in many parts of the Fort now prepared in case of an attack. Chunar is a gravelly soil over the Rock, it is particularly hot and from being so confined it is reckoned unhealthy. The Fort is Principally Garrisoned by Invalids.[136] I breakfasted with Mr Corrie and he returned with me on Board my Budgerow to call on Mrs S.

Benares may be seen from Chunar. The Mountains near Chunar have a pleasant appearance running close to the River & covered with wood, the River itself looks very pretty from the Fort. We were much pleased with Mr Corrie who was very kind to us, he remained near Three Hours with us. His Father I believe is either Rector or Curate of Stamford in Lincolnshire. We this day proceeded as far as Eight Miles above Chunar.

---

[136] Mentioned by Eric Newby in *Slowly down the Ganges*.

November 1807

We find the River getting very rapid and Shallow it was with the greatest difficulty that we advanced Eleven Miles the heat also still continues very great. The Thermometer stood at 90 in the Boat, we Anchored under a high rocky Bank

2nd The River winds now very much and is very shallow. We reached Mirzapoor this Evening which is about 10 Miles reckoning the windings of the River, we did not cross to the Mirzapoor side but I was told it is the same kind of Place as all the Rest of the Indian Bazars. Mirzapoor is near a great pass or Gaut in the mountains leading from the Maharatha Country and we have always a Small Force to watch them.

3   This morning Mr Hanson & myself got out to walk. On the Mirzapoor side, after walking between 3 & 4 Miles we came to a Garden cultivated in the European way. The Gardener told us it belonged to a Xstian Padre, probably an Armenian, here were many Remains of old buildings and Wells to all appearance as if there had been some Large Town. All that we could learn from the Dandies was that the River at One Time passed close by but the Bed is now nearly dry. This must have been the case as we found several fine flights of steps. As we came to our Boats we passed some small Temples in one of which we saw heaps of broken statues, some Large but most of them appeared to have been about 12 Inches hight. I brought away a womans head about as large as a doll's head, after embarking we saw Numbers of Persons among old Ruins performing some kind of Pooja and at a Great distance we could see a Gigantic Image of an Old Man with a long White Beard, we could also distinguish Numbers of Goats & Kids being sacrificed, their Heads being cut off. We did not proceed much further this day as the Wind rose from the N. W. but we crossed over to a sand Island & lay there very uncomfortably all night. The land was wet & the wind blew strong during the night. Col^l Mawby attempted to cross & Ran aground, but without damage.

4th The Wind came Round in our Favor & after some difficulty we had a fine Country with a sloping Bank we did not however proceed above 4 Miles today.

5th This day we reached a village caller Goo Gong in a very fine Country. We saw the Remains of a fortified village in the Fields were very large Stone Troughs or Mills to grind Corn. The Bottom one shaped like a Large Mortar and the Upper One very large & Heavy fitting in, it seemed as if it were worked round with long spars, like the Capstan of a Ship, but the difficulty of getting the upper into the Mortar or socket must be great for they were very Large. We were called away from these

3rd River Journey—Berhampore to Cawnpore 1807

Mills I stood in a Tope[137] by a Complaint that a man was distilling Rum for Sale to the Men. We found the Fellow in the short space of Time since we Anchored had erected a Compleat Still of Earthen pots and stoped them with Clay, the whole Apparatus not worth Eight Annas. He had buried the Reservoirs in the Earth. We found Three considerable Stills going. These we broke.

4th   The Breeze carried us along very well so that in spite of current in the Shallows we made 13 Miles. We anchored under a high bank my Budgerow exactly opposite a Dingle.

The Trees were covered with Birds Nests in the most curious manner, they hung by Threads from the Branches like large Fruits. This is done for fear of the Monkies. They were in such Numbers that it really appeared as if the Trees were overloaded with Fruit.

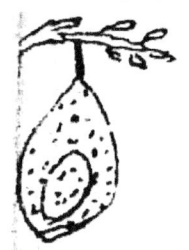

We found here great Numbers of Porcupines whose holes lay in the Side of the Steep bank.

7th. This Morning early we passed Lucker Ghee. I could not learn what it had formerly been but I have no doubt it must have been of great consequence, it seemed to be a very high hill rising perpendicularly from the River, encrusted with Brick work almost all the way up and in many places from the Top to the Bottom were earthen Jars laid over each other & fitting in in such a manner as either to have formed with them a hollow Well or else being filled with earth to have been intended as a lining for the Bank, the Boatmen say this place is remarkable for Thieves. This Evening we stoped at a Village called Seersa at the Bottom of a Bend in the River, it appears to be a place of some Trade. There were a great Many Boats on the Stocks and Several Temples, a Little further on is a small River which I believe in the Rains is navigable for a great distance into the Bundlecund. We had a prospect of a pretty rising ground or hill rising from the level Country called Parnassa. We called it Mount Parnassus.

The 8th & 9th   The Current was very strong and we only made 13 Miles in the Two days. Anchoring at Night on the Sand Bank.

Allahabad

On the 10th we reached the Old Fort of Allahabad on a point of Land formed by the Junction of the Two Famous Rivers the Ganges and The

---

[137] Tope: a clump of trees.

Jumna. As we approached we seemed to be advancing to a large old Strong Stone Castle standing in the very center of the River and shutting up the Passage but I presume when the River is full it must appear even to greater advantage. The Current of the Two Rivers mixing formed worlpools which threw our Boat round some Times.

As soon as we got completely in the Jumna the water was calm with very little Current, It was necessary to go a considerable way up the Jumna to cross it that we might not be driven back into the Two streams. We advanced I suppose about a quarter of a Mile and crossed. No sooner had the Colonel and Staff passed to the Allahabad side when a Signal was made for the remainder of the Fleet to halt on the opposite side, this I suppose was done to hinder the Men getting on Shore & running among the Artillery all over the Fort.

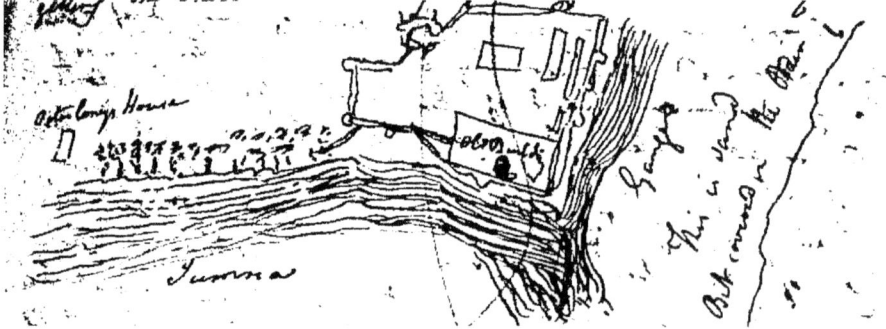

This is a very imperfect sketch & done without any kind of proportion but merely to shew how the Rivers come down. The Jumna is broader than the Ganges but, the one is at this time of the year very rapid & the other nearly dead water. We Anchored Close under Colonel Ochterloneys House which is very large. We should not find much closer space for our Boats As the Ruins have fallen into the River & make the shore difficult of access. As soon as it got cool Mr Nice & myself proceeded to view the fort. We went from the house under a Row of Trees & entered by a Sally port. We found the Fort very strong & just repaired, the walls on the River side are very high and seem strong nor could I see any height from which the fort is commanded, nor could an Enemy approach on any side under cover. They are Building new Officer's Quarters as the Old Mount Barrack both for Men & Officers are very close & not consequently very healthy. The Commanding Officers Quarters are very fine and look towards the Jumna. I have marked them. Even the old Buildings, the Ramparts are Thick and high. They are pulling down the old native Bomb proof Barracks, from the Angle of the Fort just on the Junction of the Two Rivers we had a fine view on your Right hand you see the Green Jumna coming down steadily

3rd River Journey—Berhampore to Cawnpore 1807

& quietly it is suddenly met at the Point by a Rapid dark muddy Torrent (The Ganges) Rushing with all its force against the Green Water, here & there it enters a small distance but is driven back, it appears to fight with violence for Two Hundred yards or More until the Battle draws to an Angle where the contention ends in Both Rivers joyning & becoming rapid yet the Right hand for a considerable way keeps it green color. Under the Fort just at the Angle of the junction the Hindoos come from all parts of Hindostan to Worship & devote themselves in innumerable multitudes. Many of all ages drown themselves every year some of whom come on purpose from the farthest parts of India. We had a good view of the Worshipers. It is not the Season yet however there were a great many & they made a most terrible Yelling.

N.B. Government exact a tax on all worshipers & our Servants requested a certificate from us that they were in our employ thinking & I believe justly that our name would have passed them free of Tribute but I refused to have any thing to say to it.

In the Fort there is a beautiful Granite Pillar covered with inscription but the Character is unknown. It was getting dark & I could only see it as it lay on the Ground near the Southern Gate.

The 11th   We moved from Allahabad. We passed the Junction of the Jumna & Ganges without any difficulty but about half a Mile higher up the Stream was very violent. Our Manjee[138] was prepared & we had bent new drag ropes but the water rushes down at a terrible rate. I hired 20 Additional Men to pull the Boat & the Wind Blew rather strong in our favour yet one of my drag ropes snapped & we only advanced 5 Miles by 5 o clock in the Evening, had we been in any common part of the River the wind alone would have carried us 20 Miles at least.

This morning (12th) we had a good deal of strong Water & we halted at Pahamoor to give time to the Rest of the Fleet, which did not get up until the Evening of the 14th. We saw in our Walks a strong Brick enclosure & the remains of a Palace which must have been a place of consequence in former Times. We were told the Emporer lived here when under the Protection of the English but I am not sure whether I understood right, here is a Gunpowder Manufactory. The Regiment lost some Boats getting Round Allahabad but no lives were lost.

The 15th   We moved on & halted on a low sand Bank near Coreasar. On the 16th we found the River very shallow rushing rather violently over sand banks. We were several Times aground & once we

---

[138] Manjee: boat master.

had a great difficulty in getting off. We halted again on a Sand bank in the middle of the River. The Weather gets very pleasant & Cool.

17th We advanced Better today the Country was pleasant & Woody. We passed the Ruins of some antient Town with a fine Gaut & Caravanserai of Stone. They called it Ramchowda & a little further Singhrore. The River became very shallow & we had great difficulty getting on. We halted at a pleasant village called Ianabad, here was found a Collector of the nabob of Oude Collecting the Rents, he had with him a force of 200 Seapoys 200 Matchlock Men & 100 Cavalry, it appears that the he farms the Revenue of a District & he seizes as much as he can, The Ryots have no redress & are of course very much oppressed. They fly at his approach burying all the money. We are told that the Farmers here have mostly ran away. The Farmers on this side are as bad for they never will pay their just quota except by Force. One cannot help being supprised at the absence of the Natives, for they dare not shew their Riches but bury it in the ground & they have no way of spending it. There is a great deal of Money buried in India but not much in the English Territory. We crossed & recrossed the River 4 Times on the 18th & halted near to Conkerabad. The Weather was very cold. The Country is hard rocky & dry.

On the 19th The Weather was very cold & quite unpleasant. We halted at Jumgerabad Among Old Ruins of Mosques & Pagodas. We saw the Ruin of a very large & strong Brick Fort. We inquired of the Villagers what it was but we could only learn that it belonged to a Man called Achelgree in the reign of Akbar & that it was then besieged & taken but they did not know who Achelgree was, they said he was a Fakeer. They also said that it was more compleat a short time since but that Mr Achmutly had destroyed it for the Sake of the Bricks he however found the Bricks too thin for his use. I understand that their being thin is a proof of their Age, the Wall of the Fort comes quite down to the River with Loop holes for Archers like York.

The 20th.   We walked up the Hill of Currah which must have been very strong formerly. There must also have been antiently a large Town under its protection as the whole country round for some distance is covered with Ruins. We found a great many porcupines Quils under the Fort. From the Top of the Fort of Currah we see Manikpore which much resembles it. It has a very striking appearance of Windsor Castle. We passed Manikpore with a fair Wind & we should have made a great way of the River had not been so very shallow. We halted about four Miles above Manikpore.

21st We did not collect the Regiment this Morning until nine o clock when we moved with a light wind we however passed Nabistash Ghaut about 3 Miles and halted under a Jungle full of wild Peacocks of which many were caught & shot. I presume not less than 50 by the whole Regiment. I had no Gun but I saw many.

22   We had a very fine Breeze & we reached Dalmow at One Oclock. The Fort of Dalmow like Currack & Manickpore is on a high & almost inaccessable Hill above the River. The Wind was fair as we passed Dalmow, It seems now to be a place of consequence we saw several very elegant stone gauts. We made 18 Miles today & anchored in a pretty place full of Zombie Beads. We dined with major Mansel.

23rd We had no wind & a very rapid stream in passing a point Major Mansels Horse Boat was overset but fortunately his Horse was saved, we passed an Old Brick Fort Called Hafremee & the remains of an old Fortified Village of the same name. We halted about 2 Miles above Singoore.

24th. This morning Mr Hanson & myself landed at day light & walked a very long way as far as Rampoor. The Country was in general Planted with Cotton & mustard seed for making Oil, and soon Mangoe Groves but whenever they wernt it was covered with a low thorny bush.

There is also a great Quantity of Barly & Wheat & a green called Bazra which grows much better than Wheat & has a small round Grain. We saw some beautiful Birds like Cranes but so wild we could not get near enough to shoot them.

25th We walked again as far as a place called Buxar. The Country well cultivated.

We found a Passage at Buxar and a great store of Corn of all kinds ready to be carried over the River. A Poor Man came begging he said he was a Grasscutter belonging to the Dragoons & was ill. I had no money about me but when I got on board my Boat he followed & I threw him a pice A Stout Fellow of a Fakeer came & took it away from him, nor would he give it up until I went on Shore and gave him a good beating with a Stick. My Boat Men who were Mahomedans thought it wrong to take the Pice away from so holy a man. I found out that all my Boatmen & almost all my Servants were completely drunk. The Lower Ranks of Mahomedans are great Drunkards, they all will drink any kind of Spirits & they also intoxicate themselves with Bang & Opium. They do not like wine because it is forbid by the Law & is also too cold for the Stomach, we halted opposite Suraghpoor.

—We found some difficulty getting along today the River is very shallow but we had a favourable Breeze & halted above Mijaff Ghur—

The Wind blew so strong on the 27th. That the Regiment only went its own length ie the Rear halted at Night on the same spot that the head Boat left in the Morning.

1807 November 28th   Cawnpore

On the 28th The Wind was still strong & the Banks very difficult we however reached Jaugesnow which may be called Cawnpore. Mr Hanson & myself walked into the Cantonements four Miles from our Boats. I had before written for a House & we found that it was necessary to purchase one, the 17th Regiment having left theirs not to be Let but sold. We thought that if it is necessary to buy, we had better buy one in repair. I therefore took the one belonging to the PayMaster of the 17th Regiment for 4000 Rupees or £500 Sterling this seems a great price but the Value of the Money here is not the same that it is in Europe. I paid at Dinapore Houserent in Sterling per Month £7.17.6. and at Berhampore £7-5-6 and the House not so convenient, this was 18 Per Cent for Money. Our House is a very good One. The Front Room is 56 Foot long by 12 Broad, there are besides three Sitting Rooms, Two Large Bed Rooms and Two Baths. It is compleat with Carpets for all the Rooms & Nine Pairs of Wall Shades. This is the form of the Infantry Cantonements at Cawnpore.

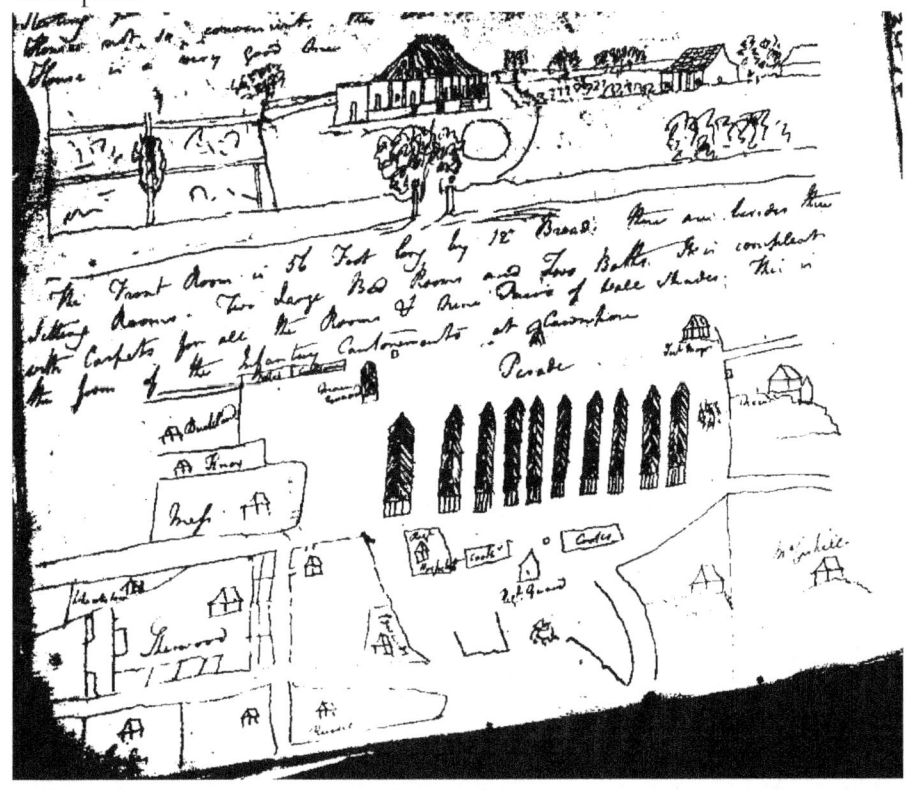

We find Cawnpore a very disagreeable Station. The Roads are up to our knees in a very light dust which is blown about by the least wind. Within the Walls of the Estates it is pleasant because the Gardens are kept well watered, my garden is in very good order, there are Six good sized Apple Trees, a very Long Vine, and Plenty of every kind of Indian Fruit, in fact when you enter the Gate it seems as if you had got into an Island from a Sea of Sand. As soon as I got settled in my house I wrote home to M^r T Butt, Mr Cameron & Mr Maskall. The weather is so cold we are glad to keep good Fires.

On the 15th We had good Peas, Carrot & Turnips in the Garden and Super Apples coming in, there is a great deal of Ice collected at Cawnpore which is preserved to Cool the Liquors of the Rich in the hot winds. The Method of Collecting it is as follows: they provide themselves with a number of very shallow Earthen jars which they grease & putting a small Quantity of Water in them leave them exposed during the Night & when the Sun warms them a little the Ice slides out which is carefully collected, but the ice is more like hoar frost, they sell Ice in the hottest season. Eight Pounds for a Rupee. I sent home a £100 but it was too late for the *General Stuart* which took the packet and the 9th Ins^t the Fleet is expected to sail in February.

My Expences last 8 Months have been as follows.

	Servants	Housekeeping & Cloaths	Houserent	Wine	Total
May	115	80	60	40	295
June	120	80	60	39	299
July	140	80	60	40	320
Aug^t	112	90	50		252
Sep^r	80	80	Boatrent 205	60	425
October	107	80	205	60	452
November	112	80	205	60	457
December	129	80	60	60	329
					2829

Receipts	Pay	Interest	Total
May	523-8	36	559-8
June	512	38-8	551
July	523-8	40-8	564
Augt	523-8	42	565-8
Sepr	542-7	42	584-8
October	563-8	43	606
November	549-	43	592
December	561	43	604
And Boat Allowance			450
Total of Receipts			5076-8

Cawnpore 1807-9

Total of Receipts	5076-8
Total of Expenditure	2829
Total of savings in 8 Months	2147-8
Total of Savings from Sepr 1805 to 1 may 1807	4750
Total of Savings in India Sicca Rupees	6897-8 or S[?] 7208
Equal in Sterling Money to	£901-

Thus ends the year 1807

But my real savings are £907-8-1 which arises from the difference of Exchanges in Rupees but this is to be understood of India alone as I had overspent from 24 Decr 1804 to 26 June 1805 £130 Therefore my saving is only £777-8-1 to take it from the beginning

January 1808

I have now nothing to relate except when I dined or what kind of Weather it is. I have not Horse & my Time is passed as follows. We do not rise until Seven o clock, take a Turn in the Garden, Breakfast at 8 and write & do my business within Doors until One then we dine read or write again until near Sun Set then to Parade, sit by the Fire till 9 & to bed and except when we are asked to Dinner in the Evening there is no change, for there is scarcely any News in the Country. On the 7th The Weather gets warmer and Pruned the Second Grape Vine, sent home a Bill on Mr Horsely of Canterbury for £60 in favor of the Rev^d T Butt. On the 9th Wind Rain Thunder & Lightning & the Weather gets cool again. The £100 Bill on Greenwood in favour M^r T Butt which I sent in Decr goes by the Ship *Marquis Welesley* on the 14th I again wrote home & begged him to Pay a Second Bale of Birch to his Wife.

On the 28th Gathered potatoes in the Garden and cabbages, Guavas coming in.

29th 30th & 31st Rain with Cold Chilly Wind. Lettuces Celery Endive Turnips Carrots Cabbage Cauliflowers & Potatoes in Plenty.

February set in Cold but towards the Middle became warmer. I must mention the only thing which now strikes one which is the continuous variation of the Price of Carried Money.[139] On Our arrival at Cawnpore the Calcutta Sicca Rupee was worth per Hundred 105. Furakabad Sicca, a Gold Mohur, Calcutta Sicca, 16. Fed Sicca 17, Pice 31 ½ per Rupee in less than a week the Calcutta fell to Par with Furakabad. The Gold Mohur to 16 Rupees to A^s Fd. The Pice to 29 Per Rupee. The Bills on Calcutta from 1 Per Cent Premium to 1 Per Cent Discount. They are all

---

[139] Some Indian states and the East India Company all minted coins. One rupee was equal to 16 annas, 64 paises or 192 pies. Rupees were silver and traded by weight and local value of silver. Mohur was gold of the same weight as the silver rupee but trading at local gold value, about 15x silver. Sicca was mint condition.

rising again now. The Arrival of our Regiment with a great many Calcutta Rupees may have affected a little in lowering their value yet there are other Reasons, as The Season for sending Cotton down. The merchants draw on Calcutta to pay for it. The labourors are so poor that the Merchant is obliged to advance before the ground is prepared & almost all this Money must be drawn from Calcutta, this happens in Decr and January at which Time Furruckabad Money is scarce & Calcutta Handdeals low but after this money not being wanted it rises & keeps up until November again. Pice vary on Account of the Pilgrims passing up & down & also about February or March by reason of the Mahomedan Mohurrum. People collect them to give to Charity at that Season.

The Nawab of Shumsheen Bahadur Pont[140] to this Station. He had been to visit his Fathers Tomb at Delhi, he halted a week & gave an entertainment to several Officers, he has a Territory in Bundlecund (Bandah). & he engaged with the Marathas in the last war but was beat by the English. He pretends to be fond of the English. He got drunk & threw away his Turban saying he would in future be an Englishman. The Throwing away the Turban or uncovering the head is one of the last things a Musulman will do. There are several Nabobs who dress in Breeches and Boots, Sandit Ali the Vizier even does but they all retain the Turban. All the Nabobs are alike in their Amusements, the same Nautches & Jesters act farces before them all & they dress most of their Time in this Manner, it rained in the Middle of February which is not reckoned good weather they say it brings on blights.

28th Feby   The Fleet for England got clear of the River on the 18th. Towards the End of the Month the Heat & wind were very uncomfortable & the Dust was blown about in great Clouds. The Brasil Cherry came in.

The Muhurram[141] began on the 27th.

March.

We were most terribly annoyed by Hossun & Hassun with the Drum & horns until the 7th. We could scarcely sleep all Night & our Servants were all drunk & fighting on the 7th. They were particularly Bad & we could get no dinner. The Guards were doubled & Pickets paraded all day & night as it is very common for the Hindoos & Mussulmen to Murder each other. Last Year a whole Brigade was obliged to march to Delhi to quell the Riots occasioned by the Religious Quarrells. When the Mahometans

---

[140] 'Nawab of Shumsheen, Bahadur Pont' Shamsher Bahadur II Nawab of Banda, Maratha.
[141] Muharram: 1st month of Islamic calendar, commemorates death of Caliph Hussain for 10 days.

had the power they were used to keep the Hindoos so low that it is not to be wondered at if quarrels arose. The Winds are very strong during the day but not so hot. We hear that a Fleet from England is arrived at Madras which left England in September, but we must wait with patience until April for our Letters. We hear that the fleet in February 1807 arrived in England in September. We gathered the first Bunch of grapes on the 24th. I wrote to Mrs Cameron with Bills Duplicates of 160 Pounds and the first of a Set on Mr Ellerton for £100. We gathered Asparagus & Artichokes. I wrote to Mr Maskall & we hear that all our Letters will go by Three Ships which are to sail in April. I sent £80 to Mr Maskall. Mrs Sherwood wrote to her Mother & Mr J. H. Brown.

April.

The Weather mild we had our Tattas on the Third but they are of little or no use. The Thermometer in the house with the doors shut not above 82 but in a Shed exposed to the wind it rose to 102, in a large house with doors open it was 90, the greatest heat is at four o clock in the Evening, on the 21st the Wind out of Doors became hot but not so bad as either at Dinapore in 1806 or Berhampore in 1807. The Thermometer in a House with the Doors shut 90 & in the Shade but exposed to the Air 100 and near a Tatta 80. The *Georgiana* Packet arrived from England I received a Letter form Lucy dated 3rd November & we also received Letters by the Fleet dated in July, all well. Marten had a Son born the 18th Augt last. Mrs Butt is gone to Live at Worcester & taken my Little Mary[142] with her. The hot winds have not set in all the Month but the Wind is Easterly & rather close & disagreable.

May.

The Weather very hot the Wind East & very slight, the days uncomfortable & long & the Nights very close & hot. The Europeans troubled with slight Fevers bur they do not last above Two or Three days. The *Procius* Sloop of War arrived from Plymouth, sailed in December. The News said to be — that the Prince Regent & the Court have abandoned Portugal & sailed for the Brasils. We have taken Madeira. We have as Enemies the whole Continent of Europe excepting Sweden & we are likely to be at War with America. On the 17th We had a heavy squall of Rain.

We are certainly the most extraordinary Regiment as wherever we go the Weather seems to alter our purpose for us, at Dinapore & Berhampore every one said what odd weather. They never saw the like before, and now every body says the same. It is usual for the Hot Winds to set in

---

[142] Mary Henrietta (1804-?), the Sherwoods' first child, left in England 1805-1816.

about the last week in March & to blow invariably from the North West as hot as Fire until the last week in June. This Years we have not had above Two days hot wind. On the 19th the wind blew with a deceatful coolness from the East, it feels as if cool, yet you perspire a cold clammy sweat which is very uncomfortable & you are always wet. The Nights are so close that we sleep as wet & uncomfortable as if water had been thrown on us & our hair is quite wet. The drops falling as from a Drip stone. The Thermometer in the shade & screened from the wind 101 & in a Room made artificially cool 87. We wrote to Lucy & Mr- Maskall on the 30th & the North West wind blew comfortably the 30th & 31st.

June.

On the 1st. The wind fell again and left a close heat. The River begins sensibly to rise on the Third I had a smart attack of Bilious Fever which lasted till the evening of the Fourth & then left me so reduced I could scarcely walk. On the 6th a heavy shower of rain from which time to the 13th a high Easterly wind with frequent lulls. The Thermometer 100 in the Shade on the 13th at Night it rained and also during the day of the 14th & 15th in occasional Showers, on the 16th it rained very violently nearly all day and on the 17th we had a few slight showers & the wind Turned to the North West but not blowing strong, the 21st it rained & then the End of the Month heavy cloudy hot disagreeable weather & little Rain.

Expences for Six Months—

1808	Servants	Housekeeping & Cloaths	Houserepairs & Interest of Purchase Money	Wine	Total
January	121	80	60	60	321
Feby	102	80	60	68	300
March	121	80	60	62	323
April	129	80	60	60	329
May	128	80	60	60	328
June	128	80	60	60	328
					1929

Receipts	Pay &c	Interest	Total		
January	561	15	576		
Feby	537	16	553		
March	561	18	553		
April	549	20	569		
May	561	22	583		
June	549	24	573		
Total Received			3433		
Total spent			1929		

Cawnpore 1807-9

Total in Six Months	1502
Saved to 31st Decr 1807	7208
Total saved to 1st July 1808	8712 or £1089 in India

I sent Home £240 Sterling which reduced The Interest received in this Country But the Real Saving in India is £1096 and the Real Saving since 25 June 1804 £964.

July 1808

On the first Second & Third it was very hot, on the 2nd in particular. The Glass stood at 92 but in a Shower fell to 84, after the Third we had no rain & the Wind changed to the North West gradually increasing in heat till the 10th When it blew a regular hot wind the Glass being as high as 98 at Sun Set. The Hot Winds continue and with great violence in so much that the Tattas which are always removed from the Soldiers Barracks on the 1st July, were brought back at a great expence. The Trees in the Garden are dying and a universal fear of Famine is spreading in the Bazar. The heat between the 10th & 24th is more than can easily be consieved. The Thermometer at Twelve at Night standing at 96. On the 24th it rained again which seems to revive nature. It rained every day the rest of the Month. Two Ships arrived from England being part of a Fleet which left England on the 6th March. They parted Company with the Fleet on the 26 March from some Reason known only the Cap^n. They do not bring any Letters & the only News which has transpired is the Death of Lord Lake & Colonel Fullarton.

August

I wrote to Mrs Cameron on the 2nd & sent it to Messrs Alexander & Co it rained every day until the 11th.

Sept^r

In this Month I sent Mr Maskall a Bill for £50 on Greenwood to pay Vernon. The weather continued wet & hot, the Glass in general 92 in the shade until the 23rd when it got cooler, on the 26th I observed the Glass fall suddenly from 87 to 80 in a Shower. We received Letters from England dated April 1807. I wrote a Short Letter to Marten on the 29th.

October

This Month was very hot. The Commander in Chief passed Cawnpore on a Tour through the upper provinces. I wrote several Letters to go by Major Buckland. The heat on the 20th was 87 after which we had no more reason to complain.

November

I wrote to Mr Maskall & sent it to Maj^r Alexanders House. On the Eleventh Major Buckland left us for England on the same day we had a good dish of Peas. We sent Letters to Mrs Butt, Mr Cameron & Mr Browne by Major Buckland & duplicate Power of Attorney to M^r T Butt. On the 26th we had a kind & Pleasant Letter from Oddingly[143] where all the family were Assembled together & were very happy, it gets so cold that we were glad of a Fire on the 30th.

December

Rumours of War & the 1st Regiment of Native Cavalry & the 2nd Native Infantry marched suddenly away. They say that Runjeet Sing the Chief of Sicks[144] has marched towards the English Territories at the head of Seventy Thousand Cavalry., The Reports which are raised are very contradictory. Sometimes we hear that the Sicks have plundered all the Country in a line from Kermand to Meerut but the report dies on a letter being received from one of the Officers who had been killed requesting a few Grose of Corks as his Madeira Wine was fit to be bottled. We however hear that the Army is in Motion & His Majestys 17th Regiment have marched towards Meerut. Reports still gain strength we are continued to be prepared to move, in consequence of which we have provided ourselves with Camels & Tents. The Seapoys are all marched away on 24th Towards Bundlecund.[145] I wrote to Marten, in hope of being in Time for the Ships which are now under dispatch.

My last 6 months Accounts as follows.

1808	Servants	Housekeeping	Houserepairs	Wine	Contingencies	Total
July	132	80	60	60		332
Augt	125	80	60	68	8	333
Sepr	126	80	60	62	19	345
October	128	80	60	60		329
Novr	128	80	60	62		330
December	128	80	60	70		338
						2008

Receipts	Pay &c	Interest		Total
July	561-10-4	50		611-10-4
Augt	561-10-4	52		613-10-4
Sepr	549-10-4	54		603-10-4
October	561-10-4	56		617-10-4
Nov	549-10-4	58		607-10-4
Decr	561-10-4	60		621-10-4

---

[143] Rev. Marten Butt, Mrs Sherwood's brother was 'mad' vicar of Oddingley.
[144] 'Ranjeet Sing' Maharajah Ranjit Singh (1780-1839) founder of the Sikh Empire.
[145] 'Bundlecund' Bundelkhand, south of Cawnpore, West of Allahabed. Maratha state, now part in Uttar Pradesh and Madhya Pradesh.

Total Received	3675-14-
Received	3675
Total Saved 6 Months	1667
My Credit 1 July	8712
	10379 In Sterling £1207

1809 This month & Year set in with very cold weather which in fact probably is as much as we feel the Cold in England. The Reports the end of the last Month were very numerous & contradictory nor do we as yet know what is going on, it however appears that we are marching an Army Towards Ludhana one of the Fords on the Sutledge the most eastern branch of the Indus it also appears that the Sick Chief Ranjeet Sing of Lahore has a large Army with him on the Western Bank but whether we are seeking to establish ourselves in his Country or whether he is troublesome we must be content to remain in Ignorance. The Newspapers are not allowed in this Country even to mention the Army if we can judge from the Reports. The great People are alarmed but of whom we know not. Two Armys have been formed. The First one under Colonel Ochterlony[146] which has advanced to Ludhana. The Second in which is H. M. 24 Lt Dragoons & 17th Foot are rather behind. We have also heard from good Authority that an order was actually written for H. M. 8th Light Dragoons & ourselves to march but a Spy came in with some news which altered the Plan. The Advanced Corps consists of One Regiment of Native Cavalry & Three of Native Infantry. The 2nd Army is encamped between Meerut & Seharampur in Latitude 30 North. We are informed also pretty good Authority that there is to be a European Regiment permanently stationed at Meerut as soon as Barracks can be built.

The Fleet for England sailed on the 23rd December. On the 7th an order arrived for the March upwards of H. M. 8th Light Dragoons and the Pioneer Corps. General St Leger[147] is also called up to the Army. We are now left alone how long we shall remain is uncertain. Reports are flying about. On the 12th the English Dragoons marched their destination is the Plain of Coel about 200 Miles to the north West of us. The probabilities

---

[146] Colonel Ochterlony: Sir David Ochterlony (1758–1825), 24th Native Infantry. Commanded four regiments in the first Anglo-Nepalese War. In 1816 made Baronet of Pitforthy, first Baronet of Ochterlony and British Resident at the Mughul Court in Delhi.

[147] Lieutenant-Colonel Arthur St Leger (1761–1823), 6th Native Infantry. Son of General Barrymore St Leger.

are so strong of our moving that we are providing ourselves with Camp Equipage & Camels. They are very scarce.

1809 January 15th Ajaighar Campaign

On the 15th An Order arrived for the Immediate March of Three Companies into Bundlecund, they are to take a strong Fort of Adgy Ghur near Callinger[148] which lies nearly West of Allahabad among the Mountains. Our 3 Companies which are now to enter on a service quite new to them & very different from European Warfare are all confusion providing themselves with Cattle & Provisions it is necessary for a Captain to have Six Camels to carry his Tent & Provisions. There are 3 Captains 6 Lieutenants & 1 Ass.t Surgeon wanting at least 46 Camels and 16 for the Privates tents – 62 Camels besides which the Men require Carts for their Baggage, which they cannot carry themselves in this Country & the Companys Provisions so that on a moderate calculation for every European leaving this, there is One beast & Six Black Men the Doctors Establishment of Doolie[149] Bearers is one Hundred altho I believe the whole Three Companies consist of no more than 250 Men the Number of camels could not be provided, nor could the Officers buy them at any Price. They marched on the 19th & we hear from them that being obliged to use Bullocks instead of Camels they are very uncomfortable. The Reports from the North West Frontier are favourable. It is said Runjeet Sing is inclined to Peace & that he will give us the eastern Bank of the Sutledge. We have now met Alexander the Great. The Reports now are sending the remainder of the Regiment into the Bundlecund after 3 Companies. I took a long walk through Cawnpore Bazar on the 20th & found it large & well supplied but what amused me most was a European Painting of Adam & Eve in Paradise which was worshiped as Maha Devi or Saib & Durga. Report is as busy as ever. We hear the French are in Persia & the Russians. We hear the Spaniards have rebelled & drove the French out of Spain & that the Spanish Fleet have come over to the English. We also hear that it is certain that there is a French Army in Cabul. We expect every Moment to receive our order for marching. We sent all over the Country for camels & I procured four & we all set to making Camel Trunks. On the 28th The Camel Agent received a Strong Letter from Head Quarters desiring him

---

[148] 'Callenger' now Kalinjar.
[149] Doolie: light palanquin stretcher hung from a pole, usually with two bearers.

to prepare for the March of the 53rd Regt we now look upon it almost as certain that we shall move. This Report of the Rising of the Spaniards is confirmed & in a very extraordinary Manner within Two days. Three different Accounts reached Cawnpore from Three Quarters of the World. From Turkey, From South America & from Madeira which brought an English Newspaper of the 8th Augt. The Bundlecund Army to which our Three Companys are Marching attacked the Fortified Hill of Chigourly belonging to Luckman Dowr the Adgyghur Rajah[150].

[Margin note: Adgyghur Invincible Fort. Luckman was a Brother to Adgydeo Persand offspring to the Invincable God Ram]

This Hill was defended by the Rajah's Uncle Adgydeo Persand who fought desperately, the Hill is represented by as cut into terrasses, one above the other & the Storming Party lost a Great Number of Men. Three Officers were wounded one Sircar dead & upwards of 100 Men. Adgadeo Persand was killed & the Enemy were frightened, abandoned the Hill in the Night. The North West Army remains at Chilkauna under Major General St Ledger. The Wife of Agadeo Parsand hearing of her Husbands death Burned herself & when going to the Pile told the Rajah Luckman that he was certain of victory provided he did not begin first & that he must allow the English to fire 5 Guns before he returned it. This might seem like a wish to be just but the fact is that it is only to deceive their followers for Luckman is a usurper & a Robber & has no right to be independent, in fact he appears to live something like the Neapolitan Bandits or Rinaldo Rinaldini. His Fort is on an almost inaccessible Rock & he rushes out at Times to Pilage the whole Country. At a few Miles distance is Callinger which is just like it & these Two Chiefs seem to rob each other & each others dependents as we read the Scottish & English Chiefs were used formerly to do. I hear that the Adgygaur Man is more enterprising & that all the Callinger Mans Villages have been destroyed. The Villages are strongly fortified with Mud but it was Adgydeo Persauds way to draw a small Gun to some neighbouring height & fire into the Villages knocking them all to Pieces. The Weather very cold.

---

[150] 'Luckman Dowr the Adgyghur Rajah' Lajshman Dada, usurper Raja at Ajaighar, about 15 miles WSW of Kalinjar.

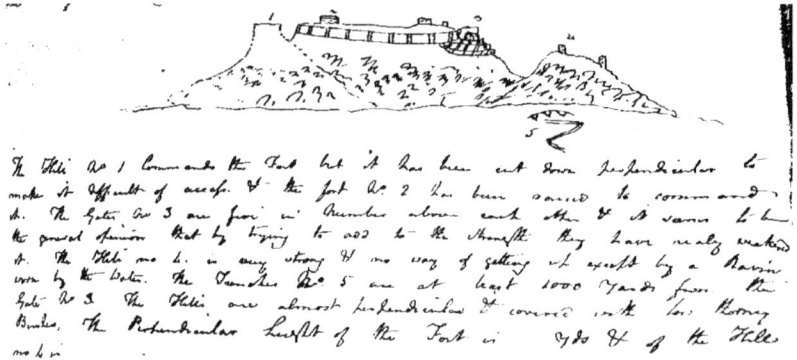

The Hill N° 1 Commands the Fort but it has been cut down perpendicular to make it difficult of access & the fort N° 2 has been raised to command it. The Gates N° 3 are five in Number above each other & it seems to be the general opinion that by trying to add to the strength they have really weakened it. The Hill no 4 is very strong & no way of getting up except by a Ravine worn by the Water. The Trenches N° 5 are at least 1000 Yards from the Gate N° 3. The Hills are almost perpendicular & covered with thorny Bushes. The Perpendicular height of the Fort is   [?]   yds & of the Hill no 4 is [sentence unfinished].

February

The Battery opened against the Fort of Adgyghur on the 4th but we understand at too great a distance. They are also in want of Mortars, the Howitzers will not admit of a proper Elevation. Our Officers write that nothing but a Bird can get in. They seem to think a Monkey would be puzzled. I wrote to Mrs Cameron on the 10th. We hear that the Hill No 4 was stormed on the 6th & altho it was so strong that the Men were obliged to lift each other up, yet the Bondelas did not fire a single shot. The party was headed by Capn Piercy (Ignes et Sanguines) The English got a Battery on the Top by the 13th on which day the Principal Fort surrendered. Our Officers think it could not have been taken had it been properly defended. I wrote to Mr Maskall. The Reports about the Regiment moving die away.

The Fleet for England left the River on the 26th. The Cold Weather continued very late this year I had a fire until the 19th. The Mohurrum & the Hoolie happened to fall together & we had plenty of confusion. We were very glad when they were over as our Servants were drunk for Ten days. The Revd Mr Jeffreys called on us on his way from Calcutta to Furruckabad to which Station he is appointed Chaplain. We were very much pleased with him. It appears that in the beginning of 1806 Three Clergymen arrived from Cambridge appointed Chaplains in Bengal. The Revd Mr Martyn of St Johns, the Revd Mr Corrie & the Revd Mr Parson.

These gentlemen are (according to the Term now used) Methodists that is exact followers of the 39 Articles. The Chaplain on the Establishment before (except Mr Browne & Doctor Buchanan) appear to have been to Socerier but I only speak from my Ideas not from any certainty. Mr Martyn's Doctrines were therefore Rather hard & he was commented on with some Bitterness by Elder Chaplains who thought Doctrines should be left out of the Question & that morality should be preached. This attack was repeated until it made so great noise & all Calcutta was in parties. Mr Jeffries never spoke on one side or the other (as he was the Military Chaplain & on a distinct service) until he was called upon to give an opinion which he did by reading the Homily instead of a Sermon. This of course went against the Moral Preachers and they were very angry with him. The Inhabitants of Calcutta were divided respecting the Propriety of reading the Homily. One of them said I wonder Mr Jeffries should read so old a Book are we not making improvements every year in the Services & of course in Religion also —

March

It rained hard the beginning of this Month. A Fleet arrived from England at Madras, left England the 17th September by which we hear that the homeward bound Fleet which sailed from this in Feby 1808 arrived in England on the 14th August. Our Three Companies which had been at Adgy Ghur returned to the Regiment on the Tenth. They gave a very pleasant account of their March. Bundlecund is not so much parched as the Dooaub and it is mountainous. The Villages are also better built being tiled instead of Thatched but by all accounts they are miserably oppressed by their Native Zemindars or Self created Rajahs who fortify every hill & pillage the Ryots & Travellers like Banditte. The Rajah of Adgyghur who was constantly at War with the Rajah of Callinger had destroyed all the Villages & cultivated fields of the latter, the poor Ryots were returning with their ploughs & a few Cows & Goats to occupy their lands when they knew that Adgyghur was fallen. To shew the manners of this Country I will only mention Luckman Dowrs history but I do not vouch for it. The former Rajah of Adgyghur had been so narrowly watched that he could not pillage the Country round & his followers began to threaten him if he did not pay them their arrears. They say that Luckman who had a few Thousand Rupees offered to pay the Troops & give him the Rupees if he would give him up the Fort. The bargain being made & the money paid, the first thing Luckman did after taking possession of the Fort was to seize the Money which he had paid for it.

1809 March 10th Cawnpore

The North West Army is to return to the Companys Territories, leaving a Force at Ludhana on the Sutledge which has been ceded to us. H. M.. 8th Light Dragoons are to return to Cawnpore. The Weather keeps very cool but the Wind begins to be disagreeable — on the 21st we received a very pleasant Letter from Mrs Butt & Mrs Cameron but on the 22 we had one from Mrs Marten Butt which gave us great uneasiness in that they had sent our poor Little Mary at <u>Four Years & a Half Old to an expensive Boarding School</u> against a positive bargain made by Mrs Cameron and also agreed by Mr Cameron before his Marriage that they never would abandon the Child. They also knew both my (& Mrs Sherwoods) rooted dislike to a Girls Boarding School. Both Mrs S & myself wrote home as strong as we could requesting that she might be taken from School & this will be an additional reason for Mrs Sherwoods return to England in this Autumn. I received a Letter from Mr Maskall dated the 23rd August mentioning that the Chancery suit was over.[151]

April

We had a very little Wind on the first & we began using our Tatas but the Wind was so light they were of very little use. My Letters which I wrote last Month go by the *Streatham* & *Lord Kieth* & we are informed that these Ships will not sail before the Middle of this Month, I therefore wrote to Mrs Marten Butt. On the 17th it rained and we were for several days very much troubled with Flies. On the 18th & 19th we had showers & the Weather much like last Year without Wind. The Army on the North West Frontier broke up the beginning of the month leaving a Detachment at Ludhana. The 24 Dragoons go to Sicunda. The 8th Light Dragoons return here & the 17th Foot go to Mattha, we expect the 8th Dragoons on the 10th May. The Hot Winds set in on the 25 & blew strong until the end of the month, on the 30th the Revd Mr Martyn arrived at my Bungalow having travelled in a Palankeen from Dinapore, the first part of his way he only Travelled by Night, but was obliged for Two days & Two Nights to sit on a Palankeen exposed to a Wind blowing like fire, he is very unwell & can neither eat or Sleep.

May

---

[151] Chancery Suit: Sherwood's father sued Mr Lilley Smith, his grandfather's executor, for maintenance of his children, Sherwood's step-siblngs, the grandchildren including Sherwood Mrs Sherwood: *Sherwood –v- Smith* established the right of children to maintenance from monies in a will trust during their minority.

The Hot Wind left us and we had a close suffocating Calm on the 2nd. Mr Martyn has been so overcome by his Journey that he cannot hold his head up from the Couch. The Thermometer is in a Bungalow close shut up, 96 & in Doctor Pollocks house which was shut up & had a partial assistance from a Tatta in another Room it was only 92 And in Colonel Mawbys where the Tattas were well watered the light excluded and a Punkah[152] at work they reduced it to 87. The Punkah or fan did assist in lowering the Mercury probably from the Dampness of the little air which entered through the Tattas. Mr Martyn fainted twice, I believe from the heat. The Hot Winds blew pleasantly from the 4th to the 12th when they fell & the Sky became overcast & altho there was only a little wind from the East it was not very hot, until the 14th when it rained a heavy shower with a Squall from the North West which was repeated on the 15th. This is again the fourth year of <u>very extraordinary</u> Weather as it may be seen by referring to June or May 1806 – 1807 – 1808 and now 1809. The Inhabitants still say what an extraordinary Year yet I found it is just like the years which are passed. These North Westers with rain every day for about a quarter of an hour at a Time, at other Times a close Easterly Wind as if steam was rising from the Ground. On the 24th the storms more frequent with a good deal of rain and also on the 25th. The 26 – 27 – 28 – 29 Dark close weather with east Wind & No rain. Mr Martyn purchased a Bungalow and left us. 30th & 31st Rain in Showers and then close Easterly Wind.

June

The Wind a little Better & on the 4th at Night it began to blow strong from the South but during the next day came again round to the East. We are informed that the Rajah of Adgyghur who surrendered himself & Fort in February last has without any known reason escaped from Bandah & gone into the Mountains, his Wifes father on hearing it stabbed all his family & then himself, this is common among the Hindoos & without any reason as the Natives as well as the Europeans always treat their prisoners Wives well. The South East Wind with very close weather stuck by us until the 16th when a very heavy shower fell & the Wind changed to the North West and on the 15th & 16th heavy rain particularly on the 16th when we had one of the most violent storms I ever saw in India. The Wind Blew from the North West getting warmer each day until the 19th when the Regular hot winds blew which continued to the 28th when we had a North East Storm but no Rain. The 29th we had a Shower & on the 30th a considerable quantity of Rain fell. A Frigate the Cornelia arrived from England sailed 29 Decr she brings accounts of

---

[152] Punkah: a hanging framed sheet operated as a fan by a servant.

the success of the French in Spain, my Last Six Months Accounts are as follows

1809

	Servants	Houserepair wear of Furniture	Housekeeping &Cloaths	Wine	Camels	Total
January	129	60	80	60		329
February	129	60	80	40	26	335
March	130	60	80	39	26	335
April	132	60	80	38	24	334
May	133	60	80	39	24	336
June	129	60	80	39	24	332
						2001

Receipts

	Pay	Interest		
January	561-10-5	62		
Feby	527-10-5	64		
March	561-10-5	68-8		
April	553-10-5	69		
May	561-10-5	74-8		
June	549-10-5	78		
	3317-14-6	416	3733-14-6	
			2001- -	
Total Saved in 6 Months			1732-14-6	
Saved to 31st December 1808			10379 -	
			12111-14-6	
			£ 1513-15-9	

Total Saved in India One Thousand four Hundred and Thirteen Pounds Nineteen Shillings and Nine pence from which deduct my Debt when I came to the Country £130 there should be upon the General Acc^t of £1383-19-9 but I always have Five Pounds more than I could Account for.

July 1809

The First week in July we had an Easterly wind with occasional light showers & dark Weather but it could not be called the <u>Rains</u> neither had we hot Winds, on the 3rd the Shower was rather heavy & again on the 7th which cooled the Earth. I had a good Complaint made to me by two of my Servants, they stated that, as they were proceeding quietly along The Road near a Village, some Men came and abused them & afterwards beat them. As I suspected that it was some very frivolous quarrel I wished to make light of it but I was told that if I did not endeavour to protect my Servants that they would not go into the Country any more & the consequence would be that my Camels would be starved as they can get nothing for them at Cawnpore. I therefore got hold of One of the Villagers & took him before the Judge, when it turned out as I had expected. That a Villager had abused but not struck one of my Men because he had left the Road & was crossing a ploughed Field. I mention this to shew how teasing they are: had I not made a bustle about this They would have refused to go into the Villages & it is very likely it was with that intention that the complaint was made. I therefore got the Judge (as a favour) to threaten to put them in Prison for bringing such a complaint & to tell them that if ever they did it again that he would certainly punish them, thus a good result came, for they are terribly frightened at a Judge.

Converts

The Revd Mr Martyn brought the new converted Arabian to see us, his Name is Sabat, of the Tribe of Koreish which is the Most Noble and of which Shah Mahomet was, indeed Sabat says he is a descendant of that imposter but I much question whether it is certain as the Mussulmans are very apt to say so & altho he is a Xtrian now, I think I can perceive a great deal of National & Family Pride in him. I heard the outline of his History from Mr Martyn & I think it curious. He was born on the Banks of the Euphrates near Bagdad. His Father died when he was very young and left him to the care of his Mother who (as he says) was a very clever & <u>Learned</u> Woman, (this is to be understood as limited probably she could read) of a Persian Family. He says they had a Number of camels & Sheep which they gave away in Feeding Mahometan Pilgrims, he left Arabia as a Soldier when very young & served against the French when they came to Palestine, he afterwards was in the Persian Services & was wounded often. One wound in his Head is still very troublesome, he left the Persian service & served as assistant Secretary to the King of Cabul, in this situation he had a friend who had some employment & was of the same Tribe, his name was Abdalla, he was very clever & a Poet (which most Arabs are). When the Wahabees took possession of Mecca he wrote to the King of Cabul & Abdalla was ordered to translate the Letter which he did, putting it into Persian verse & so pleased the King that he ordered his mouth to be filled with Pearls (this is a Custom in the Eastern Courts). Abdalla however did not seem happy, he was observed often to frequent the House of an American but the American having a handsome Daughter, it passed off as Love. He at length asked leave to retire to Arabia. Some time after this the Tartars from Bochara attacked the King of Cabul & Sabat was made Prisoner & kept as a Slave. One Day the King of Bochara passing, Sabat cried out "Justice, Justice." the King stopped & enquired why he cried for Justice. Sabat answered it is unlawful to keep a descendant of the Prophet in Slavery. The King enquired further & finding him a clever man he took him into his Service and raised him in Rank so that he travelled in a Litter & had a great Suwarree (great many Servants & equipage). One Day he thought he saw his old Friend Abdalla at Bockara and he ran at him but Abdalla endeavoured to avoid him. Sabat overtook him & observed that he had no Beard, he asked the reason & Abdalla confessed that he was a Christian & did not wish to be known. Sabat who was then a Bigoted Mahometan begged that he would not disgrace his Tribe and when he found him determined he threatened to bring him to punishment, this however had no effect and Sabat in a Rage had him seized and he was brought before the Learned Priests who wished to spare him, they therefore tried to persuade him to renounce the Xtrian Religion. When they found him determined, One said "In the Gospel of Christ is any thing said respecting Mahomet." This was done as they wished to turn the promise of the Comforters into a Prophesy of Mahomet but Abdalla Answered quoted the 7th Chap^r Matthew 15th V^{se}, on which the Principal Priest ordered him to be beat on the Mouth until Blood ran down. Sabat says he then thought of the time when he had seen the same Mouth filled with Pearls. Abdalla was then ordered to Prison and four days given him to change his Religion at the end of which in case of refusal he was to suffer Death. This was published all over Bochara and Numbers were gathered together. Abdalla was brought to the Scaffold & pardon offered but he refused to leave the religion of Christ, he then had his left hand cut off when again he was desired to save his life, they then cut off his right hand. Sabat was near him & Abdalla looked on him with a sorrowful countenance but not in Anger as much as to say why have you done this. Sabat says he looked kindly on him & he began to be sorry. They then cut Abdallas Head off. I do not know how Sabat left Bochara but he was afterwards Moola or Chief Orative Judge of the Mahometan Court at Vizagapatam, it was here that reading the Koraun he met with a passage which acknowledged that Jesus had no Father among Men but was conceived of the Spirit, this puzzled him for Mahomet never pretended to have been born unlike others. Mahomet died & was buried and it was not said that his Body rose again yet Mahomet allows this of Jesus. Sabat went to the most learned of Priests for an explanation, but they told him he must read & believe & not endeavour to find out what was above him. He was not pleased with this & he applied to an English Gentleman for a Persian or Arabic new Testament, but no copy could be got in that part of the Country. He at length procured one with much trouble & expence from Bombay and having read it he found that without understanding the Prophecies & the fall of man it was not clear., He had great difficulty in getting the Old Testament but when he had compared it he became perfectly convinced that Jesus alone was Christ. He applied to Doctor Kerr for Baptism who thought it right to delay until he had some proof of his being in Earnest. Doctor Kerr put it off so long that Sabat was impatient and at length he told him that at the resurrection he would be his accuser before God. He is now employed in Translating with the Assistance of Mr Martyn who is himself very capable of it as I understand that M^r- M- is perfectly acquainted with Greek, Hebrew, Persian & Arabic & I hear this Translation is likely to be very elegant. As I write all this from memory & having only heard it once, there may be some mistakes but I think it is nearly correct. M^r- Martyn thinks Sabat a true Convert but he is still a Child of Ismael & answers to the description in the Prophesy of Ismael. His Eye at times darts fire & he was subject to violent passions which he is getting over & I think has improved even since I knew him. He says that in Tartary and Arabia there are many persons connected & many martyrs still, for he knows of Two besides Abdalla. One of them a Relation of his own, but the proof of his conversion is not very strong for he says he neglected all Religious ceremonies & it was taken notice of & he was called before his Tribe who asked him the Reason, he said it was nothing to them & spoke like an Atheist. Some of them said it would be better to be a Xtrian than to disbelieve all Religion, therefore if you cannot be such a fool as that to believe in God probably the Speaker did this to try him. He acknowledged that he thought the Xtrian the best, but seemed undecided, however they stoned him for a Xtrian. The other was a boy at Bagdad who was converted by an American & endeavoured to escape but was caught and offered Pardon but he refused it on the condition of returning to Mahometanism.

The Weather continued Dark with a trifling shower now & then until the 24th when the Rains set in with violence. We heard on the 16th that Sir John Moore & the English had been driven out of Spain. The Fleet arrived at Madras about 12th, sailed from England the 22nd February. One of the Ships (The Warren Hastings) had reached Sangor but had been driven to Sea again however on the 31st we heard of her reaching Diamond Harbour.

Augt 1809

The Rains were heavy on the 1st & 2nd on the Latter day we received English Letters from Mrs Butt of the 29 January continued to 1st Feby and on the 4th we had Letters again from Mrs Butt & Mrs Devison but no News whatsoever except all well on the 9th The Regiment was reviewed by Generals St Leger & Fuller. On the 10th Mrs Sherwood brought to bed of a fine Little Daughter,[153] on the 12th I wrote to Mrs Butt & Mr Maskall which Letters go by the *Union*. The Flies & muskitoes very disagreeable, on the 30th we saw a very large Water Spout & some one Asked his Servant what it was, the Man said it was God's Elephant who was drinking. I immediately went to a Bramin who said it was Indras Elephant drinking but he seemed very much put out when I told him I had seen Numbers at the same Time, for Indras Elephant has no Young Ones therefore he said probably it might be something else & at last he said — foolish story —

September

Mr Martyn Xtrianed the Child Lucy Elizabeth on the 1st. M^r T Butt as Godfather & Mrs Cameron & Miss E Congreve as Godmothers. As we had determined that if I had another Child in India Mrs Sherwood should immediately return with it to Europe I asked leave to go as far as Calcutta to see her safe on Board Ship. We hear via America that the *Georgiana* Packet which sailed from Bengal in December 1808 arrived in England on the 23rd April and the *Tigris* & *Diana* & *Anne* soon afterwards but it is found Three Ships homeward bound are lost. It was very hot the middle of this month, the Glass standing at 90 in a close shade on the 20th I obtained Six Months leave of Absence to commence from the first of November. I sold my Bungalow for 3000 Rupees to Doctor Mack.

---

[153] Lucy Elizabeth (1809-1835). The Sherwoods' fourth child.

1809 October 25th   4th River Journey. Cawnpore to Calcutta, 955 Miles.

The Rains broke up with a most violent Shower on the 7th after which the weather became much cooler. I hired a Budgerow to take me to Calcutta for 300 Rupees she is large, 16 Oared. I was very busy settling my affairs & I went into the Boat on the 16th but our Friends gave us so many Invitations that we could only remain in the Boat during the Night, we passed most of our Time with Mr Martyn who was very kind to us & we met with great Civility from Col^l & Mrs Mawby, Capⁿ & Mrs Perryworth, with the latter we passed the Evening of the 23rd when they gave a party at the Christening of their little Child. The Colonel procured me leave to go away on the 25th and I only remained to muster the Reg^t on the Evening of the 24th and at half after five on the morning of the 25th we left Cawnpore. My Budgerow is to cost me 300 Rupees & my small Cooking Boat 70. We passed Nujaff Ghur at Ten & Surajpore at half after 2: we saw a very large Aligator laying on the Bank close to the Boat. They say there are no Crocodiles in the Ganges, I do not know the distinction but this I should suppose to be as large. We halted this Evening at a small Village called Buxar. Mrs Sherwood & myself took a pleasant walk in a Tamarind Grove & I enquired the Price of Grain, we found 28 Sur or 56 Pounds of Gram (a kind of Pea the principal food of the Natives & also of the Horses)[154] per Rupee, at Cawnpore there was only 21 making a Difference in 36 Miles of fourteen Pounds weight in half a Crown's worth. On the 26 we move at a quarter before Six it being day break and soon after I shot a peacock which was drinking by the Rivers side. I broke its wing but it ran like a Partridge & before we could get the Boat on Shore it had got into the Jungle. At a little after ten a strong easterly wind began to blow and it was with the utmost difficulty that we could make any way in the bend of the River, it was half after One before we arrived at the fortified Village of Hassenee. The appearance of the Village is very striking. In former times almost all the Villages were fortified & Hassenee, having a fine natural Rock, the people had fortified it very strongly but the little Hutts within are so close & small that it looks like an assemblage of Pig Sties than the habitations of Men. Since the English have been in the Country these forts are of no

---

[154] Gram: Chickpea *Cicer arietinum*.

use, the Gates are all pulled down & the mud walls suffered to go to ruin. It would appear at first sight that the country is all ruins & indeed some persons say it is since we have had posession but I think it is from the great safety of the Inhabitants who neglect their old Forts & Towns to live in villages and altho the Old stone buildings are in ruins yet the Villages flourish & the Land is cultivated & I think it must stand to reason that the People are happy for the oldest Man does not recollect War which formerly drove them into forts. They might as well say England is ruined because the old Castles are suffered to go to decay. We reached Dalmow & saw an Old man brought to the River side to be smothered, he was not dead but his relations had given him over & when that is done the Poor man in general wishes to be brought to the River to die & to make quick work of it they stuff his mouth & Ears with holy Mud & so stifle him. This is one of those things which appear continuously & cannot be denied by any defender of the Mild & Innocent Hindoos. Dalmow is the ruin of a Fine old Moorish Castle Built on a Rock & there are also some ruins of Mogul Houses with pleasant Gardens.

27th   We got on very well as far as Nabustah Gaut but the Easterly wind arose again very strong about 12 o clock and we proceeded very slowly to a little Village about Six Miles above Manickpore.

28   This day we had but little wind & we passed Manickpore at Eight. Currack at Ten and came in sight of Shazadazapoor at Eleven. This latter is not on the River except in the Rains. We passed a large Detachment of large Troops from England to Cawnpore. Colonel Wade of the 8th Light Dragoons had charge of them from Calcutta. We halted at Ramachowda Ghaut.

29th   at 7 o clock we saw Oujany and Papamow at Twelve. The Boats which we passed prepared us for very violent Water at Allahabad, it always is so but sometimes much worse than others, it is now so strong that the Boats had been 12 days coming round five Miles. We found it as they said for the Boat seemed as if it flew and at the Bastion at the Fort just at the Junction of the Jumna & Ganges notwithstanding all our exertions we were drawn against the Fort & we struck so violently that we were fortunately whirled round into the Eddy & had just time to reach the shore before the Boat was half full of Water, she had struck on a Pile and knocked a large piece out of her Bottom, had she not been new & strong there was every reason to suppose she would instantly have gone down. I immediately applied to Capn Fuller of the Artillery who has charge of the ordnance Department and he kindly sent Men down to my Assistance but we could not clear the Boat during the Night but on the

Morning of the 30th   we got into another Budgerow & brought ours down on her side. It was repaired by 12 oclock. The hole was very large & difficult to stop.

30th   In the Evening we walked in the Fort and saw Jihangiri the 2nd Son of the Mogul who is a prisoner there, he is not above 19 yet they say he is a vicious Drunken Young man, it appears that his Mother has great Influence over the King (Shah Abbas) and that she was trying every thing to get him declared heir, but the Eldest Son being in the way, he attempted to Murder him, but the present reason for his being confined is his having fired on Mr Seton the British Resident in a Drunken fit because (they say) His Father had given orders that he should have no more Spirits, but I am apt to think that it is about his Elder Brother that he did it & that this is the Story given out. I heard from good authority that the eldest & rightful Heir was obliged to claim the British Residents protection. This Mans Mother is not one of the Lawful Wives. This Young Man is a regular Descendant of Tamerlane but he is very Black.

I could not get a good sight of the Stone Pillar but I believe it to be about 48 feet Long, One Single Stone, it is covered with unknown Characters. I understand the Engineer wishes to raise it up & I hope he will succeed as it is a great curiosity.

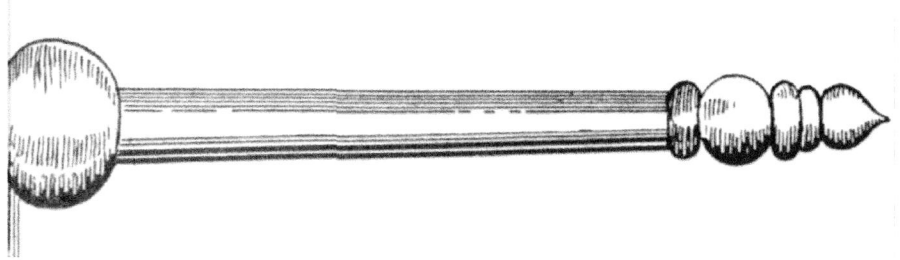

Ashoka Stambha, Allahabad.

3rd Century BC. 36 feet (10./M) long. Re-erected 1838.

We left Allahabad at the critical Hour. The Boat did not admit much water and I hope repairs will do. We reached the Village of [Doass?] at Ten o clock but now the East wind set in strong and had not the Water been so strong we could not have advanced at this Place Dum Dum there is very strong Water which I recollect in coming up in March 1807, the wind became so very strong at Two o clock that we stopped about Two Miles below Seenah.

November

We had the Easterly wind this morning before Sun rise but not very Strong we passed Luckergee at 7 and Geerah at Ten from which I should think that Luckergee is nearer to Luraa & further from Geerah than it is laid down in the Maps, we passed the Broad part of the River & halted at a Ferry on the right side of the River about Two Miles above Gooly. On the Second we reached Mirzapoor, the latter part of the way the Water was rapid & shallow. We had a Sail up. Just above Bendeh Abbassie & we ran aground with great violence but did no damage.

Suttee

We found Mr Rickets at Mirzapoor who was very kind to us and pressed us to stay a day or Two which we were obliged to decline fearing we might be to late for the fleet. Mirzapoor is situated on a very high rocky Bank & it is not far from a Principal Pass into the Maratha Country there is always a Battalion of Seapoys Kept here. We dined with M^r & Mrs Rickets, there were two Gentlemen at Dinner and the Conversation turned on the Natives. A Woman having <u>(with Mr Rickets permission)</u> burnt herself two days before and another about a fortnight before, I enquired into it and the Story I heard was this. A woman of a low Cast (a Paun Seller) went to request permission from Mr Rickets (as Judge) to burn herself <u>for the Judge if he pleases may hinder them.</u> Mr R. only sent his Servants to persuade her not and to offer Money if she was in distress, when the Money was offered she shewed her Arms which were covered with Silver rings & said what does the Gentleman mean I have plenty of Money but I wish to rejoin my Husband & if the Gentleman will not allow me to be burnt I will Poison myself. M^r Rs Servants contented themselves with prevailing on her to put it off until the next day to see whether she had been taking any intoxicating drug. The next day as she seemed determined she was allowed, when she reached the Pile she told People round her that this was the Third time she had burnt herself on the same spot & that she was to be born again & burn herself again. This seems very inconsistent as I always understood once burning was sufficient to carry her to Heaven, besides by her own Account she had lost rank, as the time before she had been a Bramin's Wife. A Gentleman who had seen a Woman burn herself related as follows. A Certain Number of Faggots mixed with Old Straw are Piled up on which the Widow is placed with the corps of her Husband on her lap she is then surrounded with other Faggots and built into the Pile, when this is finished she in general receives a Brand and sets fire to the Straw but sometimes one of her Young Children is ordered to do it, it is reckoned a good sign if she can repeat several times the Name of Sitta Ram after the pile is alight each time that she calls out the People round shout out and seem to enjoy it. This Woman repeated Sitta ram Three Times. The Gentleman remarked that when the fire reached her Cloaths she attempted to put it out & seemed uneasy. The Priests immediately set up a loud Shout & threw fat & wet straw into the flames so that she could neither be seen or heard. There is a great Reason for Hindoo Women burning themselves independent of their <u>wish</u> to join their Husbands which it is probably they would sometimes wish to avoid (as they are not remarked for being very kind to each other). This is that a Widow becomes Immediately a Slave to her own Children and all her Jewels & fine things are taken away she is if any thing worse treated than the other Slaves, but very few of the Rich or educated do it. You scarcely ever see the Widow of a Bramin or Rajepout burn themselves. They are mostly from mixed Casts.

From talking on this Head the Gent[n] told me more stories of the Natives & as they were Indigo Planters & live much among them they have better means of Information than we have. M[r] Rickets told me the following. When he was Collector of Patna a man came crying for Pardon and asking his Servants to Drive him out of the Compound but they would not being afraid of touching a Fakeer. He was therefore obliged to hear what he had to say. The man produced a Paper signed by General Clark " I release the Bearer out of Purgatory." The mans Story was that in a former State of Existance General Clark & M[r] Rickets were two holy Bramins who lived in a Tope & that he was a very wicked Man who set fire to the Tope upon which he was cursed by the Two Holy Men in consequence of which he was then born a Leper. He said he had performed Pilgrimage to all the Celebrated Temples, Jaggernaut &c but that he never should recover until General Clark & M[r] Rickets pardoned him. M[r] R. thinks this was put into his head by some of the Priest, that he seemed to believe it himself.

Aghori Sadhu

Another Gent[n] told us of a Sect or Cast of People[155] near him who make it a rule to be acted upon in every instance they are naked & never resist in the least altho they are Hindoos if you put Beef before them they will eat it or Wine they drink it, if you push them they walk if you stop them they stand still & if you knock them down they lie til some one puts them

---

[155] Aghori sect still claim to be corpse cannibals in 2015.

up again, if you took them in the River or to the edge of a Precipice & push them from it they would not endeavour to save themselves. He says they will just as soon eat Human carcases as any thing else, the other Two Gent^n agreed to it, and said that a man was taken in the Act of Eating a Body which had been stranded, he was brought before the Magistrate to be confined as a Mad Man but nothing could be made out against him, and it appeared that all the Men of his Tribe did it.

On the 3rd we left Mirzapoor & arrived at Chunar at Three o clock and were kindly received by the Revd Mr Corrie, at the same time that we arrived Cap^n McCaskell, L^{ts} Price & Nice arrived from Calcutta. We spent the Evening with Mr Corrie and left Anny & Sally[156] in charge of Miss Corrie. Anny she has undertaken to keep and Sally is to go to Mrs Robinson at Benares but M^{rs} R being now very unwell Miss Corrie will take care of her for a short time.

On the 4th we reached Sultanapoor otherwise called Choata Calcutta at 7 o clock and we came in sight of Benares at Ten but the water was very shallow & the wind rather against us we did not stop until Twelve at the River Gaut. We had expected here to have met a Buggy to take us to Mr Robinson's at Seeroli but as it was not there I put Mrs Sherwood and the Child into a Palenkeen and as the wind blew rather cool and set off walking. I did not know the exact distance but I found it five Miles and altho the wind was cool the Glare and the Suns heat were very disagreeable. I made but short marches from One Tope to another and amused myself in the Shade with looking at the Silk Winders. Their operations are so simple, they chose a large Tope and stick split Bamboos in the ground in Two rows sometimes as long as an English Rope Walk and wind the Silk round them; from off the original Reels which form the skain. The man holding a Reel in his hand to which is attached a bit of Bamboo with an Iron Eye at the end through which the Thread runs, to avoid entangling he walks all round these little sticks running off the Silk. I should conceive he must be much tired before night as he is constantly walking. The Thick shade of the mangoe and Tamarind Tree is of great use to him and appears at first sight a delightful kind of life, it would make a fine Picture, or may be compared to Mr Belshams description of Bengal in his History of George. But in reality it is very different. The heat dries up the Ground so much that the dust is driven before the wind in all directions. The Pools of Water are green & from dirty customs have

---

[156] Annie Childe, adopted by Sherwoods in 1807, remained in India. Sarah (Sally) Pownall, adopted in 1808, returned to England with Sherwoods. Adoption, as a term used by Sherwood, was what we term fostering as adoption was not legally regulated until the Adoption of Children Act, 1926.

a very strong smell, the Borders are Mud & full of all manner of insects, in fact a more disagreeable place cannot be conceived. I had advanced in this Manner about three Miles when I came to the Bank of a small River, at which Place Mr Robinsons Buggy met me. We found Mrs Robinson (who I formerly mentioned as being so like Mrs Marten Butt) very ill and I could not see her but Mr Robinson, who is a Son to Doctor R. of Leicester received me very kindly. Tecrole is the European Station which with regard to Benares what Dinapore & Berhampore are to Patna and Moorshedabad, here are Judges of Appeal, District Judges, Judges, Two battalions of Seapoys. The Country is like Cawnpore flat but broken into ravines by the heavy Rains, the soil is what is called conker being in appearance like the Rubbish of an old house, it is very porous and when wet is like a Chalk. Mr Robinson had a large Bungalow & garden & we think that he copies too much of the old Indians, his Income is scarcely half mine yet his expences exceed mine by 1/4 but a great deal is to be said for him from his Situation among the Judges &c who receive & spend 1000s for our 100s.

Hindu Muslim Quarrel

A Week before our arrival a most violent quarrel happened between the Hindoos & Mahometans in which 3/5 are said to have been killed in one day 200 of whom were Mahometans. The Quarrel arose as follows. One of Monsieur St Pierces holy and Inocent Men (who are the greatest Rascals in the World) found a little Image in the Ground and made it his God & built a little Clay platform and a little shed of straw & worshipped it. Vowing if it would be his God & send him a Child that he would build it a Puckah (Stone or Brick meaning ripe and compleat) House. As he had a Child he thought to perform his vow but he had forgot that the Land was not his. This belonged to a Mahometan mosque but was so situated that the little shed had never been remarked, however when he attempted the Puckah House the Mahometans were roused and probably some words arose. The mahometans met & their Zeal became violent. They Killed a Cow (One of the Hindoo Gods) and sprinkled its Blood over the little Bood & defiled it for ever. They then were bent on destroying Idolatry they proceeded to the Celebrated Stone which is said to have fallen from Heaven & that it was to last as long as the Hindoo Religion & Hindoo Casts were to remain. They said it had considerably decreased lately when Aurunzeb destroyed the Hindoo Temples at Benares. They say he attempted to destroy this Stone by firing his Guns at it but the shot recoiled on his Army & they say killed 1000 of his Men, others say Furious Beasts came out of it & cut 1000 of his Men to Pieces upon which he deserted. The Mahometans now Piled Wood on this Stone & set fire to it & then killed another Cow threw its Blood mixed with Water on it when hot and the Stone split into many Pieces. They then went to the celebrated Temples one of which they destroyed but fortunately for them the Seapoys arrived and saved the One <u>which was built before the flood</u> otherwise the Hindoos would never have been pacified. The Hindoos now began to collect and as they are 100 to 1 soon drove the Mahometans away into their Houses & beat their Childrens brains out against the stones in fact they acted like Devils. The Mahometans did act in this Manner, they seem of the Two much the Mildest at all times. The Hindoos pulled down one of the Mosques which is dedicated to Fatima & killed Pigs in all the Mosques the only thing which saved the Minarets was a fear of their falling on their Heads & while they were deliberating the Soldiers arrived. It was curious to see with what respect they behaved to the Seapoys fourteen of whom put to flight Thousands of men completely Armed & quiet was restored by only One man being Killed by the Seapoys. Some of them at the first attempted the House of the Princes the Sons of Jihanidar Shaw. The Eldest Son of the Late Emporer Shah Allum & as they were unprepared the foremost of the Mob had got within the Gate but the Servants killed one & fortunately succeeded in Closing the Gates. It is to be remarked that all the Natives Houses of any Rank are very Strong fortifications. The People are not yet calm & the Mahometans are all hid. It is fortunate that both sides paid such respect to the English who ran between them without fear or even danger. Mr Wilberforce Bird son of Mr Bird formerly M. P. for Coventry is the acting Assistant Magistrate, he was much employed & as I did not personally know him I did not call. The shops are still shut and no business carried on nor is any Person (except Soldiers) allowed to go into the City armed. Mr Robinson has all the wounded to take care of. Among the rest is a Boy who has some little Landed Property near Benares & was sitting Quietly in his House not knowing of the Quarrel when the Hindoos rushed him & cut him with their Salwaurs, he was unarmed and raised up his hands to defend himself, he is so severely cut that they are afraid he must loose One if not both hands. We heard here again of some well authenticated Stories of the Innocency of the Hindoos. A Woman is now in Jail for throwing her own Child into a well and the only reason she gives for it is that a Person had offended her & the Childs Ghost would now haunt him. I lately met with the Jesuits Letters, the Editor of which doubts this account of these cruelties, but I think them the best description of India I ever saw. They certainly (from their wish not to pass for Europeans) must have studied the manners of the Natives better than any other Person. I was told as a known & positive fact that there is a Feast (Poujah) in which Two of the Handsomest Children of about Two Years old personate Two of their Dieties after which they are not suffered to Live yet all this fact is known, the honor is so great that no Hindoo ever hesitates to give up his Children.

November

The Sixth.   We left Mr Robinsons on the Evening of the fifth and came to our Boat. We sailed in the Morning but owing to the great winding of the River which sometimes turned directly against the Wind we only got to within Two Miles of the Gormty River. The Country begins to be much pleasanter & we see Palm Trees but not in great numbers.

7th We went on very well to day as far as Jumersah when we were overtaken by a most violent Hurricane & we had scarcely time to get our Sail in & it was afterwards very difficult to reach the windward shore,

8   We arrived at Gazepoor at ten o clock where we stopped Two Hours to purchase cloth. I have been reading Barrows & other Persons travels & descriptions of Africa & I cannot help thinking that there must be some error in the Translating the word Peacock in the Account of Solomans sending to Ophir. As I should think there are none in Africa. I have made many enquiries but I have reason to believe it is so, and It is also remarked that altho Elephants have tusks in India yet they are often found without them & Ivory is not so common in India. I have heard it said Peacocks should be Parrots which seems more likely as Peacocks are found in Persia & therefore one would suppose no great rarity in Judea. I have been told to mention this as Tarsis was Subject of general Conversation at Cawnpore and we were all looking for it for from there also Peacocks were brought, from Gazipoor we had a strong wind, rather more than I liked which carried us to Buxar, at Six o clock having ran 38 Miles notwithstanding we halted Two Hours at Gazepoor.

9   We had a Calm all day to day & we floated down very pleasantly about 30 Miles.

10th We passed the Mouth of the Gogra at Two o clock & ran into the Choprah Nulla which was so very shallow we had great difficulty getting on. The Palm Trees now become very common & we observed the Wells to day being much nearer the surface of the Earth and the water is drawn by an inclining Pole, above this they are obliged to employ Oxen. We stopped at the Eastern End of the Choprah.

11th At half after Eleven we saw the Great House at Dinapore & at Three we stopped under Doctor McNabbs at Bankipore. Mr Robinson had written him from Benares to beg that he would vaccinate Little Lucy & he thus was prepared & promised us to do it tomorrow morning. We found them very stiff & cool but it seemed their manner as we formerly remarked the same thing.

12   We breakfasted with the McNabbs & about Eleven the Child was inoculated & at One we dropt down to Patna & halted in the Center of the City near the great Bazar, in which we took a walk, we bought 2¾ Surs of fine white Sugar for a Rupee & 23 Surs of fine Table Rice 8 Rupees.

13   We passed Mr Parson with his intended Bride & halted at the Old City of Bar being Forty Miles from Patna.

14   We had a fair Wind & we stopped a little below Surajhgurrah & about 16 Miles above Monghir.

15   At Ten oclock We stopped at Monghir for 3 Hours to buy Bread & Butter. Mrs Sherwood bought Two Chip Hats[157] for a Lady for Two Rupees Eight Annas the Pair. The Old Fort of Monghir is now in ruins, it has formerly been very large & contains a great space of ground which is very pleasant, being in small elevations & well covered with grass which appears as if newly mown. There is a Large House on One of the Hills within the enclosure which has a fine lawn from it & at the Bottom two extensive pools which appear to be kept clean, they look very pretty. Monghir formerly was the Residence of the Sabah of Bengal & it was also intended to have been again fortified by Cossim Ali Cawn but he had not time, at One we passed the Rocky Hills of Sittacund, they are nearly bare & look like a Heap of Ashes, if you may compare such large Heap of Stones to Ashes, at the foot of these Hills are two or Three Hot springs the Water of which is too hot to be touched, the Hindoos think they are Holy & tell some odd stories about Rams wife being purified here after she had been recovered from the Great Ravun.

16th We passed the Rocks of Jungara but the Wind was much against us. We found this River much altered since 1807, it has forced itself against its right or Southern Bank and almost made its principal Channel through the Boglipore Nulla. This Nulla in 1805 began a little below Jangara & opened near Calgogny, at present it is not above Five or Six Miles Long beginning about Three Miles above Boglipore & entering the Ganges about Two Miles below & even that is navigable nearly all the Year. Several Lives were lost & villages destroyed by the change. We found Doctor Glas very Civil & he pressed us to stay Tomorrow but we are fearful of being too late to get through the Hoogly at Moangonge we

---

[157] Chip: fine wood strips woven like straw.

therefore only Drank Tea with him. He was as violent as usual & seems to think that we shall all be murdered if the Missionaries are allowed to preach. Poor Man he takes up an idea so violently that it would be useless to say any thing to him, he seemed to exult in a story of some disturbance at Malda which I do not quite understand but it seems the Natives burnt the Missionaries Church down. Boglipore is close under a Ridge of fine wooded Hills inhabited by a Class of Men that seem very different from the Hindoos, they have no Casts, nor have they any of the Hindoo Religion. They have a Custom once a Year of sacrificing a Buffaloe which they do by every one plunging his Knife into the Animal and receiving the Blood in his hands drinking it up. They have a kind of Treaty with the Tigers which infest these Hills & you cannot prevail on them to break it except they are first attacked, if a Tiger destroys any thing belonging to a village, The Truce is broken & they immediately join & Kill a Tiger & then stop. They are a very Active Race & formerly were Enemies to the Natives of the Plain & disturbed them very much but Mr Cleveland prevailed upon them to make Peace & enter into our Service & we have now some Companies of them & they are found a very useful Contented Race & never hurt the Hindoos since.

17   At Eleven o clock we were within sight of the Hills of Colgory but a strong Easterly wind arose & the men were obliged to go on Shore & track down which took Two Hours for about Two Miles. The Wind fell & the Current was strong from Colgory to Pattergotly. We passed the Point at Three & Crossing the River we were among the sands until upwards of an Hour after Dark when we reached Pointy.

18   The Easterly Wind rose even before Sun rise & increased so much that we had considerable Waves & the Current could not keep us against the wind & about Nine neither the exertions of 16 Men either Rowing or Tracking could advance us we lay in this Manner until Eleven when a lull came on & we gained a Bank we were carried into the Terragully Nulla & Sheltered. We find the River is gaining on its Southern Bank here for in 1805 & 1806 The River was seven or Eight Miles from Terragully, it now runs close under the pass, we got to Terragully at four & walked up to the Mosque where we saw a fine Black Stone something like a Coffin covered with Persian Characters I should think it would be highly valued in England & it might be easily taken away if it was right. The Country starts about Sceely Gully is very Beautiful it reminds me much of the West Indies & I think the Bay between Terragully & Sceely Gully is exactly like Chock Bay St Lucia & I should suppose the River here in one Sheet of Water was at least three Miles across.

19th   We passed Rajamahal at ½ after 11 with a good North West Breeze at Two we were opposite Oudanulla. I should suppose the River to be here near four Miles a across yet Brookes Gazetteer[158] says here is an elegant Bridge across the Ganges. I believe it would be easier to Build one from Dover to Calais. Indeed The Village or Fort of Ouda is not on the Ganges but the Name Ouda Nulla means Rivulet of Ouda & I believe there is a small Bridge of One Arch. I have not actually seen the Place myself it being four Miles in Land from the Ganges but I much doubt the whole Account of it except the Victory gained by Major Adams over Cossim Ali at which time There was a Fort & a fortified line from a Lake to the Nulla. I cannot say any thing about Sultan Sujah but I believe he lived at Gour which is opposite but rather lower down & sometimes at Tandah & Panduah all of which are the most Ancient Cities in Bengall & sometimes at Monghir. We stopped this Evening near a Village called Cadgeria 2 Miles below Furruckabad & Five from the Moangonge River, but we find it closed & we must go down in hopes the Jullinghy may be open or another Six Miles lower formed itself last year.

20th   We passed the Mouth of the Noangonge River at 7 & that of Sootie at ½ after 9. I mentioned when I was at Jungipore Two Years since that the River had been encroaching to the South West and this day we halted within Six Miles of Jungipore, formerly the Two Rivers were near 20 Miles asunder as may be seen in the Maps then published.

21st.   At ¼ past Eight we passed the Mouth of the River which runs from the North passing by Malda & Dinagipoor. We passed Bogevan Gola at Eleven. This is 12 Miles from Moorshedabad and is the port to that City on the Ganges. In the Time of Alivender Khan when the Marathas were in the Cossimbazar Island, Morrshedabad was much distressed for Provisions. Alivendra Built a Wall from Moorshedabad the Bogevan Gola but whether any thing remains or not I do not know. The sands now ran so far into the River I suppose we could not be less than a Coss (2 Miles) from The Village. We halted 2 Hours at Alipoor 6 Miles lower down & afterwards made about 12 Miles halted at the beginning of an Island in very Shallow Water. We had neither wind or Current today & we advanced but slowly at One we passed the Mouth of the Jillinghy which had not above 12 or 14 Inches of Water, we therefore kept on until three when we entered a River which had formed itself last Year. We found some difficulty in getting over what I may call a Bar, after which we had plenty of Water but the river winds much and has no

---

[158] *Brookes's Gazetteer*: Richard Brookes (1721 – 1763) compiled a gazetteer of the known world published in 1763 and running to many editions into the 19th Century.

current. I shall be here completely at a loss for there is not a Village known between this & Chogda nor is there any Mark to the Channel.

22nd This River [Jellinghy R.] opens from the Ganges about 6 Miles below Jillinghy & if I understand the People, will fall into the Hoogly River about Ten or Twelve Miles above the Town of Hoogly. I think I have read somewhere or other that the Portugese had formerly a Town on a Navigable River above Hoogly but that it became dry, probably this may be it opened again. We found some difficulty in getting over what might be called the Bar at the opening of the River, but when we were once in we found no want of water. We stopped this Evening near a Village in a Marsh, there are several pretty walks about it but I suppose that it is flooded in the Rainy season. We have met Major Mansels Servant going up with his Masters effects, he has left Calcutta Eleven days & he says the Regiment is gone into the field in consequence of which Mansel has gone up to join them by Dawk (Post) I do not believe him.

23rd. We advance very slowly. There is no Village to be seen, there is scarcely any Current & the River winds very much. We halted among Bamboos & some Boats past us 8 days from Calcutta.

24 25 & 26 We had nothing but winding between high banks & here & there a plot of bamboos, but no villages. I am as much out of my Reckoning as if I was in the Deserts & the Windings are so short that I suppose I never proceed a Quarter of a Mile in one direction. At One oclock on the 26th we saw a Bazar called Kissengunge and suddenly at the turning of a Corner we found ourselves among above 100 Boats all in confusion & the Men making a great up roar. I ran on deck & saw a man dressed something like a European, he was dressed in an Old Coat waistcoat & Breeches, he had a Red Wig on covered by a Welsh Wig & that by a hat & a Parasol over all, his Beard was a fortnight old & covered with scruff, I asked what is the Matter, he answered half in English & half in Dutch that there was a narrow cut to go through & that the Water rushed by Twelve Knots an hour with another river that the passage was very narrow & the noise was made by the Boatmen. As we are what in India is called (Burrah Sahibs which is Great Gentlemen) all the boats cleared the Way for us & we rushed through a very narrow passage about twice the Breadth of a Boat & about a Quarter of a Mile in length. We continued to keep ourselves steady by the Boatmen who were on Shore Guiding the Boat by Two Ropes attached to the Stern and half our Men on each side of the River keeping us back but which was not my fancy was the name of this odd Dutch figure which they told me was Cap^n Gulaub (Rosewater). From this Pass called Kissengunge to Hansealler

which (altho the Water was Rapid) took us four Hours the Country was pretty. The river was very narrow winding every 100 Yards & the high Banks covered with wood, sometimes we were carried Round a Cape with great Rapidity & at other times we lay quite still in the Eddy water. We halted at Hanscallee which we were told is Ten coss by Land from the Hoogly.

27   We entered the Hoogly about four o clock & anchored, but a 12 at Night we had the Tide & by the help of the Ebb we proceeded as far as the Town of Hoogly where the flood Tide met us & we anchored.

28   At ½ past 8 the Ebb came on again & we passed Hoogly a Dutch settlement but now in our possession. Chendanagore French: do this seem a populous Town. Chensura was Danish & Lower down Serampore on the Right & Bankipoor on the Left of the River. Serampore is large, it is the settlement & the Residence of the Bengal Baptiste Mission, we were obliged to stop at the Turning of the Tide 3 Miles below Serampore & on the Morning of the 28th we reached Calcutta.

1809 November 28   Calcutta Holiday

The appearance of the Shipping through which you pass, something like London on a small scale brings home to your mind. My first business now was to get a passage for Mrs Sherwood to England & I called on my Agent Messrs Alexanders. I found that there were four Ships so near ready that the Captains had gone on board & that in two Days at furthest they would sail. Alexanders strongly recommended the *Ocean* & they said If I went down as Tomorrow Morning or even in the Evening I should be in time, I therefore returned to Mrs S. & consulted with her, we agreed to get her passage if possible by the *Ocean* & proceed in the Morning to the Ship as she was prepared in every thing but a few things wanting washing. I therefore wrote to M^ss Alexanders & told them to make enquiries about this passage. In answer to my Note they Offered half the Round house for 7000 Rupees. As we could not afford such recommendations I went up to enquire if there were any other & I found that there was another under the Round House for 5500. I agreed to give 4000 but the Man in Answer said that he was only the Captain's Brother he was not authorized to close the bargain under 5000, however he would advise that we should proceed to the Ship & he said that the Captain was a Man of Generosity. Now I did not like at all to put it on that footing and I told him I could not think of any thing but a regular settlement & that I would close for 4000 & go in the Morning if he gave me a decided answer. No Answer came and the Agency House of Alexanders was shut. I returned to my Boat. So far no doubt or thought had one occurred about a difficulty in parting but all was going on as a Matter of course & the bargain having been struck the Passage money must have been paid, there could not have been any alteration, how little things turn on, When I came to the Boat Mrs Sherwood met me & said that Mrs Wiley (who for her own convenience & against our Advice had determined to go to England) had changed her mind & I found her crying. All that she could say was She knew it was wrong she could say nothing in her defence, but she could not leave her Husband. I pointed out to her the great inconvenience she had put us to & the difficulty in procuring a Servant by the Morning told her of her Husbands wish that she should go & at length insisted on it. This agitated me. I went to bed & not being aware that Calcutta was more subject to Muskitoes than the upper Country, we had neglected to close the Curtains properly. I awoke in the Middle of the Night Severely bit & agitated I could not sleep. The Idea of parting came strongly upon me. I lay & fancied it in every way but at length I could bear it no longer. M^rs S was something in the same way & at length we agreed to put it off until the next fleet which sails on the 15th December, we should have time to look about & get another Servant if necessary In the Morning for we did not shut our eyes it came into our Minds that we would consult the first medical Gent^n in Calcutta & Mr Shoolbred being pitched upon, Mrs Sherwood said that as our Intention always was to do what we thought right we would whatever it cost us abide by his advice.

It is strange that we never thought of this before but it may be right to mention how we came to think of going home. Our poor Little Henry was always weakly from his Birth & therefore nothing struck us as extraordinary at his Death but Lucy was so stout & healthy until less than a Month before she died that The Country was blamed & it may be remarked as continually happening if you use an expression in grief it is resolved by those about you. As for instance, what a bad Country for Children, every body said "oh: A very bad Country for Children." In the height of Mrs Sherwood grief I had said "my Dear I will go home with you in Two years if you have another child." & I saw it comforted her & the more so when I said if I cannot go home myself If you have another Child you shall go with it & so it was settled. There was no appearance of an other for some time & the Idea had formed itself in our Minds & lay there without any more for upwards of five Month, at length Mrs S. thought of having another little one we thought the thing at a distance & drove it from our minds when we were again roused by a Letter from Mrs Marten Butt mentioning that she had taken little Mary to school for some bad conduct but not explaining what that conduct was, and a Letter from Lucy of an after date not saying a word about it but plainly hinting that Mary was neither with her or her Mother, almost made us wish instantly to return home at any rate & had it not been from considering that Mary was not four years old when she was sent to school we should have been more unhappy still. This was an additional reason for Mrs S going Home & we prepare with all despatch – collected cloaths &c &c as we thought had made our minds up. A Letter however from Lucy had in the mean time had cleared up the Mistery of Mary & altho we did not see the necessity of the Step we were convinced that it was intended for good & could not be of any Material consequence at her age, this Load was taken from our Minds & we became perfectly Easy on that head, but the original impulse still pushed us on and we left Cawnpore for Calcutta as we may say mechanically.

However I shall never forget my feelings on the Night of the 29th & 30th November. We wrote to Mr Shoolbred & he immediately came down &

we told our Story, he seemed surprized & said without hesitation that children were better in India than at home & that the risk of so long a sea voyage was much greater than any danger from the Country, but he soon stopped himself & said that from very particular circumstances he wished to call in other advice & proposed Doctor Russel which we agreed to, the circumstance which he alluded to was that he is married to a Sister of Mrs Piercy & an expression had dropped from Mrs Sherwood that Mrs Piercy had set Mr Martyn & others to prevail on her not to go & to bring up Religion as a Reason. I saw the change in Mr Shoolbred & I approved the application to Doctor Russel but on reconsidering I thought it was unnecessary however his advice was asked & was given very strongly in favour of Remaining in India.

In the course of the Day but not in the very early part of it Note came wishing to close for 4000 for the Cabin but I now declined it. We now determined to return again to Cawnpore & our minds were much more at ease.

On the first of December I went into the Bazar & purchased what things I want for The Voyage up again for it requires so much attention as going a Little Sea Voyage. I believe I never explained how we travel. I have described the Pinnace which is in fact a travelling Parlour & Bed Room besides this we have a Boat of the Burthen of about Thirty Hundred Weight or as we call it 400 Maunds. This Boat is Thatched like a Cottage and is very Roomy, here our Servants stay & it serves us as a Kitchen. On the Top we have Coops for Fowls & Ducks. We in General lay in about Two Dozen of each with Bread Butter Potatoes Charcoal, Two or Three Goats for Milk & enough to serve us Three Weeks & we trust to the Voyages for occasional assistance we are scarcely ever above a week without being able to recruit our Stock but as the Hindoos live mostly on Coarse Rice Or Peas called Gram we can only get things from Large Bazars, even Milk is not easily got altho we pass Thousands of Cows feeding on the River Banks. The Natives use the Milk themselves & some how or other they will not give any up for Money. I cannot tell the Reason whether it is that they are afraid of us or that they do not want Money or that the Servants rob them, I cannot say, but I perceive a great wish to avoid us. The Boatmen are great Thieves & always steal from the Villages if they can & I find great difficulty in restraining them. Nor are the Villagers the least backward when they are the Strongest. A European is a great safeguard to both for they know that even the worst have some Ideas of Justice & they always come & complain to them & respect their decisions. I had determined to begin our Journey up immediately but this day the (2nd Dec^{ber}) I met the Revd Mr Thomason a friend of Mr Martyns & he insisted so strongly on our staying Sunday with him & then going to pass a few days with him at a Country House which he is repairing that I could not refuse, particularly as we so seldom meet with Clergymen or Churches. We therefore went to Mr Thomasons House in the Evening & we found him preparing to examine the Children of his parish on his last Sundays Sermon, a practice which he attends to every Saturday Evening & to enable them to answer the better he has some of the principal remarks in the form of Questions & Answers printed for their use. The examination takes place in the Church.

On Sunday we had Service at Eleven & in the Evening about Eight as it is now nearly five years since we had an opportunity of going to Church or hearing a bell toll it was delightful & put us in mind of England. Mr Thomason had a Curacy near Cambridge and came out to this Country through the Interest of Messrs Grant & Piercy & rather against the wishes of the East India Directors who think that the Christian Religion is not of consequence enough to be thought about. On Monday the 4th we took all the Thomasons family into our Boat & went Six Miles down the river to a House which had been lent him by Mr Laws Brother in Law to Mr Udny while his own is repairing. Under Mr Thomasons Family there was a Miss Walters, a Young Lady rather Amiable but with high Spirits wishing to do what is right & thinking that easy to be done if she wishes it. Her education has been among the Worldly & she has been unfortunate in losing her protectors in very early life. She is as it were an isolated being. I hope she will hold fast the only true support. She seems to wish much to do what is right but Inbred Sin or Original Sin has not yet made itself known to her in its true form. We passed Monday & Tuesday pleasantly but the fatigue & anxiety I had undergone were rather too much for Me and we were obliged to go to Calcutta on Wednesday to Dine (or as it is called in India Tiff) with Mrs Shoolbreds as they had taken so kindly to us we could not well refuse. We found them very kind and as worldly People liked them very much (Do not let us judge others, I merely mean from their not Worshipping Religion) We returned on Thursday Morning to Mrs Thomasons & found that it is a Custom in their Church to have Service every Thursday Evening. We were therefore required to take part of the Family to Calcutta which we did & attended Divine Service. I must not forget the kindness and attention of a Family of the Name of Myers who are low in the World. I do not mean in Money but in Rank, being Builders. These kind & religious People hearing from our friend Mr Martyn, came & asked us kindly to their House to Breakfast &c &c would have taken little Anny Childs had not Miss Corrie done it. On Friday we returned again to the Garden reach &

Calcutta 1809

on Saturday came to Calcutta where we dined with the Shoolbreds. On Sunday we were very happy in being able to attend the Church.

It was our intention to have left Calcutta on Monday the 12th but we were so much pressed by M^r & Mrs Thomason that we could not resist & we therefore agreed to stay One other Week, it was proposed that we should go to the Garden Reach & as Mr Thomasons Town House would be repaired we should all come up together on Thursday but Mr Shoolbred insisted on our Tiffin there on Wednesday we therefore on Monday stayed in Calcutta to look about us & in the Evening went down with Mr Thomasons Children & the Children of the Revd Mr Jeffries. Miss Walters went in the Pinnace with the young Ones & Mr Thomason took us to visit Mr Harrington the President of the Colledge[159] who was very kind to us.

On Tuesday I went to Doctor Roxbury's at the Botanic gardens who appeared a very pleasant Man, he spoke to me as if we were old aquaintances & gave me four large Pots of fine Strawberry plants to take up the Country. On Wednesday Mrs Sherwood passed almost the whole day at Mrs Shoolbreds while I looked out for what I wanted to take with me. We were employed all Thursday in carrying the Family of the Thomasons to Calcutta on Friday we called on Mrs Henry & others, Mrs Dashwood &c & on Saturday Mrs Sherwood visited the China Bazar packed up a Trunk for her Sister which I saw safe to Alexanders & on Sunday we wished to do as we should do & on Monday we got into our Boat much pleased with the kindness of Mr Thomason Myers & several others during our stay at Calcutta. We met with Mr Browne, the Senior Chaplain who was kind enough to invite us to his House but it being at Serampore which is not in our way we could not accept his invitation. We also met with a Mr Bird from Warwickshire, a very amiable & religious Young Man related to Mr Wilberforce, he is not a Son of Wilberforce Bird of Coventry but Nephew. I mention this as W Birds Sons are here also, we were much pleased with Mr Bird. In the Evening of Monday I saw an embarkation of Artillery & found that they were commanded by Cap^n Samuel Shaw a friend of Mrs Marten Butt. We had already gone on board Ship & I had not the pleasure of seeing him I sent him a Message but I presume his Business was such he could not attend to us.

---

[159] Fort William College, taught Indian languages to British EIC official.

1809 December 19th   5th River Journey, Calcutta to Cawnpore, 1055 miles[160]

On The 19th we sailed from Calcutta early in the Morning to wait for the turning of the Tide. We waited a short time at Kidderpore & entered a very small Canal called Tollys Nulla[161] & were obliged to pay Eleven Rupees as a Toll for the Two Boats, we passed under Three Bridges which belong to roads leading from Calcutta. The Canal was very narrow & shallow at least when we passed it but the Tide was rising & in some places we were obliged to stop until the Tide rose. We were much crowded with Boats & even found a difficulty in passing and by the Time we advanced Ten Miles it was time to stop for the Evening but I think there was another reason which did not strike me at the time which was that as there were two Inlets to this Canal & no outlet except there, the two Tides did not meet & it happened just where we stopped for I was supprized in the Middle of the night to find we were moving and at day Light we were in a much broader River. The Banks entirely covered with Brush Wood exactly like the mangrove trees in the West Indies. I heard Guns firing which they told me were from Dum Dum where the Calcutta Artillery practice at this Time of the Year. The Place we were in is called the Sunderbunds and is very little Inhabited but mostly covered with a Thick impassible Jungle (or Forest) I did not see the least cultivated but as we proceeded at the Rate of Four Miles an hour we saw a small point here & there which I at length found is cleared because they are just where the Boatmen stop waiting for the Turning of the tides for the Angle being very Sharp & not requiring a full Tide or Tides to reach them, there are in consequence always a number of Boats either waiting to go to or coming from Calcutta.

The Brush wood coming down to the edge of the Water & the number of Angles & uncertainty of the Rapidity of the Tide made it impossible to ascertain the distances for in One Tide of Six Hours we actually passed Eighteen Points or Capes & the Next Thirteen I presume on the 19th we might have gone 10 Miles 20th between 40 & 50.

---

[160] Owing to the lack of water in the upper Hooghli and Jellinghy Rivers between January and June the Sherwoods headed east across the Sunderbunds through modern day Bangladesh to gain access lower down the Ganges from the Hoorangle River.
[161] Tollys Nulla is now the site of Calcutta Docks.

21st   We did not get above four miles this Morning when we were obliged to Anchor waiting for a Turn in the Tide, we proceeded in this Manner without being able to go on Shore. The Banks being a Black Mud & the small Trees or Brush wood interwoven with each other until the 25th in the Morning when we reached a Village called Cubia which is generally set down as being out of the Sunderbunds & we stayed all the day to prepare for the Journey against the stream. I however found that we were not out of the influence of the Tide & that by still continuing a Pilot whom I had brought from Calcutta that I might the sooner get clear of this unhealthy Country. We set off again about Six in the Morning of the 26th and advanced about Six Miles when we were again brought to by the Flood Tide, here we waited until Two when finding a good breeze & in my favour, I would not want the change of the Tide but proceeded with a fair & very fine Breeze nearly East & with a Westerly wind. The only Map I had being Rennels, points a passage towards Gapaulgunge but it is East & by South of course I expected to have had the Breeze in my favour but the Great marsh which is laid down in Rennels Map but without any River or passage through it. I am not here blaming Rennel as probably this is either opened or at least enlarged since his map was made or it was not the common way, we wound about so much from the North to East that we could scarcely see 100 Yards before us, the direction however was North East we had before us a marsh as far as the Eye could reach & nothing to break the Circle but about Three Topes of very small extent & a few Clumps of Houses as I think you may call them on little Hillocks scarcely larger than Mole Hills or four Bamboos stuck in the Ground on which was a little Hut just large enough for a fellow which was nearly under Water & to keep Birds off. The Houses in this part of the Country are singular the Ridge Pole of the Roof not strait but bent down towards each end, it is done with a Bamboo and resembles a Hogs back. I should think they are likely to resist the wind well. They have also a very neat & clean look but they are not so in reality for they are formed as if you were never to sweep or clean a place but cover it with a Coat of clean clay every day or Two. The original dust still remains it is a part of the Religion to wash their Houses with Clay & Cow Dung Mixt very often. We halted for One Tide during the Night in the marsh and in the Morning we entered a River laid down in Rennels Map as the Hoorangle. The Channel was much larger than the Hoogli at Calcutta altho it is further from the Sea. The Town of Gopaulgange was about Two Miles above the Place we entered and we reach to opposite Shore and halted about Twelve o clock, we here found a Temporary Village which I suppose is only inhabited for six months in the Year as from June to December it must be flooded or nearly so, they had formed one Street on an Eminence composed of such houses as I have described above but the Sides were covered in with matts about Three feet square which I think it is Probable they remove if the Country is flooded there then remains the roof supported on its upright Posts which is preserved until the water goes off. There were however many small cabins just large enough to sit in on their Hams, made by sticking a pliant Bamboo in the Ground & then drawing the other end down forming a 'Row of Bows' on which they fastened there some matts. They may be compared to a Tilt of a common sort in England, only scarcely so deep. From Gopaulgunge we began our old way of tracking up the River. The Tide having left us a few miles below. The Country is so low & marshy that we did not see even a Tree to break the flat for near Sixteen Miles to Radnaghur where we saw the first Grove (called a Tope by Europeans, I believe from the Portugese as it is not a Hindoo Word).

On the 29th we passed Colna which was a well wooded Village. The Country here is full of Indigo Works managed by Europeans. We saw no less than four European Houses (or Bungalows) at one time. We halted for the night under them but it was not Inhabited, it seemed like a temporary residence probably only built for an Overseer to remain in during the season of making Indigo. I understand that the way Europeans do is to contract with the natives for so many Bigahs[162] (a Land Measure) & advance Money for seed, but at the gathering they only pay for the Quantity brought but in this I am probably mistaken as I am not acquainted with any Indigo Planter & I do not understand enough of the Language to converse with the Natives. Thus far I hear that it is a very dangerous concern & they are liable to great losses.

30th   We saw nothing extraordinary today. The Country flat & like the Commons in England, we reached a little above the place marked in the Map Ragnaghur but the Bazar is not on the River, neither is Mamoudpoor.[163]

31st   We entered a very narrow Rapid Stream which winds though a marsh with great Rapidity, I am completely lost in the Map but I

---

[162] Bigha, land measure, standardized in West Bengal to 1333m², 1600m² or 1/3 acre.
[163] Although Sherwood refers to Rennell's map, his 1786 map shows both Rajanagar and Mahmudpor and the 1776 map shows the latter so Sherwood may have had another edition.

understand this same Nulla will take us past Commercolly & Custier & from thence to the River Ganges.

1st January 1810   I finished Mrs Sherwood's instructions to Mary as far as the end of Africa.[164] The River since Yesterday Morning winds exceedingly & we can see nothing but a wide marsh, Yet it seems well cultivated & fruitful bearing great crops of Rice & Gram, altho the water where the Rice grows is at least 1½ feet deep. The dikes are about 12 feet above the River & I presume the land might be drained if it was adviseable. The Country would however be always flooded in the Rains. The Stream is very Rapid & we had some difficulty in finding a secure place to stop in the Evening.

2   This Morning heavy fog, the River extremely confined & Rapid, forming whirlpools which in some places would be dangerous for small Boats, I presume that we did not advance above 5 Miles direct. We halted near some comfortable farm houses among Bamboo Trees. I had three Shots at Pigeons, the 1st Shot I killed 6 the 2nd 4 & the 3rd 1.

3   The River broader & the River less Rapid we reached within a Mile of Comercolly.

4   Before 6 we were at Commercolly & I was much disappointed at finding a poor common Village without a Bazar. There is a Commercial Residence & the Residents Communer makes a good deal of Money by selling bread to Passengers who have been without for some days. We procured 2 Rupees worth of Bread for which we paid four times as much as Calcutta & 6 times as much as we should have done at Berhampore which is the nearest Station, the Man therefore makes as least 500 p^r C^t. I found that several Boats passed the day & that Six Rupees were spent on Bread by which the Man gained 4 Rupees & a half, yet we are very glad even to be so accommodated at Two o clock Doctor & Mrs Robinson came down & halted by us, & we passed the Evening together & took back Sarah Pownel.

5   Parted with the Robinsons & advanced reached Custea at 2, but did not enter the great Ganges as I expected The River having changed its course within the last two Years. We halted two Miles above Custea.

6   The 1st Part of our Journey to day was difficult, the Stream Rapid & many Trees fallen into the Stream which renders it dangerous, at 6 o clock we had to cross & in so doing fell much down owing to the Rapidity of the Stream, at 8 oclock we had scarcely reached the bank opposite to where we halted last Night. The River has been making great

---

[164] Mrs Sherwood compiled lessons for their daughter Mary, left in England. She published *An Introduction to Geography* in 1818.

havoc on the land about here as we found from the Roots & clumps of Bamboos standing in the Stream, we found considerable difficulty in getting clear of them, we did not move at the Rate of 1 Mile p^r hour but at 12 o clock we entered the Great Ganges. The Banks had fallen in very much on the Eastern bank & seem likely so to do, we halted near Dumodepoor about 3 Miles from the small River.

7 It was very cold, the North Wind blew strong against us we halted in a pretty spot.

8 The River made a turn running from the South East & as if in opposition the South East Wind blew, we halted on a Sand bank & were trouble with Sand.

9 Coasted sand Banks with the Sand blown much about & entering our boat & our Soup & our food we reached Jellengy, a Corn Market.

10 This day we had difficult Sand Banks to pass, we halted near a large Silk Manufactory. The Smell of the dead worms was very offensive & the noise of the Children at Night troublesome. We went to see the Works, we observed a Copper like a Common Boiler, above this Copper there was a Rod with a few wore eyes to pass the threads thro, at a little distance a Reel. The natives are very ingenious we saw an invention of theirs for pounding flour which this little elegant sketch will give some Idea of. 2 Short posts driven into the Earth a Pole fixed by a pivot between them with a Heavy weight at the ends this acted as a Pestel into a Mortar made of a Solid trunk of a Tree.

A Woman sits half asleep & works this Machine by which she pounds every thing wanted. The More common way however is by grinding Corn between two Stones, about the size of our Grindstones one being laid on the Ground & another of the same size placed upon it the lower being a little concave & the upper one in the same degree convex but very slightly so. These Mills are so portable that we generally paid for a Woman to grind for us, who brings the Stones on her head & grinds Gram or other grain in our presence & having secured her pay carries her apparatus away, her wages amounts to about 3 Pence per Cw^t.[165] The Work which they do is very well done but they are so slow about it that an Englishman can scarcely refrain from anger, they will not grind more

---

[165] 1 Cwt (hundredweight) = 50 kilograms.

than 1 Cw^t per diem. In this way the Carpenters, Mason &c they will make any thing for you & not charge above 4 Pence a day, their saw is little better than an old Iron hoop jagged yet with this instrument they will make the most delicate mechanism but it is done so slow, taking up a part looking at it putting it down taking up another & so on that if you come out at the end of an hour to see them they appear to have the same piece in their hands which they had on your going in. Should you be inclined to stand by them it puts you in the fidgets, they take up the Saw, feel the teeth look along it slowly, bend it, try whether it become strait again lay it down, take up an Adze feel its edge, put it down, take up every other Instrumant & so on, I have watched them for hours.

11 This day we had many sand Banks to pass & being often obliged to cross the River in search of a proper depth of Water we stopped for the Night about 16 Miles below Bogwan Gillah.

12 Reached Alli Poor.

13 Passed Bodwan Golla & sent a Man on Shore for Butter &c while we continued our Rout but after passing the Village & finding several Streams which would be difficult to the Gentleman to pass we stopped & sent another Servant to hasten the first but he did not return & we were obliged to send a Third & he did not return, we now found that our Servants were our Masters & we were obliged to submit for the Boatmen were all in League.

14 This Morning one of the Servants had returned but I would not wait & therefore moved on. The Boatmen were very slow in their Motions, at Twelve the Servants returned. We reached the Malda River & stopped near the Monument of a Col^l Laxton erected by our old Friend Elston to his Father in Laws Memory who was <u>not</u> buried here but the place was chosen for the sake of its prominent situation putting me in mind of the description in Bridgenorth 'Here lie the Bodies of 3 Children dear, Two Buried at Oswestry & One here.'

15 A most Violent Northwester, we could not move, there were some fine pools near my Boat full of wild ducks but they were so shy I could not get one,

16 The wind strong & altho we tried we could not advance above a Mile by which we lost a snug berth & go on the Sands.

17 We reached a Spot close to the Ruins of Gour one of the oldest Cities of Bengal & I am much astonished to find that the Natives seem to know so little of it, I met a Farmer & asked him where the Ruins were & he put his hands on his hips & stood for some time staring at me then spoke as if from a vacuum "<u>Ge Saheb Kadaurand.</u>" or, "what my Lord."

with a long stupid whine. I could almost have thought of myself in some stupid place in England, we halted near Icebgunge Pokiria.

18   Moved on at 8 & as I had desired the Boatmen to ask every one they met & at length one of them came on board to say that we were now close to Gour, At first I thought that he was deceiving me because I had understood that from my conversation with the Natives Yesterday that we had passed it. I looked on & he shewed me a ruin which induced me to go on Shore & I found myself in the midst of ruins, still I was doubtful whether or not these ruins might be some more modern ruins. I enquired of every Ryot I met where is Gour & the answer invariably was here, until having walked thro Ruins for upwards of a Mile I was induced to believe that I was at Gour but after all, what was to be seen but a heap of old House in ruins in no respect differing from a Thousand other ruins & modern after all for it is not so long since Gour was abandoned notwithstanding what is said about it.

I passed under a large high Arched Gateway. The Buildings were of small brick plastered over like Stocco, the Stucco had fallen off in most places yet large spots remained which shewed how it had been covered. I entered one square some thing like the Keep of an old English Castle, on one side were there remains of Mahomedan Buildings probably barracks like those of Allahabad.

Darkhil Darwaza, brick main gate to Gour. 2015.

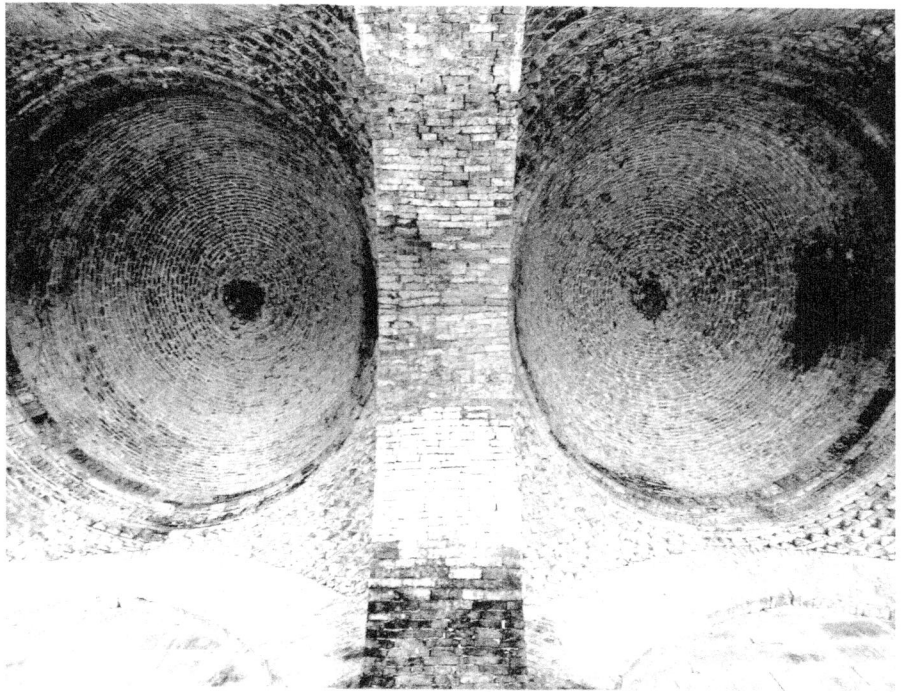

Brick arched and domed roof. Gour. 2015.

The Roof an Arch supported by Brick Pillars the Building must have been old as the Sun had corroded the Bricks, probably the Mahomedans had only altered the original building at a small distance I saw a Mosque in good repair, it was like an old Cloister but roofed as is customary with 3 Domes with a large flagged Court before it & a Hall surrounding the Court about 4 feet high upon the whole every building that I saw was Mahomedan.

One Tomb seemed superior to the rest, there were at each corner a shaft of black Marble about 6 Feet high to six Inches in diameter curiously carved but there were also many Slabs of Black Stone of various Shapes curiously carved but the general shape was that of a Sarcophagus. The Characters were almost defaced but appeared Persian.

I had not much time to look about me for the Boat was going on & in the lower part of the Country there are such numbers of Streams running into the Ganges that it would be a serious difficulty to have a River between me & the Boat indeed before I got up with my Budgerow I had to pass the Beds of two Rivers so very large that they had evidently once contained the whole body of the Ganges, one of these was dry the other had a narrow but rapid stream running thro it. I thought myself in good luck on finding Mr Ellertons Boat laying at the Mouth by which I passed over. We crossed the River & halted at a Small Village called Cadgerea. There is a Nulla here which runs to Moangonge. The Country here is a Marsh abounding with reeds but some spots growing mustard.

21 We reached Rajamahal on the 21st. Here I employed myself Sketching an old Mosque with four Tombs said to be the Tombs of Futty Jung Bohander but who Futty Jung was, the deponent said not. It being Sunday we halted all day. Plenty of Ruins but all Hindostany Ruins are alike being built of brick & the Rooms very low, the walls are about 2 Feet thick.

22 We moved & crossed the river advanced 10 Miles halted on a Sand Bank with a rapid current.

23 The Current was rapid, the wind strong we reach Seelygully at Night. This is a most beautiful spot often mentioned before, I always think it more beautiful than when I saw it last & it will seem extraordinary that its principal attraction to me was that the leaves had fallen from the Trees & were covering the Ground, the weather was cool if not cold & we thought it much like England.

24 This Morning we had great difficulty in advancing. The River was very wide but shallow & we found great difficulty in discovering the Channel by which means we were running on Sand Banks & often entered what we thought passages but having proceeded some way found that we were obliged to Return & we did not get on above 6 miles, during the Night the Wind rose & before Morning it blew a compleat Hurricane, we could not move on the 25 & 27 & were obliged to use our endeavours to keep the Budgerow from striking against the shore & bulging. We placed spare masts lashed to the sides & firmly fixed against the shore. The blows given us by the waves made the boat Tremble. On the 27th the wind abated but I could not advance above 5 miles altho it was late before I halted.

28 We had a fair day.

29th We advanced pretty well & passed Colgong—about 2 miles from Colgong is a Nulla which formerly was dry almost all the Year & I have never before found it navigable. The Year before last the River burst thro it & has formed a large & deep Channel all the way thro to Jangara, we were not aware of this & altho we made some way thro the Nulla we at last kept to the Main Channel but I went to Baglepore & called on Doctor Glass, from him I learnt that we might safely have passed thro the whole way. The Baglepore Nulla as it is called is very narrow but deep & the Island between it & the Great Ganges is not above a Mile

5th River Journey—Calcutta to Cawnpore 1809-10

across opposite Boglipore, but we lost about 2 Miles & convenience of Marketts &c, about 2 Miles below Jangara the Rivers unite, opposite the Mouth of Jangara we saw a great Multitude of Out Casts, they are the same People mentioned by the Abbè Ragnal,[166] but I must confess I never heard of them being held in such detestation as he related, but he speaks of another part of India, they are here much like Gypsies living in round Hutts & keeping many Hogs, they are extremely dirty & they eat Carrion. It is said that they eat Human Bodies which they get from the Ganges half Putrid but this wants (or rather <u>does not want</u>) confirmation & sell Basketts, Matts &c &c. They do not wash their garments but smear them with grease & their hair is matted with grease. We passé Jangarra & halted about 3 Miles above where there were plenty of Zumbee Beads growing. Numbers of Pilgrims were passing to the Ganges to Bathe & carry water to the interior I believe 20 or 30,000 must have passed us the day we halted at Gogary. It must however be observed the Villages & their Names often move in the Country as the River encroach or retires & they also extend sometimes several Miles. I think the Parishes in England often do the same.

On the 4th We reached Monghir. There are many Ruins here of brick & very dirty but we cannot know the Age, Aurangzeb's Brother lived here & the Walls must be Antient.

5th   We made a long days Journey & almost reach Surajgurry & halted at a very pleasant Village which had been granted by the Government to the Invalid Seapoys. It is remarkable how very different these Villages are to the Neighbouring ones in neatness & cleanliness.

6   We had very Rapid water near Pelileah –

7   We had a very strong North Wester & did not proceed far.

8   Reached Mooheah & were overtaken by Lieut Jeffries of the 22nd Regt Sr. I. Son of the Revd Mr Jeffries. He had left Calcutta 10 days later than we had but he was in a Small light Boat.

9th   Near Bar.

10th   Rupusgunge.

11th   to Bidygunge where are the highest Palm Tree I have ever Seen I should think them 60 feet high, I fired at a Bird on the lowest leaf & the shot fell down again scarcely touching the leaf.

---

[166] Abbé Raynal: Guillaume Thomas Raynal (1713-1796). *Histoire des Deux Indes*, 1770, a compilation of European travellers and merchants accounts.

12   To Futwah, a manufactory of Napkins & Table Cloths, we bought our Stock we paid for a Table Cloth 7 ½ Feet by 6 Feet 6/3 & Napkins from 5/- to 7/- per dozen.

13   Patna here the best Wax Candles are procured we paid 53 Rupees equal to £6-12-6 for a Maund or R 80—the Wind was high & we did not advance.

14   The Wind high, Jaffier Ali Khaun's gardens are a large enclosure but now in Ruins. It must not be expected than a common Native can tell you any historical fact, they know nothing of the Khaun & they will probably tell you that he lived before the flood, altho he has not been dead many years, so distances are little noticed: a Coss may mean 1 Mile & it may mean 4 Miles, it is a short answer "ek Coss." The great number of Boats always laying at Patna detained us very much we were half a day in passing half the City & we halted under Mr Douglass's House.

15   It is true that the Wind was very high. Mrs Sherwood sent a Book[167] with which she had entrusted to Mrs Hawkins wife of the Judge of the Court of Appeal & we thought no more of it but on return of the Messenger we received a most pressing invitation to go up to dinner & were most kindly received, Mrs Hawkins is just returned from England where she has religious friends & her mind seems seriously impressed. Mr Hawkins (a Brother of Admiral Whitehead) was extremely kind & pressed us to stay another day, desiring us to send our Boats forward & he would send his Carriage with us as far as the Road ran which would be at least a days journey & we were induced to acquiess, the Boats went on & we remained & in the Evening we followed in Mr Hawkins Carriage to Dinapore where our Boat was.

16   Notwithstanding our hurry we found our Boatmen unprepared to proceed & after waiting the whole day we found ourselves under the necessity of removing to another Boat, our own Manjee & Dandies being inclined to rest themselves for a time, this is often the Case in India where you are obliged to submit to the Caprises of the natives, it is true I might have insisted on the Boatmasters performance of his Contract but I thought it would not have been done with a good will, but this detained us all day 17th & we were hospitably entertained by the Penny's.

18   Today I cannot proceed for want of Dandies.

19   I could only reach the flag staff less than two Miles, We have now been 4 days from Mrs Hawkins & not got a Mile, these are vexatios incident to India. I began to be afraid lest Mrs Hawkins might be

---

[167] Mrs Hawkins undertook to translate Mrs Sherwood's *Little Henry and his Bearer* into Hindoostani.

offended at not hearing from us but on the 20th we set off. I received Letters from the Reg^{t168} which is now at Sangor in 24 North lat 79 East Long^{de}. They report the Probability on going to Indore, a report prevailing that Holkar[169] is dead, & his late dominion in danger from Ameer Khaun, his General.

21 We wrote many Letters, & proceeded with a fair wind, altho light & reached Cheeram at Night. We had an Easterly wind, but there was but little of it & the Stream was rapid with many Shallows. The Small Branch called the Chuprah Nulla was dry we were therefore obliged to go round the Island. There was nothing to mark our halting place.

22nd Passed the Mouth of the Gogra & soon afterwards we heard a great Shouting & saw about 50 Men with drawn Swords standing on the bank of a small ravine. This was somewhat alarming & I asked what they were about & the Answer was "Lurna Mangta" (They want to fight) on further enquiry I found that they were a set of Villagers who had quarrelled with those of another Village & were come to down to shew them Courage. I was reminded of a Print in Hudibras. I soon saw the opposite Party armed in the same way & making a Trojan Horse. Having ascended the Mast I beheld the Field of Battle, a Nulla separating the Combatants. They waved their Swords they screamed, they danced, they seemed frantic. At length one descended into the Hollow & then returned to his Companions, bye & bye one of the Enemy did the same. It put me in mind of the Game called Prison Bars. At first I felt some alarm & thought there would be a battle but my Boatmen told me it would all evaporate in words & I was more easy. This game continued as long as I could see or hear them. The Dandies tell me that at Night each Party will go quietly home. We halted about 6 Miles above Selimpore.

23 We had a very strong wind against us & were obliged to halt 3 Hours. The Wind generally rises about 9 increases to 12 & sinks at 3, this happens generally from April to July: it had begun rather Early this Year, in the Evening we proceeded & reached Chaur Ghaut, (4 Warfs)

24 The Wind Strong. The River Shallow.

25 This Evening we passed a Country now virtually acted upon by the River. I formerly mentioned this spot as very beautiful like a Nobleman's park but lately the River has encroached so much that it sweeps away a hundred Yards in a Season & nothing is so desolate as the appearance. Trees swept away. The Bank falling & houses half cut off.

---

[168] As Sherwood's regiment was still at Cawnpore, this must have been some other regiment.
[169] Holkar: Yashwant Rao Holkar, Maharajah of Indore, a Maratha, did not die until 1811.

The Natives seemingly careless, large Bodies of Trees laying in the River with a Rapid Current running of them. I despair of describing it so as to be understood. The looseness of the soil is such that if the River bends itself against a spot it immediately gives & a Channel is formed almost in a day which means Large Trees are actually deprived of their foundation & sink branches & all into the Middle of the Stream. The danger now becomes very great as Boats are swept into the Vortex & it is with the greatest difficulty that they escape, indeed numbers are destroyed every season, indeed the Trees are destroyed by some means or other in a short time but I do not know that there is any regulation ordering them to be destroyed. These Trees obstructed the Navigation for about three Miles, we could not advance above 8 Miles altho we had a Calm day & the Current generally not strong, we halted at Berea.

26   We passed Baleah which is one of the Spots where a Mela or fair is held every Year combining Religious Pilgrimage & Merchandizing.

27   To Buxar. The River near Buxar flows in one deep quiet stream & it almost appears wonderful how so great a quantity of water can be contained & flow so evenly thro so narrow a Channel, I could scarcely believe that the whole Ganges was flowing thro this Channel, it must have been very [sic] for a little above the Channel was a full Mile across with a deep channel slowly flowing & so it continued for 17 miles as far as the Mouth of the Caramassa River. This river which flows from the West is reckoned impure in so much that if a Pilgrim returning from any of the Holy places to the South should accidentally touch its waters, all his Pennance would be of no avail. Our proceeding after passing the Mouth of the Carammassa was impeded by sand banks rapids &c with high rough Conkery Banks on one side & low sandy banks on the other, the Channel sometimes following the Right hand Conkery bank & sometimes the left. This spot is always difficult to pass but I think less so than in 1807. This day we passed the false channel in which we entangled in 1807. I observed a large Tree with its roots torn bare by the Stream & threatning to fall next Rains. I observed to My Maungie that the Tree should be now cut down which might save many a boat next year. The Maungee said it was a God & must not be touched. I halted a little Below Ghazepoor.

1 March 1810. We passed Ghazepoor, Gehazepoor, we saw Boats laden with Stones for Lord Cornwallis's Monument, about 6 Miles above Gazepoor observed the Ravages of the River, a large Village on a high bank half swept away. The Hutts abandoned some of them standing on the brink with half their walls down, the bank shelf stood about 30 feet above the River.

Lord Cornwallis's Memorial. 2015.

4   On the 4th we came up with a fleet of Boats & we found that they were waiting for others a head. On going on Shore we found that the Rapids were so strong that only one Boat could pass at a time & that with the greatest difficulty, it appeared that the Boats were obliged to assist each other 3 or 4 Sets of Boatmen being employed to hale one Boat. Our Boatmen could not by any means pull us thro this strong water. I therefore paid a daily rate for assistance, the Water was not like at Allahabad that is an immense body contained in a narrow space, but a large sheet running over a very broad bed divided into innumerable small streams. By hiring assistance I got over the difficulties in a short time but it often requires the Shoulders of the men to lift the Boat almost out of the water a Budgerow is not a Keeled boat, neither is it flat bottomed one but exactly formed like a Barrel so that like a Barrel one point only touched, the means taken by the Boatmen was to turn the Boat round & round working it as you would to get a Barrel thro a passage. If with the Current the Broadside to if against it the Men placing their Shoulders under the Stern moved at first to the right & then to the left cutting (as one might say) a Channel & lifting it over /\/ .

When we had got thro our Chanell we halted at Douchanpoor, a very pretty spot calculated for wild Poultry & Peacocks. The latter in the Morning screaming like Cats. We might purchase as many as we pleased for 4 Annas about 1/4- but they are not good eating. The spot we halted at reminded me of a field near Bridgenorth on the Shrewsbury Road, a Bank with a Rivulet below, at this season there cannot be a more delightful Country than India. The mangoe Trees in Blossom shed such a fine odour & the harvest getting in. The Poor are so much better off than the poor in cold Climates, they have no fear of nakedness or Cold, food is all that they require & that is easily procured. I must not however disguise a truth that where things are easily procured there is no providence & if there should be a scarcety there is a famine, for no one thinks of stacking Wheat. The day is only thought of & the horrors of famine have been felt. No one knows the advantages of Monopoly that has not felt famine, then he will readily allow that the Monopolizer saved his life tho they probably made him pay more during a year of plenty. I often wish that things were dearer. It might induce people to provide stock, but here things are so easily procured that half & more than half the time is spent in idleness. The Native Christians, called Portugese, appear the most useful class in that respect for they rear animals & take some little foresight.

We reached Chandrolee a Mud fort but now abandoned, its situation is strong & I suppose it was formerly a place of consequence. The Country all around being covered with Brick.

6   About 12 oclock this day we met a Pinnace which we found contained Mr Parson & his new wife, on recognizing each other we stopped & passed the Evening together.

7   We passed Benares, here I observed the Boats passing had a kind of fish tail Rudder, whether this is common & that I never observed it before, or that it is new I was much amused by it the simple Boat Man uses it something like a scull & letting it fall into the water edgeways then suddenly turning it flatt he draws the head down & of course forces the boat along – The Purchase which Two Men have in drawing down the Rudder gives a great rapidity to the Boat. I was much astonished at seeing the quickness with which one man crossed the River, who appeared to me to be only steering with a very heavy Rudder.

9   Reached Chunar at 12 o clock & found Palankeens at the beech waiting to take us to Mr Corrie where we were most kindly received & where we remained the 10th & 11th, here we prepared Tattas for our Boats. Miss Corrie was unwilling to part with Anne Child we therefore left her, here we heard that the Reg^t was on its return to Cawnpore.

12   We left Chunar & reached Mirzapore the 14th. Mr Ricketts would not let us move till the 16th. The Weather which had been getting very hot now became cool again with a few Showers & I was glad to put on a cloth Jacket. This cool weather continued till the 21 when we reached

Allahabad. I employed myself copying the *Infant Pilgrim*[170] to send home, at Allahabad found many English Letters for us from Mrs Butt, Mrs M. Butt & Mrs Cameron dated in Augt. I hired 12 Additional Dandies to assist thro the Strong water. I was fortunate in having a dead Calm & with my 12 Additional Men I passed around the Rapids (about 6 Miles) in 6 Hours but, notwithstanding every thing in our favour, the Rapidity of the Current against our Boat seemed tremendous. The foam of it came up to the Bow of the boat & sometimes even broke over, I encouraged the Men & promised Buckshies if they got thro before night & kept the Dandies in good humour & did what very few do at this <u>Season</u>, pass in one day.

24   We left Passamore with a very strong Easterly wind with frequent squalls which pushed us on. The windings of the River prevented our proceeded so far as we expected, our whole days worth was only 10 Miles—to Futypoor.

25   This day we had frequent violent Squalls during which we were obliged to lay too, between the Squalls the wind was favourable. The wind was some times North & at other times South veering by the East four times we were obliged to seek Shelter from the Squalls & at night we experienced a very strong one at Ramahouda Ghaut.

26   The Wind fair & moderately strong we ran 8 Miles very pleasantly when an unfortunate bend brought us against the wind & we were two Hours in getting one Mile & even that was done with extreme exertion. We had then a fair wind again for 3 Miles in Two hours & then another run.

27   Passed Deliligunge & Currah. The wind North West (against us) halted 2 Miles above Currah.

28   Passed Maneckpore & halted at Bahaudergunge.

29   A strong North West Wind, very slow work, halted at Jurah

30   Advanced about 10 Miles halted between Dugduggy & Cootera, during the Night Two violent North Westers, the Second was so violent that we were obliged to get up, the Waves beating into the Budgerow.

31   We made but little way owing to the furious St Westers a large Cotton boat caught fire just above us, near Dalmow & burnt with great fury. 200 Maunds[171] of Cotton was destroyed & flaming Bales passed us

---

[170] Mrs Sherwood's *The Infant Pilgrim's Progress from the Valley of Destruction to Everlasting Glory* 1814.

[171] Maund: Indian weight varying from 25 to 160 pounds. Standardised in 1833 as 82 pounds.

all Night. MEM. A Bramin formerly poisoned their Father to frighten a neighbour into a cession of Property, the business tried at Mirzapoor.

1st April   Passed Dalmow but could not reach Hassenee.

2   Jingore.

3rd   Six Miles above Adampore & Three below Buxar.

4th   The water Shallow & wind Strong saw Suraj Ghur.

5   Passed Suraj Ghur & almost reached Nujuf Ghur or Negarpoor.

6.   Did not move above a Mile owing to the violence of the Wind.

7th   Worked very hard but wind against us, nearly reached Jaugemow, which is reckoned Cawnpore.

8   I arose at 3 o clock & set off on foot & reached our Barracks before sunrise, Mrs Sherwood following in the boat, we were glad to accept the kind invitation of our Assistant Surgeon Millar.

1810 April 8th   Cawnpore

Not having a house I was employed until 12 in looking for a Bungalow & in taking charge of the Regimental Accounts. The first was very difficult & I could only get a building formerly used as a shop, on the Banks of the River, we moved into it on the 19th & found it comfortable & more cool that we had anticipated. The Weather is very extraordinary as it is cool with Easterly winds & occasional NorthWesters. We sent home the first four Chapters of the *Infant Pilgrim*. Mr Martyn called & encouraged me to learn Hebrew, the same Easterly winds to the end of the Month, on the 28th a very violent Storm.

May

Dined with General St Leger on the 1st. The weather very hot, the Easterly wind continues & the Tattas are of no use. The men sickly, I feel an oppression at the Breast which is a common complaint. Two Men died. The Thermometer stood at 12 at Night at 92. On the 23rd at 3 o clock with our Tattas up & well watered the Thermometer at 96—in the outward Verandah in the Shade 124—The heat scarcely bearable but on the 27th some rain which cooled the Air. On the 28th Rain & the Glass fell to 82 but on the 29th the Heat increased & on the 31st we had the North West Wind,

June

1   The Regular Hot Winds which are a great relief for altho they are hot yet the house can be easily cooled.

2   Miss Corrie arrived

3   The Thermometer at 8 in the Morning before the Wind rose 92. On the 4th being His Majestys Birthday the General did what his majesty would not have done, that is half killed his soldiers by having a field day. It is indeed easy for a General to Canter to a field 3 or 4 Miles & back but a Soldier with his flinlock finds it hard to walk it at this Season. I As paymaster having nothing to do may be allowed to make this remark. The Station kept this day as the Jubilee & made a great to do. The weather exceedingly hot, the wind not being steady to the West, we could not keep our house at a less heat than 92 at Night & 97 in the day. This lasted all the Month. The bed at Night when you went to lie down seemed like an Ironing blanket & Mrs S & Miss Corrie walked about the

greater part of the night, it is impossible to describe it, heat alone will not, for I have often felt it hotter.

July 1810

This Month set in with exceeding heat. Captain Wallace died & many Men. The death of Captain Wallace is attributed to throwing off flannel which he could not well bear from the heat & irratibility of his Men. On the Third there was a very heavy Shower fell & the sudden change was very great viz from 96 to 86 as fast as the glass could fall. This Shower altho heavy was not followed & consequently the heat again became as bad if not worse. The dust flew again & we were every quarter of an hour anxiously looking out for Rain the Sky was dark but not a drop fell until the 16th when it rained hard all day & the Glass came to 87. On the 17 we had no rain & the Steam it was scarcely bearable the Glass standing all night at 92 & so it continued till the 23rd. The flies & Muskitoes most troublesome as they always are in damp warm weather, on the 24 Much rain fell & the Steam from the Earth like a Brewhouse the Glass from this to 31 standing at 90.

Augt

1. 2. 3. 4 No rain, I had a Bilious complaint & numbers of Boils breaking out like poor Job after that rain every day, but not refreshing as usual. The Glass was 94 Night & day. The days cloudy the Night damp.

Sepr

Mr Martyn, Mr Corrie & Mrs Sherwood hired a Pinnace & went on the River hoping for relief but found none, on the 16th It really began to rain & soon almost flooded the cantonement. The River rose higher than I had ever seen it after this the Glass stood from 81 to 85. This is comparative comfort, but the three last days of the Month it was warmer & the Glass stood at 92.

Octor

I purchased a good Bungalow for which I paid 2000 Rupees £250 on the 10th a swarm of Locusts passed over the Cantonement & almost hid the Sun, they did not alight but their body or Army must have been square of Two Miles at least & it was computed some feet deep like a shower of Snow. Where they alighted which they did about 7 Miles off they did not leave a leaf or blade remaining.

15 The Glass stood at 90 – on the 21 at 87. The Ratts got into my Pantry & eat every thing except Beef, a Plain proof that they are Hindoos & of a high Cast. Indeed the Dogs & Cats of this Country are not fond of Beef in this instance a Roast Leg of Mutton with some ribs of Beef were in the same dish, almost the whole of the Mutton was eaten but the

Beef untouched, on the 26th there was a Material change in the Weather & it became gradually cooler until the end of the Month when it became quite pleasant.

Nov^r

This Year (since April) has been much warmer than any former years & it still continues so for altho the Mornings Evenings & Nights are cool the Glass stands at 80 at 12 o'clock & the glare of the Sun is very great. The 8th the Glass was as low as 65 in the Morning.

On the 10th I went to see a Melaw at Betoor. This seems exactly to answer to an old English Wake, it is a religious festival in a Religious spot but instead of a Roman Vault here is a Hindoo River God, it also is a fair, in which Merchandise is regularly brought & wild beasts are shewn & Hurdy gurdys &c &c. The number of People assembled was immense it is said Two Millions— Here it seems that Noah was born & here his Cradle is still preserved. Lameck his Father was king of this Country &c &c &c. The Richness of the Country & the fine Crops was really surprising. This Land is in the hot weather a compleat rock so hard that it requires the hammer to break it (it is called Conker) but the instant rain falls it dissolves & becomes a Kind of Chalk, fruitful in the extreme.

As all times of Peace are uninteresting I have nothing to say except to draw the figure of my House One Room 40 feet by 22. And one 20 feet square & Three Rooms on each side, The Sleeping Bungalow 20 Feet Square.

1811

This Year not quite so hot as last Year but in the end of June the heat scarcely bearable, on the 2nd July the Rains began, Emily[172] was born on the 20th & Xtened on the 20th by Mr Corrie: Miss Corrie & Mrs Cameron with M^r- Cameron Sponsors, the first in Person the others from Letters. 3 French Frigates in these seas taken by 2 English. Finished copying Joshua & Judges into Hindoostany.

Aug^t

---

[172] Emily Sherwood (1811-1833).

A Body of Locusts appeared on the 3rd they came from the South West, they were not in a dense body but like a fall of Snow, scattered & falling like large flakes, they passed from 4 o clock till Night & how much larger I cannot say, the Birds were all alive eating them as fast as they could catch them, the Natives catching them to fry & preserve & as the People ran, two very different appearances came into my Imagination, first a very slow fall of large flakes of Snow & next of the running of a man into a wilderness of sensitive plants for the Locust has large Wings expanded & as the natives ran among them they either took flight or contracted their wings by which the spot for a few Yards round the Person seemed bare, but the Snow falling still in large flakes & seemingly with the same kind of whirling motion was the nearest resemblance. Ducks, Turkey & Fowls every animal was in Motion to catch them. I had the curiosity to measure the growth of an Aloe & I found that it grew 9 Inches in 24 Hours for 3 days following. Ruth & Samuel finished in Hindoostanee.

Sep^r

The Weather hot & moist more so than last month, I lost 6,400 Rupees or £800 by the death of my Agent M^r McLean who died insolvent. We were much troubled with opthalmea. The damp & heavy rain caused the Mud walls of our Gardens to fall which cost some money to repair. M^r McCaskell left us for England. I began to learn Hebrew with a Jew, finished Kings in Hindoostany.

Octo^r

The Nights now become cold, this is a very early season for cold. The Glass was as low as 70 in the day. Java known to have been taken.

Nov^r

Holkar died. The weather cool. Col^l Wades Court Martial.[173]

Dec^r

Five Companies of the Regiment order to take the Field again some Forts to the Westward. The Commanding Officer Colonel Mawby goes & the Staff are to go. I am preparing.

---

[173] Lt. Col. Henry Gore Wade. Cashiered—dismissed in disgrace—by court martial at Cawnpore, 1811, bribed by a sutler, a merchant allowed to sell provisions to soldiers in the Cawnpore cantonment.

1811 December 24th   Callenger Campaign March, 140 Miles.[174]

On the 24 We marched to Cultrah where we halted the 25 & 26th. As I am not obliged to conform to the Line of March I had an excellent opportunity of seeing the proceedings of an Indian Army & I can say that from the Ground on which we halted one day to the Ground we were to occupy the next was one chain of followers Hackries.[175]

A Hackery.

Men & Women on Bullocks, on foot, on Tattoos, carrying spears, Swords, Shields, Bird Cages, Puppy dogs & parrots of the Latter I observed an Old Woman riding a Tattoo (a Pony) on a Pillion was a Puppy peeping from under the Old womans cloak, a Man carrying a Parrot on his finger & teaching it to speak all the way he went, to calculate what number of followers an Army must have I can only relate my own, I have 5 Camels, 2 Drivers, 2 Tent Pitchers, Carry Basketts, Water Carrier, 1 Link Boy, 1 Sweeper, 4 Coolies, 1 Ketmedgar (Footman) 1 Horstler, 3 Grasscutts, every one of whom has a wife or something like it & some have Children — of Publick Servants it is impossible to speak & of Market People a person not having seen the thing cannot form a conception as far as the Eye can reach all round it is an Ant Hill in Motion, we have 25 Publick Elephants besides many Private ones & several Thousand Bullocks, Xerxes Army is easily accounted for. I found my Canvas Bag (Tent) very cold & uncomfortable.

[174] Callenger: now Kalinjar.
[175] Hackry: bullock cart.

27 Dec.r We Marched before day break thro a level Country & deep sand, without seeing it cannot be conceived the amazing Ant Hill in Motion we halted at Reneer.

28   Marched at day light thro the same sandy level Country, had a difficulty in finding water for an encampment, halted near Fattypoor.

29   9 Miles, halted near Packra or Pockyria, in a field in cultivation but we could find no other, Government pay for any land in Cultivation destroyed.

30   The Movement began at 3 o clock, after marching 6 Miles the Ravines of Conker broke the Ground much & confined us to our road, this was for 2 ½ Miles when we reached the River Jumna, the Jumna is here quite as broad as the Ganges, but not so rapid, as soon as we arrived on the Bank out business was to get over & then every one (independent as I was) for himself. I soon contrived to get over & with a good deal of Maneevoring & acting the old soldier contrived to get my Camels, Tent &c over by one oclock, this is no little trouble, we encamped on the Sandy bank of the Jumna & having seen all safe I walked to Calpy. It is an old fort above the River & in some respects reminded me of Bridgenorth, it was of great consequence in former times, one thing that struck me much was a well standing like a steeple out of the Ground, One side at least 40 feet high, the Earth had been washed entirely from one side & very much on the other altho the ground at a little distance was rather above its level.

31 We marched up the Hill & encamped on a kind of Common covered with Tombs about a Mile from the River. These Tombs generally enclose one sarcophagus. Here we are to halt a day or two. The Country is a hard Conkery soil with Prickly Byar Bushes & much cut up by Ravines.

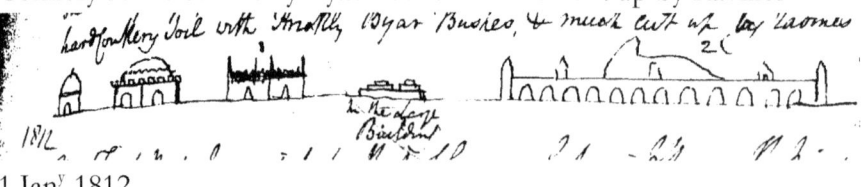

1 Jan.y 1812

This Tomb no. 1 Is said to be that of Gazy or Gehazi Khaun, the Minister who destroyed 3 Moghul Emperors. He was the Son of Nizam al Moolk, he was very famous in his time but died in distress, the Tomb is small & is only plastered. He was thought the handsomest Man in India. The Kings Mausoleum (2) is a very large Building. The Principal Dome is fallen and the natives say struck by Lightning. It is square & built in the old Cloister like form entirely open with pointed arches /\ /\ The Building is very large & must have cost a great deal of Money.

2   I busied myself in making observations on the Geography of the Country, see Map. [No map found.]

3 & 4th The same.

5   Marched. I advanced in front it was dark the first 6 Miles over a conkery Common much cut up by the Torrents in the Rainy Season, to a great depth, our direction South a little East passed a Village on the Right at 3 Miles, one Mile further a Puckah well & a Jee (or Pool) the Country level & well cultivated, halted at Moorgong or rather more than 10 Miles from Calpy, being Sunday some Soldiers came to my Tent & I read one of Burders Sermons.

6   The Road a fine rich country but apparently swampy in the Rains. The Rutts & cattle footsteps having the appearance of a Track suddenly frozen, it is dangerous to ride as there are large cracks in the soil into which a Horse putting his foot would scarcely be able to recover, fortunately the Horse are aware of this & keep a good look out, at the end of the 1st 5 Miles we had the same kind of conkery broken Ground indicating the proximity of a River, this led us to the Betwah, this River has banks about ½ a Mile asunder, but the Stream is now about 200 Paces across, the water beautifully clear, running over a Pebbelly Bottom about 2 Feet deep but rapid, the Banks being steep we had some difficulty in getting the Guns & Camels across. On the South Bank situated high is Jelalpoor an old City of some note, passing which we encamped on a Common.

7   We could not advance to day as the Artillery were not all up the bank of the Betwah, I was invited to dine with Doctor Burt.

8   Marched from Jellalpoor by Dhool, 4 Miles South by East, 3 Miles further inclining more to the Eastward passed a small River about 20 paces across, passing Bunder Choota & Burra, halted at Bewar. 12 Miles flat Country full of cracks & consequently dangerous to ride over.

9   Bewar to Benowly 3 Miles to Taire 3 Miles to Mhoodha 8 Miles to the Country beautiful, rich & level but cracked & rough, Moodha has a kind of Baby House fortification built by Shamsheer Bahadur after some droll plan of a Fort probably in a Childs picture book, the embrasure in the curtain & made of pasteboard.

10   3 Miles good ground then the appearance of approaching a river the ground much broken for 3 Miles to Chaudrour. The descent to the River very bad & the ascent almost the same, it required good driving not to overset the guns, a few Enemies might have easily impeded our passage. Halted at Cupsa. Here the foolish fellow Shumsheer Behauder had once made a Shew of assistance & by accident at a great distance shot Major Smith, but he never stood a fight, we halted at Cupsa seeing

the Hill of Bandah calculated distance 7 Miles. No wells but good Tanks at Cupsa—here we caught a young deer which we called Cupsa. This Deer became at length mischievous & was obliged to be killed.

11   From Cupsa 3 Miles in a strait Line then suddenly turning S nobody knows why (Except I presume the Commanding Officer we marched three Miles in another direction making 6 Miles of what might have been done in 4, we then moved 5 Miles again in our former direction we might easily have followed the dotted lines in the Margin— we halted on the Banks of the Cane River near Boorajhur, our Motion to day was so eccentric that our Servants having calculated according to know problems, as if a Ball was shot from such a point it would here form such a circle all naturally proceeded to Bandwah distant from our last nights station about 9 Miles, the consequence was that all the Camp followers who generally preceed found themselves at Bandah & were much surprized to find that their Masters had been at the Trouble of March Eleven Miles & were still one Mile behind in consequence of which we all suffered, by loosing our Breakfasts & some of us our dinners but in this we have an example of the advantages of secrecy for every one knew from Authority that Bandah was our point D'assis yet nobody could guess that we should make a two day march of 9 Miles & that some ingenuity was required to find bad roads, which fortunately we succeeded in. I went to Bhoraghur which is a large old fort, very imposing in its appearance but very useless.

12   Crossed the Cane River under the Walls of Borraghur. The Stream is now divided into two branches each 20 Yards across beautifully transparent & about 2 Feet deep with a strong stream. Here we begin to see very curious hills, rising out of a plain as level (except these Hills) as a sheet of water. They rise to the hight of 100 Feet or more, are formed of irregular rock, with some brushwood & Trees & Many Aloes, they are quite detached & altogether Singular, as if they had fallen from the Clouds, or like a large Haystack in a field. We were encamped near the Stables of Shumsheer Bahadur, this Man was formerly Nawaub of Bandha, Son of Ali Bahadur, a Natural Son of one of the Pushwahs by a Woman of inferior Cast & his Father knowing that his Cast would be low among Hindoos made a Mussulman of him (I do not vouch for the truth of this, I only give it as the Natives tell me) & I have no means of knowing more. Ali Bahaudur besieged Callinger (where it is presumed we are now going) & died before the Walls. Sumsheer Bahauder raised a considerable Army in favour of the Mahrathas last War but acted <u>very prudently</u> in not placing it or himself in any danger. He came near Colonel Powel's brigade & a random shot Killed a Major Smith but

afterwards he was not heard of. He is called a drunken Fellow, imitates the English in his Dress & has 3 Troops of Dragoons dressed like the 8th Dragoons.

13 We walked thro Shumsheers Stables which are on the plan of English Cavalry Stables but excessively dirty & his horses very poor. The People inclined to be insolent, but frightened at the same time. Col^l Martindale arrived.

14 We lay still, in a great measure ignorant of our destination.

15 We this day marched Southward over a fine level Country to Tingwaree 5 ½ Miles & halted.

16 To Girwah 7 ½ Miles. Two of my Camels died. Girwah is 3 Miles East of Seurah & here we see the Mountains.

17 Passed over a beautiful flatt Country with detached hills 10 Miles & encamped about 2 Miles from Pungurrah among detached Rocky Hills very beautiful. The Hills rocky with Trees growing among the Rocks, there is a spot in Lord Staffords Grounds at Trentham like it where there is a spring opening from a Valley. The Mawah or Tallow Tree forms here beautiful Groves. From a Hill in front of our Camp we can see about 12 Miles, the Range of Hills which begin a little Above Allahabad & Cross the peninsular of India, Callinga & Adgyghur are detached from this Range & advanced into the Plain.

18 The Country much worn by beds of torrents, we are now within 3 Miles of Enemies yet we advance as carelessly as ever. We have indeed every reason to suppose that the object of our Marches is not far off & that the person is aware of our views, yet not a step seems taken altho much mischief might be done by firing upon us from the Jungle particularly as the Road is often confined to the beds of torrents sometimes not 20 feet wide with high perpendicular banks & the Road shut up by falling Camels & broken Hackries, about two Miles from the River Boga, Col^l Martindale with his staff & myself were so wedged between Hackries &c &c that we could neither advance or retreat, with high perpendicular Banks on each side covered with wood. It is true that the Col^l may have Spies out, we near the River at Gorrah & altho we had only march 3 Miles, such was the difficulty of the road that much of the Baggage did not come up.

19 The Country today was beautiful & rich but not cultivated, it belongs to an Independent rajah & the contrast been an Independent Country & under the British Government is striking. This Rajah's abode is at Callenga & we were now almost certain of what we had for some time expected that we were going to attack Callinger. We advanced and

halted without the smallest interruption at about 3000 Paces from Callinger.

20   We are encamped at about a Mile & a half from Callinger & some of our Officers rode to the very foot of the Hill & Close to the Rajah's Sentries without any molestation, altho there is no doubt but that we are come to attack it. The Soldiers simply warned the Officers from approaching too near. The Hill is detached from the Main Chain & is about 750 Yards Hill & may be compared to the Wrekin in Shropshire, it is as one May say a Spade full of Earth with a little Hill made by the scraping of the Shovel. This little Hill is called Callingeree [now Kalinjar Fort] the steepness of the assent is such that there is no natural way of reaching the Top, the only path which is very narrow is by Stone Steps, there are Guns on the Top but they have all been carried by the meer strength of Men & long Bamboo Poles. We can see the Native followers of the Chief (who in Peace time inhabit the bottom of the Hill) as busy as Ants carrying their property into the Fort, yet we are so polite on both sides that a person unacquainted with India might think that we were come to pay a ceremonious visit.

21   We are quite civil as usual, possibly a Treaty is carrying on.

22   We quietly marched to the Top of Callingeree during the Night, had we had a European Enemy to contend with it could never have been done.

23   Very large detachments were at work all day making a road for Cannon to Callingeree.

24   With immense labour 2x18lbs were got up to the top of the Hill—all our Regiment was employed & they actually forced the Guns up Perpendicular heights some parts of the Road are said to be 75 degrees. No opposition whatsoever is made. This is often the case in India & we do not the less expect a severe opposition bye & bye. The Kelladar is aware that the Fort must fall, but he will make a determined stand, this is in some degree unaccountable for he is the acknowledged dependent of the Punnah Rajah, yet he would advance & fight with him, here he seems to affect a Shew of Justice, as much as to say I do not begin the War, & if we did not know better we might suppose him an Innocent oppressed Man, but the fact is that he is a robber by profession & he has some slight hopes of assistance from the Pundarries, should he see an Army of these on whom he could in any way depend he would soon alter his plan, it is something like the Armadillo, rolling himself into a Ball. They compliment the English by talking of Justice but do the same with regard to each other.

25	The Pioneers hard at work forming Roads. The Milk Men brought in a Horse which they said that they had taken from a Pindaree this may have been a simple Robbery & most likely it was, but the Cow Keepers are a fighting Cast.

26	We hear that the Rajah is in low Spirits because the Jays are departed, probably from the Noise, but a Jay appeared to day & has relieved him, this Bird is sacred to Seeb from its blue Neck. Seeb is called Neel or Seel Cund, the Blue Necked, from a Story in the Hindoo Mythology. The Bramins have decided that if the Feringees[176] fire the first Shot the Rajah will be victorious, this is very convenient for the Ferringhees for by this means they will make them approached without fear as near as they please.

27	It is reported in Camp today that a Vakeel[177] has come in.

28th	At 7 this Morning our Batteries opened & Major Kelly with a detachment of the 7th Native Infantry took possession of the Village at the foot of the Hill. In less than two Hours after the opening of the Battery from Callingery the Bastion seemed to fall very fast – I rode out this Morning to the Eastward to see what effect the Firing had had upon the Bastion. The Appearance of the Hills was thus.

29	The Firing yesterday had brought down almost all the Masonry at the Top but it all fell down the Precipice at the foot of the wall & left this difference—so that after all it was nearly as steep as ever, indeed from the distance it is impossible to judge what the degree of elevation it may be but I much doubt whether any thing but a Monkey can get in. No further impression seems likely to be made.

30	This day we kept firing but I could see no difference in the Breach as it is called. The Enemy fires only Twice which seems laughable.

31	No difference in the appearance of the Breach altho they have been firing all day.

Feby 1	On the first we heard no firing & we all believed that a Treaty was going forward but a little after the Batterys began again with as little effect as if a Person was to play a Country dance to a Milestone. The Shots strike the rock & a dust rises but that is all. It is now settled that a Storm is to be attempted tomorrow Morning.

---

[176] Feringee: Urdu: foreigner, from Farsi, Frank/French or, in India, a European.
[177] Vakeel: a representative or emissary.

2   I arose at 3 this morning & saw the Regiment march to Storm the Fort. The Quarter Master & myself walked out in anxiety till daylight, soon afterwards the Batteries opened with Shells & Shrapnels & about sunrise we heard a very heavy fire of Muskettry but we could not find the Reason for we saw no smoke in the direction of the Breach, we sent messengers for information but none returned at length the Adjutants Clashe[178] appeared & told us that his Master was killed & Captain Fraser & that Lieut Young was severely wounded, he said the Fort was taken soon after this we saw Many wounded Men brought in who confirmed the account as far as the death of Cap^n Fraser & the Adjutant but said that they neither had nor could take the fort, at length Lieut Booth was brought in wounded. He said that he thought the breach impracticable. Cap^n Cuppaidge, Lieut^s Young, Stewart Horsley, Daly & Davidson soon came in wounded. They all agree that nothing but a Monkey could get into the Fort, the lowest place is 10 feet perpendicular height which was over come by Ladders after which there was 30 feet of broken wall, ragged it is true, but leaning against a perpendicular rock. The European Soldiers having got up the first 10 feet clung to the Stones &c of the old wall, were while hanging to the brocken rock Knocked down by large Stones rolled upon them, the Breach itself was very narrow so that few could push a great quantity of Stone down & the sides were defended by Matchlock men who perfectly secure themselves could fire with the truest aim, nor do I believe that they were ever the least alarmed for their own security which often spreads terror among Defenders— About 9 o clock the Regiment Returned, bringing down the Body of Lieut & Adjutant Nice. Cap^n Fraser had advanced too far & his body was left in the breach, of 16 Officers who marched upon health, 12 were carried back, 2 Corpses. Of the Men 122 were carried back & 13 left dead.

3rd I was called upon to read the Service over poor Nice. Two Men who were brought in wounded yesterday died to day.

4th Our Fire is much slackened since our failure a Shell is now & then sent in, permission was granted to look for the dead Bodies, Another Soldier died of his wounds.

5   Poor Travers body was brought in & I read the Service over it, it seems that we were wrong in thinking that the Rajahs People had not suffered for we now find that the Rajahs Brother in law was killed, Coosla Naum Breege Laaly, and 49 of his Privates, the Wounded are in great Numbers 3 having died yesterday. It seems that the alarm was so great that many ran out of the Fort, Sixty were taken yesterday on the

---

[178] Clashe: servant.

other side & the panic is so great that we do not expect that the Rajah will risk another Storm, he is aware that we must either conquer or all Hindoostan be wrested from us— In fact before Night he sent in to surrender—At four oclock a Number of Elephants & Palankeens appeared coming into Camp. As they approached we counted four Elephants, 40 Matchlock Men & a few miserable Horse Men with the Son of Dureow Sing (The Rajah) & his Nephew, both Lads they are now hostages.

6   We continue our advances & erecting of Batteries, altho we hear that all is settled but I presume it is right to prepare in case of a change. At One o clock Gopaul Sing came into Camp, he has been for some time past a Rob Roy McGregor & has kept our Troops on the Alert for these two Years past, a Vakeel also from the Churkarry Rajah & Our Old Friend Shamsheer Bahauder in person. We have a great Many Native Chiefs in Camp.

7   This day our Bearers were employed in assisting the Rajah to convey his Women from the Fort & we looking upwards, in a vain attempt at seeing what was going forward, for they all departed by the opposite face of the Hill. The Women it is said were removed last Night & we expect to have a prossession to day. I went into the Village at the foot of the Hill & found it like all other Hindoo Villages, that is Mud built houses with Thatched Roofs, built irregularly more like wasps nests, formed the new ones against the sides of the old ones without any form & the original ones abandoned as they become full of vermin, it looks much like an old Comb of a Beehive. Their Buildings called Puckah are here not much better for altho stone is used the interstices are filled with Mud instead of lime. The very great moisture of the Rains so pervades the clay or Mud that it dries out & the Stones sink together & the Wall protrudes, looses its perpendicular & very soon falls— At 12 oclock the Fort was opened & I proceeded up the Steps for the only way up is steps. The fatigue was very great altho I have been accustomed to the Steep forts in the West Indies, our other Officers seemed to feel it more than myself & looking down the very appearance made my head giddy, it has been measured & is found to be 50 feet high the inner face of the Wall is not touched & I do believe that I could not get up now without opposition. The height from the plain is 750 feet& almost perpendicular. I was One Hour & a half in going up & down. I noted many large Tanks or reservoirs for water, some of them hollowed in the rock & beautifully clear, one in particular which was very large & had only a narrow ledge between the overhanging rock & the lower ground much resembling the opening to receive letters in an English post office.

Within was a reservoir immensely deep full of clear water, how far this went under the Hill I had no means of knowing.

9   Being Sunday read to the Men.

10   At 5 o clock I proceeded with Portbury to the Hill again we took our Breakfasts with us as we went up we examined our Road & found that there had been a good deal of damage done by the 12 Pounders from the Village, a large Tamarind Tree was much battered, several Shots had gone quite thro it. I presume the Ascent from the Village is nearly a Mile, the stepping Stones are very difficult & high but then they are not judiciously placed & there are descents & level parts. If proper Angles had been taken the Road would have been easier & yet equally as strong. The Wall is actually formed of Steps almost the whole way up. Having reached the Fort we again Descended to the Temple of Seeb cale Neel or Leel Cund (The Blue Neck). It is entirely excavated from the Rock, together with its Portico the Pillars of which are beautifully carved with wreaths, several mutilated Statues lay about, some of good Workmanship & some Monstrous in size the Stone Black & I have no doubt very hard for it is quite Marble like having a fine Polish (I believe) the simple friction of resting upon it. One of the Figures was very large & had had I think a hogs snout but it was broken off. There was a fine Stone Hog & a Reservoir hollowed in the Rock as described the other day. The Rock being above it 100 feet & 500 at least below. The opening about 8 Inches. The water running over the whole length like a small but perfect Cascade, we could observe that the inside of the Tank was formed like the Temple supported by Pillars of Carved work no doubt originally a passage had been allowed for the lower part & the Hollow was made like a Cistern & afterwards closed but no one in Europe can feel the sensation. In these hot Climates is felt on the Brow of a Hill 500 Feet or steps, when you reach a cool refreshing tank like this even should you abstain from the Water which is provident. The Sight alone cools you. The Number of Grey Monkeys about the Fort jumping from Crag to Crag is amazing. The Young ones hanging to their Mothers & Dams holding one Arm round used the 3 Legs so very well as to fly from Rock to Rock like Birds. I could scarcely believe what I saw after walking round the Hill which formed something like this [sketched oval] we could not perceive a single weak part. It is barren but there are Numbers of Tanks & Springs, I should think that water alone will be always sufficient for any Garrison & the extent of the Ground &c will always prevent its being surrounded. The View of the Country from the Hill was extremely Rich with several Streams, on the Eastern Angle the Range of Hills approaches very near but of an Elevation sufficient to over look it.

Callenger Campaign 1811-12 347

Callingery is the only place from which it can be annoyed & that can be so easily defended that it is a wonder that it was not so.[179]

11 & 12   Nothing. 13 Col¹ Mawby offered me leave to return to Cawnpore which I most willingly accepted & leave was obtained from Col¹ Martindale. I left Camp before 5 o clock Crossed the River Goora at ½ after 7 & did not overtake my Servants until I reached Gerwa at 11 o clock I believe I must have advanced 24 Miles. The Country delightful but wanting in cultivation, I overtook M' Richardson, The Agent for the Governor General which may almost be translated into the Vice Roy. He asked me to dinner & was very kind. M' Richardson insisted on my dining with him tomorrow at Bandah which place I reached at 8 & was it not for my engagement I should have proceeded.

15   I breakfasted quietly in my Routee, not showing myself for fear of an invitation from the Burah Sahib (The Great Lord) but I dined comfortably with him & moved off at 5 o clock over a Common 4 Miles to Mowae (this is a different road from which I came) 5 Miles to Lomar, I never saw a Richer Country or better cultivated as far as I could see was one level tranquilla per Alta. If I may say so, a calm sea of corn, over which one might skait 2 ½ Miles to Perperind. I was reminded of the Roads above Heidelberg towards Tuabra. The only break was here & there a grove of Mowah Trees. This Tree is very useful, oil is Procured from it & Spirits are distilled. The Towns of Mowae, Luma & Peperind are very large but I did not enter them. I pitched my Routee near Peperind at ½ after 8 o clock & breakfasted but being by myself I did not know what to do I therefore ordered Tiffin at one & intended amusing myself in feeding till near 4 but my servants knowing that I wanted to get on & being equally anxious themselves brought in Tiffin at 12 & outstood me that my watch was wrong so that I had finished my Food by 2 o clock yet seeing the sun high I lingered, but only ½ an hour when I moved & walked on quietly & slowly & contrived to reach Pullerah the Country was highly cultivated, when I got to the end of my journey & sat down I found that I had walked rather too far & I was tired & got to bed, there is a pleasure in being tired when you can get to bed. Chilla Terra.

17   At 4 o clock I moved off again & reached the Ghaut at Sun rise 8 Miles, it was quite dark the first part of my Road, towards the end I

---

[179] 'In 1812 the British troops marched into Bundelkhand. After a long battle they were able to annex the fort. The British seizure of Kalinjar proved to be a great watershed, transferring the legacy of the old aristocracy into the hands of the new bureaucracy of officials who showed their loyalty to British imperialism by damaging the captured fort. The damages caused to the fort can still be seen on its walls and open spaces.' Wickipedia.

found myself on a Common with Topes of Mowah. The former here is very narrow, the stream 300 Yards. The whole Channel not a Mile. On the North of the River a Reedy Sandy Plane 2 Miles to Lilooly which is built on the Ridge of High ground probably the Bank of the River in some former times. Here I met Chepmell going out to join the Detachment being appointed Adjutant in the Room Poor Nice & we stopped to breakfast under a Tree, after Breakfast we sat together till ten when we parted. I advanced up the Hill over a Common the Sun being very hot, but a cold wind blowing my lips much chapped. Pitched my Tent at Mahaker.

18   At four marched & after walking 8 Miles stopped to Breakfast under a Tree then to Kidgeway 6 Miles which is a large walled Town, sat myself down in the Serai, but the Fidgets coming on I enquired of the People what way there was of proceeding & was foolishly persuaded to attempt proceeding in a Bullock Hacky (Riding Post). It is true that I expected to meet a Palankeen every mile, I therefore procured a Bullock hackey such as the women ride in but as they sit cross leg'd when I got in I found myself obliged to draw myself up like a Taylor for the first Mile this seemed bearable but very soon my back began to ach & having nothing to lean against I sat like Mr Stick on his board & felt such Torment as cannot be conceived at length I was obliged to descend & walk by the side of my Chariot. Unfortunately the heat was excessive & I blamed myself much & feared that my Arms were black & blue, our Stage was to Chundkapoor 12 Miles which I reached exhausted at ½ past 2 here as I entered the Town I met my Palankeen & tumbled into it, quite delighted. From Chunderkapoor to Cawnpore 20 Miles which was performed by my Dack Bearers by 7 o clock. I found all well. Mr Corrie left us on the 27th that he might proceed to Sea for his health.

An English Officer in a Palenquin.

March Callenger to Cawnpore, 120 Miles.

March

The Weather Cool & Pleasant

April

The Heat increased the Glass standing in our Center Room on the 30th at 86

May

Towards the end of the Month the Glass stood at 91 at Night.

June

The wind at the beginning of the Month Easterly & oppressive The Rains began earlier than usual vz on the 13th & 14th & again the 16th. 24. 25. & 26 & again till the end of the Month.

July

1 week earlier with a Moist heat, the Children troubled with irruptions difficult to cure. The 2nd & 3rd week no Rain the heat scarcely bearable, on the 22nd a very violent North Wester (a Hurricane). We received orders for the Regt to go to Meerut to relieve the 17th Regt. We are succeeded by the 69th Regt

August

The Children had the Hooping Cough, but it was slight, we were however obliged to change the Air & we went to the Native Cavalry lines about 5 Miles off. No rain fell from the 21st to 26 & the heat was very great, on the 28th of flight of Locusts passed over the Cantonements in so thick a cloud as almost to cause blackness they alighted on the small shrubs & bent the Twigs & branches to the ground much like what Snow does in England. I went out in the Evening in my Buggy to the Cavalry lines & could have fancied myself in a Shower of Snow. The Locust came all round in the same manner & fell on the ground, only they rose up before my Horses. I could scarcely have believed it had I not seen it. It was equal to the heaviest fall of snow in large flakes, from some reason which I do not understand they did not destroy the vegetation but passed away harmlessly. We had hot winds the 28. 29th & 30th & we were all much troubled with Opthalmia.[180]

Sepr

1.2.3 extremely hot, no rain. The Opthalmia very painful, Mrs Sherwood had it to such a degree that she could not rest, in the course of the Night

---

[180] Opthalmia: inflammation of the eye.

I gave her 25 drops of Laudanum yet she could not rest, no rain till 5th & the hot wind blew. This is very uncommon, the 5th we had a violent wind which did damage to our thatch. At length Rain came on. Mrs Sherwoods Eyes were very bad until the 10th when the pain abated after having had 13 Leeches & two blisters. Sir George Nugents Commander in Chief arrived & we are reviewed on the 26th. The Heat at the Review was very great, a Man died there.

Oct^r

The Commander in Chief remained until the 7th when he went to Lucknow. We had not called but were surprized by receiving an Invitation to dinner which we could not decline & we experienced great civility.

11   A sudden order reached us for the Regiment to go into Camp preparatory to the March. The 8th Dragoons were also ordered to camp, this gives rise to a number of Reports.

12   The 8th Dragoons were suddenly marched away. We cannot learn what is the matter but the probable reason is to raise a report of a large Army there is actually going. We are encamped on the Race course 4 Miles from our old Lines. I remained at home but we are much alarmed not knowing whether we are to go to Meerut or be employed on an expedition. We remained in this state of doubt till the 28th when we received order to proceed to Meerut.

1812 October 30th   6th River Journey, Cawnpore to Meerut, 250 Miles.

I obtained leave to go by Water & on the 30 I advanced in my Budgerow. The Heat is not yet gone, but we find a material difference between a House & a boat, at Night it is really cool in the day dreadfully hot. At one o clock passed Betoor where Noah was born but could not pass it owing to the shallowness of the River.

31   Advanced very slowly, the River Broad & Shallow halted at Hutwah.

Novr

1   Cold Morning, Glass 72 wind against us. Halted on a Sand Bank

2   Wind against us, passed Nanamow at 12, halted at Dyepoor

3   At 12 Reached Mundghaut found the River very rapid near the old Fort but mastered the Strong Water in 2 Hours & saw Canouge at a distance before night, passed the Mouth of the Callee Middee, the Ganges ie the Great Stream does not pass Canouge & probably never did. Many Porpusses[181] but no other kind of Fish. Remark that the Eastern side of the River is invariably a Conkery Bank, The West low land & have observed the same in the Jumna as if the Stream wished for form a nearer cut to the Sea but was prevented.

4   Passed the Mouth of the Ramgunga a Stream coming from Rohelcund.

5   Strong Stream in the Morning but reached Singeram

6   Passed Singeram early, a good Stone Ghaut with a Hindoo Monastry dedicated to Baba Ram Kissen, reached the Southern extremity of Futy Ghur

7   Remained at Futy Ghur all day for Bread &c, it is a large & fine station. The Bungalows altho pleasant & beautiful seem for the most part empty. Mrs Law was there & very civil, no Potatoes yet.

8   We scarcely cleared the Station to day in part owing to a strong wind against us & in part to the Number of Boats, over whose Masts we had to pass our drag rope. The Station may extend nearly 3 Miles.

9   This day we had no wind & we advanced a fair journey to the nearest Ghaut to Amrapour.

---

[181] Gangetic dolphin, still plentiful in 2015.

10   To Bogwanpore

11th   The Stream divided & shallow with rapid water at times, we could see at 12 oclock our halting place of last night, since leaving Futtyghur we have not seen the true bank of the river, the Channel running towards the Middle of the River Bed, having long Sand Banks on both sides, with hard work & great difficulty we reached Pura. The Country here most fruitful a fine level.

12   The River rapid, the Channels broken, we halted on an ugly sand bank.

13   During the Night a very heavy squall with some Rain. The Thermometer fell very much & we felt extreme cold. We advance d very slowly

14   We passed Macbeths Castle of Cawder Gunge at 8 o clock, it is a considerable place with one old Ruinous Castle or more properly (Ruin) As this is the Country formerly belonging to Gholaum Cawder it probably took its name from him for it cannot be of such an age as Macbeth, as some suppose. We halted at Night at one of those spots where the Natives were assembled at a Religious fair.

15   High wind we scarcely moved—

16   To Peeperol, only 6 Miles.

18   We passed Husseenpore probably Husseengunge of Rennel we have reached the Real Shore again, a most beautiful level flat Country.

19   To day oh! Wonderful we saw a hill or Elevation probably 30 feet high, it is quite a novelty, called Sankyria.

20   This Evening we saw Ramghaut but could not reach it.

21   The Wind very strong all Night & with some difficulty we reached Ramghaut at ten o clock, but as our Servants wanted food we could not advance further to day, we had been looking forward to Ramghaut as a place of consequence & where we could provide ourselves with all manner of provisions but we were mistaken we found nothing here but Gram & other grain. Here we saw a large Pagoda which is now undergoing a repair with a Kind of free stone. There was nothing here to induce me to halt. The Dandies indeed found some Grog shop & it was with difficulty that I could get them on but as I knew that I must either do it to day or tomorrow. I forced them on, making my bearers take the drag rope, indeed we had some very difficult points to pass which we accomplished before night & advanced 2 Miles.

22   Reached Corrimboss. The Country very beautiful with Mangoe Topes.

23   A Strong wind reached Anopseer at Night. I was here disappointed as this fine old City is now a small bazar, the cause is that the Station for Troops is no longer here & the Neighbouring Enemies are friends, Wars sometimes cause a particular spot to flourish, indeed fortified places are no sign of the Riches of a Country.

23   Here I received a Letter from Mr Parson, but written in such a hurry that I could not make out its meaning. By it I was in doubt whether he had provided bearers to carry me by Dawk, I therefore sent on shore to the Post Master Mr Mercer to enquire, he said there was no dawk laid. Dawk is the Post of Men & Basketts like sending relays of Vegetables Horses.

24   This Morning I advanced but soon after Moving a Bearer ran after the Boat to say that a relay of Bearers were ready. Mr Mercer now knowing some friends had sent me a Horse & a Dolly.

I went up to Mr Mercers House who was very polite he said that if I departed immediately that I should reach Meerut during the Night he therefore begged I would take my Tiffin with him & proceed afterwards. I accepted his kind invitation & at Three o clock proceeded in my Palankeen. The Wind being high, I was much incommoded by the dust, my first stage to Chouta Coss about 10 Miles, which was performed in 2 ½ Hours. The Second the same distance in the same time. This Stage was to the Village of Cawnpore, here there were no bearers & the Cutwal wanted me to take an Elephant which I declined & with some difficulty I prevailed on the same Bearers to proceed another 10 Miles which they performed in 3 Hours making 20 Miles in 5 ½ Hours, from this at the Rate of 4 Miles per Hour I reached Meerut before 9 o clock, being a distance of 60 Miles. The Country Generally a fine level, but many dark jungles which are getting into cultivation. The Mud forts going to Ruin & the Inhabitants betaking themselves to a Village life or rather spreading themselves over the Country instead of retiring each night to a fort for security, during the Night I felt extreme cold. The Glass (as I found on my arrival) having been at 42. I found Mr Parson & his family well & very kind.

1812 November 24th   Meerut

25   I went round Cantonements in search of a House & by Mr Parson;s advice purchased a Bungalow of Lieut.{t} Gale 17th Regt for 2500 Rupees, it is small but 4000 Rupees are required for the next door altho not much superior. Mr Parson lent me Tents & Cattle to convey Mrs Sherwood from Ghurmucktezel Gaut where the River comes. This is nearly 30 Miles off. The Boats are not expected there till the 27th. I sent off my Suwarree & remained to dine with Col.{l} M{c}Gregor of the Native Cavalry

27th   Having sent Tents forward to meet my family at the Ghaut I proceeded in a Palankeen at 8 o clock my Road was as follows 10 Miles to Mow. The Country flat with much dock Jungle,[182] 10 Miles to Hagehaunpore the same kind of road. This is a very old City now in ruins—14 Miles to the Ghaut passing by the City of Ghur Mucklezer, I passed many delightful Mangoe Groves called Topes. The natives call them Baugechee Wallahs, Garden or Grove fellows. As I reached the Ghaut or Warf I perceived the Boat coming round a point about ½ a Mile off all well, having travelled from Anopseer in 4 Days which is reckoned by water 80 Miles.

The 28 & 29th   I was busily employed loading my goods & Chattels on which I employed Nine Hackries, on the 30th Marched to Shalychaunpore which I reached at 9 o clock the Tent was pitched ready to receive us & we found ourselves delightfully hungry.

Dec.{r} 1

Marched to Mow which we reached by 8 o clock very cold. The road very heavy, last night we were much teased by Wild dogs & Wolves. The Former were several times in the Tent during the Night, the latter attacked the Sheep, but were driven off.

2   Marched at daylight, the Country flatt, the Roads full of Ruts & from the stumps of dock great presission required in driving I nearly overturned my Gig on an old stump. Reached Meerut before Mr Parson was up. Mrs Sherwood was pleased with the House the form of which is as in Margin, [sketch obscured] vz 3 large Rooms with a verandah all round & two Baths on the North end. 1 Large Drawing Room, 2 dining, 3 Bed Room 4&5 Bathing Rooms, the Verandahs all divided into small

---

[182] Dock: Dhak or Flame of the Forest tree, *Butea monosperma*.

rooms, it must be noticed that the Servants rooms are all at a distance from the House forming separate Hutts at the Bottom of the Garden. We were much taken up the whole of this Month in paying & receiving visits & Mrs S. commenced anew her Native Schools.[183] We found a House in the Bazar built by some Privates of the 17th Reg^t as a kind of Charity in which the Revd Mr Parson performed Service on a Sunday, this I bought of these poor Men & Mr Parson was kind enough to say he would continue to do duty here to our Men "for we have no place of Worship appointed." An order has been received from the Duke of York for appointing a Schoolmaster to teach the Children of the Reg^t & as it happens that the fittest person to get the Situation is a most serious Man. We have received accounts of the Marriage of M^r & Miss Corrie, the former to Miss Myers, the latter to Mr Sherer a Civil Servant & a most excellent Match not only in a worldly way but in a Religious one as Mr Sherer is a very Religious Man.

The Station of Meerut is a perfect level the Soil Sandy & unproductive indeed it was not in a state of cultivation when the Barracks were built the most remarkable part of the soil is that the greater part is absolutely barren, not a blade of grass growing on it, while there are small spots like the oasis of Egypt beautifully green. I cannot account for this, the Natives say that it is from the quantity of Saltpeter in the Mud, but I understand that an Officer boiled the Earth in Water, but it was as bad as ever. I have spots in my Garden which have been trenched deep & manured & mixt with other Earth yet nothing will make them even produce a weed, yet they do not appear to the sight as if extraordinary. Our Quarters are built in a line as at Cawnpore viz each stroke being a range of barracks for 100 Men behind these Two Rows for subalterns and behind these one Row for Captains & in the Rear of the whole The Staff of which mine is the one marked one. In the Rear of all in the Bazar, the Subalterns have an enclosure of 60 Yards square on which

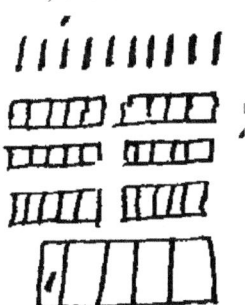

they have built houses according to their own ideas. The Captains have 80 Garden Depth & the Staff 100 in depth by 60 Broad. The Staff having a vacant space behind have all of them taken in more Ground & as they have never had a full complement they have enlarged the breath. I have 100 Yards in Breadth & 200 in depth. The buildings are very irregular every one consulting his own tastes so that some married Subalterns

---

[183] Mrs Sherwood started schools at each cantonment, initially for children of the regiment, including orphan drummer boys, but then for local Indian children as well.

built large & good houses & some field Officers a kind of Pig Stie. The consequence is that (as these houses are called private property we have purchased them according to our own conveniences. A Colonel lives in a Subalterns Room & a Horse has possession of a Field Officers Quarters but no one not belonging to the Regiment stationed in the Barracks could purchase a house without the Colonels leave. On Christmas day General Marshall (The Commanding Officer) received notice to be given that he should prepare a Room in his House for Divine Service on Sundays.

Mrs Sherwood has got 16 Children in her school for Natives. The English School consists of 64.

January 1813

The Weather is very cold with high winds. The Crops last Summer were so difficult that Gram is selling for 17 Seers a Rupee, it is generally 80 Seers, Wheat 15 Seers. The Commander in Chief arrived on the 24th & remained until the 27th.

February

We had rain on the 31st January after which the weather became warmer, the price of grain is falling vz Gram from 17 Seers to 26— Wheat from 15 to 21 Seers. The Cold again was severe from the 14th to the end.

March

This month cool & pleasant, Lucy fell from a Tonjon[184] & broke her Arm which was immediately set & did well but gave us great alarm & anxiety, the heat on the 24th was only 75. We heard of Poor Mr Martyn's death which took place at Tocat on the borders of Turkey on the 16th October.

April

The wind high but not very hot, we put up Tattas on the 7th but they made the house too cool. The Thermometer would stand at 86 but shutting the doors before Sun rise the center room is only 81. We find considerable difference in Climate between this & Cawnpore & a great change in the Animals & Birds, we have no squirrels here or Adjutants so common in Cawnpore. Cap^n McCaskell left us for England & carried Letters, it was so cool on the 12th that we were glad of warm clothing at Night but after that day it became warmer.

May

The beginning of this Month we heard of the defeat of Bonaparte in Russia. An overland dispatch mentions that the French had been obliged to retreat to Wilna not far from Konigsburg.

---

[184] Tonjon: A sedan chair carried on a single pole with 2 or 4 bearers.

The Weather gradually increased so that on 16th at 10 o clock at Night the Glass stood at 104. This is higher than I ever saw it at such an hour, at 8 o clock in the Morning of the 18th it stood at 89 in my Center Room, it was dreadfully hot all day & at 9 at Night I sent the Thermometer into the Garden & it was brought back standing at 100. 19 & 20 excessively hot, the Glass 102 at Two o clock on the 20th. The wind rose from the Eastward with dark weather & a sensible coolness during the night a Shower of rain. The Glass on the Morning of the 22 was 90, in the Evening the day having been dark there came on such a Northwester as I had never before seen or heard of. I saw the appearance of a heavy squall rising in the North West & being acquainted with the portent I ran to the house & shut the Windows expecting that the Wind would have risen with violence.

I shut all the windows & held the door in my hand to admit air but prepared to shut it should the wind become more furious. The whole air soon became a cloud of dust but without wind (of any consequence) while I held the door it suddenly became dark, so dark that I think I never saw a night so dark. I put my hand before my eyes but could not see it—in about a Minute the Light again appeared like a flame of fire. I could have thought that the whole surrounding Country was on fire, I can only conceive from this that storms in the Sandy desert can overwhelm Caravans, when I consider that this storm must have come from so great a distance & of course losing its darkness every Yard, yet with a coat of dust of a very considerable thickness, when all the doors were shut to exclude the air. After this storm we had rain & the Thermometer stood at 86 in the Morning violent North Wind squalls every Evening so violent as to turn up the Thatch of the Bungalow like the feather of a Friesland hen, the sides being carried from the outhouses, the thermometer on the end of the Month stood at 90 but the heat feeling much more oppressive that the thermometer indicated.

June

The Weather as last month very hot with a squall every evening with thick dust causing an almost total darkness between the squalls hot but not so much so as Cawnpore being generally two degrees lower, on 10-11th-12th Rather cooler with some Rain, the Nights excessively hot & what is worse we have violent squalls every hour between these squalls the heat excessive we cannot sleep without the Windows being open but when the squalls come on it is necessary to shut the Windows so that our Rest is broken, this weather lasted thus the whole Month with excessive Wind Lightnings & some drops of Rain but they were only heat. The great fatigue & uncomfortable Nights were very unpleasant.

July

Henry[185] born on the 1st Great heat with occasional Showers but we cannot call it the periodical Rains until the 12th but we had North east Toufans every Evening, the 12 & 13 it rained hard but it did not rain again until the 19th when it rained again very hard until the 22nd and indeed to the end of the Month, on the 24th the Rain prevented us from assembling at our Little Chapel as usual.

Aug^t

We had no Rain from the 26 Ultimo to 5th when we had a slight shower & harder on the 7th. 9th & 10th it was dry which is very uncommon weather. We can see the Range of Mountains to the North covered with Snow, hard rain on the 10th-11th-12th-13th-14th-15th-16th-17th-18th-19th-20th. Then dry weather as the excessive damp heat, the Glass 92 to 93. Mrs Parson confined on the 17th & going out too soon was very ill, dangerously so to the end of the Month.

September

1st No Rain. 2nd only a Slight Shower. The Fleet arrived. 3rd No Rain, 4th a Slight shower but it rained during the Night & on the 5th very hard indeed.

Within the last Year we have had many self murders among the Troops it has now taken another turn & they are killing each other! It is very extraordinary that Meerut has always been remarkable for suicide & the Common Soldiers & indeed some of the Officers also think that there is something in the Climate probably a heaviness of atmosphere causing low Spirits. The first instance of killing others was in the Artillery & the 2nd in the 4th Dragoons. These two attempts failed, the Men were tried & condemned but the 1st pardoned & the second executed on the 2nd Instant, but the very evening of the day on which the Execution took place an attempt was made in the same Reg^t but the Man missed his aim, on the 22nd The Sentinel on the Main Guard at Cawnpore belonging to the 67th Reg^t deliberately shot the Officer of the Guard while he was sleeping nor could any reason be given for it. On the 10th one of our Men Shot a Man while laying on his Cot, he did not even know the Individual whom he shot, the same day a Young man shot himself at Agra, & on the next day a Man of the 24th Dragoons snapped his Pistol (at his Comrade) 3 times before he was perceived. 13th very heavy Rain all the day, on the 21st it was very Cold. The glass standing at 78 with a great

---

[185] Henry Martyn Sherwood (1813-1912). He died at Pershore on January 21, 1912 just eighteen months short of his centenary. He had been vicar of White Ladies Aston for seventy-one years. His son and grandson were also called Henry Sherwood.

damp, on the 22nd the glass at 77. We hope the Cold is set in which is a full Month earlier than at Cawnpore, fine pleasant Weather, but growing warmer to the end of the Month, the win W. N. W. glass 85 in the Middle of Day.

October

The beginning of the Month The weather was warmer than usual, the Glass stood at 90 on the Morning of the 19th. I employed myself in copying the Stories on the Church Catachism[186] for England.

Nov^r

On the 1st The 24th Dragoons marched for Cawnpore. We sent John Adlington to Mr Corrie. This John Adlington is the Son of a Serg^t in the Regiment, born in St Vincents the very month I joined the Reg^t, his father is dead & he had been at our school till insensibly he had got into our House where he has been living two Years. Mr Corrie has kindly offered to take him from the wickedness of the Barracks.

Christian Converts

The Christian Convert Abdool Messeh came to see us, he is a fine looking Man with a long beard & puts me much in mind of an old Picture in my Bible of the Jewish High Priest he remained a Fortnight preaching in the City. He left behind him a Convert named Taleb Messeh, a Physician formerly Chief Physician to the Rajah of Bhustpore. He is a good Arabic Scholar, but knows little else & is most amazingly conceited. He is however reckoned a learned Man altho he believes the World to be balanced on a Pivot like a Childs whirligig, the Axis of which is a high Mountain.

Dec^r

Two Natives have applied for Baptism, one of them a Byragy or dervise, he lives about 12 Miles off and possesses some property, he can have no worldly object in view- The other is a Woman, She is strongly recommended by Colonel Rutledge the Native Regiment to which her Son belongs. There is also a learned Man in the Bazar, a Native of Rampour, who has been persecuted even to the confiscation of his property by the Rampoor Rajah only for speaking favourably of Xtrians, he now seems half inclined to become a Xtrian himself & is now reading the Scripture with great attention. McCaskell my oldest friend & companion is leaving us for England on account of his health. I am now

---

[186] Mrs Sherwood: *Stories Explanatory of the Church Catechism*, Calcutta 1814, London 1817.

the oldest officer but one (Buckland) in the Regiment. I received a very pleasant letter from Stuart from Madras

January 1814

The 8th Dragoons arrived on the 1st. The Weather warm with Easterly winds threatning Rain the Glass within doors 61 at 12 o clock. The rampoor Moluvee[187] seems to be deciding to brave the world & acknowledge himself a Christian, he says fear of the World is the only thing which holds him back. We hear from Agra that Mr Corrie has baptized within the last Six months 56 Native & Eleven nominal Roman Catholics but unbaptized. On the 9th the Rampoor Moluvee decided & applied to Mr Parson for Baptism. But Mr Parsons declines saying that he is not sufficiently master of the Language to reason with him & further he conceives himself to be a Military Chaplain & in no case as acting as a Missionary or having any concern for the natives. He is also afraid that the Natives may have some hope of gain by professing a Religion professed by their rulers, alas! The Rulers so far from shewing a partiality to Christians studiously avoid employing any one about them. I received a Letter from Mr Corrie stating that he would be at Dhelhi on the 13th. Saw the Rampoor Moluvee & told him I heard Mr Parson question him, his questions were to the following purport. What did our Savior mean when he said in the Gospel according to St John The Prince of the World cometh who hath no part in me first, who the Prince of the World was? Secondly if Satan was meant how could he to come who was always with us & what was the meaning of having no part in him. Mr Parson explained to his satisfaction.

The Thermometer stood within doors at 55 & out of doors at daybreak at 43. In May in the same place that it now stands at 43 it stood at 102 being I think a greater difference than ever happens in England. In April at Hardwar the Glass at daybreak stood at 55 and at 12 oclock 108 the same day. I had received no answer from Mr Corrie & I began to fear that I should not see him. The Candidates for Baptism became so anxious that they determined on going to Delhi to meet him. They set off on the 17th vz Munghool Doss, the Byragee, Munsoor the Rampoor Muluvee & Ubbadoola, the Moonshee employed by Mrs Reddie as her schoolmaster, on the 21st we received a Letter from Mr Corrie saying that he would come to us & that he had met the 3 Natives & was pleased with them, 26 Mr Corrie arrived & was deeply engaged with the above Mentioned men until the 30th when he determined to Baptise them all three gave very satisfactory reasons for embracing Xtianity, but it was

---

[187] 'Moluvee' Moolvee, a judge or learned man.

thought adviseable to delay the Baptism of Mrs Reddies Moonshee[188] for some for Family reasons, indeed he hopes to convince others in his family who live at Lahor.

The Byragee Munghool Doss gives the following account of himself. He was educated as a Byraggie or begging Dervice, in which Character he Travelled over great part of India, that some years ago he met with the Works of a satirical Poet named Cubbeer[189] who resided at Benares, this Poet lashed the Religion of his Country, both Mussulmaeen & Hindoo, without appearing to have any himself, he praised the Xtians more because they seemed to have no Religion than from getting superiority in their Creed, indeed Cubeer seems to have been a facetious Deist. It is said that his writings are much read. When the Maharattas had obtained the Common of the Doaub after the defeat of Gholaum Cauder, a Dewaun or Collector of Tribute under Scandeah & a follower of Cubeer patronised Munghoor & granted him a Jaghur[190] of 80 Bigahs of land on which he erected a house, small but substantial with open porches for Lodgings for travellers, here he remained until the English expelled the Maharattas & eventually took the Country. The poor Man still retained his land but increasing in years & unsettled in his faith he remembered the favourable report of Cubeer & wished to gain some insight into the Christian Religion. He called upon the English Resident a Mr Lister & having introduced himself, asked him if he could instruct him in the Christian faith. The Novelty of the thing & the uncouth appearance of the Man it seems offended Mr Lister & he ordered him from his presence without hearing his story. Some time afterwards he heard that a change had taken place & that Mr Guthrie had relieved Mr Lister. He then appeared again & asked the same question. Mr Guthrie did not drive him away but ordered him a present & dismissed him without an answer. The poor man received the present (some Money) but divided it at the door among Mr Guthries Servants (This is an Eastern Custom). The Man returned to his house & hearing that a Clergyman was come to the Station again returned & it was so ordained that he should fall in with Mr Bowley & ourselves, by which means he obtained a perusal of the law & the Gospel. Having considered these things for 6 Months he wishes to become a Xtian but he has of course met with slights & even insults from his friends.

The Rampour Mouluvee a Man of Quick natural parts, or considerable learning & a hasty temper has been long unsettled in his Parents Creed.

---

[188] Moonshee: Secretary or scribe.
[189] Cubbeer: Kabir (1440-1518).
[190] Jaghur: a feudal land grant.

When he first heard Abdool he perceived that the Mahomedan faith was wrong & that we want a Saviour or Redeemer which is not to be found in Mahomet, who indeed points to X^t & he now discovers that sinful Man has no substitute but Jesus. The Moonshee is a Servant of Mrs Reddie. He says that he was employed as a Copier by Mrs Reddie & that the Book of Job was put into his hands to Copy about a Year ago (The History of Job is imperfectly known to the Mahomatans) he was much struck by some expressions in it & when he had finished it he copied the Psalms, in the 120 Psalm these words struck him 'As David speaks of Two Lords vz one who is his Lord & one who sits on his Right hand. He was pondering over this when he was employed to Copy our Creed for the use of the School when he suddenly exclaimed I have found it! He then found himself more convinced by reading Isaeah of one suffering for the Sins of others. He confessed the Saviour. Abdool Messahs coming from Agra to Meerut & the answers that he was enabled to give to his enquiries quite convinced him that David in the Psalm speaks of Jesus Christ. This Man is a Native of Lahor, a Mild but reserved Character but having plain good sense.

The first Two were baptised in my little Chapel on Sunday immediately after Service & received into the Number of the outward & visible Church, all the Congregation sang 469 Hymn of Rippons Collection. The ceremony was very affecting. The Moonshee was present, Mr Corrie remained with us until the 2nd February & baptized a Woman, Miss Cox who has been with us for the last 18 Months left us with Mr Corrie.

The Moonshee who stood by & saw the others baptized is now so uneasy at having hung back that he set off to follow Mr Corrie, we have had much rain & high wind which was very unpleasant & cold.

March

March set in Cold with very heavy rain more than is commonly seen at this season the Natives are afraid of its continuance. At present there is an appearance of a very abundant Harvest. Corn is fallen one half vz. The best wheat from 15 Seers or 30lbs per Rupee of 2/6 to 30 Seers or 60lb. The Mote which sold last year 16 Seers per Rupee is now 66 Seers.

April

Fine Weather & every appearance of Abundance. The Weather very comfortable. We heard of the failure of the French in Russia.

May

Very little wind and consequently warm, a most abundant Crop of Musketoes probably owing to the quantity of Rain we have had. The Nights were cool but the glass in the day often standing in the center

Room 96. It rained on the 28th & the Night was cold & Damp the Glass having fallen to 78.

June

As the Summer advances the heat becomes great we were out as usual on the Kings birth day to fire, the fatigue was great & after breakfast we were ordered to pay of respects to General Gillespie[191] which we could have dispensed with, his house is about a Mile & a half from our Cantonements, on my return I had so severe a bilious head ach & could not sit up all day. Glass 96 heard of the Russians entering france.

July

Excessively hot on the 9th a North Wester which brought down the Glass Eleven Degrees in an instant, it Rained hard 10-11 &12 after which the glass gradually rose till the 19th when it rained again & continued to the 31st. heard of the battery of Paris & Bordeaux.

Floods at Meerut

Aug. No rain 1 to 15th & the Ground dry, with heat rained a little on the 15th no rain again till 23rd a lady described the weather as not grilling but stewing on 23rd so heavy a Shower which lasted only an hour yet set all the Cantonement afloat there was not the smallest cloud to be seen when the rain commenced, some of our Officers were in the Levies of the Native Regiment. Between which lines & ours there is a small brook, but dry except for a few Hours after rain, this swelled so suddenly that there was no possibility of return. Over this there is a Puckah Bridge of about six arches which has always appeared to us as a most useless expence as it wanted a River but now it is of no more use for it stands as an Island in the midst of a lake & is more dangerous to approach than the attempt to ford the Nullah for it seems the rapidity of the Current having met with resistance at the bridge has formed most deep ravines at each end. On the 24th it rained moderately in the Morning & I went over to the Colonels on business, while I was there it increased so much that after waiting upwards of an hour I thought it useless to remain. I returned home. My house is only 250 paces from the Colonels & the space between may be called a perfect level, except where the Wheels of Carts or the foot paths of Men may have worn the ground in a very trifling way yet my Bearers found very great difficulty in carrying me these few paces

---

[191] General Sir Robert Rollo Gillespie (1766-1814) KCB. Homicidal duellist, shipwrecked, killed six burglars by sword, acquitted of fraud, relieved Vellore mutiny, took Java, speared an escaped tiger, shot at Nalapani.

& the water was in an agitate expance up to the Middle of their legs, making an appearance of a Pond in a very heavy shower the drops causing a rising or splashing of water which multiplied the bubles in the surface of the water like a Kettle over the fire. 25 Moderate Rain, 26 about four in the Morning it recommenced most furiously 27th no Rain but the Sun most excessively ardent 28th a heavy shower 29th No Rain 30th & 31st Moderate.

Sep^r

1 Moderate Rain, 2nd Heavy rain which continued without ceasing in so much that all the Walls surrounding our Gardens began to melt being made of unburnt bricks & the upper part, being sheltered by the overhanging Burn tiles, soon became too heavy for the sodden foundations, & they commenced falling in 100 Yards at a time with a Sound like Thunder as the beating rain still continued. Our alarm became very great & having gone to Bed we became so much agitated that we arose at 1 o clock at Night waiting in anxious expectation for the Walls of our Houses giving way, every moment we heard a Crash of a falling wall & on looking out the whole place presented the appearance of a Sea in a Calm with Heavy Rain under the Line, the walls around our Garden were all down before daylight & the stable shewed symptoms of giving way, but the Rain abated. Towards Evening it ceased but it was not until the 5th in the Morning that I could get off & Immediately went to see how Mr Parson was situated, taking off my Stockings I waded to his house & found him in an out house trying to save some effects which he had in an outhouse the wall of which had fallen altho it was situated on so level a place that had I been asked before which way it inclined I could not have answered yet on looking over the broken wall there was a current or more properly a Torrent rolling by which I presume I could not have withstood, on comparing Notes with my Neighbours I have reason to be thankful my whole loss will be replaced for between 20 & 40 £ but there are some who will suffer to a large amount, one a Doctor Ruxton lost upwards of £[illegible] sterling, his new Mansion being scarcely finished was all carried. Many lost 800 Rupees worth. The Bridge is broken down & the City wall has suffered immensely, 20 lives have been lost in the Cantonement, one house destroyed 11 vz 7 Men 4 Women. The Rain continued but not so violently yet the effects are probably increasing. Major Stevenson was driven from his New Puckah built house. The Theatre is a very large & substantial house which has cost 9000 Rupees, shewed symptoms in the Morning of giving way & I went with Colonel Mawby & several Officers to examine it, we thought it much hurt but had no idea of danger yet we had not left it 5 Minutes when it fell in with

a tremendous Crash the Materials are not worth 800 Rupees. The loss of this building if loss it can be called is £1000.

On the 6th occasional showers but towards Evening the Wind came round to the westward & we had no more rain. The damage however is very great. almost all the walls are damaged some of them entirely down, others partially so, some Bungalows in Ruins & no ford as yet between the old & new Lines. On the 11th having business to transact I attempted to go to the City but could not get over in my Buggy & on the 15th when I did succeed the water was up to the axle Tree before I could reach the bridge.

On the 17 I had my congregation again in Hindoostanee. Mr Bowley had during the last year officiated he being a better Hindoo than myself, but he is now gone from the Station &^ I am again called on to officiate. There are indeed many more capable than myself but not willing. The Hindoo Service is at 7 in the Morning & I have English Service again at 9. Mungal Doss came to me afterwards. He had a Disciple with him, he talked reasonably or probably with a little too much reason. He said the Hindoos all acknowledge one God call el Quom (The Eternal) & I began to fear He had picked up some of the Theophilanthropists[192] Notions of Jehovah & Jove &c but I think our conversation that he merely meant to explain to me that the Hindoos had a kind of foundation already laid for argument in the acknowledgement of one eternal God, Superior to Idols. Indeed he said that there was more prospect of conversion of the Hindoos than of that of the Mahomedans, & as I differed from him alledging that the Mahomedans went so far as to allow the Jehovah & the Law Prophets & Gospels. He said "To be sure the mahomedans will receive your Bible & holding it in his hand will say what is this? Is it the word of God written by Moses & Moses is the Scribe of God, & this is the Gospel of Husnit Esau (Jesus) Allah, <u>Jesus Christ God</u> Jesus is Zemanee. Heavenly, Mahomet a Prophet which is Zemaunee, humane fleshly, Earthly he then immitated the Mahomedan again turned the book in his hand & said Kaugh Kaugh, Good Good, put the book down & turned away. The mahomedans said "we are like the Pharisees, They know but do no the Heart is hard."

---

[192] Theophilanthropists: A French deist sect formed late in the French Revolution.

1814-16 The Ghurka War

1814 October 12th—March to Dehra Dun, 135 Miles.

October

The end of last Month we had many flying reports about a move but they were so vague & sometimes ridiculous that altho sometimes irritated we did not give credit to them, they now gain strength but vary every day sometimes the Report says 4000 pairs of Boots are making for the Soldiers, at another time that the same number of flannel Pantaloons were making for the Soldiers that 500 Behestie Bags[193] were making in the Bazar, however on the 3rd we received an order most suddenly to march two days given for preparation. Not the slightest hint is given of our destination, there is of course a fine scene of confusion & numerous conjectures as to our destination which in many instances became affirmations most positive.

Notwithstanding the most positive orders for Marching in two days we were detained by the Contractors until the 12th when we marched without a sufficience of Camels for the Private Soldiers <u>let alone the Stores</u>. On the 12th we march & were set down at Durrowlah 9 Miles North of Meerut. These are the severe tryals of a Military Life when the Officer is suddenly ordered to leave his family, uncertain whether he will be able to return to the same place to rejoin them. The Private has fewer anxieties for the Government provide for his family (I speak of India). On our arrival at Durrowlah, the Camels which had transported the Soldiers Tents returned to Meerut & we were told & a fresh supply would be on the ground before Morning from the Westward, but none arrived & we could not move. The Country between Meerut & Durrowlah is a perfect flatt, with a quantity of Bagerah growing & many waste Dock Jungles, a kind of stumpy Tree the leaves of which are eaten by all kinds of Cattle and consequently it always looks stunted & rugged. It is a kind of Fig, there are some acacia called here baboul & a small herbaceous planted of the species of Casia & near each Village a large Grove of Mangoes with some Tamarinds, on the Western side Durrowlah looks very formidable but on the Eastern side its mud walls are washed into the Ditch & looks like a wall of Ice melting in a thaw.

---

[193] Behestie Bags: Waterproof bags or water bags, from Bheastie, water carrier.

We were obliged to stop at Durrowlah waiting for Cattle all the 13th & 14th during which time the 8th Dragoons arrived & passed us, it also rained. On the 15th the General Beat to strike tents at 3 o clock & I mounted my Horse to preceed the Throng but got beautifully involved in the thick of it. I walked leading my Horse until day light but got among crowds of Camels, Elephants, Hackries, Taltoos &c & could find no way out, until it became light when I mounted & escaped. The whole Country is Wild Jungle of Dock & wild Corinda Bushes, having cleared myself of the Throng I again alighted & strolled over the Country thro the same Dock Jungle with a few patches of Badgerea to Kutowlee 12 Miles from Durrowlah.

15 This is a large City but the Walls are in a sad state of decay. We encamped to the North of the City in a Mangoe Tope. Our Baggage was very late in coming up as it generally is on the first day.

16 I moved before the Regiment & walked 8 Miles before daylight. I understand that the Country is open & well cultivated, about 7 Miles from Kutowlee before daylight we passed thro a Village, the Road was so bad & so full of wells that it would have been a great risk advancing but I availed myself of a Lanthern carried with the Mess Utensils of the 8th Dragoons, at daylight I came to a Marshy Common with a small brook running thro it & it can scarcely be believed what pleasure such a sight gave for I had not seen a rill running thro green pastures for nearly Ten Years, about Two Miles further I came to a fortification seemingly in good repair, it was a square with four circular Towers, however on approaching found it entirely of Mud it is very imposing & experience teaches us that while it lasts it is very formidable probably more so than works of more durability. Two Miles further passed Hassenpur a Brick built walled Town of about the same size & age but more ruinous, Two Miles further to Muzzufferpoor, thro a cultivated Country. This latter place is of considerable extent & walled, the Callee Nuddee River before you reach it having a heavy fog rising over it reminds us very strongly of an English morning. Encamped in a Tope about a ¼ of a Mile from the Northern angle of the Wall. The ground very good but travelling & change of food have made me ill.

17 Marched from Muzzuffer Nugger at 3 o clock, crossed the Calle Nuddee at about 4½ Miles from our encampment. The Stream two feet deep, Narrow but with little or no stream at this season, it was quite dark when I crossed it when the day broke I had advanced Ten Miles & found myself in a well cultivayted and perfectly level Country at a ½ after six in sight of Deobund thro which our Rout lay. It is a very fine old City in which there have been many large Houses, but now these as well as the

Walls are in a state of decay. What the Towns lose the Country gains for the Villages are increasing & the grounds in high cultivation, owing to a great state of security than formerly when the Seeks & Mahrattas would plunder the open Country at their pleasure. We observed many Tanks or pools of Water generally built of Brick & very spacious, a great scarcity of Well water. The Thermometer in the Tent 90 at Three o clock but cold at Night.

18   I set off again at 3 o clock & reached the encamping ground about ¾ of an hour after daylight. The Country as usual level with small parches of wild Corindas, many Topes of mangoes, often with the small brush wood Corinda growing under.

19   This day we saw the Hills very clearly to the North. We passed by Saharapore at day light, this is a large City in which are cantonments for a Regiment of Seapoys and a Cavalry Regiment, they are Empty and ruinous. I was at a great loss to find where the Regiment was to encamp, I therefore wandered about expecting them & entered into a Grove sacred to the Monkeys. I was much pleased with the spot for a clear stream ran thro' it which is a new feature in Indian landscapes. The grove was full of Monkees with a fakeers house in the midst & these demigods were dreadfully impertinent & tame. The Regiment were particularly late today & owing to the Assemblage of so large a force the ground was not to be marked out till their arrival. I at last saw Colonel Mawby & went to his Tent to Breakfast. He is now a Brigadeer & of course the secret & of necessity as full of secrets as an egg is full of Meat & could not even look wise without exciting suspecion, I acted the Part of Marlboro for I looked over his Map & soon found our projected Rout by the fingering & he acknowledged in confidence that I was right. Indeed there is but little choice of Routs for we must either turn to the Right or left immediately if we are not to go to the Hills, after breakfast I found my Tent pitched on out proper ground & I soon heard from Col^l Mawby that he is to leave us in the Morning in command of a small Army consisting of about 1000 Men in which are two companies or about 150 of the 53rd Reg^t. He did not tell me where he was going but simply said I shall not see you again till all is over & that will probably not be until the Spring. We are expected to move Northward on the 21.

20   I was busy all day in writing letters & scarcely moved from my Tent but we hear that we are to move tomorrow, a great deal of secrecy is pretended altho every Coolie in Camp knows the Rout that we are to take. Our Rout it seems is directly north to a pass in the Mountains which leads across them to a beautiful Valley called the Dhoon, we do not know whether we are to enter the Valley, for as yet we are only sent

by report. Two days march vz 70 Coss to Kirkalee & 7 Coss to Jasmore the latter place is out of the Road to the Pass.

21   We were to have marched this Morning at ½ after five for being now in the frontier we have strict orders to proceed with caution, at ½ past five then we were paraded but our Commanding Officer Col^l B not being able to understand his Guide would not move. He asked the Man in English (which the poor fellow did not understand) whether he knew the way. The Man told me that he did but B— would not believe him because he called Naree Laree. I endeavoured to explain that N&L are often used squerimously, as Lucknow, Nucklow, but nothing would convince him & we remained till 7 o clock, however at this time he was prevailed upon to march under the Man's guidance, we soon after met the General who appeared angry & said "as you are so late you cannot take the full march to day, you must therefore halt at Magra, the Snow cap'd hills now open finely on our view, as plain & as fine as the Alps from Geneva. The Country we are in is very beautiful & finely cultivated. I saw several fields of Rice just ripe, we encamped in a ploughed field without Water, Our Rout has been almost East Thermometer 65 at 10 oclock.

22   Marched at 5 o clock this Morning this is a fine Country without any visible road, we saw foot paths but no appearance of wheel treads, we twice crossed the beds of Nullahs which had round small Stones in the beds, evidently brought down from the Mountains, there is evident appearance of vast bodies of Water passing thro them in the Rainy Season. One Bed was a full Quarter of a Mile from Bank to Bank. I rode by myself following the advanced Guard, by a narrow path thro field of Joar Badgera & Mote, to Jasmow the last Village under the Hills & in consequence our advanced post. The Villagers describe the Country between us and the Hills as a Jungle of long coarse Grass & Briar Bushes & having no road, the passes into the Dhoon lie at Right angles from us vz Timly to our left 12 Miles Keene to our right 10 Miles. The foot of the Range 6 Miles in a strait direction in front. The Mountain covered with snow in front they say is 100 Miles off. They say it is so cold on it that the Ice (Baruf) will not melt when it boils & they seem to think that the Ganges comes from it. The remaining part of the Himalaya range is hid by 1st or 2nd Range we expect to halt here. We guess that Colonel Carpenters division which left us at Seharunpore has marched up the Timly Pass & Colonel Mawby the Keerie Pass & that we are to support the one or the other as circumstances may require.

We remained here till the 28th & we were as if completely out of the World surrounded by high grass Jungle & it was only the last days that the Post found us with our Letters, we caught a young Elephant during our stay.

27   This Morning orders were received for us to march tomorrow morning towards Kerie & a rout sent but on investigation it was found that the road which was pointed out is impracticable.

28   We marched at five oclock this Morning & were obliged to return on our footsteps to a Village called Kurkullee here we joined the Main road which we left on our rout from Saharunpore, the Country from this to Kerie was most beautiful but about double the distance which we had expected. Kerie has formerly been a fortified place & now as we passed we saw Ruins, particularly two round Towers of brick standing at a distance from the Town & now in good repair. We passed Kerie about two Miles finding it difficult to meet with a spot to pitch on for fear of the dry Grass which might easily be fired, we at last encamped on the banks of a Nullah surrounded by the long dry Grass which was very dangerous our ground was very damp. The Water oozing out if dug to a Spade depth, e found it very difficult to keep our Trunks above the water for the Sand turned out to be a kind of quick sand & in the Nullah we were nearly loosing some Cattle from the Sands, we did not march less than 23 Miles, the consequence was that our sick & Baggage did not come up all Night.

29   Add to this a dispatch arrived ordering an instant advance, we therefore moved again at one o clock in the Afternoon, we crossed no less than five running Streams in the course of 15 Miles, but such was the lassitude of the Men that we heard a cry for water all along the Road & the poor fellows lay along by the side of the Road unable to move, we reached Toombarah. This beautiful spot I can hardly describe except by referring to my Letter

Letter to Mrs Sherwood, Octr 1814. Toombarrah in the Kerie Pass

We moved at one oclock to day, the Sun was not so oppressive as I had expected but still it was bad enough & made our backs pretty hot, for we were marching North Eastwards, dreadfully hot, for the first four Miles we travelled over a waste of long grass with here & there a small field which had been planted with Badgera or some grain of that kind but now cut & carried we saw several Men's nests in the trees & at the end of the distance (vz 4 Miles) we came to a Dhawk Station & the Hircarrahs[194] explained to us that the nests which we had seen in the Trees were Stations for watchmen & Hircarrahs to be out of the reach of Wild Beasts, particularly Tigers & Elephants which are very common so that they dare not sleep on the Ground but at Sun Set retire to their nests, from this we entered a kind of Forest of high Trees with very little brush wood, the Grass beneath being beautifully green & fine, about a foot in height, we here perceived a great change in the species of Trees most beautiful Trees covered with fruit. One like a small Apple but we dare not taste it, the Natives say it is only fit for horse medicine & I think it is used as a strong astringent in Blacking like Galls. Another very Elegant Tree with a Transparent fruit like a plumb. The Tree itself like a fir.

We travelled in this Forest for 4 Miles delightfully shaded from the Sun. I could almost have fancied myself in the Dingle at Badger when suddenly a most enchanting Scene opened to us at a turn we saw a Mountain in front as if on the other side of a River, not abruptly rising but apparently a gentle swelling, but to a great height green with grass & Clumps of Trees as if formed artificially. The beauty of it struck us the more as it reminded us of Europe. The River between us and the Mountain was dry but its bed was so different from the green Banks that it resembled a large River. We entered the Bed of the Torrent & almost immediately found ourselves shut out from the plain by the Mountains so high as to intercept the Beams of the Sun, the walking was now very painful as we could not leave the Bed of the Torrent which was composed of large round smooth stones about the size of a Mellon, just large enough to tempt you to place your foot on the edge & then rolling over upon you & breaking your Shews, in the Middle was a beautifully clear moving stream filtering as it were among the stones but tempting you to walk in it stepping from Stone to Stone & invariable wetting your feet every 20 Yards. Here we saw the Fir Tree & I gathered a Cone with the greatest delight, here also we saw the Willow & the Fern.

The Mountain is worn away by the passage of the Mountain Torrent and formed a wall on each side generally perpendicular always inaccessible so that should a sudden storm arise I doubt whether we could get out of the way. It reminds me of the Ravines in the West Indies, particularly Rabbacca River in St Vincents. I dismounted on entering the pass & preferred falling my own height to the greater fall from my Horse, after proceeding at a very slow pace about 4 Miles I came to Millers buggy abandoned in the Road, but uninjured, he could

---

[194] 'Dhawk & Hircarrah' Dawk Hurcura, relay post messenger.

not get it further. Nothing can be greater than the change it reminds me of Mount Jura, but my feet tell me that it is much more difficult My feet are so sore I can scarcely crawl & what is worse there is not a level piece of ground in our encampment, or any means of fixing our Tent Pins, should a Storm of wind come we shall be all blown away. We are employed picking out the softest stones & Harrington is employed boiling them hoping that they will become softer like the Pilgrims peas. We are all in good health, not one officer sick but all their feet are dreadfully sore which we expect will be well with a Nights rest.

It is a fine Moonlight Night & the beautiful appearance of our place of encampment exceeds all description, the lofty Mountains on each side, with waving woods. The Men cooking with the fires spread along the valley. The shewing of the Sentries Firelocks in the Moon light is like but very far superior to a Scene I remember in Blue Beard. I allowed my fancy to work until I expected Blue Beard to come out & sing a Song. We are now about 3 Miles from the Top of the pass & the Guides say the road becomes more difficult. As we are to advance we expect to march Tomorrow afternoon for we cannot go before. Colonel Mawby is said to be only Eleven Miles in advance & we shall join him in one march, thank Lucy for her message thro Mrs Mawby. I am afraid that dolls are not to be procured in the Dhoon I must catch her a Monkey or buy her a young Ghorkalee or a Young Dhoonee for here we find that Parents sell their Children as a common trade. She should be thankful that she is born to a different lot. I am much obliged to Mrs Mawby for her letter, but the Colonel writes me word that he shall call me to account for corresponding with his Wife in his absence. I saw Howarth completely knocked up laying by the road side Yesterday, but it is entirely fatigue, he was well enough after dinner. The less you say about our movements the better, this marching in the heat of the sun has <u>lengthened Polloks</u> face a Yard. I do not think that he will ever smile again.

Letter to Mrs Sherwood, 3 Miles from Dehrah in the Dhoon, 1st Novr 1814

Yesterday I wrote you a short & hurried note to prevent if possible exaggerated reports reaching you without your having any certain intelligence. The death of a General sometimes occasions the loss of an Army but in our case it seems the contrary, I mean not to take from General Gillespie what he really deserves vz the praise of Courage but he had risen too high in the Service. He was a good partisan but should never have had the command of an Army. His last words "We must stand, we will never retreat, Death or Victory." & as long as he had lived the Men would have remained to be killed, I mean the Europeans. He was shot thro the heart & was dead in a moment. He had advanced with a small Gun, close up to the Stoccade of a Fort & stood like a Boy shooting peas against a high wall exposed to the Fire of the Enemy without the smallest possibility of hurting them in return we have many wounded men of the Reg^t but only 8 killed, but the wounded are severely hurt, we had only two Companies engaged & the Members as belonging to them will of course be much talked of & what is exterordinary they are almost all of your acquaintance, being the religious Men of the Regiment. Lieutenants Young & Anstree are severely wounded & dear as the experience is bought we hope it may be eventually of service in restrain such foolish self confidence as our English Generals have when attacking the Natives whom they have foolishly been taught to consider as wanting in every energy, but I will begin from our termination of my last letter, which was written from Toombarrah in the Kerie Pass.

We lay there to recruit our Men until 12 o clock on the next day, indeed it was necessary, for many stragglers & particularly the sick did not arrive much before it was notified that we should march the same Evening. The Instant this was known, notwithstanding orders to the contrary, all the baggage was in motion, every one anxious to get his Tent over the Pass before it should be choked up by the Column & altho I was inclined to attend to orders I found myself insensibly drawn to leave my Tent to be struck & tacitly to authorize the removal of it when the Tent was once removed the next thought was to advance myself intending to go slowly, for why might I not sit down by the road side as well as run about the bed of the River where I was, & I therefore set off. I had not proceeded far on foot & looking into every bush for plants before I was overtaken by Colonel Buckland & Lieut^t Emery (now acting Quarter Master). They were on horseback & as the Stones were rather hard to my feet I mounted & joined them, Bucklands Horse being larger than mine contrived by taking longer steps to get over the Ground quicker than mine & would have left me behind had I not trotted after every practicable part of the pass like a dog running after his Master.

This kept my mind fully occupied in watching my opportunities as we advanced the Ravine grew narrower & the number of camels being gradually confined in a narrower space that we were obliged to dismount, & now we had a scene of the most delightful confusion. I was soon separated from my Companions & holding my horse by the bridle I crept under one camel & over another for some were fallen in the Road & literally stopped up the passage which was not 9 Feet wide with a wall like hill on each side & the ascent itself as steep as the Ridge of a House, such swearing & beating of Camels & hallowing & Echo's it was enough to stun me. I could only compare it to the Kings going to the Theater, supposing Camels & Horses were to be the Auditors, this part of the Road was about 100 Yards & after having surmounted it & being joined by Buckland & Emery we stood on the Top professedly to give advice & no doubt added to the noise by our own Shouting. The Apex of the Hill was not 5 feet wide & I could not help laughing at the Colonel who was drowned in perspiration as white as a sheet dragged up by Emery.

One Native Camel chose to fall in the narrow passage & nothing could make him rise, we were under the necessity of turning him on his back & putting a rope round him, to drag him backwards partly by his Tail till we had cleared the Road. As it grew dark I outwalked my Companions & getting down the Hill which was not so steep, I seated myself under a Tree & got a fire lighted prepared some dinner. When Buckland & Emery came they were delighted at finding me so comfortable & we drank a bottle of wine in expectation of the Moon rising, which it delayed much in doing, which gave me occasion to sing "Rise, Guthrie, Rise" in my best stile which did not a little anoy the Colonel as he felt the Cold & would much rather have been in Ibbotsons Hotel, indeed I would almost have agreed with him. We thought it not prudent to advance further. We therefore covered ourselves with our great Coats & lay under a Tree. The distance which I had marched could not get the Quicksilver out of my feet so that I was up & down every moment, at length about Ten o clock the Regiment arrived & we proceeded, it became very cold & a most heavy dew fell. It was twelve o clock before we reached Deyrah where Colonel Mawby had been encamped but on coming to the Ground we could see by the light of the Moon, the round marker made on the Ground by the Tents now removed, but no sign whatever of Man or beast. We were of course astonished, but I quietly lay Myself down to sleep while others rode about in search of our Army.

1814 October 31st   Battle of Nalapani.

Continuation of letter to Mrs Sherwood, 1st November 1814.

The Camp is as found about 3 Miles off, but it was three o clock before we reached it, we found the Camp opposite & apparently three or 4 Miles from a Fort called Kalunga situated on the Top of a Mountain no body appeared until day light & as it became light we anxiously looked out for the fort which appeared in front of us, it had no appearance of size or strength but stood on the highest part of a Ridge which had no very imposing appearance for it was only the foreground to a very high range called the Second Range & which from our Station seemed to join to it.

We heard that the forces under Colonel Mawby had attacked on the 24th but found its Natural defences so strong that he was obliged to desist after losing & one or two Men, after this he had drawn up his 2 sixpound Gallopers half way up the Ridge & formed a small Battery. Now we find this Battery occupied by some Men of the 8th Dragoons & the Two Companies of ours which left us at Seharanpore. Soon after day light Three other Companies of ours were ordered to the Battery, but the provisions had not arrived & some instructions were waiting they paraded in front of our Camp & did not march immediately. I was with them with my Glass in my hand, when suddenly I observed a large fire near the Fort & heard a heavy firing, on looking thro my Glass I observed numbers of Men jumping over the walls of the Fort. It immediately struck me that some fire had broken out within the Fort & that the Garrison were making their escape from a fear of being blown up, but I soon perceived that whatever might be the reason of their leaving the Fort it was soon over for they returned to it again & I perceived that a very heavy fire was kept up from the Fort, altho I could not see what it was directed against. We all agreed that it could not be an attempt at Storm for no Person was seen advancing towards the Wall, indeed there did not seem any break, or apparent way in & the firing continued very long, but what grieved us was that we found that our 3 Companies were expected up the Hill for some duty even before they had marched from our ground. The firing of small Arms at length ceased, but a great Gun from one of the Angles of the Fort occasionally fired being pointed outward, a plain proof that whatever had caused the firing, the Enemy had still possession of the Fort. After cessation of all firing for about half an hour it again commenced & we now plainly saw the Enemy coming out of the fort & defending themselves in great numbers behind a Stockade.

 Here the firing was very brisk, but the smoke became dense. I forget to mention that about the time that the first firing had finished two other Companies of ours had marched, & as the first two which marched this Morning must have been too late for the first firing, so the two last must have been too late for the present. While we were in anxiety about these two firings an Officer of the Native Cavalry came galloping down & said "General Gillespie is killed & the attack has failed" soon after this we saw the wounded carried into Camp both the Officers of our first Companies vz Lieutenants Young & Anstie were brought in wounded & many Men, we soon learned that three Serjeants and 8 Men were killed & that the 8th Dragoons had lost more, these attacks are described as having been conducted in a most rash manner & <u>unworthy of a General</u>. Just a few Dragoons were sent (a most unfit body for a Storm) they were followed but not near enough to support the Two Companies 53rd Reg^t. The Dragoons were unencumbered by knapsacks or firelocks & soon outran the Infantry, they were eager to enter on Action, but having only Sabres were altogether unfit for such an Attack they were fired on as they stood (as I may say) unarmed, but the Enemy, gaining courage, jumped over the wall & rushed down on them with Sword & Shield but they soon found that they had made a mistake for they were not equal to the Dragoons hand to hand & were glad to excape back again into their fort from which they could fire down while themselves were entirely covered.

 When the Two Companies 53rd Reg^t advanced they could find no means of getting into the fort which had no breach or opening & they had no ladders. The Seapoys refused to advance so that several of their Officers left them & joined the European Troops & several were Killed. The first attack was no sooner abandoned than the Second Two Companies of the 53rd Reached the Top of the Hill & they were sent. Had there been only one attack with the 4 Companies in all probability it would have succeeded. Contradictory orders had been given & the Signal for Attack having been most clearly pointed out in general orders, was so completely unattended to by the General himself that he headed an attack at least two hours before he had appointed & what was more extraordinary his own orders of the day before clearly pointed out what would be the result of such disobedience of orders.

The 7th Native Infantry had received instructions to advance on a certain signal & the Officers of that Corps had their watches in their hands waiting for the time & dare not advance for fear of disobeying positive orders & at length one division under Captain Campbell who thinking he might be mistaken advanced & was the Means of saving the Gun which the General unGenerallike had been serving with his own hands.

The General was in the act of abusing & calling the Seapoys "Cowards" when he was struck by a ball in the heart & never moved after. He repeatedly said that he would never return & when he was struck he had few except Officers near him & was within a few paces of the wall. Major Ludlow the Senior Officer ordered a retreat after the loss of nearly 500 Men Killed or wounded the 53rd Reg^t lost 107 of these, Officer killed, General Gillespie, Lieut^{ts} Ellis, Fothergill, Goselin, O Harah, Broughton. The Wounded are in great numbers & many with little hope of recovery. The events of today have thrown a damp on all, but it is the general opinion here that Gillespie's death has saved the Army.

Diary resumes.

Nov 1st This Morning at ½ after six oclock I was called on to read the Service over the Officers who were killed yesterday. Three Officers & four privates bodies have been found. A Note was sent to the Kellidar[195] to ask leave to bring away the bodies from under the Wall —in this Melancholy Affair 3 of my Congregation have fallen, viz Hays, Gill & Russel. In the Evening the Bodies of Lieut^t Goselin & several Men were brought in & buried.

2nd We understand that a Battering train has been sent for which will not arrive in much less than a Month, in the mean time were are to retreat to better ground at about a Mile from the Village of Dehrah. The Dhoon or Valley in which we lay is less than 10 Miles broad between two ranges of Hills, very rich but badly cultivated & the Inhabitants wish us success.

These Ghoorkahs or Goorkalies are the Inhabitants of a district within the Valley of Napaul their principal City is Ghoorkah & they have conquered Napaul whose Capital is Catmandhu, it is only since 1803 that they have succeeded in conquering Siringuhr & advancing along the Hills to the Sutladge but have not opposition from the Seeks, they would

---

[195] Kellidar: Kallidar, fort commander.

however in all human probability have succeeded & reached Cashmere if they had not foolishly quarrelled with the Company.[196]

3rd   We moved on the 3rd & pitched in a Cultivated field. I called on Lieuts McDonald, Tomkyns & Holland. Three Senior Officers & we agreed to have regular prayers in my Tent as long as we remain near each other. The Ghoorkas call themselves Ragepoots, but their features are flatt with prominent cheek bones, how they obtained possession of the forts I know not, probably by blockade or Treachery. This Vally is very rich but full of Stones some of a very large Size almost rocks probably washed down by dreadful Torrents in former times. There are numerous streams of pure clear water, one runs behind our Camp & turns a rude Mill, which does not grind above 80lb of wheat in a day but there is no want of Water to form a proper Mill if it was in our Territory.

Tomkyns turns out to be a Worcestershire Man & born within a few Miles of Mrs Sherwood, near Bromyard—Lieuts McDonald, Tomkyns, Hall & Keathede, Montgomery & Harrington came to Prayers but only very few Privates owing to hard duty. Babcock brought me some honey which is very fine, almost as good as English Honey & sent some bottles into Meerut & received in return Potatoes & wine. I went to see a Water Mill, it is very small, the wheel is horizontal & the water is conveyed to it by a small trough & can only force its way by turning the stone the operation is very slow & not above 80lbs of corn is ground in a day. 5 Pice is the established Price for grinding one Maund of wheat. Mr Robbie called on me. He came up the Timley Pass & left the Cavalry yesterday who are now lying at Fyzabad on the South of the Tinley pass. He travelled 48 Miles during the last Two days & he describes the Country thro which he came as rich but depopulated & covered with reeds.

My memorandum of this date expresses a great anxiety for Potatoes, talk of honey collected in the Hills & complain of the fermentation thereof. From the 15th to the 24th I further remark that our Regiment remained on the ground to which we had marched on the 3rd waiting for the Battering Train during which time little occurred. A detachment was sent to the highest part of the Ridge immediately in front of us (called Budraj) to occupy a part of the road leading from the Westward towards Kalunga (for the Roads are confined to the extreme ridge of the Hills) at Budaje the Ghoorkas have erected a Stockade & formed a link of their chain of

---

[196] In 1814 both the Kingdom of Nepal and the East India Company wished to control the border which ran along the last foothills overlooking the Gangetic plain. The Nepalis established a number of hilltop forts which the British decided to attack. Nalapani was the first battle of the 1st Anglo Nepalese or Gurkha War.

The Ghurkha War 1814-15—The Battla of Nalapani

Posts. The difficulties that the detachment met with were very great, but only the Natural difficulties of a Mountainous district.

My Beast of Burthen could be employed & water was very scarce, for the Higher Casts of Hindoos would sooner die than drink water if not drawn from the Spring or carried by themselves, yet they are too proud to carry it & consequently they suffered & indeed were useless, while the Mahomadans & lower Casts drank from Beheistic Bags which Government had provided & what was worse after the detachment had surmounted these difficulties & reached the Top they found the Stockade on fire & that there were innumerable other Roads on Paralel Ridges & having remained exposed to intense cold two days they returned having no provision. It was from the detachments suffering that I introduced the word Bawakoossee instead of Bevoack.

It happened as follows, one of our Officers enquired what the term bevouack meant, he was convinced, be awake, I said it meant be foolish, for it was a foolish business altogether without wakif, understanding.— This term became common in the Camp Bawakoofing. Captain Warner who commanded this detachment told me that looking towards the North he could see nothing but Hills piled on Hills until the view was bounded by the snow clad Himilaya. The Hill People like our Ancestors have small watch Towers on almost every Summit from which they can watch the passes, in security. The passes are only the beds of Mountain Torrents worn by the Rains— I employed myself during our inactivity in copying & comparing Maps by which I find that the Valley in which we now are called the Dhoon, which means the Valley in pre eminence is about 44 Miles & 11 Broad, its length is bounded by the Rivers Ganges & Jumna & its breadth by the first & second Ranges of Hills. In the first range which separates it from the District of Saharumpore are seven known passes, 5 of these are only for foot passengers the Remaining two for Camels. The Larger of these & the most Westerly is near the Jumna & is called Timley, from a Village of the Name within the Dhoon, it is about 7 Miles across. The other large pass is called Kerie, is situated about the Center of the range & is longer & more difficult. These are the beds of Mountain Torrents except at the very Top of the Ridge. The Road is of course difficult being either entirely rock & looses stones.

The Soil of the Dhoon is good & it is well watered but a great part lies waste probably from the Arbitrary nature of the Government of the Ghoorkas. The Revenue in 1803 was calculated at 100,000 Rupees but now it does not produce 20,000. I can only gain information of 3 Passes in the 2nd Range, the principal is near the Ganges leading from the Hurdwar by Ricketies which passes Deopraj, a celebrated Temple at the junction of the Bhaugrettee & Alkanundra Rivers which form the Ganges & leads to Siringuhr. The next is called the Tuan Torrent, & having joined the Bhaugrettee or Ganges which it crossed & again returns winding among Mountains & Valleys till it reach Shriiggur.

The Pass of Ricketies is the only practicable pass for Cattle, besides these three passes from the Dhoon proper there seems to be one immediately opposite Timley which crosses the Jumna & ascends the Mountains near Calfie & up the Tremendous Mountain of Burhaut. The pass which is immediately above us does not extend above 60 Miles before it reaches the impassable Himalaya & returns by the opposite bank of the Ganges so that the famous Story of the Cows mouth is all a Tale for so far from the Ganges crossing the Himalaya it does not even arise from that Range but from a Snowy Mountain on this side not above Sixty Miles from us.

The whole of the Country between this & the Himalaya Mountains is most rugged imaginable being scarcely any thing but Mountains, the base of one joining the base of the other, but there are some few narrow vallys which are fruitful.

24 On the 24th the Battering train arrived. The Facines & every other requisite for the construction of Batteries have been prepared so that the 25th The Infantry advanced at Daylight towards Kulinga,[197] the Doolie Bearers carrying the Gabions &c, all The Tents were left standing & I was left with the 8th Dragoons with my Money & the Colors of the Regiment in the old camp, after my Breakfast I advanced towards Kulunga taking with me a Glass, but the Army had advanced to the other side of the Hill on which the fort is situated. I could perceive nothing of them, but I found many European Fruits Trees as pears & apples & plums & several kinds of fruit of a species I had never before seen. One Tree was loaded with a fruit as large as any fist & something like a Raspberry but insipid. The Camp followers were greedily taking it, on my return before I reached the Camp I was recalled by a Sound of heavy firing & returned & seated myself under a Tree. I soon observed thro my Glass that there were red Coats running up the Hill in Two places. They took possession of a stockade apparently close to the fort I should conceive that this must be a great point gained & from the Short time employed I hope there could not have been much loss. At Night accounts came down the Hill that Captain Parker (with part of the 53rd Regt) had made good his position within 300 Yards of the Fort, from

---

[197] Khalanga, now a suburb of Dehra Dun lies below the site of the fort at the southern end of Nalapani Hill. The fort was demolished after the Battle of Nalapani but a cenotaph at the site commemorates the battle, adorned with Buddhist prayer flags. The village is still occupied mainly by Nepalese.

which position a few Shrapnels had been fired into the Stoccade. The Goorkas finding their Stoccade to hot for them had evacuated & Captain Stone had taken possession.

26 After breakfast I rode towards the Fort but could not reach the Army without being too long absent from my charge, I however got near enough to the fort to see the Stoccade & the new position which appeared to me close to the Fort & almost as high, some Guns must have been got up for I heard great Guns fired occasionally, on my Return I heard that Serjt Thompson 53rd was killed yesterday & that the 18 Pounders were expected to be got up today, every one speaks highly of Captain Parkers Conduct yesterday & of the promptitude with which his Party got possession of the Ground.

27 I rode over to the Army & found it laying to the North of the Fort in a valley under the Hill having it rear protected by a high precipice at the Bottom of which runs the Mountain Torrent the Soan which has a considerable quantity of water in it as this season(which is the driest) altho from the height of the bank on which the Camp stands it seems like a narrow blue Line running thro a Yellow bed. I presume it cannot be less than 5 or 600 feet below us. it roars over its rocky bed passing between what is called the Tivalee Range & the Detached Hill of Nalla Panee on which Kalunga stands. I had not been in the Camp above & had scarcely seen the Officers before we were roused by the Noise of Trumpets, Shawnes & enough to frighten his Imperial Majesty & on looking round we saw a body (like An Ant Hill in Motion) about half way up the first Mountain of the Tivallee range immediately opposite us across the River, we judged them to consist of about 300 Men & we supposed them to be a detachment from Nahun which is a City & Fort to the westward. Intelligence of a Party of this Number had reached our General & we are sorry that they had not got within the Fort before our Blockade as they would have eaten provisions.

Towards Evening I was obliged to return to my Money at the Old Camp, understanding that the Fort was soon to be stormed & indeed I had not advanced half way when I heard heavy firing. I was so situated that the fort was hid from my sight by the projecting hills, for it cannot properly be seen at a less distance than 4 or 5 Miles & it was not until I reached the Cavalry Camp that I could see the Fort. I found the Officers of the 7th Native Cavalry collected on a rising ground & I joined them, the firing was on the other side of the Hill, we could see nothing but smoke & as it continued for so long a time our fears told us that our Army had not succeeded. At length Lieut^t Rainey ordered his horse & galloped off to gain intelligence but as it was impossible for him to return before dark I left them. Soon after this Lieut^{t} Sneyd of the 8th Dragoons came in & told us that the attack had failed & that Captain Campbell of the 4th N.I. Lieut^{t} Cunningham 13 N. I. & Lieut^{t} Harrington of the 53rd Reg^{t} were killed & that there had been a great Slaughter among the men, that the wounded were in great numbers, Lieut^{t} Luxford of the Horse Artillery Dangerously, indeed it is said mortally.

28 This Morning a Corporal came into our Camp & brought word that of our regiment Colonel Buckland, Major Ingleby, captains Chepmell & Stone, Lieutenants Horsely, Brodie, Green & Ensign Aufrere were wounded, Horsely dangerously. The Report further states that the breach was a good one, but that on reaching the Top it was found that the inside of the Fort was sunk into the Rock & consequently lower than the Hill itself & that a stockade had been made between the Wall & the Keep immediately behind the breach, among which Spearmen & Matchlock Men were so posted as to render it impossible to descend even when the breach was gained. This Evening our order was received for the Treasure to move forward & join the Camp under Kalunga, but Cattle not being on the Spot it was almost black before the Ammunition & Treasure could move. I was riding slowly on when I overtook Lieutenant Harrington of the 8th Dragoons who persuaded me to return & dine with him & offered me a spare bed in his Tent which I agreed to & returned.

29 At Day light I left the Camp at Deyrah & reached the main Camp in Two Hours as it now seems likely that we shall remain sometime in our present Camp were pitched the Tents & took up more ground, this employed us for the day. I saw Horsely & Brodie the only two of ours who are confined from their wounds, Brodies wound is thro' the Thigh but has not broken a bone, Horselys is dreadful to behold having passed thro the Roof of his Mouth & he is a dreadful figure & cannot swallow any substance, nor can he speak, From what I hear from the Officers it seems that on approaching the Fort having mounted the breach without difficulty they found as was described that they would have to descend at least 12 feet & that there appeared a regular fence of Bamboos, thro which appeared Spears & behind these was a large fence filled with matchlocks so that it appeared absolutely like throwing themselves on spikes, to attempt to leap down Captain Parker had ran up to the breach but the Men who accompanied him being all Killed or wounded he had returned & Harrington rushed up after him, Cap^{n} Parker caught him by the sash saying it is useless we cannot get in, Harrington answered I must go & he advanced to the Top of the breach, ran along its whole breadth & then turning round lifted up his hands as much as to say you cannot

get in he waved his sword & fell dead in an instant, the Men now began to throw large stones into the Fort & seemed to do mischief by it but as they did not advance the taking of the Fort was in no wise accelerated they were called away after the fruitless attempt of Two Hours.

30th   At Two oclock in the Morning I was awakened by a heavy fire of musketry which continued so long it appeared so close that I got up & dressed myself, it continued about half an hour & then ceased, by reason of the reverberation of the Valleys I could not tell from which side it came, I lay down again when it ceased, but a little after it recommenced & continued very heavy. I again arose & went out just as I got to my Tent door I heard distant shouting & the beat of a drum, I was convinced that the Shout was English, but could not make out the beat of the drum. I went towards the quarter guard to McPherson who was the Officer & Lieut Emery having heard the firing & Shout had got there before me, they also thought that the shout was European but could not make out what the drum was, but the Men said that it was the Grenadiers March. Major Piercy now joined us & proposed going up to the Trenches, himself Emery & I set off but soon met a Seapoy looking for Colonel Mawby, he said he had been sent by major Kelly to say that the fort was <u>empty (Kali)</u> & our Troops within. Emery & myself returned with him but major Piercy proceeded.

It appeared that at two o clock the Enemy had rushed down the side of the Hill in a body, but were opposed & driven back with great loss to themselves, this was the subject of the first firing which I had heard. At three they collected again & rushed down many were Killed but in so desperate an attempt several got thro tho it is not thought that many did, while Colonel Mawby was waiting for his dispatch, I wrote to Mrs S & got my Note conveyed with the dispatch, after which I set off to the Fort & reached it just as the day was breaking, before it was light, on reaching the top of the breach I met Heathcote who caught me by the Arm as I was stepping into the Fort & told me to walk cautiously or I should tread on bodies either just dead or expiring & on looking with attention a scene of horror struck me, indeed the fort was very small & the whole space visible within was covered with the dead & dying on my right in a small redoubt were two small brass Guns near one of them a space not above ten feet long & six broad lay 7 dead bodies across each other & in going from one enclosure to another (for the place seemed all small enclosures) the same kind of objects appeared, 86 Dead Bodies lay about under our feet within the body of the fort, we heard groans & a crie of <u>Panee Panee</u> & on descending never was any thing so shocking, the whole length of a Trench which had been dug across the Fort was full of wounded, they appeared to have crept in for shelter they were calling for water & the officers were assisting them. They had lain now for three days, a Young Woman (I shall never forget her) was lying with a broken leg, surrounded by dead & wounded. She was crying for water. The difficulty was to get to her without treading on others. She held her head up without her mouth open in such an anxious way as I cannot describe. An Officer (Heathcote) poured Water in her Mouth from a distance which she received, another was unhurt & had a little Child at her breast wounded, the Mother was in the greatest distress, but the little thing took its food & did not seem to care, indeed it was not in any danger, the most affecting sight was two little Girls one about four the other only one year old, the Father & Mother had both been Killed, they were immediately taken care of but the Elder thought that she was to have been separated from the Younger & began to scream, but when told that they were to go together she was quieted. This day I saw the horrors of War & indeed horrible it is. [198]

1 December   I again went up to the fort to examine it, the dead bodies had been removed & burnt, 97 of them were collected but I could still count 30 half buried which appeared to have been put into the ground between the 31st of October & 27 November, probably who had been Killed or died since the 31st October. The Fort is small & unfinished but from the Nature of the Hill, very strong. I do not see how it is possible to take such places if properly defended for altho you knock down the Wall yet the body of the Fort being sunk within the Rock is not to be destroyed & of the Shells very few entered the Fort, altho it seems to be the fashion to say otherwise.

2nd This Morning I went to see the Soan River which runs between our position & the Tevalie Range of Mountains, from the Road we had come when advancing from Dherah all the Nullah & beds of Torrents running to the South East, it was natural to expect that the Country, if not a plain would rise as we advanced toward the Hills, but from the Rear of our Camp we look down a precipice of five or six hundred feet at the Bottom of which runs a Torrent over a rocky bed on the other side of which rise Mountains in comparison of which Kalunga is a Mole hill, the Roaring of the Torrent is clearly heard in the Camp, in the course of my walk I found a promontory clearer than the rest from Trees, from the Point of which I could see the Torrents bed, from its issuing from the

---

[198] In the town to the west is a memorial set up by the British with twin obelisks, one to Gen. Gillespie and his officers, the other to the Ghurka commander and his brave men. Following this campaign the British recruited Ghurkas into the army, honoured for their bravery.

Mountain until hid by Kalinga or Nulla Panee Hill, a course of 3 or 4 Miles, the Water whose roaring I heard seemed like a line of blue drawn by a hair pencil, the sides of the Mountains are all thickly covered with wood, great part of which is a species of Fir but very handsome, not so ragged as the Fir with us, the Mangoe is also very common but it is probably planted, directly across the River from where I stood I could distinguish a path or road but I could not trace it far from the Water, it had the appearance of a Ferry but that I conceive could not be for the Rapidity of the Stream if unfordable must preclude all Ferries neither did it appear that any person could get to the Top of the Mountain.

Cenotaph at the site of Khalunga Fort. 2015.

[Viewed from the position where Gillespie was shot. Note Buddhist prayer flags. The plaque at the fort cenotaph records British losses as 31 officers and 750 men killed and 35 and 1500 wounded. The fort was manned by 600 Ghurkas whose losses are not recorded.]

3   We left our encamping Ground to return to Dheirah, I took the road over the Hill & by the Fort, descending by the Spot where our first six pounder battery had been erected, from the 24th to the 31st of October, & by the Spot where General Gillespie fell & the road by which he brought up the Gun & I wondered how it was possible to have done what had been done, I saw the Spring about 300 or 400 yds from the Fort, from which the Garrison had been supplied with water, & by the cutting off of which the Garrison must have been forced to surrender from the first. Lower down were numbers of considerable streams one of which almost the size of a Mill Stream is said to give the name of Nullah Panne or Blue Lilla Pane to the Hill, but I think it may as well be [Urdu

script word] Lillah Pharee or Blue Hill, the Road over the Hill is not much shorter than that round the Hill, I suppose the Hill from Dheirah cannot be less than 5 or 6 Miles.

Double memorial at Dehra Dun. 2015.

[The memorial commemorates the Battle of Nalapani on the distant hill.

The three plaques on the Nalapani memorial obelisks read:

'On the highest point of the hill above this tomb stood the fort of Kalungr [sic]. After two assaults on the 31st Oct^{br} and 27th Nov^{br} it was capt^d by the British troops on the 30th November 1814 and completely razed to the ground.'

'To the memory of Major Genl Sir Robt Rollo Gillespie K.C. & Lieut^t O'Hara 6th N.I., Lieut^t Gosling Light Batt^n, Ensign Fothergill, 17th N. I., Ensign Ellis, Pioneers, killed on the 31st October 1814. Captn Campbell, 6th N.I., Lieut^t Luxford, Horse Art^y, Lieut^t Harrington, H.M. 53rd Reg^t, Lieut^t Cunningham, 13th N.I. killed on the 27th November and of the noncom^{sd} officers and men who fell at the assaults.'

'This is inscribed as a tribute of respect for our gallant adversary BULBUDDER commander of the fort AND HIS BRAVE GOORKAS who were afterwards while in the service of Runjeet Sing shot down in their ranks to the last man by Afghan artillery.'

It is worth noting that this memorial to a respected adversary was erected by the British who subsequently recruited Ghurkas into the British Army.]

4 Sunday. All the Wounded Europeans were sent to Seharunpore. I waited for the Meeting for worship, but not a private Soldier came, the duty is so hard, but Lieutenant Tomkyns & Montgomery came. In the Evening nobody came.

5 This Morning Major Piercy, Mr Price & myself went into Deirah to look after the wounded Ghoorkas, we found them in a Serai & Doctor Govan was attending them, but it was a wretched Scene, every [thing] was done for them that could be done but they were melancholy objects, I had Mr Tomkyns to dine with me.

6 Major Piercy, Price, Emery & myself went to see a famous natural curiosity called Sansadhara, or the dripping Rock, it is situated by the bed of the Soan River in the pass leading over the Second Range of Mountains, we went by the Road to our last Camp & proceeding strait to the Village Narghal came to the edge of a very steep precipice which we descended with some difficulty leaving our horses on the Top, I suppose the descent much have bee 300 or 400 Feet, when we came into the Vally it was beautiful & covered with fine Trees, & the brush wood mostly of Camdas, Biers & wild Limes, on the higher parts of the Mountain were Firs, major Piercy Emery Price, who all know Bristol said it much resembled some of the beautiful spots near Clifton but grander, our way was over the rocky bed of the Soan, jumping from rock to rock, the Roaring of the stream & echo from the Hills had something terrible in it, several flocks of Buffaloes were coming down the pass & their drivers to encourage them kept up a constant shouting, which was rendered loud by the echo, when we came to Sansadara we found it well worth seeing, it was an immense overhanging Rock, covered with Moss & Trees, & the water dripping thro it as from the thatch of a House, in a heavy shower, or great for small the squeezing of a wet sponge, & the water is of a petrifying character, & resembles the Icicles hanging to the Eves of a Thatched House, we brought away many specimens of petrifactions.

7th A very cold Rainy day,. The Rain began about 3 in the Morning and at daylight we saw some of the nearest Hills covered with Snow. At Twelve o clock the Rain increased & continued all day (oh the delight of a heavy Rain while living in a canvass bag) but ceased at Sun set, the outer fly of the Tent was completely wet thro.

8 It was dark & cloudy & cold, the Tops of the Hills at about 12 Miles distant covered with snow, at 12 the rain came on again but ceased

at Night, & began again at 12, ceased at 3, but the orders from head Quarters are so positive that we march.

1814 December 9th   March Dehra Dun to Nahan, 120 Miles.

9   At 7 o clock we left our Camp near Deirah, in passing thro the Town we could see how bad it must be in the Rains for the Mud was up to the Knees. We had but one shower on our march but the whole Horizon was covered with dark clouds & we could see it rain very hard in our front, but the clouds as they advanced towards us, broke to the Right & left & followed the Ridge of the Hills, it was very cold & damp, the Country thro which we passed was most rich & beautiful, if cultivated it might be compared to the valleys of Switzerland it is now sadly overgrown with long Jungly Grass with Villages widely scattered, there are many woods of Sissoo which would be delightful but you cannot advance into them from the height of the Grass. We halted in a Ravine close to the Arsan River, it would be a charming Spot, if it was cultivated, the River very much like the Wandbeck at Morpeth, with about the same quantity of water, it was a clear Rapid murmuring stream & the Sissoo wood on its banks like the Ladies Chapel Wood, the day was much against us & I was rather unwell.

10   We marched at 7 passing a fine level Country to Sainspore then crossing the River Arsan which has a wide bed, & rapid clear stream about two feet deep, further on we passed several other streams, the Country being covered with Jungle Grass, we began to ascend towards Timley & encamped on the Rising ground in a jungle, about five feet high & very wet, for it had rained here yesterday much more than where we were, at the rear of our Camp at a little distance was the plain over which about 10 Miles off was the 2 Range thro which issues the Jumna & Tonse Rivers which unite opposite to us in the Angle Calie, apparently very high, yet not on the Summit. Above it at a very great height several stoccades & forts pointed out at Burhaut Runtrum, & to the Right Bredraj thro every break appear the Snowy points of other Mountains but the Weather & my illness hindered me from enjoying the prospect during the Night I was very ill, & being forced to get up & go out thro the Wet grass which was as high as my head, & dropping on me as I went out of my Tent. I was seriously ill.

11   When Morning came & we were to march I could scarcely sit on my Horse & in attempting to walk, I found myself very weak,

immediately on leaving the Camp, we came to a Forest of high Trees but, tho the Road had been lately so much passed by Carriages & guns that it was very good, I reached the Summit of Trimley in 5 Miles the pass is not any thing like so difficult as Kerie, neither is it so romantic the side towards the Dhoon is a very gradual slope, wooded, but the side towards the Plain of Hindoostan is the Bed of a Torrent, there is a spring at the Top, I could not observe much but at the bottom of the pass was the remains of an old Garden called Badshah Baug, & I am told that a little way from the Road is a Palace in Ruins called Badshah Mahal. I saw a puckah Well & many Fruit Trees, the Palace is said to have been built by Shah Jehan, I was too unwell to go to it & it is said to be difficult if not dangerous of approach for the whole Country is full of wild beasts, the Jumna runs at a very little distance from Fyzabad, & I could just see its water at a distance. I could not go down, it is described by those Officers who did go down as rushing from the Hills & I heard its waters roaring thro the Night we halted at Fizabad, but the difficulties of the pass had been so great that many of our Tents, & the Hospital could not get up till late at Night & altho I was unwell I could get no Medicine. Pollock advised me to go in my palankeen in the Morning & to take some Medicine, it did not rain today but it was damp & cold.

12   I took the Doctors advice & travelled in my Palankeen. The Road was very good & full of Villages to Nanoullee near the place we had been informed that the Jumna was fordable. The Artillery had been sent in advance (while we lay at Deirah to get away our wounded Men) in order to cross the River, but no ford is to be found & they now lay at a place called Jatuwalla waiting for orders. It has been necessary to go down to the Ford which lies in the direct road from the Lower provinces of the Punjaub, the Dews fall so heavy that the outer Canauts & fly of the Tent are as wet as if it had rained & our feet get wet if we attempt to walk, this is very disagreeable as the cold of the Morning would tempt us to walk.

13   We marched thro a Marshy Country crossing several small Nullahs the Country no doubt is overflowed in the Rains, at Chilcaunah we found the ground higher, from whence we turned westward to the Jumna where is a Ferry but very few boats were found. The 7th N. I. just crossed going to join Col^l Ochterlonys Army before Ramghur. We halted on the Eastern side of the River, the 13th Native Infantry & Light Battalion crossed the River & encamped on the other side, here are only six Boats, the weather very damp, & threatning rain, & I am far from well.

14   It Rained very heavily all day & my tent being pitched rather low in a turnip Field was very uncomfortable, during the Night it rained very

hard so much so as to break down Mr Brownes Tent, with the weight of water.

15   The Guns were got over the River.

16   We crossed the Jumna but the confusion was great & the difficulty of getting the Camels into the Boats insurmountable but after fatiguing the rear Guard until Night a ford was found a few Miles higher however & advanced passing first over a low marsh with several Muddy Streams, then ascending a small Hill, I found for nearly a Mile the ruins of some old City the ground being covered with antient bricks & burial places. We are now out of the Companies Territories in the Country of the protected Seeks who are divided among innumerable Petty Rajahs acknowledging no head, & paying no tribute, they are very insolent, we came to a very large brick built Town called Boorea subject to a Sheik rajah called Gulaub Sing, here we halted in a beautiful Mangoa Grove, I had no tent up all day. Colonel Mawby took me to dinner, just at dark I heard that my Tent had fallen into the River but that a ford had been found, No Tent arrived, I got into the Mess Tent but at about 12 at Night, the Tent came up & as so few were pitched, I took it for granted that we could not march in the Morning, therefore pitched it & I had just layen down when I heard the General beat, I jumped up & calling my establishment about me we found that yesterday, had destroyed 3 of my Camels, 2 had died & one gone lame, however I exerted myself a little and partly by persuasion & partly Zuberdustee (strong hand), obtained 3 more, we marched only 3 Miles thro a most beautiful well cultivated Country to Sankeera, this Town also belongs to an independent Rajah, we could see the Fort of Jeituk & the Town of Nahun, as high as the Clouds, I felt still unwell, the weather excessively Cold.

18th   Marched 4 Coss to Belaspore, here we found Major Kelly's Battalion of the 7th N. I. in which is Lieutenant McDonald. They had left us at Deirah immediately after the fall of Kalunga & had joined Col^l Carpenter at Calei from which they had advanced up the Mountains & taken several Stoccades & forts among the Rest Burhaut which is described as immencely strong & if defended might have defied them, from this they had descended to Calai & crossing the Jumna twice, first into the Dhoon & then by Rage Ghaut into the Kardah valley & along the Galousin Pass joined us again at Belapore, Macdonald describes the fatigue as excessive, the Mountains passes difficult beyond description & the Rains very uncomfortable & unhealthy. We halted at Seidoura a large Town many Seeks came out to meet us & shew off their horsemanship, they are fine looking Men & good horsemen, & have a very strong countenance, the Turban is put on very gracefully.

19	We marched from Seidoura, the Country beautiful & unlike the plain, to the East of the Jumna, it is cultivated even to the very foot of the Hills & higher for we could see spots of cultivated Land & Villages on every Table Land, We entered the Hills by a broad Water course & advanced up its bed (thro which ran a considerable stream) for about four Miles. We then got up the bank, & found a spot for encamping close to a Village called Magincund near which was a small stockade on the Apex of a Hill, but it was evacuated before we reached the neighbourhood, & we are told that the Guard stationed therein collected the duties on Merchandise passing over these Mountains to Thibet & Tartary, but I cannot learn what are the principal articles, Cows hair is said to have been one article, in the Evening I ascended one of the Eminences which (altho no more to be compared to the Mountains around us the declivity of the River to us) yet it would be a Mountain in many parts of the World. From this we could Trace the water course to the plain, & also upwards about 3 Miles the table land on each side (which answers to the Hams near our Rivers) is finely cultivated & is of considerable breadth on each side & it appears that we might have avoided, the rugged bed of it by using the bank. The Villages are very thick & the young Corn of a very vivid green.

20th Dec^r	It was in orders last Night to move on but General Martindale arrived & took command, the order was not in force but not countermanded, so that we remained uncertain what would happen, our Camels loaded. In the Evening we hear that the Goorkahs have evacuated the Town & I went out to see the British flag flying on the Cazy's house. It is said that we shall not now go up until a road is made.

21	This Morning we hear that the Hill is so steep & the passes so difficult that it will be impossible ever to get the Guns up, & the wonder is, how the Goorkahs ever allowed our advance to reach the town, they say that the Town might have defended itself for ever, against us, it is completely separated from the Hill which is called Jeytuk not Jumptay in which is a very small strong fort appearing to us as [sketch] but altogether unconnected with, we can see stoccades innumerable in every height & we are at a loss to conceive how People like the Goorkahs who can at one moment defend themselves so well, not only with great bravery but also with great judgement should at another neglect the commonest means of defence, for here they might have defended every Inch of ground with us & in perfect security, & I do not think we ever could have advanced.

22 Our Bilders & Pioners were employed all the 22nd-23rd & 24th clearing a road & by advancing slowly our Guns to the bottom of the Hill Side we remained quietly at Mogencund.

25 On Christmas day McDonald & Tomkyns came but our Meeting was very thin & our own Officers have altogether left off coming.

26 In the Morning of the 26 we marched for Nahun, the army moved at day light but I remained until after breakfast & then proceeded by myself having heard of the difficulty of the Road, I left orders only to trunk half of my Tent & afterwards tomorrow to return with the Camels for the other half, I proceed on the plain above the Nullah but sometimes descending & crossing it as the Mountains approached the bed occasionally abruptly. The plain on each side differed much in breadth, sometimes being very narrow but it is finely cultivated & the water which should run in the bed of the Nullah has been in places artificially raised above it, by which means the plain is watered & many Mills turned, the Valley continued further than my road lay for at the end of about 4 Miles I came to the foot of the Hill on which Nahan stands, here the Artillery were encamped & here I think they are likely to remain. I now ascended the Road was very steep after which it became level, & then steep again & soon to the Top, the distance from the foot is at least four Miles some parts equal to the ascent of a Roof of a house, & full of large Rocks. I reached the Top about 12 oclock, the Town of Nahun covers a ridge on the Top of an immence Mountain yet surrounded by other the Mountains far exceeding it in height. The Point on which the Fort to which the Goorkahs are now retired (Jeytuk) stands it calculated to be 10000 feet from the level of the Plain.

Nahun has been a place of considerable consequence. The Town is full of Puckah well built houses & the Palace has been a fine building, very considerable in size & strong there are several very large Tanks, on the Top of the Hill both Puckah Hutchah & many fine cisterns & springs. About a Mile before I reached the Top I passed several fine large Tanks with springs running thro them, the Body of water carried thro which could not have been less than three Inches in diameter, three Large ones were close together near to which were dwellings for many Faqueers like Monasteries. I suppose Nahun itself must extend at least half a Mile, but the palace & the houses are in a state of decay & dangerous to live in seeming as if they had been altogether neglected since the Goorkahs had had possession & indeed the Revenues of the Country could scarcely if at all pay the Troops of the Conquering Nation, who must of necessity have greater borders that the Natives could keep up & plainly shews that the Goorkahs in keeping these hills must have had views of conquest further on, & most probably to Cashmere. The Evening came at length, but no Tent arrived so that I bewackoofed in my palanquin & was more comfortable than I had expected for altho the frost was very severe below & the ground was covered with hoar frost, yet it was here comparatively warm & without any dew.

1814 December 27th   Nahan, Battle of Jeytuk.

27 During the Night two parties advanced towards Jaytuk, the one under Major Ludlow, the other under Major Richards, the first led by our Grenadiers & staff of the Light Battalion & 6th Native Infantry. The other had our Light Infantry & the remainder of the Light Battalion with the 13th N. I. The first Party under Major Ludlow advanced up the hill to the

spot marked 1 we could se them plainly early in the Morning but we were sorry to observe even at the distance where we were, that instead of stopping at the point 1 a small irregular detachment advanced to 2 where was a small stockade, they were driving the Enemy before them, but at the same time we could see the Rear of the Column straggling over the whole side of the Hill, at least a Mile behind the advance & we could plainly distinguish that the advance had lost its support, from the Nature of the Ground, only one or two Individuals reaching the Top of the Hill at a time, & consequently they must either advance by independent files or wait a long time to form for each man had his knapsack on his back & was otherwise heavily laden. The Goorkahs appeared issuing from the Fort in great Bodies covering the whole Ridge, & soon we saw our Men retreat. At first the Retreat was slow but we were soon to see that the Rear instead of advancing to the Support of the advance immediately come down to the Road, which they had ascended but inclined to the Westward & I had hopes that their intention was to have obtained possession of other heights of which there were several but the Enemy became bold & increased in Number so that I suppose there must have been 12 or 1400 & our rear beginning to retreat, the Head of the Column at the same time commenced descending & now I expected that very few would escape, the whole forces seeming to Run & the Goorkahs to pursue them as a scattered body yet our Troops often turned & checked them, & obliged the Goorkahs to halt.

Battle of Jaytuk.

At length the Detachment reached our Camp & we had so small a loss that I could scarcely believe it only one European Officer & six Soldiers Killed; it is true that many poor Black Men suffered & many Officers & Prisoners of the Europeans were wounded but in fact the Europeans bore the brunt, Major Ludlow who was himself the cause of the overthrow, threw the blame on his Regiment they being the most unable to speak for themselves, however his Error was on the Right side. Thus ended Major Ludlow attack, we were now turning our attention to the other Column under Major Richards, composed of our Light Company some [... ?]

We had heard that very early in the Evening that the Coolies carrying ammunition had fallen in with the Enemy & had thrown down their loads to escape by which it is said that 60,000 Rounds of Cartridges are taken. It was the middle of the day before we perceived this party & it then appeared to the Right of the foot on the Hill which is detached & rather behind the Fort. At 3 oclock they seemed to have established themselves, I overheard the Commissary say that in consequence of the loss of the Ammunition & the failure of Major Ludlows party, orders had been sent for this party to Retreat, we could not perceive any regular firing but only an occasional Shot or two which continued till dinner time. I did not remain at the Mess but returned to my Tent about 8 o clock at which time they were firing very violently & I stood a long time looking that way, at length I went to bed but about 3 o clock I was awakened by a Voice calling out that a light Infantry man was come in & wanted food. I arose & found his Story to be that they had possessed themselves of a most excellent position on the Top of the Hill on which they had been attacked 9 different times by the Goorkahs, but that they could make no impression until a retreat was ordered after which from the Nature of the ground every one was obliged to look to himself. Soon after this Lieut[t] Ainslie arrived his story was much the same with that of the Private.

28th   Towards Morning (IE Daylight) The Men came straggling in with Cap[n] Parker & at length we thought all that had escaped must have come in, if our Light Infantry we miss One Lieutenant (Hutchinson) one serjeant, and 14 Privates, the Number of Seapoys is not made public. There are 8 European Officers of the Seapoys & 2 Doctors missing, every hour reports reaching us of Officers seen in the woods for we have no actual account of the death of any except Captain Warner of the 6th N. I. & Doctor Darby of the Light Infantry Battalion. The latter it is said could not get his Servants to carry his Instruments he therefore took the firelock & accoutrements of a dead man & acted as a Private until he was overpowered & cut to pieces by the Goorkahs, in this kind of uncertaincy the day passed.

29th   Early this Morning I heard a Soldier cry out "Eleven & all starving" I concluded that it must allude to our missing Men so I immediately arose & found that Lieut[t] Hutchinson with 11 of our Missing Men had returned, both the Doctors, as well the dead one as the living one & Captain Warner & three other Officers, from what we could learn from Lieut[t] Hutchinson it seemed that when the Retreat sounded they scrambled away as fast as they could but not being able to see the road a considerable party took the Northern side of the Hill & came down to a River which was very deep, they found some Villagers who called it the Ganges. It must have been the Gerry Gunga, these Villagers behaved very kindly to them, cooked them Rice & Ghee & undertook to bring them to Nahun, that on their Road they fell in with a party of Matchlock Men sitting round a fire, these Men challenged them upon which they lay down & sent the Villagers to gain intelligence. The Villagers were gone nearly three hours at the end of which time they had served them so faithfully that with great precautions they satisfied themselves who the party were & finding that they were friends they brought their Chief who had 100 Men with him, this Man escorted their party to Camp & the Villagers were rewarded, there now remain four officers & 4 Privates of our Light Infantry, these are supposed dead, for it is scarcely possible that they can have subsisted in the woods yet reports are every Moment raised of a White Man being seen.

30th The Missing Officers of Major Richards's party are Ensigns Turner, Thackery, Stolkard & Wilson. Several Seapoys came in today & spread reports concerning the Missing Officers, saying that Europeans have been seen. We know that 3 of our 4 Missing Men were Killed before the retreat, a Subador & 40 men were taken prisoners & have been released except a little Drummer who is detained to teach the Goorkahs. The Subador says there is a European Officer a prisoner, but this we do not believe.

31st Ensign Turner One of the Missing Officers was brought in by the Villagers. His story is very interesting. He was pursued by four or five Goorkahs & his only chance of safety was to throw himself down a precipice which he did & escaped unhurt, however a Goorkah even followed him there & calling him a feringhee & was in the act of making a cut at him when Mr Turner rolled down another precipice & found himself near a Cave where he hid himself. But after some time considering that he must either starve or be destroyed by Tigers he came out & perceiving some cultivated land he advanced towards it, he entered a Village where was an old Woman & two boys, her Sons, the Old woman on seeing him, without waiting until he spoke called him her Dhurrum Beta & took him into a Cow house, took off his Red Jacket and gave him a Cumbul, a kind of coarse blanket belonging to her sons, she then made an Oler cake & boiled some milk, still muttering Dhurum Beta. Mr Turner told her that he had nothing to give her, she answered that she wanted nothing, but begged his whistle as a keepsake. *(Every light Infantry Officer wears one attached to his breast plate). She kept him until the Night of the 3rd Day & then packed up his Clothes in a bundle sent her son with him to Camp – This Evening we heard of some successes of Colonel Ochterlony's Army before Ramghur.

1815 January 1st

The Body of Ensign Thackery was found by his taylor & brought in we were ordered to attend the funeral which hindered our meeting it being Sunday, but I had formed a plan for distributing some Hindoostany Gospels & after the funeral I mentioned it to Lieut^t McDonald & Tomkyns, & we went to the Principal Temple & conversed with the Mahunt or principal Priest. He very willingly accepted a Nagree Copy of the four Gospels & said that he would read it. We then went all over the Town in search of Mahomedans but could find none. We had Letters from Col^l Ochterlonys Army saying that the Goorkahs had made a very spirited Sally from Ramghaur but were beaten back with the loss of 150 Killed & twice that Number wounded, 70 dead Bodies were picked up & in consequence all the Stoccades were abandoned & they have hopes that Ramghaur itself will soon fall.

2   The Thermometer on the 2nd at Sunrise was 45 no news of any kind.

3   Every thing at a Stand, 300 Irregulars, mewattees came to join us. A Court of enquiry commenced its sittings to enquire the Reasons of the failure on the Fort of Kalunga on the 31st October & 27 November last but, like every thing else this Campaign, care was taken to issue the order in such a Manner that the Court was found to be inadequate to hear the Evidence, they themselves ie the members not being sworne, We are so still that we might fancy ourselves at Peace again we hear again from Colonel Ochterlony's Army that he has not yet succeeded in taking Ramghur its natural position is so strong.

4th   We hear all Manner of Reports, sometimes it is said that we are treating with the Goorkahs at other Times Report says that Lord Moira[199] says he will annihilate the Goorkahs if he is obliged to send every soldier in Bengal, but we do not believe half of what we hear. We are receiving Numbers of Irregulars, but think them of little use. We are I believe waiting for Reinforcements of Regulars. Colonel Ochterlony is the same.

8   Sunday after Service McDonald & myself went to the Mahunt to see what he had done with the book, he said that he had been reading it, but did not quite understand the language, being rather different, he says that there are no Mahomedans inhabiting Wakuno who can read, he seems very willing to converse.

9th to 18th   The Weather Cold & threatening Rain, nothing done, all our movements completely stopped. So are Colonel Ochterlonys, the Goorkahs are increasing the Number of their Stoccades on every Hill, & our Allies are coming in every day in Numbers, they say that they are as many as 2800 in Camp. The Weather dried up again, on the 18th I had Service in my Tent McDonald & Tomkyns came down. On the 18th a Party of the Enemy who had stoccaded themselves to the Westward destroyd the Stoccade & came over to us, & we sent a Party of 800 Irregulars to take possession of a small Pagoda called Beneta on another Range of Hills to the Westward. We heard in Camp of the loss of General Sulivan Wood in the Gorruckpore District & of General Marly

---

[199] Lord Moira: Francis Edward Rawdon-Hastings, 1st Marquess of Hastings KG PC (1754-1826), known as The Earl of Moira, Governor General of India, declared war on Nepal, the Gorkha War or Anglo Nepalese War, 1814-1816.

near Saul Forrests above Betea & of major Bradshaw & Report says that the great Lord is in a scrape. The Irregulars have been very busy in Stoccading round the small white Pagoda at Benita the place appears of great Natural Strength & of an immense height but it must be at least 10 Miles from the Fort. I do not exactly see the use of them, nor do we know whether the Ridge on which it stands is the same for there appears a break in the chain between it & Jaytuk, but we have not a good view from hence.

21   Reports reached us that Colonel Ochterlony, thro manoeuvres had caused Ummar Sing[200] to evacuate his stoccades which he was doing when the letter came away. We are very anxious to know which way Ummur Sing has marched, for we are altogether uncertain as to his Strength. Some calculate it at 2800, others as much as 6000. If he was to march this way he might at least cut off our supplies & probably take our Guns which are down in the Nullah at the foot of the Hill only guarded by a few irregulars, they are near 7 Miles off & we have not strength enough to oppose him.

22   Sunday it rained all day but we did not feel the same kind of uncomfortable feeling which we have experienced in like circumstances in the plain, indeed this seems a fine Climate.

23   News from Colonel Ochterlonys Camp, that the Colonel has marched towards Belaspore & had halted near the Sutledge, Ummur Sing had abandoned his Stoccades & followed him upon which Colonel Arnold had got possession of all the Stoccades. Ummur Sing had reached Maloan, a Strong Fort on the Top of a Hill & Colonel Arnold had taken a position to cut off his supplies. There are however some in Camp who say that Ummur Sing had marched first & had deceived Colonel Arnold, having taken up a better position

24   A Goorkah deserter came down he says that they are much pushed for provisions within the Fort & that the Villagers do not supply them.

25   Another deserter came down who gives the same Account.

26   The 26th Regiment N. I. arrived at the Foot of the Hill & there is a considerable bustle in the Army as if something would be immediately attempted. It rained most violently all the Night with Thunder & Lightning several Tents were blown down.

---

[200] 'Ummar Sing' Bada Kaji Amar Singh Thapa expanded the western boundary of Nepal up to the Sutlej River. Also known as "Living lion of Nepal". He was the Bada Kaji General of the Nepalese forces of the western front in the Anglo–Nepalese War when Nepal lost several western states.

27	In the Morning I was walking up & down opposite my Tent when Col.^l Mawby came up & addressed me "Well Mr Buckshee[201] would you like to go in to Meerut between this & next 24.th." I said why Sir, I do not think that I can well do it, & return, he said "You may have my Buggy from Sirampore." I paused a Short time & thought that as it was offered me I might as well accept it, he also hinted that I might write to him which I understood as a permission to ask for further leave as it followed these words, "You had better get Sir Wm Kerr to keep you." I answered "May I write to you on the Subject." he answered "Yes." I then accepted his offer & as there was no time to lose I began to prepare that I might go down the Hill to night & leave the Battering Train tomorrow morning. The Colonel sent for me & told me that the General, not only gave me leave but had sent a Hack & 4 Seapoys & he advised me to go immediately, so I got ready as quick as I could & left the top of the hill about 12 o clock.

[Sherwood's march to Meerut follows but he then resumes a journal of the events at Nahun while he was in Meerut.]

On my Road I overtook Lieut.^t Montgomery who was going to Seharanpore, ill, & I joined company with him from Nahun to the foot of the Hill where the Battering Train lay ie 4 ½ Miles, the Road has been cut as strait as possible & in some places it is almost perpendicular (for it is easier to drag a gun up a perpendicular than wind round a precipice) before we had reached this part of the World there was only a pathway & in some places Steps of Stone, there are however several halting places or small Table lands on the way. About a Quarter of a Mile below Nahun are some very fine Springs, the Water is collected in large Cisterns of Stone & shaded by large Trees, here several Fakeers live. On arriving at the foot of the Hill we went to Govan's Tent, hoping to advance as far as Moganund were we had been encamped from the 19th to 29th Decr but the Servants would not come on, Govan gave up his Tent to us & a dinner & we slept there & before daylight moved along the bed of the Nullah

28	but having plenty of Room we were enabled to pick our way & about a Mile from the Artillery Camp we got on the Bank & kept upon it except to cross the Ravine once or twice, until we reached Chowra Panee at the foot of the Hills, and entered on the plain which from this spot (Chowra Panee) to Chittagong or even Calcutta, by keeping the left of the Ganges there is not an Elevation higher than a house. The Mist was so thick all the way to Chowra pane that I could not see Nahun or even

---

[201] 'Buckshee' Baxee, Moghul military paymaster.

the Tops of the nearest Hills & suppose the distance from where I left the Artillery to Chowra Panee about 8 Miles making something above 12 Miles from Nahun, from this to Seidoura 6 Miles, the Country a Compleat flatt & I do not think well cultivated. Seidoura is a large City or rather three Cities each with a separate Fort acknowledgeing as Chief the Pathcally Rajah who is here encamped with a body of Cavalry to assist the English for he says (Poor Montgomery was very unwell & his Camels also sick) that this short days march was too much for them, Some Officers have complained of the impertinence of the Seeks but I saw nothing but a little inquisitiveness.

29 I was much delayed yesterday by Montgomery & As I alone had the guard I gave him the charge of it & set off at daylight with my Palankeen to sleep in, in light marching order, I <u>Walked</u> thro a rich but not well cultivated Country thro Mariwa, Belaspore, Santheera, Boorea where I stopped from 12 to 2. Boorea is a very large City with brick walls, the Present Governor is Raesh Goolaub Sing. Travellers complain of him but I met no molestation. Soon after leaving Seidoura I was joined by a Rajepoot from a Village near Chicherowly, he came up to me & we walked on conversing till we came near to Sankeera where the Road turned off between Belaspore & Sankeera I was soon after joined by another who continued with me as far as Boorea, the first addressed me saying how much the Natives were astonished at finding that the Company's Army in passing thro a Country had done no mischief while had an Army of Seeks passed thro their <u>own</u> Country they would have destroyed the whole produce & probably burnt the Villages, he was very inquisitive & fell into conversation with my Size[202] asked him who I was, how long I had been in India, how many servants I had, how much money I was worth, what wages I gave my Servants, & how I treated them, to all the Size's answers he exclaimed "Wah! Wah! Wonderful! Poodigious" & indeed the Size made me out to be a great Man from Borea it is 5 Miles to the River over a low marshy Country. I have met a detachment of our Men under a Company's Officer, he could not manage them, they were shockingly Drunk & straggling, they were ashamed when they saw me. I passed the River & slept on its banks in my moveable House (my Palankeen) near a Ferry House where were some Burkandusses collecting the Tolls.

31 5 Miles to Chilkanah over a fruitful but Marsh Country. The fog was so thick that I could not see 20 Yards. I had to ford a small Nullah & could scarcely see across it, at Chilkanah we rise again, it is a Large Town belonging to the Begum Soomno, just outside on the Seharungpore Road

---

[202] Syce: ostler.

are Cantonements for Two Battalions of the Begums Seapoys, with 4 Guns. The Cantonements are pleasantly situated with Gardens. The Troops are commanded by a European, from Chilkhan to Seharungpore is 8 Miles. On arrival at Saharungpore I was invited to dine with Mr Dyer the Field Surgeon. My Servants did not arrive till very late having been much fatigued by yesterday's long march. I went thro the Hospital & saw our wounded Men. I left Mr Dyers Tent at 5 o clock but lost my way somehow in the town but found my self at daylight near the Fort & with some little trouble got into the Road again, near the Judges House. I made use of Colonel Mawby's Buggy & drove as far as Kudgoorwallah which appeared a poor Village, I did not enter it but got my Breakfast in a mangoe Tope & waited two Hours, when I again proceeded to Deobund 14 Miles, it was very hot in the Sun altho quite otherwise in the Shade. I met a Gentleman going Dawk & before he came up a sudden thought struck me that I might have his return bearers, when he came I stopped him, but he told me that he was travelling by order of the Company & at their expence, on my arrival at Deokund I went to the Sannah Dauks house & told him that I should feel much obliged to him if he could procure me a set of bearers to carry me on & I thought I could trust to the next Tannahdar to get one, and I also promised a small present over & above the Regular hire. The Tannedar got me what I wanted namely six Bearers & a Mussaulchee, I started for Muzzufferrugger about 3 o clock, as soon as I got clear of the Town I stopped the Palanqueen & told the Bearers that I would give them an extra Rupee, if they would get me a set of Bearers at the end of the Stage, which they promptly promised to do, saying "Han, My Lord" by this additional sum given in the same day to each set I had no further difficulty I had a set at Mussuffugger, Kitowlee, Durlowlee & reached Meerut by 4 oclock in the Morning & found all well, I had got over 71 Miles in the last 24 Hours, Lord Moira was at Meerut on my arrival but went away before day light. Mr Thomason & Col^l Penson were at Mr Parson's. Mr Thomason left after tiffin.

[The following appears as an account of the battle at Nahan although Captain Sherwood was in Meerut]

The Engineer & Lieut^t Holland of the 6th N. I. having also left the Park at the foot of Nahun Hill to endeavour to find a practicable Road had suffered severely from Cold & wet & had returned without finding any Road, by which Elephants (the most adventurous Animals) could reach the top of the Ridge.

1st Feb.y On the 1st it seems that Colonel Kelly with the 7th N. I. left Nahun & found means to reach the point called Nownee, but from the 1st to the 4th the Cold & Rain was so bad that Many Seapoys Bildars & Coolies died, so that Major Ludlow was sent up with the 6th N. I. to relieve the 7th N. I. the latter being almost all sick.

5.6.7 The Weather extremely bad. The poor Seapoys suffering severely on the Hill, having only blankets laid across a Ridge to cover them from the Rain, the Officers have Chowldaries, namely a very small Tent made with bamboo sticks in the same form, It is said that 20 Seapoys have died from the Cold.

8 On the 8th it snowed very hard & in such quantities as to hang heavy on the Tents, & nearly breaking them down by its weight, the Natives almost dead, & extremely astonished, the Cattle dying & laying in all directions – 800 Sheep are Report dead belonging to our Regiment, the Troops on Nownee have now got a few's Pants, the Hill is white with Snow & the Seapoys quite Torpied. But we have got up a Six Pounder, & two Small Hill Howitzers but if the Goorkahs attack the position. I do not know what the Consequencies will be. The Europeans are now in their Element, Pelting each other with Snowballs, the Natives looking on with astonishment. When the Seapoys reached the Top of the Hill & saw nothing beyond except Hills still higher, they wondered what the Company was there for.

9 The Weather cleared a little the wind coming round to the west.

10 On the 10th it shifted to the East again with & cold weather & sickness.

11 The 26 N. I. went up the Hill to reinforce Major Ludlow.

12 The Light Infantry Battalion making a force of 1200 Seapoys & as many Irregulars, with 2 Sixpounders & 2 Mountain Howitzers. The Road to the Hill is difficult above measure, every one wishing that Lord Moira would look at it.

13 Bulbudder Tappa (The same who Commanded at Callunga) got into the Fort with 700 Men laden with grain. The Troops on the Hill are employed in making a Battery.

14 Colonel Mawby went up the Hill intending to remain & command the Troops there but the General was there & brought him back. Report says that the Belaspore rajah, a Prince whose Territory lies on the Sutledge above Malaoun & whose Daughter is Married to Ranjour has come over to our side by which it is supposed that Ummer Sing & Malaoun will be so much distressed as to enter into terms with us.

20   From the 14th to the 20th H. M. 53 Regt was employed in getting two 18 pounders from the Nullah at the Foot of Nahun to the Town & Cutting a Road from Nahun to Mut, where Major Ludlow attacked on the 27 Decr.

21   Accounts reached us of the taking of Ramghur & the small fort by Brigadier Arnold, Ummer Sing is in Malaoun, 3 Deserters came in from the Goorkah Battalion (Runjour's picked Battalion) they say that they are distressed for provisions. Mrs S. brought me a Daughter.[203] I was kindly allowed to be in Meerut at the time. The Road towards Jeytuk we hear is going forward.

23   The Irregulars to the Number 3000 Men under Lieut Young & the famous fighting Nahun prince of the Dynasty Kissen Sing were sent to intercept 500 Goorkahs, but were beaten with the loss of 180 Killed & about 100 Wounded most dreadfully, cut with Sabres. Report says that the Goorkah Chief Backlar Tappa from the Westward is coming to Jaytuk with 1000 Men. The Intelligence department say that there is but little provision in the Fort. Rice is selling at 5 Seers per Rupee. The Goorkahs cut off some Camp followers in the Ravine between Maun & Jaytuk & appeared in Numbers Commanding the Nullah, In consequence of which another Road is commenced more to the Westward, the Engineers differ in opinion as to the practicability of making a road, one saying that when they are up they can do no good by force, The Fort standing so high.

24   Colonel Mawby went up & pitched his Tent on Black Hill.

26   The Road to the westward is again abandoned, it would not answer & the old Road is recommenced. If the Goorkahs are enterprising they can at any time interrupt the Workmen.

27   The Enemy came down & fired on the Working Party & we had some casualties. A Battalion of Seapoys (15th) joined the Army. 1500 Irregulars asked for & obtained their discharge which I believe is rather the wish of our Government for we only entertain them to keep them from engaging with our Enemies & we see with pleasure that they are tired of the War they are as they say Dum Kuhed, that is they have (Eaten Fear) the Road is again abandoned—The Ravine is so much Commanded another Road about Midway is commenced. The Weather becomes warmer.

March 1st   I got leave to remain at Meerut. Report says that Runjour is fortifying a very high Mountain about 12 Coss to the North of Jaytuk

---

[203] Sophia (1815-99). Later her mother's biographer as Mrs Kelly. *The Life of Mrs Sherwood* London, 1854.

called Gumboor, this he means to retire to if we should succeed in driving him from Jeytuk.

8   Lieut' Mongommery died from his fatigues leaving me his Executor. In the Mountains of Almora, Colonel Gardiner has gained some advantages. The Kings Regiments to the Eastwards have closed in towards each other & joined Genl G. Wood vz 14th. 17th 24th Reg^{ts}.

10   Report says that 900 Men have marched out of Jeytuk but nobody presumes to say which way they have marched. At four o clock on the Evening of the 10th the Road to the Ridge was reported practicable but on the Morning of the 11th it turned out not to be so. Runjour says that he can keep possession of the Hills until the Rains set in, when we shall be obliged to leave the Country. He then hopes to recover all he has lost.

16   This day the 2: 18lbrs were got up towards the Hill with extreme difficulty.

17   In the Morning our first Batterys opened but with very little effect for the Shot went thro the Stoccades without knocking them down anything material. The Enemy had cut off the approach by digging down each side of the Ridge so as to form a compleat precipice on each side, behind which they lay covered from our shots, the lower trench is ours.

18   Scarcely any thing was done altho the 18 Pounders fired all yesterday & to day. A Deserter says that we killed 4 Men & wounded 2: after having fired several Hundred 18lbs shot, on the night of the 18th we advanced to the Trees, Col^l Buckland succeeded in reaching us, having taken two days with the Assistance of our Adjutant Surgeon & Quarter Master & a Drummer. The Stoccade now seems to be in ruins, but the Trenches cut around are so strong by Nature & Art, we are not much advanced.

20   We cannot get our Guns to bear on the 2nd Stoccade it being covered by the Hill on which the first stood, a constant Fire is kept up, but from the Nature of the Ground with little execution. Three of our Soldiers were wounded. Serj^t Burns was one who is since dead.

21   Nothing favourable. The Goorkahs are indefatigable they must have had from 12 to 1500 Men working all Night Strengthening their Trenches which are now cut down till they reach a Precipice.

22   We expected to have attempted an Attack but it was not done.

25   In the Evening a Man was brought out of the Fort facing us with his hands tied behind him & his head was cut off as if to shew us what

they were about, his body was thrown down the Hill it is supposed that He was clamorous for pay or provisions.

It is said that Runjour is straining every Nerve to procure provisions & altho he contrives to get some, yet not sufficient for his wants. General Ochterlony (it is said) has almost surrounded Ummer Sing in Mulaoun but 400 Goorkahs have attacked 1000 Irregulars (& altho the latter were stoccaded) beat them & destroyed the Stoccade. They say that Ummer Sing has cut noses of the Men composing the Garrison of Ramghur & Chumbla for giving up them. In consequence the Garrison of Tarraghur finding they could not defend themselves have deserted to us in a body. Ummer Sing is afraid of being assassinated. A Flag of Truce was sent in to Rumjour to complain that he had beheaded two Jemadaurs & to request that he would reinstate their heads, Rumjour said that it was done without his knowledge & that altho willing he could not comply with the request.

28   Reports are current in camp that General Ochterlony has taken Ummer Sing but we cannot trace from whence the Report arises. Major Richards with the Light Battalion & 13 N. I. are preparing to advance round the Fort to the Eastward, to take up a position at or near Peacock Hill. The Same spot where he (Major Richards) had got possession of on the unfortunate day of the 27 December.

Jaytuk Fort Approach Ridge. 2015.

29   Major Richards did not move, a Lieutenant of ours was shot thro the Arm, the bone broke.

30th   A Party of 500 Irregulars were surprized & beaten to the North of the Fort by the Goorkahs, Major Richards marched.

April 1st   A Report is spread in Camp which gains credit that Ummer Sing made a desperate Sally from the fort of Malaoun in 4 Columns, he himself was Killed & 3 of the Columns were destroyed, but the 4th escaped & is expected to make its way here, we are all on the Alert in consequence but it was soon found out to be a hoax, or April Fool trick of a young Cadet who actually forged a Letter from the Army of Ochterlony. This was nearly leading to something serious as our Army is so much scattered.

2   Major Richards's Party met the Goorkahs, supposed to be about 1200 strong. The Enemy shewed great judgement, remaining perfectly quiet until our troops had advanced to within 40 Yards of them. They then opened a heavy fire but very ill directed, the Seapoys fired immediately, charged & drove them from Hill to Hill until they got a good position where they Established themselves, our loss is 4 Killed & 27 Wounded, that of the Enemy 55 Killed, great Numbers wound & Prisoners, among the latter of Carnee Chumber Pund the Commanding Officer. Prisoners are being brought in every moment & the Garrison of the Fort is said to be in great alarm & we have now cut off their supplies, a Report prevails that Bulbudder was in the Action & severely wounded upon which a flag of truce was sent to offer medical assistance but it was laughed at & very properly. Bulbudder was not wounded.

9   Quiet till the 9th. The provisions most cut off from the Fort. On the 9th official reports were received that Temporary Barracks are to be built for the 53rd Regt who are to remain at Nahun during the Rains. Nothing else until the 13th when official Reports came that the 53rd Regt is to go to Calcutta by water as soon as the Rains make the River navigable. I was very unwell the 13th & 14th when finding that it was better to join the Regiment, I sent off my Servants & laid a Dawk to Saharunpore & I proceeded on the Evening of the 19th at 4 o clock, when I left Meerut, at first setting off it was dreadfully hot & I expected to find my journey very uncomfortable but it got comfortable a little after 5 o clock. I reached Saharunpore at Ten o clock on the 20th being a distance of 70 Miles.

20   Not knowing what to do with myself I plucked up a little Independence & called on Lieut Tager, a wounded Officer, to whom I had once been introduced, he gave me breakfast & Tiffin & the News vz that Genl Ochterlony had made a movement up the Malaoun Ridge to cut off the Communication between Surajpore & Malaoun, it appears that the Malaoun Ridge is enclosed between two Rivers on the Northern Extremity is Malaoun & on the Southern Furzepore. General Ochterlony has succeeded, but lost a most excellent Officer (Captain Showers 19th N.

I.) who seems to have been a serious & a Religious Officer & universally beloved. The Goorkahs lost a great many in an attempt to recover ground & amongst the rest, the famous fighting Chief Bucklar Tappa, whose wife burned herself with the Body which we sent in. The Goorkahs sent in the Body of Captain Showers, wrapped in leaves. After Tiffin about 3 oclock the weather being cool, I set off on horseback, but when I got out, the wind blew so strong that I had great difficulty in holding my umbrella & the Sun was too powerful without it. I passed Chilkanah which is 8 Miles, considerably before Sun Set, it had been my intention to have passed the Night there but having so much daylight & my Servants fresh, I proceeded to the Riverside, about 4 ½ Miles further. I passed the Night at the Custom Ghaut.

21   I crossed the River before daylight, at Six I passed Boorea, 4 Miles 2 Furlongs & advanced to a small Tope at Mankura 6 Miles before the sun was very hot, I met several Goorkah prisoners on the road & immense numbers of People returning from a Mela at Tulockpore, a place sacred to Bowaney about 6 Miles from Nahun. I got my breakfast & sat reading in the Tope where I did not find it so hot as I had expected, where a Seek came to me & was very inquisitive, about what I was reading, at 3 o clock I moved to Sankeera 2 ½ Miles but finding it warm I sat down. The Seeks surrounded me looking at every thing, saying they only came to see the Tomachee, they are very tall Men, all Armed & having their Horses Piqueted. I found myself in too publick a situation so I advanced to Belapore, 2 ½ or 3 Miles further, here I arrived before Sun Set. A Man with a sword came &asked me questions & wanted me to Doctor Him, for a pain in the Loins (Lumbago) & insisted on my reading Rollins Antient History to him, & altho I told him that I could not translate it yet he begged me to read it in English, he thought it did him good, I wished much for a Hindoostany Gospel, but my Baggage did not come up. The Man left me promising to send me Chockadaurs, but did not fulfil his promise. It being a fine Moonlight Night there was nothing to fear.

22   At four in the Morning I moved towards Seidoura the Country all Jungle but in flower & the perfume of the Wild Corinder making my head to ach. The common Dock Jungle has a very large & beautiful flower, 4 Miles from Belaspore is Marou where I ought to have come to last night, there is a good spot for me to encamp but not for any Number, from Marou to Seidoura is all Dack & Corinder Jungle, for 6 Miles till you come to Mangoe topes on both sides Seedhoura, I here met 12 Bearers sent by Emery to assist me. I stopped in a Fakeers Tope a little to the West of the Town in a very beautiful Spot under a Mulberry

Tree with Fruit Ripe & far preferable to what we got at Meerut. A Dawk Hircarrah brought me a Goorkah, one out of 20 who was caught carrying provisions to Jeytuk, from Sedourah. He says 4 more have been caught in different Villages. At 3 oclock I moved off in the Palankeen & reached Chowra Panee, The entrance of the Pass by 5. I now got out & walked to the Tope Khaunah 7 Miles, here I was preparing for the Night when Mr Allen of the Ordnance Department offered me a Tent & introduced me to Captain Warden of the 27th N. I. in Command with whom I drank Tea. They were on the Alert, expecting to be attacked & had loaded an 18 lb^r with grape & Canaster but we were left quietly.

23   At 3 in the Morning I moved to Nahun & passed the Day in the Cazees house with Mr Cook & at 3 oclock I ascended to the Camp near Jeytuk in 2 Hours hard pull up a Mountain, towards 3rd Ridge on which stands the Fort of Jeytuk. I got up on Foot for a Horse can scarcely carry itself let alone a Man & I suppose the distance to be 6 or 7 Miles, altho the exact distance from Nahun to Black Hill is under 3. In some places it is very difficult to ascend at all. I got up by 5 oclock & found our Reg^t encamped on the side of the Ridge under Black Hill. The Colonel came down & wanted me up with him to Dinner but I was too much fatigued.

24   At daylight I went up the black Hill & breakfasted with Colonel Mawby. Walked about the Ridges of the Hill. On the Top of black Hill & Nowree we are building small redoubts as a protection to our rear but the younger part of the army laugh at the precaution & called the Forts Gudder Ghur & Gudderghuree & Gabiegunge however it is but prudent to be secure for Ummer Sing might force his way from Malaoun & he is supposed to have at least 4000 Men probably even 6000 & is acquainted with Countryside. We have not 2000 Men in any one Army & they much scattered.

25   I again went to black hill which is a good pull being I believe from my Tent at least as high as the high rock at Bridgenorth & the weather is very hot. I dined with Colonel Mawby & passed the Evening. The heat is great in the middle of the day but the wind refreshing & the Night cool. Many European Fruits are now growing wild in great abundance close to our tents vz. Raspberries, Strawberries, Barrberries, Mulberries, Figs, Apples, pears. Apricots, Grapes I have not seen but I am told they will be plenty in the Season but they are wild & sour for want of cultivation. The Goorkahs desert from 10 to 15 every day.

May 1st 1815 50 Deserters came in to day.

2   A Cazee[204] came in with a letter & many deserters came in. We hear of an Action near Almorah wherein the Ghoorkahs were defeated with the loss of their General, Husta Dhill & 30 Killed the rest driven into Almorah. Hustah Dhill is Uncle to the Napaul Rajah, further accounts reached us in the Evening which mention a second Action & the Goorkahs completely defeated under Bumsah, another Uncle of the rajah & obliged to capitulate Kecholls, agree to evacuate the Whole Common District which is said to include Serinaghur. The Goorkahs during the Night sent out a desperate Attack who actually beat the 4th N. I. but they recovered themselves, these desperate sallies are very irregularly conducted, they rush out beating their Swords against their Shields & vociferously "Napaul sa Dour, Murna Zurrour." Far from Napaul, let us die all.

4th   On the Evening of the 4th About 9 oclock a most furious North wester came on which soon after brought rain and it was so cold that I was glad to get up & dress myself in warm clothes. The Wind increased so much that I was afraid of my Tent & had all of my Servants holding on to windward. Lieut' Daley was driven out of his Tent & came in. The Night was very dark but with vivid flashes of lightning & the howling of the wind was Tremendous. I wondered that the Goorkahs who know the Country did not make a sally for they have this advantage that they know their Enemy (A European) but they are themselves always able to claim kindred with the Camp followers & Natives Troops in the Color of their Skin. I was up all Night & it was intensely cold, I shivered in my Red Coat & wrapped in my Gooderie. In the Morning we saw the next Range covered with snow about 5 Miles off & apparently little higher than where we are. We now calculate ourselves 6000 feet above the plain & this is Summer.

5 to 9th We did nothing, deserters coming in all day who report the State of starvation in the garrison.

I went with Emery & Brodie to look out from our 18lb Battery on Red Hill which is calculated at 1 mile from the 1st Stoccade while standing behind & leaning on Brodie's Chair a shot passed under my Arm & struck Brodie breaking the small bone at the very joint of his Elbow. It was very painful & a dangerous wound. News from Malaoun saying that the Goorkahs have abandoned their stoccades & come in to General Ochterlony in a Body, & that Ummer Sing has not above 300 Soldiers with him in Malaoun, but these are so obstinate or desperate that it is thought he will not be easily induced to surrender, he has about a dozen

---

[204] Cazee: judge.

Wives with him & the wives of his Officers & in such circumstances they often make a large Pile & burn their women & then rush out & are killed fighting desperately. He has now sent in a Flag of Truce which looks well.

10   It seems Ummer Sing could not be brought to terms for the Guns were advanced & a breach made we are much afraid that he will burn himself & family. With us we are still staring at Jeytuk but desertions from the Enemy are becoming more common.

13   Upwards of 50 Goorkahs with several officers two of them called Adjutants deserted to us. To stop this desertion it seems that Runjour has promised to treat or fight.

14   This day two Vakeels came in but their terms could not be listened to. A dispatch towards the Evening from Malaoun saying that Ummer had surrendered. Ramdoss, Son of Ummer Sing was in General Ochterlony's Camp.

15   Today & during the night upwards of 160 deserters came in & this Evening great vakeels but we have not accepted the Terms.

16   Constant Messages passed on the 16th & 17th we can only guess that all is over.

Surrender

18   Rumjour & his General Jospow came down. A Tent was pitched for his Visit & Rumjour remained above an hour, & all was settled. He walked three times round the temple of the Goddess Jumpla & returned. As it seemed the end of our warfare I asked leave privately but got no answer.

19   I went up to Blackhill & was detained by the Colonel to Dinner & I got private leave to go to Meerut after Muster on the 24th. From the Top of Blackhill I could see the Goorkahs carrying their effects out of the Fort.

20   I wrote to the Judge at Saharunpore to lay Bearers for me, after which seeing some of our Officers strolling towards the Goorkahs advanced posts I also went. The first stockade was not so formidable as I had expected to find it & order soon came down to prevent any one going to the Goorkah works & who to hinder the Goorkahs coming to us & particularly to hinder provisions going. This is no doubt a proper precaution as famine is the Enemy which has conquered them, but the poor creatures are actually starving & several of them could scarcely be driven from our trenches. We gave a small quantity of food to them, at a

little distance lay a Woman with a Child dying, she had not strength to reach our Trenches, altho called to. We sent her some food, but it is uncertain whether or not the other starving people gave it to her. It is as yet uncertain when Runjour leaves the Fort as it is necessary that his Bramin should point out a fortunate hour.

21   I again went up to Blackhill for news & I found that it was the opinion of the Big Wiggs that the 53rd Reg^t would be at Nahun by the 24th. The Goorkahs are now wishing to enter into our service & one of their chiefs Cheet Sing, Brother to Bulbudder is come over with his Regiment, he quarrelled with Runjour & is gone to Colonel Kelly at Nahun. He received him in a most ludicrous manner sitting down on the Ground embracing him & calling each other Brothers which is called by us Bie Bunding.

The Goorkahs say that they have defended Runjour as long as they could, having eaten his Salt, but now they find that the English Salt is much sweeter. Before I left the Hills I went as far as the Enemies fourth Sroccade & was astonished at the weakness of their works but the natural strength of the Country is very great, I should almost say insurmountable, from our Trench we rose at least 45 Degrees to their Stoccade. The sides of the Ridge on each side of the path almost perpendicular, & from their Stoccade each side a Trench cut with steps from the first to the Stoccade. A very narrow path, in many places only one could pass & even then broken by rocks which required to be climbed over, from the 2nd to the 3rd Stoccade the approach was more easy at the point you descend a considerable depth till you join the Hill on which Jeytuk stands but which is so steep that you cannot ascend it in a Strait Line, the Fort is nothing if it could be reached. One Shot would destroy it. At 4 o clock, I heard that orders were in place for our Flank Companies to take possession of the Fort this Evening I therefore set off for Nahun going strait down the Water Course it was much further than I had expected & before I had got up the Hill to Nahun there was great appearance of a violent Storm & I could not enjoy the beauties of the Scenery which was very fine, for about half way down there was plenty of Water running over large rocks in a beautiful clear stream & the banks shaded by Trees, exactly like the West Indies only the Fir Tree & Oleander were common. I was obliged to walk very fast & was completely tired. On my arrival I met Veleta who took me to his quarters, the Cazee's House. I had scarcely got to the Step when the Storm burst & so violent was it that very large Hailstones flew along the Air Horizontally, we collected them in Basketts to cool our wine, Gooan came in & we had Tea. I was glad to get the cover of the House altho it looked as if it would fall every moment.

Jaytuk Fort inside. 2015.

The Interior was only about 12 x 20 metres with four corner towers and a central keep about 6 metres square.

22 Saw McDonald of the 7th. He is anxious to get Permunund the Pundit when we leave the Coun try. The Fort was given up yesterday Evening, just as the Storm began. Runjour was invited to remain but he seemed to think that it would blow over. We met a son of Sir Henry Flags famous for having Ran away with a Miss Pike & transported in consequence. He met Ranjour this Morning who (it seems) had had a very bad Night.

23 It rained most of the Night but abated at 4 in the Morning and the Right Wing of the Regiment came down. The Tents were to be removed before the other half come, Runjour remains near Nahun, with the 200 Men he was allowed to take with him but it seems these Men would prefer leaving their Commander & join themselves to the remainder of the Garrison who have entered into our Service. He has complained to them. The General of course took his part against his Men

& endeavoured to persuade Cheet Sing to return but without effect & the Son in Law of Ummur Sing has begged to be taken into our Service. Poor Runjour says that if they leave him he cannot return to Nepaul with any dignity.

24 Rained all last Night but the left Wing came down in the Morning & at 5 o clock in the Evening I mustered the Regiment, & immediately proceeded towards Meerut. I slept in my Palankeen at the foot of the Hill. It rained very hard, with high wind Thunder & Lightning. At ½ past Two it ceased, but the Tops of the Hills were covered with dark clouds.

25 I made haste to clear the Hill. The Clouds seemed to follow me & the Road was covered with water but I got out safe. At day Light I found the road very wet as far as Havillah when suddenly at one particular spot they became dry as if no rain had fallen & I had reached Seidoura. My Servants told me that they had had a very violent Toufan but no rain. I remained at Seidourah till four o clock when thinking I might venture forth I proceeded but, on getting clear of the grove in which I had been, I found the heat most oppressive. I reached Belaspore before sun set, 8 Miles, here I found several Seek Horsemen & I believe persons of some consequence. They came to me where I had determined to pass the Night (In a Babool grove) & with great Civility asked me questions. They much wished to see some wine & asked me how it was made, I produced my Wine in a Pint Bottle, all I had & with some fear offered them to taste but they declined & contented themselves with smelling it, it was uncomfortably hot during the Night. About Twelve o Clock Lieut^t Hall passed me he had laid relays of Horses. Numbers of Muskitoes but they did <u>not</u> pass me.

26 Not being able to sleep I moved off at 2 o clock & reach Booreah at 6—soon after Breakfast the Atmosphere clouded as if for a Violent Toufan, but after a little puff, the sand & dust remained floating in the Air but the wind lulled. At 12 as the Sky did not clear and the Sun did not appear, I thought I might venture to move & knowing that there were Topes (Groves) of Mangoes more than half the way I set off telling my Syze (Horsekeeper) to lead my Poney after me, it was however very hot. I sent on my Servants & when I thought that they had nearly reached a Village half way I got on Horse back holding an Umbrella & Cantered after them, here again I stopped in the shade then proceeded to the Jumna which I reached in the same Manner & getting on board the Ferry Boat seated myself in my Palankeen but we had no sooner loosed from the Bank than it began to blow from the North West most furiously (which is called a Toofan) I made my Servants get into the River which was not above 3 Feet deep & drag the Boat or we should have drifted

down. I met a boat crossing, my Molley[205] with a Dozen of Wine. He told me that Bearers were waiting for me at the ghaut. When I got on Shore the People told me that Bearers had indeed been there but they were gone back for food to a Village four Miles off. My Bearers had carried the Palankeen (Empty) twelve Miles & I felt compunction in pressing them further but they seemed to wish to get forward & persuaded me to ride to the Village mentioned, it was very hot & altho I had an Umbrella, The Wind blew so high it was not of much use.

When I reached the Village no Bearers had been heard of, they had gone to Chilkauck in all probability. I thought that as I had advanced so far I might as well advance this other 4 Miles & I reached Chilkauck very soon, I stopped at the Police Dhaur's house who denied having any Bearers Ordered & I endeavoured to prevail on him to procure me a set to Saharunpore but he said he could not do it till Night, having made up my Mind to wait I entered into conversation with him & he acknowledged that Bearers had been sent to the River for Shraub Saheb, or Mr Wine but that that Shraub Saheb had no Palankeen & the Bearers had returned. Now this Shraub Saheb turned out to be myself & that Piercy & Coultman having passed in the Night it was taken for Granted that Coultman was Shraub Saheb, for Piercy had a Palankeen but Coultman none, some mistake either wilful or otherwise brought the Bearers from their post. Who expected that Coultmans Palankeen would have been at Chilkauck but he passed on with relay Horses & they lingered round the Dawk House not well knowing what they were about. At four o clock I was packed in my Palankeen & reached Saharungpore at half past, at 7 moved again.

27   At 12 o clock in the day reached Meerut & found all well. From this to the 20th of June the day the Regt arrived we were busily employed packing & getting furniture conveyed for Sale, that the time passed without notice. The Reg^t left Nahun on the 5th and Chowrapanee on the 6th. They had rain on the 10th when they crossed the Jumna. They Reached Sahaungpore on the 12th & encamped at Abdulpoura not 3 Miles to the Eastward of Meerut on the 20th to which place I went & paid The Officers.

I had formed an acquaintance in my last trip to Meerut with Captain Arden of Longcroft near Lichfield, he is only temporarily in Meerut & has no house. I therefore offered him mine & left him in it having sent off all that I expected to want to Ghurmucklezer Ghaut on the 21st & we went over to Mr Parson's to pass the day intending in the Cool of the

---

[205] 'Molley' Mallee or mali, gardener.

Evening to set off it being full Moon & this the Dry Season, to Travel during the Night to Shagehaunpore.

1815 June 22   7th River Journey, Meerut to Berhampore, 1115 Miles.

Mr Parsons appeared really affected at Parting & expressed himself as if he had lost his only friends. The day had been uncommonly over clouded for the season with occasional Showers & it seemed so dark that we ventured forth at three o clock in the following order, Bullock Carriage, Mrs Clarke, Lucy & Emily, Mr Darby's palenkeen, Carriage Mary & Sally, Palenkeen Mrs S., Sophia, Palenkeen Dhye & Henry, Rhut, Ayah & Dhye's Child & lastly H S. P M & ASS on Horseback, behind were 17 Coolies Carrying provisions & Cloaths. Our procession advanced for about 2 Miles as far as Gwatken Lodge where the Rain began to pour not a Storm but a dead Solemn Calm. The whole Horizon being dark heavy Cloud & soon the whole plain was one continued sheet of Water. The bearers & Cattle, sliding at every step, for the Earth about Meerut being a Soapy nature, under these circumstances & knowing that the kali Nuddy lay in our Rout we judged it right to return which we accomplished with some difficulty to Mr Parson's slipping & Sliding all the way, myself wet thro & thro. It rained a good deal during the Night but about one o clock it stopped. The wind began to blow away the Clouds which passed Rapidly before the full Moon. I arose & collecting the Family moved off. The Roads were wet & slippery & we advanced with difficulty. The day broke before we reached Mow & I was glad it did for a little further on the water was between 3 & 4 feet deep. I was now very glad that we had returned last night & almost afraid that the Cattle would be knocked up. We however all got safe & Breakfast Ready. In less than an hour the rain again fell in Torrents & we congratulated ourselves on being snug. Fish actually fell from the Clouds, as we saw.

23   The Rain yesterday fell in great Quantities but also as yesterday cleared up at Midnight, at One we moved but there was a flood of water over the Country, we got on but found our baggage in different Villages, with the Cattle Tired, however as our Boat was ready to receive us, we pushed on. The Village of Douleah was so bad, that we had great difficulty in passing it. The Clouds became more dark & I was the only one exposed. Then I got to the City of Ghurmucklezer. I pushed on & was wet thro only 5 Minutes before I reached my boat, but I found a change of cloaths in my Boats. The Quartermaster who has been down some time gave us a good breakfast & except that all our Bedding is wet we are comfortable. The Sun broke out & a Westerly Wind blew for a

short time. The Thin coverings (or Gooderies) were dried & we made a better shift than we had expected.

24   The Regiment arrived completely wet & the Officers & Men say that they have never been dry since the 20th. Yet there is no more sickness than usual. It rained all day & I mustered the Men in their Tents & I procured 2 good Baggage Boats.

25   It rained to the 28th almost all the time while our Reg^t was embarked & it was very uncomfortable.

28   We sailed at ten oclock but only changed our ground for the sake of cleanliness halting on a Jewaddy Bank about 2 Miles above Phoot.

29   We were 6 Hours in going 20 Miles – 4 Miles above Andpseer.

30   A strong [wind] hindered our advance. Stopped opposite Currumboss at 8 o clock.

July 1st Passed Ramghaur at 8. The Hill at Seykeera at 10, halted 3 Miles below at 1 o clock. Heat very oppressive, a shower for the moment Relieved but it was soon hot again.

2   Symptoms of a Storm, which broke with Rain near Peiparole it lasted an hour, when we moved again & halted 4 or 5 Miles below.

3   The Wind was Easterly & Strong, saw Cawdergunge at 9, passed on 7 Miles & stopped at the usual hour on a heathy Bank.

4   The Wind East & strong which freshened to a storm, the waves rising like a Sea, stopped for an hour, it afterwards became calm & we moved on, at the usual hour halted on a heathy Bank, 18 Miles above Futtyghur.

5   Early in the Morning I ran aground & remained for above an hour in the mean time the whole fleet passed & when I came up I found them halted off Furruckabad, by leave I passed on to see Colonel Pewson, but the Rain poured so strong that I could not go out to see him.

6   The Regiment passed at day light but I remained to see Col^l Pewson, he came down & sat an hour. He begged that we would if possible see his sister Mrs Quincey at West Hay half a Mile from Mrs Moor of Barly Wood. On Colonel Pewsons leaving us we dropped down past Singrampore where the fleet was halted, we found that the Dandies being only Ghaut Men, from Ghurmucklezer had been only engaged to Futtyghur & on passing they had left the boats, we must therefore obtain many fresh ones which it is said will take 4 days. An Answer for my application for leave came, requiring a Statement of the Period to which my Accounts have been closed, also an answer from Major Lumsdaine

granting his protection to Serj.^t Cake. In consequence Cake & his wife were sent off by Col.^l Mawby in the Morning.

7   Poor Cake had been threatened on account of his Religion & was afraid that when his friends left the Reg.^t that he would be oppressed. Colonel Mawby kindly listened to our request & gave him up.

8   The Dandies did not arrive but we moved down 4 Miles.

9   At 6 we passed Kissenpore & at 10 reached Mindt Ghaut where we stopped as it is probable that the fleet will be some time in getting forward for want of dandies. Mindty Ghaut is the Warf of the Antient City of Canouge, the Ruins of which are scattered over the Country for many Miles the Buildings were erected with a very small brick scarcely thicker than Tile. The Mindy Ghaut is the remains of a large Mud Fort in which Almass Ali Khaun had drawn together a large Force & it was thought that he intended to render himself independent of the Nawab of Lucknow.

10   The Wind very high from the West which increased so much that by 10 o clock we endeavoured to reach the Western Bank for Shelter but could not. My boat drifted 3 Miles before I could gain the bank & the whole fleet was dispersed according to position they were in when the wind arose. I was by myself in a very good spot.

11   The Wind very high & we were obliged to stop at 9 o clock, opposite altho rather higher than Betoor.

12   Some of the boats which were dispersed yesterday did not get up till late this morning, consequently it was late before the regiment moved. The Wind blew strong, we halted at 10 o clock opposite to Cawnpore & I hear that we are to stop a week to receive at least 27 Lacs of Rupees from Lucknow a Loan from the New Nawaub to be carried to Calcutta.

13   this day I crossed the River to receive Money for the Regiment when I called on captain Whish, he & Mrs Whish were well but little George has been very unwell, & is not yet recovered. Mrs Whish soon after came to our Budgerow & asked us to her house which we declined but promised to pass a day with them if we could.

14   Having procured Money for the Reg.^t I returned to the opposite Bank. I should suppose the river to be 3 Miles across.

15   Leave of absence arrived for me to go to England for 12 Months.

17   The Treasure arrived from Lucknow, 25 Lacs & 2 ½ Lacs[206] from Betour this is sooner than we expected therefore to keep our engagement

---

[206] Lack: Lakh, 100,000. 27.5 lakh was an equivalent value in 1815 of about £350.000=£23,000,000 purchasing power in 2015. (measuringworth.com). 30 tons of

7th River Journey—Meerut to Berhampore 1815

with captain Whish we crossed & were kindly received & we passed the day until after Tiffin on the 18th.

18   When we returned but were caught in a squall all Night the wind being very high with heavy Rain.

19   The Wind lulled & we got off to our place, but it rained hard & nothing could be done in embarking the Treasure. It rained most part of this day.

20   The boxes of Treasure were all on board & we were told that we should move but on the 21st. Instead of moving we were told that the lids of the Boxes wanted fastening, cramping Bouyes Fixing that in case a Boat should sink a Bouy might show its place, all this day was passed.

22   In the Morning we moved at half past 5 & passed Jaugmow at 7, Kissenpore at 8, Nujufghur at 11 & halted at half past 12 a little below the Pagoda in sight of Surajpore.

23   Passed Surajpore with a strong opposing wind with occasional Showers. We had difficulty in passing a bend in the River opposite Surajpore but afterwards we proceeded better & halted at Rampore opposite Adampore.

24   We mustered the regiment before moving. It had rained during the Night & we had halted on a low Jungle which was wet & very unpleasant on Parade. At ½ after 6 we sailed but had a strong contrary wind, at 9 we were opposite Hassenee but were oblige to stop from the Violence of the wind, at 10 We moved again, passed Dalmow at ½ after 12. My boat was drawn into a small Nullah with wind & current & with great labour got out after being whirled round many times, all the fleet passed me. I at length got out & gained my place when the fleet was halted 3 Miles below Dalmow.

25   It rained very hard during the night & as day came on it blew violently & we had difficulty in proceeding, but having passed Manickpore the River became more favorable & we quickly ran to Currah & halted., Here is a manufactory of coarse Cotton Muslin called Chaurkands which we bought on an average at Two pence per Yard. The Young Officers have a good story against Col. Buckland who they accuse of a fondness for good eating. A Man came with a large Packt to the Boat side crying Chaurcauna. Col B— called him but finding only Muslin in his package, was very wrath & beat him saying "Couch Khana, Couch Khanahka Cheeze nehen." that is "You have nothing to eat." The joke lies in the words Khaunah which means food.

---

silver or 2 tons of gold. On 31 July Sherwood refers to this 27 lakh as 270,000 so the amount may have been 1/10 as much.

26   Several Boats it appears were unable yesterday to get round the point at Manickpore & one of the Treasure boats was damaged losing a Rudder, we were in consequence obliged to halt all day. There was a deep Nullah cutting off from the Main land, we could not get on Shore.

27   We moved early the wind being as usual very strong, at 6 passed Shahzadpoor, at 7 Jahpore, the wind increased so much at 9 that we were obliged to halt, soon after we tried again & were much buffeted but reached Pulhana & halted, with great confusion for each boat was obliged to stop whenever the wind drove it & we had a most delightful scene of confusion which lasted the whole day, for the fleet had been much scattered & came up very irregularly. Each boat drove at the same point & made the land almost at the same spot which was occupied by the first boats you may see in the Margin & <u>such Knocking & thumping was never before seen.</u> [obscured sketch]

28   The wind increased & blew a dreadful Gale all Night we thumped against the Conkery bank, in the Morning the waves appeared as high as those of the sea & the Ladies were sick & many of the servants, The spot near which we halted is very pretty.

29   Reached Futtypoor.

30th To Papamow where we had expected to stop & collect the fleet & receive directions before we went into the strong water of Allahabad but our Commanding officer went on & I followed, he however halted in such a dangerous situation that altho his own boat was safe, the rest of the fleet was exposed in a most unwarrantable manner. I ran to him & told him that he could not be aware of the circumstances & I stated that not 100 Yards from where he was large slices of the Bank were falling every 10 minutes which would overwhelm any Boat. He listened to reason & moved on again & we were agreeably surprized to find that the Water at Allahabad was calm & we were tracked over the same spot in which I had nearly been swamped from the Rapidity of the water last year. This is owing to the great breadth of the river at present.

31   We received 130,000 Rupees in addition to the 270,000 which we had brought from Cawnpore, we sailed at 10 o clock. The day was very calm & we passed Rapidly along until we reached Dumdum where we halted at ½ past 2 under a high bank. I bought a large Fish which fed nearly 50 of us it cost 12 Annas – 2/-

Augt 1st Calm with heavy Rain. We ran 42 Miles & halted at Jumgerabad.

2   Mirzapore. The wind high in the Morning & we halted at 9. After 12 it was quite calm but we did not proceed.

3   Very heavy Rain during the night & squalls but when dawn broke it was calm & we were carried by the stream 8 miles an hour, passed

Chunar at 9 o clock, Siltaupore at ½ past 9 it raining very hard. The Rapidity of the river at Chunar was very great forming a compleat whirlpool, ½ past 10 saw Benares. We halted opposite Benares at Eleven o clock, having run 47 Miles in 6 Hours altho during the first hour the wind was strongly against us. One Boat full of Soldiers was dashed to pieces & one Man drowned. As the Regiment was to remain here for a day to deliver Treasure I proceeded in advance to Ghazepoor on the 4th At 5 in the Morning & at 7 passed the Bend of the River where there is a Rapid & the wind being strong in opposition to the Current we had a very heavy swell. The Waves almost entering the Budgerow, at 8 we passed the Mutt (Pagoda) at Chamroutee at 9 the Mouth of the Gooratee, and reached Ghazepore (Gehaze Poor) at ½ after two – performing the distance of 60 miles in 9 ½ Hours. The Wind blowing violently against us the whole way. Lieut^t Peevor 17th Reg^t came down as soon as we arrived & carried us to see the Revd Mr Hastyns the Chaplain. Mr Hastyns is the son of the Rector of Martley near Stanford[207] he seemed delighted at seeing us & insisted on our going up to his house.

5   Peevor took us up to the School of the 17th Regiment which appeared to be in a better state than ours. The Regiment is indebted intirely to Peevor for this, it is his chief employment. It has had (it is true) greater advantages, the Masters having been left behind with the Boys during the Campain & Peevor himself remained. We dined with Mr Hastings, who was very much pleased at Meeting so near neighbours as were we also.

Sunday 6th It was very wet, I went to Church at Sunrise in the Riding School. The wind blew very strong. Mr Hastings left the Station at 10 o clock at Night for Buxar to visit Colonel Toone. We dined with a Captain Truscott a Brother of an old Friend of mine whom I left in Martinique in the year 1798. Mrs Truscott is an acquaintance of Mrs Wm Whitmore.

7   We Tiffed with Peevor & drank Tea with Truscott.

8   The Regiment did not arrive & I fear some accident as the Wind has been so high.

9   We received a Note from Captain Truscott saying that Col^l Nichol had a note from Colonel Mawby informing him that the 53rd Reg^t would not reach Ghazepoor before Tomorrow & Captain T— at the same time said that he expected us to dine with him. We declined dining but agreed to drink Tea with him. The answer was scarcely gone when the Regiment appeared & we found that the detention of the fleet had arisen from damage to some Boats about 14 Miles below Benares in the

---

[207] Stanford on Teme, Mrs Sherwood's childhood home where Dr Butt was rector.

strong water mentioned by me on the 4th. When I had seen the Colonel I proposed proceeding in advance to Buxar, my object was to get out of reach of invitations to dine. I therefore stopped at Beerpoor 16 Miles below Ghazepoor in a very beautiful spot.

10 This morning we reached Buxar about half after 6 o clock & Mr Hastings came down to ask us to Colonel Toon's. We declined but promised to go up in the Evening. This we performed & went out an Army in the Carriage. The Regiment did not appear. Mr Hastings related an anecdote of himself, which appeared to me worth noticeing. He was riding one Morning & within a mile of Buxar he found a Crowd Collected of European Invalides & Blacks, he rode up to them to enquire what they were about & was informed that there was a Tigger laying in a small Bush almost exposed. "Come here Sir & see." said one & "Come & see." said another & they pointed with their fingers. Mr H. at first told them how dangerous it was to stand so near, but after a time his own fear went off & he dismounted & gradually Approached the Bush. The Tiger which had been quiet began to shew signs of irritation & moved, upon which they all took to their Heels. The Tiger made a few bounds striking on each side & Killed five blacks with blows from his paws & had almost reached Mr Hastings when he providentially fell & The Tiger bounded over him & escaped. Mr H. got a scratch which confined him somewhat. The Tiger very seldom returns when he has missed his object.

11 The Regiment passed at Ten o clock but did not stop. Mrs Toone would not allow us to go away until after Tiffin. It was three o clock before we got off & we overtook the Regiment 8 Miles below Buxar.

12th Colonel Mawby received a dispatch by which it seems we are ordered to the Mauritius. I am uncertain whether this will be in my favor or not, but suppose that it is not of much consequence.

13 Moved at ½ past 5. Saw the House at Rivelgunge at 8- we did not pass thro the Chuprah Nulla, but halted at 12 o clock near Cheeran.

14th Reached Dinapore at 7 o clock & called on Mr Moore the Baptiste Missionary & on Doctor Gilman. We were received with great kindness by both. Doctor Gilman loaded our Boat with fresh Pork, a Ham, Bread & Butter & Fruit, Dinapore appears much as it did in 1806—the Trees do not seem grown & the Large House is not fallen, which it then threatened to do every day.

15 We dropped Down to Degab to Mr Moore's Bungalow. He was preparing that we should dine with him but we did not think it right but engaged ourselves to Tea. Major Latter came to Tea. He is a very Serious Officer, his Brother is married to Julia Jeffries, he pressed us much to pass a day with him. Ensign Pecket of the Engineers came who is also a

serious Officer & a friend of Mʳ Corrie's. We thought ourselves among our own Relations, Mʳ Moore keeps a School & has 20 Children under his Charge but they are all half Casts & illegitimate, he received for each 32 Children per Month about £100 a Year. The Girls & Boys are too much intermixed.

16   This day we saw a good deal of Major Latter, Mʳ Moore & Pecket & they were all very kind.

17   We moved down to the Nawaubs house sorry to part with our friends this is one of the trials in a Military life, you no sooner form friendship than you are hurried from them.

18   We moved early & passed Patna at 8 o clock. The Face of the Country is quite different from what it is at Meerut. Instead of Groves of Nime, we have Toddy Trees & Coco Nuts & long avenues of Palm & Mountain Cabbage, generally paralel with the River. We passed Futoah at 9 & halted at Binnipore at Ten having come 25 Miles. I fired at a Dove at the top of a Palm Tree & the Shot did not even strike the leaves on the Head of the plant, I said I thought the Hight about 60 Feet but the Officers said 90. This is of course judged by the Eye.

19   Passed Bar before 8 o clock. The Wind which had been Westerly since the 11ᵗʰ now came round to the Eastward. We halted one Coss above Deriapore = Noted for my Dispute with the Dandies about a Pig in 1805.

20ᵗʰ   The wind was easterly & very strong. We saw the Hills early & passed Suraj Ghurrah at 8 o clock, at 9 o clock we saw the Rocky Ridge at Sittacund, this Ridge is below Mongher, by the course of the River yet it is apparently nearer to us, we halted above Mongher. Here they bring for Sale Birds vz Parrots, Peroquets, Mina's & Java Sparrows, indeed all Species of Bengal Birds. They also bring Iron Wood, Joiners work & Straw work, all very well made & in immitation of English. The outward appearance almost as good.

21   It rained very hard, we moved & 7 I had prepared for very strong Water but it was not so bad as we had expected, but the heavy rain without any wind may have been favorable to us. We passed above Two Miles below Jangarra Rocks & Anchored having made 40 Miles to day.

22   We reached Boglipore at 9 o clock & halted but I know not for why. We were prevented dining with Doctor Glass by Sophia's being unwell. Pollock Lanced her Gums.

August 23   We moved at half after six & passed the Rock of Colgong at ½ after 9. The Current rushing by was most Violently Rapid, forming Whirlpools. The Budgerows as they passed were quite unmanageable twirling round several times, we halted at Pattergolly at Ten o clock soon after we had halted we had a smart storm & very heavy rain which abated at One.

24   Mustered the Regiment before we moved this Morning. At ½ after 8 passed Pointee, a very calm clear day, yet as we ran down the Eastern Bank I could not perceive houses on the Eastern nor in some places the shore itself, but a few Trees as if rising from the Water yet we cannot be less than 300 Miles from the Sea. We ran on until 4 o clock & saw Rajahmahal when we halted having come 47 Miles.

25   Soon after moving we had most heavy rain & altho we had but little wind yet we were obliged to halt, having only come 6 Miles.

26   The Rain continued heavy. Sophia very ill, with a fever. The Quarter Master shot a very large Wild Boar, of the Real kind. It was very dangerous business & had he not had a double barrelled Gun, he would have been Killed. The Animal made a charge at him & had his Gun missed Fire he must have been destroyed, the Animal weighed between 5 & 6 Cwt—Mr Donoghew sent me a small part but I could not eat & therefore am unable to say whether it was good.

27   Sophia very ill. The Weather dreadfully damp & uncomfortable. At 7 we moved & in an hour entered one of the small channels which now begin to form the Delta, this channel is called Cadgere & here we halted.

28   Sophia is better, we passed Moangunge which was in 1805 & 1807 The principal Entrance from the Hoogly to the Ganges but this channel is now closed we passed along to Seebgunge which is only 5 Coss from Jungapore where we entered the Bhaugelly by a good new Channel we reached Jungapore at 3 where we found the 66 Reg^t. At Jungapore our intention had been to stop but the 66th had occupied the whole bank of the River so that Mr Chomsery & ourselves were dissapointed, we were expecting to dine with him. We received orders to halt at Berhampore & to leave our Boats, the reason for this change is that the 59th & 71 Reg^{ts} are arrived unexpectedly at Calcutta & there is no room for us, we have had our destination so often changed that we know not what next will happen.

29   We reached Berhampore & went into the Barracks there but there is no authority for discharging Boats & the Government Boat being retained we are at a loss how to act. This ends Aug^t.

Sept^r

On the first at Night an order arrived for the Regiment to proceed immediately to embark for Madras, here is another change.

2 & 3rd All uncertainty, no new orders arrived, and the order which we received on the 1st is still in force but awaiting confirmation thro the Local Authority vz Genl Blair. Report indeed sometimes varied to take but substituting Java for Madras & then Madras for Java & sometimes Mauritius & sometimes the Cape. In the mean time continued to advance & on the 24th I mustered the Reg^t (as I suppose for the last time).

Part 6—1815 September 25th—12 Months Leave

8th River Journey, Berhampore to Calcutta, 175 Miles.

On the 25th I took my departure with some feelings of regret (for I had never left any Corps before for any length of time for 17 years & a half. I was anxious to avoid taking leave & it may be understood that I should go on the Morning of the 26th. I got under weigh at four o clock on the Evening of the 25th & halted about a Coss below the Station.

26   The Wind was so high that I scarcely moved. I stopped at Davidpoor, Davids Town.

27   We had much rain during the Night & in the Morning by which the wind was better I proceeded, passed Plassy at 9 o clock & passed Agadeep & halted near a fine old Temple, the outside inlaid with curious tiles formed in moulds.

28   From Agadeep to Culna where we halted a little before 5 here we perceived some indication of a Tide. The banks being Mudd, & damp, with overhanging Bamboos.

29th   We moved from Culna early & halted at Chandernaga[208] to prepare ourselves &c as we are to anchor at some distance from the Shore, the Maunee[209] is making the Anchor. The Maungee took four crooked bamboos, bound them with their branch outwards which formed a most clumsy four fluked Anchor, filling the shank with heavy stones he bound them tightly together & it answered very well. We in the mean time walked on the Town & saw French Men & heard French talked until I fancied myself half way to france, which curious caricature of old French Costumes reminded me of Martinique, but the recollections it brought were rather pleasing. We went into a chapel & found it full of Black Christians, I presume the descendants of Portugese who intermarried much with the Mahomedans & being in themselves over fair some accommodated to the Tropical Complection.

30th   We moved at 4 o clock & reached Calcutta before the Tide Turned but we could not pass the Shipping & were obliged to halt on the Western side of the River near the Docks from 10 to 1 o clock when the tide turning we proceeded & crossing the River soon reached Balou Ghaut where we found a Servant from Mr Sherer waiting for us & soon afterwards two Carriages came & carried us to Chowringhee we found

---

[208] Chandernagar was a French colonial town.
[209] 'Maunee' Maungee: boat master.

that Mrs Sherer had been confined on the 26th of a daughter, Mr Sherer came & Welcomed us in the Evening.

1815 October   Friends in Calcutta.

Octo^r   During this Month we were in Calcutta with Mr Sherer. The Climate is much inferior to the upper Country, damp & disagreeable. The Mosquitoes are very Troublesome & I dare not say how very much so or all the Stories that I have heard of them & which I partly believe, for why should not Mosquitoes be as intelligent as Bees. The Heat is now greater than it would have been in the upper Provinces but it is never here so hot in summer, owing no doubt to its proximity to the Sea.

We engaged our passage to England on board the *Robarts*,[210] a ship now Building of 750 Tons. We are to have a Cabin for us all Eleven feet by nine, fitted up like a Pigeon House vz Two Tiers of Holes for Sleeping in & we are to pay 6000 Rupees equal to £750. We had enough to do in making preparation for so long a voyage yet we occasionally saw Friends as M^r & Mrs Thomason, Major & Mrs Latter, Mr Davies a Clergyman going to Bombay— Mr Fisher going to Meerut, & Mr Herbert Harrington, our next door Neighbour, Mr Money, Brother to Mr W. Money whom we have known in England, Mr Loring the Arch Deacon & we have also seen the Bishop. The Regiment arrived towards the end of the Month preparatory to embarkation for Madras, but I now am on leave & therefore only visit my Friends as a Friend. Many of the Seniors are absent as Col^l Mawby, Majors Piercy & Ingleby, Cap^ns Coultman & Price, Horsely &c indeed all the Elder ones who are summarized to give Evidence on a Court Martial & it seems to me like the same Body without a Soul. I have it is true some few friends remaining but, they are but few, & from the misfortunes of the Campane, the Mess is divided in opinion, a number of Officers have joined from Spain who profess to say that if we had been at Kalunga we should have carried the Fort at once & who talked lightly of Indian Troops & old Soldiers, perhaps I do feel too acutely. The Regiment was encamped on the Glacis. Two Duels took place between the Old & New Officers, Lord Moira is aware now of his injustice & appears to wish to forget it.

---

[210] Probably built for Abraham Robarts (1745-1816) a Director East India Company was disqualified and died in 1815 so the boat might have been sold and renamed on arrival from this maiden voyage to Liverpool. In *Lloyds Register of Shipping* no *Robarts* ship is identified after arrival off Liverpool until the 1830s which may have been a later ship.

Nov^r

We heard of the Victory at Waterloo which was not well received by our Regiment who had hopes of being employed during the War. It was advised that Mrs Sherer should remove from Calcutta on account of her health & as we had completed our preparations we agreed to accompany her. Her little Girl was christened (Mrs Sherwood was a Sponsor. The Late Mr Browne had a House called Aldeen close to Serampore which is now empty & Mrs Sherer fixed on it as the most convenient situation to proceed to, we were much pleased with this arrangement as it placed us so near the Baptists Missionaries at Serampore.

On Thursday the 16th We left Calcutta with the Tide & in 3 Hours reached Aldeen. The side of the River is very delightful the whole way. Aldeen itself is very interesting as being the Spot in which was first conceived the plan of Missionaries & in which The Original Baptistes vz Mr Thomas & Mr Carey were kindly assisted. Mr Browne had an old defiled temple (Vulj Pagoda) on his Domain which he had formed into a Study & here he often prayed for Labourers & here his prayers were answered by Numbers of Workmen. Martyn, Corrie & many others not in his own Sect, but equally followers of X^t.

On the 19th We went over the Baptiste Establishment, we saw Mr Marshmans School & Mr Wards Printing House. We had been led to think Mr Marshman a proud overbearing Bigot but we found him a kind friend. Doctor Carey was a fine old Gentleman fond of Botany & ornithology. We left our poor Prisoner the Cheekor[211] in his hospitable Care, in the Evening we heard Mr Ward preach to the Workmen in the Printing house but did not understand the Language. Doctor Carey walked over his Garden with us & we drank Tea with Mr Marshman. The Missionaries tell us that they have baptized upwards of 800 Persons since their arrival in India. Mr Marshman now has one Hundred Scholars, we afterwards went to their Meeting where Doctor Carey propounded a Text & M^r preached on it, he dwelt on the <u>providence</u> of God & particularly dwelt on the Good arrisen from the French Revolution & good from evil. Mr Marshman followed dwelling on the irruptions of the Northern Nations.

Sunday 19   Mr Sherer & myself attended the Baptist Service at … ? [word missing]

Doctor Carey preached a very impressive Sermon on the Influence of the Holy Spirit. The Sermon was beautifully plain & edifying. We did not approve of a very irreverent manner among the Congregation.

---

[211] Cheekor: red lagged partridge.

20   Mr Sherer took me in his Carriage to Calcutta, we crossed over to Barrackpore & from thence to Calcutta 14 Miles. The Road is very fine being made of pounded Brick without an inequality sufficient to cause a jolt the whole way it reminded me of the German Roads, with Double Rows of Trees on each side the whole way.

In the Evening I returned by the same Road from this time to the end of the year I frequently passed between Aldeen & Calcutta with Mr Sherer. A Poor Hindoo woman burnt herself close to the Pagoda. Our Children & the Baptists ran out to endeavour to save her but it was too late.

Dec^r

We heard of Bonaparte's Capture of the *Bellepheron*. Towards the end of the Month Mrs Sherer was obliged to go to Sea for the recovery of her health & she embarked on Board the *Hastings* Pilot Schooner.

The 53rd Reg^t embarked & sailed for Madras.

1816 January 2nd Depart Calcutta for England

On the Second we left Calcutta to embark for England. I hired a Boat which was very convenient called the *Wellington* for which I paid Rupees 200—we moved after dinner & on the Third being our Second tide passed Falta where Mrs Sherwood mistook Buffaloes for Tygars in 1805. The 4th we made the Ship (*Robarts*) at Sangor, here we lay until the 11th taking in Cargoe, when we sailed but we had no wind & were afraid of attempting the Narrows without wind we therefore Anchored.[212]

12th   At daylight we sailed & at Ten We passed the wreck of the *Jassy* Pilot Schooner. Torrid N.E. by N. very slight, which soon fell to Calm at 1 we Anchored near the Reef Buoy, we got under weigh again at 8 at Night with the Turn of the Tide.

13   Calm at Night but increasing towards Morning, Lat at 12/ 20-28. Ship very low in the Water & water oozing into our ports, which is very uncomfortable.

14   More Motion than we had expected, Ladies Sick. Lat 18-36

15   Lat 16-1 Wind increased & a little Sea, made much waster thro the Scuttle.

16   Heavy swell   Lat 13-37

17   Very disagreeable, heavy swell, pump every two hours, much water from the Scuttle's & Ports very unpleasant, no observation.

18   More Moderate but still disagreeable, Lat 8-55 Long 86-9 Mrs S very unwell from Sea Sickness.

19   Weather more Moderate but the Ship Pitched very much Lat 6-18

20   Strong Easterly Wind   Lat 3-42

21   More Moderate Sunday no Service   Lat 1-42   Long 86

22   Moderate but squally Lat 0-5 Towards Evening Calm

23   Nearly Calm South   Lat 0-53

24   Cow died Eheu do   —— 1-33

25   do. Ship in sight, passed to Windward, No observation, Rain, rather heavy

---

[212] The Sherwoods were accompanied by children: Lucy, 6; Emily, 4; Henry Martyn, 2; Sophia, 6 months; and adoptees Sally Pownall and Mary Parsons; with Mary Howarth travelling in their care: all in the 11 feet x 9 feet cabin. Their servant was an injured soldier, Robinson, 6 feet tall, who was a capable nanny.

Calcutta to England—1816

26	Light Breeze. after dinner Calm	Lat 3-10 South
27	Calm with occasional Squalls, no observation	
28	do Heavy Swell	Lat 3-52 Long 84-1
29	do	——4-25 Long 83-54
30	do	——5-1
31	do—	No observation

February 1 only 54 Miles in Two days   Lat 5-55

2   6-53

3   Calm   7-4

4   Sunday 7-30 Calm with occasional squalls a very severe sudden squall at Night but it did not last

5th   Lat 8-2   Long 84-14

6   Lat 8-24— long 83-54

7th   Calm all Night at 7 in the Morning a heavy squall with a great deal of Rain. We caught 3 Butts of Water The Heat has been very great since we sailed averaging 85 but this day it is 83— great swarms of Flies have troubled us   Lat 9-5

8th   The Wind fell towards Evening but freshened during the Night
        Lat 14-4

9   We had a severe Gale from the North West with a heavy swell & Rain   No observation

10   heavy swell—   no observation

11   heavy swell—   no observation

12   do—do—little Wind, The Ship pitched & Laboured much
        Lat 16-12   Long 79-54

13   do—do—do—do   ——17-34 —79-20

14   Calm

15   do   ——18-2 —78-40

16   a light Trade sprang up before noon   ——18-38 —78-37

17   — little stronger wind   ——19-34 —75-46

18   — Wind high Sea Rough but all in our favor— 20-54 —72-56

19   — More Moderate   ——21-51 —70-25

20   — Mr Gardener a Passenger related a fact which happened under his own observation while Judge at Allahabad. Four Private Soldiers of the Honorable Company's Artillery finding themselves lonesome & wishing for Wives wrote to the Manager of the Orphan School at Calcutta for an assignment of Young Women & immediately received four Girls, on their arrival The Soldiers drew lots for First Choice & Mr

Fortesque Married the four Couple— Quere, did not the Managers of the School act without due consideration.

20	The Wind blew strong in Squalls	——22-51 —67-2
2	—do	——24-1 —64-23
2	—do	——25-8 —61-8
2	—do	——26-3 —58-26
2	—do	——26-26 —55-7
25	Fine Moderate Breezes & Smooth Sea	——26-46 —50-2
26	—do— & afterwards Calm	——27-53 —"—"
27	Calm till 10 at Night then Moderate Wind	——27-56
28	South West Wind & Cloudy.	No observation

29   A Very heavy squall without any apparent reason. S. W. wind in squalls, the Ship Labours much — Lat 28-1 heavy swell at Night

March 1   Wind from the South—   The Swell abated the Lat 28-33   Long unknown

2	Wind Moderate, Cloudy,	no observation
3	Light Wind	——30-16

4   Wind increased we find that the Captain has taken offence at some questions asked & sports the Sulky, he will not let the passengers know the Longitude we can find the Latitude without him.

5   A very fine breeze with Rain & Cloudy we ascertained the Longitude by a Lunar observation to be 39-7 we had no observation.

6   Fine day, pleasant Run   Lat 33-32   Long 32-52
We fell in with a Ship which we spoke & she proved to be the *Bengal* which sailed from Bengal on the day before we did.

7   We had expected to have some conversation (gossip) with the *Bengal* today but she ran away from us for the Night.We lost the Main Top Gallant Mast which altho in itself of no material consequence yet entangled the Rigging &c   Lat 34-34   Long 30-39
The Wind increased during the Night.

8   This Morning it blew strong form the NW. Lat 35-0   Long 27-10 The Wind inclined to the West & continuing came to the south West, we still see the *Bengal* & she does not appear to gain.

9th   The Breeze light from the South West. The Swell heavy
            Lat 35-27   Long 28-10

10th   Fine Weather We must have had a Current Setting South West which is very common here   Lat 35-48   Long 21-42

Calcutta to England—1816

11   At Daylight saw cape Agullas distant 15 Miles, Calm with Cloudy weather, we could not get a certain Mark to distinguish our position for altho the Cape Agullas is a certain point, yet without seeing a more fixed point vz the Gunners Gun, the situation is not reckoned as sufficiently ascertained. We stood off from the Land & lost sight of it before Sun Set, but about three in the Morning we were alarmed by the Roar of Breakers apparently very near. It was long before we could believe our Ears but at length we were forced to acknowledge that we were close upon some Shore. It was a dead calm, we lowered all the Boats to try & tow the ship & prepared cables &c but a light Breeze springing up we were providentially relieved from our Fears, we stood away to the South nor could we conceive how it was possible to have got so near the Land as we had had a dead Calm, not the slightest swell of a Sail & we were out of sight of land last Night. At day light we had a pleasant Breeze & we saw imperfectly the land with a long line of dreadful Breakers between us & at length we ascertained that we were off Cape Agullas, & at 12 We saw Cape of Good Hope distant about 25 Miles the Wind increasing & blowing rather strong we ran 7 Miles an hour at 4 o clock passed Cape of Good Hope & continued our course it being a fine Moon light we entered the Bay of the Cape & worked up in famous stile, anchored at Three o clock in the Morning

13   At Ten o clock I went on Shore & saw Colonel Bird, formerly a Cap^n in the 53rd Reg^t now Colonel Secretary here. Bird was very kind & wished us to go to his Country house, offered his Carriage &c, &c, we had appointed to go, but little Sophia was taken ill. Cape Town is small & nothing worth mentioning seeing there are so many descriptions of it. I walked to the Botanic garden, saw Lions, Ostriches & Ok Trees, & the Table Mountain with its Table Cloth, but we are now so near the equinox that it becomes of some consequence to watch the Weather & invariably about 11 o clock signals of storm appeared, this is a kind of white drifting cloud rolling over the Top of the Mountain which is called the Table Cloth. It is considered as an unfailing prognostic of high wind & we found it so, in so much that I could not enjoy the Shore, having those on board from whom I should not have asked to be seperate for a Night. Mrs S. went only once on Shore & she could not enjoy it fearing that the wind might rise.

20   On the 20th we got under weigh with a light southerly & breeze & we were obliged to lay to off Robbin Island (but finally sailed at 3 o clock)

21   Sailed at the Rate of 5 Knots—Cloudy & no observation

22   Wind North West, a heavy squall & wind shifted to S. W.

23 Wind more to the south   Lat 30-2
24 Wind South E.   ——28-33
25   ——26-33
26   ——24-46
27   23-19
28   Light wind   ——22-11
29   ——— a little Rain   ——20-57
30   ——19-52
31   ——18 46
April
1st   —17-42 Long 3-10W
2   In the Trades   Lat 16-54
3   We ought to have seen St Helena & indeed we do think we see it but we cannot ascertain our Longitude   Lat 16-1
4   We had so little Wind that we may almost call it a Calm Lat 15-21 From this to the 12th all was wrong in the Ship altho no words passed, the Captain looked Sulkie & we did not enquire much about the latitude pretty well understanding that we went about a Degree per Diem— On the 12 the explosion burst & it all turned out to be a simple question asked by Colonel Broughton—whether it might not be better to go more to the Westward. This question was asked about 6 Weeks since when we were on the other side of the Cape & has been ruminated on since but I hope it is now over.   Lat 3-32   Long 20 W
13   Lat 1-40 Long 21-10W
14   0-26 North   21-15
15   Lat 2-17 N
16   The Wind left us, at 12 saw Two Ships but could not get near them. 2 Portugese Schooner apparently a Slave Vessel, was brought near us in a fog & we got our boat out to ask for news, but she ran away.
17   It rained very hard all yesterday afternoon & this Morning
18   Yesterday Evening a N. E. Wind which we had hoped was the Trade but it fell at 11 at Night & we had Violent Rain till 5. Lat 5.2
19   Very heavy Rain yesterday Evening
20   The wind freshened during the Night, a Ship passed in the Morning supposed to be the *Bengal*
21   An Easterly Wind blowing Fresh in squalls sprung the Fore Top Mast. The *Bengal* came near & the Captain came on board & dined, in the Evening took leave, for England & I wrote. We reefed our Mast, that is

lowered it so as to bring the Crack below the Cap, consequently we must carry less Sail.

22   From this time we sailed pleasantly along as is observed always in these of Latitudes, we got over our pet with the Captain & learnt the Longde again,

On the 3rd of May we had reach	Lat 30	Long 26,
9th May	Lat 40 and on the	
14	Lat 47	Long 24

which brought us near our own Shores, here we fell in with *Louis le Desire* a french Ship 24 Days from Martinique, crowded with Mulatoes &c, while we were speaking to her the wind gradually veered to the East & we changed our Tack while speaking we were obliged to steer East, a little South until the

20th   in which 6 Days we approached England 60 Miles— we Wore on the 20 & felt considerable chill from the Eastwind & had still made on

21st   very little way. The Wind strong & piercing, several Land Birds came on board, Yellow Hammers, Swallows. Thus it was till the

25th when the wind veered to South West

Moderate & Cloudy

26   Dark & Cold about 10 o clock the wind suddenly arose & blew a perfect Hurricane which lasted all day but fell at Night leaving a most tremendous swell.

27   A Most dreadfull swell from N. W.

28   do— do— The swell most tremendous we suppose ourselves to be in Lat 49-30 & Long 8-20 but no sign of Land, in the Evening we saw a Ship from Waterford having lost her Topmasts in Yesterdays Gale computes her distance from Cape Clear 14 Leagues

29   Fine Moderate Weather saw The Land of Youghill & at 6 o clock yesterday in the Evening the Hook light. The Wind fell during the Night to an almost calm. At day light saw the *Tuskar*, we proceeded finely all day

30   At Day light this Morning we had a North wind which was against us & as the Tide acts here strongly we dare not venture much without a Pilot, at Ten o clock we were amused seeing Mountains right ahead apparently detached form the Main Land of England & resembling Islands. We were so unconscious of our situation that we at first took them for the Isle of Mann but as the day cleared we found ourselves in Carnarvon Bay with Holy Island ahead. The Shore in this most pleasant Season very delightful the Welsh Mountains having their Summits still covered with Snow. The day was almost Calm & the Sun rather warm,

we lost ground until Two, when the Tide Turned & we stood on and passing the Lights at Holyhead at Ten o clock, which filled our minds with pleasure.

31   At Day Light we had a heavy fog & light wind we could scarcely see the Land, but we know from the lights that we were off the Great Orme's head, a Pilot boat came on board bringing Fresh Bread, Meat, Potatoes & Butter, which was very delightful. We advanced pleasurably along the Coast of Cheshire and passing the floating light we anchored in Hoyle Lake,[213] after an absence of 11 Years.

Now all was confusion & Bustle on board & I hired a Boat to take us on Shore in the Morning We could get no sleep during the Night the noise was so great, & when I arose in the Morning not a white face was to be seen. The Lascars even were all drunk I was of course anxious to get on Shore, but the Boat which I had hired last night to carry me on Shore was gone, I asked the Tindal[214] what was become of it but I found him drunk & told him so, the Man repeated to the Officer what I had said a plain proof that he & the Officer understood each other for such a thing is never done in India. The fact turned out to be that all the Officers had been Smuggling & of course in the power of the Sailors. Some time after this a Letter came on board, but there was not an officer sober enough to read it & I was obliged to speak sharply before one could be brought up, but as they were aware of their own bad conduct, I had not incivility shewn, all that appeared was, an anxious whish to get rid of me, but now a more curious fact appeared which was that the Pilot was absent. The officer was quite drunk, the Custom House Waiters were so too & after a short time I was let into the Secret for my Boat returned with the Steward on board, & I found that they had been smuggling all night & either trusted to my not rising so early, or else they were themselves detained. I was glad to get away for from the Chief mate, to the lowest Lascar there was not one quite Sober, the Custom House Waiters as bad as any & they were very insubordinate for before we left we had two or three Battles between the Chief Mate & the private Sailors.

June 1st We got off as soon as we could & reached Liverpool by 12 & soon passed our Baggage got quietly to the Inn & had a good fresh Dinner, the Children being very delighted with the Fresh Vegetables, Emily asked her Mamma if the Chambermaid was a woman —[215]

---

[213] Hoyle Lake: a safe mooring in a lagoon off Hoylake on the south side of the Mersey estuary.
[214] Tindal: Petty officer or bosun's mate.
[215] Lloyds Register of Shipping reports *Robarts* off Liverpool on May 31st and *Bengal* docking at Liverpool on June 1st 1816. They were the first EastIndiamen permitted to

from this to Trentham, Snedshill & Worcester[216] & so ends for the present the Voyages of Travels of H. S.

---

land at Liverpool and the Sherwoods were greeted by bells ringing and followed by a curious crowd. They were all still in their Indian clothes.
[216] Mrs Sherwood had relatives in Trentham, Snedshill and Worcester.

1816 to 1849   Epilogue

The Sherwoods set up home close to Worcester and Captain Sherwood decided to retire from the army on half pay, transferring his nominal rank to the Brunswick Hussars in August 1818.

Mrs Sherwood became a successful author of over 300 books for children. They established a boarding school for young ladies at their home. With an inheritance each from their grandfather they were able to buy property and to travel on the Continent. Captain Sherwood established a school for boys.

In old age they moved to Twickenham where he died on December 5th 1849, aged 72, and Mary died on September 22nd 1851, aged 76.

The following monumental inscription was to be found at Oak Lane cemetery, Twickenham, London, United Kingdom, circa 1930. The Cemetery is now closed, and many of the monuments have now been so damaged by time and weather erosion that they are illegible (including this one):

> Sacred to Henry Sherwood of Lower Wick
> formerly Captain of His Majesty's 53rd Regiment of Foot
> and late Captain in the Brunswick Hussars
> who died in this parish on the 6th of December 1849 in the 73rd year of his age.
> Blest are the dead which die in the Lord, ever so saith the spirit for they rest from their labours. Rev 14. v.13.

By Sherwood's will he left several properties, Lower Wick Estate, Bedwordine, Worcester including tenanted cottages and lands, the substantial Georgian house at Brittania Square, Worcester where the family had lived, a house at Salwarpe, Worcester and at Rainbow Hill, Worcester, miscellaneous real estate, money and investments in trust for his wife and children and grand-daughter and £4000 divided between a son-in-law, his son and grand-daughter.

The Sherwoods' daughter, Sophia, born in Meerut in 1815 continued her mother's writing of children's books as Mrs Streeten and later as Mrs Kelly. She also published an edition of her mother's life including purported extracts from Captain Sherwood's diaries, all paraphrased in her own style.

Kelly, Sophia, ed. (1854, & 2nd ed. 1857). *The Life of Mrs. Sherwood, (chiefly autobiographical) with Extracts from Mr. Sherwood's Journal during his Imprisonment in France & Residence in India Edited by Her Daughter.* 1st & 2nd editions differ. London: Darton & Co.

Other Biographies of Mrs Sherwood including her life with Henry Sherwood:

Darton, F. J. Harvey, ed. (1910). *The Life and Times of Mrs Sherwood.* London: Wells Gardner, Darton & Co. Based on Kelly with some additions.

Eaton, Barbara. (2016) Francis Boutle Publishers, London. *Mrs Sherwood 'so rich in children.'*

The Sherwoods' son Henry Martyn Sherwood, born in Meerut in 1813, died in 1912 just short of his centenary after 72 years as rector of White Ladies Aston, Worcestershire.

Note in the hand of Sherwood's great grandson, also Henry Sherwood (1896-?), inserted in the 2nd diary:

> The IXth Battn, The Middlesex Regt. sailed in Oct 1914 in HMS DILWARA & DONGOLA for INDIA and on arrival there HQRS + A & B Companies were stationed at DINAPORE which was reached on 3 DEC while C & D Companies moved to BARRACKPORE & DUM DUM respectively.
>
> While I was confined to bed in MARCH 1915 with a badly poisoned thigh (poison from a saddle) I received by mail from my father at home extracts from this diary which I was persuaded to send to the Statesman (cutting above).

[The cutting shows an much edited, very brief version of the diary. Ed.]

> Resulting from its publication I learnt from the wife of a retired judge from Patna that my great grandmother founded a home in CALCUTTA in 1815—the year the Sherwoods returned to ENGLAND—for the sons and daughters of soldiers with the object of keeping them away from barrack room life![217]
>
> Later I received an invitation to go to CALCUTTA to be shown over this building which was then celebrating its centenary but under existing conditions I did not feel justified in accepting.
>
> I also received an invitation to BERHAMPORE where a public memorial to "little Henry"[218] existed.
>
> Henry Sherwood.

---

[217] Mrs Sherwood had been instrumental in the foundation of the European Female Orphans Asylum in Calcutta for the children of European soldiers whose wives had died.

[218] Little Henry, the Sherwood's first son (25 Dec 1805, Dinapore-25 Mar 1807, Berhampore, inspiration for Mrs Sherwood's bestseller *Little Henry and his Bearer* published in 1814.

The editor, Tim Eaton, with his wife, Barbara, author of *Mrs Sherwood: 'so rich in children'*, at the Ghurka memorial, Jaytuk, near Nahan, Himachal Pradesh, India, 2015, when they also visited the site of the Battle of Nalapani at Dehra Dun and travelled by boat down the Ganges from Varanasi (Sherwood's Benares) to Calcutta.

Acknowledgements

I am most grateful to my wife, Barbara, whose research for her biography *Mrs Sherwood 'So Rich in Children'* led us to Henry Sherwood's Diaries in the Shropshire Archives at Shrewsbury where the Archivist, Sarah Davis kindly allowed me to photograph and transcribe the diaries and offered useful advice on publication. Her staff, including Liz Young and Nat Stevenson were most helpful. Having read the diaries for references to Mrs Sherwood and her life with Henry, my wife encouraged me to make a full transcript which has fascinated me, first as a 'raw' transcript and later as a text to edit and publish.

Across the road from the Archives, at Shrewsbury Castle, Mr Duckers, Curator of the Shropshire Regimental Museum was most helpful in showing me, and allowing me to photograph, material relating to Captain Sherwood's service career.

Having enjoyed many touring holidays in India we decided to visit some of the places mentioned by the Sherwoods for which David Pettitt and Peter Holroyd of Pettitts, most efficiently, as usual, made all our travel arrangements, and Pettitts India, the ground arrangements where Bobby, Pettitts India driver and guide deserves special thanks. Assam Bengal Navigation's on-board tour manager, the ever-helpful Kumal, and his friendly staff and crew of *MV Rajmahal* provided a delightful river journey taking three weeks from Varanasi (the Sherwoods' Benares) to Kolkatta (Calcutta).

Thank you all.

Illustrations

Henry Sherwood's Miniature. William Naish. 1798.	Title page
Engraving from *Pacification of the Maroon Negroes*. Agostino Brunias.	58
Off Madeira. Thomas Daniell. 1810.	68
Fort Duvernet. 2014.	80
St Lucia, Piton. 2014	126
A Fleet of East Indiamen at Sea. Nicholas Pocock. 1803	200
Madras Landing. Engraving after J B East. 1856.	210
Old Fort Gaut, Calcutta. T & W Daniell. 1810.	215
A Pinnace with a Panchway in front. Balthazar Solvyns. 1807.	218
Cremations, and remnants, on the Ganges. 2015.	219
Near Gangwaugh Colly on the River Hoogly. T & W Daniell. 1810.	225
Augustus Cleveland's house, Bhaghalpur, now a university faculty. 2015.	229
Jangara by Sherwood above. In 2014 below.	232
Golghar Granary at Patna, built 1776 for 138,000 tons of grain. 2015	237
A Budgerow. Balthazar Solvyns. 1807.	241
Charack Puja	253
Gateway at Ramnagar Fort. 2015.	268
Ashoka Stambha, Allahabad.	299
Darkhil Darwaza, brick main gate to Gour. 2015.	322
Brick arched and domed roof. Gour. 2015.	323
Lord Cornwallis's Memorial. 2015.	329
A Hackery.	337
An English Officer in a Palenquin.	348
Cenotaph at the site of Khalunga Fort. 2015.	385
Double memorial at Dehra Dun. 2015.	386
Battle of Jaytuk.	394
Jaytuk Fort Approach Ridge. 2015	405
Jaytuk Fort inside. 2015.	412

Photographs 2014 and 2015 by Tim Eaton.
Sherwood's diary sketches are not listed.
Other illustrations internet open sourced.

Henry Sherwood's Timeline

Born at Wood Street, London to Henry Marten Sherwood (1754-1803) and Margaret (nee Maskall) (? -1778)	January 1	1777	Age
Mother dies at birth of sister Margaret	April	1778	1
Father remarries—stepmother rejects Henry and Margaret			
Free school in Kidderminster, living with Butts	1788		11
Merchant Taylor's School, Ashford, boarding		1789	12
Account of life between 13 and 18 in a letter to Cousin Mary Butt			
To father's family in Calais	April	1790	13
With family to St Valery sur Somme	August	1790	
Working on father's ship L'Etoile Mignion		1791	14
Sail for Marseilles	July 22	1792	15
Arrive Marseilles	August 24	1792	
Sail from Cette for Dieppe	January 7	1793	16
Arrive Fecamp for St Valery	February 22	1793	
Navigation School, St Valery		1793	
Arrest as alien, Imprisoned	September 22	1793	
Free but destitute, cannot travel	December 23	1793	
Escape: Passport to Amiens & family	March 28	1795	18
Paris	April 4	1795	
Geneva, in funds	June 6	1795	
Germany, destitute	August	1795	
By sea to England	October	1795	
Inherits at 21	January	1798	21
1st Journal	March 12	1798	
Ensigncy purchased in 45th Foot	April 25	1798	
Lieutenancy purchased in 53rd Foot	April 28	1798	
Depart Portsmouth for the West Indies	May 15	1798	
Service in St Vincent, St Lucia and Martinique	1798 to 1802		
Lands back at Portsmouth	Dec 13	1802	25
Marries his cousin Mary Martha Butt	June 30	1803	26
(1st cousin Mary Martha Butt 6 May 1775 – 22 Sep 1851)			
Paymaster, Captaincy, 1st Batt 53rd Foot	May 1	1804	27
Regimental Paymaster Gazetted	June 1	1804	
1st Journal ends.	April 23	1805	28

2nd Journal starts	April 23	1805	28
Sails with wife and regiment for India	April 24	1805	
Service in India based at Dinapore, Berhampore, Cawnpore and Meerut			
See separate table of travels in India.			
Battles at Ajaighur, Callinger, Nalapani and Jaytuk	1805-15		
A year's leave of absence to England	Sept 25	1815	38
2nd Journal ends, arrives in England	June 1	1816	39
Retires to Worcester on half pay		1816	
Brunswick Hussars half pay	August	1818	41
Dies	Dec 5	1849	72

Captain Sherwood's Travels in India—1805-1816

23 April 1805   Embarkation from Portsmouth, England for Bengal
       ^ upriver   v downriver   <u>Miles   Days   m/day</u>
24 Aug to 2 Sep 1805 Madras
10 Sept 1805   Sangor Island, Mouth of Hooghli River, India
                                     11,400   4.5 months
14 Sept 1805   Arrival at Calcutta   120   4   30^
<u>1st River voyage—with regiment—Calcutta to Patna Dinapore</u>
13 Oct 1805   Depart from Calcutta by Rivers Hooghli & Ganges
31 Oct 1805   Passing Berhampore
10 Nov 1805   Enter Ganges: the current strong
3 Dec 1805   Arrival at Dinapore, near Patna   550   51   11^
<u>2nd river voyage —with regiment—Dinapore Patna to Berhampore</u>
1 July 1806   Depart Dinapore
16 July 1806   Arrival at Berhampore   365   16   23v
<u>3rd river voyage —with regiment—Berhampore to Cawnpore</u>
9 Sep 1807   Depart Berhampore
8-11 Oct 1807 Patna, visit Dinapore
27 Oct 1807   Benares
28 Nov 1807   Arrival at Cawnpor   780   76   11^
<u>4th River voyage— Sherwoods alone—Cawnpore to Calcutta</u>
25 Oct 1809   Depart Cawnpore for Calcutta
2 Nov 1809   Mirzapore
4 Nov 1809   Benares
11 Nov 1809   Dinapore
22 Nov 1809   Ganges to Jillinghy River
27 Nov 1809   Enter Hooghli
28 Nov 1809   Arrival at Calcutta   955   34   28v
<u>5th River voyage—Sherwoods alone—Calcutta to Cawnpore</u>
19 Dec 1809   Leave Calcutta eastward through Sunderbands
6 Jan 1810   Enter Ganges from Sunderbands
13 Feb 1810   Patna
7 Mar 1810   Benares
14 Mar 1810   Mirzapore

9 April 1810   Arrive Cawnpore   1055   111   9.5^

24 Dec 1811-18 Feb 1812 Callingery [Kalinjar] Campaign

<u>6th River voyage—with regiment—Cawnpore to Meerut</u>

30 Oct 1812   Depart Cawnpore for Meerut by river

24 Nov 1812   Arrive Meerut   240   25   10^

12 Oct 1813   March for Nepal: Kalunga Campaign (Battle of Nalapani) & start of Jeytuk Campaign

31 Jan 1814   On leave in Meerut during preparations at Jeytuk

19 April 1814   Jeytuk Campaign

27 May 1815   Return to Meerut

<u>7th River voyage—with regiment—Meerut to Berhampore</u>

22 June 1815   Leave Meerut for Calcutta

1 Aug 1815   Benares

14 Aug 1815   Dinapore

28 Aug 1815   Leave Ganges

29 Aug 1815   Arrive Berhampore   1115   96   11.5v

26 Sep 1815   Leaves 53rd Regiment after 17 years service.

<u>8th River voyage—Sherwoods alone— Berhampore to Calcutta</u>

25 Sep 1805   leave Berhampore

30 Sep 1815   Arrive Calcutta   175   5   35v

<u>9th River voyage—Sherwoods alone—Calcutta by Hooghli to *Robarts*</u>

2 Jan 1816   Leave Calcutta down Hooghli

4 Jan 1816   Board *Robarts*   <u>70</u>   <u>2</u>   35v

                                River totals   <u>5425 m   488</u> days

River voyages 1805-16 total 16 months being 13% of their 10 years 3 months in India

<u>Sea voyage to England</u>

11 Jan 1816   Sail for England

31 May 1816   Arrive Liverpool   11,400   4.5 months

Maps

Henry Sherwood's France and Escape through Germany	450
Henry Sherwood's West Indies	451
Title Panel from William Faden's 1786 Edition of Rennell's Survey	452
William Faden's 1786 Edition of James Rennell's Survey of the Ganges Basin	453
Key to Detailed Extracts 1 to 11 and Sherwood's Sketch, 12	453
1 Hoogly River—Calcutta—Culna	454
2 Sunderbans—Gopalgang, Hoorangle River—Custea, Ganges	455
3 Hoogly R—Culna—Jungipur—Ganges & Jellingy R—Ganges	456
4 Ganges—Jungipur—Monghyr	457
5 Ganges—Monghyr—Dinapur	458
6 Ganges—Dinapur—Benares	459
7 Ganges—Benares—Allahabad	460
8 Ganges—Allahabad—Cawnpur	461
9 Adgygaur and Callenger Campaigns	462
10 Ganges—Cawnpur—Caudergange	463
11 Ganges—Cawdergange—Gurmacteasle for Meerut	464
12 Sherwood's Sketch Map of the Himalayan Foothills.	465

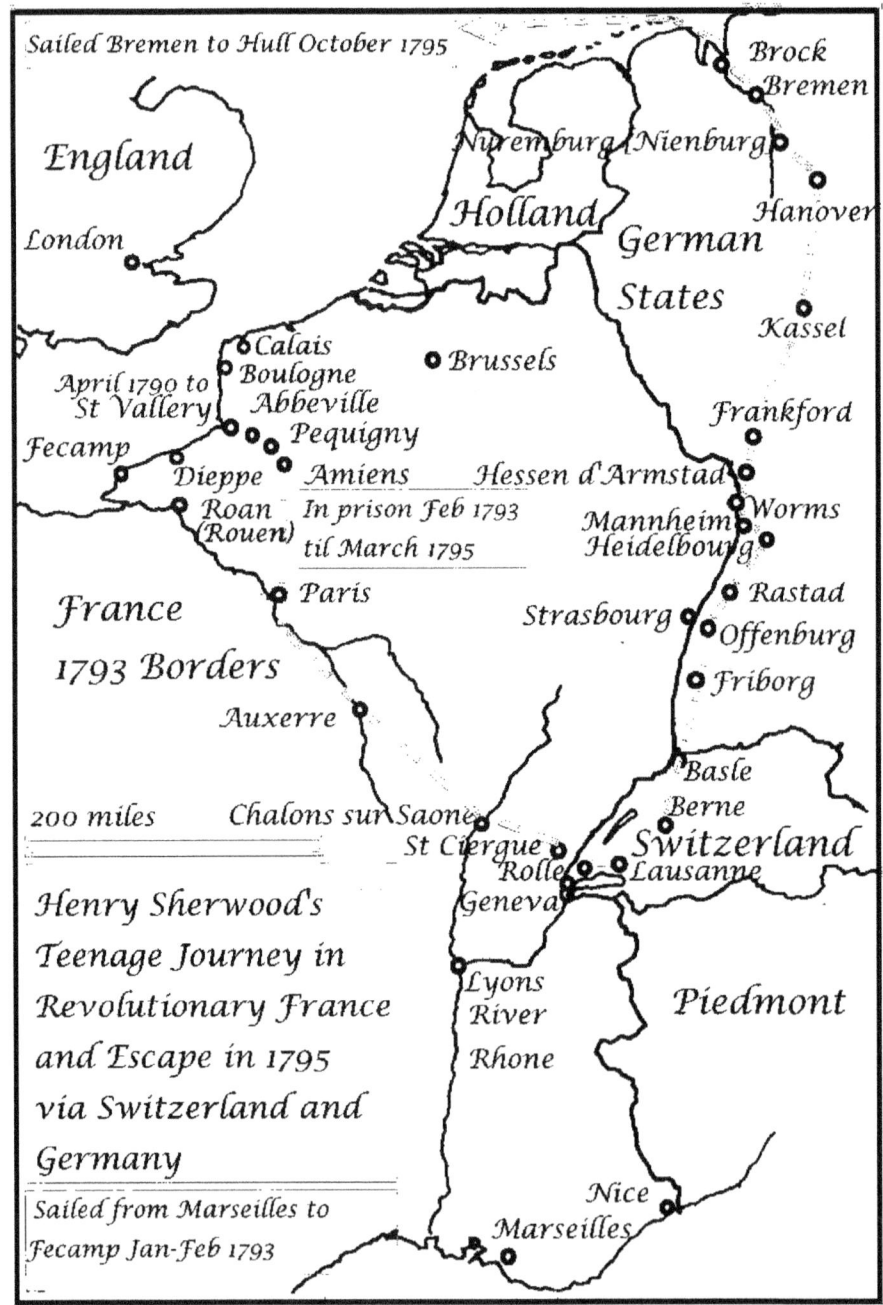

Henry Sherwood's France and Escape through Germany

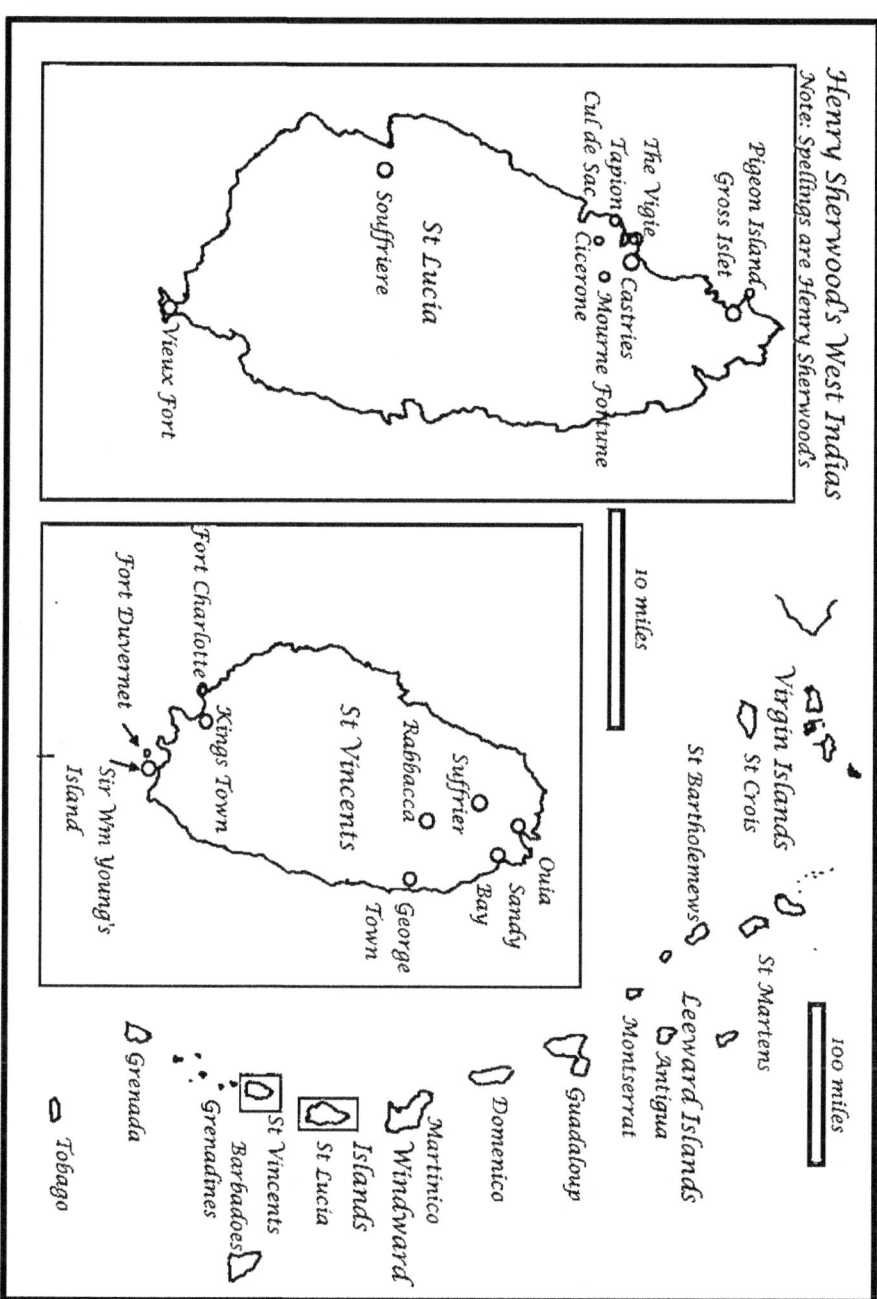

Henry Sherwood's West Indies

Title Panel from William Faden's 1786 Edition of Rennell's Survey

Sherwood refers to 'Rennells map' during his river journeys. Several maps based on Surveyor-General James Rennell's survey of the Ganges Basin were available to Sherwood including Andrew Dury's 1776 edition, William Faden's 1786, both showing the same extent, Dury's 1777 of the eastern part, and an 1806 edition showing the whole of India. Some place-names are omitted in various editions and many are spelt erratically. Extracts of Faden's 1786 map are reproduced here for consistency.

For much of its length the Ganges is one to five miles wide with a flood plain of level sandy ground. The course varies widely from year to year. The level varies as much as 50 feet (15M) from the summer floods to winter dry season when the navigable channel may be very shallow. Before the 20th Century barrage at Farraka the access to the Hoogly, Jellingy and other distributaries varied annually necessitating winter access by the tidal mangrove swamps of the Sunderbands.

Maps 453

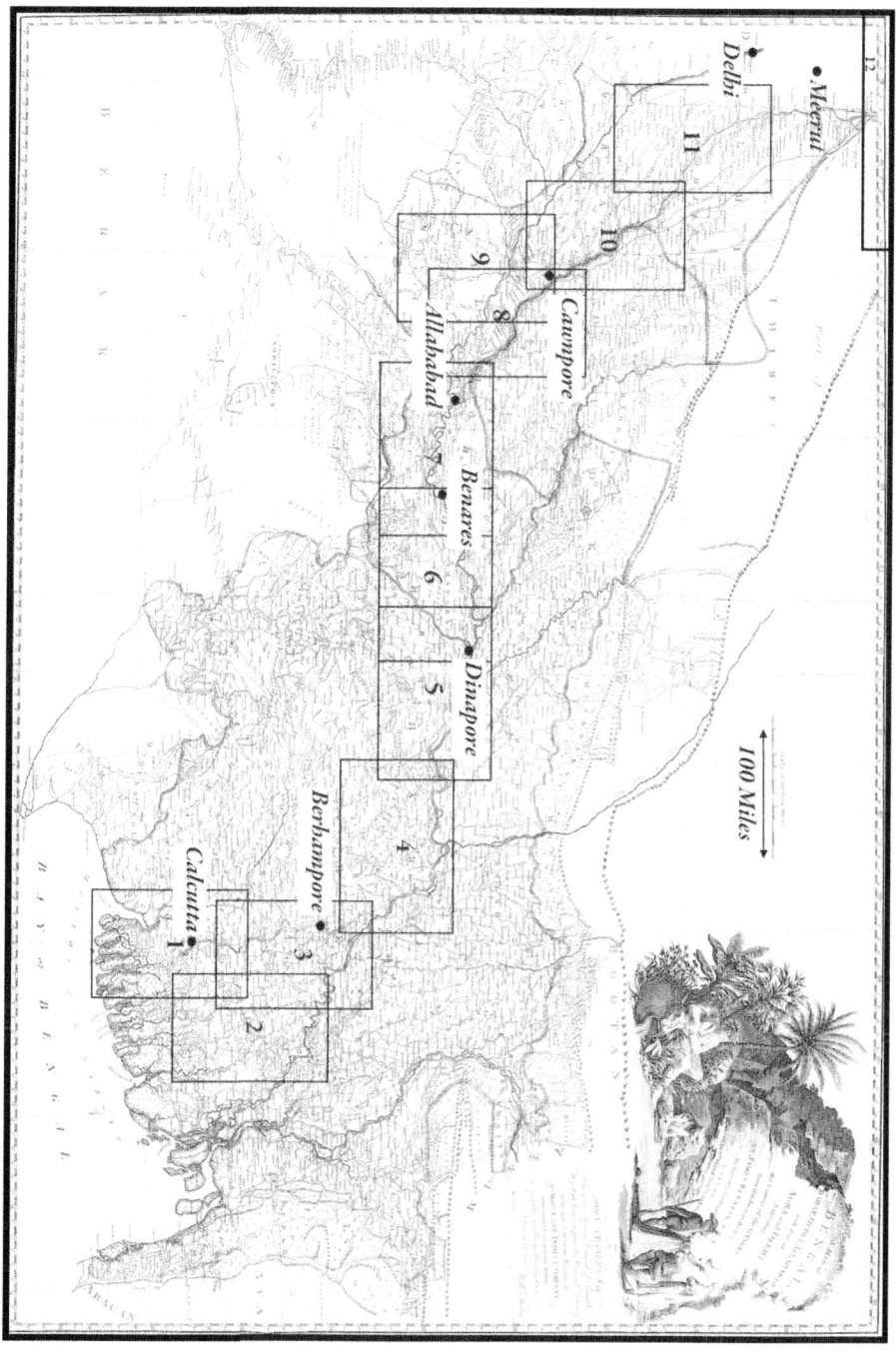

William Faden's 1786 Edition of James Rennell's Survey of the Ganges Basin.
Key to Detailed Extracts 1 to 11 and Sherwood's Sketch, 12

1 Hoogly River—Calcutta—Culna

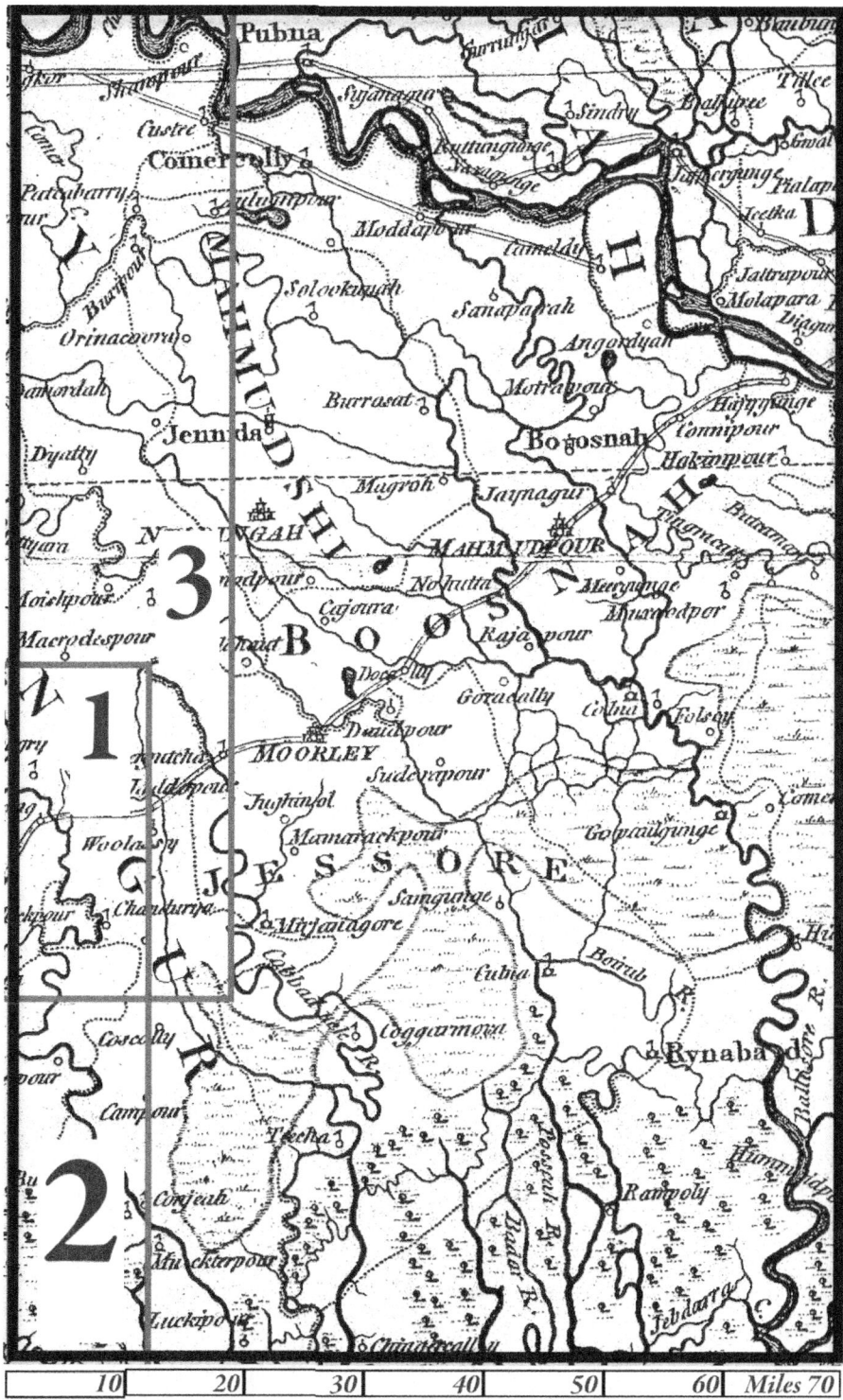

2 Sunderbans—Gopalgang, Hoorangle River—Custea, Ganges

3 Hoogly R—Hoogly—Culna—Jungipur—Ganges & Jellingy R—Ganges

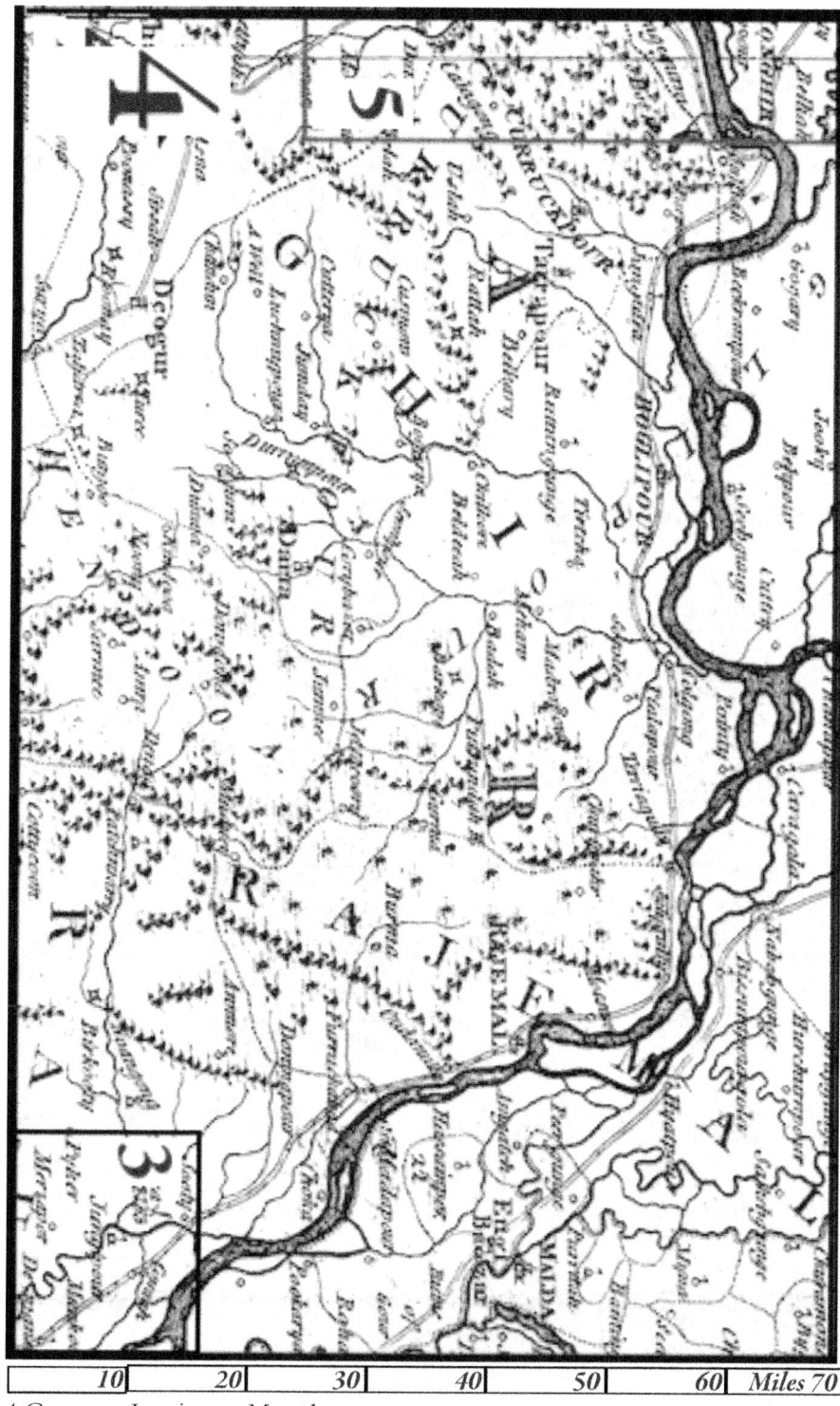

4 Ganges—Jungipur—Monghyr

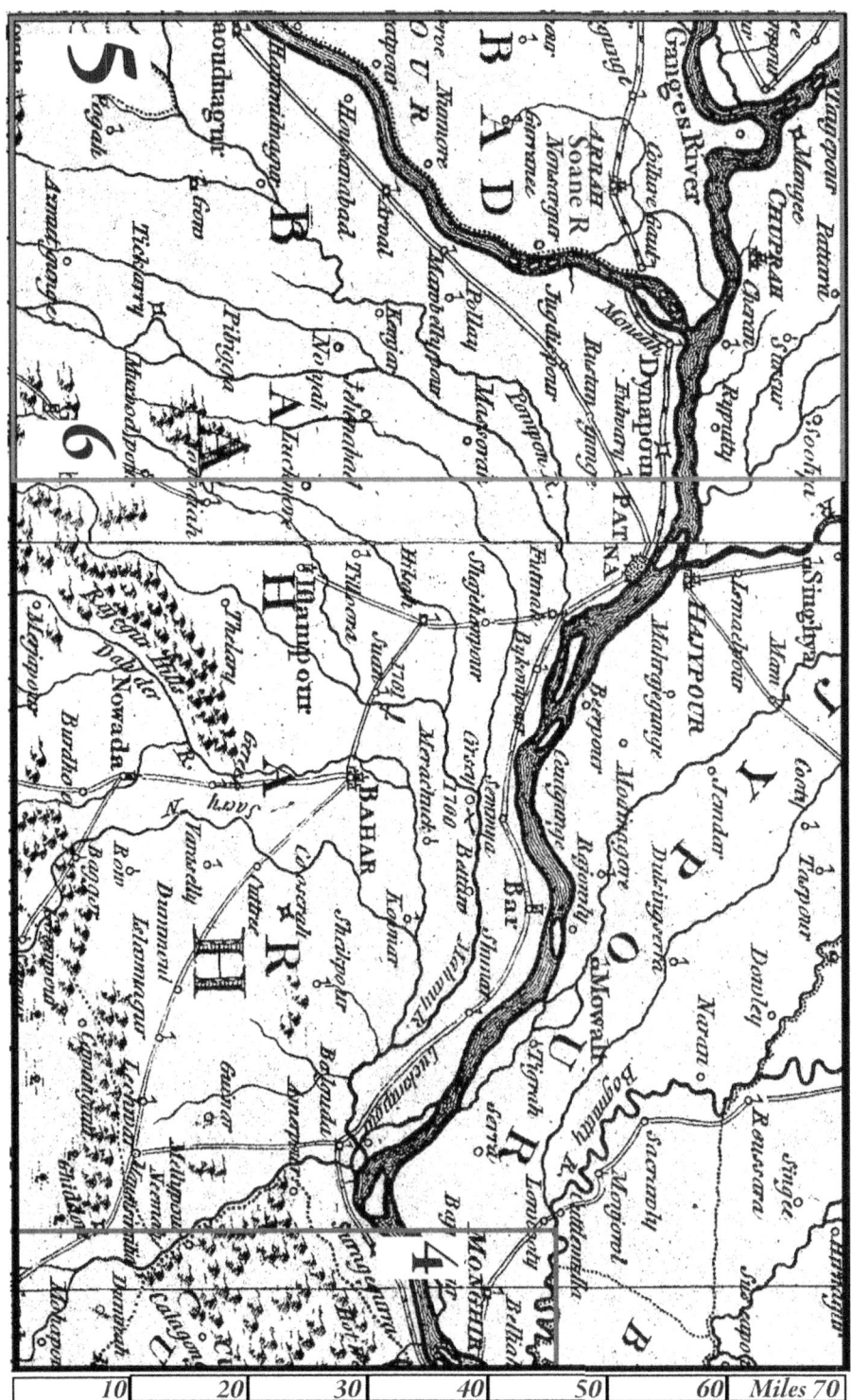

5 Ganges—Monghyr—Dinapur

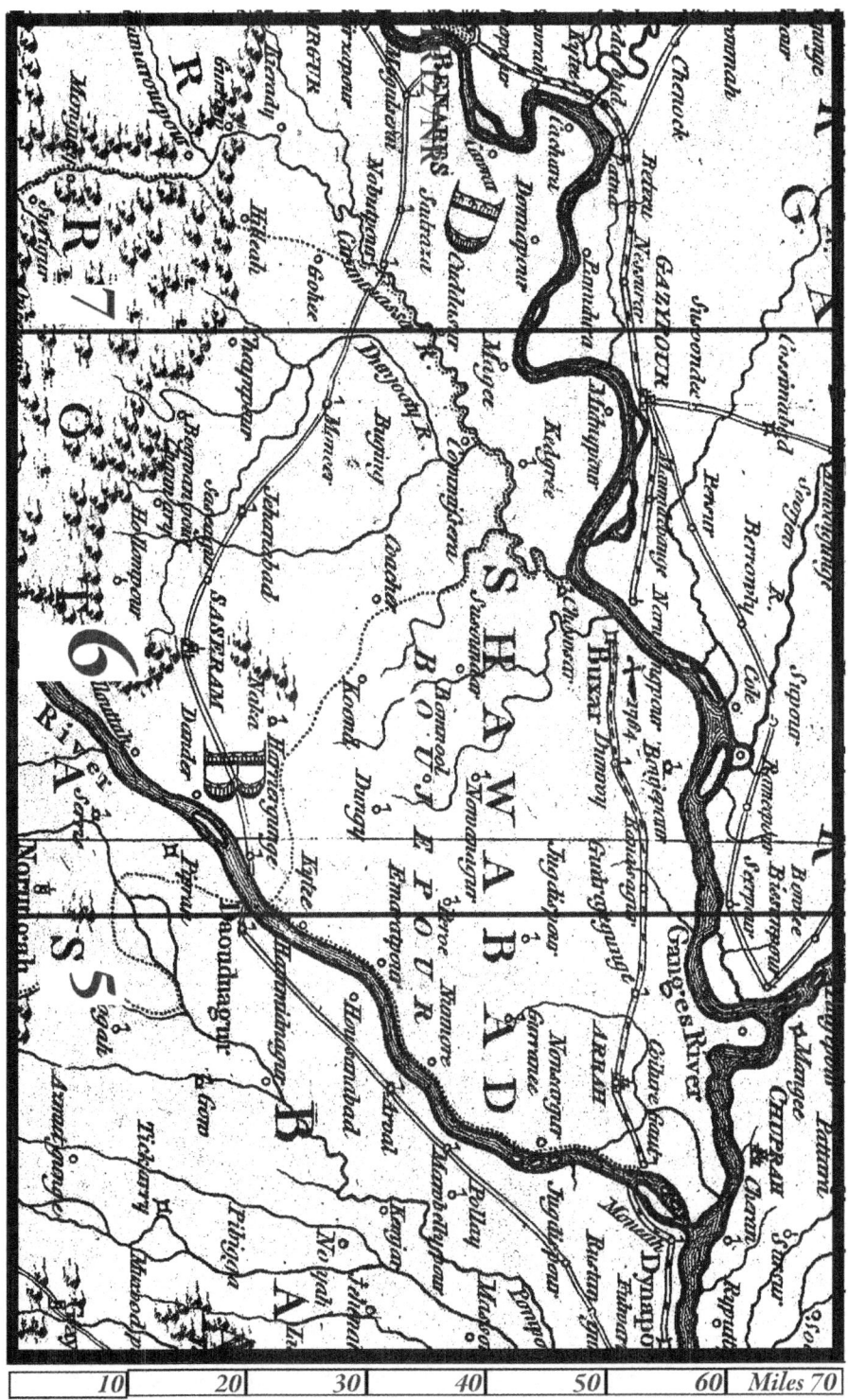

6 Ganges—Dinapur—Benares

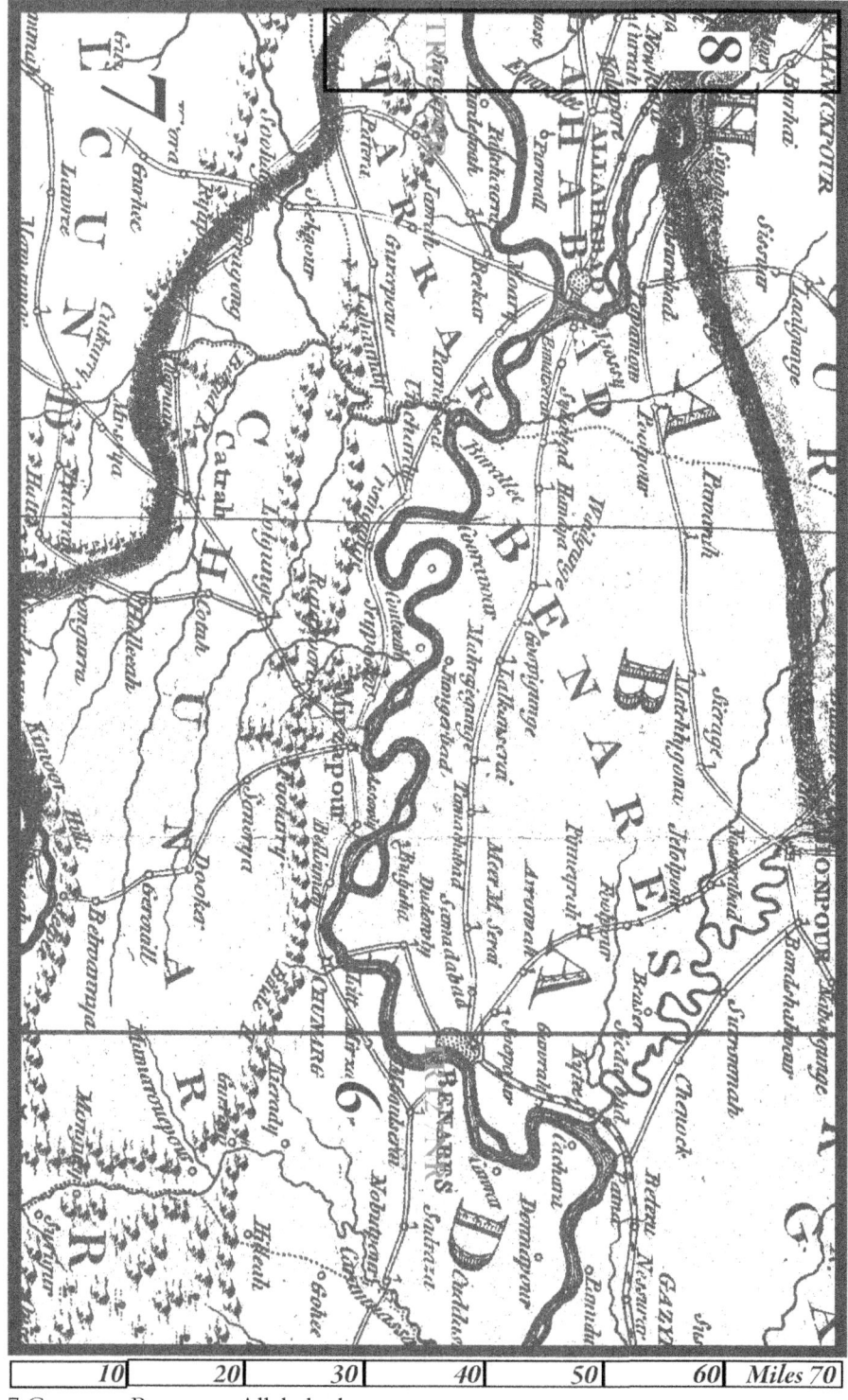

7 Ganges—Benares—Allahabad

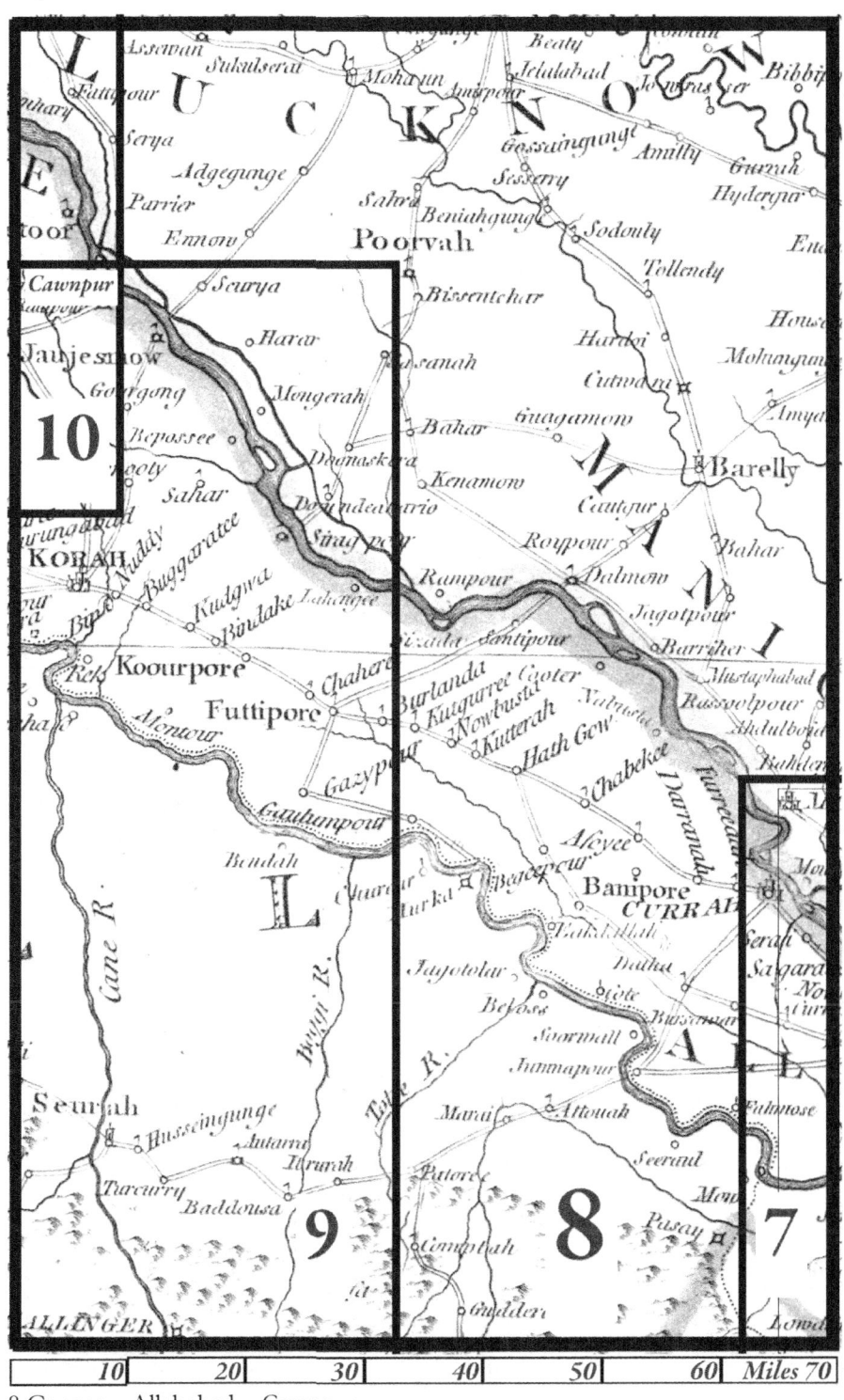

8 Ganges—Allahabad—Cawnpur

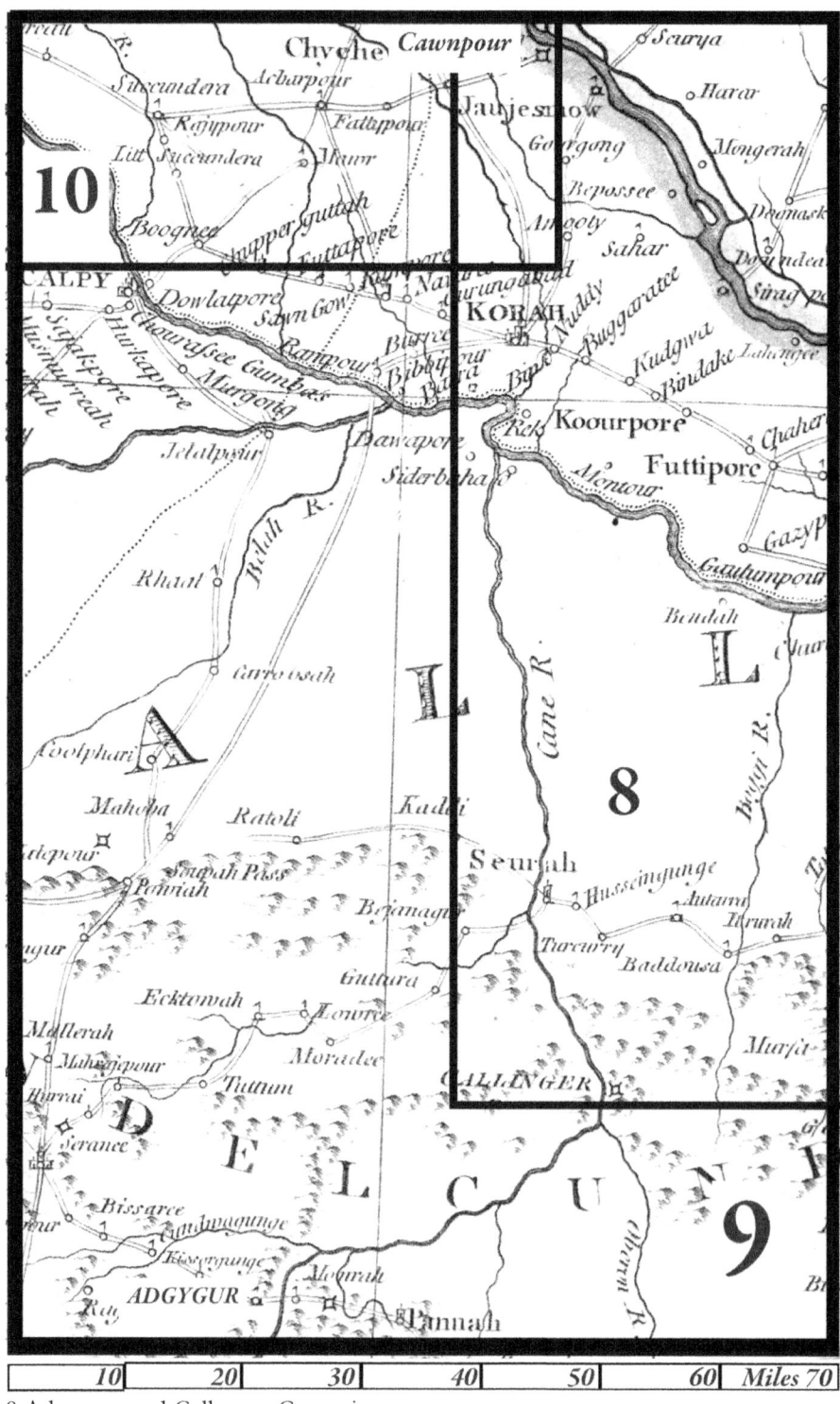

9 Adgygaur and Callenger Campaigns

Maps

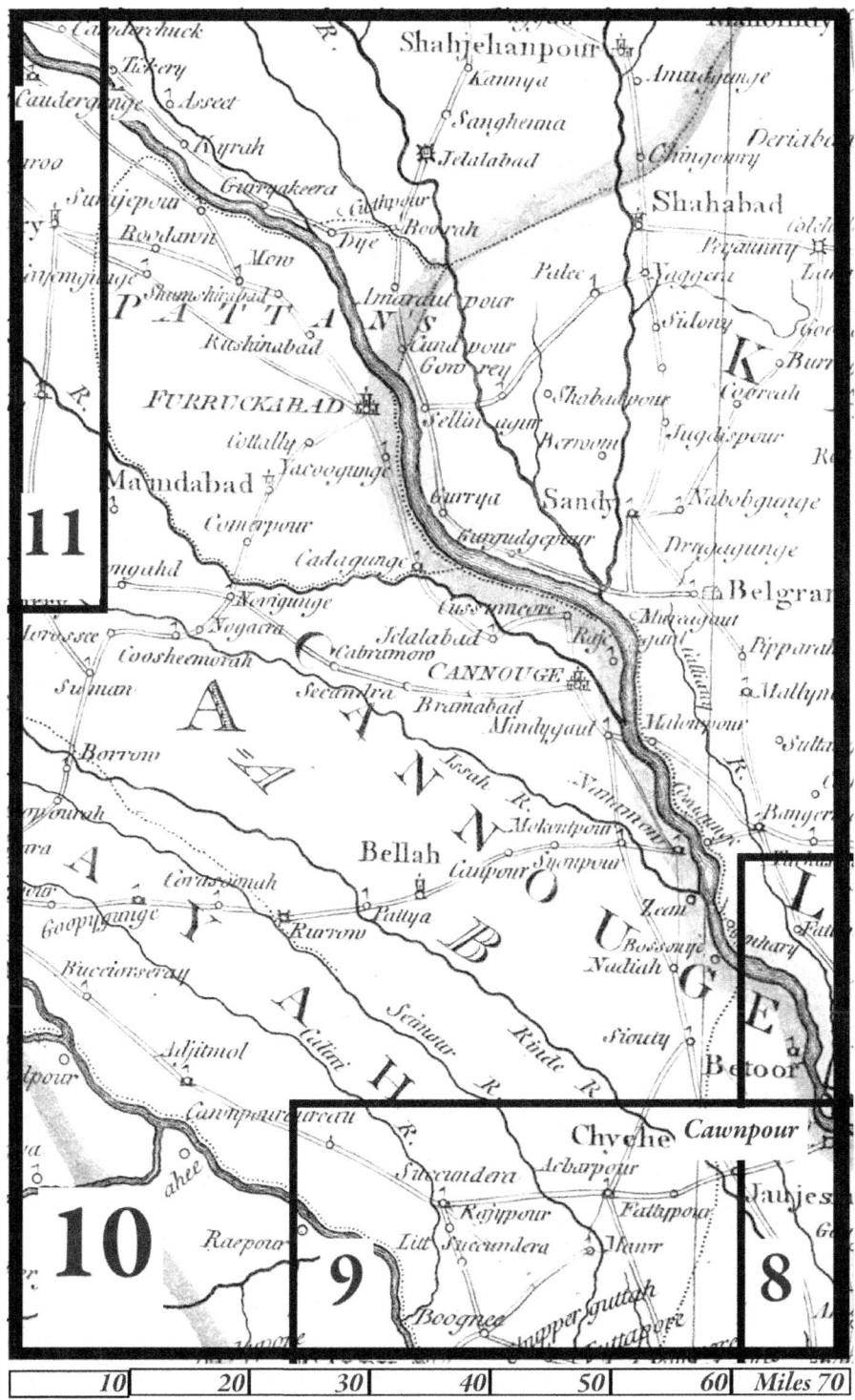

10 Ganges—Cawnpur—Caudergange

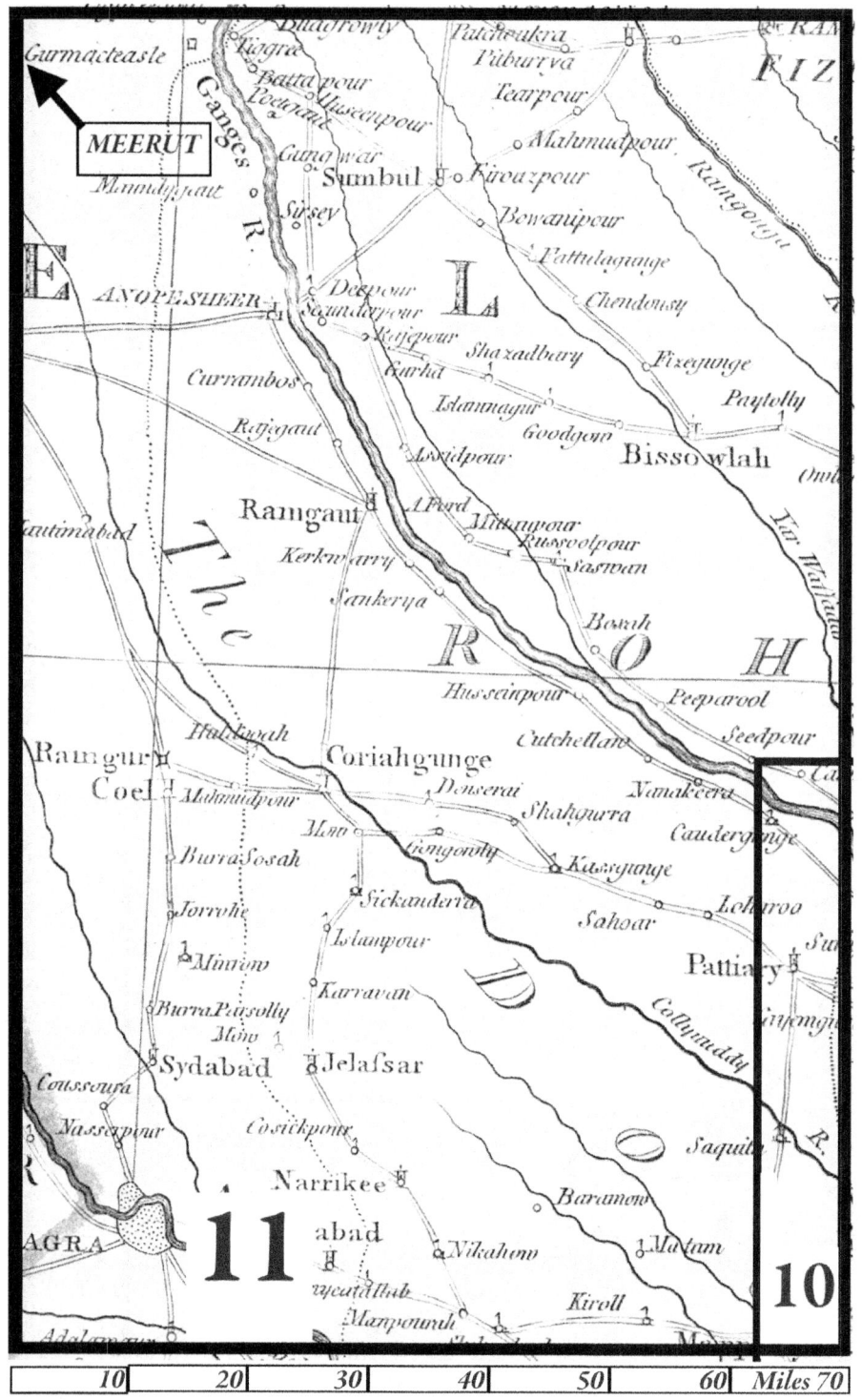

11 Ganges—Cawdergange—Gurmacteasle for Meerut

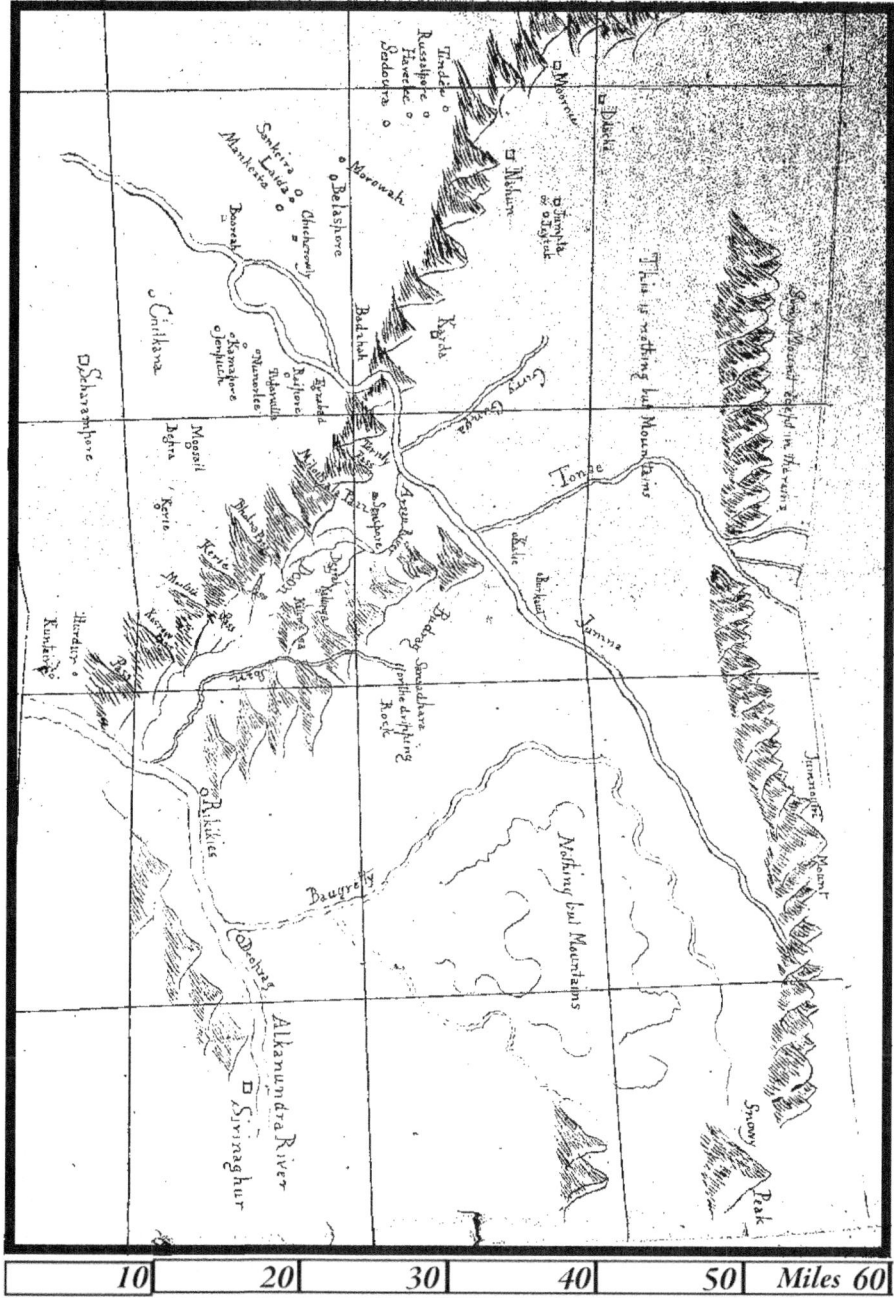

12 Sherwood's Sketch Map of the Himalayan Foothills.
Scale very approximate

Sources and Bibliography

Original Sources

Diaries of Henry Sherwood. Original handwritten foolscap sheets pasted into two leatrherbound letterbooks, about 400 sides. Shropshire Archives, Shrewsbury. 5624/1 and 2.

Henry Sherwood's Notebook. A photocopied collection of popular contemporary songs in Sherwood's hand, with a few notes of personal debts. Shropshire Regimental Museum, Shrewsbury.

Bibliography

Belsham, William. 1793-1801 *Memoirs of the reign of George III*, 6 Volumes, London.

Brookes, R. 1794 *The General Gazetteer; or, Compendious Geographical Dictionary*. London: B Law & Son.

Brown, William Wells. 2014 *Clotel and other Writings*. New York: Literary Classics of the United States.

Buckley, R N. 1998 *The British Army in the West Indies*. University of Florida Press.

Cannon, R. 1849 *Historical Record of The Fifty-Third Regiment of Foot containing an Account of the Formation of the Regiment in 1755 and of its Subsequent Services to 1848* in the series *Historical Records of the British Army*. London: Adjutant General's Office.

de Courcy, Anne. 2012. *The Fishing Fleet, Husband-Hunting in the Raj*. London: Weidenfeld & Nicholson.

Darton, F. J. Harvey, ed. 1910 *The Life and Times of Mrs Sherwood*. London: Wells Gardner, Darton & Co. Based on Kelly with some additions.

Eaton, Barbara. 2005 *Letters to Lydia 'Beloved Persis'* Hypatia Publications, Penzance. A biography of Henry Martyn in India.

Eaton, Barbara. 2016 *Mrs Sherwood 'So Rich in Children'*. London: Francis Boutle Publishers. A biography of Mrs Sherwood.

Kelly, Sophia, ed. 1854, & 2nd ed. 1857 *The Life of Mrs. Sherwood, (chiefly autobiographical) with Extracts from Mr. Sherwood's Journal during his Imprisonment in France & Residence in India Edited by Her Daughter.* 1st & 2nd editions differ. London: Darton & Co.

Newby, Eric. 1966 *Slowly Down the Ganges.* London: Hodder and Stoughton.

Paley, William. 1803 *Natural Theology or Evidences of the Existence and Attributes of the Deity.* London: J Faulder.

Roberts, David. 1815 *The military adventures of Johnny Newcome, with an account of his campaign on the Peninsula and in Pall Mall and notes, by an officer.* With fifteen coloured sketches by Thomas Rowlandson.

Yule, Henry and Burnell, Arthur Coke. 1886. *Hobson-Jobson: being a glossary of Anglo-Indian colloquial words and phrases and of kindred terms etymological, historical, geographical and discursive.* London: John Murray. New edition. (1994). Sittingbourne: Linguasia.

Printed in Great Britain
by Amazon